History of Labour in
the United States

History of Labour in the United States

By

John R. Commons
David J. Saposs   Helen L. Sumner
E.B. Mittelman   H.E. Hoagland
John B. Andrews   Selig Perlman

With An Introductory Note
by
Henry W. Farnam

Volume II

BeardBooks
Washington, D.C.

CONTENTS

INTRODUCTION
By John R. Commons

PART I. COLONIAL AND FEDERAL BEGINNINGS
(TO 1827
By David J. Saposs

CHAPTER I
ORIGIN OF TRADE UNIONS . . . . I, 25

CHAPTER II
DEVELOPMENT OF BARGAINING CLASSES . I, 32

CHAPTER III
THE MERCHANT-CAPITALIST . . . . . . I, 88

CHAPTER IV
EARLY TRADE UNIONS . . . . I, 108

CHAPTER V
CORDWAINERS' CONSPIRACY CASES, 1806-1815 I, 138

CHAPTER VI
SIGNS OF AWAKENING, 1820-1827 . . . . . I, 153

PART II. CITIZENSHIP (1827–1833)
By Helen L. Sumner

CHAPTER I
CAUSES OF THE AWAKENING . . . . . . I, 169

CHAPTER II
RISE AND GROWTH IN PHILADELPHIA . . I, 185

CHAPTER III
WORKINGMEN'S PARTIES IN NEW YORK . . I, 231

CHAPTER IV
SPEED OF THE MOVEMENT . . . . . . I, 285

CHAPTER V
NEW ENGLAND ASSOCIATION OF FARMERS, MECHANICS AND OTHER WORKINGMEN I, 302

CHAPTER VI
RESULTS OF THE AWAKENING . . . . . I, 326

PART III. TRADE UNIONISM (1833–1839)
By Edward B. Mittelman

CHAPTER I
THE TURN TO TRADE UNIONISM . . . . I, 335

CHAPTER II
THE CITY TRADES' UNION . . . . I, 357

CHAPTER III
TRADE UNIONISM IN ACTION . . . . . . I, 381

CHAPTER IV
THE NATIONAL TRADES' UNION . . . . . I, 424

CHAPTER V
PREMATURE NATIONAL TRADE UNIONS . . I, 439

CHAPTER VI
DISINTEGRATION . . . . I, 454

APPENDICES

I FIRST DATES ON WHICH TRADE SOCIE-
TIES APPEARED IN NEW YORK, BAL-
TIMORE, PHILADELPHIA, AND BOS-
TON, 1833–1837 . . . . I, 472

II STRIKES, 1833–1837 . . . . I, 478

PART IV. HUMANITARIANISM (1840–1860)
By Henry E. Hoagland

CHAPTER I
DEPRESSION AND IMMIGRATION . . . . . I, 487

CHAPTER II
ASSOCIATION AND CO-OPERATION . . . . I, 493

CHAPTER III
THE NEW AGRARIANISM . . . . I, 522

CHAPTER IV
THE TEN-HOUR MOVEMENT . . . . . . I, 536

CHAPTER V
THE INDUSTRIAL CONGRESSES . . . . . I, 547

CHAPTER VI
CO-OPERATIVE UNIONISM . . . . I, 564

CHAPTER VII
THE NEW TRADE UNIONISM . . . . . . I, 575

PART V. NATIONALISATION (1860–1877)
By John B. Andrews

CHAPTER I
ECONOMIC CONDITIONS . . . . II, 3

New Conditions. Railway construction, 3. Through-freight lines, 4. Railway consolidations, 4. Appearance of the wholesale jobber, 5. The first national trade unions, 5.

The Moulders. William H. Sylvis, 6. The effect of the extension of the market on the moulder's trade, 6. The national union, 7. Its weakness, 7.

The Machinists and Blacksmiths. Evils in the trade, 8. The national union, 9. Strike against the Baldwin Locomotive Works, 9. Outbreak of the War depression, 9. Other national unions, 10.

Unemployment and Impending War. The workingmen's opposition to war, 10. Louisville and Philadelphia, 10. Fort Sumter and labour's change of attitude, 11.

CHAPTER II

THE WAR PERIOD, 1861–1865 . . . . **II, 13**

War and Prices. The lethargy of the trade unions, 13. Legal tender acts, 14. War prosperity and its beneficiaries, 14. Cost of living and wages, 15.

The Labour Press. *Fincher's Trades' Review*, 15. The *Workingman's Advocate*, 16. The *Daily Evening Voice*, 16. Other papers, 17.

Local Unions. The incentive for organisation, 17. The wave of organisation during the war, 18.

The Trades' Assemblies. Progress of the trades' assemblies, 22. Strikes, 23. Functions of the trades' assemblies, 23. The Philadelphia trades' assembly, a typical assembly, 24.

Employers' Associations. Local and national associations, 26. The Employers' General Association of Michigan, 26. The reply of the trade unions, 29. Richard F. Trevellick, 29. New York Masters Builders' Association, 29. Master Mechanics of Boston, 30. The associated employers and the eight-hour movement of 1872, 31. The attempted " exclusive agreement," 32. Attitude towards trade agreements, 33.

International Industrial Assembly of North America. The national trade unions and federation, 33. The trades' assemblies and federation, 34. The Louisville call, 34. The convention in Louisville, 35. Assistance during strikes, 36. Attitude towards co-operation and legislation, 37. The constitution and the national trade unions, 37. Politics, 38. Causes of failure, 38.

Distributive Co-operation. Cost of living, 39. Thomas Phillips, 39. The Rochdale plan, 40. The turn towards productive co-operation, 41.

CHAPTER III

THE NATIONAL TRADE UNIONS, 1864–1873 . . **II, 42**

Causes and General Progress. Effect of the nationalisation of the market, 43. National trade unions in thirties, 43. The effect of national labour competition, 44. Effect of employers' associations, 44. Effect of machinery and the division of labour, 44. Organisation of national trade unions, 1861–1873, 45. Growth of their membership, 47. The national trade union — the paramount aspect of nationalisation, 48.

The Moulders. Epitomise the labour movement, 48. Activities during the war, 48. Beginning of employers' associations, 49. Lull in the organisation of employers during the period of prosperity, 49. West and East, 50. American National Stove Manufacturers' and Iron Founders' Association, 50. Apprenticeship question, 50. The strike in Albany and Troy, 51. Withdrawal of the Buffalo and St. Louis foundrymen from the Association, 51. The general strike against wage reductions, 51. Defeat of the union, 52. Restriction on strikes by the national union, 52. Turn to co-operation, 53. Sylvis' view on the solution of the labour question, 53. Co-operative shops, 53. The Troy shops, 54. Their business success but failure as co-operative enterprises, 54. Disintegration of the employers' association, 55. Revival of trade unionism, 55.

Machinists and Blacksmiths. The intellectual ascendency in the labour movement, 56. Employers' associations, 56. Effect of the depression, 57. Effect of the eight-hour agitation on the union, 57. Revival in 1870, 58.

Printers. The National Typographical Union, 58. " Conditional membership," 58. The national strike fund, 59. The persistent localist tendency, 59. Northwestern Publishers' Association, 61.

Locomotive Engineers. The cause of nationalisation, 61. Piece work,

62. Brotherhood of the Footboard, 62. Brotherhood of Locomotive Engineers, 62. Charles Wilson and his attitude towards public opinion, 63. Strike on the Michigan Southern, 64. The railway's blacklist, 64. The brotherhood's attitude towards incorporation, 65. The brotherhood conservatism, 65. Discontent of the local branches, 66. Wilson's incorporation move, 66. Failure in Congress, 67. Growth of the opposition to Wilson, 67. His removal from office, 67. P. M. Arthur, 67. The benefit system, 68.

Cigar Makers. Effect of the war revenue law, 69. Growth of the international union, 1864–1869, 70. The introduction of the mould, 71. The strike against the mould, 72. The attitude towards the mould of the conventions of 1867 and 1872, 72. Failure of the anti-mould policy, 73.

Coopers. Effect of the machine, 74. Martin A. Foran, 75. Career of the International Coopers' Union, 75. Robert Schilling, 76. Co-operative attempts, 76.

Knights of St. Crispin. The factory system, 76. " Green hands," 77. Aim of the Crispins, 77. Crispin strikes, 78. Their principal causes, 78. Attitude towards co-operation, 79.

Sons of Vulcan. The puddler's bargaining advantage, 80. The sliding scale agreement, 80.

Restrictive Policies Apprenticeship. Beginning of restrictive policies, 81. Effect of the wider market on apprenticeship, 81. Effect of the increased scale of production, 81. " Botches," 82. Sylvis' view, 82. Limitation of numbers, 82. Policies of the national trade unions, 83. Regulation of apprenticeship in the printer's trade, 83.

CHAPTER IV

THE NATIONAL LABOR UNION, 1866–1872 .   . II, 85

The Labour Movement in Europe and America. Eight-hour question, 87. Ira Steward and his wage theory, 87. Stewardism contrasted with socialism, 90. Stewardism and trade-unionism, 91. Stewardism and political action, 91. Boston Labor Reform Association, 91. Grand Eight-Hour League of Massachusetts, 92. Massachusetts labour politics, 93. Labour politics in Philadelphia, 93. Fincher's opposition to politics, 93. Return of the soldiers — a stimulus to the eight-hour movement, 94. The question of national federation, 94. The move by trades' assemblies, 94. New York State Workingmen's Assembly, 95. The move by the national trade unions, 96. The compromise, 96.

Labour Congress of 1866. Representation, 96. Attitude toward trade unionism and legislation, 98. The eight-hour question at the congress, 98. Resolution in political action, 99. The land question, 100. Co-operation, 101. Form of organisation, 101.

Eight Hours and Politics. Congressional election of 1866, 102. Independent politics outside Massachusetts, 103. Eight-hours before Congress, 104. Eight-hours before President Johnson, 104. Eight-hours before the General Court of Massachusetts, 105. The special commission of 1865, 106. The commission of 1866, 107. E. H. Rogers, 107. Eight-hour bills in other States, 108. Causes of the failure, 109.

Co-operation. Co-operative workshops, 111. Productive co-operation in various trades, 111.

Labour Congress of 1867. Activity of the National Labor Union during the year, 112. Address to the Workingmen of the United States, 113. Viewpoint of the " producing classes," 114. Representation at the Congress of 1867, 115. The constitution, 116. The immigrant question and the American Emigrant Company, 117. The question of the Negro, 118.

Greenbackism. The popularity of greenbackism among the various elements at Labour Congress, 119. A. C. Cameron, 119. Alexander Campbell, 120. The " new Kelloggism," 121. Greenbackism contrasted with socialism and anarchism, 121. Greenbackism as a remedy against depressions, 122. "Declaration of Principles," 122. The depression, 1866–1868, 123. Progress of co-operation, 124.

Eight Hours. Government employés and the eight-hour day, 124. The Labour Congress of 1868, 125. The conference on the presidential election, 125. Representation at the congress, 126. Women delegates, 127. Discussion on greenbackism, 128. Discussion on strikes, 129. The first lobbying committee, 130. Sylvis' presidency, 130.

The International Workingmen's Association. International regulation of immigration, 131. Sylvis' attitude towards the International, 132. Sylvis' death, 132. Cameron's mission to Basle, 132.

Labour Congress of 1869. Representation, 133. Effect of Sylvis' death, 134.

The Negroes. Invasion of industries, 134. Causes of their separate organisation, 135. Maryland State Coloured Labour Convention of 1869, 136. Supremacy of the politicians, 137.

Politics in Massachusetts. New England Labour Reform League, 138. American proudhonism and the intellectuals, 139. The Crispins and politics, 140. The State Labour Reform Convention, 140. The Crispins and incorporation, 140. The State campaign of 1869, 141. Boston municipal election, 142. Wendell Phillips and the State election of 1870, 143. The end of labour politics in Massachusetts, 144.

Labour Congress of 1870. The Negro question, 144. Decision to call a political convention, 145. Changes in the constitution, 146.

Chinese Exclusion. The industrial situation in California during the sixties, 147. Early anti-Chinese movement in California, 147. The Mechanics' State Council, 148. The effect of the transcontinental railway on the California industries, 148. The National Labor Union and the Chinese question in 1869, 149. The North Adams, Mass., incident, 149. The Burlingame treaty with China, 149. The National Labor Union and the Chinese question in 1870, 150.

Revival of Trade Unionism. Stopping the contraction of the currency, 151. Eight-hour strike movements in 1872, 151. New and aggressive leaders, 152. Abandonment of the National Labor Union by the national trade unions, 152. The Crispins — the exception, 152.

Politics and Dissolution. Horace H. Day, 153. The "industrial" convention of 1871, 153. The political convention, 154. Nomination for President, 154. Failure and dissolution, 155.

CHAPTER V

DISINTEGRATION, 1873–1877 . . . . II, 156

Industrial Congress and Industrial Brotherhood, 1873–1875. The fresh impulse towards national federation, 157. Joint call by the national trade unions, 157. Guarantee against politics, 158. The circular, 158. The Cleveland Congress, 159. Representation, 159. The trade union nature of the proceedings, 159. The constitution, 160. Attitude towards co-operation, 161. Attitude towards politics, 161. Effect of the financial panic on the new federation, 161. Congress in Rochester, 161. Representation and the secret orders, 162. Debate on the constitution, 162. The minority recommendation of secret organisation, 163. Defeat of secrecy, 163. The Industrial Brotherhood, 163. The *Preamble*, 164. Robert Schilling, 164. The money question, 164. Arbitration, 165. Other demands, 165. Politics, 165. The Congress in Indianapolis, 166. The dropping out of the national trade unions, 166. The new constitution with organisation by States as its basis, 167. End of the Industrial Brotherhood, 167.

Greenback Party, 1874–1877. Patrons of Husbandry, 168. Anti-monopoly political movement, 168. The Indianapolis convention, 168. The Cleveland convention of farmers and mechanics, 169. The "Independent" or Greenback party, 169. The anti-monopoly convention, 169. National conference in Cincinnati, 169. Fusion with the Greenback party, 170. The nominating convention of 1876, 170. Representation, 170. Greenbackism — a remedy against depression, 170. Peter Cooper's candidacy, 171. The campaign, 171. Results, 171.

Sovereigns of Industry. Co-operation, East and West, 171. William H. Earle, 172. Elimination of the middleman, 172. Constitution of the Sovereigns of Industry, 173. Membership, 1874–1877, 173. Activities, 174. Relation to trade unions, 174. Relation to the Industrial Congress, 175. Failure of the Sovereigns of Industry, 175.

National and Local Unions. The weak points in the trade unions of the sixties, 175. The depression, 175. Labour leaders and politics, 175. The westward migration, 176. Decrease in membership, 1873–1874, 176. The trades' assembly, 177. The cigar makers' strike against the tenement house system, 177. Strikes in the textile industry, 178. The Amalgamated Association of Iron and Steel Workers, 179. The trade agreement, 179. Bituminous coal miners' organisation, 179. John Siney, 179. Mark Hanna, 180. The trade agreement, 180. The umpire's decision in 1874, under the trade agreement, 180. Failure of the agreement, 180.

The Molly Maguires. Trade unionism *versus* violence, 181. The Ancient Order of Hibernians, 182. Influence over local politics, 182. Crimes of the Mollies, 183. James McParlan, 184. The "long strike," 184. The wrecking of the union, 185. Growth of the influence of the Mollies, 185. Arrest and trial of the Mollies, 185.

The Great Strikes of 1877. Reduction in wages of the railway men, 185. The Brotherhood of Locomotive Engineers, 185. The Trainmen's Union, 186. Robert H. Ammon, 186. The plan for a strike, 187. Failure, 187. The unorganised outbreak, 187. The Martinsburg and Baltimore riots, 187. Pittsburgh riots, 188. State militia, 189. Federal troops, 190. Effect of the strikes on public opinion, 190. Effect on subsequent court decisions in labour cases, 191.

PART VI.   UPHEAVAL AND REORGANISATION

(Since 1876)

By Selig Perlman

CHAPTER I

SECRET BEGINNINGS . . . . II, 195
Employers' opposition to trade unions during the period of depression, 195. Necessity for secrecy, 195. Beginning of the Knights of Labor, 196. Uriah S. Stephens, 197. Assembly 1 of Philadelphia, 197. "Sojourners," 198. Ritual and principles, 198. Additional assembles, 199. District Assembly 1 of Philadelphia, 199. District Assembly 2 of Camden, New Jersey, 199. District Assembly 3 of Pittsburgh, 199. Recruiting ground of the Knights, 200. Strikes and strike funds, 200. Rivalry between District Assembly 1 and District Assembly 3, 200. The issue of secrecy, 201. Attitude of the Catholic Church, 201. Junior Sons of '76 and their call for a national convention, 201.

CHAPTER II

REVOLUTIONARY BEGINNINGS . . . . . II, 203

The International Workingmen's Association. Its emphasis on trade unionism, 204. Its attitude towards political action, 205. Lassalle's programme and the emphasis on political action, 206. Forerunners of the International in America, 206. The Communist Club, 206. F. A. Sorge, 207. The General German Workingmen's Union and its Lassallean programme, 207. The Social party of New York and vicinity, 208. Failure and reorganisation, 209. Union 5 of the National Labor Union and Section 1 of the International, 209. New Sections of the International, 209. The Central Committee, 210. The native American forerunner of the International, 210. Section 12, and its peculiar propaganda, 211. Rupture between foreigners and Americans in the International, 211. The Provisional Federal Council, 212. Two rival Councils, 212. Decision of General Council in London, 213. The American Confederation of the International and its attitude on the question of the powers of the General Council, 213. The North American Federation of the International, 214. The Internationalist Congress at The Hague and the defeat of Bakunin by Marx, 214. Transfer of the General Council to New York, 215. Secession of a majority of the European national federations, 215. Section 1 of New York and the Local Council, 216. Abolition of the Local Council, 216. Secession of six sections, 217. The national convention of 1874 and the resolution on politics, 218. Adolph Strasser, 218. The panic and unemployment, 219. Organisation of the unemployed, 219. The riot on Tompkins Square, 220. John Swinton, 220. Organisation among the unemployed in Chicago, 220. Section 1 of New York and the struggle for the control of the *Arbeiter-Zeitung*, 221. The United Workers of America, 222. P. J. McDonnell, 222.

The International and the Trade Union Movement. Lack of response among the native American workingmen, 223. Success among the Germans, 223. *Die Arbeiter-Union*, 223. Adolph Douai, 224. Temporary sway of greenbackism among the Germans, 224. Victory of the ideas of the International, 225. The Franco-Prussian War and the discontinuance of *Die Arbeiter-Union*, 225. Organisation of the furniture workers, 225. The German American Typographia, 226. The Amalgamated Trades and Labour Council of New York, 226.

Lassalleanism and Politics. The effect of the industrial depression on the spread of Lassalleanism, 227. The Labor party of Illinois and its form of organisation, 228. Its attitude toward trade unionism and politics, 228. Temporary Lassalleanisation of the sections of the International in Chicago, 229. The Labor party of Illinois in politics, 229. Overtures to farmers, 230. The return to the principles of the International, 230. The Lassallean movement in the East — The Social Democratic party of North America, 230. The first national convention, 231. Peter J. McGuire, 231. Reasons for Strasser's joining the Lassalleans, 231. The *Sozial-Demokrat*, 232. The change of sentiment in favour of trade unionism, 232. The second convention of the Social Democratic party and the partial return to the tenets of the International, 233. Attempts towards unification, 233. The remaining divergence of ideas, 233. Preparations for the national labour convention in Pittsburgh, 234.

CHAPTER III

ATTEMPTED UNION — THE PITTSBURGH CONVENTION OF 1876 . . . . II, 235

The preliminary convention at Tyrone, Pennsylvania, and the two reports on a platform, 235. Discontinuity of the Pittsburgh convention from all preceding labour conventions, 236. The socialist draft of a platform, 237. The Greenback draft by the committee on resolutions, 237. Victory of the greenbackers and the withdrawal of the socialists, 238. Other planks in the platform, 238. Negative attitude towards politics, 238. Recommendation to organise secretly, 239. Failure to establish a permanent national federation of all labour organisations, 239.

CHAPTER IV

THE GREENBACK LABOR AGITATION, 1876–
1880 . . . . II, 240

The change in labour's attitude towards politics produced by the great strikes of 1877, 240. Organisation of the National party, 241. Fusion with the greenbackers, 241. State labour ticket in New York, 242. The "Greenback and Labor" combination in Pennsylvania, 242. Success of the Greenback party in the West, 244. The "national convention of labour and currency reformers" and the formation of the National party, 244. Predominance of the farmers, business men, and lawyers, 244. Platform, 245. Further Greenback successes, 245. T. V. Powderly, 245. Congressional election of 1878, 245. Obstacles to a unified movement in New York City, 246. "Pomeroy Clubs," 246. The organisation of the National Greenback Labor Reform party, 246. State election in Pennsylvania, 247. Analysis of the vote, 247. State election in Ohio, 248. Successes elsewhere, 248. Effect of the returning industrial prosperity, 249. Effect of the resumption of specie payment, 249. Tendency to fuse with the Democrats, 249. National pre-nomination conference, 249. Denis Kearney and Albert R. Parsons, 249. National nominating convention, 250. Labour demands, 250. Failure of the movement, 251.

CHAPTER V

THE ANTI-CHINESE AGITATION IN CALIFORNIA . . . . II, 252

Class struggle *versus* race struggle, 252. The depression in California, 253. Socialists and the strike movement, 253. The anti-Chinese riot, 253. Denis Kearney, 254. The Workingmen's party of California, 255. Its platform, 255. The sand-lot meetings, 253. Arrest of Kearney, 256. Nomination of delegates for the State constitutional convention, 256. Threats of riots and the "Gag Law," 257. Kearney's acquittal, 258. The state convention of the Workingmen's party, 258. First successes in elections, 259. Election for the state constitutional convention, 260. Alliance of the workingmen with the farmers, 260. The anti-Chinese clause in the Constitution, 260. Adoption of the constitution by the people, 261. The workingmen's success in the state election, 261. Success in the San Francisco municipal election, 261. Movement for the enforcement of the anti-Chinese clause in the state constitution, 262. Success in the state legislature but failure in the United States Circuit Court, 262. Second arrest of Kearney, 262. Beginning of the disintegration of the Workingmen's party, 263. Defeat in elections, 263. Relation to the national Greenback movement, 263. The end of the party, 264. Spread of the anti-Chinese movement among small employers, 264. The question before Congress, 265. The Congressional investigating committee, 265. Increase in the Chinese immigration during the early eighties, 266. The Representative Assembly of Trade and Labor Unions, 266. The white label, 266. The state labour convention, the League of Deliverance, and the boycott of Chinese made goods, 267. The Chinese Exclusion Act, 267.

CHAPTER VI

FROM SOCIALISM TO ANARCHISM AND SYN-
DICALISM, 1876–1884 . . . . II, 269

The Nationalised International. The preliminary union conference of all socialist organisations, 269. The Union Congress, 270. The Workingmen's party of the United States, 270. The resolution on political action, 270. Plan of organisation, 270. "Trade union" and "political" factions, 271. Phillip Van Patten, 272. The New Haven experiment with politics, 272. The Chicago election, 273. Factional differences, 273. Struggle for the *Labour Standard*, 274. Douai's effort of mediation, 275. Effect of the great strike of 1877 on the factional struggle, 276. The part played by the socialists in the strike movement, 277.

The Rush into Politics. Election results, 277. The Newark convention, 277. Control by the political faction, 278. The Socialist Labor party, 278. Strength of the trade union faction in Chicago, 279. Success in the Chicago election, 279. Failure in Cincinnati, 279. Van Patten's attitude towards trade unions, 280. Workingmen's military organisations, 280. Autumn election of 1870, 282. Chicago — the principal socialist centre, 282. Influence in the state legislature. 283. Chicago municipal election of 1879, 284. Persistent pro-trade union attitude of the Chicago socialists, 284. Effect of prosperity, 284. The national convention at Alleghany City, 284. Differences of opinion on a compromise with the greenbackers, 285. National greenback convention, 285. The "socialist" plank in the platform, 286. The double revolt: the "trade union" faction and the revolutionists in the East, 287. Attitude of the *New Yorker Volkszeitung*, 287. Referendum vote, 288. The decrease in the greenback vote, 289. Struggle between the compromisers and non-compromisers in the socialist ranks, 289.

The Evolution towards Anarchism and "Syndicalism." Chicago and New York, 291. The national convention of revolutionary socialists, 291. Affiliation with the International Working People's Association in London, 291. Attitude towards politics and trade unionism, 292. August Spies, 292. The proposed form of organisation, 292. Political action in Chicago once more, 292. Reorganisation in Chicago along revolutionary lines, 292. Johann Most and his philosophy, 293. The Pittsburgh convention and *Manifesto*, 295. Crystallisation of a "syndicalist" philosophy in Chicago, 296. Attitude towards the state, trade unionism politics, and violence, 296. A model "syndicalist" trade union, 296. The Red International., 298. Burnette G. Haskell and Joseph R. Buchanan, 298. Ebb of the Socialist Labor party, 300.

CHAPTER VII

THE NEW TRADE UNIONISM, 1878–1884 . . . II, 301

From Socialism to Pure and Simple Trade Unionism. Two lines of trade union action, 302. The plan for the organisation of the unskilled — The International Labor Union, 302. "Internationalism" and stewardism, 302. Trade unionism and eight-hour legislative action, 303. Programme of the International Labor Union, 303. Success among the textile workers, 304. First convention, 305. Steps towards an international trade union organisation, 305. Failure of the International Labor Union, 306. International Cigar Makers' Union — the new model for the organisations of the skilled, 306. Strasser and Gompers, 307. Crystallisation of the pure and simple trade union philosophy, 308. The railway brotherhoods, 309.

The First Successes. Trades' assemblies and their functions: economic, political, and legislative, 310. The building trades' councils, the first move toward industrialism, 312. The federations of the water-front trades in the South, 312. The Negro, 312. The formation of new national trade unions, 313. Their increase in membership, 1879–1883, 313. The control over locals, 314. Their benefit features, 314. Their attitude towards legal incorporation, 314. Predominance of the foreign-speaking element in the trade unions, 315. The charge that the foreigners in the trade unions deprive the American boy of his opportunity in industry, 315. Strikes in 1880 and 1881, 316. The iron workers' strike in 1882, 316. The boycott, 316. The New York *Tribune* boycott, 317.

Towards Federation. The attempts towards national federation since 1876, 318. The part played by the Knights of Labor in the last and successful attempt, 318. The Terre Haute conference, 318. Call for a convention, 320. Trade unions in the eighties and trade unions today, 320. The Pittsburgh convention of 1881, 321. The cause of the large representation of the Knights of Labor, 321. The formation of the Federation of Organised Trades and Labor Unions of the United States and Canada, 322. Attitude toward organising the unskilled, 323. Subordination of the city trades' assembly to the national trade union, 323. Legislative committee and the legislative programme, 324. The incorporation plank, 325. The shift from the co-operation argument to the one of trade agreements on the question of incorporation, 326. Second convention of the Federation, 326. Absence of the Knights of Labor and the iron and steel workers, 326. Lack of interest in the Federation on the part of the trade unions, 327. Convention of 1883, 328. The first appearance of friction with Knights of Labor, 329. Attitude towards a protective tariff 329. Miscellaneous resolutions, 330. Failure of the Federation as an organisation for obtaining legislation, 331.

CHAPTER VIII

END OF SECRECY IN THE KNIGHTS AND DEVIATION FROM FIRST PRINCIPLES, 1876–1884 . . . . II, 332

Secrecy and the movement for centralisation, 332. District Assembly 1 and the convention at Philadelphia, 1876, 333. The National Labor League of North America, 333. District Assembly 3 and the convention at Pittsburgh, 333. Lull in the movement for centralisation, 334. The Knights and the railway strikes of 1877, 334. Other strikes, 334. The General Assembly at Reading, Pennsylvania, January 1, 1878, 334. The Preamble, 335. First principles: education, organisation, and co-operation, 335. Form of organisation, 337. Special convention on the secrecy question, June, 1878, 338. Referendum vote, 338. The Catholic Church and secrecy in the Knights, 339. The compromise in 1879, 339. Final abolition of secrecy in 1881, 339. Growth and fluctuation in membership, 1878–1880, 339. The resistance fund, 340. Claims of the advocates of co-operation and education, 340. The compromise, 341. Compromise on political action, 341. Demands of the trade union element within the Knights, 342. National trade assembly, 343. Growth and fluctuation of membership, 1880–1883, 344. Component elements of the Knights, 344. Unattached local unions, 344. Weak national organisations, 345. Advantages to an incipient trade movement from affiliation with the Knights, 346. T. V. Powderly — Grand Master Workman in 1881, 347. Enthusiasm for strikes, 347. The telegraphers' strike in 1883, 348. Unorganised strikes, 349. The freight handlers' strike in New York, 349. Failure of the strikes conducted by the Knights, 349. Its effect on the fluctuation of membership, 350. Political faction, 350. Nonpartisan politics, 351. Partiality of the general officers for co-operation, 351. Independent politics in the West, 352. Co-operative beginnings, 352. Attitude of the trade unions towards the Knights, 352. Their endeavour to turn the Knights back to "First Principles," 352. General summary, 1876–1884, 353.

CHAPTER IX

THE GREAT UPHEAVAL, 1884–1886 . . . . II, 356

The New Economic Conditions. The difference between the labour movements in the early and the middle eighties, 357. The unskilled, 357. Extension of the railways into outlying districts, 358. Resultant intensification of competition among mechanics, 358. The industrial expansion, 358. Growth of cities, 359. Extension of the market and the supremacy of the wholesale jobber, 359. The impossibility of trade agreements, 359. Pools, 360. Immigration, 360. Exhaustion of the public domain, 360. Peculiarities of the depression, 1883–1885, 361. Reductions in wages, 361. The effect of the depression on the other economic classes, 362. Anti-monopoly slogan, 362.

Strikes and Boycotts, 1884–1885. Fall River spinners' strike, 362. Troy stove mounters' strike, 363. Cincinnati cigar makers' strike, 363. Hocking Valley coal miners' strike, 363. Vogue of the boycott, 364. Extremes in boycotting, 365. Boycott statistics, 1884–1885, 365. Resumption of the strike movement, 366. Saginaw Valley, Michigan strike, 366. Quarrymen's strike in Illinois, 367. Other strikes, 367. Shopmen's strikes on the Union Pacific in 1884, and the Knights of Labor, 367. Joseph R. Buchanan, 367. The Gould railway strike in 1885, 368. Gould's surrender, 369. Its enormous moral effect, 370. The general press and Order, 370. Keen public interest in the Order, 370. The New York *Sun* "story," 371. Effect on Congress, 372. The contract immigrant labour evil, 372. Situation in the glass-blowing industry, 372. The Knights and the anti-contract labour law, 372. "The Knights of Labor — the liberator of the oppressed," 373. Beginning of the upheaval, 373. Unrestrained class hatred, 374. Labour's refusal to arbitrate disputes, 374. Readiness to commit violence, 374.

The Eight-Hour Issue and the Strike. Growth of trade unions, 375. New trade unions formed, 1884–1885, 375. Convention of the Federation of Organised Trades and Labor Unions in 1884, 376. Eighthour issue, 376. Invitation to the Knights to co-operate, 377. Referendum vote by the affiliated organisations, 377. Advantage to the trade unions from the eight-hour issue, 378. Lukewarmness of the national leaders of the Knights, 378. Powderly's attitude, 378. Enthusiasm of the rank and file, 379. Pecuniary interest of the Order's organisers in furthering the eight-hour agitation, 379. Marvellous increase in the membership of the Knights, 381. Membership statistics for various States, 381. Racial composition, 382. Composition by trades, 382. The pace of organisation in Illinois by months, 382. The Southwest railway strike, 383. Its cause, 383. Its unusual violence, 383. Its failure, 384. The eight-hour strike, 385. Degree of its immediate success, 385. Its ultimate failure, 385. Unequal prestige of the Knights and the trade unions as a result of the strike, 385.

The Chicago Catastrophe. Effect of the Haymarket bomb on the eighthour strike, 386. Spread of the "syndicalists" influence among the German trade unions in 1884, 386. Formation of the Central Labor Union, 387. Its relation to the "syndicalists," 387. Its declaration of principles, 388. Relation of individual trade unions to the "syndicalists" in Chicago and St. Louis, 388. Agitation among the English speaking element, 389. *The Alarm*, 389. Strength of the Black International in Chicago and elsewhere, 390. Attitude of the Chicago Central Labour Union towards the eight-hour movement, 391. Eight-Hour Association of Chicago, 391. The McCormick Reaper Company lockout, 392. Beginning of the eight-hour strike in Chicago, 392. Riot near the McCormick works, 392. The "revenge circular," 392. The meeting of protest on Haymarket Square, 393. The bomb, 393. The trial, 394. Attitude of labour organisations, 394. Governor Altgeld's *Reasons for Pardoning Fielden, etc.,* 393. Judge Gary's reply, 393.

CHAPTER X

THE AFTERMATH, 1886–1887 . . . . II, 395

The Knights and the Federation. New National trade unions, 396. Efforts of the Knights to annex the skilled unions to strengthen the bargaining power of the unskilled, 397. Resistance of the skilled, 397. Situation in the early eighties, 397. Beginning of aggression, 398. District Assembly 49, of New York, 399. Conflict with the International Cigar Makers' Union, 399. The split in the latter, 399. Support of the seceders by District Assembly 49, 400. The strike in New York in January, 1886, 400. The settlement with District Assembly 49, 400. The fusion of the secessionists from the International Cigar Makers' Union with District Assembly 49, 401. Widening of the struggle, 401. Gompers' leadership, 402. General appeal to the trade unions, 402. Conflicts between the Knights and other trade unions, 402. Trade union conference in Philadelphia, 403. The "address," 404. The proposed treaty, 405. Reply of the Knights, 406. Refusal of the skilled trades to be used as a lever by the unskilled, 407. Further negotiations, 408. Declaration of war by the Knights, 408. Impetus for the complete unification of the trade unions, 409. Convention of the Federation of Organised Trades and Labor Unions in 1886, 410. The American Federation of Labor, 410. Its paramount activity — economic, 410. Another effort for a settlement, 411. The outcome, 411. Arbitrary action of District Assembly 49 of New York, 412. Return of the secessionist cigar makers to the International Union, 412. The Order's new conciliatory attitude, 412. Non-conciliatory attitude of the unions, 413.

The Subsidence of the Knights. Beginning of the backward tide in the Order, 413. The employers' reaction, 414. Forms of employers' associations, 414. Their aim, 414. Their refusal to arbitrate, 415. The means for the suppression of the Order, 415. The Knights' and the employers' attitude towards trade agreements, 416. The control over strikes in the Order, 416. The control over boycotts, 417. The strikes during the second half of 1886, 417. The Troy laundry workers' lockout, 418. The knit-goods industry lockout, 418. The Chicago packing industry lockout, 418. Powderly's weakness, 420. The 'longshoremen's strike in New York in 1887, 420. Its spread, 420. Its consequences, 421. The falling off in the Order's membership, 422. The recession of the wave of the unskilled, 422. Growing predominance of the middle-class element in the Order, 423. Success of the trade unions, 423. Chicago bricklayers' strike, 423. The employers' association and the trade agreement, 424. The situation in the bituminous coal industry, 425. The National Federation of Miners and Mine Laborers, 425. Relations with the Order, 425. The "interstate" trade agreement, 426. Drift towards trade union organisation within the Order, 427. History of the national trade assemblies, 1880–1885, 427. Fluctuation of the Order's policy, 427. Its cause, 427. Victory of the national trade assembly idea, 427.

CHAPTER XI

THE FAILURE OF CO-OPERATION, 1884-1887 . II, 430

The attitude towards co-operation of the several component elements of the Knights of Labor, 430. The inheritance from the sixties, 430. Powderly's attitude, 431. Co-operation in the early eighties, 431. Centralised co-operation, 432. The change to decentralised co-operation, 432. Statistics and nature of the co-operative enterprises, 433. Sectional distribution, 434. Co-operation among the coopers in Minneapolis, 434. The General Co-operative Board, 435. John Samuel, 435. Difficulties of the Board, 435. Participation by the Order, 436. Failure of the movement, 437. Its causes, 437. Lesson for the future, 438.

CHAPTER XII

THE POLITICAL UPHEAVAL, 1886-1887 . . . II, 439

The Greenback Labor party, 439. The Butler campaign, 440. New political outlook, 441. New York Central Labor Union, 441. Its radical declaration of principles, 442. Early activities, 442. The conspiracy law, 443. Campaign of 1882, 444. The Theiss boycott case, 444. Decision to go into politics, 445. Henry George's life and philosophy, 446. Comparison with John Swinton, 447. California experiences, 447. The "new agrarianism," 448. Availability as a candidate, 448. The platform, 449. Attitude of the socialists, 449. The Democratic nomination, 450. George-Hewitt campaign, 450. The *Leader*, 451. The general press, 451. Hewitt's view of the struggle, 452. George's view of the struggle, 452. Reverend Dr. McGlynn, 453. Attitude of the Catholic Church, 453. Powderly's attitude, 453. The vote, 453. Effect on the old parties, 454. Beginning of friction with the socialists, 454. Choice of a name for the party, 455. The "land and labour" clubs, 455. The county convention and the party constitution, 455. The call for a state convention, 456. Opposition of the socialists, 456. Their capture of the *Leader*, 456. The *Standard* and the attack upon the Catholic hierarchy, 456. The Anti-poverty society, 456. George's attitude towards the purely labour demands, 457. McMackin's ruling on the eligibility of socialists to membership, 457. The struggle in the assembly districts, 458. Attitude of the trade unions, 458. Gompers' attitude, 458. Unseating of the socialist delegates at the state convention, 459. The new platform, 460. The revolt of the socialists, 460. The Progressive Labor party, 460. Swinton's nomination, 461. The vote, 461. Causes of the failure of the movement, 461. The political movement outside New York, 461. The labour tickets, 462. The labour platforms, 462. Success in the elections, 462. Attitude of the Federation, 463. Powderly's attitude, 464. Efforts for national organisations, 464. The national convention in Cincinnati, 465. National Union Labor party, 465. Labour's attitude towards the new party, 465. Spring elections of 1887, 466. Autumn elections of 1887, 466. Spring elections of 1888, 467. Chicago socialists, 467. The Union Labor party presidential nomination, 468. United Labor party, 468. Predominance of the farmers in the Union Labor party, 468. Apostasy of many labour leaders, 469. Powderly's secret circular, 469. The vote, 469. The Order of the Videttes, 469.

CHAPTER XIII

REORGANISATION, 1888-1896 . . . . II, 471

The Perfection of the Class Alignment. Decreased influence of industrial fluctuations, 472. The trade-agreement idea, 472. The huge corporation, 472. The courts, 473.

CONTENTS   xix

The Progress of the Trade Unions. New unions, 473. The increase in
membership, 474. Strikes during 1888, 474. The Burlington strike,
474. Resumption of the eight-hour struggle, 475. Action of the convention of the Federation in 1888, 475. The agitational campaign, 476.
Selection of the carpenters as the entering wedge, 476. Their success,
477. The unwise selection of the miners to follow the carpenters, 477.
End of the eight-hour movement, 478. General appraisal of the movement, 478. Backwardness of the bricklayers on the shorter hours question, 478. The trade-agreement idea in the building trades, 479. The
closed shop, 479. The stove moulders' agreement, 480. Peculiarity of
the industry from the marketing standpoint, 480. Stove Founders' National Defense Association, 480. The St. Louis strike, 481. Further
strikes, 481. The national trade agreement of 1890, 481.
The Liquidation of the Knights of Labor. The decrease in membership, 1886–1890, 482. Relative increase in importance of the rural
membership, 482. Increasing aversion to strikes, 483. Relation to the
Federation, 483. Grievances of the trade unions, 483. Rival local trade
organisations, 483. Mutual " scabbing," 484. Refusal of the Order to
participate in the eight-hour movement of 1890, 485. Final efforts for
a reconciliation, 486. Their failure, 486. Withdrawal from the Order
of the national trade assemblies, 486. The shoemakers, 486. The machinists, 486. The spinners, 486. Situation in the coal mining industry,
487. United Mine Workers of America, 487. Situation in the beer
brewing industry, 488. Increasing predominance of politics and of the
farmer element in the Order, 488. The Southern Farmers' Alliance, 488.
The pivotal rôle of the merchants in the southern economy, 488. The
Northern Farmers' Alliance, 489. The Shreveport session of the Southern Alliance, 1887, 490. The Agricultural Wheel, 490. The session
of the Southern Alliance in 1889 and the abandonment of co-operation
for legislative reform, 490. Alliance with the Knights of Labor, 491.
The common programme, 491. The middle-class character of the Knights,
492. Political successes in 1890, 492. The Knights and an independent
reform party, 493. The Cincinnati convention in 1891 and the People's
party, 494. The Omaha convention in 1892, 494. The election of J. R.
Sovereign as Grand Master Workman of the Knights, 494. His farmer
philosophy, 494.
The Reverses of the Trade Unions. Neglect of legislation by the Federation, 495. The Homestead strike, 495. Negotiations for a new scale of
wages, 496. Battle with the Pinkertons, 496. Defeat of the union and
the elimination of unionism, 497. The miners' strike at Coeur d'Alène,
497. Quelling the strike, 498. The switchmen's strike in Buffalo,
498. Its failure, 498. The coal miners' strike in Tennessee, 498. Its
failure, 499. The lesson, 499. Gompers' view, 499. The stimulus to industrial unionism, 500. Eugene V. Debs and the American Railway
Union, 500. The panic of 1893, 501. Gompers' hopeful view, 501.
Trade Unions and the Courts. The miners' strike, 501. The Pullman
strike, 502. The general managers' association, 502. Court injunctions,
502. Violence, 502. Arrests for contempt of court, 502. The Pullman
boycott, 503. Attitude of the Federation, 503. End of the strike, 503.
Court record of the labour unions during the eighties, 503. Evolution
of the doctrine of conspiracy as applied to labour disputes, 504. The
real significance of Commonwealth v. Hunt (1842), 504. The first injunctions, 504. The legal justifications, 505. The Sherman law and the
Interstate Commerce Act, 505. Stages in the evolution of the doctrine
that the right to do business is property, 505. The part of the doctrine
of conspiracy in the theory of the injunction, 507. Injunction during the
eighties, 507. The " blanket injunction," 507. The Ann Arbor injunction, 507. The Debs case, 508. Statutes against " labour conspiracies," 508.

The Latest Attempt Towards a Labour Party. Causes of the change on the question of politics, 509. Convention of the Federation in 1892, 509. The "political programme," 509. Gompers' attitude in 1893, 510. The disputed plank 10, 511. Referendum vote, 511. Sporadic political efforts, 1894, 511. Their failure, 512. Gompers' attack on the "political programme," 512. The "legislative programme" at the convention in 1894, 513. Attitude of the convention in 1895, 513. The Federation and the campaign of 1896, 514.

The Socialists and Labour Organisations. The factional struggle, 1887–1889, 514. Final victory of the trade union faction, 515. Its hope of winning the Federation over to socialism, 516. Relation to the New York Central labour bodies, 516. Central Labor Federation, 516. The socialist question at the convention of the Federation in 1890, 517. Daniel De Leon and the new tactics, 517. The United Hebrew Trades, 518. Socialists and the Knights of Labor, 519. Socialist Trade and Labor Alliance, 519. Concluding summary, 519.

CHAPTER XIV

RECENT DEVELOPMENTS (FROM 1896) . . II, 521

Industrial Prosperity and the Growth of the Federation. The extension into new regions and into hitherto untouched trades, 522. Lack of success among the unskilled, 523. Industrial Workers of the World, 523. The floaters and the non-English speaking workingmen, 523. The success of the miners, 523. The garment workers' unions, 524. Progress of the trade-agreement idea, 524. Its test during the anthracite miners' strike in 1902. 525. The manufacturers' control over access to the market, 525. The trust and its effect on unionism, 526. The "open shop movement," 526. The structural iron industry, 526. The trade-agreement outlook, 527. The awakening of the public to the existence of a labour question, 527. The evolution of public opinion since the eighties, 528. The public and labour legislation, 528. Organised labour's lukewarmness toward labour legislation, 529. Its cause, 529. Its effect on the administration of labour laws, 530. The courts, 530. The Danbury Hatters', the Adair, and the Buck's Stove and Range cases, 530. The failure of lobbying, 531. "Reward your friends and punish your enemies," 531. The alliance with the Democrats, 531. The socialists, 532. The effect of the litigation and politics on economic organisation, 533. Problem of the unskilled, 533. Three forms of industrialism, 533. The "one big union," 533. Industrialism of the middle stratum, 534. "Craft industrialism," 534. The National Building Trades' Council, 535. The Structural Building Trades' Alliance and the theory of "basic" unions, 535. The Building Trades' Department, 536. Other departments, 536. Forced amalgamations, 537. New conception of "craft autonomy," 537. The probable future structure of American labour organisations, 537. The "concerted movement," 537.

BIBLIOGRAPHY

BIBLIOGRAPHY . . . . II, 541

General Survey, 541. Colonial and Federal Beginnings, 548. Citizenship, 555. Trade Unionism, 561. Humanitarianism, 566. Nationalisation, 571. Upheaval and Reorganisation, 576.

PART FIVE

NATIONALISATION (1860–1877)
BY JOHN B. ANDREWS

HISTORY OF LABOUR IN THE UNITED STATES

CHAPTER I

ECONOMIC CONDITIONS

New Conditions. Railway Construction. Through freight lines, 4. Railway consolidations, 4. Appearance of the wholesale jobber, 5. The first national trade unions, 5.

The Moulders. William H. Sylvis, 6. The effect of the extension of the market on the moulder's trade, 6. The national union, 7. Its weakness, 7.

The Machinists and Blacksmiths. Evils in the trade, 7. The national union, 9. Strike against the Baldwin Locomotive Works, 9. The outbreak of the War and depression, 9. Other national unions, 10.

Unemployment and Impending War. The workingmen's opposition to War, 10. Louisville and Philadelphia, 10. Fort Sumter and labour's change of attitude, 11.

WHILE the country was engrossed in Civil War and Reconstruction, the American labour movement developed for the first time, almost unnoticed, its characteristic national features. This period witnessed the distinctly American philosophies of greenbackism and the eight-hour day; the rise of the agitation for the exclusion of Oriental labour; the invention of the trade union label; the first national trade agreement; the establishment of the first government bureau of labour; the organisation of the first permanent labour lobby at Washington; the enactment of the first eight-hour legislation and the earliest laws against "conspiracy" and "intimidation." The period also saw the organisation of the first national employers' association, and the first national labour party. Pre-eminently, it was the period of nationalisation in the American labour movement. Back of it all lay the nationalisation of the economic life of the country.

The fifties had been a decade of extensive construction of railroads. There was an increase from but 8,389 miles of railway in 1850 to 30,793 in 1860.   Before 1850 there was more traffic by water than by rail.   After 1860 the relative importance of land and water transportation was reversed.

Furthermore, the most important railroad building during the ten years preceding 1860 was the construction of east and west trunk lines.   There were seven such roads: the Western & Atlanta connected the seaboard cities of Georgia with the Tennessee River in 1850; the New York & Erie was opened in 1851; the Pennsylvania, in 1852; the Baltimore & Ohio and the Canadian Grand Trunk, in 1853; the New York Central, as a result of consolidation, in 1854; and the Virginia system was connected with the Nashville & Chattanooga and the Memphis & Charleston roads in 1858.   The western ends of these lines were still points like Buffalo and Pittsburgh, rather than Chicago or St. Louis, but alliance with contemporaneously constructed roads of the Middle West gave practically all of them an outlet in the far West.   During the sixties, owing to the War, railway construction fell off to 16,090 miles, as against 22,404 during the preceding decade.   Yet these years marked developments in the railway business which, from the standpoint of the nationalisation of the market and the increase of competition between manufacturing centres, were no less epoch-making than the construction of the trunk lines.   These were the establishment of through lines for freight and the consolidation of connecting roads.

The through-freight lines came into existence soon after the beginning of the War, with the discontinuance of the Mississippi River as an outlet for western products and the necessity of sending shipments eastward by rail.   These lines, whether the cars belonged to separate companies established for that purpose, or to co-operating railway companies, greatly hastened freight traffic by abolishing the necessity for transshipment.

The most notable consolidations were those of three important trunk lines: the Pennsylvania, the Erie, and the New York Central & Hudson River.   The Pennsylvania then purchased the roads running west of Pittsburgh and thus obtained direct connections with Chicago, Cincinnati, and St. Louis. The New York Central consolidated with the Hudson River & Harlem Road at its eastern end, and in the West with the Lake

Shore & Michigan Southern, forming direct connection between New York and Chicago. The Erie increased its length from 459 miles to 1,355. Important consolidations were also made by the Philadelphia & Reading and the other anthracite roads. Among the western and southwestern lines which rapidly increased their mileage were the Chicago & Northwestern, the Burlington, and the Milwaukee & St. Paul.

Arteries of traffic had thus extended from the eastern coast to the Mississippi Valley. Local markets had widened within fifteen years to embrace half a continent. Stoves manufactured in Albany were now displayed in St. Louis by the side of stoves made in Detroit. Competition had increased and intensified.

This intensification of competition and the separation of producers and consumers resulted in the development of the middleman as the dominant figure in industry. Through his extensive purchasing opportunities and his specialised methods of reaching customers, he possessed a kind of " intangible " capital by which he dominated the market and, in consequence, credit.

The existence of this common oppressor — the wholesale jobber or middleman — was felt both by wage-earners and by employers, while farmers were in addition oppressed by the railroads. As a natural consequence came the coalition of the " producing classes " against " capital."

Spectacular also were the direct effects of the Civil War upon labour in transforming an army of productive labourers into an army of non-productive consumers, and then at the end of four years suddenly pouring them back from the fields of battle upon the fields of industry. But still more sweeping were the indirect effects of unprecedented fluctuations in prices and the cost of living, which were closely linked with inflation and contraction of the paper currency.

The industrial depression which followed the panic of 1857 destroyed almost completely the modest beginnings of labour organisation made during the preceding years. A large number of the trade unions went under. Those, however, which were able to withstand the stress were forced to combine with similar organisations in the same trade and to form national unions. The two important national trade unions which were born under these circumstances were the Molders' International Union and the National Union of Machinists and Blacksmiths, both established in 1859.

The leading spirit in the moulders' union was William H. Sylvis, afterwards the first great figure in the American labour movement. His career was typical of the period. Born in the little village of Armagh, Pennsylvania, in 1828, his father's failure in the business of wagon maker in 1837 forced him early into apprenticeship in a foundry. First as journeyman, then part proprietor of a foundry, then again as journeyman in Philadelphia in 1852, he typified during this period in his life the easy shift between skilled mechanic and small master.[1]

The conditions which forced the moulders' union to the front and made Sylvis the recognised head, not only of his own union, but also of the entire movement of the sixties, are described by Sylvis himself. Speaking of the intense competition brought on by the extension of the railway to the West, and immediately preceding the formation of the national union of moulders in 1859, he said:

" They [the employers] saw in the future a possibility of monopolizing almost the entire trade of the country, and set themselves about doing so. In the first place, it was necessary for them to mark out a line of policy, which, if closely followed, would insure this result. This they did, and the first act of the drama (I might, perhaps, more properly say tragedy, for it resulted in squeezing the blood and tears from its victims), was to reduce their margin of profits to the lowest possible standard, that they might go into the market below all others. Owing to fluctuations in the price of material, their profits would sometimes disappear entirely. This they used as an argument to their workmen, telling them that owing to the unfair competition of other manufacturers, they were unable to advance their selling prices, and that being unable to compete without loss they must either close up or reduce wages. The men being unorganised and supposing that they were being honestly dealt with, readily submitted to a reduction. This reduction of prices was small, but after being repeated two or three times, the men became restive and disposed to complain. A few were bold enough to remonstrate, but a guillotine had been prepared, and their heads immediately dropped into the basket. . . . To effectually smother in its infancy any disposition the men might have to fraternize . . . they commenced to work upon their prejudices. They succeeded in a short time in arraigning the representatives of one

1 See J. C. Sylvis, *The Life, Speeches, Labors and Essays of William H. Sylvis.*

religion or one nation against those of another. . . . This accomplished, they found no difficulty in the further prosecution of the nefarious plans. Then commenced the contract system . . . Next, each man was required to furnish his own tools at their prices. . . . Next came the Order System. . . . Simultaneous with this was introduced the 'helper system' . . . [and] the stoves were cut up, that is, each man made one piece. . . . Thus this system went on until it became customary for each man to have from one to five boys; and . . . prices became so low that men were obliged to increase the hours of labor, and work much harder; and then could scarcely obtain the plainest necessaries of life. . . ." [2]

The iron-moulders of Philadelphia organised their first trade union in 1855, but Sylvis did not join until 1857, after a strike in the foundry where he worked. He was soon elected recording secretary of the union and his career as a trade unionist had begun.

The conditions in the moulders' trade became so desperate that a strong sentiment developed among the various local unions in favour of a national organisation. The union in Philadelphia took the lead, and a national convention, composed of thirty-five delegates representing twelve unions, met July 5, 1859, in Philadelphia, largely as a result of Sylvis' efforts. The convention established a national organisation with limited powers.

Although it could not levy an assessment, the national union conducted to a successful issue the strike which broke out in Albany at the time the convention was in session. The organisation made good progress and organised forty-four locals during 1860. Strikes, however, became so numerous and the demands upon National Treasurer Sylvis for assistance became so frequent that the third [3] national convention, which was held in Cincinnati, January 8, 1861, was obliged to adopt a stringent resolution against careless strikes by locals.

The other union which furnished the most consistent trade union leader of the sixties, Jonathan C. Fincher, was that of the machinists and blacksmiths. Here, again, the greatest leader of the organisation has described the development of his craft, and the reasons for the organisation of the union.

[2] *Fincher's Trades' Review*, July 18, 1863. Cited hereafter as *Fincher's*.
[3] The second convention was held in Albany six months after the Philadelphia convention.

Fortunately, it is possible to give much of the story in Fincher's own words. Writing in 1872, he said; [4]

" Still within the recollection of grey-headed machinists and blacksmiths [are] the days when a machinist was a compound of handiwork, a kind of cross between a millwright and a whitesmith, a fitter, finisher, locksmith, and so forth. But building of cotton machinery, steam engines, etc., required steady employment at what is now called machine work, and it soon led to the acknowledgment of the craft as a special trade or calling. . . . The machinists began to consider themselves a branch of the great industrial family of civilization. They took part in the struggle for the ten-hour system, and suffered in common with other mechanics in all the fluctuations of trade. Several attempts at organisation were made in the principal seaboard cities, but were short-lived and restricted in their sphere.

" Unfair dealing on the part of the employers had long been a grievance with the men. The baneful system of paying in orders was common. The taking on of as many apprentices as could possibly be worked was considered the indubitable right of every employer. . . . In dull times, men with families to support would find themselves out of work, while the shops were filled with apprentice boys. . . . The writer of this was one of some twenty young men kept at work after the great financial crash of 1857, while there were sixty apprentices employed. . . . Over one hundred and fifty journeymen had been discharged from the shop within two months. . . . A marked difference had come over the employers during the same time. In the early days of mechanism in this country but few shops employed many men. Generally the employer was head man; he knew his men personally; he instructed his apprentices and kept a general supervision of the business. By that means every workman knew his employer, and if aught went astray, there was no circumlocution office to go through to have an understanding about it. But as the business came to be more fully developed, it was found that more capital must be employed and the authority and supervision of the owner or owners must be delegated to superintendents and under foremen. In this manner men and masters became estranged and the gulf could only be bridged by a strike, when, perhaps, the representatives of the workingmen might be admitted to the office and allowed to state their case. It was to resist this combination of capital, which had so changed the character of the employers, that led to the formation of the union. . . . Competent journeymen counselled together . . . in private parlors of the different members of the proposed union. Some favored embracing all forms of iron workers; others

4 *Machinists' and Blacksmiths' International Journal*, February and March, 1872.

desired to restrict it to only machinists; finally it was decided that the machinists and machine blacksmiths were the only trades whose interests were inseparable, hence the union of the M. & B's." [5]

Beginning with 14 members, the first union of these combined crafts, formed after the panic, was established in Philadelphia, in April, 1858. During the following summer the membership grew to 300. One year later there were unions organised in 5 cities of three different States, which on March 3, 1859, sent 21 delegates to the first national convention in Philadelphia, where they established the national union. The number of local unions increased to 12 during 1859 and, at the time of the convention of November, 1860, there were 57 unions in the organisation, covering all sections of the country,[6] with a total membership in good standing of 2,828.

In March, 1860, the union was forced to call a strike in the Baldwin Locomotive Works, Philadelphia, against a proposed reduction of wages and the payment of arrear wages in the company's stock at extortionate terms. The strike lasted four months and although the employers did not give in, the fruit of victory was with the men. The prestige of having combatted the greatest shop in the country to a drawn conclusion proved that the organisation was a power in the land and that its resources were not to be despised.

Secretary Fincher, who was to become one of the most influential figures in the whole labour movement in the later developments of the sixties, was ripening into confident trade union leadership. " Little dreamed that crew of the fearful gales they were to encounter, and the terrible shipwrecks they were to witness in their eventful voyage," wrote this same leader when looking back upon this period in later years.

Meanwhile, the political troubles of the country multiplied and so embarrassed the business of the nation that it was impossible to forecast the future for even a day. Following the breaking out of the War of the Rebellion in the spring of 1861, the union suffered severely in the loss of members who volunteered, as well as in the loss of all locals in the Southern States,

---

[5] During the first year it was a secret organisation and the full name of the union was carefully suppressed.

[6] Of these there were 7 in New York State, 12 in Pennsylvania, 6 in Illinois, 5 in Massachusetts, 3 in New Jersey, 2 in Ohio, and 7 in States which later seceded from the Union.

so that the summer of that year was most gloomy. At one time the secretary reported 87 unions on the list of active working organisations; but the convulsions of this year brought the number down to about 30, with a greatly diminished membership, and the tendency was continually down. At the national convention in the fall of 1861 delegates were present from only 4 States, Massachusetts, Missouri, Wisconsin, and Kentucky. So discouraging was the prospect that the president of the union declined to go to the convention as he did not believe that a session would be held.

Other national trade unions which came into existence before the War were the typographical, organised in 1850, with a membership of 2,182 in 1857; the stonecutters, organised with 13 locals and a total membership of 3,500 in 1853; and the national union of hat finishers, organised in 1854.

With only these few national trade unions in existence in 1860, the labour movement of the period had not really begun. The mass organisation of labour occurred later when the unprecedented prosperity during the War had forced up the cost of living.

UNEMPLOYMENT AND IMPENDING WAR

Lincoln's election was immediately followed by a period of severe unemployment, and wage-earners generally felt that their immediate interests were made to suffer by the prospective war. Open opposition began in the border States with the moulders of Louisville, Kentucky. A workingmen's mass meeting was called on December 28, 1860, which was addressed by William Llorian, Robert P. Gilchrist, and others, friends of W. H. Sylvis. A resolution was carried declaring the allegiance of the workingmen to the Union and the Constitution. It laid the blame for the present political crisis upon the politicians of both sides, affirming that workingmen had no real or vital interest in the mere abstract questions used to divide the masses. It also called for general organisation of the workingmen and for a national workingmen's convention to decide what concerted action should be taken in order to avert the crisis.[7]

7 Sylvis, *Life, Speeches, Labors and Essays*, 42–46.

A similar movement led by Sylvis was started in Philadelphia. A delegate body was organised in January, which gave its endorsement to the Crittenden compromise [8] and sent a committee of thirty-three to present a memorial to the State legislature in Harrisburg and to both houses of Congress.[9] The committee was favourably received by the legislature, and in Washington the Pennsylvania members of Congress promised their support to the Crittenden resolution. In Newark, New Jersey, a mass meeting of unemployed likewise indorsed the compromise.[10] A similar movement was on foot in Reading, Pennsylvania; in Norfolk, Petersborough, and Richmond, Virginia; Louisville, Cincinnati, St. Louis and in many localities in the States bordering on Pennsylvania.[11]

The national convention of workingmen met in Philadelphia on February 22, 1861. It contained representatives from several States, though it was not as well attended as had been expected. It was called to order by Sylvis, who took an active part in the discussion.[12] The convention was preceded by a procession of workingmen and by a public meeting at which the delegates furnished the chief speakers. The resolutions adopted at the meeting probably represent the best available statement of the attitude of workingmen with regard to the War. They read:

" *Resolved,* That we earnestly invoke zealous and energetic action at once by Congress, either by the adoption of the Crittenden, Bigler or Guthrie amendments, or by some other full and clear recognition of the equal rights of the South in the Territories by such enactment for constitutional action as will finally remove the question of slavery therein from our National Legislature. . . .

" *Resolved,* That our Government never can be sustained by bloodshed, but must live in the affections of the people; we are, therefore, utterly opposed to any measures that will evoke civil war, and the workingmen of Philadelphia will, by the use of all constitutional means, and with our moral and political influence, oppose

---

8 The chief provisions of the compromise introduced in the House of Representatives by Crittenden, of Kentucky, in January, 1861, were that in all territories acquired now or hereafter north of latitude 36° and 30', slavery should be prohibited, but south of this line it should be allowed by Congress and protected as property. States formed from territory north of that line should be free or slave as they might provide in their constitutions.

9 Philadelphia *Enquirer,* Jan. 8 and 28, 1861.

10 New York *Tribune,* Jan. 10, 1861.

11 Philadelphia *Enquirer,* Feb. 18, 1861.

12 Sylvis, *Life, Speeches, Labors and Essays,* 43.

any such extreme policy, or a fratricidal war thus to be inaugurated." [13]

Before adjourning, the convention made the committee of thirty-three permanent and charged it with continuing the agitation and organisation. It held several meetings and its corresponding secretary, Sylvis, who, through his prominent position in the moulders' national union possessed wide connections over the country, devoted his time to this work.

On April 12 the first gun was fired on Sumter, and thereupon peace agitation was at an end. The War once broken out, the northern wage-earners abandoned their former opposition and vied with the farmers in furnishing volunteers. Entire local unions enlisted at the call of President Lincoln, and Sylvis himself assisted in recruiting a company composed of moulders, of which he became orderly sergeant. [14]

13 Philadelphia *Enquirer*, Feb. 23, 1861.

14 The time for which they enlisted permitted them to do little but assist in protecting Washington from threatened invasion by General Lee. Sylvis then returned to Philadelphia.

CHAPTER II

THE WAR PERIOD, 1861–1865

War and Prices. The lethargy of the trade unions, 13. The legal tender acts, 14. War prosperity and its beneficiaries, 14. Cost of living and wages, 15.

The Labour Press. *Fincher's Trades' Review*, 15. The *Workingmen's Advocate*, 16. The *Daily Evening Voice*, 16. Other papers, 17.

Local Unions. Incentive for organisation, 17. The wave of organisation during the War, 18.

Trades' Assemblies. Progress of the Trades' assemblies, 22. Strikes, 23. The functions of the trades' assemblies, 23. The Philadelphia trades' assembly — a typical assembly, 24.

Employers' Associations. Local and national associations, 26. The Employers' General Association of Michigan, 26. Reply of the trade unions, 29. Richard F. Trevellick, 29. The New York Master Builders' Association, 29. Master mechanics of Boston, 30. Associated employers and the eight-hour movement of 1872, 31. Attempted "exclusive agreement," 32. Attitude towards trade agreements, 33.

The International Industrial Assembly of North America. The national trade unions and federation, 33. The trades' assemblies and federation, 34. The Louisville call, 34. The convention in Louisville, 35. Assistance during strikes, 36. Attitude towards co-operation and legislation, 37. The constitution and the national trade unions, 37. Politics, 38. The causes of failure, 38.

Distributive Co-operation. Cost of living, 39. Thomas Phillips, 39. The Rochdale plan, 40. The turn towards productive co-operation, 41.

WAR AND PRICES

THE first effects of the War were the paralysis of business and the increase in unemployment.[1] The combined effect upon the existing labour organisations, both of the industrial disturbance and of the enlistment of their members, was demoralising. At the convention of the machinists and blacksmiths held in Pittsburgh in November, 1861, National Secretary Fincher, the only officer present, reported that the membership in good standing had decreased from 2,717 to 1,898 during the six months from April to October of that year, and that the subordinate unions betrayed but little activity.[2] The effect

---

[1] Rhodes, *History of the United States*, III, 122, 162, 171.

[2] International Union of Machinists and Blacksmiths of the United States of America, *Proceedings*, 1861, p. 21.

upon the moulders' organisation was still more demoralising. The national union seemed to have ceased existence by the middle of 1861, and the national convention, which was to be held in January, 1862, failed to meet. This period of industrial stagnation, however, lasted only until the middle of 1862.

The legal tender acts of February 25, and of July 11, 1862, threw $300,000,000 of greenbacks into circulation. As a result, prices began rapidly to increase, causing a revival in industry and creating ample employment for those wage-earners who did not join the army. The further issue of greenbacks to the amount of $750,000,000 authorised by Congress in January and March of 1863 added to the impetus of the upward move- ment of prices. This, acting together with the enormously grown demand upon industries for the supply of the army, brought on an unprecedented degree of prosperity. Wholesale prices, during 1863, increased 59 per cent above the level of 1860, 125 per cent during 1864, and 107 per cent during 1865.[3]

The fruits of prosperity were shared unequally by the four industrial classes, the merchant-jobber, the employing manu- facturers, the farmers, and the wage-earners. Merchants who contracted in advance for the output of manfacturers were the largest beneficiaries of the rapidly rising prices. Many of them were able to realise enormous profits on government con- tracts so that the foundations of numerous great fortunes were laid during this period. The manufacturer and the farmer benefited perhaps more moderately. The high war tariff which was adopted originally as a revenue measure enabled the manu- facturer to begin to accumulate capital and was thus a potent factor in building up a class of capitalistic employers. The farmers were equally benefited by the tide of prosperity. The prices of their products having risen on an average 143 per cent from 1860 to 1864, they forgot their grievances against the railroads and the middlemen and relinquished the small attempt at organisation which they had made in the years im- mediately preceding the War.

3 " Wholesale Prices," in United States Bureau of Labor Statistics, *Bulletin*, No. 114, p. 149. See above, chart, I, 11.

The only class which suffered rather than benefited from the
wave of prosperity was the wage-earning class. It is true that
opportunities for employment increased and by that much the
wage-earner was a direct beneficiary of the high prices. But,
on the other hand, the cost of living was rapidly increasing
while wages were lagging approximately six months behind.

In July, 1862, retail prices in greenbacks were 15 per cent
above the level of 1860 and wages remained stationary; in July,
1863, retail prices were 43 per cent above those of 1860 and
wages only 12 per cent above; in July, 1864, retail prices rose
70 per cent and wages to 30 per cent above 1860; and in July,
1865, prices rose to 76 per cent and wages to only 50 per cent
above the level of 1860.[4] The unequal pace of the two movements inevitably led the wage-earners to organise along trade
union lines in order to protect the standard of living.

THE LABOUR PRESS

It was this period of nationalisation in the American labour
movement that witnessed the establishment of a labour press
upon a lasting foundation. No less than 120 daily, weekly,
and monthly journals of labour reform appeared during the
decade 1863–1873.[5]

Perhaps the most influential labour paper of the period —
certainly one of the best labour papers ever published in the
United States — was *Fincher's Trades' Review,* published at
Philadelphia. The first issue appeared as a four-page paper
on June 6, 1863, and it continued weekly during the following three years. As secretary of the most important national
trade union, that of the machinists and blacksmiths, Fincher
had already established, in January, 1862, a regular monthly
journal for his own organisation, and was in close touch with all
the active labour leaders throughout the country. This enabled
him to make his paper a true mirror of the national labour
movement, a truly national labour paper. Advertising was
ignored from the first, and financial support was entirely dependent upon subscriptions and donations from trade unions.

4 Mitchell, "Gold. Prices and Wages
under the Greenback Standard," in University of California, *Publications*, I, 279.

See also *Doc. Hist.*, IX, 67, on the cost
of living.
5 *Doc. Hist.*, X, 142.

Beginning with a circulation of less than 5,000 copies, the paper gradually extended its field of influence until, at the end of the first year, it had doubled both in size and sales. At the end of two and one-half years (December, 1865) over 11,000 copies were printed. The territory covered included 31 out of the 36 States, the District of Columbia, 3 provinces of Canada, and 8 cities in England. The paper thus became a powerful organ for the propaganda of trade unionism, co-operation, and shorter hours. Among its colabourers were the most prominent labour leaders of the time, William H. Sylvis, Richard F. Trevellick, Thomas Phillips, and Ira Steward.

A few labour papers had been published in the years immediately before the War. The *Mechanics' Own* was published in New York for eleven months during 1859–1860, and advocated arbitration. Another paper by the same name was published in Philadelphia a little later. The *New England Mechanic* appeared in 1859, and in New York during the same year the *American Banker and Workingmen's Leader* was published for a short time. The need for a German labour press had been keenly felt in New York City and the *Arbeiter* and the *Soziale Republik* appeared in 1858. None of these papers, however, survived the depression which immediately followed the beginning of the War.

The principal labour papers during the war, beside *Fincher's,* were the Chicago weekly *Workingman's Advocate* and the *Daily Evening Voice* of Boston. The *Workingman's Advocate* was founded in July, 1864, during a printers' strike and was edited during all of the thirteen years of its existence by Andrew C. Cameron,[6] who from the standpoint both of length of service and ability as a practical writer was the greatest labour editor of his time. The *Workingman's Advocate* was the official organ of the Chicago Trades' Assembly and later also of the National Labor Union. In its editorial columns it reflected the views of the western labour movement, which inclined more than the eastern to active participation in politics.

The *Daily Evening Voice* of Boston, the official organ of the workingmen's assembly of Boston and vicinity, was of still

6 In the year 1906 the son of Mr. Cameron presented a file of this paper to the Wisconsin University Library.

greater importance. It was started early in December, 1864, by the locked-out printers of Boston, and continued by the various local unions on a co-operative basis until its suspension in October, 1867. During the last twenty months it was supplemented by a weekly edition. The *Voice* was not only a labour paper but also an interesting general paper; it contained telegraphic news and gave much space to general local news; it also differed from the other labour papers by its large amount of advertisements. The *Voice* enjoyed a large circulation in the New England States and accurately reflected the movement of that section, which was strongly influenced by the agitation for shorter hours.

Another noteworthy paper, the *Weekly Miner,* was established at Belleville, Illinois, by John Hinchcliffe, as the official organ of the American Miners' Association, on May 23, 1863, one week before the appearance of *Fincher's Trades' Review*. It lasted until 1865, when a libel suit led to its removal to St. Louis, where it survived one more year under the name *Miner and Artisan*. About the same time, 1864–1866, a second labour paper by the name of *Daily Press* was published in St. Louis. It was established, as were many labour papers of this period, on a co-operative basis, by striking printers. The editors of nearly all of these labour papers believed themselves pioneers in the field, so completely had the movements of the thirties and the forties been forgotten.

LOCAL UNIONS

The organisation of local trade unions probably began in the second half of the year 1862, but reliable information concerning the movement can be secured only from the beginning of June, 1863, when Fincher began publishing his weekly, *Fincher's Trades' Review*.

The question of wages played a large part in the organisations which took place during this period, though demands for wages were not the only cause of organisation. *Fincher's* says that although wages were good, in fact, had risen from 25 to 50 per cent, this did not mean that there were more opportunities for the workingman to save; for prices had risen to a still greater extent than wages. Further, when the War ceased, there was likely to be considerable unemployment, and the proper way to meet the situation was to organise. With this warning to the trades, organisations increased at a rapid pace.[7]

Another incentive given to the organisation of locals was the organisation of trades' assemblies. In Albany, New York, the printers' union flourished, but organisation was not confined to the printers alone. Other unions were doing as well, or better. New unions composed of members of occupations which never before thought of such a thing in their trade, were organised and joined the trades' assembly. The constitution of the assembly provided that any organised trade with twenty-five members, which sent duly accredited delegates to the assembly, would receive the support of all unions there represented.[8] What was true of this assembly was no doubt true of others.

The wave of organisation is shown by the growing size of the trade union directory printed in Fincher's paper. Occupying but half a column in June, 1863, it grew to a full column during the next month, to two columns six months later, to four columns in July, 1864, and finally to a seven-column page in May, 1865. At the end of each half year during the first eighteen months, beginning with June, 1863, the record thus preserved was 20 trades embracing 79 unions in December, 1863; 40 trades and 203 unions in June, 1864; and 53 trades embracing 207 unions in December of that year. In November, 1865, there were 61 different trades organised with approximately 300 unions.

The following table shows the number of unions reported in *Fincher's* up to December, 1863, and the increase during the next year. The year 1864 saw the number of unions increased from 79 to 270. By November, 1865, but 8 more trades were organised and something like 30 locals added; so that the year 1863–1864 represents the most marked growth of local organisation.

7 *Fincher's*, July 4, 1863.   8 *Ibid.*, Aug 6, 1864.

Table Showing Growth of Local Organisation from December,
1863, to December, 1864

State	Dec., 1863	Dec., 1864
Connecticut	2	6
Delaware	..	1
Illinois	1	10
Indiana	3	17
Kentucky	2	8
Maine	1	7
Maryland	..	1
Massachusetts	17	42
Michigan	4	9
Missouri	4	9
New Hampshire	3	5
New Jersey	4	10
New York	16	74
Ohio	4	16
Pennsylvania	15	44
Rhode Island	1	7
Tennessee	..	2
Vermont	1	..
Virginia	1	1
Wisconsin	..	1
Total	79	270

Of the trades in 1863, the machinists and blacksmiths had
the largest number of unions, 29, and following closely were
the moulders with 24. Then followed the carpenters and joiners with 4, and other trades with numbers ranging from 1 to 3
each. These 79 unions were scattered over 16 States. New
York, Pennsylvania, and Massachusetts being the leading industrial States at this time, it is only natural that they should
have the largest number of unions. They lead with 48 out of
the 79 unions, or 60 per cent of the whole. The unions were
pretty evenly divided among these three States, Massachusetts
having 17, New York 16, and Pennsylvania, 15. Virginia,
the most southerly State, had 1, Maine, the most northerly, 1,
and Missouri, the most westerly, had 4. So up to 1864, unionism was confined, with one exception, to the region east of the
Mississippi River and mainly to the northeastern and central
part of that region.

The beginning of 1864 showed a phenomenal activity among wage-earners. *Fincher's Trades' Review* for March 12 of that year gives an account of labour activities for New York and vicinity, which was typical of other places:

" The Slate and Metal Roofers are organising and it is thought they will demand $3 per day. The Segar makers are preparing to secure better wages. The Longshoremen have demanded $2.50 per day of nine hours, from the 7th inst. The Jewellers have decided to add 25 per cent to their wages. The Bricklayers demanded $2.50 per day, House Carpenters demand $2.50 per day, Painters $2.50 per day, Dry dock practical painters $2.50 per day, Plumbers $2.50 per day, Blue Stone cutters and Flaggers, $2.50 per day. The Piano Forte makers demand an increase of 25 per cent on former wages. The Iron Moulders ask for 15 per cent advance. The Cabinetmakers and Tailors are also moving. The Carvers ask 15 per cent addition. The Shipwrights are preparing for a struggle. The Brush makers have been conceded 25 per cent advance in New York by all employers but three. Wheelwrights and Blacksmiths are in council. The Bookbinders are organised. The Coopers have obtained their increase recently sought, and will make no immediate demand for change. The Coach Painters and coach Trimmers will shortly remodel their list of prices. Several of the trades mentioned above have obtained the wages sought by amicable treaty; and let us hope that all may succeed without the resort of a strike."

As might be expected from the foregoing, the year 1864 was a year of rapid increase in the number of local unions. The number of trades increased to 53 and the number of unions to 270. Some of the unions showed a big increase over 1863. For instance, the machinists and blacksmiths' locals increased from 29 to 46, the carpenters and joiners from 4 to 17, and several of the other unions in proportion. But the greatest increase in any trade was among the moulders, who increased their local organisations from 24 to 65.

As in 1863, the States having the largest number of locals in 1864 were New York, Pennsylvania, and Massachusetts, and the percentage which they had of the whole remained about the same.

The number of States in which locals were organised did not increase greatly; in fact, but four States were added to the list and these with a total of but five unions. Furthermore, unionism was not extended any farther westward, and Virginia still continued to be the most southerly State.

The following list of 61 trade unions is presented in the chronological order in which the union notices appeared in *Fincher's Trades' Review,* between June, 1863, and November 25, 1865.

Machinists and Blacksmiths, Moulders, Carpenters and Joiners, Painters, Plasterers, Printers, House Carpenters, Cabinetmakers and Carvers, Tin Plate and Sheet-Iron Workers, Tailors, Upholsterers, Bricklayers, Garment Cutters, Shipwrights, Tinsmiths, Coopers, Steam Boiler-makers, Boiler-makers and Shipbuilders, Varnishers, Sparmakers, Shoemakers, Cigar makers, Fancy Chair Makers, Freestone Cutters, Wheelwrights, Curriers, Engineers, Collar Makers, Horseshoers, Labouring Men, Druggistware Glass-Blowers, Brotherhood of Locomotive Engineers, Seamen, Ship-Carpenters and Caulkers, Granite Cutters, Window Glass-Blowers, Gilders, Brush Makers, Coach Makers, Harnessmakers, Boot and Shoemakers, Bookbinders, Brass Founders and Finishers, Sewing Machine Operators (Women), Axemakers, Pattern Makers, Trunk and Bag Makers, Saddlers, Gas and Steam Fitters, Saddle and Pad Makers, Stove Mounters, Marble Cutters, Puddlers, Iron Rollers, Morocco Finishers, Plumbers, Hat Makers, Ship Painters, Ship Fasteners, Heaters, and Ship Joiners.

These unions were scattered over a wider territory than had ever before been organised, and the numerous and general efforts at organisation justly deserve to be called a " movement " ; for not only did they comprise every trade, but the various trades in the more important localities soon gave concrete expression to the prevailing sentiment of the solidarity of labour and federated into trades' assemblies.

TRADES' ASSEMBLIES

The local trades' assembly,[9] and not the national trade union, was the common unit of labour organisation during the period

---

[9] The springing up of national trade unions during the fifties, like the molders' national union, made it necessary for the local trades' unions, or unions of trades, in the sixties, to forbear designating themselves by the name union, and they generally chose "trades' assembly," and almost monopolised the word "trades." The word "trades," "trades' " or " trade " during the sixties seldom appeared in the names of unions of single trades which generally bore names like painters' union, ship carpenters' and caulkers' protective union,— and the same was true of the national unions which were named: Iron Molders' International Union, Machinists' and Blacksmiths' International Union. But still we find in

of the War. Transportation by rail, which had established a national market for industries producing a standardised commodity like stoves, had not yet consolidated the markets of a very large number of industries. In these competition remained substantially local and called for a merely local union. Another factor was the novelty of organisation itself and the difficulty in establishing connections with fellow craftsmen in other cities, due to insufficient channels of communication. This was later amended to a large degree by the trade union directories printed in the labour press.

The first trades' assembly of the war period was organised in Rochester, New York, in March, 1863. Boston and New York followed in June of the same year. Albany, Buffalo, Louisville, Philadelphia, Pittsburgh, St. Louis, and San Francisco likewise had trades' assemblies by the end of 1863. At the end of the War, trades' assemblies existed in every important industrial centre. The trade assembly endeavoured to do for the local trade unions what the American Federation of Labour is at present doing for the national trade unions. The powers of the assembly were merely advisory, but since the membership was made up of the most influential men in every local union, the influence of the assembly was great. The assemblies carried no strike funds [10] and distributed no strike benefits, but served as publicity agencies in case of strikes. They aided the striking union in the collection of funds, and through connections with assemblies of other cities counteracted the efforts of employers to hire strike-breakers from outside the strike area. Another important function was the organisation of boycotts, known then as " non-intercourse." A delegate to the St. Louis Trade-Union League wrote of the methods of that organisation as follows: [11]

" We do not propose to do this [to aid labour against capital] by pecuniary aid, but by the moral force of numbers and active sympa-

1866 a House Carpenters' Trades' Union in Washington, D. C., as an exception to the rule. Speaking, however, of unions of single trades in the generic sense, they were frequently referred to as trade unions or even trades' unions. Thus Fincher speaks of " National Trade Unions " and the directory of trade unions (local, national and trades assemblies) which ap-

peared in the paper was headed " Trades' Union Directory." When the trades' assemblies created, in 1864, the International Industrial Assembly, it was sometimes referred to as " The International Trades' Union."

10 The Trades' Assembly of Rochester was an exception to the rule.

11 *Fincher's*, Nov. 28, 1863.

thy. To illustrate: We will suppose a boss tailor refuses to pay the prices established by the Tailors' Union. It is the duty of the tailors to inform the general society, through its delegates, of the facts in the case, whereupon it becomes the duty of the delegates from each of the other Unions composing the general society, to inform their particular organisation, and each member of all the societies is then under obligation to refuse to patronise the shop so refusing to pay the established rates, and to counsel their friends to do the same. In this way we expect to bring an influence that no proprietor can ignore."

Throughout the period of the War, the number of strikes was comparatively small, considering the incessant readjustment of wages to prices. The number of strikes mentioned in the three leading labour papers was 38 in 1863, affecting 30 trades; 108 in 1864, affecting 48 trades; and 85 in 1865, affecting 46 trades. In numerous cases the mere organisation of a union was sufficient to secure the demands.

The trades' assemblies devoted their main efforts to the work of organisation and agitation. They appointed special agents to form trade unions in the unorganised trades; they also agitated the idea of organisation at mass meetings called for this purpose. The trades' assembly further assisted in the establishment of co-operative stores, frequently appointing special agents to set the business on foot. The assemblies of Albany, Boston, Chicago, and Troy were instrumental in the establishment of such stores as dealt in groceries alone. In addition to this, the Troy Assembly also maintained a " workingmen's emporium," which was well patronised by the union men. Free libraries and reading rooms were established by the trades' assemblies of Chicago (German), Philadelphia, and Troy. The trades' assembly also was an organisation for "lobbying." When a bill, directed against picketing, was introduced in the legislature of New York in the winter of 1864, the trades' assemblies of New York,[12] Brooklyn,[13] and Buffalo[14] passed strong resolutions and saw that the bill was defeated.[15]

[12] *Fincher's*, Apr. 16, 1864.
[13] *Ibid.*, Apr. 23, 1864.
[14] *Ibid.*, Apr. 16, 1864.
[15] Sylvis explained to the moulders' convention in Chicago in January, 1865, that the primary object of this bill was to de- feat the moulders' and machinists' unions at Cold Springs, N. Y., which were on strike against R. P. Parrott, a shot and shell manufacturer for the army. The strike was broken up through the inter-

The support of the labour press was regarded as an important duty by the trades' assemblies. Frequent references may be found during the later issues of *Fincher's Trades' Review* to the aid received from various trades' assemblies. In St. Louis, the trade union league subscribed $1,000 toward the establishment of the St. Louis *Daily Press*.[16] The Boston *Daily Evening Voice* and later the Chicago *Workingman's Advocate* were also aided by the assemblies.

The proceedings of the Philadelphia Trades' Assembly have been much more fully preserved than those of any other, and a survey of its history will give an idea of the career of the average organisation.

The Philadelphia Journeymen House Painters' Association seems to have taken the initiative in bringing about the organisation of the assembly. In September, 1863, the members of this union offered the use of their newly erected hall for meetings of all trades. At the first meeting on October 27, nine trades were represented and Jonathan C. Fincher delivered an address on " Combination." At a second meeting held on November 10, six additional trades were represented, but it was decided to effect a permanent organisation at the next meeting to which all the various trade associations in the city were to be invited. At the same time it was announced that the federation of all trades would bring together 30,000 organised workingmen.[17] At a meeting held on December 8, the trades' assembly was organised, but the adoption of a permanent constitution was delayed for several months.

At a meeting held January 12, 1864, resolutions were adopted urging the immediate establishment of a library and free reading room, the support of *Fincher's Trades' Review*, and the necessity of securing a charter.[18] At the same meeting the strike and boycott policy was defined in the following resolution:

" That the different organizations herein represented, be requested to report to the Trades' Assembly all grievances that can in any way be affected by public opinion: and where the complainants make

vention of the militia. *Fincher's*, Jan. 14, 1865.

[16] Boston *Daily Evening Voice*, Jan. 17, 1865.

[17] *Fincher's*, Dec. 19, 1863.

[18] There is no evidence that the matter of incorporation was ever brought before the assembly again.

good their claim to the general sympathy of their fellow working-men, the Trades' Assembly shall request of the various Unions represented, that they adopt a specified course of action, calculated to secure the success of their brother workmen, either by expression of opinions, non-intercourse, or in event of a severe struggle with capitalists, pecuniary relief." [19]

The constitution, which was finally adopted at a meeting on March 8, 1864, recognised only the power of recommendation and provided for the admission of three delegates from each organised trade. The expenses of the organisation were to be paid from annual dues of $10 from each local union having more than 200 members; $8 from each local with a membership of less than 200 and more than 100; and $5 from unions with less than 100 members. Intoxication, or the use of profane or indecent language, subjected the offender to a fine and to expulsion from the meeting. A by-law expressly provided that " no subject of a political or religious nature shall at any time be admitted."

At the first election in April, 1864, W. B. Eckert was elected president and John Samuel, vice-president.[20] James L. Wright was made treasurer.[21] and William H. Sylvis and Jonathan C. Fincher were elected to the board of trustees.

Within a year from the date of its organisation, the assembly represented twenty-eight local trade unions and was the strongest trades' assembly in the country.

It has been shown how the trades' assembly mirrored and focussed the labour movement during this period. Each assembly with its affiliated trades was a world in itself, maintaining but loose and irregular diplomatic relations with the other thirty or forty similar worlds. No serious attempt was

---

[19] *Fincher's*, Jan. 23, 1864.

[20] John Samuel was a druggist-ware glass-blower, born in Wales, Feb. 3, 1817. He came to America in 1832 and served his apprenticeship in Philadelphia. He took part in the general strike of 1836 in Philadelphia during the fourth year of his apprenticeship. In 1857, he organised the glass workers in Philadelphia and vicinity. Later he became a member of the editorial staff of *Fincher's Trades' Review*. After that time his chief interest was the encouragement of co-operation. He was placed at the head of the co-operative board of the Knights of Labor in the eighties. In 1907, at the age of ninety, he presented his collection on trade unionism and co-operation to the University of Wisconsin. He died in 1909.

[21] Wright was born in Ireland in 1816 of Scottish-Irish ancestry and came to Philadelphia in 1827. In 1836 he became a member of the tailors' benevolent society; in 1854, manager of a large clothing house; in 1862, he helped to organise a garment cutters' association of which he was president for many years; and in 1868, with six others, he founded the Knights of Labor.

made to confederate these independent organisations until the middle of 1864.

EMPLOYERS' ASSOCIATIONS

The aggressive trade union movement during the War period gave rise to a no less aggressive movement for organisation among employers. In one trade, stove moulding, the employers organised on a national scale just as their employés had done some years earlier. However, the typical employers' association of the period was local, embracing the employers of one or more trades in the locality. These organisations expressed the employers' reaction against the wide-spread growth of local unions and trades' assemblies. In counteracting these organisations they often were even more successful than their own interests demanded, for in a large number of trades, by forcing labour to take the next step and to organise national trade unions, they unwittingly helped to strengthen a still more formidable adversary than either the local union or the trades' assembly. Where, as in the moulders' and the machinists' trades, national trade unions had already been in existence, the employers' associations helped to keep them intact against disrupting forces from within. However, during the War period proper, it was not so much the struggle against the national trade unions, spectacular though it was, that described their most typical activity but primarily the neutralisation of the local trade unions and the trades' assemblies.[22]

Most of the information about the employers' associations comes from the labour press of the time. The employers themselves preferred secrecy. Nevertheless the records show the existence of such organisations in every important locality and in nearly every trade. A most complete development of the idea of organisation among employers was the general city federation.

An example of an employers' association including representative employers of several different trades is clearly outlined in the Detroit *Tribune* of July 25, 1864. This organisation was known as the " Employers' General Association of Mich-

[22] The employers' associations which were especially active against national trade unions will be treated in the following chapter.

igan." It consisted of a general association and of various auxiliary associations. Each auxiliary was composed of the owners and managing agents of some particular line or branch of manufacturing or mechanical business. For example, the iron workers formed one auxiliary; the carpenters and joiners, another; the ship-builders, another; sawmill men, another, and so on. Each auxiliary was empowered to fix, grade, and regulate, from time to time, the maximum rates of wages to be allowed and paid to the different classes of employés in its particular branch of business; and also the minimum prices to be charged for different kinds of articles and work. The General Association was composed of the members of the various auxiliaries, not, however, in the character of delegates, but in their original and primary capacity. It was the province of the General Association to see that each of the various auxiliaries observed its constitution and by-laws filed with the general secretary as a prerequisite of membership, and also to act as a kind of court of appeal in cases arising from disputes between one auxiliary and another, and between an auxiliary and any of its members. The constitutions of the general and auxiliary associations were printed with proper blanks, the same as a deed, so that they answered for one place and for one branch of business as well as for another. They were ample in their provisions and carefully drawn. Particular care was taken to provide all needed funds.

The preamble to the constitution of the Michigan employers' union stated that the workingmen had for a long time been associated together in trade unions which had lately come to assume a dangerous attitude. " As a natural result of this system of general and persistent interference," said the employers, " our business is thrown into a condition of much uncertainty. . . . Business-like calculations and arrangements, especially such as involve prices for work, and time of completion and delivery, are thus rendered quite impracticable. . . . If continued for any considerable time, it must result in wide-spread beggary, with all its attending evils — suffering, bread-riots, pillage and taxation."

The employers' document further regretted that well-disposed workmen were not left to act freely, and charged their disaffection to the work of the leaders among them. " They come in contact," said the employers, " with others of a different make and temper — uneasy spirits, pregnant with the leaven of discontent, and whose words, constantly dropping, are full of the seeds of trouble." To the work of these "uneasy spirits" was ascribed the entrance of workmen into unions, where, according to the report, they were led on from one step to another, and finally went on strike. " These men go with the rest," said the preamble, " being hurried on by the excitement of the occasion, by the maddening influence of sympathy, or by ill-regulated zeal for a common cause. A strike follows. . . . These men are idle. Their wages are already nearly or quite consumed. The wants of a wife and children press upon them, as well as their own. . . . They desire to return to work at former rates. . . . But now up steps a ringleader, and with threats and abuse dilates on their duty of fidelity to the ' Unions '— reproaches them with odious epithets, calling them cowards, sneaks, traitors, and threatening to break their heads or burn their houses if they go to work on terms different from those decreed by the Union. They are intimidated and shrink back."

In the concluding introductory paragraph, the employers' association included the following sentiment which was singled out and highly commended by the editor of the Detroit *Tribune*: " We cordially accept the principle that ' the laborer is worthy of his hire '— that he should be remunerated for his labour, and so treated and provided for in general arrangement of society and of the body politic, as to enable him by diligence and fair economy to place himself and those dependent on him on a footing of intellectual and social equality with others." [23]

The great majority of employers and establishments engaged in manufacturing and mechanical business in Detroit had already connected themselves with these associations. The same was the case in several other cities both in the East and in the West, and the organisers firmly resolved to make such employers' associations general throughout the United States and Canada.

This public announcement of employers' association activity,

23 Detroit *Tribune*, July 25, 1864, quoted in *Fincher's*, Aug. 13, 1864.

as might be expected, brought a counter thrust from the trade unions. At the next meeting of the Detroit Trades' Assembly Richard F. Trevellick was instructed to publish a reply. The answering article appeared in the *Advertiser and Tribune* of August 1. Trevellick referred to the action on the part of the employers as "both wise and laudable, if carried out in the right spirit." But, he said, "labour should be free to seek the best market." He charged that employers sought to destroy this market, and had said: "If you leave my employ you can't work in this town." He declared further that certain employers even followed men who left their employ and caused their discharge from good situations merely to gratify a malignant spirit of revenge.[24]

With the multiplicity of organisations of employers of separate trades, and the combination of two or more trade divisions of an industry when largely controlled by the same capitalists, came still further consolidation into associations of employers of many closely related trades. Perhaps the best early example of this was the New York Master Builders' Association which in the spring of 1869 represented employers in the fol-

---

[24] Trevellick himself had suffered much from the blacklist on account of his trade union activity. He was a Cornishman, born May 20, 1830, on St. Mary's Isle, some thirty miles off Land's End, England. At the age of fourteen he started out to learn the ship carpenter's trade, and when twenty-one he went to work in the Southampton shipyard. He early distinguished himself in debates with his fellow-workers on the eight-hour question. In 1855 he visited Australia, where he joined the labour movement, and to him is said to belong the credit for the adoption of the eight-hour day. Shortly afterwards he came to New Orleans, where he was made president of the ship carpenters and caulkers' union, and through him that union secured the nine-hour day. When the Civil War broke out, he moved to Detroit, Mich., which city he made his home for the remainder of his life. He was elected president of the local carpenters' and caulkers' union, and later, in 1865, president of the International Union of Ship Carpenters and Caulkers. In 1864, when the Detroit Trades' Assembly was organised, he was elected president and in the same year was sent as delegate to the Louisville convention. Beginning with 1867, he attended the congress of the National Labor Union each year. He was president in 1869, 1871, and 1872. In 1867 he was elected as delegate to the International Congress at Lausanne, but on account of lack of funds, he did not go. In 1867 and 1868 he made 270 speeches in the West and organised 47 unions of labourers. He was an ardent advocate of temperance and delivered many lectures in favour of abolition of the liquor traffic. In 1869 he spent 169 days travelling and making speeches in behalf of labour. In 1870 he travelled over 16 States, helped to form 3 state labour unions and over 200 locals. In 1872, when the National Labor Union split into two sections, one industrial and the other political, he attended the meetings of both and was nominated as the candidate for the presidency in the latter but refused to accept the nomination. He favoured greenbackism and helped to form the Greenback party and in 1876 was a delegate to the convention that nominated Peter Cooper and Samuel F. Cary at Grand Rapids. In 1880 he was president of the convention which nominated General Weaver for president of the United States. His contemporaries gave him unstinted praise for his devotion and for his ability as an orator and an organiser. He died Feb. 14, 1895.

lowing trades: painters, blue-stone cutters, granite cutters, marble cutters, roofers, stone setters, stair-builders, sash and blind makers, and stone workers.[25] Four years later this employers' association was represented by a conference committee of three which met several times with a like number of representatives from the Carpenters and Joiners, the Amalgamated Carpenters and Joiners, and Stair-Builders' Unions. It was proposed at this time to make the conference committee a permanent institution to settle future trade disputes in an amicable manner without recourse to strikes.[26] But the uncertain success of the system did not lead to its adoption until later.

An adjourned meeting of the Master Mechanics of Boston, called togther by a committee appointed at a mass meeting held February 12, 1867, met on March 7 following and adopted a preamble and resolutions. An executive committee of thirtysix members, indicating the composite nature of the organisations, was drawn from the employers in fourteen different trades.[27] The secretary, Thomas D. Morris, said he had never been able to see the justice and reasonableness of the eight-hour system. It seemed to him that it was a practical dictation on the part of the employés, whether or not he should continue in his business more than eight hours.

These " Master Mechanics " asserted their readiness and willingness to do everything in their power to advance the condition of their employés. But they unanimously resolved that in their observations as to the effect of labour upon the physical or mental faculties of mankind they had yet to find that ten hours of diligent, faithful labour is a burdensome tax upon the vitality or energies of any class of men. They also announced it as their " sincere conviction that any general reduction in the number of hours of labor for a day's work would prove ultimately injurious " and that " on these grounds we shall be persistent in exacting ten hours labor for a day's work." [28]

" Very disinterested and important testimony! " exclaimed

25 *American Workman*, Apr. 24, 1869.
26 Chicago *Workingman's Advocate*, Apr. 19, 1873.
27 Masons, plumbers, plasterers, painters, slaters, freestone cutters, carpenters, granite cutters, machinists and boiler-makers, blacksmiths, founders, marble workers, copper and tin roofers, and coppersmiths.
28 Boston *Daily Evening Voice*, Mar. 8, 1867; quoted from the Boston *Daily Advertiser*, Mar. 8, 1867.

the labour editor of the Boston *Voice*.[29]   "As if the fisherman should testify that it did not hurt eels to be skinned!"

On June 19, 1872, 400 employers in New York held a conference to secure concerted action for the maintenance of the ten-hour system, and during the same year in some places the manufacturers combined, binding themselves in one instance to the sum of $1,000 each, to break up the organisations of the workingmen.[30] In July, 1872, the Employers' Central Executive Committee of New York, which, according to several labour sources, was "nothing else than a trade union of employers," sent into the industrial districts a great number of circulars containing a list of eleven questions concerning the possibilities of employers' associations. The fifth and sixth questions were as follows:

"5. Would a combination of employers engaged in *one* business be able to successfully overcome a strike of their workmen if the strikers were supported by means of assessments levied upon workmen of *other* trades, then in employment?

"6. Would a General Combination of Employers, representing diverse business interests, be successful in such a case as is supposed in the last question?"

The circulation of such a list of questions certainly indicates more than ordinary eagerness for information. One of the other questions suggests activity of a kind not elsewhere indicated. It is this: "Would it be possible to enact and enforce laws, *without encroaching upon the liberties of the people,* that would wholly or at any considerable extent, prevent the interruption of industry and the other evil consequences of strikes?" [31]

Without going further into the details of employers' association activity at this time, it may be said in conclusion that a large number of early examples might be added to the illustrations given above. Each additional case but corroborates the impression already given.

But there were several instances which prove that, hostile

29 *Ibid.*, Mar. 9, 1867.
30 McNeill, *The Labor Movement: The Problem of To-day,* 143, 146.
31 Chicago *Workingman's Advocate,* Nov. 23. 1872: *Address to the Intelligent Workmen of the United States,* by the New York Employers' Central Executive Committee, 1872. (Pamphlet in New York Public Library.)

as the typical employers' associations of the period were toward labour organisations, yet they occasionally found that their relations might be made mutually profitable.

The relatively high stage of organisation, among both workmen and employers, demonstrated to each element the advantages of united action. And it naturally suggested the next step. If individual workmen, by submerging their little differences in union agreements, secured exclusive privileges in bargaining; and if individual employers by uniting in turn relieved competition among themselves, what could be more natural than a desire to unite the two organised elements for the purpose of securing still greater benefits? The associated employers might agree to hire none but union men, providing the union men would agree to work exclusively for the associated employers. This would tend to force outsiders of both elements into the organisations with a practical monopoly of the trade, the employers could raise wages and at the same time increase profits by exacting higher prices from the public. And this form of understanding, now notable in the building trades of several cities under the name " exclusive agreement," was attempted as early as 1865. One of our earliest examples, too, is among the building trades. This interesting overdevelopment of the trade agreement beyond its legitimate scope of protecting labour and equalising the competitive labour conditions of employers, occurred among the bricklayers of Baltimore. The journeymen bricklayers of this city had been organised nearly a year, when, in the spring of 1865, their employers had the first serious trouble in arranging satisfactory terms. About the first of February the employers received official information of an intended demand for an increase in wages. This increase was to take effect April 1. They were invited by the journeymen to attend a special meeting or conference for the purpose of arranging matters to the satisfaction of both parties. At this meeting the Master Bricklayers' Association agreed to continue their policy of employing strictly union men. After the journeymen had withdrawn from the conference the employers revised their old scale of prices, and at a later meeting took measures to secure its general enforcement upon the building public. This plan was reflected in a resolution requesting the journeymen not to work for any employer that failed to join the employers' association. But the journeymen refused to do this on the ground that such an agreement would force all small contractors to abide by the advanced list. They felt that the blame for an exorbitant book of prices would be thrown upon the journeymen's union by the Baltimore public. In order to punish them for this refusal the employers reduced wages 50 cents per day, whereupon the journeymen struck. The disclosure of the employers' association plan for an " exclusive agreement " came to light during the strike.[32]

But while occasionally employers may have been willing to give recognition to the trade unions for the purpose of crushing competition, there was little desire to recognise them for the legitimate purpose of entering into trade agreements.

While the principal labour leaders expressed a willingness — almost an eagerness — to meet the employers in conference for the settlement of disputes, the officers of employers' associations generally discouraged such meetings by refusing to recognise the labour unions. In fact they tried to break them up by blacklisting and refusing to give employment to union members.

The employers had yet to overcome the feeling that meeting committees of their own workmen on a basis of business equality was " beneath the dignity " of employers.

INTERNATIONAL INDUSTRIAL ASSEMBLY OF NORTH AMERICA

The idea of a national federation of labour was agitated at the national convention of the machinists' and blacksmiths' union in November, 1860. President Isaac S. Casson suggested in his address " the co-operative alliance of all trades, and the erection of Trades' Assemblies to represent them, subordinate to a National Trades' Congress." [33] And again, at the convention the following year, resolutions were adopted favouring the appointment by the various trades having national organisations, of a committee which should meet and form a national trades' assembly.[34] These attempts, made at

---

32 *Fincher's*, May 6 and 13, 1865.
33 National Union of Machinists and

Blacksmiths of the United States of America, *Proceedings*, 1860.
34 *Ibid.*, 1861, p. 25.

a time when the few existing national trade unions lay prostrate under the stress of unemployment and of the general disturbed conditions, naturally remained fruitless.   When the next serious effort to create a national organisation was made in the spring of 1864, it emanated not from the national trade unions but from the trades' assemblies.   In April, 1864, the corresponding secretary of the assembly at Louisville issued a letter to the trades' assemblies of the United States and Canada, asking for their views with regard to the calling of a national convention and suggesting that the convention should be held in the city of Louisville in July of that year.[35]

The answers to this letter were few, and another appeal was made in August.   The president of the Louisville[36] assembly issued a call setting the date of the convention for September 21.   This call indicates clearly the trade union situation at the time.   Although addressed " to the officers and members of the Trades' Assemblies," its authors appreciated the necessity of national trade unions, for they proposed that the trades' assembly should become the agent " to organise the mechanics of every branch, and, if necessary, labouring men into protective unions and draw these unions into international bodies, such as moulders, machinists and blacksmiths, printers, etc." That the proposed international federation of labour was intended to embrace these international trade unions is evident from the advantages that would result therefrom.   " Should the employers by combination attempt to overthrow any one branch of the trades, the other branches or organisations of mechanics would make the cause of the trade or branch struck at, their cause, and would lend their aid and sympathy to the trade." [37] It is apparent, therefore, that the Louisville trades' assembly desired to see in the future an organisation similar to the present General Confederation of Labour in France in which trades' assemblies (*Bourses du Travail*) and national trade unions are represented on an equal footing.

Another more important advantage to be derived from a na-

---

35 *Fincher's*, Apr. 30, 1864.

36 The president was Robert Gilchrist, who had started the anti-war agitation in Louisville in 1860. He was later appointed chief of police of that city.

37 This could not refer merely to a mutual protection of trades within one trades' assembly, because that would be no innovation and it would not require any national federation.

tional federation, according to the call, would be the final abolition of strikes and the establishment of trade agreements. The combination would become so powerful " that the capitalists or employers will cease to refuse us our just demands, and will, if we make any unreasonable demands, condescend to come down on a level with us, and by argument and positive proof, show to us that our demands are unjust, but this would have to be explained to the satisfaction of the trades' assembly of the city in which the demand was made." The last sentence shows that the authors recognised the local trades' assembly as more influential than the national trade union.

The call ended with an expression of the belief that " there are over two hundred thousand [38] mechanics now represented in protective unions in the United States and Canada, and that they could be brought under the jurisdiction of the international trades' assembly in less than six months."

On the appointed day twelve delegates met in the trades' assembly hall in Louisville. They represented trades' assemblies of eight cities in as many States. [39] Richard F. Trevellick, of Detroit, was the only delegate who later achieved national prominence in the labour movement.

The delegates at first apparently had no clear conception of the purpose of the meeting. [40] A committee of eight, one from each State represented, was appointed to draft a constitution and the remaining delegates were appointed on a committee on resolutions. The two committees soon worked out a plan of organisation based on the principle of trade unionism.

The preamble to the constitution, in its final form, called attention to the fact that the capitalists had banded themselves together in secret organisation, " for the express purpose of crushing out our manhood "; that " capital has assumed to it-

[38] This is doubtless above the actual figure.

[39] Buffalo, Detroit, Louisville, Boston, Cincinnati, Chicago, Evansville (Ind.), and St. Louis. For complete list of delegates and reprint of " the Call," the resolutions and the constitution, see *Doc. Hist.*, IX, 118–125.

[40] Whittier, the delegate from Boston, who was elected chairman of the convention, said in his report to the organisation which he represented: " It is well known to you, gentlemen, that at the time I was chosen to represent you in the Convention at Louisville, you were in comparative ignorance as to what was intended to be accomplished at that session. Accordingly, your delegate experienced no small degree of embarrassment on entering the Convention on the morning of its assembling. But when the Convention had assembled and became duly organised, I found that all the other delegates were like myself, *they had no definite idea of what was intended to be done.*" Boston *Daily Evening Voice*, Dec. 30, 1864.

self the right to own and control labour," and that "experience has demonstrated the utility of concentrated effort in arriving at specified ends." For this purpose the "International Industrial Assembly of North America" was formed. Its chief object was "to use every honourable means in our power to adjust difficulties that may arise between employers and workmen, to labour assiduously for the development of a plan of action that may be mutually beneficial to both parties; to use our influence to discountenance strikes, except when they become absolutely necessary, and to devise the best means of supporting such organisations as may be driven to the necessity of resorting to such means to force a recognition of their rights." That this support was intended to be more than merely nominal is derived from the following clause: "In order to create a fund for the practical benefit of any organisation of workingmen which may be struck by the capitalists unjustly, this assembly may at any stated and regular meeting levy a per capita tax of five cents on every organised workingman through the various trades' assemblies of America and to be kept in their treasuries subject to the order of the International body."

The principle of conciliation was affirmed in the words of a special resolution proclaiming the right of the workingmen to be the judges of the value of their labour and that as " the creators of wealth they are entitled, equally with capital, to a fair and equal participation in its benefits, . . . but while thus clearly defining our fundamental rights, as a measure of courtesy and mutual confidence, we would recommend in the adjustment of wages, as a preliminary step, consultation with employing capitalists, with a view to the adoption of a scale of wages which may be mutually satisfactory to both parties."

The other resolutions relating to trade union action were one recommending that the various trades' assemblies should employ, in order of precedence according to the date of their organisation, salaried travelling organisers, subject to orders from the International Assembly; one urging that the local trades' assemblies come to the aid of the sewing women; and one offering support to the members of the Chicago Typographical Union, recently discharged by the proprietors of the Chicago *Times,* and affirming that this effort was the result of a combination of capitalists, known as the Northwestern Publishing Association, to break up the typographical union. [41]

Attention was also given to legislation, and the trades' assemblies were urged to work for laws prohibiting the store-order system and abolishing the competition of prison labour. They were also " to agitate the justness to all who labour for support that eight hours should constitute a legal day's work."

The movement for consumers' co-operation was highly recommended and the trades' assemblies were advised to establish stores for groceries and provisions. [42]

The next meeting of the international assembly was set for Detroit, in May, 1865, but the meeting did not occur.

The exclusive prominence given by the convention to trade union action reflects the prosperous conditions of industry and the prevailing success of local trade unions in securing higher wages. Less significant is the form of organisation adopted for the International Industrial Assembly. The plan proposed in the Louisville call, looking forward to a mixed organisation of trades' assemblies and national trade unions was evidently abandoned, for the convention made no provision for the representation of the existing national trade unions, to say nothing of aiding in the establishment of new ones. The local trades' assembly was to be the only unit of organisation, each assembly having one vote in the international assembly. The Chicago *Workingman's Advocate,* commenting upon the Louisville convention, found the International Industrial Assembly superior to the national trade union because " there are thousands of mechanics and workingmen on this continent who never have been, and never will be, represented in an International Union of their particular branch of Labor," and because it was less expensive to support.[43]

Thus the American labour movement in 1864 found itself little further advanced in the form of organisation than the movement of the thirties. The national trade unions which

[41] This association was organised primarily as a news agency similar to the Associated Press, but evidently it performed functions of an employers' association, at present performed by the American Newspaper Publishers' Association.

[42] A resolution was also passed urging upon the workmen of the country the duty of sustaining *Fincher's Trades' Review,* the *Workingman's Advocate,* and the Buffalo *Sentinel,* and censuring the Chicago *Times* for its persecution of the members of the typographical union.

[43] *Fincher's,* Oct. 22, 1864.

were in existence in 1864 were unable to compete with the trades' assemblies for the honour of establishing a national federation of labour. They were too few in number, too weak, and too much occupied in their struggle with employers' associations.

While the Louisville convention was clearly an attempt of the scattered trades' assemblies in the country to form a national federation on a purely trade union basis, an effort was made to inoculate it with politics, although this does not directly appear in the proceedings. The following occurs in Whittier's report to the Boston Trades' Assembly, from which we have already quoted: " Considering that there were some objectionable sections in the Constitution as adopted, and frankly stating that the Boston Assembly would object to being hampered with anything of a political character on the eve of a presidential election, the vote was reconsidered and on my earnest representation, the objectionable features were stricken out." [44]

The political tendency was evidently represented by Blake, the delegate from Chicago and publisher of the *Workingman's Advocate*. He had read the majority report of the committee on constitution in which Whittier must have found the objectionable political features, and, after a prolonged discussion, the minority report, presented by Whittier, was adopted by the convention, and the majority report was not printed.

The Louisville convention brought no practical results, mainly because the organisations that composed it did not yet feel the pressing need of a national federation. The movement for higher wages was carried on almost universally with success by the local trade unions assisted by the local assemblies. In view of this success the need of favourable legislation, which two years later forced the formation of the National Labor Union, was not yet felt. At the same time, there was no necessity of a national agency for the purpose of deciding jurisdictional disputes — an important function of the American Federation of Labor at a later time — because the sphere of action of each trades' assembly was well defined by geographic boundaries and the jurisdictional disputes arising between the trade unions in each city could be settled by the trades' assembly. This ac-

44 Boston *Daily Evening Voice*, Dec. 30, 1864.

counts for the lukewarm attitude of the trades' assemblies toward the idea of a national federation.

There was yet another cause. The Philadelphia Trades' Assembly, the strongest in the country, refused to send delegates to the Louisville convention. When the letter from the Louisville assembly, inviting delegates to meet in their city, was presented to the Philadelphia assembly, a committee composed of Sylvis, Fincher, and Graham was appointed to consider the matter,[45] but the committee apparently never reported. The reason is not difficult to guess. Sylvis and Fincher were officers of the two strongest national trade unions, the moulders', and the machinists' and blacksmiths', and a national organisation with a trades' assembly as its unit could not appeal to them. After the convention, the Philadelphia assembly adopted the view that, since the local assemblies possessed only advisory powers, the delegates to the international assembly had overstepped their powers in providing for the levy of a tax upon members of local unions.[46]

DISTRIBUTIVE CO-OPERATION

Following the upward sweep of prices, workmen had begun toward the end of 1862 to make definite preparations for distributive co-operation. They endeavoured to cut off the profits of the middleman by establishing co-operative grocery stores, meat markets, and coal yards. The first substantial effort of this kind to attract wide attention was the formation in December, 1862, of the Union Co-operative Association of Philadelphia. The prime mover and the financial secretary of this organisation was Thomas Phillips,[47] a shoemaker who came

[45] *Fincher's*, June 4, 1864.

[46] *Fincher's*, Oct. 22, 1864. This view was not entirely correct, because the assembly of Rochester was empowered to levy strike assessments.

[47] Thomas Phillips was born in 1833 on a farm in Yorkshire, England. At the age of sixteen he became apprenticed to a shoemaker in a small town in Lancashire, where he soon joined the union of which his boss was secretary. He also joined the Chartist movement. In 1852 he bought his liberty before his term of apprenticeship was over and came to America. Here he moved for a time from city

to city working at his trade, engaging in a strike as a picket during the first year. He was active in organising his trade and became interested in co-operation upon reading Holyoake's *History of Co-operation in England*. He started in Philadelphia the first co-operative association in America, the Union Co-operative Association, on the Rochdale plan. This association failed in 1866 after it had branched out, contrary to Phillip's advice, into four stores.

Phillips was closely identified with the Knights of St. Crispin, the national union of the shoemakers which existed from

from England in 1852, fired with the principles of his brother craftsmen, the Rochdale pioneers. One year after the Philadelphia store was opened Phillips could write: " One of the brightest spots on earth to my vision, is the little dingy one-story co-operative shop, 917 Federal Street, Philadelphia. Its very reticence throughout the day and through all but three nights in the week, is pleasing to me. . . . They adhere to the rigid old Rochdale system." [48]

Starting in this small way, the pioneer Philadelphia experiment expanded with several small branches in various parts of the city. Toward the end of its second year, it planned, although it never carried into effect, a series of wholesale distributing centres including country storehouses for farm products and city wholesale establishments for direct distribution to its retail stores.

Meanwhile Phillips, over the name of " Worker," contributed to the columns of *Fincher's Trades' Review,* the national labour weekly, a series of enthusiastic letters in which he explained the Rochdale plan and enlarged upon the possibilities of co-operation in America. Twice during the first year, to meet urgent demands for information, *Fincher's Review* found it necessary to reprint in full the rules of the Rochdale Equitable Pioneers' Society, then beginning its twentieth year in England. Letters of inquiry poured in upon the editor from all parts of America, and before the end of 1863 notices of the organisation of similar co-operative grocery stores had been received from Buffalo, New York; Susquehanna Depot, Pennsylvania; and from Lawrence

1867 to 1878, and especially in the work of furthering productive co-operation. He favoured a co-operative factory open to all Crispins rather than one controlled by a small group. His idea prevailed and the enterprise began with $20,000 capital, each member having to pay in $200 at $1 per week, the profits to be divided between the interest on capital, labour, and custom. After four years, partly as a result of the opposition of the disappointed Crispins who desired a limited group in control, the enterprise failed. Phillips was organiser of the Sovereigns of Industry in the late seventies and at an earlier date he had been the first shoemaker to join the Knights of Labor. He was elected to represent his local in District Assembly 1, and was placed in charge of the labour column which the organisation se-

cured with the daily *Public Record,* at a salary of $1,000.

In 1876 Phillips became president of a co-operative company started by the local assemblies of District Assembly 1. At the same time he was engaged in the Peter Cooper presidential campaign. In 1887 he ran for mayor of Philadelphia on a labour ticket. In 1889 he was elected president of the Boot and Shoe Workers' International Union.

While still working in a Philadelphia shoe factory, he presented, in 1905, his valuable collection of rare labour papers, including a complete file of *Fincher's Trades' Review,* to the University of Wisconsin Library. He died in 1916 at the age of eighty-four.

[48] *Fincher's,* Dec. 3, 1864.

and Charleston, Massachusetts. During 1864 stores were opened in Providence and Woonsocket, Rhode Island; in Springfield and Fitchburg, Massachusetts; in Albany, Troy, Ilion, Brownsville, and Schenectady, New York; and farther west in Cincinnati, Ohio and Detroit, Michigan. The following year witnessed the spread of distributive co-operation from Biddeford, Maine, to Carondelet, Missouri, with new stores announced also in Worcester, Pawtucket, Bridgeport, New York, Trenton, Baltimore, Pittston, and Evansville. The agitation continued and in the early months of 1866 stores were added in Lowell, Chelsea, Taunton, Cohoes, St. Clair, Cleveland, Kensington, and Chicago.

There was continued writing and speaking on the subject during the following year, and the movement had extended until practically every important industrial town between Boston and San Francisco had some kind of distributive co-operation. Disastrous failures, however, toward the end of 1865 foreshadowed the end of the movement in the sixties. With the fall of prices immediately after the close of the War, accompanied not only by a lessening of interest in co-operative grocery stores but also by the failure of strikes, there developed suddenly, as we shall later see, a pronounced movement toward productive co-operation.

CHAPTER III

THE NATIONAL TRADE UNIONS, 1864–1873

Causes and General Progress. Effect of the nationalisation of the market,
43. National trade unions in the thirties, 43. Effect of national labour
competition, 44. Effect of employers' associations, 44. Effect of machinery
and the division of labour, 44. Organisation of national trade unions,
1861–1873, 45. Growth of their membership, 47. The national trade union
— the paramount aspect of nationalisation, 48.

The Moulders. The epitomisation of the labour movement, 48. Activities during the War, 48. Beginning of employers' associations, 49. The
lull in the organisation of employers during the period of prosperity, 49.
West and East, 50. The American National Stove Manufacturers' and
Iron Founders' Association, 50. The apprenticeship question, 50. Strike
in Albany and Troy, 51. Withdrawal of the Buffalo and St. Louis foundrymen from the Association, 51. General strike against wage reductions,
51. Defeat of the union, 52. Restriction on strikes by the national
union, 52. The turn to co-operation, 53. Sylvis' view on the solution
of the labour question, 53. The co-operative shops, 53. The Troy
shops, 54. Their business success but failure as co-operative enterprises,
54. Disintegration of the employers' association, 55. Revival of trade
unionism, 55.

Machinists and Blacksmiths. Intellectual ascendency of the machinists
in the labour movement, 56. Employers' associations, 56. Effect of the
depression, 57. Effect of the eight-hour agitation on the union, 57. Revival in 1870, 58.

Printers. The National Typographical Union, 58. " Conditional membership," 58. National strike fund, 59. Persistent localist tendency, 59.
The Northwestern Publishers' Association, 61.

Locomotive Engineers. Cause of nationalisation, 61. Piece work, 62.
Brotherhood of the Footboard, 62. Brotherhood of Locomotive Engineers,
62. Charles Wilson, and his attitude towards public opinion, 63. Strike
on the Michigan Southern, 64. Railways' blacklist, 64. Brotherhood's
attitude towards incorporation, 66. Brotherhood's conservatism, 65. Discontent of the local branches, 66. Wilson's incorporation move, 66. Failure
in Congress, 67. Growth of the opposition to Wilson, 67. His removal
from office, 67. P. M. Arthur, 67. The benefit system, 68.

Cigar Makers. The effect of the War revenue law, 69. Growth of the
international union, 1864–1869, 70. Introduction of the mould, 71. Strike
against the mould, 72. Attitude towards the mould of the conventions of
1867 and 1872, 72. Failure of the anti-mould policy, 73.

Coopers. Effect of the machine, 74. Martin A. Foran, 75. Career of
the International Coopers' Union, 75. Robert Schilling, 76. Co-operative
attempts, 76.

Knights of St. Crispin. The factory system, 76. "Green hands," 77. Aim of the Crispins, 77. Crispin strikes, 78. Their principal causes, 78. Attitude towards co-operation, 79.

Sons of Vulcan. The puddler's bargaining advantage, 80. The sliding scale agreement, 80.

Restrictive Policies — Apprenticeship. The beginning of restrictive policies, 81. Effect of the wider market on apprenticeship, 81. Effect of the increased scale of production, 81. The "botches," 82. Sylvis' view, 82. Limitation of numbers, 82. Policies of the national trade unions, 83. Regulation of apprenticeship in the printer's trade, 83.

CAUSES AND GENERAL PROGRESS

In a sense every period in the industrial development of a country may be called a period of transition. However, this characterisation would apply with greater strength than usual to the sixties. At the present time, when Marx and Sombart have been popularised, we generally think of technical evolution alone when we speak of the evolution of industry. Yet we forget that no change in technique, not including even the utilisation of steam as a motive power, has ever had so simultaneous an effect upon all industries as had the sudden extension of the market due to the railway consolidation of the fifties, an effect which awaited only the years of prosperity of the sixties to become visible. Steam had revolutionised the textile industry at an early date, but for a long time it had left the other industries almost unaffected. The creation of a national market fundamentally changed the price-fixing forces in the majority of the industries, and therefore could not help producing a most thoroughgoing effect upon the struggle between industrial classes.

In the field of trade unionism the nationalisation of the market gave birth to the national trade union. To be sure, there had been some attempt at "national" trade unions during the thirties, such as the national conventions of the printers and cordwainers. It is nevertheless true that it was only during the sixties that labour organisations began to think and act on a lasting national basis. Moreover the "nation" over which the unions of the thirties had spread their activities was, properly speaking, nothing more than a region of neighbouring towns such as the "greater industrial New York" of to-day.

There were four distinct sets of causes which operated during the sixties to bring about nationalisation: two grew out of changes in transportation, and two were largely independent of such changes.

The first and most far-reaching cause, as illustrated by the stove moulders, was the competition of the products of different localities side by side in the same market. Wherever that was the case, nationalisation was destined to proceed to its utmost length. In order that union conditions should be maintained even in the best organised centres, it then became imperatively necessary to equalise competitive conditions in the various localities. That led to a well-knit national organisation to control working conditions, trade rules, and strikes. In other trades, where the competitive area of the product was still restricted to the locality, the paramount nationalising influence was the competition for employment between migratory out-of-town journeymen and the locally organised mechanics. This describes the situation in the printing trade, where the bulk of the work was still newspaper and not book and job printing. Accordingly, the printers did not need to entrust their national officers with anything more than the control of the travelling journeymen, and the result was that the local unions remained practically independent. The third cause of concerted national action in a trade was the organisation of employers. When the power of a local union began to be threatened by an employers' association, the next logical step was to combine in a national union. Thus it transpired that the numerous local employers' associations which sprang up during 1864 and 1865 gave the impetus to the nationalisation of the labour movement.

The fourth cause was the application of machinery and the introduction of division of labour, which split up the old established trades and laid industry open to invasion by " green hands." The shoemaking industry which, during the sixties had reached the factory stage, illustrates this in a most striking manner. Few other industries experienced anything like a similar change during this period.

Of course, none of the causes of nationalisation here enumerated operated in entire isolation. In some trades one cause, in other trades other causes, had the predominating influence. Consequently, in some trades the national union resembled an agglomeration of loosely allied states, each one reserving the right to engage in independent warfare and expecting from its allies no more than a benevolent neutrality. In other trades, on the contrary, the national union was supreme in declaring war and in making peace, and even claimed absolute right to formulate the " civil " laws of the trade for times of industrial peace.

Although some nationals were organised before 1864, it is at this time that an appreciable movement started towards nationalisation. Four nationals were organised in this year as compared to two organised in 1863, none in 1862, and one in 1861. A call was also issued from the tin, sheet iron, and copper workers, the upholsterers, and house painters, but there is no evidence that these unions met. The nationals organised before the War took a leap forward. The National Typographical Union at its session of 1864 reported 14 new charters issued, against 6 reported in 1863 and 1 in 1862. No convention was held in 1861.[1] The Iron Molders' Union reported in that same year (1864) 46 new charters and a total membership of 6,778 as compared to 3,500 in 1863.[2] The Machinists and Blacksmiths' Union was the only national that did not recover the strength it enjoyed prior to the War, having 87 locals before the War commenced and reporting in 1864 a smaller representation than in former sessions.[3]

This process of nationalisation once started, lasted for ten years, the number of nationals cropping up and the number of members gained by those already in existence varying with the prosperity or depression in business during that time. During the period of intense business activity which lasted from 1863 to 1866, caused by the inflation of greenbacks and the demands of the War, ten national unions sprang up in two years: the Plasterers' National Union, National Union of Journeymen Curriers, the Ship Carpenters' and Caulkers' International Union, National Union of Cigar Makers in 1864, and the Coach Makers' International Union, the Journeymen Painters' National Union, National Union of Heaters, Tailors'

---

[1] National Typographical Union, *Proceedings*, 1864, including the tenth, eleventh, and twelfth sessions, held at New York, Cleveland, and Louisville, Ky., May 5, 1862, May 4, 1863, and May 2, 1864.
[2] Iron Molders' International Union, *Proceedings*, 1865.
[3] See above, II, 9.

National Union, Carpenters' and Joiners' International Union, Bricklayers' and Masons' International Union in 1865.

In 1866 industry entered upon a period of depression, but recovered in 1868. The flush times of the Civil War had passed. Large and profitable contracts no longer existed and, in addition, prices fell, owing to the contraction of the greenbacks by Congress in the early part of 1866. This condition was reflected in the labour movement. Not a single national was organised in 1866; the spinners alone appeared in 1867. In 1868 the Knights of St. Crispin and the Grand Division of the Order of Railway Conductors organised, and in 1869 the wool hat finishers, the Daughters of St. Crispin, and the Morocco Dressers — a total of 7 nationals in 4 years, compared with 10 in the preceding 2 years. The unions already in existence, although they gained, did not gain as rapidly as in the previous period. At the convention of the Iron Molders held in 1865, the president, Sylvis, reported 53 locals chartered; in 1866 he reported 38; in 1868, 32; and in 1870, 14. The number of locals organised by the printers shows a similar decline. In 1866, 18 were reported organised during the previous year; in 1868, 14; and in 1870, 11. Not only were fewer locals organised than in the previous years, but many more were suspended for non-payment of dues, for " ratting," and for being composed of "unfair" men. Actual figures of the number dropped are not available, but that they left a big gap in trade union ranks may be gathered from the general amnesty laws passed a few years later by most nationals. The national union of the machinists and blacksmiths fell off to about 1,500 members in 1870.

In the summer of 1870 business, which in the preceding two years had been normal or slightly above normal, became good and remained so for approximately three years — until the panic of 1873. Nine nationals appeared in these three years — the telegraphers', and the International Coopers' Union of North America in 1870; the painters' in 1871; the woodworking mechanics, and the Brotherhood of Iron and Steel Heaters, Rollers, and Roughers of the United States in 1872; the National Union of Iron and Steel Roll Hands of the United States, the furniture workers, the Miners' National Association and the Brotherhood of Locomotive Firemen in 1873. This period, however, is marked by the internal growth of the unions that organised in this and in previous periods. The machinists and blacksmiths, who had 1,500 members in 1870, had 18,000 members at the end of this period. The Sons of Vulcan, who had 1,260 members in 1870, had 3,048 members in 1873. The coopers, who organised in 1870, had a membership of 10,050 [4] at the end of two years. The Brotherhood of Locomotive Engineers, whose membership in 1869 was 4,108, had 9,000 in 1873. The anthracite miners grew to about 30,000 in this period, and the Knights of St. Crispin reached the unparalleled membership of 50,000. The cigar makers alone showed no gain.

An estimate of the total trade union membership at one time, in view of the total lack of reliable statistics, would be extremely hazardous. A rough estimate made in August, 1869, by a correspondent of the New York *Herald,* resulted in a total of approximately 170,000.[5] A labour leader [6] claimed at the same time that the total was as high as 600,000. It appears that it would not be far from the truth to put the membership during 1870–1872 at about 300,000, a figure which seems to provide amply for the increase after 1869.

Thus, during this ten-year period there were organised twenty-six national unions. Taking into consideration those that appeared before 1864, namely, the International Typographical Union, 1850, Machinists' and Blacksmiths' International Union, and the Iron Molders' International Union in 1859, the American Miners' Association in 1861, the National Forge of the Sons of Vulcan (boilers and puddlers), 1862, the Grand National Division of the Brotherhood of Locomotive Engineers in 1863, there were altogether thirty-two nationals

---

[4] *American Workman,* Feb. 10, 1872.

[5] The membership was apportioned as follows:

Trade	Branches	Members
Carpenters and Joiners....	77	6,000
Cigar Makers	95	5,000
Bricklayers	70	15,000
Typographical Unions	112	17,000
Knights of St. Crispin.....	147	50,000
Coopers	20	5,000
Plasterers	18	2,500
Iron Molders	204	17,000

Trade	Branches	Members
Machinists and Blacksmiths	120	10,000
Grand Forge of the U. S...	78	1,600
Engineers	11	621
Tailors	35	2,000
Locomotive Firemen	35	3,000
Masons	8	2,000
Painters	3	1,500
Metal Workers	5	850
Cigar Packers	25	2,500
Miners	30	30,000

[6] A. C. Cameron.

in existence during the ten years. Most of them called themselves " nationals." Those that prefixed the " inter " did so on the claim of a few locals in Canada.

It was the national trade union rather than any other form of nationalisation, such as the formation of a political National Labor party, that gives us the right to call the period of the sixties the period of the " nationalisation " of the labour movement. The national trade union of the sixties marked a lasting change in the basis of trade union action, a change in the daily activity of union officers and members, and one necessarily accompanied by a change in their mode of thinking.

THE MOULDERS

The stove moulders have epitomised the American trade union movement not only throughout the sixties, but even to the present day. Owing to the standardised nature of their product, they were the first to feel the depressing influence of a national market and we have consequently seen them driven to organise a national union as early as 1859. But that was not the only respect wherein the moulding industry formed the vanguard: The national organisation on the side of labour was soon followed by an attempted national organisation on the side of the employers. Eventually, after the two had measured strength and had found that neither could completely subdue the other, they did the logical thing and, in 1890, developed the trade agreement system, which became the prototype for all other industries. But confining ourselves to the period, there is still another reason why the moulders' history is of the greatest interest. If their development had been strictly along the road of trade unionism, without deviating either to the side of productive co-operation or to that of political action, they would, to be sure, have epitomised the American labour movement in its broadest aspects, but, at the same time, we could hardly have considered them a typical labour organisation of the sixties. That they did not follow such a straight line of development, at one time almost wholly abandoning trade unionism for co-operation and general labour reform, marks them as part and parcel of the general labour movement of the sixties.

As soon as the industrial depression which had been precipitated by the War had worn away, President Sylvis of the Molders' International began an active campaign of organisation over the country. His weekly letters, which ran in *Fincher's Trades' Review* through the latter part of 1863 as well as through 1864, described his impressions of the various cities he visited, and bear ample testimony to his untiring activity. The trade was so prosperous that it was sufficient merely to organise in order to obtain concessions from the employers. Consequently the union was not only successful in raising wages but also in enforcing its trade rules, especially with regard to apprenticeship. But the very great initial success was responsible for creating a new set of circumstances in the trade which made it the arena of the hardest fought labour conflicts of the period, namely, the organisation of a national employers' association, the first ever organised in this country.

As early as September, 1863, a group of iron founders from Louisville, New Albany, and Jeffersonville, Ohio, met and organised the Iron Founders' and Machine Builders' Association of the Falls of Ohio and adopted the following principles: "We deny the right of the 'Iron Moulders' Union' to arbitrarily determine the wages of our employés, regardless of their merits and the value of their services to us. . . . We deny the right of the 'Iron Moulders' Union' to determine for us how many apprentices we should employ. According to . . . their constitution they dictate to their employers that no more than one apprentice shall be employed in each machine foundry and one to every fifteen moulders in each stove foundry."

They stated their grievances and adopted the following course of action:

"The corresponding secretary of the 'Iron Founders' and Machine Builders' Association of the Falls of Ohio' shall put himself into communication with all the parties of the principal cities of the United States engaged in similar business to that of the members of the Association and suffering under the same grievances. . . . He shall endeavor to cause the interested parties to form similar associations to ours. . . . In case no association can be formed . . . the Corresponding Secretary shall correspond with individual firms of other cities. . . . Should the employees in any of our establishments stop work in order to force their employers to submit to unreasonable demands, the . . . Association . . . shall not employ any man engaged in such strike. The names of the parties engaged in any attempt to force their employers to submit to unreasonable demands shall be sent in circular at the expense of this Association to all the other Associations in order that they may be prevented from getting employment until they withdraw from the ' Moulders' Union,' or cease to attempt the enforcing of their unjust demands." [7]

In 1863 the West thus took steps towards nationalisation and formed the association of the Falls of Ohio. In 1864 an attempt was made in a similar direction in the East.[8] Employers here too felt that the International Iron Molders' Union interfered with the management of their business, and to protect each other they issued a call to all interested to meet at New Haven in March to form an " American Iron Founders' Association." A number of men met but, without doing very much, adjourned to meet at the Astor House, New York, in the latter part of the same month. The invitation was extended to a larger number of employers covering a larger territory, and, accordingly, at the New York meeting we find representatives from New England, New York, New Jersey, and Pennsylvania. Employers of both bench and floor moulders were admitted to membership.

This was the end of this association as far as a national body is concerned; it never got farther west than the Atlantic coast. Times were too good in 1864 to fight the workmen. It was not therefore until 1866 that a real national association appeared. Times had grown dull at the close of the War and it was an opportune time to strike a blow at the union which had grown so powerful in the last few years. Delegates representing both sides of the Alleghanies met in Albany, March 4, and formed themselves into the American National Stove Manufacturers' and Iron Founders' Association. They drew up a constitution and adopted a set of resolutions declaring in the main that they organised to resist any and all actions of the moulders' union, to employ as many apprentices as they deemed fit, and to exclude shop committees.[9]

These resolutions they posted in the different foundries of

7 *Fincher's*, Oct. 3, 1863.   8 *Ibid.*, May 28, 1864.   9 *Fincher's*, Mar. 31, 1866.

Troy and Albany, where there were about 600 moulders employed. The resolutions caused a considerable stir. A large meeting of the moulders was held and a determination was evinced to fight the matter out. It was decided to stop work at once and stay out as long as the circulars remained posted. They communicated the trouble to Sylvis who, in a short time brought the entire resources of the national union together at this centre. The fight lasted for several months. The International was as strong as the employers' association was weak and came out of the struggle with a complete victory. It was a fight for union principles and no effort or money was spared to bring the matter to a successful determination. They retained their shop committees, continued to regulate apprenticeship, and forced the removal of the obnoxious posters.

This was by no means the end of the employers' association. It extended its operations to other cities so as to include chiefly Ironton, Covington, Cleveland, Cincinnati, Indianapolis, Richmond, Buffalo, and St. Louis. The fight lasted for several months and ended favourably to the unions. In most places they won and in others some had to submit to reduction of wages.[10]

In February, 1867, the Association met in Cincinnati and determined to continue the fight. But here already we find an element of disruption. The Buffalo and St. Louis founders withdrew and reached an agreement with their workmen at a reduction of 30 per cent on their former wages. The rest of the Association voted a reduction of 60 per cent and decided to start their work in Cincinnati.[11] Although prices were at their lowest in this year, such a large reduction was announced primarily to force a fight. Sylvis who appeared on the ground was willing to concede a reduction of 30 per cent, but that was not the issue.

The strike started in February and lasted for fully nine months. It was this protracted struggle that almost broke the union. On February 16, 1867, Sylvis issued a circular submitting the question of a special tax of 5 per cent on the earnings of the members of the local unions. The circular was re-

10 Iron Molders' International Union, *Proceedings*, 1867.
11 *Ibid.*, 1868.

turned with 99 for the tax and 42 opposed. In April he issued another circular asking for an increase of the special tax and it was returned with 78 in favour and 57 opposed. Still a third request was issued on July 30, but this time the vote was 63 in favour and 70 opposed. These figures show the downward tendency of the strength of the union. Many of the locals that voted in favour of the tax sent in words of caution that a further increase and an effort to collect it would break the union. Others returned circulars with a statement that rather than pay the tax they would give up their charters. In addition to tax exactions, times were hard. Sylvis in his annual address to the convention of 1868 says that trade conditions were exceptionally hard, that almost half of the members were out of work and many worked on part time or small piece work, while the necessaries of life were dear. A man at full time could not do more than take care of his running expenses.[12]

The immediate effect upon the union of this successful onslaught by the organised employers, coupled with the hard times, was to discourage strikes. At the convention of 1868, the Iron Molders' International Union adopted a measure which required a favourable vote of two-thirds of all the locals in the union to permit another local to enter into a strike and receive strike benefits; and further, that it should not be permitted to go on strike unless it had in the treasury the amount of its indebtedness to the International. This made strikes almost impossible. From 1868 to 1870, 37 locals issued strike circulars and only 7 of these were authorised.[13]

The cumbersomeness of these regulations was obvious two years after they were made, especially when business was picking up. Circulars sent out to locals for their vote were very often never returned, and if returned it took two weeks before the vote could be announced, and another two weeks passed before financial aid could be given. In spite of this unsatisfactory condition the only change made in the constitution at this session was to require a one-third negative vote to withhold authority from a local to strike instead of requiring a two-thirds positive vote to give it authority to strike.

[12] *Ibid.*   [13] *Ibid.*, 1870.

But the defeat of the union gave rise to even a more fundamental change in policy than the temporary abandonment of strikes.   The very foundations of the trade union philosophy came to be questioned and the view gained currency that, after all, the principal goal of the labour movement must be to find a way of escaping the wage system.   Productive co-operation was to become the substitute for trade union action.

"At last," exclaimed Sylvis in the summer of 1867, "after years of earnest effort and patient waiting, and constant preaching, co-operation is taking hold upon the minds of our members, and in many places very little else is talked about." [14] A year later he declared that the co-operative stove foundries "marked the beginning of a new era" in his trade.

The first of these foundries, established at Troy in the early summer of 1866, was quickly followed by one in Albany and then during the next 18 months by 10 more — 1 each in Rochester, Chicago, Quincy, Louisville, Somerset, Pittsburgh, and 2 each in Troy and Cleveland.   The original foundry at Troy was an immediate financial success and was hailed with joy by those who believed that under the name of co-operationists, the baffled trade unionists might yet conquer.

But the remarkable hold that co-operation was getting over the moulders is best attested by the fact that the Molders' International Union at its convention in September, 1868, changed its name to "Iron Molders' International Co-operative and Protective Union."   This step was due to Sylvis.   In the presidential report to this convention, he reiterated in much stronger terms than ever before his disbelief in trade unionism and his faith in co-operation.   "Combination," he said, "as we have been using or applying it, makes war upon the effects, leaving the cause undisturbed, to produce, continually, like effects. . . . The cause of all these evils is the WAGES SYSTEM. . . . We must adopt a system which will divide the *profits* of labor among those who produce them. . . . Should we adjourn without such legislation as will restore confidence, renew hopes, and give a reasonable promise of ultimate and final success, and freedom from strikes and taxation, more than fifty unions will return their charters before the close of

14 *Weekly Voice*, Aug. 22, 1867.

1868. . . ." [15] The report further said that there were 11 co-operative iron foundries in the country: 1 in Troy and 1 in Albany, both established in 1866 and giving employment to 130 moulders, and 9 established in 1867: 2 more in Troy, 2 in Cleveland, and 1 each in Rochester, Chicago, Quincy, Louisville, Somerset, and Pittsburgh. The last named was established as an " International Foundry," which meant that the president and the treasurer of the international union were ex-officio directors and shared authority with the directors chosen by the stockholders.

But the results of the Troy experiment, typical of the others, show how far productive co-operation was from a successful solution of the labour problem. At the end of the third year of this enterprise, the *American Workman* [16] published a sympathetic account of its progress, disclosing unconsciously, however, its fatal weakness. The " Troy Co-operative Iron-Founders' Association " was planned with great deliberation and launched at a time when the regular stove manufacturers were embarrassed by the strikes. It was regularly incorporated with a provision that each member was entitled to but one vote whether he held one share or the maximum of fifty. Yet it failed, as did the others, in furnishing permanent relief to the workers as a class. On the contrary, the co-operators quickly adopted the capitalist view. The sympathetic account mentioned above quotes from these co-operators to show that " the fewer the stockholders in the company, the greater its success." That these capitalistic co-operators were less eager for leisure to improve body and mind than they had been as trade unionists, is apparent from the statement that " the holidays do not interfere to keep them idle at the whim of the ironmaster who chooses to close up his foundry on such days." The foundry had recently made 1,100 stoves on contract at a low price for a local stove manufacturer. When delivered ahead of contract time, the purchaser expressed astonishment not only at the promptitude with which the order had been filled, but its cheapness. Totally disregarding the effect on moulders employed by competing manufacturers, the co-operators quoted

---

15 Sylvis, *Life, Speeches, Labors and Essays*, 265.
16 Jan. 8, 1870.

with satisfaction the statement of this manufacturer, who said: " I wish you would let my patterns stay at your place. . . . I can buy my stoves of you and do better than if I manufactured them myself." Membership in the moulders' union was still maintained by these co-operationists, " but," they said, " the trade-unions here are of no use now, really."

But trade union action did not remain hopeless. The cohesive qualities of the employers were after all inferior to those of the workingmen. The scramble for the ever-widening market, generating as it did the keenest kind of competition among the manufacturers, could not help but weaken the bands which held them together as employers in opposition to a common enemy — the moulders' union. As soon as it was apparent that there was no longer any great danger from the union, individual and sectional interests began to assert themselves. The very strike in Albany and Troy in 1866 had demonstrated the lack of unity in the employers' association. The western founders saw early in the strike that it would be to their advantage to withdraw from the association and reach some adjustment with their workingmen. Stoppage of work in the East to some extent removed competition from that direction in the West and the manufacturers there lost no time in taking advantage of the troubles. Meanwhile, business conditions became better, prices went up, and the founders' prime interest now became the market rather than labour. This seems to have removed for a time the need of an association, and we do not hear of a national stove manufacturers' and iron founders' association after that time until about 1872, when it reorganised as a price-fixing organisation, and without the features of an employers' association.

The return to prosperity in 1869, the disappearance of employers' organisations and last but not least the failure of co-operation as a panacea turned the moulders' union again into the groove of trade unionism. The negative attitude towards strikes disappeared. The president at the convention of 1872 reported that nine authorised strikes had occurred during the past two years, and went on to say that unauthorised strikes are beneficial in many cases and should not be interfered with. At the biennial convention in July, 1870, the International

Molders' Union changed policies. The "International" co-operative foundry, Sylvis' pet child, had gone to pieces, and the tide turned against co-operative ventures in general. The *Workingman's Advocate* reported: "The legislation of the moulders in this session undoes much that was considered good under the administration of the lamented Sylvis," [17] and further that "Saffin — a thorough trades-unionist," formerly recording secretary under Sylvis, was chosen president.

During the three following years the moulders, while fully sharing in the prosperity, lost their place as the paramount national trade union, and came to be overshadowed by others, especially the Crispins.

THE MACHINISTS AND BLACKSMITHS

If the moulders were the highest expression of practical militancy in the movement of the period, the machinists occupied in it the place of idealists and theorists. Beginning with the upward swing during the early sixties and ending with the melancholy years of the late seventies when the rising star of the Knights of Labor was the only cheerful appearance on the labour horizon, it was always a machinist who pointed the way for the general labour movement. Fincher, the versatile labour journalist, Ira Steward, the eight-hour idealist, and Powderly, the exponent of the ideas of the American mechanics of the sixties during a later and more confused period, mark the theoretical ascendency of the machinists. With the best minds in the trade devoting themselves to the general movement of labour reform, it is not surprising that the machinists' union, for a long time, lagged behind others in the everyday practical struggle for betterment in the trade.

During the War the machinists were the beneficiaries of the universal prosperity like any other trade. A true index of the success of the activity of the machinists' national union may be found in the activities of the employers' associations in the trade.

A secret circular [18] issued by the "Association of Engineers of New York" includes a preamble and resolution adopted

---

[17] July 23, 1870.   [18] Quoted in *Fincher's*, Dec. 5, 1863.

at their regular monthly meeting held November 27, 1863. In this preamble they announced that they were "opposed to every combination which has for its object the regulation of wages," and that they resolved to refuse to raise the wages of machinists for thirty days. In a separate resolution they let it be known that "for the next ninety days, the proprietors of each establishment represented in this Association refuse to employ any machinists other than those now employed in their respective establishments excepting any one who shall bring a recommendation or statement from his present employer that he has been honourably discharged." The only machinists exempted from this blacklist were recent immigrants. The special cause of the whole announcement was a demand for higher wages on the part of the New York machinists, who were organised under the name, "Finishers' Protective Union." Representatives of nineteen New York firms signed the circular, and the secretary, W. A. Searer, was ordered to print 250 copies for the use of the members of the Association.

These resolutions were likewise adopted by the iron manufacturers of Boston and vicinity, as their "future rule of action," and were signed by the representatives of twenty-two Boston firms.[19] February 15, 1864, the international secretary of the Machinists and Blacksmiths Union issued a proclamation [20] to the membership throughout the continent of North America, calling upon them to be in readiness to act with their brother workmen in New England, where the employers had adopted measures to keep down wages. "The employer will not hire an applicant," said this official, "unless he can produce a recommendation from his last employer stating that the *latter* is content to *allow* him to leave his employ. And further the recommendation must state the wages the applicant has been receiving,— also what his general character is."

During the years of depression after the end of the War the machinists' national organisation suffered a much greater setback than the moulders' or even some of the national unions of more recent origin. The demand for a universal eight-hour law then suddenly came to the forefront in the general labour

---

19 Reprinted entire fifteen months later in the Boston *Daily Evening Voice*, Mar. 11, 1865.

20 *Fincher's*, Feb. 20, 1864.

movement and, since the leading machinists were the original spokesmen of that movement, the activities of the union in the purely economic field were allowed to decline.   It was, therefore, not until the return of prosperity that the machinists' national union, now under different leaders, took on new vigour. In 1872 the *American Workman* reported that "the Machinists and Blacksmiths' National Union has had a year of great prosperity.   Something less than a hundred new unions have been established, thus trebling the membership in twelve months, while the trade journal has 2,500 subscribers and a surplus of $8,000 has accumulated in the treasury." [21]

THE PRINTERS

The extension of the market for their product brought into existence the iron moulders' union.   The extension of the market, not for what labour produced but for what it sold, namely, labour, brought into existence the National Typographical Union.   The typographical union appeared as early as 1850. The desire to prevent the movement of printers from one locality to another brought about an elaborate system of "conditional membership."   At the convention of 1864 President Carver presented a scheme which met the approval of the delegates.

A conditional membership card was prepared, the holder of which did not belong to a union, but it entitled him to the membership and good offices of all the unions under the jurisdiction of the National Typographical Union.   On the other hand he had solemnly to pledge his honour to "maintain and enlarge the union influence which exists in this country and by similar efforts to influence fellow craftsmen to avail themselves of the privilege of membership," and also, "not to respond to any advertisement for printers from a locality where there is a union without having first ascertained . . . that such response would not be incompatible with the interests of the craft."   Such a card could be obtained by the payment of one dollar.   It entitled the bearer to the privileges above mentioned

21 Jan. 6, 1877.

for one year, when it could be renewed upon payment of another dollar and so on for each succeeding year.

For the purpose of bringing the scheme into operation the country was divided into seven districts: New York, New England, Pennsylvania, Ohio, Illinois, Missouri, Tennessee, and California. Each local union was required to amend its constitution so as to levy upon each member a ten-cent monthly tax which should constitute a " conditional membership fund." The union in each district which had the largest number of members in good standing was to elect a " district canvasser," whose duty it was to supervise his territory.[22]

At the session of 1865 it was reported that only five unions applied for certificates of conditional membership. It was thought that, because the power to do the active work was delegated to the largest local within the district, others failed to do their duty. The act was therefore amended so that each local was constituted a district whose jurisdiction extended to one-half the distance between it and the next union. But that did not bring better results. In the conventions of 1866 and 1867 no material progress was reported. In 1868 the conditional membership was not even mentioned and no trace of it is found thereafter.

The prevalence of a localist tendency among the printers is further illustrated by the vicissitudes of the proposal for a national strike fund. The typographical was the only large union which failed to create such a fund. It had been urged for many years and in the convention of 1866 the secretary-treasurer in his annual report said, " It is just now, more than ever before, the great *desideratum*. . . . Others have already tried it successfully, why cannot we establish the same object. . . . The various subordinate unions are the treasurers of their own contributions . . . collected in the same manner as the regular dues, and reserved for the specific object. . . ."[23] A resolution was adopted at this convention that the delegates upon returning home should lay this matter before their respective locals and report the result to the national president who in

22 National Typographical Union, *Proceedings*, 1864, p. 81.

23 National Typographical Union, *Proceedings*, 1866.

turn should report the action taken at the next annual convention.

The result of the vote reported showed all unions voting in favour of it with the exception of Cincinnati and of Philadelphia. The latter gave no specific reasons. Cincinnati argued that to make the fund valuable it would have to be very large and, since the union was not incorporated, no legal responsibility would attach to the treasurer for money placed in his hands; that it would be necessary to clothe the dispenser of the fund with power to pass on the legality of strikes before rendering assistance; that vesting power in a central head would be detrimental to the interests of those engaged in a strike on account of the time that would elapse before the central could be heard from. Cincinnati was powerful enough to swing the convention her way and the question was laid over to the next session, which was to adopt or reject it by a vote of delegates.

The convention of 1868 met and the proposition with other matters was referred to a committee. It received a favourable report. The objection now raised by the opposition was that it was not introduced in the manner provided by the constitution. It was then placed before the committee of the whole which reported that it be spread on the minutes for consideration at the next session. This was the regular constitutional procedure for all amendments — that they lie over for one year.

At the 1869 convention the committee in charge failed to report it back, and in 1870 it reported favourably upon it but added that the time was not sufficient to discuss it and recommended that it lay over to the next meeting. In 1871 a motion was adopted that such a fund was inexpedient.

This persistent localism of the printers is especially interesting in view of the several attempts towards a more or less widely extended employers' association.

In May, 1864, a union printer from Albany, New York, declared that " a powerful organisation exists among the newspaper publishers of this and Western States, having for one of its objects the extinction of Typographical Unions. The simultaneous introduction of female compositors at various points, shows the line of policy adopted." [24]   Another instance of this more or less well-founded suspicion appears in the report of the convention proceedings of the International Industrial Assembly which met at Louisville, Kentucky, in September, 1864. A lockout of the union printers of the Chicago *Times* was under discussion. The Chicago representatives of organised labour believed the lockout was for the purpose of breaking up the Chicago Typographical Union. The convention went further and said: "There is good reason to believe that this effort is the result of a combination of capitalists known as the Northwestern Publishers' Association, to break up the Typographical Unions of the country, and control their employés to such an extent as to dictate to them the prices and conditions of labor." [25]   That this opinion was not without some foundation is evidenced by the report of the Cincinnati Convention of the Western Associated Press which met in May, 1864. This meeting was composed of representatives from thirteen leading establishments in Cincinnati, St. Louis, Detroit, Louisville, Dayton, Indianapolis, and Wheeling, while Chicago publishers pledged acquiescence. Resolutions adopted by this convention suggested a degree of organisation among the employers somewhat similar to that already described in the case of the stove foundrymen.[26]   But it is probable that these early publishers' associations dealt only incidentally with labour questions, and they are not to be compared with the more modern Newspaper Publishers' Association or with the Typothetæ.[27]

THE LOCOMOTIVE ENGINEERS

If most of the national trade unions sprang into existence only indirectly as a result of railway consolidation, the national union of locomotive engineers was its direct outgrowth. When a small road was merged with a larger one the engineers and shopmen had to come under the system of pay and work of the latter road. The men who suffered from the change sought by combination to control the larger employer under whom they

24 *Fincher's*, May 21, 1864.
25 *Fincher's*, Oct. 15, 1864.
26 The *Printer*, July, 1864.
Fincher's, June 4, 1864.

27 See above, I, 451 *et seq*. The problem of apprenticeship in the printing trade will be treated later.

were now to work.   " Since the consolidation the Northwestern Company has been the worst managed corporation of its size in the country. . . . At the very outset of the consolidation the salaries of the officials and hangers-on were increased and the wages of the poor labourers and others were correspondingly lowered. . . ." 28

The special grievance of the engineers was that during the sixties the railroads, for the first time, tried to force piece work upon them.   Prior to this period each engineer was paid according to the time he put in.   Now the railroad proposed to pay him according to the run he made, no matter how much time it took him to make it.   When we remember the delays incident to travelling on railroads in the sixties, the new system was a just cause for complaint.   It meant a reduction of pay considering the time.   At the convention of May, 1863, held in Detroit, where the Brotherhood of the Footboard was organised, which a year later became the Brotherhood of Locomotive Engineers, it was declared that the delegates met and organised because of " the disposition of the superintendent of motive power on that Road [Michigan Central] to wage a remorseless war upon the best interests of labour, and especially his encroachment upon the established rights and usages of the engineers in his employ and the reduction in their pay. . . ." 29

This was in 1863; by 1865 we find that the movement to introduce the run or piece system became quite general.   A correspondent of *Fincher's* in October of that year writes the following:

" Noticing an article in your issue signed by ' An Engineer of the Eastern Division of the Erie Railway,' setting forth the dissatisfaction existing on that Division among the Engineers, I thought I would drop you a few lines concerning the Engineers of the Susquehanna division; and, as we are fully as bad off concerning pay and allowances as they are, it will be at least consoling to the Engineers of that division to know it, and to know that they are not going into any battle of right without a fair prospect of receiving re-enforcement.   Engineers on this Division, previous to the advent of the present management, were paid for the time they were run-

28 Chicago *Workingman's Advocate,* Mar. 28, 1865.
29 Grand International Division of the

Brotherhood of Locomotive Engineers, *Proceedings,* 1864, 5.

ning on the road over schedule hours; but as soon as the new dis-
ciples [30] took hold of the reins they said at once a stop must be put
to this . . . and from that time we have ceased to receive pay for
extra hours on the road, and, as a consequence, the Engineer's time
is figured right down to a day and a half for running the Division
(140 miles), whether it is done one day, or three days and nights." [31]

The "Brotherhood" soon found that the railways were resolute in their attitude even to the extent of co-operating with
other railways. This came to light in 1864 after a strike by
engineers against the Galena and Chicago Union Rail Road
Company when the management of that road publicly expressed
its thanks to other roads for co-operation in resisting the union.

In spite of all its grievances, the Brotherhood of Locomotive Engineers was a militant organisation for just one year
from August 17, 1863, when it was organised, to August 17,
1864, when enough changes were made in its structure to make
it an entirely new organisation. W. D. Robinson, the enthus-
iast who had placed his entire soul and energy at the service
of the organisation, was dismissed as grand chief engineer on
personal charges preferred by his enemies. The new head was
Charles Wilson, an engineer on the New York Central & Hudson River Railway. This corporation had been for some years
in favour of a conservative organisation among its engineers.
To emphasise the complete breach with the past, the name
was changed from the Brotherhood of the Footboard to the
Brotherhood of Locomotive Engineers. The policy of the
union now was to win the good graces of the employers through
elevating the character of its members and thus raising their
efficiency as workmen. The employer would be so well pleased
with their work that he would of his own free will provide
better recognition of labour and higher pay. But in case that
should not follow, they would, at the same time, turn their attention to public opinion which they hoped to enlist in case of
difficulties.

The reason for the desire to enlist public opinion may be
ascribed to the fact that the service of engineers directly affects the public. The ordinary passenger who is in great haste

---

30 This refers to a new superintendent put on that division, *Aschcroft's Railway
Directory*, 1865, 55; 1866, 52.
31 *Fincher's*, Oct. 28, 1865.

to get to his destination, finding his train stopped, puts the blame on the immediate cause — the engineer who refuses to run it. An unsigned article in *Fincher's* for July 17, 1865, says:

" To possess the mere power to suspend the operation of a road, is not sufficient. That, without the clearest evidence of the justice of the stoppage, begets towards the organisation the hostility of the travelling public, the stockholders and the public at large; for we are apt to judge harshly if any class of men who, although struggling for *their* rights, in the least encroach on the comforts or conveniences; and the traveller, finding a road over which he must travel not in operation on account of a disagreement between the officers and employés, very naturally takes sides with the arbitrary power, from the fact that he feels within himself a disposition to compel somebody to carry him on his journey. And who is more likely to be the recipient of his ill wishes than the man who should run the engine, but who declines doing so, on account of a disagreement between himself and the officers of the road? . . . The most essential point here is to be made in convincing the victim that the fault lies with officers. . . ."

In the following year the Brotherhood was given an opportunity to state definitely its position. On January 17, 1866, the engineers and firemen entered upon a strike against the introduction of a new system of work and pay on the Michigan Southern & Northern Indiana Railway. The strike was a protracted one. The railroad was not very much affected. It hired new men and blacklisted the old ones.[32]

The blacklist, however, aroused a good many locals to action, especially those which were affected by the introduction of similar systems in the previous year. A special convention of the Brotherhood was called to discuss the difficulty. Fifty-seven delegates convened June 12, 1866, at Rochester, New York, and, of their number, twenty-six were appointed a committee to consider the blacklist. But it was Wilson's committee, and as a result of its deliberations, it drew up the following appeal to the railroads of the United States, which the convention endorsed:

" . . . do you think it right to have these men proscribed by the different Railroad officials because they are in difficulty with one

32 *Fincher's*, Feb. 3, 1866.

Company. . . . There seems to be a determination not only to pursue these men to the bitter end, but to break up an organisation that they happen to belong to, but which had no more to do with this trouble in the commencement than the most distant thing imaginable. To this we wish to enter our united protest, and appeal to you for help to avert so terrible a calamity as must ensue in the attempt to break up or destroy our organisation. We cannot believe you will consent to any such conspiracy . . . if you fully understand our object and future intentions. We have reliable information that lists of names of all the men in any way connected with this strike are in the possession of most of the Railroad Companies throughout the country and that some of the officials have given out word that not one of these men can get a job on their Road. . . . We do not wish to be understood as claiming the right to dictate who shall be hired by any Company. . . . If the Michigan Southern Railroad Company thinks it to their advantage to employ such men [scabs] to run their engines as they have employed since the strike, then we are forced to admit they have the right to employ them. . . . We appeal to you as men who profess to be willing to do right to use your influence to harmonise this difficulty, and to prevent the unwarranted interference of any outside parties." [33]

At this convention also they approved and incorporated in their proceedings a letter sent to them by the superintendent of motive power on the Erie Railway which in part is as follows: " The *ostensible object* of your organisation, I understand, is *to advance the moral, social, and intellectual condition of the Locomotive Engineers,* and to thereby elevate their standard of character as a profession. . . . Any attempt on the part of your members of your organisation to place your body in antagonism to your employers . . . should be promptly and immediately checked, and such evil disposed persons cured of their error, or summarily expelled from your deliberations. . . ." [34]

Many events occurred during the following four years that testify to the conservatism of the Brotherhood. At the convention of 1867, Wilson thanked the public press, the railroad officials, the clergy for recognition of his organisation as a factor of moral uplift and went on to say that to his mind the success of the Brotherhood depended upon a basis different than

[33] Grand International Division of the Brotherhood of Locomotive Engineers, *Proceedings,* Special Session, Rochester, June, 1866, 9, 10.
[34] *Ibid.,* 18.

that of other labour organisations. The success of the plans
of the trade union might be carried by virtue of the force of
numbers without any regard to the character or ability of their
members, but that could not be true of the Brotherhood. Its
foundation as an organisation rested upon the character and
ability of the members.[35]

At the convention of 1868 the question of endorsing a strike
entered into by the St. Louis division came up. Wilson urged
that if the national body endorsed it, it would be held responsible for it and advised that the best plan would be to let the
local division fight it out for itself.[36] The following year he
went on a trip south to organise branches. On reaching New
Orleans, he found the railroad officials opposed to such an organisation. He left after advising the engineers that they
should not organise until the prejudice had been removed. At
the convention of 1870, he again took occasion in his annual
address to declare the unity of interest between employer and
employé.

Many objections to this policy were registered during these
years by local branches which felt aggrieved over the treatment
they received at the hands of railroad officials. This was especially true among the western subdivisions which were continually in financial trouble through strikes. To prevent this, at
the session of 1871 held at Toronto, Wilson aimed to clamp
the organisation so as to make local action impossible. The
movement for incorporation was strong among most of the
national unions and Wilson saw in incorporation a possibility
of carrying his policy to a conclusion. He took the American
Railroad Association into confidence and drew up articles of
incorporation which contained the following clause: " Be it
further enacted, That any Sub-Division organised under this
act, . . . who shall, by advice or counsel, induce any Engineer,
or Engineers, to interfere, by a *strike* with the transportation
of the mails or other Government property, or who shall refuse
to expel any of their members who shall so interfere shall for-
feit their Charter, and all the rights and interests they may

35 Grand International Division of the Brotherhood of Locomotive Engineers,
Minutes, October, 1867, 11.
36 *Ibid.,* October, 1868, 8.

have in any common fund of this Brotherhood that may be accumulated at that time." [37]

The convention adopted the measure bodily, but when it was introduced in Congress there still existed enough opposition against legalisation of labour organisations to defeat it. The proposal of such a measure had its effect, however. It called forth a great deal of condemnation from the other large unions. Many of them saw in it "enslavement" of the Brotherhood, and Wilson came in for his just share of reproach.

This, no doubt, started the opposition to him which culminated in 1874 by his removal from office. It might have occurred before that time, but the country just then had entered upon a period of prosperity shared by the railroads, which lasted to the middle of 1873. The panic changed matters. In November, 1873, the engineers declared that railroads had combined to force a reduction of wages on account of a decrease in business. They did not believe the reason given as true and took steps to resist a reduction on the principal roads. The Pennsylvania Road was the chief offender. It ordered a reduction of pay within a day's notice in spite of the fact that it had an agreement to pay a certain price. The engineers resented the action and, the railroad failing to restore the wages, they struck. Wilson denounced them through the public press for their hasty action. This so enraged the Brotherhood that it called a special meeting at Cleveland, February 25, 1874, and forced him to resign.[38]

At this session William D. Robinson was present and saw the removal of his rival from office by an almost unanimous vote. Robinson had been reinstated in his old local in May, 1873, and, by urgent request of the Brotherhood, attended this national meeting. He sat silent throughout the proceedings. After the election of the new grand chief engineer, P. M. Arthur, he was called upon to address the convention, which he did in a dramatic speech that called forth cheers of vindication though he did not once mention the name of Wilson.[39]

P. M. Arthur, though elected as an insurgent against Wilson's pacifism, soon adopted the very same policies which he

[37] *Engineers' Journal*, V, 506.
[38] McNeill, *Labor Movement: The Problem of To-day*, 322.
[39] Chicago *Workingman's Advocate*, May 2, 1874.

had condemned in his predecessor. The excellent strategic position of the engineer in the railroad industry forced the employers to grant him and his organisations a degree of recognition which in those days was almost unthinkable in other trades. Arthur thus found that more could be accomplished through peaceful pressure than through strikes. In his hands conservatism was made the permanent and distinctive characteristic of the Brotherhood, a policy which was deliberately broken on only one occasion, the strike against the Chicago, Burlington & Quincy road in 1888.

A distinctive feature of Wilson's policy had been the early development of a benefit system. The chief incentive was the extremely hazardous nature of the work of the engineer which made insurance in private companies prohibitively high if not altogether impossible. As early as 1866 at its regular convention in Boston, the Brotherhood adopted the widows', orphans', and disabled members' fund.[40] This measure was referred to a vote of the subdivisions where it received a two-thirds majority vote and was adopted.[41]

About the same time (1867) the Locomotive Mutual Life Insurance Association was created. None but members of the Brotherhood could join it, and membership was optional. Those who joined paid a small initiation fee and assessments upon the death of members. The total insurance derived by beneficiaries depended upon the numerical strength of the association and upon the rate of assessment. As the membership increased, the assessment was lowered. During two years of the existence of this scheme, 1867–1869, the smallest amount paid upon the death of a member was $1,110, the largest was $1,856, at a cost of from $20 to $30 per year, which was considered good insurance.[42] It was not however until the decade of the nineties that the insurance feature of the Brotherhood became established on a firm and broad basis.

THE CIGAR MAKERS

The history of the cigar makers during this period may be summarised as the history of organisation against large shops

---

[40] *Proceedings*, 1866, 23.   [41] *Ibid.*, 1867, 17.   [42] *Engineers' Journal*, III, 505.

in the sixties and against the introduction of the " mould " and division of labour in the seventies.

Prior to the War the cigar trade was in the one-man shop stage. The master mechanic worked for himself, owned the tobacco, made the cigars, and sold them to customers in the community in which he worked. He was the ordinary workman with small means. He could buy tobacco in small quantities as he needed it. He needed practically no tools and worked in or about the place in which he lived. With the Civil War came a change. Congress introduced a system of taxation which favoured large manufactories. This at once took the control of the trade out of the workman's hands and placed it in the hands of an employer.[43] With the rapidly changing condition in the sixties it took only a few years for the larger shop to replace the little ones and to gather in the small masters to work for wages. In the East, instead of going into large factories, the trade passed into contractors' sweatshops. The cigar maker who had worked in his house for himself before the sixties now worked for some one else.

At the first national convention held in New York City, June 21, 1864, out of 21 locals represented, 12 were from the State of New York.[44] At this convention a strict trade union policy was adopted indicative of the cigar makers throughout their history. After resolving that they united themselves for better protection of their trade and requesting that all cigar makers organise themselves, they " resolved that no cigar maker coming from any city, county or district, who is not a member of a union, if any exists from whence he came, be allowed to become a member of the union where he has come to obtain employment or be allowed to work in said city, county or district, until he has been admitted a member in the place from which he came." The resolution went further " to discountenance the practice of any union allowing any of its members to work in a shop or manufactory that employs no union [sic] men working for them out of the shop or manufactory." [45] The latter part of the resolution shows the prominence of the New Yorkers and their hostility to the sweatshop.

43 Ohio Bureau of Labor Statistics, *First Annual Report*, Columbus, Ohio, 1878, 199–201.

44 From typewritten record at Johns Hopkins University Library, 1864–1867.
45 *Ibid.*

The national once organised grew rapidly, although it only gained 5 locals during the first year, June, 1864, to September, 1865. It gained 37 locals during the following year. At the convention of 1860 held at Baltimore, 49 delegates were present, representing Canada and distant points as far south as Maysville, Kentucky, and as far west as Leavenworth, Kansas. The strike-benefit feature, which has always been an important pillar in the structure of the cigar makers' organisation, appears here in its elementary form. Locals in case of difficulty could appeal to the national president who then sent out a notice for contributions. The returns were forwarded to the strikers.

At the Buffalo session in the following year, the organisation was more thoroughly developed. The name was changed from National Union of Cigar Makers to Journeymen Cigar Makers' International Union, so as to include the Canadian locals. Strike benefits were definitely prescribed. If a local entered into a strike with approval of the international president, the members were to receive $8 per week if married and $5 if single, out of a fund created by a tax upon the membership of the entire union.[46]

During 1868 and 1869 the union continued to grow, reporting 84 locals in the former year and 87 in the latter. The problem which agitated it during these years was the Kingston conspiracy case. A member of the Kingston local, New York, was designated by the other members as a " rat " and denied the privileges of the union. He brought suit against the individual members as conspirators and the circuit court fined each member $20. The International pledged the last cent in the treasury of its local unions, if necessary, to sustain the Kingston union which appealed the case to the State Supreme Court. At the convention of 1869 it was reported that the case was to be tried in the latter part of September. Nothing further is heard of it, however. It may have been dropped. Considerable feeling against conspiracy laws had grown up in the country by this time, as is evidenced by the number of state legislatures that were considering bills to repeal the laws in

46 *Ibid.*

so far as they affected labour. New York repealed its law, March 24, 1870.[47]

Thus far in its history the national met with few obstacles. The advent of the large shop, while it diminished the bargaining power of the cigar makers, did not affect the trade itself and the workman was still protected by his skill. A large organisation with a considerable strike fund was very effective in counteracting the large employer. In the five years of its existence the cigar makers' national grew to about 5,000 members, which compares favourably with other nationals at this time (1869).

But in 1867 the mould was invented, which undermined the trade itself. Before the introduction of the mould each cigar maker made the whole cigar. He was the " bunch breaker " or, as he was then known, the " filler breaker " and also the " roller." He made the bunch and rolled it himself. He had to mould it in his own hands and roll it immediately. That method was changed for most cigars as soon as the mould was introduced. The mould, however, was not a machine, but a mere press for shaping cigars by hand.

The effect of this change was threefold. It split up the trade. Instead of one man making the whole cigar, one man now made the bunches and another rolled them. It was easier to make a bunch when the mould shaped it than it was when it had to be shaped by hand, and it was also easier to roll it after it was smoothed off. This quickened the process. There was no time lost in changing from bunch making to rolling and vice versa.

The moulds, apparently, were first introduced in the Cincinnati shops. In October, 1869, the cigar makers of that city asked for an increase of $1 per 1,000. The employers assented to the demand, but immediately after Christmas announced a reduction of $2 per 1,000. This started one of the most bitter strikes in the history of the union. Three hundred men were involved. The executive committee of the International called in the strike funds from the locals and in February levied an extra fifty-cent tax upon each member. The

47 Chicago *Workingman's Advocate*, Apr. 2, 1870.

employers were likewise busy in the struggle. They sent out circulars to employers in other cities, requesting them not to employ Cincinnati men and above all not to pay more than their prices.[48]

The strike lasted eighteen weeks, finally concluding with a victory for the cigar makers. But the victory soon turned into failure. At the end of the strike the employers introduced the mould, and the union, foreseeing a reduction in wages and fearing another struggle, voluntarily reduced the price it had thus secured after a long fight.

A succinct statement of the reasons why the cigar makers objected to the use of the mould is given in the *Report* of the Bureau of Labour Statistics of Ohio (1878):

" In 1870 a cigar machine [the mould] was introduced into the town of Cincinnati. The men claimed that it did not save labour but instead added thereto. One firm purchased fifty of the machines and their employees refused to use them and the result was that men were discharged to the number of seventy-five and girls and boys were hired in their places, and this was the commencement of the female cigar workers in Cincinnati. A cigar machine company then came into operation having men, at first, but as there was no extra profit in their labour they were discharged and women and girls were brought to make cigars, they in turn being discharged for other learners receiving but little if any wages. By this means a so-called large number of female cigar makers were competing with the men for the privilege of work. Wages rapidly fell until a week's wages were not sufficient to pay the board of a single man. . . ."

In October the cigar makers held their convention at Syracuse. It was the largest convention since 1867. The mould question was settled by adopting a constitutional amendment stating that " no local union shall allow its members to work with a filler breaker."[49] The provision was more far reaching than it really seems. It meant that the national took a stand against splitting up the trade between bunch breakers and rollers. It also really meant a stand against the introduction of the mould which invariably was worked by filler break-

48 Chicago *Workingman's Advocate,* Feb. 5, 1870.
49 Constitution, 1870, Art. XI, Sec. 4;
Chicago *Workingman's Advocate,* Nov. 5 and 12, 1870.

ers. Legislating against the filler breaker thus meant legislating against the mould.

But the union was too weak to enforce its rules everywhere. Many locals permitted their members to work with "filler breakers" in spite of the law and grew lukewarm towards the International. At the convention of 1870, 42 locals were represented; 2 years later only 17 sent delegates. At this latter convention of 1872 the president, Edwin Johnson, in his annual address foretold the inevitable. "I admit it is a great evil to the trade this filler breaking system, but a minority can never accomplish anything in the way of breaking up this way of working. While we have the large majority outside of our organisation, working directly in the opposite all the time, I can see but one way of accomplishing anything that will be beneficial to our trade generally . . . Let us lay aside a little of our spirit of selfishness, make our laws liberal, and our platform broad enough to hold all, and let us endeavour to unite the whole into one grand organisation." [50]

In spite of this advice when the question of the filler breaker rule came up for consideration, whether it should be retained or dropped, the sentiment was strongly in favour of retaining it. What is more, the rule was amended so that it became more restrictive than before. As amended, it read: "No local union shall allow its members to work with filler breakers or non-union men." "Or non-union men" was added now and the whole adopted, thirteen votes in favour and four against. The strike fund was also increased. Instead of 2 cents per member, each month, 10 cents were to be levied thereafter.

These measures were of no avail. The mould came to stay. The hostility towards it was continued for another year, when at the convention of 1873, with other changes in the constitution, the filler breaker clause was amended so as to read, "Local unions may allow their members to work in shops where filler-breakers are employed, provided that no member of the union has permitted himself to work in conjunction with filler breakers." The constitution as revised and including this clause was sub-

50 Chicago *Workingman's Advocate*, Oct. 1, 1872.

mitted to a vote of the locals and was returned 60 in favour and 17 opposed.

The adoption of this amendment was a virtual acceptance of the mould. Although the union man could not work in conjunction with a filler breaker, the mould was admitted into the shop and once there it gradually replaced hand work for the great bulk of cigars made.

THE COOPERS

Another cause which brought large nationals into existence, especially in the latter part of the ten-year period, was the introduction of machinery. The unions that sprang up as a direct result of the change in the methods of manufacture were particularly the Knights of St. Crispin and the coopers.

The effects of machinery on the coopers' trade may be seen from the following extract taken from the *Coopers' Monthly Journal,* October, 1872, in a series of articles entitled " What I know about Machinery." " Whenever our craftsman demanded an increase of wages and it was refused, some employers would buy barrel machinery because they would not strike." The article then goes on to give an account of a cooperage works in St. Louis. " Some two years ago a company was started in St. Louis under the name of the St. Louis Barrel Works for the manufacture of pork barrels. The stockholders were men of means and money was not sparingly used to furnish the factory with all the modern improvements. The barrels were raised by boys, clamped and trussed by machinery; the heads were turned by machines and put into the barrels by boys, and there was nothing left for the coopers to do but plane, shave up and hoop the package. When a barrel was finished, it generally leaked at every joint. . . . But the staves were kiln dried and by pouring from one to four pints of water in each barrel . . . it could be made to pass. All this was very well and as the company warranted every package they were not in want of a market."

The effect of such a change in making barrels is obvious. The cooper was now deprived of the protection afforded by his skill. His part in the process now was trimming the barrel instead of making it. The importance of a large, powerful organisation to counteract the advantages which the employer gained over him through these improvements is plainly to be seen. On March 19, 1870, when the nation was about to start on a three-year lap of prosperity, Martin A. Foran, then president of the Central Union of Ohio, sent a call to the coopers to meet in Cleveland, May, 1870. The Cleveland coopers had just gone through a strike — that fact and the powerful personality of Foran account for the calling of a convention at this time and place.[51] Suggestions for a national union had been made as far back as the spring of 1868, when a correspondent of the *Advocate* reported the coopers in New York on a strike and expressed surprise that "with the number of coopers in the United States . . . they do not take steps to organise a national union." [52]

The international was organised and grew very rapidly. The first convention met in May, 1870, with 13 delegates representing 1,576 members. Five months later another convention was held in Baltimore. Here 41 unions were represented with a membership of 3,350.[53] But circulars sent out by Foran to locals which allied themselves with the national show returns of 142 unions in good standing embracing a membership of 6,723. The next convention was held in 1873 after the panic. Here 157 locals were reported in good standing. Seventy-two unions were organised or reorganised during these 2 years, but 72 disbanded, which left the international just about where it was in 1871.

In spite of its rocket-like career the coopers' national union permanently influenced the labour movement. It brought to the front in the labour ranks its second president, Robert

51 The career of Martin A. Foran of Cleveland is a prominent example of an American labour leader. Born in Susquehanna County, Penn., Nov. 11, 1844, he received a public school education and the beginnings of a higher education. He was a cooper by trade, but he had also taught school for three years. Having achieved prominence in the labour movement, first as the president of the Coopers' International Union, which he organised, and later in 1872, as the foremost leader in the movement for a federation of the national trade unions, he entered politics as a member of the Ohio constitutional convention in 1873. During the next year he was admitted to the practice of law and in 1874 was elected, on the Democratic ticket, city attorney of Cleveland. He was elected to Congress in 1884 and was several times re-elected. He never lost connection with the labour movement and remained a champion of labour bills throughout his congressional career.

52 Chicago *Workingman's Advocate*, May 9, 1868.

53 Coopers' International Union, *Proceedings*, 1871, 10, 11.

Schilling, of Cleveland, and later of Milwaukee, who became so impressed with the inadequacy of the existing basis of the movement that, according to his own statement, he formulated a new set of principles which in 1878 came to be adopted as the Preamble of the Order of the Knights of Labor.

In still another respect the coopers anticipated during this period the labour movement of the eighties.   In 1870 a number of unionised coopers in Minneapolis, after several attempts, succeeded in organising a co-operative association for the making of barrels.   The example was soon followed by others and there were altogether seven co-operative shops which manufactured the bulk of the barrels demanded by the flour mills in that city.   When the Knights of Labour revived the co-operative movement during the middle of the eighties, they could well keep in mind the successful example of the Minneapolis coopers.[54]

THE KNIGHTS OF ST. CRISPIN

The shoemakers' organisations reached their greatest strength in 1869 and 1870.   During the preceding years machinery had exercised but little influence on the labour movement, either in this or in other occupations.   As a rule skilled labour remained the basis of industry, and although the mechanic suffered from evils which were serious enough, no one questioned that he was indispensable.   However, there were three notable exceptions: the textile, cooperage, and shoe industries.   In the textile industry machine production had been introduced as early as the thirties; the shoe industry entered upon the factory stage of production in the sixties; and the cooperage in the early seventies.

The first step toward a factory system in the shoe industry came with the invention in 1846 and utilisation in 1852 of a sewing machine for stitching uppers.   But the invention destined to revolutionise the industry occurred in 1862, when McKay succeeded in perfecting a pegging machine.   Between 1860 and 1870 the utilisation of these machines and of other inventions proceeded at a rapid pace, and the skilled mechanic

---

[54] See Shaw, " Co-operation in a Western City," in *American Economic Association Publications*, I, 129–172.

was being displaced by the unskilled in great proportions. The situation in the shoe industry during the sixties is of special interest, as it represented the first encounter on a large scale of the skilled American mechanics with machine competition.[55] Indeed the shoemakers were called upon to meet the same sort of a situation which thirty years later was settled satisfactorily in the printing industry, when the latter was revolutionised by the invention of the linotype. As is well known the printers warded off the menace of " green hands " by agreeing to accept the linotype on the condition that it should be operated exclusively by skilled workmen. The shoemakers of the sixties advanced the same solution but, instead of finding the employers ready for a compromise, they were compelled to " fight it out." The " green hands " menace is the key to the understanding of the meteoric career of the Order of the Knights of St. Crispin.

This union was organised as a secret order on March 7, 1867, at Milwaukee, Wisconsin, by Newell Daniels, formerly of Milford, Massachusetts, and six associates. It spread rapidly- in all shoemaking districts, especially Massachusetts. Eighty-seven lodges were formed before the first meeting of the International Grand Lodge at Rochester, New York, July, 1868; 204 before the second, at Boston, April, 1869; 327 before the third, at Boston, April, 1872. The membership was estimated at about 50,000 in 1870. The Order was then by far the largest labour organisation in the country.

The Order of the Crispins differed in nature from other unions. As said above, its object was not so much to advance wages and to shorten hours as to protect the journeymen against the competition of " green hands " and apprentices. The constitution made resistance to green hands and the defence of the Order the only purposes for which the strike funds of the International Grand Lodge could be used. Wage conflicts and trade agreements were to be treated as purely local matters.

The Crispins conducted strikes with varied success. They were hampered by an inefficient revenue system and by the general looseness of their organisation, particularly by the lack of central control over subordinate lodges. The strikes were

[55] This was not the case in the textile industry, where on the whole, the machine competed not with the skilled workman in the shop but with the work of the woman in the household.

generally successful in 1869 and 1870. In Lynn, the Order was even able to force the manufacturers to sign an agreement governing wages for the twelve months following July 21, 1870, and the agreement was renewed for another year. This success, however, forced manufacturers in various localities to organise and to attempt to break up the union. In 1869 such conflicts occurred on a large scale in San Francisco and, in 1870, in Philadelphia and Worcester. But the Order was able to hold its own until the unsuccessful strike at Lynn, Massachusetts, which lasted during the spring and a part of the summer of 1872. This strike occurred following the break-up of the trade agreement when, as a result of cutthroat competition among the manufacturers, wages were reduced. The Crispins lost and were compelled to disband the hitherto powerful lodge at that place. During 1872, 1873, and 1874 the manufacturers seldom failed in their efforts to destroy the organisation.

Five principal causes of Crispin strikes may be distinguished: resistance to green hands, defence of the Order, opposition to wage reductions, refusal to work with non-Crispins, and attempts to abolish contractors. The green-hands' strikes naturally occurred primarily in the factories, but strikes in defence of the Order were common both in the factories and in merchant capitalist establishments. The Crispins embraced in one organisation shops selling in opposite kinds of markets and using opposite systems of production: the "bespoke" shop as well as the wholesale speculative shop and factory, the handicraft custom-order shop and merchant-capitalist establishments, as well as the machine-operated factory. Strikes against wage reductions, though occurring in every type of manufacture, were most marked in the merchant-capitalist shops. The latter were in a difficult position. The factories, with their machinery and green hands, were lowering wholesale prices. The custom shops, with their individual markets, were keeping up wages. The merchant-capitalists had to meet the price competition of the factory and the quality competition of both the factory and the custom shop. To compete with the one they had to reduce labour costs, to compete with the other they had to employ skilled workmen.

The Crispins, even during the period of their most successful strikes, did not turn away from co-operation altogether. "The present demand of the Crispin is steady employment and fair wages, but his future is self-employment," [56] said Samuel Cummings, grand scribe of the Order. The Crispin was less confident of his power as a wage-earner than the bricklayer or machinist. Even though winning the strikes, he knew that he was losing the mechanics' safest bulwark against encroachment — his skill. This was indeed demonstrated by the fact that the Order began to suffer defeat in 1872, when prosperity was at its height. Each Grand Lodge had a special committee on co-operation, and in 1870 this committee recommended that the grievance funds be invested in co-operative manufacture, under the supervision of the committee appointed by the Grand Lodge from among the members of the local lodge. The recommendation was not adopted, the Grand Lodge feeling that it was not expedient to take the control of co-operation out of the hands of the locals. But in 1869 and 1870 the Grand Lodge of Massachusetts made a vigorous effort to secure from the legislature an act of incorporation for the purpose of conducting co-operative stores for purchasing supplies. This was their main object in entering politics in that State, and their charter actually passed the lower house, but was rejected in the senate. In 1870 the New York State Grand Lodge recommended to its subordinate lodges co-operative workshops. These co-operative shops became numerous after 1870, and there were established also between thirty and forty co-operative stores, which soon, however, went to pieces.

In 1875 an attempt was made to revive the Order. The issue, however, was no longer "green hands," but arbitration. The second Order of St. Crispin led an anæmic existence until 1878. The Crispins later furnished a number of active members to the Knights of Labor. Charles H. Litchman, at one time grand scribe of the Crispins, later became the head of the District Assembly of Massachusetts and then general secretary of the Knights of Labor.[57]

[56] *American Workman*, June, 1869.

[57] For the detailed history of the Crispins upon which the foregoing account is based, see Lescohier, "The Knights of St. Crispin, 1867–1874," University of Wisconsin *Bulletin*, No. 355. See also *Doc. Hist.*, III, 51–54.

THE SONS OF VULCAN

The organisation of the iron puddlers, known as the "Sons of Vulcan," came into existence in 1858. It styled itself a national organisation but, as a matter of fact, its field was restricted to the Pittsburgh district. Although it was only a small organisation, it deserves attention altogether out of proportion to its numerical strength, for it offers the first instance of a trade union entering into a trade agreement with an employers' association based upon the sliding scale principle of fixing wages. The puddlers enjoyed a bargaining advantage with their employers which seldom fell to the lot of other wage-earners. The basis of this advantage was the high skill required of a puddler, and, second, the extreme localisation of the iron industry, which facilitated organisation. Accordingly, the associated employers early came to recognise the necessity of a permanent working agreement with the union, and the trade agreement of February, 1865, was the result. This wage agreement fixed the scale of prices to be paid for boiling pig iron. But it lasted only a short time. The workmen soon demanded higher pay. In 1867 another conference was held and a new sliding scale was agreed upon. This second agreement lasted seven years, until the industrial depression led the employers to reduce wages. The resulting strikes were settled by employers individually signing special wage agreements. The Amalgamated Association of Iron and Steel Workers of the United States, formed in 1875 as an amalgamation of the workmen's unions in this industry, found its principal strength in the Sons of Vulcan.[58]

RESTRICTIVE POLICIES — APPRENTICESHIP

What distinguished the permanent labour organisation of the sixties from the more ephemeral efforts of earlier periods, was a conscious endeavour to maintain certain fixed trade rules even during times of industrial peace. The beginning had been made from 1850 to 1854, when the labour movement had for the first time discarded productive co-operation for trade union-

[58] Industrial Commission, *Report* XVII, 339.

ism, but on account of the ensuing panic and industrial depression it was not before the sixties that these characteristics came into high relief. When a trade union of skilled mechanics begins to set up permanent trade rules, it is usually to apprenticeship that it turns its first attention. Thus it was that during the sixties the rules of apprenticeship, or restrictions on the entrance to a trade, became probably the subject of paramount interest to unionists in the vast majority of the trades.

It was not surprising that apprenticeship should reach an acute stage at this time. The wider market, which resulted from through railway transportation, forced the employer to give increased attention to his functions as a merchant, and correspondingly decreased the amount of time which he was able to devote to his duties as the instructor of his apprentices. Naturally the training of the apprentices was bound to suffer. Nor was that all. The keen competition in the national market made it imperative upon the employers to reduce operating costs. They therefore dismissed some of their journeymen and filled their places by cheaply paid boys whom they styled apprentices.

Closely parallel was the attempt to reduce manufacturing costs by introducing a more or less minute division of labour. This resulted in splitting up the old established trades into independent branches, each apprentice specialising in only one branch and learning little beyond that.

But apprenticeship broke down not merely because the employer succumbed to the temptation of exploiting cheap boy labour. Under the new conditions he could not teach them the trade properly even if he had the best intention of doing so. The increase in the scale of production had transformed him from a mere master workman of a small shop into a superintendent of an industrial plant, with the result that he had lost the old-time intimate contact with his journeymen and apprentices. Thus between the newly enhanced merchant function and the enlarged duties of general supervision he had no time left for teaching apprentices, and, if he continued taking them, he had to delegate their instruction to his foremen. Now the foreman had contracted no personal obligations towards the apprenticed boy, but was instead possessed of a keen interest to enlarge the output of his department. Consequently, it was only natural that he tended to keep the boy indefinitely at the first operation which he had thoroughly learned rather than to shift him from one operation to another until he mastered the whole trade. Often the boy brought the apprenticeship to a premature end by running away. If he was not of the adventurous type, he stayed until his term expired. But in either case he remained only partially trained and a competitive menace to the all-round mechanics.

The situation called for preventive action, namely the enforcement upon the employer of stringent apprenticeship rules. But with the means of communication revolutionised by the railroad, the menace no longer was local in its nature. The fact was that it was possible to mobilise the army of " botches " at short notice at any point where the workmen threatened to go on strike, and it was utterly beyond the power of any one locality to control the situation short of violence. There was needed an agency which should be able to extend its authority into every locality in order to stop the breeding of " botches " at the very source. The national trade union of the sixties was endeavouring to meet this need.[59]

The unionists of this period had two demands to make with reference to the apprentice question. They repeated the demand made by their predecessors in the earlier decades that no one should be allowed to enter a trade except as an indentured apprentice for a term of years, generally five; that the employer should be obliged to teach them the entire trade, and that the number of apprentices admitted to a trade should not exceed a fixed ratio to the number of journeymen. They claimed that such a limitation of numbers was essential to good

[59] The evils which came to be connected with apprenticeship were described by Sylvis as follows: " Recently this ' boy system ' has been introduced in its worst features in the city of Philadelphia; in four shops there is on an average about ten boys to one journeyman, and these are almost entirely without instruction. They are taken without regard to age or any other qualifications necessary to make them ornaments to the mechanical community. A large number of them are indentured, but the agreement is so one-sided that the boy has no guarantee whatever that he will be made a workman. They are to serve the two or three years, without any assurance whatever that at the end of that time they will know a trade. . . . Should they then have manly independence enough to demand their just dues, they will be turned away, and other boys put in their places. Being without a knowledge of the trade, and outside of the organisation, they will be unable to procure employment anywhere in those shops, where they will remain not as masters of their own business, but as slaves." *Fincher's*, July 18, 1863.

training and in a measure they doubtless were right.   Yet it
is not open to doubt that their intention was restrictive.

The national trade unions tried to handle apprenticeship in
various ways, sometimes by forcing the employer to live up to
the regulations they prescribed, sometimes by appealing to
state legislatures, and sometimes by offering to take the employer into counsel.   In any case, it was a difficult task to
force regulations upon the employer.   When times were good
and more men were needed, the workmen could not stand in
the way of the employment of more men.   When times were
bad and the unemployed numerous it was difficult to force the
employer to live up to regulations.   Through legislation they
tried to revive the old indenture system.   Bills were introduced
in Pennsylvania in 1864, Massachusetts in 1865, New York
and Illinois in 1869.   The Massachusetts bill was the only one
that passed.   The objects sought in all of them were legally to
bind apprentices for five years, to compel the master to teach
him the entire trade, to make the master responsible for his
moral training, and to prescribe the ratio of apprentices.[60]

The employing printers were the only ones that paid any
attention to the solicitations of the union for an adjustment of
the apprenticeship system.   It was to their interest to do so.
No material changes occurred in the printing trade, yet the
chances for learning it were poorer than they had ever been
before this time.   Printed matter must come up to a certain
standard, below which it attracts the attention of the public to
the detriment of the publisher.   Employers felt this and were
willing to improve the skill of their workmen.   At the convention of the Typographical Union held in 1865, a resolution
was adopted that subordinate unions be requested to make
regulations concerning apprentices and, inasmuch as employers
and journeymen were mutually interested in framing such
regulations, that the employers be invited to participate with
a view of harmonising interests and preserving good feeling.[61]
This effort brought no results, for in the following convention
it was reported that the question of apprenticeship referred to
subordinate unions did not receive much consideration.

60 Wright, *Apprenticeship System in its
Relation to Industrial Education*, U. S.
Bulletin of Education, No. 6, 25–27.

61 National Typographical Union, *Proceedings*, 1865, 19.

The result was that trade unions kept on regulating apprenticeship, each in its own way. In most instances the matter was left to the locals. The nearest the nationals ever got to regulating apprenticeship was by prescribing the requirements of candidates for membership. The machinists and blacksmiths, the coopers, and the cigar makers, for instance, required that they should have worked in the trade for three years. The Knights of St. Crispin required two years. The ratio of apprentices to journeymen in a shop varied with the condition of trade depression or prosperity. When times were good more apprentices were allowed than when times were bad. During the war times the moulders permitted one to each shop and one additional for every six and a half journeymen. In 1866 with the coming of hard times they changed the ratio to one apprentice to every eight journeymen in addition to one allowed each shop.

The machinists and blacksmiths had a unique apprenticeship problem of their own. In the early part of 1871, Charles Wilson, the Grand Chief Engineer of the Brotherhood of Locomotive Engineers, published an article in the *Engineers' Journal* asking the railroads to permit engineers to work in the shops while their engines were in repair. Wilson claimed that he proposed his plan not because he intended that engineers should learn the machinists' trade, but rather that they might get familiar with every part of the engine, so that in an emergency they would know just what to do. There is no evidence to show that the engineers ever worked in the shops, but it was sufficient to make the apprenticeship question for the machinists a paramount one. It caused considerable agitation in their ranks and may have had something to do with the rapid growth of the union at this time.[62]

[62] See Motley, *Apprenticeship in American Trade Unions*, in *Johns Hopkins University Studies*, ser. XXV, Nos. 11-12, pp. 37-41, for a general discussion of apprenticeship during this period.

CHAPTER IV

THE NATIONAL LABOR UNION, 1866–1872

The Labour Movement in Europe and America. Eight-hour question, 87. Ira Steward and his wage theory, 87. Stewardism contrasted with socialism, 90. Stewardism and trade unionism, 91. Stewardism and political action, 91. Boston Labor Reform Association, 91. The Grand Eight Hour League of Massachusetts, 92. Massachusetts labour politics, 92. Labour politics in Philadelphia, 93. Fincher's opposition to politics, 93. Return of the soldiers — a stimulus to the eight-hour movement, 94. The question of national federation, 94. The move by trades' assemblies, 94. New York State Workingmen's Assembly, 95. The move by the national trade unions, 96. The compromise, 96.

Labor Congress of 1866. Representation, 96. Attitude toward trade unionism and legislation, 98. Eight-hour question at the congress, 98. Resolution on political action, 99. Land question, 100. Co-operation, 101. Form of organisation, 101.

Eight Hours and Politics. Congressional election of 1866, 102. Independent politics outside Massachusetts, 103. Eight-hours before Congress, 104. Eight-hours before President Johnson, 104. Eight-hours before the General Court of Massachusetts, 105. Special commission of 1865, 106. The commission of 1866, 107. E. H. Rogers, 107. Eight-hour bills in other States, 108. Causes of the failure, 109.

Co-operative Workshops. Productive co-operation in various trades, 111.

Labor Congress of 1867. Activity of the National Labor Union during the year, 112. *Address to the Workingmen of the United States*, 113. Viewpoint of the "producing classes," 114. Representation at the Congress of 1867, 115. The constitution, 116. The immigrant question and the American Emigrant Company, 117. The question of the Negro, 118.

Greenbackism. Popularity of greenbackism among the various elements at the Labor Congress, 119. A. C. Cameron, 119. Alexander Campbell, 120. The "new Kelloggism," 121. Greenbackism contrasted with socialism and anarchism, 121. Greenbackism as a remedy against depressions, 122. "Declaration of Principles," 122. The depression, 1866–1868, 123. Progress of co-operation, 124.

Eight Hours. Government employés and the eight-hour day, 124. Labor Congress of 1868, 125. Conference on the presidential election, 125. Representation at the congress, 126. Discussion on strikes, 129. The first lobbying committee, 130. Sylvis' presidency, 130.

The International Workingmen's Association. The international regulation of immigration, 131. Sylvis' attitude towards the international, 132. Sylvis' death, 132. Cameron's mission to Basle, 132.

Labor Congress of 1869. Representation, 133. Effect of Sylvis' death, 134.

The Negroes. Invasion of industries, 134. Causes of their separate organisation, 135. Maryland Colored State Labor Convention of 1869, 136. Supremacy of the politicians, 137.

Politics in Massachusetts. The New England Labor Reform League, 138. American proudhonism and the intellectuals, 139. The Crispins and politics, 140. The State Labor Reform Convention, 140. The Crispins and incorporation, 140. State campaign of 1869, 141. Boston municipal election, 142. Wendell Phillips and the State election of 1870, 143. End of labour politics in Massachusetts, 144.

Labor Congress of 1870. The Negro question, 144. Decision to call a political convention, 145. Changes in the constitution, 146.

Chinese Exclusion. The industrial situation in California during the sixties, 147. The early anti-Chinese movement in California, 147. Mechanics' State Council, 148. Effect of the transcontinental railway on the California industries, 148. The National Labor Union and the Chinese question in 1869, 149. The North Adams, Mass., incident, 149. The Burlingame treaty with China, 149. The National Labor Union and the Chinese question in 1870, 150.

Revival of Trade Unionism. Stopping the contraction of the currency, 151. Eight-hour strike movement in 1872, 151. New and aggressive leaders, 152. Abandonment of the National Labor Union by the national trade unions, 152. The Crispins — the exception, 152.

Politics and dissolution. Horace H. Day, 153. The "industrial" convention of 1871, 153. Political convention, 154. Nomination for President, 154. Failure and dissolution, 155.

THE National Labor Union was the successor in the sixties of the National Trades' Union of the thirties, and the predecessor of the Knights of Labor and the American Federation of Labor. Its organisation, policies, and final dissolution reflect the new nation-wide problems brought on permanently by railroad transportation and the telegraph, and temporarily by paper money. Its attempt to regulate immigration through a voluntary arrangement with the International Workingmen's Association of Europe indicates also the first conscious recognition of the international competition of labour. It is more than a coincidence that the famed International, the creature of Karl Marx and the British trade unions, should have risen and disappeared in the same years as the attempted national organisation of all labour in the United States. The year 1864, which witnessed the meeting at Louisville of the Industrial Assembly of North America, witnessed at London the preliminary conference of the International Workingmen's Association. In the year 1866 the National Labor Union was organised at Baltimore and the International held its first meeting of delegates from different countries at Geneva.   In 1867 the American organisation met at Chicago, the European at Lausanne; in 1868 the one met at New York, the other, at Brussels.   In 1869 the one that met at Philadelphia was represented by a delegate to the other at Basle.   In 1870 the Franco-Prussian War interrupted the European congress, and the next two years witnessed the dissolution of both organisations through similar internal dissensions — the American organisation through the antagonism of " political actionists " and trade unionists, the European through the antagonism of socialists and anarchists.

The first great object of the International was the support of strikes and trade unions through the control of migration across the frontiers of European nations, and its later shift, in 1867, to socialism and anarchism coincides with the shift of the National Labor Union to greenbackism.   It was the national and international competition of labour, the weakness of trade unionism and the depression of industry following a period of expansion, that furnished the economic conditions underlying both movements.   That the one in America should have dissolved in greenbackism, the other in socialism and anarchism, was due to political and economic conditions peculiar to each.   Modified in this way, the attempted nationalisation of American labour movements, regardless of State lines, was the reflection of conditions that in Europe led to the attempted internationalisation of movements regardless of national lines.   The two lines of agitation that dominated the National Labor Union were eight hours for work, and greenbackism. The first prevailed in 1866, the second took possession in 1867.

The first authentic instance of the actual adoption of the eight-hour day was that of the ship carpenters and caulkers in the Charlestown, Massachusetts, navyyard in 1842.   The joiners, in the same navyyard, secured the adoption of the same system in 1853.[1]   But it was not until Ira Steward, the Boston machinist, brought forward his " philosophy " of the eight-hour day that the impulse toward a national movement was given. Steward converted it from the isolated efforts of local unions to a

1 Autobiography of Edward H. Rogers, MS. in possession of the American Bureau of Industrial Research, Madison, Wis.

general demand for State and national legislation. Steward was born in 1831, and at nineteen years of age, while learning his trade as a machinist's apprentice and working twelve hours a day, he began his agitation for shorter hours.[2] From the beginning of widespread agitation for the eight-hour day in the early sixties until his death in 1883, he was so much a part of that agitation that the man and the movement are inseparable. He was essentially a man of one idea, and, in fact, was sometimes called the "eight-hour monomaniac."[3] For this one idea he lived, worked, and fought with almost fanatical zeal. After 1863, Steward was a contributor to nearly every reform paper then published. Each article emphasised his one thought, and many were his public lectures on the subject. "Meet him any day, as he steams along the street (like most enthusiasts, he is always in a hurry)," said a writer in the *American Workman*,[4] " and, although he will apologise and excuse himself if you talk to him of other affairs, and say that he is sorry, that he must rush back to his shop, if you only introduce the pet topic of ' hours of labor,' and show a little willingness to listen, he will stop and plead with you till night-fall."

Private letters tell us something of the discouraging struggles of that time. Like every other reform that is hampered by lack of funds, the eight-hour movement lacked workers. In a letter to F. A. Sorge,[5] on March 1, 1877, Steward says: " Years ago Mr. McNeill[6] and I used to pray for the third helper. Finally he came in Mr. George Gunton. Since then we have been dreaming and longing and praying for the fourth one. Perhaps you are the one."

Steward, although self-educated and influenced in his philosophy by what he saw among his fellow-workmen rather than by what he read, was familiar with the works of John Stuart Mill. He was successful in attracting to his educational campaign such men as Wendell Phillips.[7] In 1876 he joined the Work-

2 Chicago *Tribune*, July 5, 1879.
3 Chicago *Workingman's Advocate*, Mar. 30, 1872.
4 June 19, 1869.
5 Letter in Sorge Collection, University of Wisconsin Library.
6 See below, II, 92.
7 Wendell Phillips, prominent abolitionist, orator, and champion of labour re-

form, was born in Boston of wealthy parents in 1811. He was educated at Harvard, and admitted to the bar in 1834. Three years later he joined the abolitionists and devoted much of his time during the next twenty-five years to the antislavery propaganda. With the emancipation of the Negroes he turned his attention to the relations of capital and labour, and

ingmen's party in Massachusetts and the following year helped
to form the International Labor Union.

It was at the first convention of Steward's union, the machinists' and blacksmiths', in 1859, that a resolution had been
adopted recommending the discussion and agitation of a change
of hours of labour.   This was reaffirmed by the succeeding convention.   The argument at that time had been the wage-fund
doctrine of " making work " by reducing the supply of labour.
But in 1863 Steward's ideas were enthusiastically adopted.
A committee was elected with him as chairman to confer with
a similar committee appointed by the Boston Trades' Assembly
and to arrange jointly for an agitational campaign for the
eight-hour law.   Each of the two organisations appropriated
$400 to cover expenses.   The resolution, evidently drafted by
Steward, read as follows:

" *Resolved,* That from East to West, from North to South, the
most important change to us as workingmen, to which all else is
subordinate, is a permanent reduction to Eight of the hours exacted
for each day's work.

" *Resolved,* That since this cannot be accomplished until a public
sentiment has been educated, both among the employers and the
employés, we will use the machinery of agitation, whether it be
among those of the religious, political, reformatory or moneyed enterprises of the day, and to secure such reduction we pledge our
money and our courage.

" *Resolved,* That such reduction will never be made until overwork, as a system, is prohibited, nor until it is universally recognised that an increase of hours is a reduction of wages. . . .

" *Resolved,* That a Reduction of Hours is an increase of
Wages. . . ."

The essence of Steward's theory [8] was the principle that
wages do not depend upon the amount of capital or the supply
of labour, but upon the habits, customs, and wants of the working classes.   The productiveness of capital, he held, was increasing at an enormous rate through invention.   By encourag-

---

as early as 1863 advised the formation of
a separate labour party.   In 1869 he encouraged both the establishment of the
Boston Eight Hour League and the Massachusetts Bureau of Labor Statistics.   Liberal financial contributions were made by
him to funds for the publication of eight-
hour literature and frequently he ad-

dressed legislative committees in support
of labour legislation when no other man of
note could be found to do so.   In 1870 he
was the candidate of the Labor Reform
party for governor of Massachusetts.
Later he worked for the Greenback party.
He died in 1884.

8 *Doc. Hist.,* IX, 24–83, 284–329.

ing machinery, the labourer could increase this surplus, and then could get such share of it as was required to support his standard of living. The standard of living could be raised by increasing his wants and necessities, and these have an expansive and indefinite limit, provided the labourer has the leisure that awakens desires, broadens opinions, improves habits, and multiplies wants. But such an increase of wants would not be possible if the competition of low-standard labour was permitted to drive out the labour of higher standards. It was not necessary to prohibit immigration, and it was inadequate to depend on trade unions. It was necessary only to adopt a universal eight-hour law which would compel the low-standard labourer, who already could barely live on his ten- and twelve-hour wages, to demand the same daily pay for eight hours. Soon this compulsory reduction of his hours would increase his wants and compel him to demand still higher pay, which, again, the growing surplus of machine production would permit the employer to pay. As a concession to the prevailing labour theories of the injustice and needlessness of interest and profits, he predicted that ultimately the labourer's rising standards of living would take both interest and profit away from the capitalists and thus gradually introduce the co-operative commonwealth.[9]

Such a philosophy was somewhat less revolutionary and utopian than the theories of socialism, but, like socialism, it was a clear-cut and unmixed doctrine of wage-consciousness and wage-solidarity. As such it is distinctly the American counterpart of Lassalle's "iron law of wages," differing radically from the latter in its emphasis on the psychological wants that elevate labour above the animal, instead of the merely physiological wants that maintain only life and the species — not an iron law, but a golden law of wages. It was this very optimism of the doctrine that gave it enthusiastic acceptance and made it henceforth a true watchword and rallying cry for labor.[10] Its revolutionary character consisted in its disregard

[9] Steward's philosophy was afterwards taken up by George Gunton and made the basis of his book, *Wealth and Progress . . . the Economic Philosophy of the Eight Hour Movement.*

[10] It was Steward's wife who framed up the jingle:
"Whether you work by the piece or work by the day,
Decreasing the hours increases the pay."
Spencer, *Address Before Prospect Union.*

of trade union action and its reliance on universal state and Federal eight-hour laws enacted and enforced by the labour vote. When later its impracticability became evident, and labour began to fall back on the strike and trade unions for securing the eight-hour day, the less ambitious and more spurious argument of " making work " for the unemployed was found to be more in harmony with the other restrictive arguments of trade unionism.

Since Steward's scheme was legislative, it required a plan to secure legislative influence. As outlined by him, it was similar to the one adopted by George Henry Evans in promoting his land reform schemes:

" The basis of operation for the reformer," said Steward, " is a certain amount of PUBLIC OPINION. With this he bids for the aid and power of those who will do nothing *without it*. The Labor Reform enterprise makes this bid. It expects to be served by men who at heart want nothing but position, power, pay and honour ; for it cannot succeed without them. . . . The men to take council together, are those who have *created* a public opinion powerful enough to attract politicians. Politicians are wanted, not in *council* but in *action!* In *council* a ' yes ' or ' no ' programme should be written, adopted, and submitted to them in the briefest possible terms. . . . Present this to all candidates for official position, from Governor down to city and town officials. . . . ' Will you, if elected to the office for which you have been nominated, vote for this bill ? ' " [11]

In 1864 the first independent eight-hour organisation had been created by Steward and his associates in Boston. Its first name was the Workingmen's Convention, which was soon changed to Labor Reform Association. It was composed of members of trade unions in the city, and a writer in *Fincher's* openly accused it of being " the result of a clique, who, finding that in the Workingmen's Assembly they could not rule that body to their thoughts, nor had patience enough to ' work and wait ' for fair results, resolved they would ' withdraw,' in other words ' secede ' . . . and endeavour to carry out their view of the idea." [12] The association was composed largely of machinists and blacksmiths who had always been the most ardent advocates of the eight-hour system. In its general policy, the

[11] *Fincher's*, May 13, 1865. [12] *Ibid.*, July 16, 1864.

association followed the principle of legislative action as laid down by Steward, rather than that of direct trade union action. The Grand Eight-Hour League of Massachusetts, organised in 1865, with its subordinate leagues in the State, followed exactly the line of action proposed by Steward. Next to Steward, George E. McNeill [13] was most prominent as an eight-hour propagandist. The eight-hour leagues in Charleston, Chelsea, Medford, and East Boston, sent delegates in September, 1865, to the Republican state convention to demand the inserting of an eight-hour plank in the platform, in which effort they succeeded. The Republican nominee for governor likewise declared himself in favour of an eight-hour law. Only in a few localities, as in Fitchburg,[14] where the Republican politicians paid no attention to the eight-hour demand, were independent labour candidates for the legislature nominated. The outcome was disappointing. The new legislature contained only twenty-three members pledged to an eight-hour law. The *Daily Evening Voice* openly expressed dissatisfaction with Steward's policy of exacting pledges from political candidates: " We learn one important lesson from our experience so far, and this is, that the workingmen must stand out as an independent party organisation, and make no more attempts to control the action of other parties." [15]

During the municipal campaigns in the various towns in Massachusetts, which followed closely upon the general election, the eight-hour men tried independent political action in Boston (in co-operation with a dissatisfied faction in the Republican party) and in Lowell, and met with encouragement. They

13 George E. McNeill was born in Amesbury, Mass., in 1836. His father, a friend of John G. Whittier, was one of the early anti-slavery propagandists. As a boy he worked in woollen mills and later also at other occupations. He first became known as a writer in connection with his work for the Boston *Daily Voice* during the middle sixties. About the same time he espoused Ira Steward's eight-hour philosophy and was president of the Boston Eight Hour League for eight years. In co-operation with Wendell Phillips and others he succeeded in bringing about the establishment of the Massachusetts Bureau of Labor Statistics. Upon its organisation in 1869 he was made

deputy chief, but was displaced for political reasons in 1874.

During the seventies and the eighties, McNeill continued to be active in the labour movement and retained throughout all these turbulent years the full confidence of all factions and opposing organisations. He published a history of the American labour movement in 1887, entitled, *The Labor Movement: The Problem of To-day*. He died in 1906.

14 Boston *Daily Evening Voice*, Nov. 15, 1865. The independent candidates, one for the senate and three for the assembly, carried the town, but were defeated.

15 Boston *Daily Evening Voice*, Nov. 8, 1865.

elected in the former city one-third of the aldermen and one-fourth of the council, and in the latter, three aldermen and sixteen councilmen. In Charleston, Roxbury, and New Bedford, Steward's plan of action through the existing parties was followed and there also met with considerable success.[16]

However, the object which drove the eight-hour men into municipal politics, the attainment of an eight-hour law for city employés, was not realised. Nor did they at that time succeed in getting an eight-hour law through the Massachusetts legislature.

Similar political attempts were made by the workingmen in New York, and in Newark, New Jersey,[17] but without results. Cameron, of the Chicago *Workingman's Advocate,* favoured independent political action.[18] This, however, did not prevent him from accepting the Democratic nomination for the assembly, to which, however, he was not elected. Fincher, always the consistent trade unionist, opposed politics, and his opposition was based on experience and observation in his own city of Philadelphia.

In 1863 a workingmen's party had been established in Philadelphia and it nominated a ticket for the municipal election of that year. Speaking of the ticket, *Fincher's* said: " The only thing patent in the whole batch, was to secure the election of this or that man to this or that Legislature, or this mayoralty, and he would do all in his power for the workingmen. . . . But the entire absence of all proposed measures for their relief, was to us conclusive evidence that all proffered reforms were only to accrue to the advantage of workingmen in nomination for office." [19]

Again Fincher stated his grounds of opposition to politics in the following graphic manner:

" Once absorbed in politics. the day passes in the workshop, with but little anxiety for aught else, save the anticipated indulgence in political scenes at night. The duties of block, ward, or township committees absorb the time that should be devoted to the family and to the Trades' Union. The rights of labor are made subordinate to the claims of this or that candidate. He has not the courage to

16 *Fincher's*, Dec. 30, 1865.   18 *Fincher's*, Apr. 22, 1865,
17 Boston *Daily Evening Voice*, Dec. 8,   19 Nov. 28, 1863,
1865.

demand his rights in the shop, because he is a companion of his boss 'in the cause.' He is flattered and cajoled by his employer, because his vote and his influence is needed among the 'hard-fisted mechanics and workingmen' at the coming election — and a fraternal feeling is thus awakened by mutual devotion to politics, which restrains him from asserting and maintaining those rights so essential to the comfort of himself, his family, and his fellow-workingmen." [20]

Thus, while the eight-hour agitation was broadening out and preparing the way for a unification of all labour forces in the National Labor Union, it was bringing with it the radical differences that were later to separate the politician and political actionist from the trade unionist.

With the return of the soldiers and the slackening of prosperity toward the end of 1865, trade union action no longer brought its former successful results.[21] A New York correspondent writing in the Boston *Weekly Voice* on May 10, 1866, enumerated 40 strikes, largely in the building trades, which had recently taken place in that city, of which but 7 were totally successful, and 8 partly successful.

This state of affairs aided in bringing the demand for an eight-hour law to the foreground and thereby helped to bring to a head the attempts to unify the labour movement into a national federation. A simultaneous agitation was begun by the leading organisations of every type for a national labour convention, but, before anything practical could be accomplished, it was necessary to overcome the friction between the different organisations. There existed among them a practically unanimous agreement with regard to the necessity of some form of a national federation which should place the demand for an eight-hour law at the head of its programme. But considerable difference of opinion prevailed as to the most desirable composition of such a federation. The trades' assembly of Buffalo issued, in May, 1865, an address calling for a " Trades' Congress," to meet in Buffalo, to be composed " of delegates from the various Local Unions of every branch of industry," the object being " to preserve the many interests of the labouring

---

20 *Fincher's*, Oct. 10, 1863.
21 A correspondent wrote in *Fincher's* for June 17, 1865: " As was to be ex- pected, the returned soldiers are flooding the streets already, unable to find employ- ment."

classes of the Continent and establish our just rights through Legislative action."

Early in February, 1865, the New York State Workingmen's Assembly issued a call inviting all workingmen's assemblies, and, where no assemblies existed, each local organisation, to send five delegates to a national convention to be convened in the city of New York, on the second Tuesday in July, for the purpose of " devising the most eligible means to secure to the workingmen eight hours' labour as a legal day's work." Its foundations were laid at a conference of the trades' assemblies of Troy and Albany in February, 1865, at which an address was drafted calling " for a state convention of the different Trades' Assemblies and Workingmen's Organisations in the State," to meet at the city of Albany and to petition the legislature to reduce the hours of work and to protect free labour against prison labour. The convention was also to take into consideration the propriety of forming a state organisation.[22] This address was favourably received and the state assembly was created.

Organisations similar to the New York Assembly in object, though not in composition, were the state eight-hour leagues. These organisations were not strictly workingmen's organisations but included also a number of sympathising non-wage-earners. A call for a national labour convention was also issued by one of these. In November, 1865, a " Workingmen's Convention " was held in Indianapolis, at which a Grand Eight Hour League of the State of Indiana was formed, with John Fehrenbatch as secretary. Before adjourning, this organisation passed a resolution recommending all associations of workingmen in the United States to hold state conventions and elect delegates to a general national convention.[23] But the real rivals for the leadership in the movement for a national federation were the city trades' assemblies on one side and the national trade unions on the other.

The national union of machinists and blacksmiths had agitated the idea of a national federation of trades as early as 1860, but nothing practical resulted, although the moulders' convention in January, 1864, received the proposal favourably.[24]   Two years later the Bricklayers' International Union, in session in Philadelphia, appointed its officers as delegates to assist in calling a " Convention of International Unions."

In February, 1866, William Harding, of Brooklyn, president of the Coachmakers' International Union, met Sylvis in Philadelphia and the result of this conference was a preliminary meeting in New York, March 26, 1866, of representatives of all trades except two that were organised nationally.   At this meeting it was resolved that a national convention be held in Baltimore, August 20, 1866.   Each local organisation was to be allowed one representative, and each trades' assembly two, and it was also voted that " the consideration of the Eight-hour question should be the principal business of the convention." [25] A committee was appointed to confer with the Baltimore Trades' Assembly on the necessary arrangements.

But this was insufficient to allay the rivalry of the trades' assemblies.   The Workingmen's Union of New York City indignantly repudiated the action of the officers of the national unions with reference to holding a " National Convention of Trades " as an assumption by a few individuals.[26]   Finally, a compromise was struck.   The call for a national congress was issued jointly by the above committee and the Baltimore Trades' Assembly, but all organisations of labour, " Trade Assemblies, Workingmen's Unions, eight-hour leagues, 'and Labour Organisations throughout the United States," were invited to send representatives.

LABOR CONGRESS, 1866

The convention met in Baltimore, August 20, 1866.   Seventy-seven delegates came from 13 States and the District of Columbia.   Of this number 50 delegates represented an equal number of local trade unions and 17 represented 13 trades' assemblies.[27]   Seven of the delegates were sent by 5 of the eight-hour leagues,[28] and 3 delegates by 2 of the national trade

24 International Iron Molders' Union, *Proceedings*, 1864, 12, 25.
25 *Doc. Hist.*, IX, 126.
26 Boston *Daily Evening Voice*, Mar. 30, 1866.
27 Boston, New Haven, Norfolk, New York, Rochester, Buffalo, Philadelphia, Wilmington, Baltimore, Pittsburgh, New Albany, Chicago, and St. Louis.   " Proceedings," in *Doc. Hist.*, IX, 127–141.
28 Two city eight-hour leagues, Buffalo, and New Haven, and three Grand Eight-Hour Leagues, Illinois, Michigan, and Iowa.

unions.   Most in evidence among the locals were the building
trades with delegates from 19 unions.   Next in point of representation were the moulders, machinists, and ship carpenters,
with 7 delegates each.   The Coachmakers' International Union
was represented by 2 delegates, and the National Union of
Curriers by 1, but the real representation of the national unions
was much stronger.   All presidents and secretaries of national
unions were invited to seats on the floor of the convention with
the right to speak but not to vote.   Under this provision Jonathan C. Fincher and William C. Otley, secretary and president
respectively of the machinists', and John A. White, president
of the International Union of Bricklayers, became participants
in the debates.   Furthermore, four delegates who bore credentials from minor organisations were at the same time officers
of national unions, like Alexander H. Troup, treasurer of the
National Typographical Union, and T. E. Kirby, secretary of
the International Union of Bricklayers.[29]   The representation
from national trade unions on the floor thus really amounted to
ten.   Other labour leaders widely known were A. C. Cameron,
the editor of the *Workingman's Advocate,* representing the Chicago Trades' Assembly and the Illinois Grand Eight Hour
League; John Hinchcliffe, the joint representative of the Railroad Men's Protective Union, the Printers' Union, the Machinery Molders' Union of St. Louis, and the Miners' Lodge
of Illinois.   Important leaders not present were Sylvis, who
was prevented from coming by illness, and Richard Trevellick.

The convention elected Hinchcliffe temporary chairman and
spent the first day in completing its organisation.   Hinchcliffe
was re-elected permanent chairman and on the second day he
appointed the following committees: on " Eight Hours in all
its respects," on " Trades' Unions, Organisation and Strikes,"
on " Co-operation and Convict Prison Labour," on a " National
Labor Organisation," on " An Address to the Workmen
throughout the Country," on " Permanent National Organisation," on " Public Lands and the National Debt," and a committee " to confer with the President of the United States in
relation to the Reform Movement."

29 The remaining two delegates of this
group were Richard Emmons and James
Ashworth, first and second vice-presidents,
respectively, of the Machinists' and Blacksmiths' International Union.

The sentiment of the convention is gauged best by the attitudes respectively on trade unionism and legislative action. The committee on trade unions, consisting of three representatives of trades' assemblies, Cameron, of the Chicago Trades' Assembly, Roberts, of the Philadelphia Trades' Assembly, and Baldwin, of the Mechanics' Association of Norfolk, Virginia, and of two delegates from local unions, Reed, of the house carpenters in Washington, and Auld, of the shipwrights in Baltimore, presented a report which was adopted without debate. It recognised that " all reforms in the labour movement . . . can at present best be directed through the Trades organisations," and recommended " the formation of unions in all localities where the same do not exist, and the formation of an international organisation in every branch of industry as a first and most important duty of the hour," and further also the organisation of the unskilled in " a general workingmen's association " directly affiliated with the " general organisation." It also embodied the trade union recommendation of a more rigid enforcement of the apprenticeship system. " With regard to the subject of strikes," the report continued, " your committee give it as their deliberate opinion that they have been productive of great injury to the labouring classes, and would therefore discountenance them except as dernier resort." It further advocated arbitration as a substitute for strikes and advised " the appointment by each Trades' Assembly of an arbitration committee to whom shall be referred all matters of dispute arising between employers and employés." When we consider that this was a period of phenomenal growth of fighting associations of employers, it becomes evident that by deprecating strikes and by recommending arbitration the convention showed how little faith it had that results could be attained through trade unionism.

The debates which centred around the eight-hour question indicated that legislative action had taken the first place which, in the international assembly of 1864 had belonged to trade unionism. The committee of 14, 1 for each of the 13 States and the District of Columbia, consisted of 8 delegates from trades' assemblies, 1 from a Grand Eight Hour League, and 5 from local trade unions. The report set forth that " there comes from the ranks of labour a demand for more time for moral, intellectual and social culture," which is the " result of that condition of progress in which the workingmen of this nation are prepared to take a step higher in the scale of moral and intellectual life." But this at first went no further than the resolution to recommend " agitation and organisation " as " the two great levers by which we are to accomplish the great result," and to state that " as far as political action is concerned, each locality should be governed by its own policy, whether to run an independent ticket of workingmen, or to use political parties already existing, but, at all events to cast no vote except for men pledged to the interests of labor."

After its reading, the report was hastily adopted, but opposition immediately developed. It was begun by Alexander Troup, representing the Boston Workingmen's Assembly, who moved to recommit the report to the committee on resolutions. Phelps, of the New Haven Trades Union, defended the report. He said that " he found in the meeting of the committee all diversities of political sentiment, and many who desired to make this congress a political congregation. All had been harmonised." Hinchcliffe and Roberts, likewise, defended the report, but Harding of the coachmakers said that it " would be absurd in him to return to the body which sent him to the convention to agree upon a course of action and tell them they must make their own plans." Schlägel, a follower of Ferdinand Lassalle, was the first one to urge upon the convention the desirability of an independent labour party. His forceful appeal decided the matter in favour of the opposition to the report, and A. C. Cameron was delegated to compose another. " The history and legislation of the past," said this report, " has demonstrated that no confidence whatever can be placed in the pledges of existing political parties so far as the interests of the industrial classes are concerned. *The time has come when the workingmen of the United States should cut themselves aloof from party ties and predilections, and organise themselves into a National Labor Party,* the object of which shall be to secure the enactment of a law making eight hours a legal day's work by the National Congress and the several State legislatures, and the election of men pledged to sustain and represent the interests of the industrial classes."

The report was at first adopted by a vote of 35 to 24. The opponents of independent political action were the Philadelphia delegates, headed by Roberts, who were clearly under the influence of Fincher, the delegates from Virginia, and the entire delegation from Maryland. The last named explained that they deemed it inexpedient for them to engage in the formation of a national labour party forthwith, as they feared it would prevent them from regaining the suffrage which had been denied them in recent years. On the fourth day, however, the vote was reconsidered, and the report recommitted " to meet the objections of the delegates opposing it." The committee recommended the addition of the qualifying words " as soon as possible " after the words declaring for the organisation of a national labour party, and the report, with this amendment, was adopted with one negative vote.

Interesting conclusions suggest themselves when a comparison is drawn between the mutual suspiciousness during the previous years of the trades' assemblies and the national trade unions, and the harmonious unanimity with which the convention passed upon questions of prime importance, like trade unionism, eight hours, and politics. The fact that attention was transferred from trade unionism to legislation made it possible to relieve the convention of the embarrassing task of co-ordinating the work of trades' assembly and national trade union on the economic field, where, at that time, both possessed equal strength and had overlapping jurisdiction. It was resolved instead to create a third organisation, the National Labour party, into which the centre of gravity should be carried. There are no indications that this outcome was the result of any premeditation, but it is nevertheless true that the antagonism between the trades' assemblies and the national labour unions was to a very large degree allayed until the time when economic action again assumed prime importance in the struggle between labour and capital.

The question that loomed up as second in importance was the land question. A lengthy report was presented. It argued that the public domain was extensive enough to give every man a farm sufficiently large for his sustenance and for the support of government, and that the whole public domain should be disposed of to actual settlers only. It proposed the following motto: "The tools to those that have the ability and skill to use them, and the lands to those that have the will and heart to cultivate them."

Relatively little attention was given to the subject of co-operation, although the co-operative movement was then at its height. So exclusively was the convention's attention centred upon legislative action that it did not go beyond a general endorsement of co-operative stores and workshops and a recommendation to agitate for the passage by the various States of co-operative incorporation acts without specifying what these acts should contain. The committee which reported on co-operation also reported on convict labour and recommended agitation for laws fixing the price of the contract labour of convicts so as to equal the wages of workers outside the prisons. The assignment of these two totally unrelated subjects to one committee is in itself some indication of how little, it was thought, co-operation demanded the concerted action of the national labour movement.

The convention recognised the problem of women in industry, and pledged to the "sewing women, factory operatives, and daughters of toil, individual and undivided support. No class of industry is in so much need of having their condition ameliorated" and "we would solicit their hearty co-operation," said the committee on resolutions. Coupled with this was a resolution calling attention to the subject of tenement houses and declaring that vice, pauperism, and crime were the invariable attendants of the overcrowded, illy ventilated dwellings of the poor.

The convention worked out no comprehensive plan of national organisation. It merely announced the organisation of a national labour union to meet in annual congresses, in which "every Trades' Union, Workingmen's Association and Eight-Hour League" should be entitled to one delegate for the first 500 members or less, and for every additional 500 or fractional part thereof, one additional delegate, and every national or international union should be represented by one delegate. The staff of officers elected consisted of a president, one vice-president at large, one vice-president for each State, territory, and district, a treasurer, four secretaries, and a finance committee of three. The president, recording secretary, corresponding secretary, and vice-president at large, constituted the executive board, which had the power to levy an assessment of 25 cents a year upon each member. J. C. C. Whaley, of the Washington Trades' Assembly, was elected president, E. Schlägel, the Lassallean Socialist,[30] of the German Workingmen's Assembly in Chicago, vice-president at large, and C. William Gibson, of the eight-hour association, New Haven, secretary.[31]

EIGHT HOURS AND POLITICS [32]

The Baltimore convention, although it took no decisive steps to form a national labour party, gave an additional impetus to independent political action in the States and municipalities. In fact, throughout the existence of the National Labor Union, from the time when a national labour party had been first suggested, up to 1872, when it was finally consummated, the labour movement was continually engaged in local politics. Massachusetts, the original stronghold of the eight-hour movement, naturally shared very prominently in this political agitation. In August, 1866, the Boston *Voice* started an energetic campaign to send Wendell Phillips to Congress. "What John Bright is to Parliament, the workingmen of the third Massachusetts district [33] can make Wendell Phillips to Congress," [34] was the enthusiastic motto.

The outcome of the congressional campaign made the *Voice* sceptical as to the expediency of the early formation of a national labour party. The Chicago *Workingman's Advocate,* on the other hand, was urging it with great enthusiasm, and accused the *Voice* of lukewarmness to the political interests of labour. In reply, the *Voice* said: "We perceive, indeed, that workingmen in Illinois, Michigan, and other Western

---

30 His name is .sometimes written Shläger.

31 *Doc. Hist.,* IX, 129, gives list of the remaining officers.

32 In the preparation of this section the author drew largely from an unpub-

lished monograph by Lorian P. Jefferson, *The Movement for Shorter Hours, 1825– 1880.*

33 This district covered a part of Boston.

34 Boston *Weekly Voice,* Aug. 23, 1866.

States, have more zeal and show a stronger front at the polls than their brethren in the East have ever done." It further called attention to the great enthusiasm shown in some parts of Pennsylvania, particularly in Alleghany County, and concluded with the recommendation to organise a labour party whenever it could prove a success, but implied that a national labour party was doomed to fail.[35]

Independent political action was resorted to less prominently by labour than the method of pledging the candidates of the established parties. This was practised with success in Connecticut, in Illinois, and in many other states. Likewise a lobbying activity was kept up before Congress and the state legislatures. The following more or less detailed account of the vicissitudes of the eight-hour measure at the hands of the president, Congress, and the state legislatures, will give an idea of the difficulties the labour leaders encountered, and will shed light upon the causes of the abrupt turn taken by the labour movement in the following year.

Before adjourning, a committee consisting of one representative from each State, headed by John Hinchcliffe, the president of the convention, arranged to meet President Andrew Johnson in Washington. Hinchcliffe presented to him in a speech the subjects of hours of labour, public lands, protection against importation of foreign pauper labour, and convict labour. The president replied, pointing to his past political record, to his work on behalf of an anti-prison labour law in Tennessee, and to his pioneer efforts to pass a homestead law, but remained diplomatically silent on all the other propositions. He stated, however, in general that he had "said something on all the propositions" and had himself "started most of them."

But if the president chose to be noncommittal on such important questions as an eight-hour law, the labour organisations did not fail to push the measure vigorously upon Congress and the state legislatures.

The Government of the United States had previously taken action on the question of hours on government work, when, in July, 1862, a bill was passed providing that the hours and wages of employés in government navy yards should conform

35 *Ibid.*, Sept. 26, 1867.

as closely as possible, consistently with public interests, to those of similar private establishments.[36] The eight-hour question, however, did not appear until December, 1865, when Senator Gratz Brown, of Missouri, offered to the Senate a resolution instructing the committee on judiciary to inquire into "the expediency and rightfulness" of enacting a law providing for eight hours on all government work, the committee to report by a bill or otherwise. The same question was also presented in the House of Representatives, and the workingmen from various sections of the country sent delegates to give evidence before these committees.[37] There is no evidence, however, that the resolution was adopted in either house. A similar resolution was introduced in the House early in the session of 1866 by Congressman William E. Niblack, of Indiana, and it was adopted, but nothing further seems to have been done.[38]

In March of the same year, Congressman Rogers of New Jersey presented to the House a bill providing for eight hours as a day's work for all labourers, workmen, and mechanics employed by or on behalf of the Government.[39] This bill never came back from the committee. On March 17, Senator Brown of Missouri again came forward and introduced into the Senate a bill providing that " in all cases in which any labourers, mechanics, or artisans shall or may be employed by or on behalf of the Government of the United States, or in any place which is within the exclusive jurisdiction of Congress, eight hours' labour shall be taken and construed to be a day's work, any law, regulation or usage to the contrary notwithstanding."

The friends of this bill in Congress were reticent about it and deemed it wise not to argue in its favour before any audience. But they sent appeals to its supporters among their constituents, urging, " if you want these bills reported upon and passed, ' pour in your memorials.' "[40]

While the bill was still under discussion, President Johnson expressed himself as favourably disposed to the measure and said that he would endeavour to bring it to pass in case Congress should fail to enact the desired law. He did not, however,

36 *United States Statutes at Large*, 37 Cong., 2 sess., chap. 184, p. 587.
37 Boston *Daily Evening Voice*, Dec. 18, 1865.
38 *House Journal*, 39 Cong., 1 sess., 62.
39 *Ibid.*, 288.
40 *Fincher's*, Mar. 24, 1866.

consider that such a law, which he assumed would be applicable to the District of Columbia alone, would have any noticeable effect in securing it for the country at large.[41]

Three months later, when the committee of the National Labor Union called on President Johnson, chiefly in the interest of this measure, he expressed the meaningless generality that he was in favour of the "shortest number possible [of hours] that will allow of the discharge of duty and the requirements of the country." [42]

Congressman Ingersoll, of Indiana, succeeded in having the House pass a resolution calling upon the committee for the District of Columbia to report a bill limiting the hours in the District to eight. The committee, however, never reported and the matter was dropped for that session.[43] On March 14, 1867, Congressman Julian introduced a bill making the same provisions for the eight-hour day on government work as those in the Rogers bill of the previous session. The bill was referred to the committee on judiciary and ordered printed.[44] The committee reported favourably on the bill and on March 28 it was passed by the House and sent to the Senate.[45] The Senate took no action upon the matter and the bill was lost. Thus the year 1867 went by and the eight-hour measure was no further advanced than it was at the beginning of the agitation two years before.

The efforts to secure eight-hour legislation from the state legislatures were disappointing in many States, but successful in six States, although as we shall presently see, these were empty victories. The movement was at its strongest, and the hopes for a successful outcome at their highest, in the State of Massachusetts. A joint committee of both houses had stated in its report at the close of the session in May, 1865, that the limited testimony before the committee was in favour of a general reduction to eight hours, and recommended that an unsalaried commission be appointed by the governor to in-

---

[41] Boston *Weekly Voice*, May 17, 1866.
[42] Chicago *Workingman's Advocate*, Sept. 1, 1866. Writing of this interview, Ira Steward made the criticism that the committee erred in not presenting the case to the President in such a form as to require a definite "Yes" or "No."

[43] *House Journal*, 39 Cong., 1 sess., 563.
[44] *House Journal*, 40 Cong., 1 sess., 43.
[45] *Ibid.*, 135.

vestigate more thoroughly the merits of the question, and to report to the legislature at its next session.[46]

The report created great enthusiasm among the labour organisations. Ira Steward called upon every trade union to extend a vote of thanks to the committee. He concluded his jubilant appeal with the couplet:

"Let all now cheer, who never cheered before,
And those who always cheer now cheer the more." [47]

Acting upon the recommendations of the committee, the governor appointed a commission, which soon issued a circular asking, from every one interested, information on the number of working hours required in any and all occupations; the hours of employment for children, their schooling, and their wages; the occupation and wages of women, especially needle women; the mental and physical results of overwork; the means for the profitable use of the extra time to be gained by a reduction of hours; the effect of shorter hours on business; and whether a reduction of hours by law would lead to special contracts.[48]

Responses were received from various organisations and individuals. The commission presented a lengthy report to the legislature at its next session. They reviewed "the conditions and prospects of the industrial classes," showing that violations of the child-labour law were frequent, and that the usual time was eleven hours. They however opposed an eight-hour law, but favoured a reduction from eleven hours. Their reasons for opposing the eight-hour movement were stated:

"1. Because they deem it unsound in principle to apply one measure of time to all kinds of labour.

"2. Because, if adopted as a general law, in the way proposed, it would be rendered void by special contracts, and so add another to the dead laws that cumber the statutes.

"3. Because a very large proportion of the industrial interests of the country could not observe it.

"4. Because, if restricted as some propose, to the employés

46 Massachusetts, *House Document*, 1865, No. 259.
47 *Fincher's*, May 13, 1865.
48 Massachusetts, *House Document*, 1866, No. 98.

of the state, it would be manifestly partial, and therefore unjust." [49]

Feeling, however, that they had been unable to do full justice to the question of the hours of labour, the commission suggested that a paid commission be appointed to continue the investigation.

Accordingly, a resolution of the legislature, May 28, 1866, provided for a commission to be appointed by the governor for the purpose of investigating the subject of hours of labour, "especially in its relation to the social, educational, and sanitary condition of the industrial classes, and to the permanent prosperity of the productive interests of the state." [50]

Following the example set by the earlier commission, this body, consisting of Amasa Walker, the economist, William Hyde, and Edward H. Rogers, issued a circular asking for information from corporations and individuals in various occupations throughout the State.

The report returned by this commission was not unanimous. Walker and Hyde sent in a majority report which recommended that no law restricting the hours of labour be enacted for the adult population.[51]

E. H. Rogers' minority report was a very careful and able discussion of the investigations made, and in it he reviewed the early struggle for a reduction of hours, the recent efforts of the caulkers and ship carpenters of Boston to gain the eight-hour day, and the eight-hour philosophy. He recommended the adoption of a law limiting hours to eight per day, in the absence of a contract to the contrary. No law was enacted, however.[52]

Meanwhile the question was not neglected in other States. A bill providing for eight hours was introduced in the Pennsylvania house of representatives in February, 1866. It passed, but was lost in the senate.[53] The Ohio house of representatives in the same month passed a similar bill by a vote of 70 to 14. The senate made some trifling amendments to the bill

49 *Ibid.*
50 Massachusetts, *Acts and Resolves*, 1866, chap. 92, 320.
51 Massachusetts, *House Document*, 1867, No. 44.
52 *Ibid.*
53 *House Journal*, 1866, 769.

and passed it.   But the house refused to concur in these amendments and the bill was lost.[54]

New Jersey's legislature was no longer favourable to the eight-hour system, and the bill there introduced was likewise lost.[55]   Illinois enacted an eight-hour law,[56] but it was not enforced.   Wisconsin, by a law enacted in 1867, provided for the eight-hour day for women and children,[57] but it laid a penalty only upon an employer who should *compel* any woman or child to work more than eight hours a day.

The nation-wide agitation for an eight-hour law met with some measure of success in California, which had passed a ten-hour law in 1853.   In January, 1866, a concurrent resolution was adopted by the legislature providing for the appointment of a committee, consisting of three members from the senate and two from the house, to investigate the proposition to change the hours of labour in the legal day.[58]   No record is obtainable of the report of this committee, but at the session of 1868 a bill was passed providing for the eight-hour day in all cases unless otherwise stipulated by the parties contracting. Eight hours was made the legal day for all public employment, and a fine of from $10 to $100 was imposed upon the employer who should employ a child at any work for more than eight hours in any one day.[59]

Connecticut had, in the meantime, enacted a law establishing eight hours as the legal day for all persons, unless other hours were agreed upon by the parties concerned.[60]   The immediate success in this State was mainly due to the efforts of Phelps, vice-president of the National Labor Union for that State and president of the trades' union of New Haven.

A victory, which later however proved futile, occurred in the State of New York.   Here William Jessup, the president of the state workingmen's assembly, led in the fight.   He was the first labour leader to appreciate the value of exact statistical data in support of labour's demands before the legislature.

54 *House Journal*, 1866, 195, 420.

55 Ninetieth General Assembly of New Jersey, *Minutes of Votes and Proceedings*, 1866, 653.

56 Illinois, *Public Laws*, 1867, 101.

57 Wisconsin, *Laws*, 1867, chap. 83, p. 80.

58 California, *Laws*, 1865–1866, chap. 2, 882.

59 *Ibid.*, 1868, chap. 70, p. 63.

60 Connecticut, *Laws*, 1867, chap. 37, 23.

An eight-hour bill was introduced in the assembly in the spring
of 1867. This passed both houses,[61] and was signed by Governor Fenton. He refused, however, to see that it was properly enforced. Every law, he said, was obligatory by its own
nature, and could derive no additional force from any further
act of his.[62]

The question was brought before the legislatures of Michigan, Maryland, Minnesota, and Missouri. But with the single exception of the last named State, the bills were defeated.[63]

A feature which characterised all of these measures, whether
enacted or merely proposed, was the permission of longer hours
than those named in the law, provided they were so specified
in the contract. A contract requiring ten or more hours a
day would be perfectly legal. The eight-hour day was the legal
day only " when the contract was silent on the subject or
where there is no express contract to the contrary," as stated
in the Wisconsin law. None of the laws provided for the protection of agricultural labour, and most of them did not include
domestic service.

The movement for eight-hour laws thus, on the whole, proved
futile. How the advocates of this legislation viewed the results was clearly expressed in 1867 by the committee on eight-
hours at the second convention of the National Labor Union
which said: " Your committee wish also further to state that
Eight Hour laws have been passed by the legislatures of six
states, but for all practical intents and purposes they might as
well have never been placed on the statute books, and can only
be described as frauds on the labouring class." [64]

The causes were several. First, the American Federal system made it necessary to break the movement up into as many
independent parts as there were state legislatures. In England, a legislative movement had the advantage that Parliament
was the only body upon which labour needed to bring pressure
in order to attain results. In the United States, Congress could
pass a shorter hour law only for the District of Columbia, the

61 *Laws*, 1867, chap. 856.
62 Chicago *Workingman's Advocate,*
Oct. 12, 1867.
63 Missouri, *Laws*, 1867, 132.

64 " Proceedings " (1867), in Chicago
Workingman's Advocate, Aug. 31, 1867;
Doc. Hist., IX, 169–194.

territories, and for the wage-earners directly or indirectly in the employ of the Federal Government.

Another cause was the inexperience of the labour leaders in dealing with legislative matters. They were easily be-fuddled by skilful politicians, who, while in many cases willing to pass the desired legislation, at the same time craftily omitted to provide for the means of its enforcement; and, when asked to see that their own laws were enforced, they made, like Governor Fenton of New York, the meaningless reply that " every law is obligatory by its nature."

Meanwhile, the contraction of the paper currency continued. The conditions of industry grew more and more depressed. Unemployment rapidly increased and, in the face of a falling market, strikes were doomed to failure. Some prompt and fundamental measure was required to meet the situation. This brought on a rapid growth of the movement for productive co-operation.

CO-OPERATION

As early as 1863, when retail prices began to rise far more rapidly than wages, a substantial movement for distributive co-operation on the Rochdale plan as well as on the purely joint-stock principle started. That movement continued with varying success, but about the middle of 1866 there came a strong current in favour of productive co-operation. Distribu-tive co-operation, in fact, had been regarded as merely a be-ginning, and Thomas Phillips, one of the foremost leaders in this movement, had urged in his letters in *Fincher's* that co-operation should not stop at store associations; they should be a foundation for the rest. The store should be started first, in order to get the capital and experience necessary to manage manufactures, agriculture, and general commerce.[65]

The Lawrence, Massachusetts, association, which did a flour-ishing business for several years, was fairly typical of the early efforts on the part of consumers to extend the co-operative prin-ciple through distribution to production, and illustrates well the beginnings of transition in the movement. On account of the high cost of provisions, it was organised in November, 1863, to conduct a co-operative grocery store which was opened the following January with a stock of goods worth $1,400. In less than a month the company was obliged to add another " store man "; in April they opened a meat market; in July another man was put to work and a little later still another clerk was added. In January, 1865, a shoemaker was hired, and arrangements were made for " a female to make children's clothes and to superintend the dry-goods department." They had purchased a new store building, 4 stories high, 40 feet by 30 — the cellar for a meat market and stock room, the first floor for groceries, the second for dry goods, boots, and shoes, and the top floors for work-shops and shoemaking.

Agricultural co-operation also had its early adherents. In May, 1865, news came to *Fincher's* of the establishment of a co-operative farming and manufacturing company at Foster's Crossing, Ohio. Here, too, the promoter of the enterprise had been active first in a co-operative grocery store (at Cincinnati) and in addition had already commenced the publication of a little paper called the *Co-operative Record*.[66]

But the co-operative experiments which attracted special attention during the three years following the summer of 1866, were the efforts of workmen to carry on in their own shops a form of productive co-operation which would give to them the whole product of their own labour. Such attempts were made by practically all of the leading trades including the bakers, coach-makers, collar makers, coal-miners, shipwrights, machinists and blacksmiths, nailers, foundry-workers, ship-carpenters and caulkers, glass-blowers, hatters, boiler-makers, plumbers, iron-rollers, tailors, printers, needle women, and moulders. A large proportion of these attempts grew out of unsuccessful strikes during the period of depression in 1866 and 1867. Most important among these were the co-operative stove foundries established under the direct encouragement of William H. Sylvis, president of the Molders' International Union, of which a full account was given above.[67]

The machinists, too, throughout this period, took an active interest in co-operation. The national convention, which met in October, 1865, appointed a committee of five to report on

---

[66] *Ibid.*, May 6, 1865.   [67] See above, II, 56–58.

a plan of action to establish a co-operative shop under the auspices of the international union. This plan, however, which was later adopted by the Knights of Labor under the title of "integral co-operation," was not adopted at this time, but there was a fair number of machinists' shops on the joint stock plan.

The taking up of productive co-operation brought the workingmen face to face with the credit problem. For, granting that they had sufficient to start the shops, they needed capital to finance their output. This need of a credit system naturally led to monetary reform which, as we shall presently see, was placed by the National Labor Union at the head of its platform in 1867.

LABOR CONGRESS OF 1867

The chief hindrance to the success of the National Labor Union was the lack of adequate provision for revenue to cover expenses. The executive council had been authorised to levy a tax of 25 cents on each member of the National Labor Union, but the officers confessed their inability to determine who were "members," as the constituency of that body had been "indistinctly defined and but questionably established." The lukewarmness of the affiliated organisations in providing revenue should not, however, be interpreted as a disagreement with the principles of the National Labor Union. President Whaley reported at the next convention that the platform had been invariably adopted by all unions before which it was brought for ratification.

Secretary Gibson,[68] within a month after the first convention in 1866, issued notices for subscriptions to the proceedings of that convention, but financial returns were insufficient to warrant their publication in pamphlet form. Treasurer Hinchcliffe received from the local tax for running expenses only $205.21 and disbursed $187.25.

The three States which had made substantial progress in the

---

68 Evidence of his zeal is found in the records of his correspondence during the year. Without clerical assistance he wrote 1,387 letters, and received 956. He also distributed 2,157 printed letters, and 5,816 addresses and circulars. Meanwhile he received only $75.38, and expended $791.62.

work of organisation during the year, were New York, under
the leadership of William J. Jessup,[69] Connecticut, under Alfred W. Phelps, and California, under A. M. Kennady. These
were the States which passed eight-hour laws.

An important event in the year's work was the issuing of an
Address to the Workingmen of the United States by the committee, of which A. C. Cameron was chairman, appointed for
that purpose by the last convention. Realising that their address would be subject to the " criticism of the entire capitalistic press " of the country, and in order that it might be
"catholic in spirit, comprehensive in scope, simple in dic-
tion and unanswerable in argument," the committee had
asked for two weeks' time in which to prepare it for the
public. But it was not ready until July, 1867. The address,
while probably not " unanswerable in argument," doubtless was
" comprehensive in scope." It dealt with every problem that
affected labour,[70] eight hours, co-operation, trade unions, the
apprentice system, strikes, female labour, Negro labour, the
public domain, and political action. Eight hours was declared
to be " engrossing the attention of the American workman, and,
in fact, the American people," and the arguments in its favour
were substantially the same as at the first convention. But the
subject of co-operation was given much more prominence.
After reciting the success of co-operation in England, it stated
that " there are special reasons and needs for the existence of
co-operative efforts in this country, for here there is less disposition on the part of capital to combine and co-operate with
labour, than elsewhere, in consequence of the excessive accumulations of capital *by the great rates of interest which prevail in this country."* This was the first suggestion in American trade union documents of what the next year became the
accepted platform of greenbackism.

On the subjects of the public domain, trade unionism, strikes,
and apprenticeship, the address differed little from the declara-
tions of the convention, although with regard to the last named,
the doctrine of vested rights in a trade was more clearly applied.

---

69 Jessup contributed individually toward the expenses of the organisation.

70 It was printed in pamphlet form and
widely distributed. *Doc. Hist.*, IX, 141–
168.

But Negro labour and female labour were elaborately treated. The Negro problem was discussed both from the economic and the political side. Attention was called to the recent case of the importation of Negro caulkers from Portsmouth, Virginia, to Boston during an eight-hour strike, and the need of a general consolidation of labour regardless of race was deduced. But still greater attention was called to the coming importance of the Negro as a voter and the question was squarely put: " Can we afford to reject their proffered co-operation and make them enemies ? " The address concluded on this question that " the interests of the workingmen in America especially requires that the formation of Trades' Unions, Eight Hour Leagues, and other labour organisations should be encouraged among the coloured race."

With reference to the subject of female labour, the address conceded that in many trades women were qualified to fill the positions formerly occupied by men, but demanded that they should also get the same compensation as men.

The last and the most important section of the address dealt with " political action." Like the platform adopted at the convention, it called upon the workingmen to " cut aloof from the ties and trammels of party, manipulated in the interest of capital " and to use the ballot in their own interests. However, unlike the convention, the address did not treat political action in connection with the eight-hour law, but linked it with the abolition of " our iniquitous monetary and financial system," which reduced the " producing classes " to a state of servitude.

This change is an indication that the labour movement of the sixties was already abandoning wage-consciousness for the consciousness of the " producer," embracing alike wage-earners, small manufacturers, and farmers.

The adoption by the labour movement of the point of view of the " producer," took place at a time when the movement of discontent spread all along the line of the " producing classes." As shown in the preceding chapter, the wage-earners were the only class obliged to organise during the years of war prosperity. The farmers were reaping the benefits of high prices and had no incentive to organise. But the falling prices after the War affected the farmer and the wage-earner alike. They meant unemployment and low wages to the latter and operation at a loss to the former. The wage-earners felt the turning tide sooner on account of the return of the soldiers to industry, and they hastened to start a movement for remedial legislation — an eight-hour law. By the year 1867 the farmers began keenly to feel the depression and we consequently find them joining with the wage-earners in a movement for legislation that would benefit the " producer " instead of the " capitalist."

When the second convention of the National Labor Union met in Chicago, August 19, 1867, it contained four delegates from three anti-monopoly associations in Illinois [71] and two representatives from land and labour leagues in Michigan. All of these organisations represented the farmers' interests and were but a small fraction of the numerous farmers' political clubs, which were then rapidly forming in the agricultural States of the West.[72]

The representation of the purely wage-earners' organisations had undergone some change since the Baltimore convention. The number of national unions which sent delegates had grown from 3 to 6,[73] the number of trades' assemblies had decreased from 11 to 9, and local trade unions from 41 to 33, but the eight-hour leagues increased from 4 to 9 and there was 1 state organisation.[74] The total number of organisations was 64, and of delegates, 71. The well-known leaders were nearly all present. There were Gibson and Whaley, Sylvis and Trevellick, Hinchcliffe and Cameron, Jessup and Phelps. The Lassalean Schlägel, although not a delegate, was seated by a special resolution. Prominent absentees, who had been present at Baltimore, were Fincher and Troup, but their absence was more than balanced by the presence of Sylvis and Trevellick. The important fact was the larger representation of national trade unions, showing that legislative action had found adherents among all forms of labour organisations.

President Whaley's report pointed out that the lack of a

---

71 A. Campbell, later of " greenback labour " prominence, represented the Illinois State Anti-monopoly Association. See " Proceedings," in *Doc. Hist.*, IX, 169–194.

72 J. L. Coulter, " Organization among the Farmers of the United States," in *Yale Review*, XVIII, 277–298.

73 The bricklayers', the coachmakers', the moulders', the tailors', the typographical, and the American miners' associations.

74 The Illinois State Workingmen's Convention, represented by A. C. Cameron.

steady source of revenue accounted for the inactivity of the organisation. He dwelt on the importance of the Negro question and emphatically declared that co-operation was "the great panacea for the evils complained of by the working classes on account of an unequal distribution of the profits arising from their labour."

Secretary Gibson, in his report, suggested a more closely knitted organisation and called upon the convention to evolve a plan of action which should be not only national but international, because "there is much activity and intelligent enterprise beyond the waters, and we may gain much strength and encouragement from them, while our free institutions should shed their light upon the darkness of usurpation and monarchical oppression." He also laid great stress upon the currency question.

The first important work of this convention was the adoption of a constitution. It was worked out by a committee consisting of Isaac J. Neal, W. H. Sylvis, William Harding, W. J. Jessup, and D. Evans. The characteristic feature that distinguished this constitution from the old temporary one, was the greater amount of recognition granted to national trade unions. It provided that "every International or National organisation shall be entitled to three representatives and a Vice-President at large, State organisations to two, Trade Unions and all other organisations to one representative in the National Labor Congress." Dues were apportioned according to membership, with a maximum of $6 for organisations with more than 500 members. Provision was also made for a salary for the president.

The discussion on the subjects of trade unionism, apprenticeship, eight hours and public lands contained little of original merit. A resolution deplored the fact that "the various industrial organisations now comprising the National Labour Organisation for all practical purposes, embracing labour compensation, the hours of labour, and the matters affecting the rights of the employer and employé, are acting independently under the jurisdiction of their National and International Unions," [75] and recommended more uniformity among these organisations. The National Labor Union, of course, would not undertake that, since it was not an economic but a legislative organisation. However, on the related subject of prevention of the importation of strike-breakers from Europe, the convention decided that the National Labor Union should take the matter into its own hands.

In July, 1864, an act of Congress had been approved, giving validity to contracts made in foreign countries "whereby emigrants shall pledge the wages of their labor for a term not exceeding twelve months, to repay the expenses of their immigration," and providing that the contract should operate as a lien on any property acquired by the immigrant.[76] Following this act the American Emigrant Company was incorporated in Connecticut "to import laborers, especially skilled laborers, from Great Britain, Germany, Belgium, France, Switzerland, Norway and Sweden, for the manufacturers, railroad companies and other employers of labor in America." The company's authorised capital was $1,000,000, of which in 1865, $540,000 was paid up. Among its incorporators were bankers, employers, and politicians, and the company referred as its endorsers to such public men as Chief-Justice Chase, of the Supreme Court of the United States, Gideon Welles, the secretary of the navy, Henry Ward Beecher, Charles Sumner, Henry C. Carey, and a long list of governors, senators, bankers, and editors. The advertisements stated that the company had "established extensive agencies" throughout foreign countries, and that it "undertakes to hire men in their native homes and safely to transfer them to their employers here." "A system so complete," said the advertisement, "has been put in operation here that miners, mechanics (including workers in iron and steel of every class), weavers, and agricultural, railroad and other labourers, can now be procured without much delay, in any numbers, and at a reasonable cost." [77]

Naturally this organisation called forth vigorous protests in the labour papers, and it became a subject of excited discussion at the meetings of the National Labor Union. It was not, however, until the depression of 1866 and 1867, that serious effort was made by the convention to counteract the efforts

[76] United States, *Session Laws*, 38 Cong., 1 sess., chap. 246, p. 385.
[77] New York Chamber of Commerce, *Special Reports*, 1864–1865, 21; New York *Herald*, July 31, 1865; *Doc. Hist.*, IX, 74–80.

of employers and the Emigrant Company. The discussion at the convention of 1867 brought out a number of facts relating to the activity of the American Emigrant Company in providing strike-breakers for employers as well as the part which American consuls abroad were playing in it. The convention appointed Richard Trevellick a delegate to the congress of the International Workingmen's Association in Europe with instructions to find a remedy. Trevellick, however, did not make the trip, but the agitation started at this time doubtless led to the repeal of the act of 1864, which had legalised alien contract labour. This repeal was effected by a rider attached to another bill.[78]

It is significant that, when speaking of trade union action, the convention mentioned only national trade unions and omitted trades' assemblies. On the vital subject of the Negro in industry the convention chose to remain noncommittal. A committee, with A. W. Phelps chairman, was appointed to consider the subject, but their report showed an unwillingness to deal with the matter. Phelps said it was so involved in mystery and so diverse were the opinions of individual delegates that the committee regarded it as inexpedient to take action at that time. Sylvis insisted that the issue had already been raised in the South by the whites striking against the blacks, and predicted that " the Negro will take possession of the shops if we shall not take possession of the mind of the Negro. If the workingmen of the white race do not conciliate the blacks, the black vote will be cast against him." Trevellick affirmed his faith that " the Negro will bear to be taught his duty." Nevertheless, the convention avoided the question by adopting the report of the committee, which stated, " that after mature deliberation they had come to the conclusion that the constitution already adopted prevented the necessity of reporting on the subject of Negro labour."

Nothing new was added on the eight-hour question; it was, however, quite evident that this measure had ceased to occupy the foreground. The discussion on co-operation likewise occupied little time, but it was recognised that co-operation was " a sure and lasting remedy for the abuses of the present in-

78 United States, *Statutes at Large*, 40 Cong., 2 sess., chap. 38, p. 58.

dustrial system, and that until the laws of the nation can be remodelled so as to recognise the rights of men instead of classes, the system of co-operation carefully guarded will do much to lessen the evils of our present system." A permanent committee was appointed to investigate the various systems of co-operation.

GREENBACKISM

But if the convention did not give much time to purely labour questions like strikes, trade unionism, eight hours, and apprenticeship, it did not fail to devote great attention to questions in which the farmers' representatives shared a like interest with the labour delegates. These questions were currency, taxation of United States bonds, and political action. The pre-eminence given to these questions was not due to the numerical strength of the farmers' delegates, for they numbered only ten, but to the intense interest which these questions aroused among the labour delegates. We find, indeed, that there were no more interested participants in the discussions on currency and state finance than the representatives of national trade unions, which the convention declared in one of the adopted reports as the "highest form that labour associations have hitherto taken." These representatives were men like Sylvis of the moulders, Harding of the coachmakers, and Lucker of the tailors. In fact, the labour movement in the national field had abandoned its wage-earners' demands and had come to identify its interests with those of the "producer," the farmer, and the small business man.

A. C. Cameron was the chief spokesman of money reform at the convention. As the author of the *Address of the National Labor Congress to the Workingmen of the United States,* issued in July, preceding, he had shown his adherence to money reform. Now, as the chairman of the committee on political organisation, he came forth with a scheme which was an ingenious adaptation of Edward Kellogg's *New Monetary System* to the conditions created by the Civil War.

Kellogg was a small merchant in New York who had lost his property in the panic of 1837. Thereafter he developed his plan of financial reform, which he published first in 1848

under the title, *Labour and Other Capital.*[79] It was based on a
" labour theory " of interest, namely, the notion that any rate of
interest in excess of the labour-cost of carrying on the banking
business was robbery. The physical wealth of the country, as
Kellogg found from statistics, was accumulating at the rate of
about 1¼ per cent a year, but money, " the representative of
wealth," was increasing at the rate of 12 per cent. If the
government, then, would issue legal tender currency on real
estate mortgages at the labour-cost of conducting the business,
namely 1.1 per cent, the mortgagor could use it himself or lend
it to others at slightly more than that rate. In case the market
rate should fall below 1 per cent the mortgagor could return
the money to the government and receive a government bond
bearing 1 per cent interest, thus preventing the fall of interest
below that rate. If the market rate rose above 1 per cent he
could return the bond and get the money. By means of this
" interconvertible bond " the rate of interest would be kept
close to 1 per cent.

In 1850, Kellogg had presented his plan to the Industrial
Congress of New York, to which he was a delegate, and it had
been favourably reviewed in the *Tribune.*[80] But it was not
until the greenback period of the War that his followers multiplied. Alexander Campbell, a delegate to the National Labor Union, published a pamphlet in 1864 entitled, *The True
American System of Finance; . . . No Banks; Greenbacks
the Exclusive Currency,* which was reprinted in 1868 under
the title, *The True Greenback, or the Way to Pay the National Debt Without Taxes and Emancipate Labor.* Cameron, in his report as committee chairman at the Congress of
1867 had already adopted Campbell's modification of Kellogg's
scheme. The modifications were simple. The war debt was
to be transformed into the interconvertible bonds and the rate
of interest was to be 3 per cent instead of Kellogg's 1 per cent.

Of course, the greenbackers of the National Labor Union
did not overlook the inevitable inflation of prices that would

79 The subtitle continued as follows:
" The rights of each secured and the
wrongs of both eradicated; or, an exposition of the cause why few are wealthy
and many poor, and the delineation of a
system which, without infringing the
rights of property, will give to labour its
just reward."
80 See above, I, 556.

follow this scheme, but that was not a matter of concern when prices were already falling tremendously because of the retirement of the greenbacks then persistently carried on by the secretary of the treasury. But more important to them than the effect on prices was the effect on rates of interest and on the credit that could be advanced to producers. The scheme was quite similar to that of Ferdinand Lassalle in Germany, wherein the government was to lend money to workingmen to finance their co-operative undertakings. It differed only in that the money was to come from inflation of greenbacks rather than taxes. The greenback theory was also on a par with all anarchistic and socialistic theories, since it held that interest was robbery to the extent that it exceeded the labour-cost of conducting the loan transactions. Its confusion was parallel with the double meaning of the term "value of money." Kellogg and the greenbackers of the National Labor Union looked upon the market rate of interest as the market value of money. The market value would be reduced if the government entered the field as a lender of its own legal tender money. After 1872, this aspect of greenbackism was abandoned for the most part, and the sole argument for inflation was the other aspect which defined the "value of money" as its power of exchange against commodities, and which turned on the practical object of keeping up the level of prices.

But "Kelloggism," in the form advanced by its founder, was more than price inflation — it was a revolutionary philosophy of social reform, entitled to rank with the similar philosophies of anarchism and socialism. It was in harmony with the efforts of the time to finance co-operation, to expel the middleman and financier, and to raise the small producer to a position of independence. From 1867 to 1872 may be designated as the social reform period, or the wage-earners' period of greenbackism, as distinguished from the inflationist, or farmers' period that followed. Not that discussion touching the latter was absent prior to 1873. In fact the legislation of 1868,[81] which stopped further retirement of the greenback, was carried

---

[81] United States, *Statutes at Large*, 40 Cong., 2 sess., chap. 6, p. 34. This act fixed the minimum amount of treasury notes at the quantity then outstanding, namely, $356,000,000. Knox, *United States Notes*, 140.

through Congress as a preventive of that contraction which was reducing the prices of commodities. But it stopped short of the interconvertible bond and the government loans for private business, which were the machinery of the revolutionary scheme to abolish interest on money.

In logical consequence of its espousal of greenbackism, the committee on political organisation modified the declaration of the Baltimore convention, which had set forth that workingmen of the United States should organise themselves into a national labour party, by substituting the term " industrial classes " for " workingmen." It also recommended the local nomination of workingmen's candidates, and presented a lengthy platform as a basis of such political action. This platform, or *Declaration of Principles,* modelled after the Declaration of Independence, was a document of about 3,000 words and dealt in about two-thirds of its space with financial reform.[82] It declared that the law creating the so-called national banking system was a delegation by Congress of the sovereign power to make money and to regulate its value to a class of irresponsible banking associations, and " that this money monopoly is the parent of all monopolies — the very root and essence of slavery — railroad, warehouse and all other monopolies of whatever kind or nature are the outgrowth of and subservient to this power." Also, as a remedy against this money monopoly, the platform set forth at great length the scheme of interconvertible bonds and legal tender paper money and, as auxiliary to the latter, the repeal of the exemption from taxation of bank capital and government bonds. The question of the taxation of government bonds was again considered by a special committee composed of A. Campbell, R. Trevellick, and A. J. Kuykendall, and they found the question " one of very grave importance," and the exemption a " burden imposed on labour for the benefit of capital." In addition to the pivotal question of financial and fiscal reform the declaration of the congress pronounced against land monopoly, in favour of an eight-hour law, co-operation, improved dwellings for workmen, and mechanics' institutes; it expressed sympathy with the working women and recommended to the unemployed that they

82 *Doc. Hist.,* IX, 175.

"proceed to the public lands and become actual settlers."
Finally, there was a plank deprecating strikes.

Thus, the National Labor Union, having already abandoned
trade union action for the legislative method of shortening hours,
now took up greenbackism. This followed naturally the state
of trade from 1866 to 1868. The government's policy of contracting the greenback currency brought its effect in the fall
of prices and severe unemployment. The general level of prices
fell in 1866 to 18 per cent below the level of 1864, and in 1867
to 27 per cent. The fall in 1868, after the anti-resumption
act of February of that year, was only 1 per cent.

The total lack of any reliable statistics on labour matters
(the first labour bureau, that of Massachusetts, was established
in 1869) greatly aided the formation of what were doubtless
exaggerated conceptions on the matter and tended to spread
much gloomier views than the situation warranted. William
Jessup, in his report to President Whaley, which the latter
presented to the convention held in New York, September,
1868, estimated the number of unemployed at one time during
the preceding winter at 20,000 in New York City alone. In
Buffalo, the report stated, the stream of Canadian immigration
had completely destroyed the twenty existing trade unions. All
of the coachmakers' unions in the State, except two, had disappeared. The ship carpenters' and caulkers' and the woolen
spinners' unions had also become much demoralised. The whole
number of trade and labour unions in the State had, however,
slightly increased, and reached 285 in September, 1868. The
moulders were engaged in a severe and protracted struggle in
Rochester against a reduction of 20 per cent in wages. But the
most important strike of the year was the one of the bricklayers
in New York City for the eight-hour day. It began on June
22 and was still in progress in Poughkeepsie and Buffalo at the
time of the convention of 1868. The trade unions throughout
the country were giving the strikers generous support. But
the prospects were evidently not bright, for the weight of a
legal prosecution had been added to the strength of the employers. A lawsuit for $10,000 damages on the ground of
conspiracy was pending against Samuel R. Gaul, president of
the union in New York, and other prominent members. While

trade unionism was thus, on the whole, unsuccessful, co-operation was making headway in the State of New York. Jessup's report enumerated successful co-operative foundries in Albany, Troy, West Albany, and Rochester; there were also successful carpenters' shops. On the other hand, but three co-operative stores had survived in the State. They were located at Albany, Lockport, and New York, and Jessup said that "as a general thing they are not as successful as other co-operative enterprises."

EIGHT HOURS

While the year 1868 was thus marked in the labour movement with but poor success in the field of trade union action, the efforts for legislative reforms were crowned, if not with complete, yet with considerable, success. In June, Congress enacted into law for government employés the chief demand of the Baltimore convention — the eight-hour day.

The passage of this measure was due considerably to the indefatigable efforts of Richard F. Trevellick. Some months before the date of enactment, he was sent to Washington on behalf of the National Labor Union, and he stolidly adhered to his post although he was obliged to pay a large part of his expenses from his own pocket.

This, however, did not end the battle for the eight-hour law. The various officials in charge of government work put their own interpretation upon the law and some held that the reduction in working hours must of necessity bring with it a corresponding reduction of wages. Most notable was the order of the secretary of war to this effect. A committee of workingmen of Washington presented to President Johnson a vigorous protest against this order, and asked that the President seek the opinion of the attorney-general.[83] The President complied with this request, but Attorney-General Evarts in his opinion, November 25, upheld the action of the secretary of war. On April 20, 1869, Attorney-General Hoar handed down a similar opinion. The matter was finally settled by President Grant, who, moved by the storm of protest from the working people led by Sylvis, Cameron, Trevellick, and Jessup, issued on May 19,

1869, a proclamation [84] directing the heads of departments that no cut in wages should accompany the reduction of hours. Since the department heads did not generally obey the order, a second proclamation [85] was issued by the President on May 11, 1872, reiterating the same order. On May 18, 1872, the year of the presidential election, Congress enacted a law [86] which provided for the restitution to all workmen employed by the Government between the date of the first passage of the eight-hour law and the date of President Grant's first proclamation, of such sums as had been withheld from them because of the reduction of hours of labour.

LABOR CONGRESS OF 1868

The law prohibiting the further contraction of the currency, which met half way the demand of the convention of 1867, was passed by an almost unanimous vote of both houses and became a law on February 4, 1868. Since the " producing " classes, business men, farmers, and workingmen were almost a unit in urging its passage, no further obstacles were laid in its way, and the country began rapidly to recover from the effects of the late depression. The restoration of prosperity could not fail to affect the labour movement, and we shall presently see how it affected the National Labor Union.

Meanwhile, the time for the presidential election was drawing near, and it became imperative to take a definite stand on the question of a labour party.

The *Workingman's Advocate* urged Samuel F. Cary of Ohio as a fit candidate for president. The *Welcome Workman,* while discouraging the principle of independent politics, proposed Sylvis as the vice-presidential candidate, but added rather sardonically, " Still we do not see our way clear to more than about fifteen hundred votes for our ticket anywhere in these United States, including Alaska." [87] The *People's Weekly,* of Baltimore, which advocated the platform of the National Labor Union but supported the Democratic party, urged the nomination by that party of George A. Pendleton and Sylvis.

---

[84] United States, Session *Laws,* 41 Cong., 1 sess., Appendix, III.
[85] United States, *Statutes at Large,* 42 Cong., 2 sess., Appendix, 955.

[86] *Ibid.,* 134.
[87] Mar. 17, 1868.

Sylvis was also mentioned as the running mate for Chase.[88] President Whaley called a special conference of prominent labour leaders, which met on July 2, 1868, in New York City. Among those invited were Phelps, Gibson, Jessup, Lucker, Troup, H. H. Day, S. R. Gaul, Sylvis, Trevellick, Campbell, Hinchcliffe, Mary Kellogg Putnam, and Ezra A. Heywood.[89] Heywood was practically the only one present who urged that the National Labor Reform party should put a candidate for president in the field.

The conference passed a set of resolutions reiterating the various planks of the platform of 1867 and concluded by recommending the holding of mass meetings to ratify the principles of that platform, and " to vote only for those candidates who endorse them." The resolutions continued: " Unless these principles are adopted by one of the two great parties, we care not which, we advise the National Labor Union, at its annual convention, soon to be held in this city, to put in nomination an independent labour candidate for the presidency, and rally the masses to his support." [90]

The convention met September 21, 1868, in New York City. The tide of organisation seems to have reached its height for the period. All the important leaders were present and Sylvis estimated that fully 600,000 organised workmen were represented. Five national unions were represented by 8 delegates: the typographical by Alexander Troup and Robert McKechnie, the carpenters and joiners by Phelps and 2 other delegates, the bricklayers by Samuel R. Gaul, the machinists and blacksmiths by Jonathan C. Fincher, and the moulders by Sylvis. Five state organisations sent 7 delegates; the New York State Workingmen's Assembly, 2; the Massachusetts State Central Organisation of the Industrial Order of the People, 2; the Labor Union of Indiana, 1; the Workingmen's Union of Missouri, 1; and the Michigan Labor Union was represented by Trevellick. Six trades' assemblies were represented by as many delegates and 52 local unions by 53 delegates.

A significant change in the composition of the convention

---

88 Sylvis, *Life, Speeches, Labors and Essays*, 75.

89 See below, II, 138, note, for his connection with Josiah Warren.

90 Chicago *Workingman's Advocate*, Aug. 22, 1868.

was due to the non-appearance of farmers' representatives. The farmers' agitation had apparently subsided after the passage of the currency act. Neither was there any representation from eight-hour leagues. They were replaced by delegates from three new types of organisations: "labour reform leagues" and "labour unions," both purely political local organisations, and working women's organisations. Of the first kind there were three delegates from as many organisations, notably Ezra A. Heywood, from the Worcester Labor Reform League. Their presence indicated that the labour movement had absorbed a portion of the radical intellectuals. The "labour unions" apparently did not differ in their composition from the former eight-hour leagues. They were preponderately workingmen's organisations with a purely political purpose, and numbered four delegates in the convention from as many unions.

Finally, the presence of delegates from women's organisations heralded the appearance of the "woman question." Two New York working women's protective associations were respectively represented by Susan B. Anthony, the famous woman suffragist leader and editor of the *Revolution,* and Mrs. Mary Kellogg Putnam, daughter of Edward Kellogg. A third organisation, the Woman's Protective Labor Union of Mt. Vernon, New York, was represented by Mrs. Mary McDonald. The appearance of the women delegates meant more than a stronger emphasis upon "female labour," a subject which had been frequently discussed at previous conventions. This was apparent from the fact that the women's unions were the only ones in which the leaders did not come from the rank and file but had to be drawn from the better situated classes, the educated women. The convention faced the subject soon after it had organised.

The credentials of Elizabeth Cady Stanton, signed by Susan B. Anthony, secretary of the Woman Suffrage Association, were presented and were reported formally by the committee. A heated debate arose on the ground that the suffrage association was not a labour organisation as stipulated in the by-laws. After speeches and motions in favour by Sylvis, Lucker, Phelps, Miss Anthony, and others, and in opposition by several delegates, the credentials were accepted, yeas 94 and nays 19. The next day eighteen delegates threatened to resign if Mrs. Stanton were a recognised delegate. In order to appease them a diplomatic resolution was adopted, which said that the admission of Mrs. Stanton did not mean that the convention gave indorsement to her " peculiar ideas," but " simply regarded her as a representative from an organisation having for its object the amelioration of the condition of those who labour for a living."

At the same convention the unanimous thanks of the congress was tendered to Miss Kate Mullaney, chief directrix of the Collar Laundry Workingwomen's Association of Troy, for her " indefatigable exertions in the interest of workingwomen." President Sylvis afterward appointed her assistant secretary of the National Labor Union,[91] " to correspond with and aid the formation of workingwomen's associations throughout the country, and bring them in co-operation with the National Labor Union."

The convention of 1868 added little of original merit to the discussion of the important questions which were agitating the labour movement. It left unaltered the position previously taken on greenbackism, co-operation, land, trade unionism, and eight hours. Greenbackism remained the foremost demand, the indispensable prerequisite before co-operation could proceed. The discussion of the platform serves to illustrate how practically unanimous the delegates were with regard to the supreme importance of currency reform. L. A. Hine, a member of the committee on platform, who had been a prominent lecturer in the land reform movement of the forties, submitted a minority report in which he opposed the currency scheme of the committee, favoured gold and silver, and contended that the real remedy needed was land limitation. Fincher was the only speaker who sustained him in his opposition to currency reform. Fincher, however, did not advocate land reform as the substitute. He remained true to his position in favour of a strong trade union organisation and an eight-hour law, the latter to be attained by a policy of pressure upon the old political parties. He attacked the scheme of interconvertible bonds and paper money on the ground that it would " give the bond-holders the power of making the amount of currency optional with them-

91 *Proceedings*, 1868.

selves, for they could contract it at any time to answer their own purposes." Immediately the whole phalanx of leaders — Cameron, Trevellick, Whaley, Susan B. Anthony, Sylvis, and others — rushed to the defence of the pet scheme. Sylvis, however, made the only real attempt to answer Fincher. He said that the danger Fincher saw was merely an illusion, because the greenback measure would "kill the bankers entirely." Under the new system, he contended, "we will borrow money from the government of the United States, not from bankers; and we will get it at one or one and one-half per cent."

The clause of the platform which deprecated strikes caused a long discussion. A delegate from New York moved that the clause be stricken out, because it might have an injurious effect upon the bricklayers of New York indicted for conspiracy. This offered the opportunity to the women delegates to come out in favour of strikes. Mrs. McDonald offered a resolution recognising the "right of the workingmen and workingwomen of this nation to strike, when all other just and equitable concessions are refused." The convention adopted it unanimously for the sake of the striking bricklayers.

No other changes were made in the platform or constitution. The only important new demand made by the convention was the one for a department of labour, introduced by Sylvis. This was the first appearance of a resolution of this character in a labour convention. The resolution specified, " said department to have charge, under the laws of Congress, of the distribution of the public domain, the registration and regulation, under a general system, of trade unions, co-operative associations, and all other organisations of workingmen and women having for their object the protection of productive industry, and the elevation of those who toil." A supplementary resolution demanding that in the act for the approaching census Congress should order the taking of comprehensive industrial statistics, was also adopted.

On the all-important question of political action, the convention reiterated the necessity of immediate organisation of a labour party, "having for its object the election to our state and national councils of men who are in direct sympathy and identified with the interests of labour." But it cautiously added, " provided, this shall not be understood as contemplating the nomination of presidential electors in the states during the pending presidential campaign."

Congressman Samuel F. Cary, of the second congressional district of Ohio, was endorsed for re-election as an advocate of the principles of the National Labor Union, and the " action of our fellow workingmen of said district in making him their candidate " was " fully endorsed."

The convention adjourned after electing Sylvis president for the next year.

After the New York convention in 1868, the National Labor Union entered upon the most fruitful year of its existence. Sylvis now introduced systematic methods and persistent efforts into the management of the affairs of the National Labor Union. He at once established a vast correspondence with men interested in the movement, and issued several circulars, which were widely distributed. The second circular contained the following characteristic passage: " There are about three thousand trades'-unions in the United States. . . . *We must show them that when a just monetary system has been established, there will no longer exist a necessity for trade unions.*" [92] Shortly after the convention had adjourned, he appointed a committee of five to reside in the city of Washington during the session of Congress, whose duty it was " to watch over the interests of our Union, lay our plans and objects before Congressmen and Senators, and take advantage of every opportunity to help along the work." [93]   This was the first permanent lobbying committee established at Washington by a labour organisation. Congressman Cary, who was again elected in the fall of 1868, introduced on January 5, 1869, a bill embodying the principle of interconvertible bonds and legal tender paper money, and was supported by Benjamin F. Butler, of Massachusetts.

In spite of the shortage of funds in the treasury of the National Labor Union, Sylvis, in company with Richard Trevellick, undertook, in February, 1869, a propaganda trip through

92 Sylvis, *Life, Speeches, Labors and Essays*, 81.
93 " Presidential Report," in Proceedings of the Convention of 1869, *Doc. Hist.*, IX, 232.

the South. He took advantage of every opportunity to bring the principles of the National Labor Union before the people. He addressed meetings, wrote letters to and obtained numerous interviews with public men,[94] and printed articles in the *Workingman's Advocate,* of which he had several years previously become joint proprietor.

THE INTERNATIONAL

Sylvis was the first American labour leader to endeavour actively to establish relations with the European labour movement; namely, with the International Workingmen's Association, the European contemporary of the National Labor Union. During the first three or four years of its existence, from the date of its establishment by Marx and the British trade unionists in 1864, the International had been primarily an economic organisation. Its main function was to assist trade unions in the various countries during strikes, either by preventing the importation of strike-breakers from abroad, or by collecting strike funds. This suggested the value of this organisation as a regulator of European migration to the United States and led to a series of attempts on the part of each, the National Labor Union and the International, to establish a permanent mutual relationship. However, little was accomplished prior to Sylvis' election to the presidency. The Baltimore convention had adopted a resolution inviting the International to send a delegate to the next convention in Chicago, since it was too late to send a delegate to the congress of the International at Geneva. At the Chicago convention, the question of immigration was discussed. Trevellick had been named as a delegate, but it was too late for him to attend. In 1868 Eccarius, general secretary of the International at London, again invited the National Labor Union to send a delegate to the congress at Brussels, but this could not be done on account of lack of funds. In 1869 the general council of the International addressed a memorial to the National Labor Union regarding

[94] He had a rather interesting encounter with Attorney-General Hoar, to whom he wrote a letter severely censuring him for his opinion upholding the reduction of 25 per cent in wages on public work, following the introduction of the eight-hour system. Hoar replied by a brief, haughty note, and Sylvis in turn retorted by a second letter written in a similar vein. A letter from Sylvis to Grant, while acknowledging the merits of the President's proclamation of May 21 re-establishing the old rate of wages, was framed in a similar independent style.

the impending war between England and the United States. The International advised the simultaneous agitation by the working people of both countries in the interests of peace. Sylvis replied by a forcible letter: " Our cause is a common one. It is war between poverty and wealth. . . . This monied power is fast eating up the substance of the people. We have made war upon it, and we mean to win it. If we can, we will win through the ballot box: if not, then we shall resort to sterner means. A little blood-letting is sometimes necessary in desperate cases." [95]

Sylvis died suddenly on July 27 following. Had it not been for this loss of its leader the alliance of the National Labor Union with the International, judging from Sylvis' correspondence, would have been speedily brought about. A letter from Eccarius was read at the convention of 1869, again extending an invitation to send a delegate and proposing the establishment of an international bureau of immigration. This time A. C. Cameron, editor of the *Workingman's Advocate,* and an ardent greenbacker, was sent as a delegate to the congress of the International at Basle, his expenses being paid by Horace H. Day. Cameron took small part in the work of the congress.[96] On his way home, he attended a meeting of the General Council of the International in London and discussed the establishment of an international bureau of immigration. Nothing practical, however, resulted from Cameron's mission, except that the National Labor Union at its next annual convention in Cincinnati, in 1870, adopted a resolution in favour of affiliating with the International. But this belated affiliation had no practical significance.

[95] Both the call and Sylvis' letter, dated May 26, were printed in the *Vorbote,* organ of the I. W. A., published at Geneva, Switzerland, September, 1869. See also *Doc. Hist.,* IX, 833–350.

[96] However, some of the observations he made in his letters from Europe to the *Workingman's Advocate* on the nature of the European labour movement merit attention. In the issue of Nov. 6, 1869, he said: " One important fact, however, must not be overlooked — that while the institutions and state of society prevailing in Europe are a legitimate offspring — the inevitable offshoot of despotism — in the other it is a perversion — a maladministration of the spirit of our institutions which has created the evils of which the American workman complains. In the one case a thorough reconstruction is imperatively demanded; in the other a just administration of the fundamental principles upon which the government is founded alone is required." He went on to apologise for the extreme radicalism of the International. " Land monopoly in Europe," he said, " is as money monopoly in the United States, the matrix of all evil; the demand, therefore, of the International to abolish private property in land is just as legitimate as the demand of the National Labor Union to abolish monopoly of money." *Doc. Hist.,* IX, 341–350.

LABOR CONGRESS OF 1869

Sylvis did not live to see the large representation at the convention of 1869 from the numerous labour organisations which his efforts had brought within the fold of the National Labor Union. This convention met in Philadelphia, August 16, 1869. The representation numbered 142 and included delegates from 3 international trade unions — the moulders, printers, machinists and blacksmiths, and from the national carpenters' and joiners' union; from 2 state trade organisations — the Pennsylvania Grand Lodge of the Knights of St. Crispin and the United Hod Carriers' and Labourers' Association of Pennsylvania; from 3 state federations — Pennsylvania, Kansas, and California; from 6 trades' assemblies — New York, Bridgeport, Camden, Springfield, Washington, D. C., Monroe County (Rochester), New York; from 53 local trade unions; from 10 labour unions (directly chartered by the National Labor Union); and from a few miscellaneous benefit and reform associations. Significant was the appearance for the first time of Negro delegates. All of the prominent leaders, Jessup, Troup, Trevellick, Cameron, and Campbell, were present. Objection was made by Walsh of the typographical union to the admission of Susan B. Anthony on the ground that the Workingwomen's Protective Association, of which she was president, was not a *bona fide* labour organisation; and that she had striven to procure situations for girls in printing offices at lower wages than those received by men who had been discharged. Trevellick, Cameron, and several others favoured her admission, but after a prolonged debate her credentials were rejected on a vote of 63 to 28.[97]

President Lucker of the tailors' national union, who had taken Sylvis' place, spoke in his report of the revival of the conspiracy laws; the imprisonment of two men in Schuylkill County, Pennsylvania, "simply because they were members of a workingmen's union"; the progress of eight-hour legisla-

---

[97] The convention was not opposed to the admission of women, as there was a woman delegate from a Crispin lodge. Even the typographical union had at this time opened its doors to women, reluctantly to be sure, and had established a woman's local in New York City. See Andrews and Bliss, *History of Women in Trade Unions*, Sen. Doc., 61 Cong., 2 sess., No. 645, vol. X, 87, 103.

tion; the revival of the coolie trade; the failure of co-operative enterprises to take that "hold among the producers that their importance entitles them to." He endorsed the formation of a national labour party "to capture Washington, not with bullets, but with ballots, in 1872"; recommended the appointment of a delegate to the international congress in Basle; and reported the formation of twenty-six labour unions located mostly in the western and southern States and "in the main composed of those who are not directly connected with any trade union."

The nature of the work of the convention bears ample testimony to the loss that the labour movement had sustained through the death of Sylvis. No longer guided by his systematic constructive mind, the convention added practically nothing new to the work of the previous conventions. The platform was rewritten, but not with intention "to change or modify the existing declaration of principles, but to reaffirm the same, and for practical use enunciate the substance thereof in a more convenient and concise form, with some additional resolutions."

THE NEGROES [98]

The questions of co-operation, trade unionism, and politics received but scant attention. Some consideration was given to the eight-hour question. The president and the executive committee were instructed to draft a plan for state centralisation of trade unions for the purpose of enforcing by a general strike the eight-hour law in States where such a law had been passed. A committee on the constitution submitted a plan of organisation with the state labour union as the unit, but the whole matter was ignored by the convention. Only the problem of the Negro fared somewhat better; a permanent committee was appointed to organise the Negroes in Pennsylvania and coloured delegates from every State in the union were invited to come to the next convention. This was doubtless due to the presence of four Negro delegates, which indicated plainly that the Negro could no longer be ignored.[99]

[98] In the preparation of this section the author has drawn largely from an unpublished monograph by H. G. Lee, *Labor Organizations Among Negroes*.

[99] The other acts of the convention in the main consisted in the passage of a resolution condemning anti-conspiracy laws; urging affiliated labour organisations to report labour statistics to the executive committee, appointing a committee

Notwithstanding the efforts of the National Labor Union, the Negroes chose to organise separately from the whites. The reasons for this discontent were several, but the chief one was the " exclusion of coloured men and apprentices from the right to labour in any department of industry or workshops . . . by what is known as ' trade unions.' " [1] Clashes between black and white labourers were not infrequent during the period of the sixties.[2] When, during the same decade, the Negro began to invade the trades and superior positions, the opposition to him was no less strong.[3] Numerous instances might be brought in illustration. The bricklayers' union in Washington, D. C., forbade their men to work alongside coloured men. Four white union men were found to be working with some Negroes on government work, and the union decided unanimously to expel them from the union.[4] A Negro printer, Louis H. Douglass, in 1869 was refused admission to the local union in Washington, D. C., in spite of the fact that the constitution made no discrimination against coloured men. This case attracted great attention, since an appeal taken to the convention of the National Typographical Union had been unsuccessful and consequently offered the Negro workmen an unmistakable gauge of the sentiment of organised skilled mechanics in the country.[5]

Another cause of the separate organisation of the Negroes was their divergence in interests from the white wage-earners. Greenbackism and the taxation of government bonds presented very little interest to them. Instead, they laid emphasis upon

to appeal for funds, one-half of which should go to erect a monument to Sylvis and one-half to his family; defending the locked-out miners of Pennsylvania and charging the mining monopolies, transportation monopolies, and city speculators with responsibility for the high price of coal; advocating thorough organisation of female labour, " the same pay for work equally well done," " equal opportunities and rights in every field of enterprise and labour "; demanding eight hours for convicts and the system of prison labour now known as " public account " instead of the contract system; condemning the " alliance of the Associated Press and the Western Union Telegraph Company "; and demanding a government telegraph. Richard Trevellick was elected president for the next year, H. J. Walls, secretary; and A. W. Phelps, treasurer.

1 Chicago *Workingman's Advocate*, Jan. 1, 1870; *Doc. Hist.*, IX, 250.

2 *Fincher's*, for July 11, 1863, gives an account of a bloody fight between white and black stevedores in Buffalo. The employers attempted to supply the places of the whites by Negro workmen. The fight resulted in the drowning of two black men, the killing of another, and the serious beating of twelve more.

3 *Fincher's* for Nov. 6, 1865, tells of a strike of caulkers in Canton, Ohio, against a Negro foreman.

4 Washington *Daily Chronicle*, June 19, 1869.

5 *Ibid.*, May 21, 1869. The coloured convention of the National Labor Union especially commented upon this case.

education, and their chief legislative demand was for a liberal homestead policy in the South for freedmen. To cap it all, the platform of the National Labor Union was absolute in the condemnation of the Republican party and advocated independent political action. Such a policy not only ran counter to the sentiment of loyalty felt by the rank and file of the Negroes for the Republican party, but was extremely unsuited to the ambitious aspirations of the coloured leaders, who, like their ablest representative, J. M. Langston, a lawyer from Ohio, staked their future upon the destinies of that party.

The first attempt of the Negroes to organise on a national scale was at the national coloured convention held in Washington in January, 1869. It had a large attendance of about 130 delegates, including a large number of politicians and preachers, nearly all from the northern and border States, and was purely political in its nature. Full confidence was declared in the Republican party, but provision was made for a national committee to be composed of one from each State and territory and for subordinate state committees to " take general charge of the interests of the coloured people." Equal political rights, education, and free land for freedmen were the only topics discussed. No mention was made of the relation to white labour.[6]

The first coloured state labour convention was held in Baltimore in July, 1869. It appointed a committee to report at another state convention to be held two weeks thereafter. The report set forth that in many instances white men refused to work with Negroes and recommended thorough organisation of Negro labour throughout the country. The convention appointed five delegates to the Philadelphia convention of the National Labor Union and issued a call for a national coloured labour convention to be held in Washington in December, 1869. The union of the employés of the Chesapeake Marine Railway Company in Baltimore, all coloured men, held a meeting in November, endorsed the call for the national convention, and appointed its secretary as delegate.[7]

The national convention met December 6, attended by 156 delegates from every section of the country. Richard Trevel-

---

6 *Ibid.*, Jan. 12–16, 1869.   7 *Ibid.*, Nov. 9, 1869.

lick was present on behalf of the National Labor Union. The object of the convention stated in the call was to " consolidate the coloured workingmen of the several states to act in co-operation with our white fellow workingmen in every state and territory in the union, who are opposed to distinction in the apprenticeship laws on account of colour, and to so act co-operatively until the necessity for separate organisation shall be deemed unnecessary," and to petition Congress for the exclusion of contract coolie labour. The politicians in the convention immediately made their presence felt. Langston, of Ohio, warned the delegates against the white delegates from Massachusetts (Cummings of the Crispins and several others) whom he accused of being the emissaries of the Democratic party. The land question and education were the chief topics, and Congress was memorialised to pass a special homestead act for the Negroes in the South. The convention created a coloured national labour union with Isaac Myers, a Baltimore caulker, president, and adopted a lengthy platform. This differed in many respects from the platform of the white National Labor Union. It carefully omitted all matters such as green-backism and taxation of government bonds, taxation of the rich for war purposes, independent political action, restoration of civic rights to southerners, which might give offence to the Republican party. It omitted, also, several measures, the importance of which the Negroes did not appreciate, such as the incorporation of unions, a department of labour, convict labour, and the solidarity of men and women workers. It gave mere mention to eight hours and co-operation, but it added with strong emphasis the demand of equal rights for white and black labourers to jobs. The two platforms fully agreed that strikes were useless and that Chinese contract labour should be excluded.

After the Philadelphia convention in 1869, the National Labor Union made somewhat slower progress than during the preceding year. President Trevellick was an excellent agitator and organiser, but he did not possess that unequalled combination of breadth of vision and strong practical sense which was characteristic of Sylvis. He travelled 169 days of the year in New England, in the Middle States, in the South, and in the West; and, accompanied by John Siney, their rapidly advancing leader, he visited the anthracite miners in Pennsylvania, who were then on a prolonged and bitter strike for the further existence of their union.[8] As a result of these trips, 127 charters were issued to local organisations, but the finances of the organisation did not improve.

POLITICS IN MASSACHUSETTS

The centre of independent political action was transferred during 1869 from the West to the East.[9] In Massachusetts the movement had retained in the person of Ira Steward and his friends a strong wage-conscious nucleus. Massachusetts was also the only important section of the nation in which the labour movement came directly in contact with a reform movement of intellectuals. The majority of these intellectuals advocated Proudhon's scheme of mutual banking and thus were in closer harmony with the greenbackism of the labour movement at large than were the followers of Steward. The attendance at the convention of the New England Labor Reform League, held in June, 1869, included representatives of both brands of labour reform. The intellectuals present were Wendell Phillips, Josiah Warren, Ezra A. Heywood,[10] E. H. Rogers, Dr. William H. Channing, Albert Brisbane and John Orvis.[11] The labour representatives were Samuel P. Cummings and President William J. McLaughlin of the Knights of St. Crispin, Ira Steward, George E. McNeil, Jennie Collins,[12] and many others.

President Heywood in his opening address laid stress upon the financial question, and a series of resolutions

8 A brief history of the organisations in that region will be found below, II, 184. These organisations, known as the Miners' and Laborers' Benevolent Associations of Luzerne and Schuylkill Counties, respectively, showed but little interest in the National Labor Union.

9 Congressman Cary of Ohio was defeated for re-election in 1868.

10 See above, I, 511. Heywood was a devoted adherent of Josiah Warren, the first American anarchist, and took him into his home in his old age and cared for him until his death. Heywood published various pamphlets on "mutualism," or anarchism.

11 Orvis had been at Brook Farm and was organiser for the Sovereigns of Industry.

12 Jennie Collins of Boston was a young woman "of high culture and independent social position" who, in 1868, espoused the cause of women strikers in a textile mill in Dover, N. H., and rallied to their defence the factory women of New England. She succeeded in establishing a union of women factory workers, which, however, disappeared soon after the unsuccessful outcome of the strike. (Andrews and Bliss. *History of Women in Trade Unions*, Sen. Doc., 61 Cong., 2 Sess., No. 645, pp. 102, 103.)

was offered in which it was declared that " the use of one's credit as of his conscience or his vote, is a natural right, antecedent to, and independent of government," but that the government by " its claim to dictate the nature and amount of money, especially to restrict it to gold and silver, naturally scarce, and easily hoarded, enables the privileged few in control to make interest and prices high, wages low, and failures frequent, to suit their speculative purposes." The remedy advanced was the withdrawal of the notes of the national banks and the substitution of treasury certificates of service, receivable for taxes and bearing no interest; and the provision of free banking in the States, whereby money, based on commodities, might be furnished at cost. Declaring the solidarity of the league with the National Labor Union, the resolution finally declared that " the principles and measures here announced are no idle theories, but living issues to be made test-questions at the ballot-box; and whether it may be expedient to support our friends in either existing party . . . we pledge ourselves to make the interests of labour paramount to all other considerations in political action." [13]

Such was the position of the large majority of the intellectuals. As can readily be seen, their programme was Proudhon's scheme [14] of free banking supplemented by the greenbacker's idea of government money and political action. The league advocated currency reform in preference to any other reform. On the other hand, Steward and McNeill moved as a substitute a resolution declaring that " the whole power and strength of the labour-reform movement should be concentrated upon the single and simple idea of first reducing the hours of labour, that the masses may have more time to discuss for themselves all other questions in labour reform."

Thus the alignment stood: non-wage-conscious currency reform versus wage-conscious eight-hour reform. The line was not, however, drawn strictly, the intellectuals on one side and the wage-earners on the other. On one hand the wage-earner element found no less valuable a supporter than Wendell

---

13 *American Workman*, June 5, 1869.
14 The spiritual heir of these New England intellectuals during the eighties, Benjamin R. Tucker, the editor of the Boston

Liberty, was a strict follower of P. J. Proudhon. He translated *What is Property?* by Proudhon into English.

Phillips; and on the other hand, currency reform was defended by the representatives of the largest labour organisation then in existence, McLaughlin and Cummings, of the Crispins. The representatives of the cotton and woollen operatives and of the working women's organisations were against the currency issue and were unanimous for the eight-hour issue.

Three months later, failing in the attempt to swing the New England Reform League to the side of the eight-hour reform, Steward and McNeill established, in August, 1869, the Boston Eight-Hour League, a direct successor of the defunct Massachusetts Grand Eight-Hour League.[15] But the Crispins were not inclined to espouse the eight-hour cause in Steward's dogmatic manner. They called a state labour reform convention on September 9 to lay the foundation of a state labour party upon a broad programme of labour demands in accordance with the decisions of the recent Philadelphia convention of the National Labor Union and the recommendations of the New England Labor Reform League. The Crispin delegates formed an overwhelming part of the well-attended convention. A few delegates from the Amalgamated Ten-Hour Association, and several intellectuals like Colonel William B. Greene[16] and John Orvis were present also. The platform dealt particularly with demands that were of vital interest to the Crispins. It declared that the workingmen "will not support for any public office, candidates who do not unequivocally recognise the right of associated labour by legislative recognition and encouragement for all legitimate purposes." The Crispins had already at the session of the legislature in 1869 presented a bill for incorporation. This was again pressed in 1870 in connection with public hearings where the proposition was strongly opposed by employers and defeated.[17] The prominence given to the demand for a favourable incorporation law is explained in another resolution: "We regard co-operation in industry and exchange, as the final and permanent solution of the long conflict between labour and capital." The argument for incorporation of trade unions, at that time,

15 *American Workman*, Aug. 21, 1869.
16 Greene was a Proudhonist anarchist and published several pamphlets and a book entitled *Socialistic, Communistic,* *Materialistic and Financial Fragments* (1875).
17 *American Workman*, Mar. 5, 1870, gives an extended report of the hearing.

was based on the fact that trade unions were swinging toward productive co-operation, while "co-operation in exchange" was simply the co-operative warehouse. An emphatic condemnation of the importation of Chinese coolies and of the existing contract system in the state penal institutions likewise bear the earmarks of a strong influence of the Crispins, who were suffering particularly from these evils. The demand for a ten-hour legal day was put in the platform, but the money question was not elaborated, indicating that, although the leaders of the Crispins were strong advocates of financial reform, the rank and file were lukewarm toward this measure.

With regard to the immediate formation of a political party, much opposition had to be overcome. The success of such a party was viewed with doubt. But it was finally decided in the affirmative after the proposed name Workingman's party had been changed to Independent party. A nominating convention was held on September 28, and all but two counties were represented by 281 delegates. It substantially readopted the platform of the previous convention, but added a plank requiring the payment of the national debt in legal tender money and protesting against the exemption of United States bonds from taxation. This showed a closer endorsement of the principles of the National Labor Union. A full state ticket of relatively unknown persons was nominated, headed by E. M. Chamberlin.

The successful issue of the election proved a surprise to both foes and friends. An editorial in the New York *World,* then especially friendly to labour, called attention to the fact that the workingmen without newspaper support and political skill had, with an organisation but three weeks old, succeeded in electing twenty-one representatives and one senator, and had polled a vote of 13,000 in the State, over one-tenth of the total vote. It added: "The parties are so divided there that at the next election it is probable that the Labor party will be found to hold the balance of power and to secure the election of either of the other State tickets by giving it their support." [18] In a public meeting Cummings, the president of the Labor party, attributed their success mainly to the financial planks in

18 *American Workman,* Nov. 20, 1869.

the platform; Stillman B. Pratt, a member of the central committee, stated that the impulse given to the Massachusetts labour movement by the Philadelphia convention of the National Labor Union had accelerated the formation of the Labor party at least one year.[19]

That the political labour movement in Massachusetts had espoused the cause of financial reform is further attested by the election of William B. Greene, the money reformer of the Proudhon stripe, as president of the Massachusetts Labor Union. McLaughlin, the president of the Crispins, and other prominent members of the same organisation, were on the executive committee. On the whole, it may be said that the successful election was due to the support of the Crispins, then in their highest ascendency.

But the success of the party was short-lived. During the following month the municipal election was held in Boston. The Labor party nominee, N. G. Chase, ran on a platform of an eight-hour day for city employés, municipal ownership of the gas plant, and the speedy payment of the municipal debt. He was disastrously defeated, polling only 206 votes. The *American Workman* said in explanation that "the movement did not spring from the people, in any sense of spontaneity. The affair was much less an announcement of principles, accompanied by a bold and sturdy vindication of the same, than a game of manipulations in the interest of real or would-be ward politicians." [20]

The second convention of the Labor Reform Party was held in Worcester on September 8, 1870. A platform similar to the one of the previous year was adopted, but with a stronger type of eight-hour philosophy. An eight-hour day for public employés was demanded, since that would "establish the preliminary claim necessary to prove finally that they mean a better paid and better educated labor." [21]   George E. McNeill was on the committee on resolutions, and this recognition of Steward's doctrine was doubtless due to his efforts. Wendell Phillips was nominated for governor by acclamation, but even his immense popularity was insufficient to resuscitate the movement. The *American Workman* said in comment upon the outcome of the election: " The campaign of 1870 found one-third of our original force placed *hors de combat* by moral cowardice. We had neither the impetuous enthusiasm of the young convert, or the trained valour of the veteran." [22]

The prosperity of the early seventies made the time unpropitious for any independent political attempts on the part of labour. The third convention of the Labour Reform party met in South Framingham in September, 1871. Cummings was temporary, and Wendell Phillips permanent, chairman. The platform was drawn up in abstract style, and resembled in its thought as well as phraseology the platforms of the New England Labor Reform League. The gubernatorial nomination was contested by Benjamin F. Butler, but Chamberlin was renominated. In spite of Phillips' energetic agitation, the outcome was fruitless. By 1872 the political labour movement in Massachusetts had dwindled down to two small mutually hostile groups: the Labor Union led by Phillips, and the Eight-Hour League led by Steward and McNeill. The bone of contention was, of course, the eight-hour question. To Steward this was the only question, but Phillips advocated a broader programme, with money reform at the head of the list. Personal criminations and recriminations became frequent. The bitterness reached its height in July, 1872, when both organisations held their conventions. A resolution was offered by Phillips, indorsing the work of the labour bureau and its chief, General Oliver, but omitting to mention the assistant chief, McNeill. Into this resolution Steward read a sinister meaning and made Phillips the subject of an unmerciful attack.[23]

The cheerless result of the political movement caused Phillips to write, in a letter to Holyoake, the British worker for cooperation: " Your ranks are infinitely better trained than ours to stand together on some one demand just long enough to be counted, and so insure that respect which numbers always

---

[22] *Ibid.*, Nov. 19, 1870.

[23] Steward said: " In 1866 he [Phillips] said in Faneuil Hall, ' Don't meddle with ethics, don't discuss debts, keep clear of finance, talk only eight-hours,' and continued to speak in this strain until 1870. We adhere to that advice. No one accounts for his change though many recognise it; and in that change, he has lost the confidence of some of the most thoughtful friends of the movement." *Commonwealth*, June 29, 1872.

command in politics, where universal suffrage obtains."[24]
The failure of the political movement in Massachusetts was only a part of the general loss of interest in labour politics during 1870. But the political activity of labour doubtless brought the other parties to a keen recognition of the labour vote. In 1869, Massachusetts created the first bureau of labour statistics and within three years the legislature enacted the first effective ten-hour law. Massachusetts became the recognised leader of all American states in labour legislation.

THE CONGRESS OF 1870

The National Labor Union held its fifth convention at Cincinnati, August 15, 1870. The number of delegates had fallen from 192 to 96, and the number of organisations represented from 83 to 76. The stronger political trend is apparent. State labour unions now numbered 7[25] instead of 4 as in 1869, and local labour unions 18 instead of 13. The purely trade union representation, although it had fallen off numerically from 62 to 41, had rather gained than lost in weight, as the number of national trade unions remained 3 as before,[26] and the trades' assemblies were increased from 4 to 8.[27] Only the local trade unions diminished from 53 to 31. In addition there came 1 delegate from the Agricultural Labor Association in Virginia, 7 delegates from as many miscellaneous organisations,[28] and Isaac I. Myers from the national coloured association with headquarters in Baltimore.

The Negro question at once supplied a cause for controversy. A motion was carried to tender S. F. Cary, the ex-labour congressman and a Democrat, the privileges of the floor. Im-

24 *Equity*, December, 1874. Phillips' philosophy was set forth by him in this letter to Holyoake as follows: "But I suppose all this [the political inconsistency of labour in America] is familiar to you; as well as the strength which we expect from related questions — finances, mode of taxation, land tenure, etc. There'll never be, I believe and trust, a class party here, labor against capital, the lines are so indefinite, like dove's neck colors. Three-fourths of our population are to some extent capitalists, and again all see that there really ought always to be alliance, not struggle, between them. So we lean chiefly on related questions for growth; limitation of hours is almost the only special measure."

25 New York, California, Massachusetts, Kansas, Indiana, Missouri, Illinois.

26 The Crispins', Molders', and Typographical.

27 Cincinnati, Syracuse, New York (German), Indianapolis, Detroit, New York, San Francisco, and Newport, Ky.

28 Among these two co-operative associations,— coloured teachers' co-operative association, Cincinnati, and workingmen's co-operative association of Chicago.

mediately a motion was made to tender the same privilege to
J. M. Langston, the noted coloured lawyer of Ohio and a Republican office-holder. Troup, of New York, and Cummings,
of the Crispins, protested, the latter calling attention to Langston's endeavours to estrange the coloured labourers from the
whites at the last coloured national convention. After a lengthy
discussion in which the coloured delegates, Weare and Myers,
participated in the defence of Langston, the motion to exclude
him was carried by a vote of 49 to 23.

The Cincinnati convention merits an equal rank in the history of the National Labor Union with the Baltimore and
Chicago conventions. At Baltimore, the need for independent
political action was first proclaimed, at Chicago the fundamental principles of the labour platform were formulated, and at
Cincinnati practical steps were finally taken to create the labour party. Cummings, of the Crispins, proposed a plan of
separating industrial from political organisations; the National
Labor Union to remain an industrial organisation and to hold
annual conventions as such, but the president and a committee
of one from each State to call a political convention in order
to complete the organisation of a National Labor party. Opposition to this proposal came from two sources, for diametri-
cally opposite reasons. The coloured delegates, who were under
the influence of the Republicans, opposed it. Weare, the coloured delegate from Pennsylvania, argued that no reform movement had ever gained by attempting independent politics, but,
on the contrary, its strength lay in keeping out of party politics. Isaac Myers, the delegate of the coloured national labour
union, stated that all reforms could be obtained through the
Republican party. The Negroes were severely criticised by
Gilchrist,[29] of Louisville, and by Cameron. The other source
of opposition was among some of the trade unionists. Collins,
of the typographical union, demanded that, if some of the delegates present wanted to organise a labour party, it should be
done wholly independently of this congress, which was, first of
all, a trade union congress. But the resolution was finally carried by 60 to 5.

Having decided to call a special political convention to form

29 He had been active in the antiwar movement in 1860.

a national labour party, the constitution of the National Labor Union was modified so as to constitute a purely industrial body. It provided for the state labour union composed of local labour unions as the basis of the organisation and, to this end, state organisations were to be organized as speedily as possible. To conciliate the trade unionists, however, representation was also allowed to trade unions, national, state, and local. Revenue was to be derived from the state labour unions by an annual tax of 10 cents on each member. It is clear that the organisation so planned could never become an economic organisation like the present American Federation of Labor, since the State is not an economic unit. Its highest achievement would be a forum for the discussion of measures that should be enacted through the medium of its political counterpart, the national labour party. This indicates again the grip of the idea of legislation, to the exclusion of every other idea, on the minds of the leaders of the National Labor Union.

The resolution favouring active politics cost the National Labor Union the affiliation of the coloured organization. At the next and last national coloured convention, confidence was expressed in the Republican party and total separation from the white labour movement was declared, for the reason that the whites " exclude from their benches and their workshops worthy craftsmen and apprentices only because of their colour, for no just cause." [30]

CHINESE EXCLUSION [31]

Another form of race problem — the Chinese — was dealt with by the convention of 1870. This question had appeared at the congress of 1869, but was not then recognised as one of national importance. When, however, in June, 1870, Chinese coolies from California appeared as strike-breakers in Massachusetts, the question of Chinese exclusion ceased to be merely local.[32]

In California agitation against the Chinese was carried on simultaneously with the eight-hour movement, but subordinate to it. There, as in other States, the prosperity of the War had

30 Doc. Hist., IX, 256.
31 Compiled from manuscript by Professor Ira B. Cross, of the University of California.
32 Doc. Hist., IX, 84–88.

induced a movement for higher wages. The San Francisco Trades' Assembly was established in 1863. After the War, when the soldiers had returned to industry, the California movement had taken up enthusiastically the agitation for the eight-hour day. A. M. Kenaday,[33] president of the trades' assembly, went to the capitol at Sacramento in the winter of 1865 in the interest of an eight-hour law, but the bill failed in the senate after passing the lower house. President Whaley, of the National Labor Union, 1866, appointed Kenaday vice-president for California, and later, at the convention of 1867 in Chicago, highly commended his work.

Unlike the East, California did not experience the industrial depression that came upon the heels of the war prosperity. In that State, therefore, the trade unions attempted to gain the eight-hour day through strikes and were eminently successful in 1867 in the majority of the building trades. Eight-hour leagues multiplied among the various trades in the early months of 1867 and operated with such remarkable success that on June 2, 1867, the San Francisco *Morning Call* stated that " despite the existence of eight-hour laws in other communities, the fact exists that the eight-hour system is more in vogue in this city than in any other part of the world, although there are no laws to enforce it."

A workingmen's convention, composed of 140 delegates, representing the various trades, as well as anti-coolie clubs, met in San Francisco, March 29, 1867, formulated demands for a mechanics' lien law, an eight-hour law, and the repression of coolie labour, and decided to take part in the primary state election with the object of nominating candidates who favoured these measures. This move was singularly successful, and at the session of the legislature in 1868 the eight-hour and mechanics' lien laws were passed. The workingmen's convention had expelled Kenaday from its membership because he advocated its affiliation with the National Labor Union, and the

---

[33] Alexander M. Kenaday was born in 1829 in Wheeling, W. Va., of Irish parentage. He learned the printer's trade in St. Louis. He enlisted twice in the Mexican War and distinguished himself by bravery. After the War he went to California and, having no success as a prospector, he went to San Francisco and took up his trade as a printer. After leaving the labour movement in 1867, he devoted his time to the organisation and management of the National Association of Mexican War Veterans. He died in 1897.

leadership in the labour movement then passed to A. M. Winn,[34] who was the head and heart of the Mechanics' State Council established in August, 1867. This was a non-political organisation, but was organised primarily for the purpose of questioning candidates for legislative offices regarding labour measures. It was so careful in maintaining its non-political character that it did not affiliate with the National Labor Union until 1869 for fear of becoming involved in labour politics. It showed, however, great zeal in securing eight-hour legislation by non-political methods. Winn went to Washington in 1869 and spent some months in an unsuccessful effort to secure the passage of a law which should positively require that all public work, whether done by the day or under contract, should be subject to the eight-hour work-day requirement.

Greenbackism and other middle-class philosophies never acquired a foothold in this State. California, having held to the gold currency, had not experienced the acute depression which prevailed in the East during 1867 and 1868 as a result of the contraction of paper currency. The labour movement, therefore, was not forced to seek succour in co-operation or in the greenbackism that followed in its wake.

A change for the worse in the industrial situation came in 1869 at the time when the East was recovering from the depression. The opening of the first transcontinental railroad in that year not only threw many thousands of both Chinese and whites out of work, but it brought on a local depression by enabling the cheaper products of eastern manufacture to compete with those of California. Besides, railroad communications caused a large influx of workingmen from the East. The depression and the tremendous amount of unemployment increased the demand for Chinese exclusion. The Chinese now came to be regarded as the supreme cause of unemployment and of the destitute condition of the white workingmen. They had first appeared in the mining regions in the early fifties and the first measures took the form of local expulsion

---

[34] A. M. Winn was a native of Virginia, and went to Vicksburg, Miss., thence to California in 1848, and was the first president of the Sacramento City Council. He was a contractor and builder and on coming to San Francisco engaged in the planing mill business and was comparatively wealthy. He died in 1883.

from miners' communities. The objections raised against the presence of the Chinese were the competitive menace of their extremely low standard of living and their apparent inability to rise to the American standard. The state legislature was, of course, powerless under the constitution to prevent Chinese immigration.

The attitude of California on the Chinese question was reflected in the convention of the National Labor Union in 1869. A. M. Winn represented the California Mechanics' State Council, but he had been given little opportunity to impress the California demand of Chinese exclusion upon the convention. The committee on coolie labour, with Cameron as chairman, and the socialist, Adolph Douai, a prominent member, made a report, condemning the importation of contract coolie labour, calling for the rigid enforcement of the law of Congress of 1862 prohibiting coolie importation, but affirming " that voluntary Chinese emigration ought to enjoy the protection of the laws like other citizens." The report brought out considerable debate and was finally recommitted, three men being added to the committee: Winn, Cummings, of the Crispins, and Jessup, of the New York Workingmen's Union. The committee, however, did not report again, and the platform adopted by the convention contained a plank in the sense of the above report.

The order of the Knights of St. Crispin at this time was practically the only important labour organisation outside of the coast region in sympathy with the policy of exclusion. During a wage dispute with the Crispins, a shoe manufacturer of North Adams, Massachusetts, had by contract imported from California — 3,000 miles — seventy-five Chinese to take the places of the strikers.[35] The general agitation which this action provoked among all classes of labour served to bring the national labour movement into closer sympathy with the California point of view. At the next convention of the National Labor Union in 1870 the general labour movement was ready to take the step from merely advocating the prohibition of Chinese importation to demanding total exclusion.

While the workingmen's sentiment was thus maturing in this direction, the Burlingame treaty was signed between the

[35] *Doc. Hist.*, IX, 84–88.

United States and China, November 23, 1869. The treaty of 1844, followed by that of 1858, had opened some of the ports of China to the merchants of the United States and had secured from them the privileges of trade and commerce. In addition to this, protection was guaranteed the lives and property of American citizens within that country. The Burlingame treaty, however, went further and declared that " Chinese subjects visiting or residing in the United States, shall have the same privileges, immunities and exemptions in respect to travel or residence as may there be enjoyed by the citizens or the subjects of the most favoured nation." It was this sentence which caused the greater part of the trouble in California during the next thirteen years.

At the convention in Cincinnati, in 1870, Trevellick in his presidential address declared against the importation but not against the free immigration of the Chinese. The committee on the presidential address refused concurrence on this point and was sustained by the convention. The spokesman from California was W. W. Delaney, sent by the Mechanics' State Council, and he was made chairman of the committee on coolie labour. The committee's report stated that " the importation and the present system of the immigration of the coolie labour in these United States is ruinous to the life principles of our Republic, destroying the system of free labour which is the basis of a republican form of government . . . [and further] that this National Labor Congress demands the abrogation of the treaty between the United States and China, whereby Chinese are allowed to be imported to our shores."

The debate which followed evinced but little opposition to the proposed measure. Particularly emphatic in his support of the report was Cummings, the representative of the Crispins. Even Trevellick changed his original position. The resolution was adopted and Delaney returned to California well satisfied with the results of his mission.[36]

Chinese exclusion continued to furnish the sole basis of the

[36] Delaney was given a commission to organise branches of the National Labor Union in his State. Several such branches were formed during the following year, but were short-lived. They met frequently, discussed various issues, and passed resolutions upon the questions of labour, capital, land, taxation, and other matters, but accomplished nothing whatsoever of any importance. In January, 1872, the organisation held a state convention in San Francisco, adopted a plat-

California movement during the seventies and early eighties, until the passage of the Federal Exclusion Act of 1882. The national labour movement consistently gave California its support on this momentous problem.

REVIVAL OF TRADE UNIONS

In 1870 the conditions surrounding the national labour movement had radically changed. After the law of February, 1868, prohibiting further contraction of paper currency, industry began slowly to recuperate, and with this the prospects of successful trade union action considerably improved. Added to this was the fact that practically all of the co-operative ventures had by this time failed, and others, like the co-operative foundry in Troy, had lapsed into ordinary joint-stock companies. The consequence was a new and vigorous development of trade unions, accompanied by an aggressive policy towards employers.

Viewed from the standpoint of the form of organisation, the revival of trade unionism in 1868 was unlike the revival during the time of the War, in that the national trade unions, and not the trades' assemblies, were now the chief beneficiaries of the heightened wave of organisation.

The high water mark was reached by the revived trade union movement in the spring of 1872, when it surpassed by its universality and uniform success even the movement of the days of war prosperity. In March, 1872, a vast number of workingmen of New York City, mostly in the building trades, struck for the eight-hour day. The number of strikers was estimated at 100,000. The strike lasted three months and ended very successfully. The eight-hour day was gained by the bricklayers, carpenters, plasterers, plumbers, painters, brown and blue-stone cutters, stone-masons, masons' labourers, paper hangers (when working by the day), and plate printers.[37] On May 22, 1872, Horace Greeley wrote that the dissatisfaction had extended into all the leading mechanical trades,

form, and decided to enter politics. It faithfully supported the national organisation in the experiment of the presidential nomination in 1872, and together they went down in defeat.

[37] McNeill, *The Labor Movement: The Problem of To-day*, 143.

and in almost every instance the employers had acceded to the demands of their men.

As trade unionism again came to occupy the foreground and greenbackism receded to the background, the national trade unions grew estranged from the National Labor Union. This expressed itself most conspicuously in the changes in leadership. Sylvis, who combined in himself the business unionist and the social reformer, was dead. The older leaders remaining, like Trevellick, Hinchcliffe, and Cameron, had become primarily political agitators, and their places at the head of the aggressive trade union movement were taken by men like Foran, of the coopers, Saffin, of the moulders, and Siney, of the miners. These men, although professing faith in cooperation and greenbackism as a concession to the spirit of the time, were yet primarily trade unionists. The Bricklayers' International Union,[38] by its strike in 1868 for the eight-hour day in New York, had been among the first to show the returning reliance upon strikes. At its national convention in 1870, it passed a resolution calling upon President O'Keefe to correspond with the other presidents of national trade unions with the object of establishing a national labour federation to consist of national trade unions only.

The breach was made still wider by the fact that the National Labor Union had finally reached the logical end of its political evolution and had become a national labour party. The cigar makers, in special session in October, 1870, decided to have no further connection with the National Labor Union, because it had become "an entirely political institution." The list of delegates to the National Labor Union in 1871 contained not a single representative of a national trade union. The workingmen's assembly of New York received from Jessup "an interesting, and at times highly amusing account of his experience at the National Labor Congress," held in Cincinnati in 1870.[39] As a result, the assembly sent no delegate to the congress held in St. Louis in 1871.

A notable exception among the national trade unions was the Order of the Knights of St. Crispin. Co-operation kept

38 At its Washington convention in 1869, delegates from 62 unions represented a constituency of 10,000 members.

39 Chicago *Workingman's Advocate,* Feb. 18, 1871.

alive the interest of the Crispins in the financial question and made them more amenable to the political influence of the National Labor Union than the other national labour organisations. As already stated, the Crispins were the main support of the political movement in Massachusetts, and their leaders, McLaughlin and Cummings, remained true to the labour reform party as long as it existed.

POLITICS AND DISSOLUTION

The history of the National Labor Union after 1870 deserves but scant treatment. The large labour organisations having seceded, its convention continued to be attended only by a handful of leaders, like Trevellick, Cameron, Hinchcliffe, and several others. These had come forward at a time when the trend of the movement had been predominantly legislative and political, and now continued to travel in the same direction. As the *bona fide* labour representatives dropped out, a number of intellectual and semi-intellectual reformers came into the National Labor Union. Their presence did more to discredit the organisation before the labour unions than did its persistent political programme. Most prominent among this element was Horace H. Day, of Brooklyn, a wealthy man and doubtless an aspirant for the presidential nomination of the labour party.[40]

In pursuance of the resolution adopted by the convention of 1870, President Trevellick appointed a committee to make plans for the formation of a labour party. This committee met in Washington in January, 1871, and fixed the rate of representation in the political convention. Each State was to be entitled to one delegate for each member of the House of Representatives and of the Senate, and one delegate was to be allowed the District of Columbia and each territory. The convention was set for the third Wednesday of October, 1871, in Columbus, Ohio, for the purpose of nominating candidates for president and vice-president of the United States. Meanwhile, the time arrived for the regular convention, which met August 19, 1871, in St. Louis. The delegates present repre-

40 *Ibid.*, May 11, 1872.

sented for the most part "labour unions," *i.e.,* local political clubs organised by and affiliated with the National Labor Union. The genuine labour representatives of reputation were Cameron, Siney, Trevellick, and Ben F. Sylvis — the brother of William H. Sylvis. The remaining dozen delegates were either new in the movement or such non-labour reformers as Horace H. Day, of New York, who represented the financial reform association of that city. This convention adopted the suggestion which Cummings of the Crispins had made in 1870, that of forming a double organisation, one industrial and one political, entirely distinct from each other, and holding two conventions, one political and one industrial. The special nominating convention, which had been set for October, 1871, was thus made the regular convention of the "political" National Labor Union and the date of its meeting was changed to February 21, 1872.

It met in Columbus on the appointed day. Among the delegates who had attended preceding conventions were Troup, now of Connecticut; Campbell, Cameron, and Hinchcliffe, of Illinois; Cameron, of Kansas; Chamberlain and Cummings, of Massachusetts; Trevellick and Field, of Michigan; Day, of New York; Davis, Fehrenbatch, Lucker, and Sheldon, of Ohio; Siney and J. C. Sylvis, of Pennsylvania. Other States represented were Arkansas, Iowa, Mississippi, Missouri, and New Jersey. Charges were made that control of the convention had been sought in order to influence the nominations of the Republican and Democratic parties, and that the full delegation from Pennsylvania was able to attend "through the courtesy of Thomas Scott," of the Pennsylvania Railroad Company. It was voted that the delegation from each State should cast the full electoral vote of each State, on the ground that Pennsylvania and Ohio had full delegations, while others had not had the facilities or means of travel. John Siney was elected temporary chairman, and Edwin M. Chamberlin, of Massachusetts, permanent chairman. The platform of preceding years was adopted. Resolutions were offered by John T. Elliott of New York, favouring government ownership and the referendum, but were voted down. On the first formal ballot for nomination for president of the United States, the votes were: Judge David Davis, of Illinois,

88; Wendell Phillips, 52; Governor John W. Geary, of Pennsylvania, 45; Horace H. Day, of New York, 8; Governor J. Parker, of New Jersey, 7; George W. Julian, 7. On the third ballot Davis was nominated. The nominee for vice-president was Governor Parker. The platform of the National Labor Union was adopted as the platform of the National Labor and Reform party. Judge Davis gave a qualified acceptance, but, after the Democratic convention he declined, explaining his action as follows: "Having regarded that movement as the initiation of a policy and purpose to unite the various political elements in a compact opposition, I consented to the use of my name before the Cincinnati (Democratic) convention, where a distinguished citizen of New York (Horace Greeley) was nominated." A meeting of the executive committee at Columbus in August decided it was too late to renominate candidates.[41] This unfortunate experiment practically ended the existence of the National Labor Union.[42] The Industrial Congress, which was to be the economic branch of the National Labor Union, met at Cleveland, September 16, with only seven persons present, Trevellick, Cameron, Foran, J. C. Sylvis, Sheldon, Fay, and Manly.

[41] Chicago *Workingman's Advocate,* Aug. 25, 1871.

[42] A discussion in the columns of the Chicago *Workingman's Advocate* in February, 1873, throws light upon the relations between the national trade unions and the National Labor Union. H. J. Walls, a national officer of the iron molders' union, stated in an open letter to Cameron that the cause of the withdrawal of the national trade unions was the fact that the National Labor Union had become, after the Cincinnati convention, a political organisation. Cameron replied in the next issue that it had been a political organisation from the first Baltimore convention and that it had nevertheless had the warm adherence of men as prominent in their respective national trade unions as Sylvis and his opponent, Walls himself, of the molders, Kirby and Browning, of the bricklayers, Trevellick, of the ship carpenters and caulkers, Jessup, of the New York State Workingmen's Assembly, Siney, of the miners, and a score of other prominent trade union leaders. Cameron was undoubtedly right, because the National Labor Union, while composed, up to 1870, of industrial organisations, had never been an industrial organisation itself. It was legislative and political.

CHAPTER V

DISINTEGRATION, 1873–1877

Industrial Congress and Industrial Brotherhood, 1873–1875. Fresh impulse towards national federation, 157. Joint call by the national unions, 157. Guarantee against politics, 158. The circular, 158. The Cleveland Congress, 159. Representation, 159. The trade union nature of the proceedings, 159. The constitution, 160. Attitude towards co-operation, 161. Attitude towards politics, 161. Effect of the financial panic on the new federation, 161. The Congress in Rochester, 161. Representation and the secret orders, 162. Debate on the constitution, 162. The minority recommendation of secret organisation, 163. Defeat of secrecy, 163. The Industrial Brotherhood, 163. The *Preamble*, 164. Robert Schilling, 164. The money question, 164. Arbitration, 165. Other demands, 165. Politics, 165. The Congress in Indianapolis, 166. The dropping out of the national trade unions, 166. The new constitution with organisation by States as its basis, 167. End of the Industrial Brotherhood, 167.

Greenback Party, 1874–1877. Patrons of Husbandry, 168. The antimonopoly political movement, 168. The Indianapolis convention, 168. Cleveland convention of farmers and mechanics, 169. "Independent" or Greenback party, 169. Anti-monopoly convention, 169. National conference in Cincinnati, 169. Fusion with the Greenback party, 169. The nominating convention of 1876, 170. The representation, 170. Greenbackism — a remedy against depression, 170. Peter Cooper's candidacy, 171. The campaign, 171. Results, 171.

Sovereigns of Industry. Co-operation, East and West, 171. William H. Earle, 172. Elimination of the middleman, 172. Constitution of the Sovereigns of Industry, 173. Membership, 1874–1877, 173. Activities, 174. Relation to trade unions, 174. Relation to the Industrial Congress, 175. Failure of the Sovereigns of Industry, 175.

National and Local Unions. Weak points in the trade unions of the sixties, 175. The depression, 175. Labour leaders and politics, 175. Westward migration, 176. Decrease in membership, 1873–1874, 176. The trades' assembly, 177. The cigar makers' strike against the tenement house system, 177. Strikes in the textile industry, 178. Amalgamated Association of Iron and Steel Workers, 179. The trade agreement, 179. Bituminous coal miners' organisation, 179. John Siney, 179. Mark Hanna, 180. The trade agreement, 180. The umpire's decision in 1874, under the trade agreement, 180. Failure of the agreement, 180.

The Molly Maguires. Trade unionism *versus* violence, 181. Ancient Order of Hibernians, 182. Influence over local politics, 183. Crimes of the Mollies, 183. James McParlan, 184. The "long strike," 184. The wrecking of the union, 185. Growth of the influence of the Mollies, 185. Arrest and trial of the Mollies, 185.

The Great Strikes of 1877. Reduction in wages of the railwaymen, 185. Brotherhood of Locomotive Engineers, 185. The Trainmen's Union, 186. Robert H. Ammon, 186. The plan for a strike, 187. Failure, 187. Unorganised outbreak, 187. Martinsburg and Baltimore riots, 187. Pittsburgh riots, 188. State militia, 189. Federal troops, 190. Effect of the strikes on public opinion, 190. Effect on subsequent court decisions in labour cases, 191.

INDUSTRIAL CONGRESS AND INDUSTRIAL BROTHERHOOD, 1873–1875

THE disintegration of the National Labor Union did not end the effort to form a national federation. Shortly after the panic of 1873 a fresh attempt was made. It came from the national trade unions, which, having withdrawn from the National Labor Union at the time when it resorted to politics, now proceeded to evolve a national federation. This was the first appearance of an organisation similar in object and structure to the present American Federation of Labor. National trade unions were its basic units, and it was economic in character, but with legislative demands.

On May 3, 1873, a call appeared in the *Workingman's Advocate,* signed by William Saffin, president of the Iron Molders' International Union; by John Fehrenbatch, president of the Machinists' and Blacksmiths' International Union; by M. A. Foran, president of the Coopers' International Union; and by John Collins, secretary of the International Typographical Union. It called attention to the " rapid and alarming concentration of Capital, placed under the control of a few men," and to the fact that " almost the entire legislation of the country, both state and national, is in the interest of this concentrated capital, giving it almost imperial powers," a development which the authors declared was causing " a rapid decrease of our power as Trade Unions in comparison with that of Capital." " Already the farmers of the West and Northwest," the call continued, " are driven to desperation by the bold, barefaced robbery of the fruits of their industry by legalised monopoly, and have organised powerful State organisations," but the trade unions still remain disunited. " Let not the failures of the past deter us from making renewed efforts, but profiting by our dear bought experience build up and perfect an organisation such as was contemplated in Baltimore in 1866." The call further extended the invitation to "every Trade organisation in the United States, be it local, state, or (Inter) National, and every anti-monopoly, co-operative, or other association organised on purely protective principles, to send *bona fide* delegates to a Convention to be held in Cleveland, Ohio, on the 15th day of July, 1873." The signers pledged themselves "that the organisation, when consummated, shall not, so far as in our power to prevent, ever deteriorate into a political party, or become the tail to the kite of any political party, or a refuge for played out politicians, but shall to all intents and purposes remain a purely Industrial Association, having for its sole and only object the securing to the producer his full share of all he produces."

Another circular [1] addressed "To the Organized Workingmen of the United States" presented a list of grievances of labour as viewed by the signers of the original call. "We desire it distinctly understood that we have no Agrarian ideas; we neither believe or preach the doctrine that capital is robbery." All connection with the "Commune" was likewise disclaimed. While having no plan of action to dictate, the signers declared the following as the causes of their evil condition: The law, instead of fostering trade unions, treats them as conspiracies; while wages of labour are being reduced on the plea that the supply thereof far exceeds the demand, the country is slowly but surely being overrun by imported Chinamen, brought here in vessels subsidised by the general government; labour has not benefited from the improvement in machinery, but it has suffered from increased unemployment, because the "same number of hours must be worked to-day that were worked in a day thirty years ago"; the growth of huge monopolies has put restrictions upon the channels of trade with the result that the cost of living has risen; labour has no reliable information about its condition, such as would be furnished by a Federal bureau of statistics.

The other points which the circular mentioned briefly were that "co-operation has no legal recognition or assistance," that the "country is without an apprentice system," and that consideration should be given to arbitration.

1 Chicago *Workingman's Advocate,* July 5, 1873.

The circular was clearly a trade union document. Financial reform was not even mentioned, and co-operation received only slight attention. The officers of the four national unions intended to establish an organisation on strictly trade union principles.[2]

The congress met July 15 [3] with 70 delegates present. Six national trade unions were represented: the coopers' by 13 delegates (Foran, Schilling and Pope coming from the International Union); the machinists' and blacksmiths' by 20 (Fehrenbatch, Bucholtz and McDevitt from the International Union); the iron moulders by 5 (Saffin from the International); the Sons of Vulcan 4 (Hugh McLaughlin from the Grand Forge); and the Knights of St. Crispin by 2 (William Salter from the Grand Lodge).

The other trade unions which were represented, though not nationally, were the miners, numbering 5 delegates under the leadership of John Siney; 2 typographical local unions, 1 of cigarmakers, and 1 tobacco workers' union. No less than 5 trades' assemblies sent delegates: Columbus, Cleveland, Indianapolis, and 2 minor cities. The representation of the labour unions, the creatures of the old National Labor Union, numbered only 5, 1 of which was the National Labor Reform Union, Plymouth, Pennsylvania, and another, the Tennessee State Labor Union. The congress also seated a delegate from the Pittsburgh National Protective League. And, finally, the old leaders, Cameron and Trevellick, were, without much enthusiasm and without a vote, admitted to seats. They, however, took little part in the proceedings, as the congress was clearly under the domination of the purely trade union leaders.

The opening address made by Foran reiterated the ideas expressed in the call, and, by electing Fehrenbatch as permanent chairman, the congress organised for work. The proceedings resembled more a convention of the later American Federation of Labor than a convention of the old National Labor Union. The list of questions as outlined in the circular was fully discussed and little time was given to non-trade-union questions.

---

[2] The old leaders, like Cameron and Trevellick, took scant part in the movement. Cameron, though not openly condemning the plan, was lukewarm in his praise.

[3] "Official Proceedings," given in Chicago *Workingman's Advocate*, July 26, 1873.

Arbitration was recommended to the trade unions as a substitute for strikes, a vigorous anti-contract immigration resolution was adopted, the abrogation of the Burlingame treaty with China was urgently demanded, and the contract system of prison labour was condemned. On the apprenticeship question the report of the committee was adopted, which recommended that a committee be appointed to correspond with the officers of the national trade unions and with firms employing apprentices, and to report at the next congress. The demand for a general eight-hour day was reiterated, without specifying, however, whether it was to be attained by legislation or by trade union action; and, finally, the establishment of a national labour bureau was urged.

The trade union character of the congress is best shown, however, by the constitution. It provided that "whenever the President of this Congress has been officially notified of the existence of a difficulty between Labor and Capital, which has resulted in a strike, or lock-out, and has evidence that the labour interests have endeavoured by arbitration to settle such difficulty, it shall be his duty, if assistance is required, to lay the facts by circular, before the various Trade and Labor Unions of the Country, calling upon them for pecuniary assistance, sufficient to sustain the Labor so striking, or on lock-out." The dominance of the national trade unions over the federation being practically assured, the constitution liberally provided also for the representation of the other types of labour organisations, as follows: "Every International or National Organisation shall be entitled to three representatives; State or Local Trade Assemblies, to two; Trade Unions and all other protective organisations of labour to one each, provided that representatives shall derive their election direct from the organisations they claim to represent, and are members thereof, except where a delegate is elected at a joint meeting of two or more organisations, but no delegate shall be entitled to more than one vote." The revenue of the federation was to be derived from a 2 cent per capita tax upon local organisations, an annual tax of $10 each upon national organisations and a fee of $5 upon each new charter issued to a subordinate organisation.

Further to accentuate the trade union nature of the congress, co-operation was given but a brief endorsement, and the financial plank in the platform, embodying the interconvertible bond and paper money system, was put in only after a heated debate and a roll call. The congress was wage-conscious in its programme for action, but it still chose to give indorsement to a set of non-wage-conscious principles, provided they were relegated to a purely theoretical position.

True to the pledge of the signers of the call, the congress adopted a negative attitude towards independent political action. The platform declared that, " while we recognise in the ballot-box an agency by which these wrongs can be redressed when other means fail, yet the great desideratum of the hour is the organisation, consolidation, and co-operative effort of the producing masses, as a stepping stone to that education which will in future lead to more advanced action, through which the necessary reforms can be obtained."

The officers elected for the year were Robert Schilling, of the Coopers' International Union, Cleveland, president; S. Keefe, of the Philadelphia Coopers' Union, secretary; and James A. Atkinson, of the Cleveland Iron Molders' Union, treasurer.

Had industrial prosperity continued, the new federation undoubtedly would have attained an important place in the labour movement, but having been launched only two months before the panic and the ensuing depression, it was doomed to failure. During the nine-month interval between this and the next congress,[4] charters were issued to only 13 mixed local unions (industrial unions), to 2 city councils (industrial councils), and to 2 small national trade unions, the Associated Brotherhood of Iron and Steel Heaters, and the Rollers', Roughers', Catchers', and Hookers' National Association. The heaters' organisation was the only one that availed itself of the right granted by the constitution to apply for a circular in aid of a strike, but was denied assistance, as it had not complied with the provision concerning arbitration.

Nevertheless, the national trade unions, which had called the congress into existence, still retained a sufficient interest in the matter to be represented by delegates in the next congress,

---

4 " Official Proceedings," given in Chicago *Workingman's Advocate*, Apr. 25, 1874.

which met in Rochester, New York, April 14, 1874. The machinists' and blacksmiths' union was represented by President
Fehrenbatch and 2 more delegates, while 17 local unions sent
12 delegates; the Coopers' International Union, by 3, of whom
Schilling was 1, and by delegates from 5 locals; the recently
organised Grand Division Conductors' Brotherhood, by 5 delegates. William Saffin and John Siney, presidents respectively
of the Iron Molders' International Union and of the Miners'
National Association, were admitted to seats. The trades' assemblies of Milwaukee, Indianapolis, Louisville, and Rochester
were represented, as well as the Labor Council of Boston,
by George E. McNeill, the Workingmen's Central Council of
New York, by George Blair, later a prominent Knight of
Labor, and the Industrial Council of Cuyahoga County
[Cleveland], by 2 delegates. Eighteen local trade unions, besides those above mentioned, were represented by delegates, and
2 secret organisations, the Industrial Brotherhood, by A. Warner St. John, of Missouri, Horace H. Day, of New York, and
Drew, of New Jersey (who represented also the Patrons of
Husbandry); and the Sovereigns of Industry, by 4 delegates,
of whom President W. H. Earle of Massachusetts was the spokesman in the conference. Finally, the ever faithful A. C. Cameron was admitted to a seat without a vote.

The differences at the congress arose in the debates on the
constitution. The trade unionists wanted the strictest possible
exclusion of all non-trade-union elements. Thus A. M. Winn,
president of the Mechanics' State Council of California, in a
communication criticised the old constitution as throwing the
doors wide open to all industrial organisations. He advocated
national organisation of mechanics and miners, to which state
councils, assemblies, and other state representative bodies and
all orders of mechanics could send delegates, provided they
endorsed the constitution and paid fees. The latter provision
was intended to prevent the creation of organisations for political emergencies. H. J. Walls, of the Molders' International Union, sent in a communication, also favouring restriction to " state representatives and delegates from National and
International Trade Organisations " which endorsed the constitution, with the main object of organising local trades' as-

semblies and local unions of the several trades.[5] President
Schilling, on the other hand, in his report favoured an organisation similar to the Patrons of Husbandry with beneficial features and secrecy, and an " intimate co-operation with the Farmers' movement." He was not at all afraid of political action,
which he held to be " indispensably necessary," and he affirmed
the need of a " redoubled emphasis " on the financial plank —
a programme altogether different from the trade union programme of the congress of the year before.

The committee on constitution handed in two reports, a majority report signed by George E. McNeill, George Blair, and
M. H. Smith, and a minority report signed by W. H. Earle.
The majority report proposed to retain temporarily the present
constitution with some changes, but recommended the appointment of a new committee of seven, composed " of the President
of the Congress, two presidents of international unions, two of
national trades unions, and two persons not members of trades
unions, who shall prepare a definite plan of organisation, with
constitution and by-laws for national and State Congresses and
subordinate industrial unions." The minority report recommended a secret organisation on the pattern of the Patrons of
Husbandry and pointed to the order of the Sovereigns of Industry as meeting these requirements. It advised the merging
of the Industrial Congress with that organisation. Prolonged
debate occurred, in which Earle defended his proposition, and
St. John explained at length the objects of the Industrial
Brotherhood. Schilling, although favouring the model of the
Patrons of Husbandry, opposed the merging of the Congress
with any organisation, and was supported by Siney. Finally,
the majority report was substantially adopted and the following
were named on the committee: Fehrenbatch, Foran, Cannon,
James, Earle, St. John, and Beck.

The Sovereigns of Industry remained dissatisfied with this
decision. On the other hand, the representatives of the Industrial Brotherhood [6] agreed to fuse their organisation with
the congress and they contributed its name and ritual,[7] so that

5 He stated that the number of trade
unionists in the country was " not less
than 200,000."
6 Powderly states that the Brotherhood
had at the time about forty branches in
existence. *Thirty Years of Labor*, 120.
7 *Ibid.*, 120–123.

when the constitution was printed it bore the name of the " Industrial Brotherhood."

But if the delegates at the congress had vague ideas as to how the labour movement should be organised in order to attain its demands, there existed no such indefiniteness as to the nature of the demands themselves.   The " Preamble " to the " Industrial Brotherhood," drawn up by Robert Schilling, stated so fully the demands of labour at that period that it was later adopted, with some modifications, by the Knights of Labor at their first national convention (General Assembly) in 1878.

The declaration of principles referred to " the recent alarming development and aggression of aggregated wealth," and the imperative necessity of a system which could " secure to the labourer the fruits of his toil."   The organisation and direction, by co-operative efforts, of the power of the producing masses for their substantial elevation, was regarded as " the great desideratum of the hour," yet the ballot-box was recognised as the great agency through which wrongs could be redressed. The objects of the Industrial Congress were submitted to the people of the United States as follows: thorough organisation of every department of productive industry, a just share of the wealth created, more leisure, the establishment of national and state bureaus of labour statistics, the establishment of productive and distributive co-operative institutions, the public lands for actual settlers, the abrogation of class legislation, the removal of unjust technicalities and delays in the administration of justice, measures for the promotion of safety and health, monthly wage payments, wage-lien laws, the abolition of the contract system on public work, a system of public markets, cheap transportation, the substitution of arbitration for strikes, the prohibition of the importation of servile races, equitable apprentice laws, abolition of convict contract labour, equal pay for equal work, the eight-hour day, and finally a national greenback currency issued directly to the people and interchangeable for government bonds bearing not over 3.65 per cent interest.

As at the preceding congress, the money question was the cause of a prolonged and heated debate.   The wage-conscious McNeill opposed the adoption of greenbackism as being extraneous to the labour movement. But the congress was overwhelmingly in favour of greenbackism, and the financial plank was adopted by all but two votes (Stevens, of New York, and McNeill).

The other important resolutions advocated voluntary arbitration between employers and employés, but stated that "it would be imprudent at present to advocate the passage of a law in Congress, making it compulsory for employers and employés to settle their grievances by arbitration alone"; demanded the enforcement of the eight-hour law for government employés and shorter hour legislation, for, the resolution said, "factory operatives, the employés of steam and horse-railroad companies, steam-boat companies, saloons and places of amusement, clerks in stores and others, can only secure the reduction of their excessive hours of labour by effective legislation"; demanded abolition of the contract system on government work, and the right of incorporation for trade unions; urged the granting of a national charter to the moulders' union, which had applied for it to Congress; recommended to the constituent organisations that they should make temperance a condition of admission (a resolution adopted as a substitute to one which apparently endorsed prohibition); opposed the importation of Chinese and other servile labourers, "making importation a criminal offence," and demanded the "repeal of the Burlingame treaty" and the withdrawal of the subsidy to the Pacific Mail Steamship Company; and finally advocated bureaus of labour statistics.

On the important question of political action the congress resolved to disregard all claims of political parties and to vote "only for those persons who agree with us in our principles."

Robert Schilling was re-elected president; A. W. St. John, J. H. Wright, T. C. Clarkson, Christopher Kane and O. F. Powers, vice-presidents; Byron Pope, secretary; and P. K. Walsh, treasurer.

After the congress adjourned, Schilling sent a circular to "all labour organisations" announcing that "an organisation among workingmen somewhat similar to that of the Grangers had been provided for," urging the call of mass meetings to protest "against the action of United States Supervising Architect Mullett in virtually making the eight-hour law a dead letter " and particularly to bring the financial resolution of the Industrial Congress before the people. He also selected a list of deputies for each State to carry on the work of organisation for the Industrial Brotherhood, among whom we find the name of Terence V. Powderly,[8] a machinist, recommended to Schilling by Fehrenbatch to take the place of Siney, resigned.

But the trade unions — national as well as trades' assemblies — were in no condition to heed the appeal of the Industrial Congress. The unprecedented depression brought on a simultaneous struggle for life all along the lines of organised labour. The trade unions were obliged to strain all their efforts to resist the cuts in wages which followed one another in close succession, and naturally all attempts at such a time to secure a national federation were bound to fail. This applied with additional strength to the Industrial Congress with its unfinished constitution and undecided programme of action. At the next and last congress,[9] which met in Indianapolis, April 13, 1875, we find that the national trade unions and the trades' assemblies, with the exception of the International Typographical Union, were unrepresented, and that the twenty-three delegates present came either from the " industrial unions " or " industrial councils " created by the national organisation.

Schilling and Cameron were the only prominent leaders among the delegates. The president, Jackson H. Wright (Robert Schilling having resigned), opened the congress and especially advocated arbitration and resistance to conspiracy laws " now so much resorted to "; he favoured non-partisan political action, co-operation, regulation of apprenticeship and technical education, and bureaus of statistics, and commented on the " terrible condition of the industrial world."

The preamble and platform remained essentially the same, with the addition chiefly of a plank condemning the use of the militia during labour disputes. The adoption of a constitution was the main work of the congress. The committee appointed at the Rochester Congress reported that it found " that a unification of the existing labor organisations was an impossibility,

---

[8] This appointment marked the first appearance of Powderly as an organiser in the labour movement.

[9] " Official Proceedings," given in Chicago *Workingman's Advocate*, Apr. 24, 1875.

as none of the organizations represented had instructed their delegates in this respect, and for other reasons obvious to all who will investigate the matter closely." In consequence it prepared an entirely new constitution which could be adopted by the organisations in existence. The committee then outlined a plan, with the state organisation as the basic unit and with city and county industrial councils subordinate to it. It was, however, stipulated that each national trade union might elect a special secretary to look after its interests in the congress. This constitution was adopted and the congress adjourned, having previously adopted a series of resolutions; one designating July 4, 1876, as the date for the eight-hour system to go into effect by a " united movement on the part of the working masses of the United States "; another requesting aid for the striking anthracite miners and Sons of Vulcan; still another instructing the executive committee to correspond with the head officers of labour organisations throughout the world; and finally one designating arbitration and co-operation as " subjects for special discussion and action at the next session of the Industrial Congress." A set of officers was elected with Jackson H. Wright, of Ohio, president, and an executive board composed of Cameron, Schilling, Ben Johnson, of Pennsylvania, H. J. Walls, of Ohio, and James Connelly, of New York.

There is no evidence that the organisation continued to exist after this congress. In 1876 at Pittsburgh, another attempt was made toward the unification of the labour movement, but it came from a different source and belongs to the events of the succeeding period. Thus, in the period of long and severe depression the attempt to form a national federation of trade unions terminated as did the National Labor Union. It gave way to a new form of greenbackism.

THE GREENBACK PARTY, 1874-1877 [10]

With the rapid disintegration of trade unions during 1874 and 1875, the initiative of a political party had to come from another and more self-confident factor. This was the independent political organisation of the farmers.

[10] In the preparation of this section the author drew from an unpublished mono- graph by Louis Mayer, *The Greenback Labor Movement, 1874–1884.*

Growing out of the agitation conducted by the Patrons of Husbandry there arose by 1874, in many States, farmers' parties, known variously as " anti-monopoly " or " reform " or "independent " parties. These were playing an important part in the states of Illinois, Indiana, Wisconsin, Minnesota, Iowa, and California and, to a lesser degree, in Kansas, Nebraska, Oregon, and Michigan. In only two states, Indiana and Illinois, did the movement rest upon the principle of greenbackism, in the other States it was directed against railroad and warehouse monopolies. However, the continued depression, which affected agriculture and other industries alike, turned attention to the prospects of a national greenback party, and the convention of the farmers' party in Indiana, August 12, 1874, issued an invitation for a national conference to meet in Indianapolis in November.

Among the labour men invited were A. C. Cameron; Alexander Troup, then editor of the New Haven *Union;* Robert Schilling, president of the Coopers' National Union; Richard Trevellick; J. H. Wright, president of the Indianapolis Trades' Assembly and of the National Industrial Congress; and finally Horace H. Day, the philanthropic labour reformer, formerly active in the National Labor Reform party.

The conference met November 25. It was presided over by James Buchanan, an Indianapolis lawyer who was to play a prominent part in the greenback movement throughout its duration. All but four people in attendance came from Indiana. From among the labour men only Schilling and Day were present.

For a preliminary national convention to be held early the next year at Cleveland, the conference formulated a " basis of union," which exclusively dealt with the money question. It declared that " the solution of the money question more deeply affects the material interests of the people than any other questions in issue before the people," demanded the payment of the national debt in greenbacks, and the issue of interconvertible legal tender currency and bonds bearing not more than 3.65 per cent per annum.

A committee on organisation was appointed consisting of two labour men, Schilling and Trevellick (the latter being ab-

sent), and of a member of the executive committee of the Illinois
State Farmers' Association. Notwithstanding this, Horace H.
Day protested that the conference was not sufficiently representative of labour, and withdrew. He was apparently already
laying plans for the conference of farmers and mechanics, which
came together as a result of his efforts a year later.

The convention met in Cleveland on March 11, 1875. It
contained representatives from every State in the region bounded
by the Hudson, the Ohio, and the Mississippi, and in addition
also from Virginia, West Virginia, Iowa, and Missouri. The
platform was not altered. The name " Independent " was decided upon for the new party, and it retained that name,
formally, till 1878. It was from the first, however, known as
the Greenback party. The labour men present were Cameron,
Schilling, J. H. Wright, McDevitt (a prominent member of
the Machinists' and Blacksmiths' Union), Foran (formerly
president of the Coopers' Union, now a lawyer), John Siney
(president of the Miners' National Association), Reverend H.
O. Sheldon, of Oberlin, Ohio, one of the three men who had
attended every national labour congress since 1866, and finally
a Negro, C. W. Thompson, member of the Tobacco Laborers'
Union of Richmond, Virginia. It is significant that practically
all of these were labour leaders whose organisations had gone
to pieces. Siney and another less important labour man, who
was absent, were elected on the executive committee.

The " anti-monopoly " convention called by Horace Day met
at Harrisburg, Pennsylvania, March 3, 1875. It was made up
of " representatives from all the labour organizations of New
York and Pennsylvania, including the Grangers and retail coal
dealers," [11] 256 in all. It decided to call a national conference
of representatives to assemble about the first of July from all
parts of the country. It was agreed to leave to the conference
itself whether it should organise a new political party or confine
its actions to other matters in order to promote the interests of
American workingmen.

This conference assembled in Cincinnati, in September, the
labour reformers attending in force. Siney was chosen chairman. The platform adopted did not differ materially from the

11 New York *Times*, Mar. 4, 1875.

one adopted by the Independent party at Cleveland; it omitted the plank no longer an issue which declared against the granting of the public lands to any but actual settlers, but included a plank opposing the granting of any privileges to corporations. In addition, it contained a plank that was to be incorporated in every greenback platform until 1879 — a demand for the immediate repeal of the specie payment act which had been passed January 14, 1875.

The main discussion turned on whether a new party should be formed or whether fusion should be effected with the Independent party. Day represented the former view, and Siney and Schilling, the latter. Schilling's resolution providing for fusion was adopted. Thereupon Day withdrew and did not afterwards take part in the greenback movement. The fusion was effected, and a call was issued for a national convention to be held in Indianapolis the following May.[12]

The convention met on May 17, 1876. Trevellick, Troup, and Hinchcliffe were the only labour representatives who took part. The proceedings were opened by Moses Field, a wealthy Detroit manufacturer, who had served in the House of Representatives on the Democratic side. Ignatius Donnelly was temporary chairman; Thomas Durant, of Washington, D. C., a lawyer and former Republican politician, was permanent chairman; Wallace P. Groom, editor of the New York *Mercantile Journal* and a personal representative in the convention of Peter Cooper, was secretary; while S. M. Smith, of the Illinois State Farmers' Association, was acting chairman. This list gives a fair idea of the composition of the convention — farmers, lawyers, and a few labour leaders, with a sprinkling of former old party politicians.

The platform adopted is unmistakable evidence that the greenbackism professed by the party was different from that of the National Labor Union. Instead of a remedy against the exploitation of the " producing classes " by " capital " it became a plan to relieve the industrial depression. It primarily concerned itself, not with the rate of interest on money borrowed, but with the general level of prices. The Independent party declared for the immediate and unconditional repeal of

12 Chicago *Workingman's Advocate*, Dec. 4, 1875.

the specie resumption act and against the policy of contraction of the greenbacks. The belief is also again expressed that interconvertible "United States notes will afford the best circulating medium ever devised." The emphasis on specie resumption was made largely through the efforts of Groom, who carried a promise of financial assistance to the party from Peter Cooper.[13]

Peter Cooper was chosen presidential candidate of the Independent party.[14] For vice-president the convention nominated Newton Booth, senator from California, a Greenback-Democrat, who declined, and in his place the national executive committee chose General Samuel F. Cary, of Ohio, the former congressman supported by the National Labor Union.

The national campaign was not conducted with vigour. The party had little organisation and no funds except a sum of money contributed by Cooper. No attempt was made to interest labour organisations. In addition to the national ticket, there were state tickets in every State north of the Virginia line, except Rhode Island and Colorado. Congressional candidates were nominated in thirty-six widely scattered districts.

The total vote cast in the election was about 100,000, and came practically from rural districts. The largest state vote, 17,233, was in Illinois, but only 684 were cast in the counties where the larger cities were located. The aggregate vote in Kansas, Nebraska, Iowa, Illinois, Michigan, Indiana, Minnesota, Missouri, and West Virginia was 63,000. As yet, labour was indifferent to third-party politics.

THE SOVEREIGNS OF INDUSTRY

The order of the Sovereigns of Industry was the form assumed by the co-operative movement in the seventies. Unlike the movement during the later sixties, it took for its starting

---

[13] *Pomeroy's Democrat*, Sept. 22, 1877.

[14] He was born in New York City in 1791 and started his career as a journeyman carriage maker. Gradually, however, he took up one enterprise after another, with continuous success. In 1830 he established the Canton Iron Works, at Canton, Md., where he constructed from his own designs the first locomotive made in the United States. He built three blast furnaces in Phillipsburg, and conducted other similar enterprises. Deeply interested in the free education of the working class, he gave the money for and laid the cornerstone of the Cooper Union in New York, in 1854, and saw its completion in 1859, to be "forever devoted to the instruction and the improvement of the inhabitants of the United States in practical science and art." He died in New York City in 1883. See his *Autobiography* in *Old South Leaflets*, gen. series, VI, No. 147.

point the distribution of necessaries of life among wage-earners, although it held a vague ideal of the ultimate production of articles for the general market. Accordingly, the seat of the movement was not in the West, with its working class striving after immediate self-employment, but in Massachusetts where the workingman felt reconciled to a more or less permanent wage-earning status, and endeavoured to reduce his living expenses by excluding the middleman's profit. It was this New England co-operator and not his western colleague who bore a close resemblance to the Rochdale pioneers.

The order of the Sovereigns of Industry grew out of the Patrons of Husbandry, which had been organised in 1868 by the government clerk, O. H. Kelley, for the education and mutual aid of farmers. The Patrons started as a secret organisation, and the Sovereigns copied its secrecy. When Dudley W. Adams, of Waukon, Iowa, was elected master of the National Grange of the Patrons, he asked William H. Earle, an old schoolmate, to take charge of the work in Massachusetts. After organising granges for a time, Earle began to question the justice of excluding all but farmers from the Order. He felt that such an organisation should include all classes of workingmen. Accordingly, early in January, 1874, he called a meeting at Springfield of persons known to be favourable to organisation upon these broader lines. Only fifteen men responded to the call, but these were in earnest. They worked together for over a week, framed a constitution and ritual, organising as the National Council of the Order of Sovereigns of Industry, with Earle as president.[15]

The purposes were set forth by its founder:

" Our Order is for the purpose of elevating the character, improving the condition, and, as far as possible, perfecting the happiness of the laboring classes of every calling. Our Order will aim to cultivate a generous sympathy among its members, and a supreme respect for the rights of others. We propose to have Purchasing Agencies, through which consumers reach the producer direct, without so many needless ' middlemen,' who do nothing to merchandise *but add to its cost*. We think ' middlemen ' have grown rich enough already. ' Middlemen ' not only exact a tax from every consumer, but they are responsible for ' shoddy-goods,' ' short weights,'

15 *Equity*, October, 1874.

and adulterations. We are determined to secure *pure goods at lower prices.* . . . We pay cash and combine our orders in large numbers, and are saving from ten to fifteen per cent on our purchases. . . . In short, the Order is for the hard hand-workers, the real producers of wealth,— and its purpose is to enable them to control the *whole* of what they produce, and exchange it as near as may be even with other hand workers, thus saving to themselves the fortunes which those who are devoted to manipulating other people's labour, and to getting rich thereby, have heretofore taken by extortion." [16]

The constitution provided for national, state, and subordinate councils, the national council to be composed of two representatives from each state council, with power to issue, suspend, or revoke charters for state and subordinate councils, receive appeals and complaints, and redress grievances. The chief function of the national council, however, was agitational; it employed with great success John Orvis, a former member of the Brook Farm community, as national lecturer from 1874 to 1876. The Order was maintained by an annual *per capita* tax of 20 cents, with an initiation fee of 25 cents, and $15 for subordinate charters.

" Any person engaged in industrial pursuits, not under sixteen years of age, of good character, and having no interests in conflict with the purposes of the Order," was eligible to membership. The charter members, numbering 60 representatives from 8 States and the District of Columbia, included 21 women. The list of members seems to have included no one who had been interested in any previous national organisation, except O. H. Kelly, founder of the Patrons of Husbandry. The Order spread rapidly at first, taking root in nearly all of the northern States. The membership of the councils which reported was 21,619 in 1874; 27,984 in 1875; 16,993 in 1876; 9,673 in 1877; and 6,670 in 1878. The total membership in 1875–1876 was reported to be 40,000, of whom 75 per cent were in New England and 43 per cent in Massachusetts.[17] In 1875, 101 local councils reported as having some method of supplying members with goods, and of these 46 operated stores, 20 upon the Rochdale system and 26 upon the system of selling

16 *Ibid.*
17 Bemis, *Co-operation in New Eng-*   *land* in American Economic Association, *Publications,* I. 93.

at cost to members only.   The remaining councils had agreements with private traders for rebates to members.[18]   At the congress in 1876, President Earle estimated the annual trade at $3,000,000.

The Order co-operated in some instances with the Patrons of Husbandry, and in at least one case it united with the Patrons to maintain a co-operative store.[19]   In Vermont the state agent of the Patrons was instructed to give to members of the Sovereigns the same advantages in matters of trade that were given to the members of the granges.[20]

During the period of its ascendency, from 1874 to 1876, the Order absorbed many independent labour organisations.   Several independent co-operative purchasing societies became local councils.   Other labour organisations identified themselves with it.   In New Jersey, the lodges of the Industrial Brotherhood passed resolutions requesting their officers to ascertain whether their organisations in the State might be incorporated with the Sovereigns of Industry, and this arrangement was finally made.[21]

The Sovereigns even succeeded in engulfing some of the trade unions, whose members organised as lodges.   This alarmed the trade unionists, and their chief organ, the *National Labor Tribune,* of Pittsburgh, began in October, 1875,[22] a systematic attack on the Order, stating that "the only object of the Sovereigns is to buy cheap, if they have to help reduce wages to a dollar a day to do it," and that "the Sovereigns do not make the protection and elevation of labor's interest cardinal doctrines."   To the first accusation the Sovereigns replied that "the great mass of those comprising the Order, work for wages, and are as greatly interested in high wages, as any persons can be," but they desire to "buy without paying unnecessary profits to middlemen."   It is, moreover, not true, they said, that the Order does not make "the protection and elevation of labor's interest cardinal doctrines," for "we mean to substitute co-operation, production and exchange, for the present competitive system," and "we war with the whole wage system, and demand for labor the entire results of its beneficial toil; . . . the Sov-

18 *Ibid.,* 44.
19 E. M. Chamberlin, *Sovereigns of Industry,* 151.
20 *Ibid.*
21 *Ibid.,* 150.
22 Oct. 9, 1875.

ereigns have no contest with any existing labor organisations, we are jealous of none, envious of none." [23]

It was stated above that representatives of the Sovereigns tried to merge the Industrial Congress of April, 1874, into the Order, but failed. At this time the Sovereigns of Industry was at its height. During the next year, however, the Order began rapidly to decline. The chief cause was the hard times, which made cash payment impossible for many and resulted in a general falling off of the membership, and, in many instances, in a change to the credit system with an even more disastrous outcome for the Order. Frequently added to this was incompetent or dishonest management and, in the case of stores which sold at cost, a fierce competition of private dealers that eventually led to bankruptcy. Last, but not least, the jealousy, or, at the best, the indifference of the trade unions, was one of the causes of the downfall of the Order in 1878.

NATIONAL AND LOCAL TRADE UNIONS

The trade unions established during the sixties were peculiarly unfit successfully to weather the stress of unemployment and wage reductions. The national trade union remained a decentralised body, a loose federation of virtually autonomous locals, each enforcing its own standard rates, apprenticeship regulations, and working rules independently of the national office. With unimportant exceptions [24] there were no national benefit systems. The outcome was that the hold of the trade union upon its membership was dependent solely upon the measure of success with which it increased wages or decreased hours. At the same time, the prevailing low dues did not permit the accumulation of strike funds sufficient for resistance under adverse conditions.

Another cause of weakness lay in the general fact that during the period of depression the tendency increased among labour leaders, who possessed a wide reputation, to forsake the labour movement for politics. Fehrenbatch, president of the

---

[23] *National Labor Tribune*, Oct. 23, 1875.

[24] A death benefit for the moulders had been started in 1870 and a superannuation benefit in 1874. Both were discontinued after 1882. The cigar makers nominally paid $50 death benefit. See Kennedy, *Beneficiary Features of American Trade Unions*, in *Johns Hopkins University Studies*, XXVI, 55.

machinists' and blacksmiths' national union, was elected to the
Ohio legislature in 1876 and two years later accepted a Federal position; H. J. Walls, the secretary of the moulders' national union, became in 1877 the first commissioner of the
Ohio Bureau of Labor and Statistics. Foran, the president
of the coopers, was admitted to the bar in Cleveland in 1874
as a prelude to a subsequent career in Congress. A much
longer list might be given, but it would enumerate many persons
not otherwise mentioned here at this time. The great West,
too, was still drawing off the more energetic members of the
unions. When the labour movement again started, after 1877,
we seldom encounter the old familiar names we used to meet
on the pages of *Fincher's Trades' Review,* the *Workingman's
Advocate,* and the other labour papers of the sixties and early
seventies. And even the *Workingman's Advocate,* which, under the editorship of Andrew Cameron, had survived through
thirteen years and had chronicled the death of the other labour
papers of the period, was itself snuffed out in 1877.

It is no wonder, then, that the trade unions were on the down
grade. The *New York Times*[25] estimated that the trade union
membership for that city had decreased 25 per cent (from 44,-
950 to 35,765) during the year preceding December, 1874.
In 1877 it further dwindled to approximately 5,000.[26] The
same held true of the West; in Cincinnati the entire trade
union membership in 1878 was not above 1,000.[27] The number of the national trade unions decreased from approximately
30 during the early seventies to 8 or 9 during 1877.[28] The
membership of the cigar makers' national union fell from 5,800
in 1869 to 1,016 in 1877, that of the coopers from about 7,000
in 1872 to 1,500 in 1878,[29] and the machinists' union lost two-
thirds of its members.[30] The Order of the Crispins, with a

---

[25] Dec. 11, 1874.

[26] Waltershausen, *Die nordamerikanischen Gewerkschaften unter dem Einfluss der fortschreitenden Productionstechnik,* 202.

[27] United States Senate Committee on
Education and Labor, *Report on Relations
between Capital and Labor,* 1885, I, 411.

[28] The *Labor Standard* (New York)
listed in its trade union directory in the
first part of 1877 nine national or international unions of the following occupa-

tions: moulders, locomotive firemen,
miners, coopers, iron and steel workers,
granite cutters, machinists and blacksmiths, cigar makers, and carpenters and
joiners (the British organisation).

[29] Farnam, "Die Amerikanischen
Gewerkvereine," in *Schriften des Vereins
für Socialpolitik,* XVIII, 23.

[30] The pattern makers and blacksmiths
were added in 1877 and the name was
changed to "Mechanical Engineers of
North America." *Ibid.,* 13.

membership of approximately 50,000 in 1871, had virtually gone out of existence in 1878. The bricklayers dwindled from 43 locals, with 5,332 in 1873, to 3 locals in 1880,[31] and the typographical, the oldest national union, which had 9,797 in 1873 was reduced to 4,260 in 1878.[32] Gompers, some 20 years later, estimated the total membership of all trade unions in 1878 at 50,000.[33]

With the distintegration of the labour organisations disappeared the bulwark against wage reductions, and the gains of shorter hours made in the eight-hour movement of 1872 were swept away.

The weakening of national organisation in nearly every trade and its disappearance in many added to the relative prominence of the city trades' assemblies, even though the latter now existed in fewer localities and had fewer affiliated unions than in the years preceding the crisis. Strike assessments for the benefit of affiliated unions were levied by them in place of the national unions. The constitution of the assembly in New York,[34] for example, provided for a weekly per capita assessment upon the affiliated unions, to be paid out in strike benefits not to exceed $3 per week to each striker. In addition it provided that " a permanent strike fund should be formed through an assessment of ten cents per member and, in case an affiliated union fell four weeks behind in its payment, it should be suspended and it should not be entitled to benefits during a whole month after the back dues were paid." [35]

The retrogression of labour organisation was accompanied by a series of bitterly fought strikes, mainly against wage reductions. The industries most strongly affected were cigar making, the textiles, and coal mining.

The cigar makers in New York had first become active on a large scale during the eight-hour strike in 1872. Division

---

31 From an unpublished manuscript history.

32 Barnett, *The Printers*, 375.

33 Industrial Commission, *Report*, 1901, VII, 615.

34 Quoted by Waltershausen, *Die nordamerikanischen Gewerkschaften*, 138, from the *Gewerkschaft-Zeitung* (New York) for July 20, 1880. The New York Trades' Council was reorganised in April, 1877. *Labor Standard*, Apr. 20, 1877.

35 In 1881 strike contributions were made voluntary by the New York Assembly, each union to decide for itself upon the amount of its contribution. Waltershausen, *Die nordamerikanischen Gewerkschaften*, 138. The national trade unions, at that time, had arisen in a sufficient number of trades to relieve the trades' assembly from conducting and financing strikes.

of labour and child and woman labour were introduced first in this city and the local union therefore decided to organise on an industrial basis by taking in the rollers and the bunchers, who were excluded from membership by the vote of the international union. In the winter of 1873 the union consisted of about 1,700 members. Soon thereafter it went out on strike against a large concern, which resulted not only in a severe defeat for the strikers, but also in a complete revolution in the method of production. It stimulated the employers to transfer their work from the large shops to the tiny tenement house shops operated by docile labour. Within one year over one-half of the cigars manufactured in New York were made in tenement houses. An unsuccessful appeal for interference was made in 1874 to the New York Board of Health. In the summer of 1875 the union, which had lost under the adverse conditions nearly all of its members, was reorganised. Henceforth the work of organisation proceeded steadily until the fall of 1877, when a general strike of all cigar makers in the city for the abolition of the tenement house system was declared. Nearly 7,000 struck, including a large proportion of tenement house workers. The strike attracted attention in the country and considerable aid was secured from the outside, but after 107 days of hard struggle work was resumed under the old conditions and the tenement house system was fastened upon the trade.[36]

In the textile industry the most severe and prolonged strikes during this period occurred in Fall River, where the industry had grown during the years of prosperity faster than in any other textile centre, and consequently rested upon a less firm basis. In addition to this, a series of defalcations perpetrated by the treasurers of several corporations in that city further contributed to the disorganisation of the industry, and according- ingly increased the pressure upon wages. Between 1873 and 1880 wages were reduced 45 per cent. These periodic cuts occasioned hard and bitterly fought strikes which were uni-

---

[36] *Vorbote*, Nov. 6, 1875, Nov. 3, 1877, and Feb. 9, 1878; and McNeill, *The Labor Movement: The Problem of To- day*, 591.

In 1883 New York passed a law pro- hibiting the manufacture of cigars or any other form of preparation of tobacco in tenement houses, but in 1885 the highest court in the State declared it unconstitu- tional on the ground that " it is plain that this is not a health law, and that it has no relation whatever to the public health." In Matter Jacobs, 98 N. Y. 98.

formly unsuccessful, French-Canadian immigrants taking the places of the strikers.[37]

Disintegration, however, was not the rule in all labour organisations. In the iron industry [38] an amalgamation took place in 1876 of three heretofore separate craft organisations, the United Sons of Vulcan (puddlers), the Associated Brotherhood of Iron and Steel Heaters (roughers, rollers and catchers), and the Iron and Steel Roll Hands, under the name of the Amalgamated Association of Iron and Steel Workers. The puddlers, who had had a trade agreement with the employers upon the sliding scale principle since 1866 — the first national trade agreement in American labour history — constituted 85 per cent of the membership of the new organisation. It had about 3,000 members in 1876 and only 3,755 in 1877, but increased rapidly after this year, reaching the 20,000 mark in 1882.[39] So effective was this organisation that its pioneer trade agreement of 1866 was continued in most of the mills for a quarter of a century, and in a few of the remaining iron mills continues even down to the present time.

The development in the bituminous coal mining industry during this period is of especial interest, since it represented the first introduction of the written trade agreement into that industry.

The bituminous miners had been without a national organisation since the end of the War. But in October, 1873, John Siney resigned his position as president of the anthracite miners' union and, at a convention in Youngstown, Ohio, combined the several state miners' unions into a miners' national association, modelling it upon the pattern of the British organisation of the same name.[40] In spite of the depression the membership reached 21,000 one year later. Like the Brit-

---

[37] For an excellent account of the strikes against the periodic cuts and for a return to the old wages, see McNeill, *The Labor Movement: The Problem of To-day*, 221, 233.

[38] There were still other exceptions to the rule. The highly skilled but small National Trade Association of Hat Finishers of the United States of America retained the closed shop throughout the depression. The granite cutters, who formed their national union in 1877,

aimed at the eight-hour day. Farnam, *Die Amerikanischen Gewerkvereine*, 8, 25, 26.

[39] Fitch, "Unionism in the Iron and Steel Industry," in *Political Science Quarterly*, XXIV, 57-79.

[40] Siney was assisted by John James, the president of the Illinois Miners' Union, who had been associated with Alexander McDonald, the well-known miners' leader in Scotland.

ish association, the new organisation aspired toward conciliation or arbitration in settling labour disputes. As soon as the
general office was opened in Cleveland, Siney began making
overtures to the coal companies in that city in the direction
of conciliation. He was, however, refused by all except Mark
Hanna, who was the largest operator in the Tuscarawas Valley. The principle of arbitration was given a trial in December, 1874, when the employers in the Valley resolved upon a
reduction of the mining rate from 90 to 70 cents, and demanded a conference with the union to settle the matter peace-
ably. The union chose three representatives, the operators
three (Hanna was one), and Judge S. J. Andrews was selected
by them as the umpire of the board. The decision handed down
by Judge Andrews went entirely against the miners, the basic
rate being fixed at 71 cents, doubtless for no other than the
obvious reason that the state of the industry was depressed. The
miners acquiesced, but, as is usually the case when the conditions of wage agreements are determined by an impartial umpire
instead of the relative bargaining power of both parties, they
felt that they could have attained better results if they had
struck. One mining company had previously appealed to the
employers' association to start a general lockout against the
demand for a check-weighman and had been refused. Soon
after the award had gone into effect, this company offered, in
revenge upon the other operators, to·pay its men 80 cents, besides allowing a check-weighman. Of course, the offer was accepted. The union miners, who had accepted the cut of 19
cents, immediately appealed to the general officers of the association to be absolved from the award. John Siney called a
session of the permanent board of appeals,[41] which, upon hearing the representatives of the miners, granted the request.
The employers were obliged to grant the increase to 80 cents.
As a result of this failure of the union to live up to its agreement, another ten years passed before arbitration and conciliation was given another trial in the bituminous coal industry.[42]

41 This board had been created upon the
suggestion of Mark Hanna.
42 *Miners' National Record* (Cleveland), May, 1875. The miners' association numbered 35,000 at the close of 1875,
but it went to pieces the next year due to

several causes, the most important being,
first, the uncontrollable passion of the
members to strike against every reduction
in wages, irrespective of circumstances
and against the wishes of John Siney and
the executive board; and, second, the ar-

In anthracite mining the trade agreement system which had existed upon the basis of a sliding scale since 1869 was broken up in 1874 after the "long strike" of seven months' duration against a reduction of the wage scale. The strike ended in defeat in August and the once powerful Workingmen's Benevolent Association was so completely demoralised that it went to pieces [43] and was followed by the "Molly Maguires."

THE "MOLLY MAGUIRES"

In no industry did the failure of trade unionism in the seventies lead to such serious results as in anthracite mining, where it left an opening for renewal of the murderous activity of the secret society known as the "Molly Maguires." Indeed, we find that, beginning with the early sixties, when the society first became known, until 1876, when it was finally stamped out, its criminal activity varied inversely in frequency and violence with the fortunes of the anthracite workers' union. The *Miners' Journal* of March 30, 1867,[44] published a list of fifty murders committed in Schuylkill County alone between January 1, 1863, and March 30, 1867, a period during which unionism was weak. On the other hand, little was heard of lawlessness between October, 1868, and December, 1871,[45] the period of the greatest strength of unionism and of the trade agreement between the anthracite board of trade and the Miners' and Laborers' Benevolent Association. Crimes, however, began to occur frequently after 1871. But only after the "long strike," which lasted from December, 1874, to June, 1875, and ended in a total destruction of the union did a "crime wave" sweep the anthracite counties.

"Mollie Maguires" was the name used for the secret ring that controlled the lodges of the fraternal organisation of the

rest of Siney and Parks for conspiracy and inciting to riot in Clearfield County, Penn., in June, 1875. Although Siney was acquitted by the jury of the charge of conspiracy and Parks alone was sentenced for inciting to riot, this trial brought on the disintegration of the association. At the next session of the legislature of Pennsylvania, a law was passed exempting combinations to raise wages from the charge of conspiracy. Roy,

History of the Coal Miners of the United States, 175, 178. Siney died in 1880.

43 *Ibid.*, 99.

44 Quoted in Martin, *History of the Great Riots, together with a full History of the Molly Maguires*, 466; see also, Rhodes, "Molly Maguires in the Anthracite Region of Pennsylvania," in *Amer. Hist. Review*, XV, 547–561.

45 *Ibid.*

Ancient Order of Hibernians in the anthracite counties, and directed and perpetrated the crimes.

The Ancient Order of Hibernians was organised in Ireland as a means of opposing the encroachments of the landlords, but in the United States it was maintained in an effort to control the relations between the miners and the mine operators. The Irish organisation was composed of men who, in their own country, had lived through a period of storm and stress that had made them lawless and tenacious of their rights. The membership was composed entirely of Irish Catholics, but the Order never had the sanction of the Roman Catholic Church, and it was, in fact, the object of strenuous opposition on the part of the clergy. It is known to have existed in this country as early as 1852, appearing first in Pennsylvania, where it was always to be found in its greatest strength. Although the fact was not known until a decade later, the Order resorted to violence as early as 1862, and from that time until the crushing of the organisation in 1875 and 1876, deeds of violence were increasingly common. Its members opposed the enlistment of soldiers by draft in some parts of Pennsylvania, threatening, and in one case, at least, maltreating, the officials of the draft.

The outbreak of the Civil War caused an increased demand for coal, and consequent increase in the demand for miners. More Irishmen came over to meet this demand, and the Ancient Order of Hibernians grew accordingly. The Order was incorporated under the laws of Pennsylvania in 1871, and of several other States to which it spread. According to the constitution under which it was incorporated, the Hibernians were humane, charitable, and benevolent. They seem to have been controlled by a " Committee of Erin " with headquarters in Great Britain. There were, besides the national organisation, state, district, and local divisions, each with its own officials.

With added strength it began to take on more of the characteristics of the secret orders of Ireland, the Molly Maguires and Ribbonmen. The name in this country was gradually changed to " The Molly Maguires," although there is no evidence that there was any connection between this Order and the Irish society of that name.

The Molly Maguires early became strong enough to form a

powerful factor in local politics, in some places being able to assert complete control. They sought especially the offices of county commissioner, tax collector, school director, and others which handled money. Having secured the election, they proceeded to exploit the office to the fullest extent without regard to the welfare of the public. There were said to be 6,000 local lodges of the Order throughout the country, and, according to testimony of members when brought into court, the "entire organisation from the Atlantic to the Pacific, and from the Gulf of Mexico to Maine, is criminal in its character."[46] Whether this was true or not, it seems to be an established fact that there came no word of protest against the outrages commonly committed by the Pennsylvania members, except from a part of one local lodge in Philadelphia.[47]

The depredations of the Mollies were usually directed against the mine owners or bosses, but seldom on general grounds. The victim had usually offended some individual member of the Order and he was punished for this, rather than for a principle. In some cases the punishment meted out was severe handling, or destruction of property, but, believing that "dead men tell no tales," the murder of the offender became the common form of punishment.

The method employed in administering these punishments was calculated to protect the murderers from detection. When the death of an offender had been decided upon, a notice was sent from the Molly district in which the victim resided to the officers of another district, asking that men be detailed to come over and do the deed. These men were unknown to the victim and to the district generally. After the murder they were helped to escape by members of the local order. The local lodge receiving the favour was placed under obligation to that which granted it and might be called upon at any time for a return of the accommodation.

In the rare cases when a murderer was arrested it was easy to prove an alibi, and this became the favourite defence of the Mollies when in trouble. Perjury was obviously no obstacle to men who had so little regard for law and life, and they always

<hr />

46 Dewees, *The Molly Maguires*, 39.   47 *Ibid.*, 98.

produced as many witnesses as were necessary to swear that the accused was elsewhere at the time the crime was committed.[48]

In 1869 Franklin B. Gowen, formerly attorney for the Philadelphia & Reading Rail Road Company, became president of the road. Having been a resident of Schuylkill County for a decade, he was as familiar with the history of the Molly Maguires as was any outsider at that time. As president of the railroad, which, like most of the transportation companies of that region, was also a mining company, he realised that mining operations must be carried on at a disadvantage as long as the depredations of this criminal organisation were permitted. To end this he conferred with the Pinkerton detective agency, and a man was sent into the mining region to learn what he could about the crimes committed.

This man was James McParlan, an Irishman and a Catholic. He lived among the miners, sought the company of the roughest, declared himself a fugitive from justice, and pretended that he was even then living by passing counterfeit money. By this means he won for himself the friendship of the Molly Maguires, was initiated into the Order, and even made secretary of his district.

McParlan, or McKenna, as he was known among the Mollies, came to the anthracite region in October, 1873. He was made the confidant of many a criminal and was able to warn a number of proposed victims. When, in December, 1874, " the long strike " for higher wages began, many of the leaders and the better men in the Miners' and Laborers' Benevolent Association were opposed to it; but the Molly Maguires were in control and the strike was called. After the strike had been in progress for several months, suffering became common among the miners. Many of them would have returned to work, but fear of the Mollies prevented. The employers declared a reduction of wages necessary, but the association was firm in maintaining that at least the old wages should be paid. Much feeling manifested itself on both sides, and at last the great coal-mining companies refused to treat with the association at all. About

48 The object of these murders was usually, as has been stated, vengeance for some act of a mine owner or boss, but there was a period in 1866 and another in 1868, when a large number were committed for the purpose of robbery. There is little doubt that these were perpetrated by the Molly Maguires. *Ibid.*, 61.

June 1, 1875, the operators won, and the miners' association was crushed. The leaders advised the members to make the best terms possible with their individual employers. The Molly element in the union opposed such action, and, by intimidation, prevented a resumption of work for some time. An attempt to open the collieries of the Philadelphia & Reading Company, under promise of protection to the men, resulted in a riot. The militia was called out and the disturbance quelled. The mines began operation, the miners' union was wrecked. The Molly Maguires, on the contrary, had grown stronger and more offensive and crime followed crime in rapid succession. But it was soon to end. James McKenna had accumulated a mass of evidence against the Mollies, individually and collectively, and in the fall of 1875 arrests were made and trials were begun. These trials dragged on until late in 1876, when, with the conviction of 24 criminals, the Order was crushed. Fourteen were committed to prison for terms varying from 2 to 7 years and 10 were executed.

THE GREAT STRIKES OF 1877

Notwithstanding all optimistic expectations for an industrial revival in 1877, the depression reached its lowest point in that year. This led to further reductions in wages in the majority of industries. But in no other industry did these reductions cause so much bitterness and resentment as on the railroads. In the first place, the railroads were the largest employers in the country, and a cut in railroad wages simultaneously affected large numbers of people; and, second, the general feeling in the community against railroad·corporations made the grievances of the men appear especially huge. The Pennsylvania road had reduced wages 10 per cent soon after the panic of 1873, but it declared another general reduction of 10 per cent to take effect June 1, 1877. The other competing roads followed the example. The New York Central declared a similar reduction to go into effect July 1 and the Baltimore & Ohio, July 16.[49]

The situation of the railway unions was precarious. The Brotherhood of Locomotive Engineers had in 1874 deposed

49 *Report*, of the committee appointed by the Pennsylvania General Assembly to investigate the railroad riots in July, 1877, p. 2.

Grand Chief Engineer Wilson, who was accused of siding with the railroads, and his place was taken by the " insurgent," P. M. Arthur, who was then still in favour of an energetic policy against the companies. The Brotherhood conducted two strikes in April, 1877, one against a reduction on the Boston & Albany, and another against the Pennsylvania railroad, but both were failures. President Gowen, of the Pennsylvania & Reading, encouraged by his successful operations against the Molly Maguires and fearing a strike by his locomotive engineers, ordered them upon the penalty of discharge to withdraw from the Brotherhood. They reluctantly submitted, but decided to surprise the officials by a sudden strike at midnight on April 14. This plan was frustrated, however, through the activity of the Pinkerton detectives, and the railroad, by securing a sufficient number of strike-breakers to take the places of the men,[50] was fully prepared for the event. The Brotherhood of Railway Conductors (established in 1868) and of the railway Firemen (organised in 1873) were weak and remained quiet throughout the period of the strikes.

When the Pennsylvania declared the reduction in wages to take effect in June, the employés selected a committee composed principally of engineers, which, in the latter part of May, waited on Thomas A. Scott, the president, and accepted his explanation and promise to return to the old scale when business improved. The engineers acquiesced, but the other trainmen charged openly that the committee, because it was composed mainly of engineers, had acted merely in their own interest. Thereupon, the employés of railroads having their termini in Pittsburgh began organising a secret Trainmen's Union to resist the reduction.[51] The leading spirit was a young brakeman, Robert H. Ammon, who organised the first lodge in Alleghany City, June 2, 1877, and thereafter acted as the general organiser. In a short time he had extended the union on the divisions of the Baltimore & Ohio, the Pennsylvania and its leased lines radiating east and west from Pittsburgh, as well as on the Erie and the Atlantic & Great Western.

50 *Ibid.*, 25: Pinkerton, *Strikers, Communists, Tramps and Detectives*, 112 *et seq.*
51 *Report*, Pennsylvania, etc., 2.

The union "aimed to get the trainmen — comprising engineers, conductors, brakemen, and firemen, on the three grand trunk lines of the country — into one solid body " and to strike simultaneously. The original intention was that the strike should break out on June 27 at noon, and forty men were dispatched from Pittsburgh to notify the various divisions when the signal was given. However, dissension occurred at a meeting on the night preceding the day set and a portion of the leaders went west, declaring that the strike would not be declared. This caused the whole movement to collapse.[52]

The organised attempt at resistance thus failed, but the employés' accumulated feeling of resentment against the railroad was sufficiently strong to cause a spontaneous and unorganised outbreak at the least provocation. The events of the next month can be understood only by recalling that the four years of acute depression had created a large element in society which was ever ready to take advantage of any big disturbance to steal, plunder, and destroy. Allan Pinkerton in his book, which appeared in 1878, said that " while he, the tramp, is commonly the outgrowth of conditions of society which will never materially vary, the severe and unprecedented hard times that have lately been experienced, and which still seem to girdle the entire globe, have manufactured tramps with an alarming rapidity. Where they previously existed as single wandering vagabonds, they now have increased until they travel in herds, and, through the dire necessity of their pitiable condition, justly create some anxiety and alarm." [53]

The first outbreak occurred on the Baltimore & Ohio at Martinsburg, West Virginia, on July 17, the day after the 10 per cent reduction had gone into effect. The trainmen refused to allow freight trains to leave the station either east or west unless their wages were restored. The lodge of the Brotherhood of Locomotive Engineers refused to take an active part, but, their sympathies being with the strikers, they made only half-hearted attempts to move the trains. The local state militia was called out, but could hardly be relied upon to enforce the rights of the railroad at the sacrifice of the lives of their rela-

---

52 *Ibid.*, 671.
53 Pinkerton, *Strikers, Communists, Tramps and Detectives*, 42.

tives and friends. Consequently the strikers held full sway for two days, until the arrival of 200 Federal troops, which had been dispatched by President Hayes upon the request of Governor Matthews. Immediately the strike ceased and the trains began to move freely in and out of Martinsburg.

The strike spread like wildfire over the adjacent sections of the Baltimore & Ohio, the strikers assuming absolute control at many points, notably Cumberland, Maryland. At Baltimore, in order to avoid trouble, the management stopped running freight trains. Governor Carroll, of Maryland, profiting by the experience with the militia in Martinsburg, ordered Baltimore regiments, the Fifth, and two companies of the Sixth, to proceed to Cumberland July 20. The Fifth Regiment arrived safely at the Camden depot, where the militia was to board a train for Cumberland. The two companies of the Sixth, however, were beleaguered in the armory by an ever-increasing mob determined to prevent their departure. Gaining egress, the companies marched under a hail of brickbats and revolver shots to the depot, freely replying from their guns. The fury of the mob increased as night arrived and a successful attempt was made to set fire to the depot. The mob threatened the lives of the firemen who attempted to extinguish the fire, and the militia would have been in a very sorry plight had not a strong force of police arrived at this moment and driven the mob from the fire engines. This broke the spirit of the mob and the disorder immediately ceased. On the following day, Federal troops arrived at Baltimore and other threatened points in the State and effectively put an end to the strike.

The occurrences in Martinsburg and Baltimore, however, fade into insignificance when compared with the destructive effects of the strike on the Pennsylvania road in and around Pittsburgh. On this road the reduction in wages had gone into effect June 1, with no immediate disturbance except a small strike at Alleghany, which was unsuccessful. The outbreak of violence had a different cause. The introduction of " double headers," or freight trains composed of thirty-four cars instead of seventeen in a single train, and drawn by two engines, was designed to economise labour and throw out of work a large number of conductors and brakemen. The order for " double

headers " was issued some time in July, to take effect on the
19th of the month.   On the very day when the management
attempted to carry out the order the strike broke out.   The
strikers took possession of the switches over which the trains
would have to move, and refused to let any trains pass out.
Their number was constantly becoming larger and their bearing
more threatening.   The mayor of Pittsburgh, upon whom the
railway management called for help, gave a perfunctory reply
and very little help.   It was evident that practically all the inhabitants of Pittsburgh believed that the city was being discrim-
inated against by the Pennsylvania road in the matter of freight
rates and were on the side of the strikers.   The sheriff acted
in the same perfunctory manner, but appealed, nevertheless,
to the governor for state troops.   Several local regiments of
the national guard were immediately ordered out, but, fearing that the Pittsburgh militia sympathised with the strikers,
600 troops were also ordered from Philadelphia and arrived
at the union depot at noon, July 21.   This being on Saturday, when the mills shut down at noon, the ranks of the
strikers were swelled by large numbers of sympathisers from
the mills.   The Pittsburgh militia, as was expected, fraternised
with the strikers, but the Philadelphia troops seriously attempted
to clear the track for the movement of trains.   They succeeded
in dispersing a large mob at 26th Street crossing, killing twenty-
six, but the movement of the trains was given up and the troops
were ordered into the lower roundhouse and machine shops.
Meanwhile, upon the advice of many influential citizens, who
insisted that the presence of the troops would exasperate the
mob and aggravate the situation, the general in command disbanded the remainder of the Pittsburgh troops, who had not
yet gone to their homes of their own accord.   Thus the Philadelphia troops were left to their own fate in the face of an
armed mob, which grew to enormous proportions as darkness
set in.   The mob soon began a real siege of the roundhouse
which held the soldiers.   About ten o'clock the cars and the
shops were set on fire and soon the conflagration threatened the
roundhouse.   The soldiers fought against the mob and the fire
till half past seven in the morning when, in obedience to orders,
they marched out and began a retreat out of the city, being

subject to constant fire from all sides until they left the city limits. This left the mob the unhindered master of the situation, free to burn, destroy, and to loot. The rioting lasted another day and finally spent itself, after nearly $5,000,000 worth of railroad property had been destroyed. When a group of professional and business men, alarmed over the vast destruction of property, improvised a small band of militia and appeared at the union depot, it found only a small crowd of looters, which was easily dispersed. The great riot had ended of itself.

The mob was made up of some railroad men, mill men, boys, roughs, and tramps. It is noteworthy that at Alleghany City, a railroad centre just across the river from Pittsburgh, neither rioting nor destruction of property occurred. Here the trainmen's union survived the unsuccessful attempt to strike in June, and Robert A. Ammon, the head of the union, taking control of the situation, managed the division four days without mishap.[54]

Disturbances occurred also at Harrisburg, Philadelphia, Reading, Altoona, Scranton, and several minor points. In the first two cities they were easily quelled by the police and the militia. In Reading, however, the militia, as in Pittsburgh, fraternised with the strikers and order was restored only by the arrival of 300 Federal troops. At Scranton the coal miners were more active in the strike than the trainmen. The strikers were dispersed by a posse of citizens headed by the mayor, who enforced order until the troops arrived.

The strike spread to the Erie road and the principal disturbances occurred at Hornellsville, New York, and Buffalo. The other cities to which the strike spread were Toledo, Louisville, Chicago, St. Louis, and San Francisco.

The strikes failed in every case, but the moral effect was enormous. For the first time a general strike movement swept the country. Heretofore, the general eight-hour movement in New York City in the spring of 1872 had been the largest strike on record. But now the labour problem became a matter of nation-wide and serious interest to the general public. Fundamental changes followed. The inefficiency of the militia

54 He operated passenger and mail trains, the strike affecting only the move- ment of freight trains. *Report* of Penn., etc., 22.

showed the need of a reliable basis of operation for the troops, and the construction of numerous and strong armories in the large cities dates from 1877. The courts began to change their attitude toward labour unions; the strikes and riots brought back from oblivion the doctrine of malicious conspiracy as applied to labour combinations. The legislatures in many States enacted conspiracy laws directed against labour. But the strongest moral effect was upon the wage-earning, class. The spirit of labour solidarity was strengthened and made national. This was the first time in the history of the American labour movement that Federal troops were called out in time of peace to suppress strikes. Nor had the state militia ever been used for the same purpose on so large a scale. The feeling of resentment engendered thereby began to assume a political aspect, and during the next two years the territory covered by the strike wave became a most promising field for labour parties of all kinds and descriptions. On the side of trade union organisation the effect of the strike appears to have been more remote. Nevertheless, it can safely be stated that there was a direct connection between the active coming forth of the unskilled during the strike and the attempts, so largely secret, that were made immediately after to organise this class of labour.

PART SIX

UPHEAVAL AND REORGANISATION
(Since 1876)

By SELIG PERLMAN

CHAPTER I

SECRET BEGINNINGS

Employers' opposition to trade unions during the period of depression, 195. Necessity for secrecy, 195. Beginning of the Knights of Labor, 196. Uriah S. Stephens, 197. Assembly 1 of Philadelphia, 197. "Sojourners," 198. Ritual and principles, 198. Additional assemblies, 199. District Assembly 1, of Philadelphia, 199. District Assembly 2, of Camden, New Jersey, 199. District Assembly 3, of Pittsburgh, 199. Recruiting ground of the Knights, 200. Strikes and strike funds, 200. Rivalry between District Assembly 1 and District Assembly 3, 200. The issue of secrecy, 201. Attitude of the Catholic Church, 201. The Junior Sons of '76 and their call for a national convention, 201.

THE business depression of 1873 to 1879 was a critical period in the American labour movement. The old national trade unions either went to pieces, or retained a merely nominal existence. Employers sought to free themselves from the restrictions that the trade unions had imposed upon them during the years preceding the crisis. They consequently added a systematic policy of lockouts, of blacklists, and of legal prosecution to the already crushing weight of hard times and unemployment. Speaking of this period, McNeill says " a great deal of bitterness was evinced against trades union organisations, and men were blacklisted to an extent hardly ever equalled," [1] so that it became " very difficult to find earnest and active members who were willing to serve on committees." [2]

It became clear that the " open union " was not an effective means of combatting the tactics of capital. Hence " labor leaders met silently and secretly," [3] and advocated an organisation " hedged about with the impenetrable veil of ritual, sign grip, and password," so that " no spy of the boss can find his way in the Lodgeroom to betray his fellows." [4]   By the require-

---

[1] McNeill, *Labor Movement: The Problem of To-day*, 154.
[2] *Ibid.*, 398.
[3] Quoted in the Pittsburgh *National Labor Tribune*, Oct. 8, 1880, from a speech by William M. Davis, state secretary of the Ohio Miners' Union.
[4] *Ibid.*, July 9, 1881, from the Chicago *Progressive Age*.

ment that each applicant should take the oath they hoped to shield the organisation from the indiscretion of some of its members.[5]

" When the commercial interests," said the *National Labor Tribune* of April 24, 1875, " combine to exact the greatest share of profits of labor and give labor the least, even to the verge of starvation, when all attempts of labor to *openly oppose and defeat* the efforts of these combinations are made the pretext for still further oppression and persecution, it is time for the people to unite together for their individual and common safety. . . . These considerations have prompted men in all trades to have recourse to secret organisations."

One of the secret organisations was the Molly Maguires.[6] But terrorism could not lastingly succeed. The great railway strikes of 1877, which, in their violent methods, were akin to the Molly Maguires, were also doomed to fail. The typical organisation during the seventies was secret for protection against intrusion by outsiders, but it differed from the Molly Maguires in its peaceful methods. One of this type, the Knights of Labor, became the leading organisation of the following decade. Others were the Sovereigns of Industry, modelled after the Patrons of Husbandry of the farmers, and the Industrial Brotherhood, which captured the National Labor Congress in 1874.[7] Still another was the Junior Sons of '76. Allan Pinkerton[8] also mentions the Universal Brotherhood and the Ancient Order of United Workmen. The former might refer to the Industrial Brotherhood but the latter was a purely fraternal order, organised in 1868.

The depression also cleared the field for a revolutionary movement. Socialism emerged for the first time from the narrow circle of the refugees from Europe, extended its organisations, and made its appeal to the American workingmen. It found, however, that in order to succeed it had to dislodge the philosophy of greenbackism which the American wage-earning class was recognising as its official expression of opinion. Although the secret organisations, unlike the remnants of the trade unions of the sixties, refused to join the farmers in the " Independent "

5 *Doc. Hist.*, X, 23.
6 See above, II, 181 *et seq.*
7 See above, II, 171 *et seq.*

8 Pinkerton, *Strikers,   Communists, Tramps and Detectives*, 89.

or " Greenback " party which was formed in 1875, still the sway held over them by the greenback philosophy was none the less effective. In the Pittsburgh convention of 1876, to be mentioned below, both groups of organisations, the secret and the socialist, came together in an endeavour to consolidate the labour movement.

The Noble Order of the Knights of Labor, although it first became important in the labour movement after 1873, was formed by Uriah Smith Stephens in 1869. From that year until 1878 it maintained extreme secrecy. Stephens was born in 1821 at Cape May, New Jersey, and, although educated for the Baptist ministry, was compelled to learn the tailoring trade for a living. He also taught school for a time. His intellectual experience was broadened by a journey to Europe in the sixties and there he doubtless came in touch with the Marxian Internationalists.[9]

Stephens organised the first assembly in Philadelphia, December 26, 1869. He and the others were members of a garment cutters' union organised in 1862 or 1863. It seems that, after exercising " considerable influence in the trade," the union declined.[10] Stephens contended that the union could regain its old standing by shielding the organisation and its members with the veil of secrecy.[11] With this purpose in mind, he attempted to secure the dissolution of the old open union of the tailors, and to form, with those who cared to join, a new secret society.[12] The rivalry became so intense that the old union forbade any of its members to join any other association of their branch of trade, open or secret, under penalty of expulsion.[13]

As a preliminary attempt at organisation, Assembly 1 (this was the designation adopted for the local bodies and was retained throughout the existence of the Order) allowed men of all callings to join, receiving the same privileges as the garment

---

[9] In the eighties there was a "legend" current among the American socialists, saying that the Internationalist, J. George Eccarius, had supplied Stephens with a set of Marx's writings, including the *Communist Manifesto*. It is plain, however, that he did not adopt the essential ideas of Marx. But see *Der Sozialist* (New York). Mar. 3, 1888.

[10] McNeill, *Labor Movement: The Problem of To-day*, 397.

[11] Powderly, *Thirty Years of Labor*, 134.

[12] McNeill, *Labor Movement: The Problem of To-day*, 401.

[13] *Ibid.* This union, four years later, joined the Knights of Labor.

cutters, except that they were not allowed to participate in trade matters. Neither were they required to pay dues. It was expected that these " sojourners " would act as missionaries and organise and instruct their fellow tradesmen. The decision to admit non-garment cutters to membership was a compromise, as the most radical members wanted the assembly " thrown open to workingmen of every trade or calling." [14] For the succeeding year and a half this new secret society, through its mysterious action, attracted more attention than its membership or accomplishments warranted. [15]

The principles of the Order were set forth by Stephens in the secret ritual. " Open and public association having failed after a struggle of centuries to protect or advance the interest of labor, we have lawfully constituted this Assembly," and " in using this power of organised effort and co-operation, we but imitate the example of capital heretofore set in numberless instances," for, " in all the multifarious branches of trade, capital has its combinations, and whether intended or not, it crushes the manly hopes of labor and tramples poor humanity into the dust." However, " we mean no conflict with legitimate enterprise, no antagonism to necessary capital." The remedy consists first in work of education : " We mean to create a healthy public opinion on the subject of labor, (the only creator of values or capital) and the justice of its receiving a full, just share of the values or capital it has created." The next remedy is legislation : " We shall with all our strength, support laws made to harmonise the interests of labor and capital, for labor alone gives life and value to capital, and also those laws which tend to lighten the exhaustiveness of toil." Next in order are mutual benefits. " We shall use every lawful and honorable means to procure and retain and employ for one another, coupled with a just and fair remuneration, and, should accident or misfortune befall one of our number, render such aid as lies within our power to give, without inquiring his country or his creed." [16]

From the beginning up to July, 1872, all attempts at organis-

14 Powderly, *Thirty Years of Labor*, 143.

15 Meetings were announced by five stars, a circle enclosing a triangle being marked on sidewalks, fences, and walls.

At other times a call for a meeting would appear in a newspaper anonymously signed.

16 *Doc. Hist.*, X, 23, 24.

ing additional assemblies proved unsuccessful. However, by May, 1873, six assemblies were organised, most of them composed of textile workers and all located in Philadelphia. [17] In order to secure concerted action on matters pertaining to the "welfare of the whole," a committee on "good of the Order" was established.[18] This was the precursor of the "district assembly."

With the expansion of the Order outside Philadelphia and into bordering States, the need for a permanent central body began to be felt. So on Christmas day of 1873, District Assembly 1 was founded with thirty-one assemblies attached to it. The ritual and other work of the Order were now put into written form, and the organisation was complete.

Henceforth the growth of the Order in the East was steady and promising. The desire of the leaders to make the Order universal prompted them to turn westward. Here they interested John M. Davis, editor of the *National Labor Tribune,* of Pittsburgh, who took up the work west of that city. In the meantime (October 4, 1874) District Assembly 2 of Camden, New Jersey, was founded, and on August 8, 1875, District Assembly 3 of Pittsburgh was organised. This planted the Order in the industrial section of the United States and enabled it to reach wage-earners everywhere. It is very difficult to estimate the membership, as no provision was made for any central record, each district assembly having absolute control of its membership. The Order may have counted about 5,000 members, but the membership at this time, as well as throughout the existence of the Order, fluctuated enormously. Individuals or trade unions would join, and finding that the organisation could not or did not help them, they lost interest in it. John McBride, who was the paramount miners' leader during the eighties and early nineties and became president of the American Federation of Labor during 1894, corroborates this statement as follows: "Miners organised very generally into it for a while, in localities, but as it never seemed to show, on the surface, of anything being done to raise the price of mining, they fell off about as rapidly as they organised." [19]

---

[17] Powderly, *Thirty Years of Labor,* 183.

[18] *Ibid.,* 164.

[19] McNeill, *Labor Movement: The Problem of To-day,* 251.

The Knights of Labor received their recruits from two sources. With the disruption of most of the national trade unions in 1873, many of the surviving locals found it to their interest to affiliate with the Knights of Labor. This was true of an especially large number of locals which formerly belonged to the Miners' National Association,[20] the Machinists and Blacksmiths' national union, the Knights of St. Crispin, and the Ship Carpenters' and Caulkers' national union. The other sources of strength were in unattached locals which never belonged to a national trade union, such as silver gilders, brush makers, stationary engineers, cooks, garment workers, and carpet weavers. Most of these locals existed before the Knights came on the scene, although some were organised through their efforts.

The data as to the activities of the Knights during this period are meagre. The membership clustered mainly around the industrial centres of Pennsylvania, Indiana, Ohio, Illinois, Maryland, New York, New Jersey, and Massachusetts, but did not extend further west than the region of Pittsburgh.

Most of the district assemblies had compulsory strike funds, and as strikes, in the coal region especially, were resorted to frequently, these funds must have been used considerably. Patrick McBride, in his history of the coal miners,[21] gives two instances in which district assemblies resorted to strikes during this period.

It was understood from the outset among all who owed allegiance to the Knights of Labor that sooner or later a national organisation was to be formed.[22] In the meantime, District Assembly 1 of Philadelphia, was, by tacit consent of the other branches, to be recognised as head of the Order.[23] However, District Assembly 3 of Pittsburgh, owing to its location and leaders,[24] as a matter of course became at first the chief representative of the Order in the West. Later, meeting with " phenomenal success in organising new assemblies, and districts," [25] it began to consider itself not only equal to Dis-

---

20 *Ibid.*, 251.
21 *Ibid.*, 252, 261.
22 Powderly, *Thirty Years of Labor*, 192.
23 General Assembly, *Proceedings*, 1878, p. 3.

24 John M. Davis, editor of the *National Labor Tribune*, at this time one of the most influential labour papers, was chief organiser and district master workman of District Assembly 3.
25 Powderly, *Thirty Years of Labor*, 192.

trict Assembly 1, but even superior. As time went on, this feeling of disunion was accentuated, since the officers of District Assembly 3 were obliged to make their own " passwords, and in many other ways . . . to depend on themselves for aid which should come from the officers of District Assembly 1, who were too busily engaged in the work of organising the eastern cities and towns." [26] Resulting from this rivalry the first attempts to establish a national organisation proceeded simultaneously from two independent centres, each claiming to be the legitimate head of the Order.

One of the important issues which forced to the front the matter of national organisation was the question of secrecy. The disadvantages of absolute secrecy began to tell in the middle of the seventies when the criminal activities of the Molly Maguires threw an odium upon secret labour societies in general.

The Catholic Church, especially in that region where the Molly Maguires operated, also joined the employers and the public in opposing the " extreme " secrecy of the Order. At the same time complaints were made in some sections of the Order that secrecy was hindering the work of organisation. As early as 1875, District Assembly 1 received a petition from the flint glass-blowers' Local Assembly 82, of Brooklyn, picturing the difficulties under which " it laboured in securing members," and winding up by asking that District Assembly 1 " take steps to make the name of the Order public, so that workingmen would know of its existence." [27]

However, before the Knights definitely decided for independent national organisation, they were active participants in an attempt to bring together all labour orders for the purpose of creating a consolidated national organisation. The initiative for this move came from another secret organisation, the Junior Sons of '76.

This was a " partially secret " order, organised in Pittsburgh in May, 1874.[28] It purported to be a national organisation, but in reality its membership was practically confined to the State of Pennsylvania. Like all labour reform organisations of the time, it placed the demand for money reform at the

26 *Ibid.*, 191, 192.
27 *Ibid.*, 224.

28 Pittsburgh *National Labor Tribune,*
Oct. 31, 1874.

head of its programme.[29] The other issues specifically mentioned were the recall of public officials and opposition to the militia. The tariff policy was left to the different congressional districts to decide for themselves. The Junior Sons of '76 advocated independent political action, and, to this end, the constitution provided for organisation by political units, local lodges, county assemblies, district assemblies, State conventions, and the national convention of the Junior Sons of '76 of the United States of America. Each subdivision " when compatible with the public good and the best interest of the Order," was to nominate candidates for public office, from the president of the United States down to county officers. To guard against destruction coming from within, it was provided that " no strictly professional person, practical politician, speculator, corporator or monopolist, be admitted without a four-fifth vote of all the active members of the lodge." The leading spirits in the Order were John M. Davis, the editor of the Pittsburgh *National Labor Tribune,* and D. D. Dunham, Altoona, Pennsylvania.

The sphere of activity of the Order as such seems to have been limited, but, since it counted among its members a number of the prominent labour leaders in Pennsylvania, its influence was not inconsiderable. It thus took the initiative in bringing together all of the existing labour organisations and called a national convention to meet December 28, 1875 at Tyrone, Pennsylvania.[30]

The invitation was accepted, not only by the Knights of Labor, but also by the Social Democratic party of North America. This was the first appearance of socialism as an active participant in the American labour movement, after many years of struggle within the ranks of socialists on points of doctrine and methods of organisation. These struggles, although unknown to the public and even to the labour movement at the time, were important on account of their ultimate effect on trade unionism and the labour movement.

29 The platform, however, did not advocate Kellogg's scheme of interchangeable bonds and paper money. It merely set up the demand for an " enlightened system of financial management in harmony with the interests of the producing masses . . . [as being] of absolute importance and as the only means of averting coming disaster to the industrial and commercial interests." *Constitution of the Junior Sons of '76* (Leaflet).

30 Pittsburgh *National Labor Tribune,* Jan. 8, 1876.

CHAPTER II

REVOLUTIONARY BEGINNINGS

The International Workingmen's Association. Its emphasis on trade unionism, 204. Its attitude towards political action, 205. Lassalle's programme and the emphasis on political action, 206. Forerunners of the International in America, 206. The Communist Club, 206. F. A. Sorge, 207. The General German Workingmen's Union and its Lassallean programme, 207. The Social party of New York and Vicinity, 208. Failure and reorganisation, 209. Union 5 of the National Labor Union and Section 1 of the International, 209. New sections of the International, 209. The Central Committee, 210. The native American forerunner of the International, 210. Section 12, and its peculiar propaganda, 211. Rupture between the foreigners and Americans in the International, 211. The Provisional Federal Council, 212. The two rival Councils, 212. Decision of the General Council in London, 213. American Confederation of the International and its attitude on the question of the powers of the General Council, 213. The North American Federation of the International, 214. The Internationalist Congress at The Hague and the defeat of Bakunin by Marx, 214. Transfer of the General Council to New York, 215. Secession of a majority of the European national federations, 215. Section 1 of New York and the Local Council, 216. Abolition of the Local Council, 216. National Convention of 1874 and the resolution on politics, 218. The secession of six sections, 217. Adolph Strasser, 218. Panic and unemployment, 219. Organisation of the unemployed, 219. The riot on Tompkins Square, 220. John Swinton, 220. Organisation among the unemployed in Chicago, 220. Section 1 of New York and the struggle for the control of the *Arbeiter-Zeitung*, 221. The United Workers of America, 222. P. J. McDonnell, 222.

The International and the Trade Union Movement. Lack of response among the native American workingmen, 223. Success among the Germans, 223. *Die Arbeiter-Union*, 223. Adolph Douai, 224. Temporary sway of greenbackism among the Germans, 224. Victory of the ideas of the International, 225. The Franco-Prussian War and the discontinuance of *Die Arbeiter-Union*, 225. Organisation of the furniture workers, 225. German-American Typographia, 226. Amalgamated Trades and Labor Council of New York, 226.

Lassalleanism and Politics. Effect of the industrial depression on the spread of Lassalleanism, 227. The Labor party of Illinois and its form of organisation, 228. Its attitude toward trade unionism and politics, 228. Temporary Lassalleanisation of the sections of the International in Chicago, 229. The Labor party of Illinois in politics, 229. Overtures to farmers, 230. Return to the principles of the International, 230. The Lassallean movement in the East — The Social Democratic party of North America, 230. The first national convention, 231. Peter J. McGuire, 231. Reasons for Strasser's joining the Lassalleans, 231. The *Sozial-Demokrat*, 232. Change of sentiment in favour of trade unionism, 232. The second convention of the Social Democratic party and the partial return to the tenets of the International, 233. Attempts towards unification, 233. The remaining divergence of ideas, 233. Preparations for the national labour conventions in Pittsburgh, 234.

THE INTERNATIONAL WORKINGMEN'S ASSOCIATION

MODERN American socialism began after the Civil War. The socialistic movement during the fifties among the early German immigrants, the so called "forty-eighters," had been on the whole no less utopian than the native American Fourierism during the forties. The Weitling movement,[1] which started in 1850 with the idea of a central bank of exchange, changed during the next year to a programme of socialistic colonisation upon the Fourierite pattern. Similarly, a German Workingmen's Alliance, which grew out of the movement of the unemployed in 1857, in so far as it possessed a programme of action, aimed to bring about a co-operative social order through an appeal to all, without distinction of classes. Only for a short time during 1853 and 1854, which coincided with a period of general aggressive trade union movement in the principal cities, did the Marxian conception of the aims of a labour movement occupy the foreground among the German immigrants of this country. The short-lived General (or American) Workingmen's Alliance, which was established by Joseph Weydemeyer, a close friend of Karl Marx, in April, 1853, in New York City, was based upon the principle of class struggle and recognised the necessity of trade unionism and of political action.

The anti-slavery movement and the War absorbed all that remained of idealism of the "forty-eighters," and the socialist movement was obliged to begin over again in the sixties. The new movement, however, was radically different from the old, not only in its continuous existence, but also in its very nature. It received its impulse from two new sources in Europe: the International Workingmen's Association, founded by Karl Marx in London in 1864, and the Lassallean agitation in Germany, begun in 1863. The first was economic, the second political. The International is generally reputed to have been organised

[1] See above, I, 512 *et seq.*, 567 *et seq.*

by Karl Marx for the propaganda of international socialism. As a matter of fact, its starting point was the practical effort of British trade union leaders to organise the workingmen of the continent and to prevent the importation of continental strike-breakers. That Karl Marx wrote its *Inaugural Address* was merely incidental. It chanced that what he wrote was acceptable to the British unionists rather than the draft of an address representing the views of Mazzini which was submitted to them at the same time. Marx emphasised the class solidarity of labour against Mazzini's harmony of capital and labour. He did this by reciting what British labour had done through the Rochdale system of co-operation without the help of capitalists, and what the British parliament had done in enacting the ten-hour law of 1847 against the protest of capitalists. Now that British trade unionists in 1864 were demanding the right of suffrage and laws to protect their unions, it followed that Marx merely stated their demands when he affirmed the independent economic and political organisation of labour in all lands. His *Inaugural Address* was a trade union document, not a *Communist Manifesto*.[2] Indeed not until Bakunin and his following of anarchists had nearly captured the organisation in the years 1869 to 1872 [3] did the programme of socialism become the leading issue.

The philosophy of the International at the period of its ascendency was based on the economic organisation of the working class in trade unions and co-operative societies. These must precede the political seizure of the government by labour. Then, when the workingmen's party should achieve control, it would be able to build up successfully the socialist state on the foundation of a sufficient number of existing trade unions and co-operative societies.

This conception differed widely from the teaching of Ferdinand Lassalle. Lassallean socialism was born in 1863 with Lassalle's *Open Letter* to a workingmen's committee in Leipzig. It

---

[2] See Jaeckh, *Die Internationale.* Karl Marx, in his letter to F. Bolte, says: " Die Internationale wurde gestiftet, um die wirkliche Organization der Arbeiter-klasse für den Kampf an die Stelle der sozialistischen oder halbsozialistischen Sekten zu setzen. Die ursprünglichen Statuten wie die Inauguraladresse zeigen dies auf den ersten Blick" (*Briefe und Auszüge aus Briefen von Joh. Phil. Becker . . . Karl Marx und A. an F. A. Sorge u. Andere*, 38).

[3] For an excellent account of this struggle, see Hunter's *Violence and the Labor Movement*, 154–193.

sprang from his antagonism to Schulze-Delitzsch's system of voluntary co-operation. In Lassalle's eagerness to condemn the idea of the harmony of capital and labour which lay at the basis of Schulze's scheme for co-operation, he struck at the same time a blow against all forms of economic organisation of wage-earners. Perhaps the fact that he was ignorant both of the British trade unions and of workingmen's co-operation in England accounts for his insufficient appreciation of the economic organisation of wage-earners. But no matter what the cause may have been, to Lassalle there was but one means of solving the labour problem — political action. When political control was finally achieved, the labour party, with the aid of State credit, would build up a network of co-operative societies into which eventually all industry would pass.

In short, the distinction between the ideas of the International and of Lassalle consisted in the fact that the former advocated economic organisation prior to and underlying political organisation, while the latter considered a political victory as the basis of economic organisation. These antagonistic starting points are apparent at the very beginning of American socialism as well as in the trade unionism and socialism of succeeding years.

Two distinct phases can be seen in the history of the International in America. During the first phase, which began in 1866 and lasted until 1870, the International had no important organisations of its own on American soil, but tried to establish itself through affiliation with the National Labor Union. The inducement held out to the latter was of a practical nature: the international regulation of immigration.[4] During the second phase, the International had its sections in nearly every large city of the country, and the practical part of its work receded before its activity on behalf of the propaganda of socialism.

While the International, in the second phase of socialist propaganda, did not establish itself on American soil until 1870, there had been several forerunners. They were of two distinct classes: German and native American. The earliest German forerunner was the Communist Club in New York, a Marxian

4 See above, II, 131, 132.

organisation based on the *Communist Manifesto* and established
October 25, 1857. The membership was not large, but it comprised many who subsequently made themselves prominent in
the American International, such as F. A. Sorge,[5] Conrad
Carl, and Siegfried Meyer. The club kept up connections with
the communist movement abroad, and among its correspondents
we find men like Karl Marx, Johann Philipp Becker of Geneva,
and Joseph Weydemeyer, the last named then residing in this
country. The Club declared itself a section of the International in October, 1867.[6]

The most important German forerunner of the International
was the General German Workingmen's Union (Der Allge-
meine Deutsche Arbeiterverein), which became subsequently
known as Section 1 of New York of the International. It is
noteworthy that it owed its origin to followers of Lassalle, for it
was formed in New York in October, 1865, by fourteen Lassalleans.

The original constitution declared as follows: "Under the
name of the General German Workingmen's Union are united
all Social-Republicans, particularly those who regard Ferdinand
Lassalle as the most eminent champion of the working class, for
the purpose of reaching a true point of view on all social questions. . . . While in Europe only a general revolution can form
the means of uplifting the working people, in America, the education of the masses will instill them with the degree of self-
confidence that is indispensable for the effective and intelligent

5 Sorge was the father of modern socialism in America. Born in Saxony, he
took part in the revolution in Baden in
1849, after which he lived as a refugee in
Switzerland for two years. In 1851 he
went to London and thence to New York.
He earned his living as a music teacher.
At the congress of the International at
The Hague in 1872, Sorge formed a lifelong friendship with Marx and Engels and
became their authorised interpreter in
America, a position which he kept until
his death in 1906. He contributed a
series of articles in the *Neue Zeit* (Stuttgart) during 1890–1895, on the history
of the labour movement in America.

6 *Protokoll des Kommunistischen Klubs
in New York* (1857–1867). MS. in
library of the Rand School of Social Science in New York. The constitution said
that the members "recognise that all men

are created equal regardless of colour or
sect — and that they therefore aspire to
abolish the so-called *bourgeois* property,
both inherited and acquired, in order to
replace it by a reasonable participation in
earthly enjoyment, accessible to all, and
satisfying the needs of all." During the
campaign of 1868 the Club supported the
Social party of New York and Vicinity
which was formed by the Lassallean General German Workingmen's Union, and
Sorge even became president of the Social
party. The last session reported in the
book of minutes was of Oct. 25, 1867.
Evidently the Club did not thrive after
the failure of the Social party, for we find
that in November, 1869, it transferred its
library to the General Workingmen's Union which was then Section 1 of the International in America.

use of the ballot, and will eventually lead to the emancipation of the working people from the yoke of capital." It further provided that "in case of the dissolution of the Union, all Union property shall revert to the General German Workingmen's Union in Germany."

It appears, however, that the New York Union was not very orthodox in its Lassalleanism, for the proceedings show that an address, which was sent in October, 1866, to the Union in Germany, was objected to by a member as smacking too much of the principles of the International. A month later, the Union received an invitation from the county committee of the Republican party to send a delegate to the county nominating convention. The invitation was accepted, and President Weber was elected delegate, but it was made plain to the county committee that the Union would not allow itself to be used as a tool in their hands. In July, 1867, a delegate was sent to the United Cabinet Makers in New York to urge this body to send a delegate to the National Labor Union Congress in Chicago.

In the fall of 1868, the Union, in conjunction with the Communist Club, formed the Social party of New York and Vicinity, with Sorge as president. The party was not an avowedly socialistic party; instead of the abolition of the wage system, it demanded a series of social reform measures, such as the progressive income tax, the abolition of national banks with the right to issue paper money reserved only to the government of the United States, the repeal of all Sunday laws, and an eight-hour law. The constitution provided for two branches of the organisation: an Anglo-American and a German-American. Each branch elected an executive council and the two councils formed the chief executive of the party. The unit of organisation was a ward, club, or trade union. Trade unions were especially requested to join the party, and in case they refused, new trade unions were to be organised in their places.

The duty of the executive council was to promote the organisation of trade unions in trades where none existed, and also of co-operative societies in the field of production and distribution.

The candidates nominated by the Social party evidently made a poor showing in the election of 1868, for there can be found no further trace of the party's existence. Nor can it be definitely established whether the English-speaking working-men, on whose account, evidently, the platform had been toned down, really took part in the organisation. In January, 1869, the Social party reorganised under the old name.[7] It became Union 5 of the National Labor Union in February, and Section 1 of the International in December, 1869. It was also represented by delegates in the German trade union federation of New York — the Deutsche Arbeiter Union.[8]

After the reorganisation, the work of the Union was devoted largely to self-education, propaganda, and especially to the study of *Das Kapital* by Marx, which had just appeared. At the weekly meetings, social and political questions were discussed, and the Union's attitude was expressed in the form of resolutions. One of these resolutions stated that trade unions were extremely useful in preventing further degradation of the working class, but in their present form could not effect radical changes in the social order. Siegfried Meyer was sent as a delegate to the National Labor Union convention in Philadelphia in 1869 with instructions to advocate the eight-hour measure. At that time there were thirty-nine members in the union. Sorge was the representative at the next annual convention of the National Labor Union in Cincinnati and was successful in forcing the passage of a resolution in favour of affiliation with the International. On all other matters, particularly on the eight-hour question, Sorge's resolutions attracted but little attention.

Toward the end of 1870 several other foreign sections of the International were formed. One was French, counting from sixty to seventy members, and another was Bohemian. The three sections drew up a provisional constitution for a central committee and adopted it for one year, beginning with the middle of December, 1870. This gave an impetus to the growth of the International. New sections were formed in New York, Chicago, and Williamsburg.

In New York, the German Social Democratic Workingmen's

[7] Sorge joined at this time. He found it difficult to gain admission, not being a wage-earner, but, once admitted, he soon became the leading spirit.

[8] *Protokoll Buch des Allgemeinen Deutschen Arbeiter Vereins.* MS. in library of the Rand School of Social Science, New York.

Union, which had been formed in September, 1870, by George C. Stiebeling, a prominent socialist journalist, also joined the International as Section 6. Thus in April, 1871, F. A. Sorge, the corresponding secretary of the central committee, was able to report to London the existence of 8 sections with 293 members.[9]

Besides the radical immigrants there was another class of people who welcomed the agitation of the International in America. This was a group of native American intellectuals among whom socialist sentiments had lingered from the Fourierist movement in the forties. In 1869 they formed an organisation called New Democracy, or Political Commonwealth. The principles expressed in their platform dated back to 1850, when one William West, who now became their corresponding secretary, had advocated, in the New York *Daily Tribune,* the referendum and voluntary socialism as the true methods of social reform. The platform of the "New Democracy" likewise laid special stress on the referendum, but the socialism it advocated was not voluntary but state socialism.

The New Democracy sent William West as a delegate to the Philadelphia convention of the National Labor Union. He tried to press the referendum upon the convention, but met with no success. On October 11, 1869, the New Democracy sent to the General Council of the International in London an address, drawn up by Stephen Pearl Andrews,[10] the American anarchist. In it he pointed out that the National Labor Union was twenty years behind the times, and that the New Democracy was the only organisation in the field that understood the situation: "Our organisation can rightfully claim, both through ideas and by immediate personal affiliations, to be the direct successor, if not the actual continuator, of the industrial congress and labour and land reform movement of twenty and twenty-five years ago in the country." [11]

The New Democracy disbanded in 1870, and its members organised in the summer of 1871 two native American sections of the International, No. 9 and No. 12, both in New York City. The latter, headed by two sisters, Victoria Woodhull and Ten-

9 *Copy-book of the International in North America,* 4.

10 *Revolution* (New York), Oct. 28, 1869, p. 260.

11 See above, I, 547 *et seq.*

nessee Claflin, notorious advocates of woman suffrage and "social freedom," became the leading American section, and ultimately caused a split between the foreign and the native American branch of the International.

The Provisional Central Committee of the International Workingmen's Association in America was in the beginning highly successful in centralising and furthering the internationalist propaganda. It was particularly fortunate in its secretary, F. A. Sorge, whose reports [12] to the General Council in London show a thorough understanding of current American events, and particularly of the labour movement. He established intimate connections with the State Workingmen's Assembly of New York, of which William J. Jessup was then president. Friendly relations were also formed with the Miners' Benevolent and Protective Association in the anthracite district of Pennsylvania, which was then involved in a prolonged strike. But the success of the propagandist work among the labour organisations was soon imperilled by the activity of Section 12 and allied English-speaking sections.

In the report to the General Council, dated August 6, 1871, F. A. Sorge said: "Section 12 is rather *diligently* discussing the subject of universal language and working through the press." [13] In the report dated October 1, 1871, he stated: "Section 12 is rather zealous in spreading *its* ideas of the I. W. A. abroad through the medium of 'Woodhull and Claflin's Weekly' and trying to create a favourable public opinion in the circles reached by the above 'Weekly.'" [14] In the letter to R. T. Hinton, corresponding secretary of American Section 26 at Washington, D. C., dated October 10, 1871, it was said: "The manifesto signed by William West and published in a certain 'Weekly,' in behalf of Section 12 of New York City, was published and issued *without* the authority or consent of the Central Committee." [15] In the report to London, dated November 5, 1871, the same writer stated: "A lively and warm discussion has been going on in the different sections in relation to an 'Appeal' issued by Section 12." [16] He described the character of this appeal as follows: "The Woodhull-Claflin

---

12 *Doc Hist.*, IX, 353–370.
13 *Copy-book*, 35.
14 *Ibid.*, 68.
15 *Ibid.*, 55.
16 *Ibid.*, 71.

Section (No. 12) issued a call to the 'citizens of the union' full of empty phraseology. Section 1 protested against it — in vain so far. The right of woman to vote and to hold office, the freedom of sexual relations, universal language, pantarchy were preached by Section 12 and slanders were thrown against all opponents." [17]

The newspapers took it up and the country rocked with laughter. A rupture between the German and American elements in the organisation became imminent. Each tried to win over the General Council in London to its side. Section 12 petitioned the General Council for a permit to constitute itself as the leading section in America, a position hitherto occupied by German Section 1 of New York. The General Council in London rejected the petition, though several of its members, notably John Hales and J. George Eccarius sympathised with the petitioner.

Finally came the split. On November 20, 1871, the delegates of fourteen sections (8 German, 3 Irish, 2 French, and 1 American) met separately and dissolved the Central Committee. Two weeks later they organised a Provisional Federal Council, with a constitution identical with that of the old Central Committee; and finally decided to call a national convention in July to legalise the *coup d'état*. The delegates of Section 12 and certain sympathising sections protested vigorously, and claimed, for a time, to be the regular Central Committee. The other side offered to reunite under the following conditions:

" 1. Only the labor question to be treated in the organisation.

" 2. Only new sections to be admitted, when at least two-thirds of their members are wage laborers.

" 3. Section 12 and sections formed on its 'appeal' to be excluded, as being strangers to the Labor movement." [18]

These conditions, of course, were not acceptable to Section 12 which was entirely composed of intellectuals. It organised, therefore, with the aid of other sympathising sections, a Federal Council of its own. This organisation held meetings sometimes on Prince Street and sometimes on Spring Street, and was

17 Becker, Dietzgen, Engels, Marx, Sorge und andere, *Briefe und Auszüge aus Briefen*, 31.
18 *Copy-book*, 83.

accordingly known either by the name of the Spring Street Federal Council, or the Prince Street Federal Council. The General Council at London appointed a special committee to investigate the state of affairs in America, and, in March, 1872, the decision was handed down ordering the expulsion of Section 12 and the calling of a Union Congress in July, 1872.[19]

Section 12 and adhering sections refused to abide by the decision and called a national conevntion of their own.[20] It met in Philadelphia on July 9, 1872, thirteen sections, mostly English-speaking, being represented, and organised the American Confederation of the International. The following announcement was made to the General Council in London, which put the new " Confederation " squarely in opposition to the Marxians: ". . . While proclaiming ourselves to be in harmony with the working people of the world, we reserve to ourselves the right to regulate this branch of the International Workingmen's Association without dictation from the General Council in London, England, except so far as its decrees may be consistent with the orders of the General (or Universal) Congresses of the Association, in which we may be represented as from time to time they may be held." The opposition to the General Council did not, however, mean an endorsement of the anarchistic views of Bakunin, although the division in America between Sorge and the American believers in extreme freedom was similar to that in Europe between Marx and Bakunin. The Americans believed in politics and made ready for participation in the next political campaign. A delegation of three, headed by William West, was selected to represent the Confederation at the next general congress at The Hague.[21]

19 The conditions prescribed by the decision were as follows:

1. Both councils should unite into one Provisional Federal Council.
2. New and small sections should combine for sending delegates to the central body.
3. On the first of July, a general congress of the International in America should be held.
4. This congress should elect a Federal Council with a right to adopt new members.
5. It should also firmly establish the rules and regulations of the Federal councils.
6. Section 12 should be expelled until the next general congress, to be held at The Hague.
7. Each section must be composed of at least two-thirds of wage-earners.

From the original communication found among Sorge's Mss.

20 John Hales, a member of the National Council for Great Britain, sent a letter to Section 12 with his approval of that course. *Woodhull and Claflin's Weekly*, June 15, 1872.

21 First Congress of the American Confederation of the International Workingmen's Association, *Proceedings*, 1872.

The convention of the regular (Marxian) organisation met a few days later in the same city with 25 delegates from 22 sections, having a total membership of over 900. It declared itself to be in complete harmony with the General Council and emphasised the necessity of a strongly centralised organisation. The constitution, accordingly, gave the Federal Council the power to suspend sections until the next congress, and prescribed that local councils be formed in cities with three or more sections in order further to centralise the propaganda. In contradistinction to its rival, this convention did not recognise the time as ripe for political action, but affirmed in a general way that the duty of the North American Federation of the International was " to rescue the working classes from the influence and power of all political parties and to show that the existence of all these parties is a crime and a threat against the working classes "; and " to combine the working classes for independent common action for their own interest, without imitating the corrupt organisations of the present political parties." [22]   Sorge and Deveure were elected delegates to The Hague.

At the Congress of The Hague, in 1872, only Sorge and West represented their respective organisations; the other delegates could not be present on account of lack of means. The Americans received more than their share of the attention of the struggling factions. The Bakuninists attacked Sorge's credentials but he in turn denied West's right to take his seat. The committee on credentials, which was packed by Marx's supporters, reported favourably on Sorge and threw out West's credentials. West appealed to the Congress, and in the discussion which ensued Sorge gave as the reason why the native American sections were not entitled to representation that the native Americans were practically all speculators, while the immigrants alone constituted the wage-earning class in America. [23]

West did not take his seat. The Marxists carried the congress and expelled Bakunin from the International. Realising, however, that the control was already slipping from their hands,

22 *Copy-book*, 132–141.   *ciation* (The Hague, September, 1872),
23 *Protokoll des 5ten Allgemeinen Kon-*   47, 50. Sorge Mss.
gresses der Internationalen Arbeiter Asso-

they transferred the General Council from London to New York, away from Bakunin's influence, and into the hands of the trustworthy Sorge. It is true, the honour thus conferred upon the American Federation was but empty, for, after this congress, the International rapidly disintegrated in Europe, in consequence of the secession of the various national federations. Still, it helped considerably to prolong the life of the American Federation, and from this point of view the gift was a real one.

While Sorge remained in Europe during the summer and autumn of 1872 the American Federation showed but few signs of life. Matters became more active on his return. He was elected, as a matter of course, general secretary of the International, and went earnestly to work to prevent the seemingly inevitable disintegration of the organisation entrusted to his care. But his duties were far from pleasant. The federations which held the Bakuninist view on organisation felt little inclined to acquiesce either in the expulsion of Bakunin by The Hague congress, or in the transfer of the General Council with enlarged powers to New York. One after another they repudiated the decisions of that Congress, and to Sorge fell the dreary duty of expelling them from the International. The Jurassian Federation, Bakunin's stronghold, set the example of repudiation, and was followed by the federations of Spain, Italy, Belgium, and Holland. In England, likewise, a part of the Federation seceded under the leadership of Hales and Young and formed a rival Federal Council. The Danish Federation decided to remain neutral, but refused to transmit dues. In Germany, the Eisenacher (Marxian) faction of the socialist movement, though it adhered to the International, was too much absorbed in the problems of the German movement to pay much attention to the International with its transatlantic headquarters. In Austria the movement became divided into two struggling factions, and the General Council could expect but little support from this direction. Thus the influence of the General Council in New York hardly extended to the other side of the Atlantic. In September, 1873, the last congress of the International was held in Geneva. The General Council was financially unable to be directly represented, and the Congress adjourned without accomplishing anything.[24]

While in Europe the situation was more than gloomy, in America it looked at first very encouraging. In February, 1873, the German sections of the country had established a weekly paper in New York called the *Arbeiter-Zeitung* which helped to put new life into the work of the Federation. The annoyance from the rival Confederation also ceased, for the latter soon fell into a state of lethargy and died a peaceful death after two more years of nominal existence. However, peace did not last long, for war soon broke out within the Federation. The trouble began over the domineering attitude of Section 1 towards the remaining sections. This section was the oldest in the Federation and controlled all the administrative bodies. It had a clear majority in the General Council and in the board of directors of the *Arbeiter-Zeitung*. The two editors of the paper, Carl and Starke, as well as Sorge, the general secretary, were members. In the Federal Council it had no definite majority, but, since the two Irish members, Cavanaugh and Blissert, owed their seats to Section 1 and voted as it desired, its control of the Federal Council as well as of the General Council, was undisputed. The Irish members had no sections to represent, but were taken in merely in order not to lose complete contact with the Irish workingmen.

Of the central bodies in the various cities, the only one which Section 1 was unable to control was the Local Council in New York City, composed of 5 members, one from each of the 5 sections in the city (Numbers 1, 6, and 8, German, No. 2, French, and No. 3, Scandinavian). Consequently, on July 17, 1873, Section 1 submitted to the Federal Council, to be further submitted to a referendum vote by the sections, a resolution to the effect that there should be no local council in the locality where the Federal Council resided. Meanwhile, it was decided by the sections, upon the recommendation of the Federal Council, that there should be no convention in 1873, and the New York sections elected in August a new Federal Council, with Bolte, of Section 1, as corresponding secretary and Stiebeling,

<hr>

24 The hard uphill fight which Sorge conducted in order to keep the International from falling to pieces is amply attested by his voluminous correspondence with Europe during the time of his tenure of the office of general secretary.

of Section 6, as treasurer. On October 9, the result of the referendum vote became known. It was as follows: ten in favour of the abolition of the Local Council, four against, and two not voting. The four negative votes came from the New York sections. These sections decided to disregard the referendum vote and to retain the Local Council, claiming that the Federal Council had no right to call a vote on a constitutional amendment. As a consequence, the Federal Council suspended Section 8, which contained the leaders of the opposition. The situation became more complicated when it was known that the International Congress in Geneva had decided to leave the General Council in America, and the New York sections were obliged to make nominations for a new General Council. Section 1 tried to postpone the nominations because it felt that the control was slipping away from its hands. When that failed, Bolte resigned as secretary, and Stiebeling took over his duties. The next move of Section 1 was to impeach the Federal Council before the General Council in which it had a safe majority. The General Council responded to the appeal; it set aside the Federal Council and took over its functions until the next national convention, which was set for April 11, 1874, to meet at Philadelphia. It affirmed the suspension of Section 8, also suspended Section 6, and finally ended by expelling Dr. Stiebeling from the International because he, as treasurer of the new Federal Council, had refused to surrender its property.[25]

At the national convention Section 1 was in complete control, for of the 19 sections represented, only Sections 2, 4, 5, 6, and 8 of New York and Section 1 of Williamsburg belonged to the opposition. So that the action of the General Council was upheld and Sections 2 and 5 were suspended. The spokesman for the opposition was a recent immigrant from Germany by the name of Adolph Strasser,[26] the man who, upon becoming president of the Cigar Makers' International Union in 1877, was the first to start a revival in the trade union movement.

[25] Stiebeling, *Ein Beitrag zur Geschichte der Internationale in Nord America;* also *Copy-book,* 326–333.

[26] Adolph Strasser represented Section 5 of New York, which was formed by a secession from Section 1. Strasser had probably participated in the labour movement in Germany. He came to America in the early seventies.

The convention changed the form of the organisation by permanently abolishing the Federal Council and putting its functions in the hands of the General Council. A commission of control was established with its seat in Baltimore. These drastic measures were hardly conducive to harmony. The opposition permanently left the International and, as will be seen, formed, in conjunction with a number of Lassalleans, the Social Democratic party of North America, with Strasser as national secretary.

If the convention in Philadelphia failed to reconcile the contending factions, it nevertheless established a landmark in the history of American socialism. For it formulated a position on political action which throughout the seventies one important faction in the movement considered as the classical statement of its position on the question. The resolution was as follows:

" The North American Federation rejects all co-operation and connection with the political parties formed by the possessing classes, whether they call themselves Republicans or Democrats, or Independents, or Liberals, or Patrons of Industry, or Patrons of Husbandry (Grangers), or Reformers, or whatever name they may adopt. Consequently, no member of the Federation can belong any longer to such a party, and whosoever may accept a place or position of one of these parties, without being authorised by his Section and by the Federal Council, will be suspended during the time he keeps this place or position.

" The political action of the Federation confines itself generally to the endeavor of obtaining legislative acts in the interest of the working class proper, and always in a manner to distinguish and separate the workingmen's party from all the political parties of the possessing classes.

" As proper subjects of such legislative action may be considered: The normal working day, the responsibility of all employers in case of accidents, the securing of wages, the abolition of the working of children in manufactories, sanitary measures, the establishment of bureaus of statistics of labor, the abolition of all indirect taxes.

" The Federation will not enter into a truly political campaign or election movement before being strong enough to exercise a perceptible influence, and then, in the first place, on the field of the municipality, town or city (Commune), whence this political movement may be transferred to the larger communities (Counties, States, United States), according to circumstances, and always in conformity with the Congress Resolutions.

" It is evident that during such a municipal or communal movement, demands of a purely local character may be put forth, but these demands must not be contrary in anything to the general demands, and they are to be approved by the Federal Council.

"Considering: That the economical emancipation of the workingmen is the great end to which every political movement ought to be subordinated as a means." [27]

During the later seventies the injunction not to enter " into a truly political campaign or election movement before being strong enough to exercise a perceptible influence " was generally understood by its advocates to mean that no participation in elections should be attempted before a sufficient number of trade unions had been organised and formed into a labour party. The systematic emphasis which, since the time of its first formation in 1864, was laid by the International upon the supreme importance of organising trade unions, proves that to put this construction on the words of the resolution of 1874 was substantially correct.

The strife within the International during 1873–1874 prevented it from taking a leading part in the labour movement which grew out of the financial panic of September, 1873. The agitation among the unemployed became strong in New York towards the end of October. Had the International been harmonious within, it could have led the general movement in the city. However, knowing well its limitations, it took no action as a body. But the Federal Council in an advisory capacity worked out a plan by which its members might effectively assist in the work of relief. The plan suggested that the field should be limited at first to the wards inhabited by the German workmen, which should be organised to demand from the municipality: 1. Employment on public works at customary wages; 2. Advances of either money or food sufficient to last one week to all who suffer actual want; and, 3. That no one shall be ejected from his dwelling for the non-payment of rent. The workingmen in the tenth ward organised on this basis, and began to collect data on unemployment and want. Not all members of the International, however, agreed to this modest plan. Some of them wanted to organise the entire city, and, for this purpose called a mass meeting. The meeting, mostly

[27] Leaflet.

German, could hardly claim to represent all the workingmen of New York, but, nevertheless it elected a Central Committee. Contemporaneously, a meeting of the English-speaking workingmen elected a Safety Committee in which the hitherto slumbering Spring Street Federal Council of the International was largely represented. The Central Committee and the Safety Committee agreed to co-operate, and, after several mass meetings had been held, they called a gigantic demonstration in the form of a procession of unemployed for January 13, 1874.. It was the original plan of the Committee that the parade should disband after a mass meeting in front of the city hall, but this was prohibited by the authorities, and Tompkins Square was chosen as the next best place for the purpose. The parade was formed at the appointed hour, and by the time it reached Tompkins Square it had swelled to an immense procession. Here they were met by a force of policemen and, immediately after the order to disperse had been given, the police charged with drawn clubs. During the ensuing panic, hundreds of workmen were injured.[28] The brutal conduct of the police on Tompkins Square left an indelible impression upon the mind of the main speaker at the meeting, the journalist, John Swinton,[29] and strengthened his already awakened sympathies for the cause of labour. The riot practically put an end to the movement in New York.

A similar movement was started in Chicago by the International sections in conjunction with a few other labour organisations. A grand procession of unemployed was held on December 12, 1873, but without the atrocities of the New York police. The city council promised to do all in its power, but did not

28 New York *Arbeiter-Zeitung*, Jan. 24 and 31, Feb. 7 and 14, 1874; *Copy-book*, 326–333; New York *Times*, Jan. 14, 1874.

29 Swinton was born in 1830 in Scotland and was brought to America at the age of thirteen. He learned the printer's trade in Montreal. In 1850 he removed to New York, where he studied law and medicine, while engaging as a printer. He soon progressed from the composing room to the editorial chair. He was managing editor of the New York *Times* during the Civil War. In 1870 he joined the staff of the New York *Sun* and became in 1871, chief writer on that paper. Fol-

lowing the Tompkins' Square riot, he was nominated by the working people for mayor of New York, but received only a few hundred votes. During the great strikes of July, 1877, he addressed a huge mass meeting in Union Square. In 1880 he made a trip to Europe and met Karl Marx in London. In 1883 he started a weekly paper, *John Swinton's Paper*, for the purpose of advocating the cause of labour. After its discontinuance in 1887, he continued in the field of journalism and remained a champion of labour to the last. He died in 1901.

keep its promise, so that the movement had no practical results, except that it led, as will be seen, to the formation of the Labour party of Illinois, with a Lassallean programme.

No sooner had the strife between Section 1 and the other New York sections been allayed than a new and more serious conflict broke out. The International was suffering the fate of every revolutionary organisation of immigrants who, feeling unable to bring any power to bear upon the government and ruling classes, eventually turn against each other. This time the rebels were members of Section 1, who turned against Sorge on account of the changes he made in the editorial personnel of the *Arbeiter-Zeitung*. Sorge felt dissatisfied with the colourless matter with which the editors, Carl and Starke, filled the columns of the paper, and therefore, persuaded the board of directors to engage Wilhelm Liebknecht to send bi-weekly correspondence from Germany at $10 per month. Carl felt incensed over Sorge's meddling, and began to look for an opportunity to overthrow his influence. The opportunity came with a letter published in *Die Gleicheit* (Vienna), the organ of the Austrian socialists, in which the General Council was accused of having aided by its inaction the faction led by one Oberwinder, later shown to have been a government spy. Carl embraced the chance and accused Sorge of having betrayed the interests of the workingmen in the Austrian controversy. Sorge became weary of the permanent strife and resigned both from the General Council and the board of directors of the *Arbeiter-Zeitung*. However, at the next meeting of the board of directors, he was induced to withdraw his resignation and was promised more influence on the paper. This led Carl and his followers to arrange for a *coup d'état*. They declared the paper to be under the protection of Section 1, and the latter gave Bolte a guard of ten men to defend its possession by force. In retaliation the General Council suspended Section 1, and expelled Carl and Bolte from the International. At the same time it brought action in court against Carl for unlawfully taking possession of the property that belonged to all the German sections in the country. The court decided, January, 1875, against Carl, but the paper was discontinued two months later for lack of support.[30]   The outcome was that the paper was discontinued in March, 1875, and the organisation of the International was wrecked to such a degree that it practically ceased to exist.   No convention was therefore held in 1875. The only encouraging event to the International during 1875 was the affiliation of the United Workers of America, a small organisation of Irish workingmen, headed by J. P. McDonnell,[31] with General Rules identical with those of the International.[32] McDonnell and his associates played an important part in the socialist movement of the next few years, and he became, like Adolph Strasser, one of the pioneers of the new trade union movement. In all other respects the International was rapidly breaking down. Throughout the European countries the workingmen were building up political parties in place of the federations of the International.   In America, the same tendency towards a political party was manifesting itself, so that there was nothing left for the International but to merge itself in such a party.

On July 15, 1876, a congress attended by delegates from nineteen American sections met in Philadelphia and officially dissolved the International Workingmen's Association.[33]

30 *An die Leser und Theilhaber der Arbeiter-Zeitung.* (Pamphlet signed by the board of directors and the Commission of Control of the paper, New York, 1874.)

31 J. P. McDonnell was born in Dublin, Ireland, in a middle-class family. He took part in the Fenian movement and suffered repeated imprisonment, and was closely related to Marx and the International after 1869. He went to The Hague as a representative of Ireland at the Congress of the International, and from there to New York to settle in America. With the dissolution of the International, McDonnell joined its Americanised successor, the Workingmen's party of the United States, and assumed the editorship of the official English organ, the New York *Labor Standard.* In 1877, when the party became the Socialist Labor party, devoted exclusively to politics, he broke away and moved his paper first to Fall River and then to Paterson. In 1878 he organised the International Labor Union with a programme of organising the unskilled. About the same time he became involved in a libel suit for applying the name " scab " to strike-breakers in connection with a textile strike in Pater-

son, and was sentenced to two months' imprisonment and a fine of $500. The latter was promptly paid by a subscription among the workingmen of Paterson. He was again arrested and sentenced to a short term of imprisonment in 1880 for publishing a letter disclosing the terrible conditions existing in the brick-making yards in Paterson. McDonnell remained the foremost leader in the labour movement in New Jersey. He organised the New Jersey State Federation of Trades and Labor Unions in 1883, of which he was chairman for fifteen years, and the trades' assembly of Paterson in 1884, and was responsible for the Labor Day law of the State in 1887, the first law of the kind in the United States. He was a member of the Anti-Poverty Association organised in 1887 by Henry George and Doctor McGlynn. He died in 1906.

32 *General Rules of the Association of United Workers of America* (Pamphlet, New York, 1874) ; *Doc. Hist.*, IX, 376–378.

33 Internationale Arbeiter-Association, *Verhandlungen der Delegirten-Konferenz zu Philadelphia, 15 Juli, 1876* (Pamphlet, New York, 1876).

THE INTERNATIONAL TRADE UNION MOVEMENT

True to its philosophy, the International, as soon as it became firmly established in America, began a campaign having as its object the organisation of new trade unions and the propagation of its principles among the unions that already existed. The success met with among the English-speaking workingmen was anything but gratifying. The strong prejudice aroused by the Commune in Paris was soon turned against the International in this country, and this became mingled with the mocking contempt for the notorious exploits of Section 12. On the other hand, among the non-English-speaking wage-earners, particularly among the Germans, the ideas of the International soon became a potent force. But even there a certain amount of passive resistance was met with on one side from a survival of the Schulze-Delitzsch ideas of voluntary co-operation, which had attained popularity in 1864,[34] and, on the other side, from a strong disposition in favour of greenbackism that proceeded from the general labour movement of the period.

The principal centre of the German trade union movement was New York, where a German trades' assembly called Die Arbeiter Union was formed early in 1866,[35] and became affiliated with the National Labor Union. In June, 1866, several of the largest unions [36] established an *Arbeiter-Union* Publishing Association and issued a paper of the same name, with one Doctor Landsberg as editor. During his brief period of editorship the philosophy of the paper was a curious mixture of trade unionism and the Schulze-Delitzsch system of voluntary co-operation seasoned by a strong aversion to political action.[37] Dr. Landsberg resigned in October,[38] after the New York convention of the National Labor Union had declared for the immediate formation of a labour party. The new editor was a

[34] During 1864–1865 some of the German trade unionists in New York became interested in voluntary co-operation. They established a paper, the *New Yorker Arbeiter-Zeitung*, which espoused the tenets of Hermann Schultze-Delitzsch, who was then at the height of his popularity in Germany as the "apostle of voluntaryism."

[35] Boston *Daily Evening Voice*, Mar. 7, 1866.
[36] The United Cabinet-makers with 2,000 members, the marble cutters' union with 400, the German varnishers, the piano makers, and cigar makers No. 90. *Die Arbeiter-Union* (New York), June 13, 1866.
[37] *Ibid.*, July 11 and 25, 1868.
[38] *Ibid.*, Oct. 31, 1868.

man who subsequently became the most interesting personage in the American socialist movement, Adolph Douai.[39] Under Douai's careful editorship the paper became a real mirror of trade conditions and of the labour movement. It summed up the year 1868 as one during which " labor had wrested bigger concessions than in all of the ten years preceding." [40] His general philosophy was at this time in essence the greenbackism of the National Labor Union. He declared that the chief enemy of labour was capital in the fluid state of money capital, bearing an exorbitant rate of interest.[41] Yet the remedy he offered, while based on Kellogg's idea, was very different from the one officially adopted by the National Labor Union. He insisted that " the government should first raise by a resumption of specie payment the value of the greenbacks to a par with gold and only then install the scheme of the interchangeable bonds and greenbacks," whereby he said, " it would be possible, first, gradually to reduce the rate of interest upon the present national debt without any losses, and second, to protect the value of the new paper money." [42]

Meantime, the influence of the International was growing in the German trades' assembly, being propagated by Sorge and

[39] Adolph Douai was born in 1819 at Altenburg, Germany, in a poor family of French émigrés. He studied in the gymnasium and university and graduated as " candidate in theology." But being too poor to get established as instructor in the University of Jena, his original plan, he accepted a position as a private tutor in the family of a rich Russian land owner and passed the examination for the doctor's degree at the University of Dorpat, Russia. He then returned to Altenburg and established a private school. This idealistic educator was at the same time an ardent social and political reformer, so that the year 1848 found him the leading spirit of the revolution in Altenburg. After the victory of the counter revolution, he successfully defended himself in a trial for high treason, but was obliged immediately thereafter to spend a year in prison for an attack he made upon the government in the press. Coming out of prison he was not allowed to continue his school and therefore migrated to Texas in 1852 and established a small paper in San Antonio. His paper being of the abolitionist tendency, he was obliged to leave San Antonio after three years of hard struggle and went to Boston, where he

established a three-graded school with a kindergarten, the first kindergarten tried in America. However, an imprudent speech made at the commemoration of the death of Humboldt, in which the latter was given special praise for atheism, forced him to leave Boston for Hoboken, N. J., where he became director of the newly founded Hoboken Academy. But his advanced views again prevented a successful teaching career and he soon left and established a school of his own in New York. While in this position, he assumed the editorship of *Die Arbeiter Union,* which he conducted until it went under in 1870, and after eight more years of teaching he became coeditor of the *New Yorker Volkszeitung* at the time of its foundation in 1878. He kept this position until his death in 1888. He became Marxian in the early seventies and was the first populariser of Marxism in America. He enjoyed an authority in the socialist movement second only to that of Sorge. See his autobiography in the *New Yorker Volkszeitung,* No. 4, 1888.

[40] *Die Arbeiter Union,* Jan. 2, 1869.
[41] *Ibid.,* Apr. 3, 1869.
[42] *Ibid.,* Jan. 16, 1869.

Carl, delegates from the General German Workingmen's Union. Douai also fell under their influence and the paper began to print extracts from Marx's *Das Kapital,* along with selections from Kellogg's *Money and other Capital.* Finally, in the summer of 1870 the trades' assembly decided to affiliate with the International in Europe, mainly because this would give it a degree of control over immigration.[43] Furthermore, the delegates to the convention of the National Labor Union of that year were instructed to work for the incorporation into the platform of the demand for government ownership of all means of transportation. However, the instructions included also an endorsement of Kellogg's greenbackism.

The breaking out of the Franco-Prussian War caused strife and confusion in the German movement. The socialistic element placed itself in opposition to the war, in accordance with the manifesto issued by the General Council of the International, and was strongly supported by Douai in his paper. The trades' assembly took the same attitude and issued an address against the war to the " workingmen of New York and vicinity."[44] The separate unions, however, were almost evenly divided on both sides, and the paper, which practically depended only upon private subscriptions, was made to bear the brunt of the fight waged by the patriotic workingmen, and finally succumbed in September, 1870. The last issue named the war as the cause of its death.[45] The dissensions had a similar effect upon the trade unions themselves. Sorge stated in his monthly report to the General Council of the International at London for July, 1871, that " Trade Unions in general hold their own except the German unions, which are unfortunately losing ground presently."[46] The report for October mentioned that " seven German Unions have combined again to maintain the Arbeiter-Union, and the Cabinetmakers' Union (German) of New York City have taken energetic steps to inaugurate an 8-hour movement in their trade and to organise and combine their fellow tradesmen all over the country on a firm basis."[47]

The organisation of the furniture workers was under the complete control of the International. The first national con-

43 *Ibid.,* May 11, 1870.
44 *Ibid.,* July 30, 1870.
45 *Ibid.,* Sept. 17, 1870.

46 *Copy-book,* 33.
47 *Ibid.,* 70.

vention which met in Cincinnati in July, 1873, fully embraced the philosophy of the International in a resolution which " recommended to the workingmen first to organise into trade unions, then to form a labor party in order to elect representatives of the working class to the highest political offices." [48]   The convention declined, however, to accept the proposal made by the cabinetmakers of Liège, Belgium, and transmitted through Sorge, for the international organisation of the trade.   It was feared that the name " International " might carry with it associations which would frighten away from the organisation many American cabinetmakers, who had a strong prejudice against the International Workingmen's Association. [49]

In 1877 the Furniture Workers' National Union had 13 locals in 11 cities with 1,369 members, [50] and the statistics gathered from its members by the largest local, No. 7 of New York, show an average weekly wage of $11.87 [51] with only 1.7 per cent of the total number receiving the wage that was prevalent before the crisis, the remaining 98.3 per cent having their wage reduced 10 to 50 per cent. [52]   In other words, this socialist union fared in the depression no better and no worse than the other trade unions in the country.   The national executive board of the union admitted in the annual report for 1877 that the union had followed a mistaken policy of conducting its agitation only among the Germans. [53]   The other German national union, the German-American Typographia, also organised in 1873, was a non-socialist union, notwithstanding that its official organ expressed sympathy with socialism. [54]   One-third of the membership in Chicago were socialists. [55]

The Trades and Labour Council of New York was reorganised in April, 1876, upon the initiative of the German trade unions.   J. G. Speyer and J. P. McDonnell, both members of the International, were the leading spirits in the new body.   It is significant that in order not to frighten away the American unions, no socialist phraseology appeared in the Declaration of Principles.   This once more bears out the contention that the

48 New York *Arbeiter-Zeitung*, July 26, 1873.
49 *Ibid.*
50 Chicago *Vorbote*, Dec. 15, 1877.
51 Of its members, 47½ per cent had steady work.
52 *Ibid.*, Feb. 4, 1876.
53 *Ibid.*, Dec. 15, 1877.
54 *Ibid.*, Jan. 6, 1877.
55 *Ibid.*, May 16, 1876.

International in America placed the organisation of workmen into trade unions above the interests of the socialist propaganda.[56]

LASSALLEANISM AND POLITICS

As shown above, the first Lassallean organisation was formed in this country in 1865, but in 1868, after an unsuccessful first attempt in politics, it reorganised as a section of the International. The great prosperity from 1869 to 1873 and the rapid growth of the trade unions during these years, which was true equally of the industries employing immigrant German, French, or Bohemian labour, and native American labour, minimised the influence of the Lassallean ideas among the immigrant masses. Accordingly, as already stated, the International held undisputed sway over the foreign labour movement during these years. The crisis of 1873 brought a radical change in the situation. The rapid disintegration of the trade union movement tended to throw discredit upon the possibilities of trade unionism in general and correspondingly brought into the foreground the idea of political action. The beginning of Lassallean influence, therefore, dates from the year 1873. The organisations which were more or less tinged with Lassallean ideas were the Labor Party of Illinois in the West and the Social Democratic Party of North America in the East.

The socialist movement in Chicago after the Civil War was second in importance only to that of New York. During the fifties, Joseph Weydemeyer had formed there a small Marxian group, which was represented at a congress of German radicals in 1863. But the subsequent arrivals from Germany turned the movement into the Lassallean channel. At the convention of the National Labor Union in Baltimore in 1866, a delegate of a German workingmen's union in Chicago, Schläger,[57] spoke in favour of political action in the Lassallean sense. Nevertheless, the same organisation joined the International in 1870, as did another similar organisation in Chicago in the same year. The movement of the unemployed during the winter of 1873, and the slight consideration received at the hands of the city

56 New York *Sozial-Demokrat*, Apr. 29, 1876.
57 *Doc. Hist.*, IX, 128.

government, strengthened the feeling in favour of political action, and led to the formation of the Labor party of Illinois in January, 1874. In the following month, the party began to publish a weekly paper called *Vorbote*,[58] under the editorship of a Lassallean, Karl Klinge. The platform of the party[59] contained, among the typical labour demands such as child labour and prison labour laws, a demand for the state owner-ship of the means of transportation, the abolition of monopolies and, most important of all, the purely Lassallean demand for state aid to co-operative societies.

In form of organisation, the Labor party resembled the International. The smallest unit was a section of at least twen-ty-five persons speaking the same language, of whom two-thirds must be workingmen. The sections were grouped in divisions by locality or language, a local committee heading the organisa-tion where there was more than one division in the city. Prac-tically the total membership lived in Chicago, composing twen-ty-two sections, fifteen German, three Polish, three Bohemian, and one American at the time of the first convention in March, 1874. The executive committee was likewise composed, with only one exception, of persons of foreign birth.

The attitude toward trade unionism bore the stamp of ex-treme Lassalleanism. The *Vorbote* declared in the first issue that " in Chicago, organisation into societies similar to gilds is entirely abandoned, for it is generally conceded that it never led to any lasting betterment for the workingmen in the several trades. It is now therefore being attempted to work through socialist labour clubs." Also overtures were made to the farm-ers as possible political allies.[60]

The General Council of the International, in the report to the second national convention in Philadelphia, wrote as fol-lows regarding the Chicago situation: " The movement in Chicago is hardly flowing in our channel, since the demands

---

[58] The paper still exists in Chicago as the weekly edition of the *Chicagoer Ar-beiter-Zeitung*.

[59] Chicago *Vorbote*, Feb. 14, 1874.

[60] In the first issue, Feb. 14, 1874, the Chicago *Vorbote* said: " The German la-bour movement in the cities sympathises with the farmers' unions and will aid to enact into law their just demands." And in the issue for May 16 following, it said: " Let all narrow minded people . . . decry the alliance of the direct slaves of capital [the wage-earners] with its indi-rect ones [the farmers] as a small master compact; our movement will continue to grow in spite of the protests of these ex-ceedingly orthodox people."

which it puts forth bear only a slight proletarian character, and the local paper promises a policy of either passing the trade union movement by in complete silence, or even attacking it." [61] Evidently, the few International sections in Chicago which still retained their allegiance to the International also became imbued with the Lassallean faith. In reply to a protest made by Section 3, Chicago, against the charge of having forsaken the workingmen's movement, the General Council pointed out in a letter dated June 3, 1874, that the demand for anti-monopoly legislation did not sufficiently differentiate a labour party from other master workman parties, and added the following characteristic passage:

" It appears strange that we should have to point out to a section of the International the usefulness and extraordinary importance of the trade union movement. Nevertheless, we shall remind Section 3 that each of the congresses of the I. W. A., from the first to the last, diligently occupied itself with the trade union movement and sought to devise means of furthering it. The trade union is the cradle of the labour movement, for working people naturally turn first to that which affects their daily life, and they consequently combine first with their fellows by trade. It therefore becomes the duty of the members of the International not merely to assist the existing trade unions and, before all, to lead them to the right path, *i.e.*, to internationalize them, but also to establish new ones wherever possible. The economic conditions are driving the trade union with irresistible force from the economic to the political struggle, against the propertied classes,— a truth which is known to all those who observe the labour movement with open eyes." [62]

The points in controversy between the Internationalists and Lassalleans in America hardly require a better illustration.

The Labor party of Illinois entered upon its political career in the municipal election in Chicago in the spring of 1874. Candidates were nominated only for the north side, in order to concentrate the forces on a small area. But the success was only moderate. The ticket did not poll more than a thousand votes. However, the *Vorbote* claimed that this was largely in consequence of fraudulent practices by the old parties. Two months later, in June, the Labor party sent, upon invitation, three delegates to a farmers' convention at Springfield with in-

61 New York *Arbeiter-Zeitung*, May 9, 1874.
62 Sorge's correspondence, 177.

structions to effect a working agreement with the farmers' organisations.[63]   The convention, however, proved a disappointment. It was dominated by professional politicians and greenbackers who opposed an agreement with the Labor party.[64]

At the congressional election in the autumn the Labor party nominated a full ticket, and again the official returns gave it only 785 votes instead of the 2,500 it claimed to have cast. Despair began to take possession of the most active. The membership began to fall off and eight sections dissolved during the next four months. The *Vorbote* still continued to agitate for co-operative societies with state credit, but the prevailing disappointment with politics soon brought on a reaction from Lassalleanism to the principles of the International. In April, 1874, the Lassallean editor of the *Vorbote,* Karl Klinge, was retired and Conrad Conzett,[65] a member of the International, was elected in his place. With the advent of Conzett, the paper substituted the advocacy of trade unionism for Lassalleanism, with the outcome that its circulation immediately began to go up. In June a joint committee was elected by the Labor party on the one hand and by the two surviving sections of the International on the other, to draw up conditions of fusion. It drew up a platform wholly in the spirit of the International, which was ratified by the Labor party, notwithstanding the opposition of the Lassalleans. The participation in the elections of the past was declared to have been a mistake in tactics, and political action was deferred to such a time as the party should be sufficiently strong to make a respectable showing.[66] Accordingly, the united party took no part in the fall election of 1875.

The experiment with Lassalleanism in the East, the Social Democratic party of North America, founded in May, 1874, bore a less pronounced Lasallean character than the Labor party of Illinois. As was seen, it grew out of a combination of a few sections which formed the opposition at the second national convention of the International and several Lassallean groups, including the newly established Labor party of Newark,

63 Chicago *Vorbote,* June 6, 1874.
64 *Ibid.,* June 20 and July 18, 1874.

65 Conzett was a printer by trade and migrated to the United States in 1859.
66 Chicago *Vorbote,* June 5, 1875.

New Jersey. The party held its first convention in New York in the beginning of July following, at which the Lassallean philosophy predominated. Not only was it fully agreed that the workingmen must centre their efforts upon political action, but the platform included a plank demanding the " abolition of all monopolies in transportation, commerce, industry, mining and agriculture, and their operation by democratically constituted co-operative associations with the aid of the credit and supervision of the state." [67] Two men, who later achieved the greatest prominence in the trade union movement, were chosen national officers of the party: Adolph Strasser, cigar maker, was made national secretary, and P. J. McGuire, carpenter,[68] member of the executive board.

Strasser's defection to the Social Democratic party might be interpreted as a repudiation of the principles of the International. In reality, however, he never had forsaken the trade union tenets of the International, but doubtless was driven into the arms of the Lassalleans by many considerations, some of them of a positive, others of a negative character. His practical mind certainly could not help tracing the incessant internal strife within the International to its true source, namely, its nearly complete isolation from American life. He must have felt that, above all, the movement needed to be Americanised: first, in order that it might be restored to a normal life and, second, and by far the more important consideration, that it might be made attractive to the American wage-earners. His allies, the Lassalleans, starting out from their philosophy of political action, were just as keenly alive, if for a different reason, to the necessity for nationalising the movement. Consequently, they were in perfect agreement as far as first steps were concerned. Furthermore, since Strasser was firmly convinced that the need for trade unions was inevitably dictated by the exigencies of American working-class life, it is not at all un-

[67] New York *Social-Demokrat*, Nov. 28, 1874.

[68] *Ibid.*, Dec. 12, 1874.

Peter J. McGuire was born in New York City in 1852, of Irish parents. He received an education above an average workingman's, having studied nights in the Cooper Institute and also in an evening high school. In 1867 he became apprenticed to a wood-joiner and in 1872, joined the union of his trade. Here the able young Irishman fell under the intellectual influence of the German-speaking socialists and started on his remarkable career as one of the small circle of leaders to whom the American Federation of Labor owes its life and success. He died in 1914.

likely that he felt certain of his ability to convert the Lassalleans to trade unionism by compromising with them on the question of political action.

P. J. McGuire was but a young man of twenty-two, when he joined the Lassalleans, and was only learning his first lessons about the labour movement. The fact that at this time he became affiliated with a political party which held a negative attitude towards trade unionism does not particularly call for a reconciliation with his later purely trade union career.

Soon, however, the party's attitude on the crucial questions of trade unionism and politics began to give trouble. Dr. G. C. Stiebeling was the spokesman for the Internationals. He stated his point of view in the *Sozial-Demokrat,* the official party organ, appearing in New York, as follows: "We possess here complete freedom of speech, press and meeting; consequently, we may carry on our agitation untrammelled. Let us Germans set the good example. Let us organise a political party and try, in accordance with our means, to draw our English-speaking brethren with us." So far all agreed, but there was no such general agreement upon what he further proceeded to say: "At present we have an official organ and an executive committee, which is elected by the membership of the Social Democratic party. If, however, this will have to be changed when the trade unions will become more numerous and better organised, then the movement will be absolutely directed from the Central Committee of the Amalgamated Trade Unions." [69]

The executive board was pro-trade union, although the convention had passed the question by in complete silence. October 27, 1874, it passed a resolution asking the trade unions for their close co-operation with the party.[70] On the other hand, the editor of the paper, Gustav Lyser, was a dogmatic Lassallean and hostile to trade unions. Lyser's position became untenable from the standpoint of the party when it at last succeeded in establishing friendly relations with the National Furniture Workers' Union,[71] and he was in consequence removed by the executive board in March, 1875. The paper changed under the new management from hostility toward trade unions

69 *Ibid.,* Jan. 3, 1875.
70 *Ibid.,* Dec. 12, 1874.
71 The New York *Sozial-Demokrat* be-
came the official organ of the union after the discontinuation of the New York *Arbeiter-Zeitung* in January, 1875.

to friendliness, but the essentially Lassallean overtures for the political support of the small property owners continued as before.

The next convention met in July, 1875. Delegates came from New York, Philadelphia, Brooklyn, Newark, Williamsburg, Cleveland, Detroit, and Evansville. The convention adopted a positive trade union policy in the following words: " The convention declares that under the present conditions the organisation of working people into trade unions is indispensable, and that each party member is obliged to become a member of the union of his trade or to aid in establishing a trade union, if none exists." [72] Furthermore, the convention expelled Lyser from the party in punishment for his attack on trade unionism in the Milwaukee *Sozialist,* of which he had in the meantime become editor. The convention also decided to found an English paper as soon as possible and to choose a Marxian, Dr. Otto Walster, of Dresden, as permanent editor of the *Sozial-Demokrat.*[73]

Thus, by the middle of 1875, the secessionist movement, both in Chicago and the East, had travelled a considerable distance back to the original ideas of the International. The time was ripening for a reunion of the factions of the socialist movement.

Attempts at unification began during 1875. In Chicago, this was practically accomplished between the sections of the International and the Labor party of Illinois as early as the middle of 1875, and the union committee of that city tried repeatedly to crown its work by bringing about union on a national scale. In New York, general conferences were held between the International, the United Workers, and the Social-Democratic party.

The International and its English-speaking branch, the United Workers, desired to maintain an international form of organisation while the Social-Democratic party contended that no advantage was to be derived from international affiliations.[74] Again this difference was caused by a more fundamental difference of opinion on the question of labour tactics. The International, primarily bent on building up strong trade unions, wished to establish an organisation that would do for them pre-

[72] New York *Sozial-Demokrat,* July 25, 1875.

[73] *Ibid.*

[74] Chicago *Vorbote,* Dec. 25, 1875.

cisely what the old International had done for the trade unions in England; that is, protect them from the international competition of cheaper labour. On the other hand, the majority among the Social Democrats for the present continued to think in terms of the Lassallean philosophy on the question of labour politics and aimed at immediate political action. Consequently, they found that a strictly national form of organisation would better suit their purpose. No agreement could be reached, and the fusion of the organisation would probably have been postponed, had it not been for the approaching national labour convention in Pittsburgh. The good prospect of a socialist victory at that convention impelled the contending sides to unite in order to force an entering wedge for socialism into the English-speaking labour movement. The *Sozial-Demokrat* [75] proposed that the united socialists should offer for acceptance by the congress a strictly Lassallean platform, but, at a joint conference which was held in Pittsburgh several days before the opening of the convention, a programme of action as advocated by the International gained the upper hand.

75 Feb. 20, 1876.

CHAPTER III

ATTEMPTED UNION — THE PITTSBURGH
CONVENTION OF 1876

The preliminary convention at Tyrone, Pennsylvania, and the two reports on a platform, 235. Discontinuity of the Pittsburgh convention from all preceding labour conventions, 236. The socialist draft of a platform, 237. The Greenback draft by the committee on resolutions, 237. Victory of the greenbackers and the withdrawal of the socialists, 238. Other planks in the platform, 238. Negative attitude towards politics, 238. Recommendation to organise secretly, 239. Failure to establish a permanent national federation of all labour organisations, 239.

THE national convention met at Tyrone,[1] Pennsylvania, on December 28, 1875, as specified in the call issued by the Junior Sons of '76. It was well attended, 132 delegates being present.[2] The spokesman of the socialists was P. J. McGuire, of Connecticut, while George Blair, of New York, appeared for the Knights of Labor. But apparently nearly all the delegates came from Pennsylvania and all of the elected officers, notably the chairman, John M. Davis, a Knight of Labor, and editor of the *National Labor Tribune,* were from that State. This probably explains why it was that the committee on amalgamation recommended the calling of a second convention to be held in Pittsburgh, April 17, 1876, to which " all organisations having for their object the elevation of labor " should be invited. To this all consented, but it was nevertheless decided to adopt a platform. The committee on platform presented two reports. The text of the minority report did not appear in the proceedings, but, as it was written by McGuire, it can safely be presumed that it was imbued with the socialist spirit. The majority report was drafted in the phraseology of the platform of the Junior Sons, yet it differed materially from the latter. The financial plank was comprehensive; it included the scheme of

[1] Official Proceedings are given in the Pittsburgh *National Labor Tribune,* Jan. 8, 1876.

[2] They claimed in a resolution to represent 120,000 organised workingmen, which doubtless was a gross exaggeration.

interconvertible bonds and paper money, advocated the restoration of the depressed industries through the immediate repeal of the resumption act, demanded the repeal of the legislation creating the national banking system and the redemption of all national bank currency in legal tender greenbacks. Other conspicuous demands were for civil damages as the only punishment for persons indictable under the law of conspiracy,[3] the extension of debtor's exemption to $1,000, and the enactment of a law that would prevent employers from excluding unionists, known as an anti-ironclad law. After electing two Knights of Labor, John M. Davis and George Blair, president and secretary, respectively, of the temporary national executive committee, the convention adjourned.

The Pittsburgh convention [4] apparently failed to attract other labour organisations than those which had been represented at Tyrone. The trade unions were not represented,[5] except for the indirect representation by the socialists who were also largely trade unionists. To them, however, the interest of socialism was paramount. The discontinuity of this convention from all previous national attempts is further illustrated by the fact that only four of the delegates had been present at any one of the previous national conventions. None of the old leaders was present. The delegates numbered 136 and came from 20 States, Pennsylvania having a majority. The Order of the Knights of Labor, through John M. Davis, James L. Wright, George Blair, and others, apparently dominated the convention. James L. Wright, one of the founders of the Knights, was elected temporary chairman and John M. Davis, the leader of the Knights in the West, permanent chairman. But the socialists were also a force to be reckoned with. They and their sympathisers numbered about thirty.

The object of the convention, as the leaders saw it, was to formulate a set of legislative demands, to decide upon a political policy and to recommend to the workingmen a form of in-

3 This demand was evidently inspired by the recent Siney and Parks conspiracy case. See above, II, 180, note.

4 Official Proceedings in the Pittsburgh *National Labor Tribune*, Apr. 22, 1876.

5 The list of delegates is given in the *Proceedings* by States without mentioning the organisations. The only instance of any trade demarcation was a special conference held by the coal miner delegates from Pennsylvania, which declared war on any state senators who should vote for striking out the penal clause in a ventilation bill which was at this time before the upper house of the Pennsylvania legislature.

dustrial organisation. The controversy chiefly centred around the platform, and the contestants were the socialists on the one side and the greenbackers on the other. The socialists had firmly decided to capture the convention for their policy.

On the first day, Otto Weydemeyer read, on behalf of the twenty-one socialist delegates, an address which was drawn up in the spirit of the International.[6] It declared that the abolition of wage slavery ought to be the goal of the labour movement; it pointed out the need for international trade unions to guard against the importation of European strike-breakers; it advocated the establishment of a political party by the trade unions, but emphatically declared that no part in elections should be taken until the party was sufficiently strong to make its influence felt;[7] and it concluded by emphasising the fact that economic organisation must precede and form the basis of political organisation.

For a while victory smiled upon the socialists, for the convention adopted, by a vote of 67 to 27, a resolution introduced by P. J. McGuire, favouring state aid to co-operative societies. But the greenbackers then realised that under the circumstances [8] the resolution meant an indorsement of socialism, and, upon a motion to reconsider, the resolution was recommitted, never to return.

The open breach came when the committee on resolutions presented its first report. The committee, which was composed of 15 greenbackers and 6 socialists, reported in favour of the repeal of the resumption act, advanced the scheme of interconvertible bonds and paper money, and, the majority being from Pennsylvania, demanded of Congress " a strong protective tariff " and " that all tariff duties be so regulated as to protect home labor and home industries and the products thereof from foreign competition." [9] They also condemned " the tinkering of the gentlemen now staying in Washington at the government's (the people's) expense." The report was adopted by a

6 Chicago *Vorbote*, Apr. 29, 1876.
7 At this point the address reiterated the resolution on political action adopted by the second national convention of the International.
8 Government credit to co-operative societies was advocated by William H. Sylvis

as constituting a part of the greenback scheme, but when it was proposed by a socialist, it assumed a new aspect.
9 Especial attention was called to the " printed matter clause " which the report asserted did not offer " sufficient protection to printers and bookbinders."

vote of 59 to 46. The socialists offered an angry protest and withdrew as a body from the convention.

Having decided in favour of greenbackism, the convention then proceeded to run the full gamut of labour and anti-monopoly resolutions which were the order of the day at every labour convention. "Co-operation for trading and manu-facturing" was held to be the means by which the working classes "will eventually emancipate themselves from the wage system," and Congress was requested to grant a loan on easy terms for a co-operative mine. They further demanded the abrogation of the Burlingame Treaty with China, the enforce-ment of the eight-hour law and its passage by the various state legislatures, a liberal homestead policy to enable wage-earners to settle upon public land, a liberal policy of internal improve-ment, stringent usury laws, the prohibition of the "truck" system and of the contract convict system, the prohibition of discrimination by common carriers, a change in the postal laws, making it obligatory upon the manufacturer to publish the cost of manufacturing patented machines, mechanics' lien, the attachment of penalty clauses to labour protective laws, and, finally, "suitable apprentice laws that will insure competent workmen in various industries, by serving a regular apprentice-ship of at least three years."

On the question of political action, both socialists and green-backers on the committee of resolutions were in favour of an independent workingmen's party, but the convention dealt with this matter very cautiously. The discussion was postponed until the last day, for fear the heated discussion which it would arouse might render futile all efforts at consolidation. Finally, the conservative element carried the day and forced through a substitute, which declared that "independent political action is extremely hazardous and detrimental to the labor interests"; that it ought to be preceded by "education and discipline" through organisation, and that "the existing political parties can be made the vehicle for the attainment of their [the work-ingmen's] ends by personal and organised efforts at primary elections of both parties and through the primaries in the nomi-nating convention."

The convention recommended a plan of labour organisation

which showed distinctly that it was under the strong influence
of the Knights of Labor.   It called attention to the prevailing
system of blacklisting " all earnest workers in the cause of
labour and unionism," and, therefore, urged " upon the workingmen and working women of the country to organise under
one head, each for all and all for one, upon a secret basis, not
antagonistic with the duty they owe to their families, their
country and their God."

The leaders of the convention seriously desired to establish
a permanent national federation.   Accordingly, it was decided to create a permanent committee of fifteen to enforce the
recommendations of the convention, and to " call from time
to time annual conventions from *bona fide* labor organisations
and prepare a basis of representation and tax, the same to be
forwarded to all Trades Unions throughout the United States,
and to place themselves in communication with the Trades
Unions of the world."

It is not surprising, however, that no consolidation of the
labour forces was achieved.   The convention gave full satisfaction to practically no one.   The socialists were driven out
by the adoption of the greenback platform, the trade unions
could but feel estranged by the advice to workingmen, " to
organise under one head upon a secret basis," and the believers
in political action were repulsed when independent political
action was rejected in favour of a policy of pressure upon the
old parties.   Thus was brought to a close the era of the general
labour congresses.   Henceforth for many years the labour
movement continued to be divided.   The Knights of Labor
established their national organisation in 1878, the trade unions
in 1881, and the socialists did the same in 1876, practically
during the Pittsburgh convention just described.

CHAPTER IV

THE GREENBACK LABOR AGITATION, 1876–1880 [1]

The change in labour's attitude towards politics produced by the great strikes of 1877, 240. Organisation of the National party, 241. Fusion with the greenbackers, 241. State labour ticket in New York, 242. The "Greenback and Labor" combination in Pennsylvania, 242. Success of the Greenback party in the West, 244. National convention of labour and currency reformers and the formation of the National party, 244. Predominance of the farmers, business men, and lawyers, 244. Platform, 245. Further Greenback successes, 245. T. V. Powderly, 245. Congressional election of 1878, 245. Obstacles to a unified movement in New York City, 246. "Pomeroy Clubs," 246. The organisation of the National Greenback Labor Reform party, 246. State election in Pennsylvania, 247. Analysis of the vote, 247. State election in Ohio, 248. Successes elsewhere, 248. Effect of the returning industrial prosperity, 248. Effect of the resumption of specie payment, 249. Tendency to fuse with the Democrats, 249. National pre-nomination conference, 249. Denis Kearney and Albert R. Parsons, 250. The national nominating convention, 250. Labour demands, 250. Failure of the movement, 251.

DURING the campaign of 1876 the greenback movement was purely a farmers' movement. The workingmen cast hardly any votes for Peter Cooper.[2] The great strikes of July, 1877, changed the situation completely. Their suppression by Federal troops and state militia brought labour face to face with an openly hostile government. Immediately after the strikes workingmen's parties began to spring up like mushrooms. There was probably no important centre between New York City and San Francisco in which some movement toward a party was not begun. The movement reached its height in Pennsylvania, Ohio, and New York, where strong state organisations were formed. In every instance where the workingmen took to political action they established workingmen's parties independent of the Greenback party.

In Ohio an unpromising greenback state convention met in

---

1 In the preparation of this chapter the author drew largely from the unpublished monograph by Louis Mayer, *The Greenback Labor Movement, 1874–1884*.
2 See above, II, 167 *et seq.*

June, 1877, and nominated a state ticket. One week after the July strike, Robert Schilling published the first copy of the *Labor Advocate* in Cleveland and began a vigorous agitation for a workingmen's party. Since the strike had affected the entire State, it received wide response. On September 13 a workingmen's state convention was held at Columbus and organised a National party upon an almost wholly greenback platform. There were planks demanding an income tax, non-sectarian schools, and the reservation of the public domain for actual settlers, but the only distinctly labour plank was one demanding legislation against truck stores. The part of the platform devoted to currency reform is noteworthy in that it first, among all greenback platforms, failed to incorporate the interconvertible-bond feature of the greenback scheme. Thus it distinctly separated itself from the idea of regulating the rate of interest through control of the currency. It simply declared that " the legal tender currency is the safest and most satisfactory paper money attainable," and demanded " that it be fully restored and made a full legal tender and continued without contraction of volume." It likewise demanded the substitution of legal tender notes for all outstanding national bank notes and the remonetisation of silver.

The National party entered into an agreement with the greenbackers whereby their nominee for governor, Stephen Johnson, a retired lawyer and farmer, was retained on its state ticket, but the rest of the candidates were replaced by new men: one machinist and two farmers. Of the 10 candidates on the county and city tickets at Columbus, 4 were workingmen.

The vote polled by Johnson was about 17,000 — over 5 times as large as the greenback vote of the preceding year. Over half the votes came from the counties in which were located the cities of Toledo, Cleveland, Youngstown, Canton, and Columbus. Another quarter of the vote was concentrated in the railway towns and manufacturing counties of the northeastern part of the State. In Toledo the municipal ticket and a part of the county ticket were elected to office by a plurality, as well as two members of the lower house of the legislature. In the agricultural counties, the vote was, on the whole, light.

In New York a similar movement resulted in a state convention held in Troy early in October, 1877, and attended by a large representation of labouring men.[3] The first plank of the platform adopted declared in favour of " a currency of gold, silver, and United States treasury notes . . . and the retirement of national bank bills." This mild demand was all that the platform contained with reference to currency. The remainder was devoted to a miscellaneous assortment of labour reform planks, the reduction of the hours of labour, the establishment of bureaus of labour statistics, the abolition of the contract system of prison labour, the provision of factory inspection, and the prohibition of manufacture in tenement houses.

The candidates nominated for the two highest offices on the ticket, secretary of state and state controller, were John J. Junio of Syracuse, a cigar maker, prominent in trade union circles, and George A. Blair, of New York City, a leader in the Knights of Labor.

The party polled in the election over 20,000 votes, ten times as many as the Greenback party in 1876. One assemblyman was elected for Elmira. The vote was drawn mainly from the " southern tier " of counties of New York — the region traversed by the Erie Railroad, which alone of the railroads passing through New York had been seriously affected by the strike of July. Elmira, Oswego, and Hornellsville, the chief scenes of the railroad troubles, were the centres of activity. The leader of the party in this region was the candidate for State senator, Ralph Beaumont, a shoemaker, who later achieved prominence as a Knight of Labor. Rochester and Albany were other important centres. The vote in New York and Buffalo was small.

In Pennsylvania the ball was set in motion by a workingmen's meeting held in August, 1877, at Pittsburgh, at which it was resolved " to organise an independent movement to be called the Greenback Labor party," [4] for the purpose of choosing men for the different offices.

A meeting was held also in Philadelphia, owing to the efforts of the members of the Typographical Union, and William B.

3 *New York Times*, Oct. 10, 1877.
4 This is the first mention of the term "Greenback Labor" that has been found.

Stechert, for many years president of this union in Philadelphia, presided. As a result, no doubt, of these and other similar meetings, a so-called Union Labor or United Workingmen's convention was held at Harrisburg about a month later. Nearly all of the 30 or 40 delegates present came from Philadelphia and Pittsburgh — a few from Scranton, Reading, and Allentown. The platform adopted was prefaced by a long preamble calling attention to the depressed state of economic life of the country and condemning in general terms the vicious legislation and financial management which had induced the depression. It contained in its first plank a demand for "the abolition of the national banking system, the unconditional repeal of the Specie Resumption Act, and the issue of currency by the government upon the wealth of the whole nation." Following this was a long list of purely labour demands. The highest places on the ticket, namely those of auditor-general and treasurer, were given to two Knights of Labor leaders, John M. Davis, of Pittsburgh, and James L. Wright, of Philadelphia.

A week later the Greenback party accepted these nominations, and thus was formed in Pennsylvania the so-called "Greenback and Labor" combination. It polled the very considerable vote of 52,854, amounting to nearly 10 per cent of the total vote cast. Its stronghold was in the anthracite region where the towns of Wilkesbarre, Columbus, and Scranton were situated. Alleghany County, with the cities of Alleghany and Pittsburgh, contributed one-seventh of the total greenback labour vote, nearly a quarter of the total vote cast in the county. Schuylkill County cast 9,000 votes and Philadelphia, 5,000. The eastern manufacturing centres cast a small vote and the rural sections a negligible one. The regions found to be the strongholds of the new political movement were the identical regions in which the strength of the Knights of Labor was at this time concentrated. There can remain but little doubt that the Order stood at the helm of this movement.

In Massachusetts no workingmen's party was started, so that the field belonged undisputed to the Greenback party. The vote was negligible and came only from the rural sections. In some of the western agricultural States, however, the Greenback party vote was considerable: 15 per cent in Wisconsin; 14 per cent in Iowa; and 4.75 per cent in Kansas.

The alliance of the workingmen with the greenbackers in Ohio and Pennsylvania and the growing Workingmen's party in New York naturally suggested to both greenback and labour party leaders the desirability of effecting on a national scale a union of the forces of all parties. Accordingly a call was issued for a " national convention of labour and currency reformers " to be held at Toledo in February, 1878. It was signed by a number of prominent greenbackers, mostly of the journalist-politician type, and had been prepared by D. B. Sturgeon, of Toledo, the chairman of the state executive committee of the National party in Ohio.

Pursuant to this call, there assembled in Toledo some 150 delegates, coming chiefly from Pennsylvania, Ohio, Indiana, and Illinois. In all, delegates from twenty States were present, but only one from beyond the Rockies. Richard Trevellick was made temporary chairman. The permanent chairman chosen was Francis W. Hughes, a lawyer and former judge of Pennsylvania. Those who took prominent part were E. P. Allis, of Wisconsin, the head of an extensive steel manufacturing plant in Milwaukee and Greenback candidate for governor of the State in the preceding year; E. A. Boynton, Massachusetts, a large manufacturer of boots and shoes; ex-Congressman Alexander Campbell, of Illinois, a manufacturer, and in 1863 author of *The True Greenback,* who had attended several conventions of the National Labor Union; General S. F. Cary; W. P. Grooning, of New York, secretary of the New York Board of Trade; Robert Schilling; Ralph Beaumont, a Knight of Labor; Uriah S. Stephens, the founder of the Knights of Labor; and a score of lawyers. The evidence furnished by this list points to the conclusion that, however strong the working-class element in the new party, the actual direction of its national affairs was in the hands of farmers, radical business men, and lawyers.

The convention launched into existence the National party and adopted a platform containing the typical greenback demands. The preamble states that "throughout our entire country the value of real estate is depreciated, industry paralysed, trade depressed, business incomes and wages reduced, unparalleled distress inflicted upon the poorer and middle ranks of our people, the land filled with fraud, embezzlement, bankruptcy, crime, suffering, pauperism and starvation," and that " this state of things has been brought about by legislation in the interest of and dictated by money lenders, bankers and bond holders." Following this statement were four labour demands. They called for legislation reducing the hours of labour, for both national and state bureaus of labour and industrial statistics, the prohibition of the contract system of prison labour, and the suppression of the importation of servile labour into the United States.

Although the winter of 1877–1878 marked perhaps the point of its greatest intensity, and the summer of 1878 saw the beginning of its end already in sight, the depression continued with marked severity throughout that year. Naturally, therefore, the greenback movement was growing apace. One of the notable successes in the spring of 1878 was the election of Terence V. Powderly,[5] later grand master workman of the Knights of Labor, as mayor of Scranton.

The congressional election in the autumn of 1878 marked the zenith of the movement. The aggregate greenback vote cast in the election exceeded a million, and fourteen representatives were sent to Congress. In New England the movement was strong enough to poll almost a third of the total vote in Maine, over 8 per cent of the total vote in both Connecticut and New Hampshire, and from 4 to 6 per cent in the other States. In Maine, the greenbackers elected 32 members of the upper house and 151 members of the lower house, and one congressman, Thompson Murch, of Rochland, who was secretary of the

[5] Terence Vincent Powderly was born at Carbondale, Penn., in 1849, of Irish parents. At the age of thirteen he became a railway switch tender and four years later entered a railway machine shop. In 1870 he joined the Scranton local organisation of the Machinists' and Blacksmiths' National Union. In November, 1874, he joined the Knights of Labor and soon brought his union into the Order. In 1877 Powderly became secretary of the newly organised District Assembly 5 (District Assembly 16 since 1878) of Scranton. In 1879 he became master workman of this district assembly. In 1878 he was chosen mayor of Scranton and was again elected in 1882 and 1884. Powderly was grand master workman of the Knights of Labor from 1879 to 1893. In 1894 he was admitted to the bar, identified himself with the Republican party, and stumped for McKinley in 1896. In 1897 he was appointed commissioner general of immigration by President McKinley, serving until 1902. Since 1907 he has been Chief of the Division of Information in the Bureau of Immigration and Naturalization at Washington.

National Granite Cutters' Union. However, the bulk of the vote in that State was obviously agricultural. In Massachusetts, the situation was dominated by Benjamin F. Butler, lifelong Republican politician who had succeeded in getting the Democratic nomination for governor and was endorsed by the Greenback convention. He received a large vote but was defeated for office.

In New York where, during the preceding year, the movement had been divided between the Greenback party and the Labor Reform party, a convention was called to meet at Auburn in July, 1878, to effect a fusion and to bring the movement in line with the National party formed at Toledo. In New York City there were three groups struggling for control: the Pomeroy group, the National group, and the Junio-Blair group. Mark M. Pomeroy was an ambitious, radical editor of a weekly paper, *Pomeroy's Democrat,* which he had been publishing in New York since 1869, but he had moved to Chicago shortly before the campaign of 1876. He succeeded in organising throughout the country a large number of Pomeroy Clubs with the prime object, apparently, of furthering the circulation of the paper as well as his own fortunes. The national group was the direct successor of the Greenback party of 1876, and, after the Toledo convention, declared itself a branch of the National party. The Junio-Blair group represented the Labor Reform party.

Outside New York City there existed no obstacle to fusion. At the state convention all three New York City delegations were rejected, and their exclusion was looked upon as a triumph of the labour reform element. Similarly, the case of the contesting delegations from Albany was decided in favour of that element. Thereafter it allowed the greenbackers to run the convention. The platform was thoroughly greenback and contained fewer labour demands than that of the Labor Reform party of the preceding year. The name adopted for the new party was the National Greenback Labor party, and adhesion to the National party formed at Toledo was declared. The nominees were Gideon J. Tucker, a well-known lawyer, for judge of the Court of Appeals, and candidates in 30 of the 33 congressional districts, 3 of the nominations, however, being in fusion with the Democrats. The vote for Tucker was over 75,000, about 9 per cent of the total vote of the State. If, however, only the State outside of New York and Brooklyn be considered, it was slightly less than 12 per cent of the total. The vote was localised in the counties contiguous to Pennsylvania. No definite conclusion can be reached with regard to distribution between city and country. On the contrary, the conclusion seems to be warranted that the distribution was regional rather than occupational, that in the region in which the vote was heavy it was contributed to about equally by farmers and workingmen, and that in the region where it was light, the lack of support was common to both agricultural and industrial areas.

In Pennsylvania, an alliance between the Workingmen's party and the greenbackers had already been completed in 1877. In 1878 the two movements were entirely fused. At the state convention, the workingmen favoured the nomination for governor of Thomas Armstrong, then editor of the Pittsburgh *National Labor Tribune,* but the greenbackers succeeded in nominating Samuel Mason, a lawyer. James L. Wright received the nomination for secretary of internal affairs, and Uriah S. Stephens was nominated for Congress in the Fifth Congressional District, a part of Philadelphia. The vote for Mason for governor reached almost 82,000, being nearly 12 per cent of the total vote cast. Still larger, however, was the congressional vote, which reached almost 100,000, or over 14 per cent of the total. The movement was relatively weak in Philadelphia, the vote in each of the 3 congressional districts where nominations were held being only 7 per cent of the total. The general conclusion to be reached with regard to the distribution of the vote over the State is that the strength of the Greenback Labor party was chiefly located in the anthracite coal mining region and to a less extent in the coal mining and manufacturing region of the West. The economically diversified northern belt was a secondary region of strength, while the overwhelmingly agricultural sections were about uniformly weak in greenback labour support, a weakness which (as in New York) was also evident in the largest industrial centre of the State — Philadelphia.

In Ohio, conditions during the year 1878 did not undergo material change. The alliance of the Greenback and Labor Reform parties continued. Andrew Roy, prominent in the coal miners' organisation and more recently a state inspector of mines, was the nominee for secretary of State — the highest office to be filled at the election. The vote for the State was 38,332, and for the city of Cleveland over 5,500.

In spite of the considerable increase over the vote for 1877 in New York, Pennsylvania, and Ohio, the strongest greenback States remained, as in that year, the agricultural States of the Middle West and the Southwest. The vote in Illinois was 15 per cent of the total, in Texas almost a quarter, in Iowa it was 22 per cent, in Kansas over 19 per cent. In Wisconsin, candidates for Congress were nominated in only 4 districts, and in Milwaukee County the vote was only 7 per cent of the total. In Missouri the movement over the State as a whole was very strong, the vote in St. Louis reaching 17 per cent of the total, but in Kansas City less than 8 per cent. In Colorado the movement was not strong, polling 8 per cent of the total. In California no election was held.

Having reached its highest point in 1878, the greenback movement began rapidly to disintegrate in the next year. The month after the election of 1878 witnessed the disappearance of one of the chief demands of the party, the repeal of the resumption act. January 1, 1879, was the date fixed by the act for resumption, and on December 17, 1878, the premium on gold disappeared. From that day on, the resumption policy became a dead issue.

Still more significant for the future of the party, however, was the renewal of industrial activity which set in with the new year. Even before the election it had become apparent that an industrial revival was at hand, and by the middle of 1879 it was in full swing. Another factor of great importance was the large increase in the volume of the currency. In 1881 the currency, which had averaged about $725,000,000 for the years 1876–1878, reached over $1,114,000,000.[6] Under these conditions, all that remained available to the platform

---

6 Hardy, "Quantity of Money and Prices," in *Journal of Political Economy,* 1894–1895, III, 156.

makers and propagandists of the party was their opposition to
the monopolistic national banks with their control over currency, and to the refunding of the bonded debt.

The disappearance of the financial issue snapped the threads
which had heretofore held together the farmer and the wage-
worker. So long as depression continued, the issue was financial and the two had a common enemy — the banker. The
financial issue once settled, or at least suspended, the object of
the attack by labour became the employer, and that of the attack by the farmer, the railway corporation and the warehouse
man. Prosperity had mitigated the grievances of both classes,
but while the farmer still had a great deal to expect from politics in the form of state regulation of railway rates, the wage-
earners' struggle now became entirely economic and not political.

Another weakening influence was the tendency towards
fusion with the Democrats. The splendid showing made by
the Greenback Labor party in the elections of 1878 filled the
leaders with hope, while at the same time it inspired many of
the old party leaders, particularly Democratic leaders, with
fear. The natural result was for both classes of leaders to look
to fusion — the former to secure personal advantage and pre-
ferment, the latter to save their organisation. The only States
in which fusion was actually accomplished in 1879 were Michigan and Massachusetts, but in every State in which a state election was held, fusion had its advocates and the controversy over
the question, of necessity, greatly weakened the party.

A few weeks after the election of 1879, the chairman of the
national committee, F. P. Dewees, a Washington lawyer, and
T. P. Murch, the chairman of the congressional committee,
issued a call for a conference to be held at Washington on
January 8, 1880, for the purpose of arranging for a national
nominating convention later in the year. The call was addressed not only to the regular greenback organisation but to
the national committee of the Pomeroy faction, which had
seceded in 1878, and to representatives of labour organisations.
Denis Kearney, the leader of the Workingmen's party of California, issued a similar call about the same time,[7] but an un-

_____
[7] See below, II, 263.

derstanding was reached whereby he agreed to attend the conference called by the greenbackers.

The conference was also attended by Albert R. Parsons,[8] representing the Chicago Eight-Hour League, and by Charles Litchman, of the Knights of Labor. It drew up no platform, but merely appointed a committee to issue a call for a national convention to which any delegates coming from organisations in sympathy with the Greenback Labor party might be admitted.

The call, which professed to have been issued on behalf of the " representatives of the Grangers and Farmers' open clubs, labour organisations, the Workingmen's Party of California, clubs and other organisations of the National and Greenback Labor parties, and Union Greenback-Labor party [Pomeroy's party], united with the committees of the National party and the congressional committee of the Greenback Labor party."

Besides delegates from greenback organisations and Kearney, there were also in attendance at the convention, delegates from the Workingmen's party of Kansas and the Chicago Workingmen's Union and forty-four socialists. The platform adopted demanded the abolition of the note-issue power of the national banks, the substitution of greenbacks for the outstanding national bank-notes, and the payment of outstanding bonds therewith. Granger sentiment was appealed to by planks demanding congressional regulation of interstate transportation and the reservation of the public domain to actual settlers. A bid for the labour vote was made by including the principal labour demands, such as the enforcement of the national eight-hour law by stringent factory inspection, the regulation of prison

8 Albert R. Parsons, the only American among the Chicago anarchists, condemned to death in 1887, was born in 1850 in Montgomery, Ala., of parents with a pre-revolutionary ancestry. He was successively a printer, Confederate soldier and Federal office-holder under Grant. His attention was first drawn to the labour problem in 1874, when the working people in Chicago united to compel the " Relief Aid Society " to render an account of the several million dollars collected to relieve the distress occasioned by the big fire of 1871. Parsons joined the Workingmen's party of the United States in 1876 and became a member of the Knights of Labor in the same year. He ran repeatedly for office on the socialist ticket between 1877 and 1879. In 1879 he was secretary of the Chicago Eight-Hour League, which invited Ira Steward to speak under its auspices in the fall of that year. At the second convention of the Federation of Organized Trades and Labor Unions in 1882, he sent in a resolution from this organisation advocating the eight-hour day upon the grounds of Ira Steward's theory that " a decrease in hours means an increase in wages " and ultimately co-operation.

labour, the establishment of a bureau of labour, the prohibition of child labour under fourteen years of age, the payment of wages in cash, and the immediate abrogation of the Burlingame Treaty with China.   However, no special effort was made to reach the labour vote.   Weaver, the nominee for president, spent most of his time in the South.   The vote in New York fell to 12,000.   In Pennsylvania, although the leaders of the Knights, such as Powderly and Wright, were present at the convention of 1880, by far the greater part of the workingmen in the coal regions of the East and the iron and steel region of the West, which had polled so heavy a vote for the party in 1878, deserted it in 1880, and the vote fell to 20,000.   A careful study of the vote for Weaver in 1880 [9] reveals the fact, that, with the exception of an industrial section running through seven counties in central Michigan, the greenback movement in 1880 presents itself as a distinctly agricultural movement, drawing the bulk of its strength from the agricultural States east of the Mississippi, and the remainder from the agricultural areas of the West.   With insignificant exceptions, the desertion of the greenback cause by workingmen seems by 1880 to have been well nigh complete.

[9] Libby, " A Study of the Greenback Movement, 1876–1884," in Wisconsin Academy of Sciences, Arts and Letters, *Transactions*, 1898–1899, XII, 530–543.

CHAPTER V

THE ANTI-CHINESE AGITATION IN CALIFORNIA

Class struggle *versus* race struggle, 252. The depression in California, 253. Socialists and the strike movement, 253. The anti-Chinese riot, 253. Denis Kearney, 254. The Workingmen's party of California, 255. Its platform, 255. The sand-lot meetings, 253. Arrest of Kearney, 256. Nomination of delegates for the state constitutional convention, 256. Threats of riots and the "gag law," 257. Kearney's acquittal, 258. State convention of the Workingmen's party, 258. First successes in elections, 259. The election to the state constitutional convention, 260. Alliance of the workingmen with the farmers, 260. The anti-Chinese clause in the constitution, 260. Adoption of the constitution by the people, 261. Workingmen's success in the state election, 261. Success in the San Francisco municipal election, 261. Movement for the enforcement of the anti-Chinese clause in the state constitution, 262. Success in the state legislature but failure in the United States Circuit Court, 262. Second arrest of Kearney, 262. Beginning of the disintegration of the Workingmen's party, 263. Defeat in elections, 263. Relation to the national greenback movement, 263. End of the party, 264. Spread of the anti-Chinese movement among small employers, 264. The question before Congress, 265. Congressional investigating committee, 265. Increase in Chinese immigration during the early eighties, 266. The Representative Assembly of Trade and Labor Unions, 266. The white label, 266. The state labour convention, the League of Deliverance, and the boycott of Chinese-made goods, 267. Chinese Exclusion Act, 267.

In California,[1] as in the eastern industrial States, the railway strikes of 1877 precipitated a political labour movement. California had retained gold as currency throughout the entire period of paper money, and the labour movement at no time had accepted the greenback platform. The political issue after 1877 was racial, not financial, and the weapon was not merely the ballot, but also "direct action"— violence. The anti-Chinese agitation in California, culminating as it did in the Exclusion Law of 1882, was doubtless the most important single factor in the history of American labour, for without it the entire country might have been overrun by Mongolian labour, and

---

[1] This chapter is condensed and largely quoted from the manuscript of Ira B. Cross, University of California, on the *History of the Labor Movement in California*.

the labour movement might have become a conflict of races instead of one of classes.

When the news of the strikes and of the labour riots in Pittsburgh reached California, the business situation in that State was at its lowest ebb. Depression had set in there later than in the other States, so that in the three years, 1873, 1874, and 1875, approximately 150,000 immigrants from the East had entered the State.[2] Consequently, when the crisis came, in 1877, the usual number of unemployed, always to be found in San Francisco, was augmented many fold. The greatest unrest and discontent prevailed among this class. At that time no city or state central labour body existed. The national socialist organisation, which then bore the name of Workingmen's party of the United States,[3] was the only one in touch with the national labour movement. Thus it was that a meeting was called under the auspices of the party to agitate the labour question, and to be held on the vacant lots in front of the new city hall in San Francisco, known as the " sand-lots," [4] on the evening of July 23.

On the day of the meeting, rumors were spread that a riot was being planned, with the object of burning the docks of the Pacific Mail Steamship Company,[5] and of pillaging the Chinese quarter. Nevertheless, the police granted a permit to hold the meeting. At least 8,000 people gathered on the sand-lots in the evening. The crowd was addressed by several socialists who spoke on the labour question, but said nothing of the Chinese. Everything was orderly until an anti-coolie procession pushed its way into the audience and insisted that the speakers say something about the Chinese. This was refused and thereupon the crowd which had gathered on the outskirts of the meeting attacked a passing Chinaman and started the cry, " On to Chinatown." This marked the beginning of a two-day riot during which more than $100,000 worth of property belonging to Chinamen and others was destroyed, and four men were killed. The disturbance was quelled by the united

---

2 *San Francisco Bulletin*, Jan. 10, 1876.
3 See below, II, 269 *et seq.*
4 The sand-lots, for many years, had been the gathering place for speakers, street fakers, phrenologists, tramps, and others of like stamp who had no trouble at any time in getting a crowd of idlers to listen to their harangues, or to buy their novelties.
5 The Pacific Mail Steamship Company's vessels brought the largest portion of Chinese immigrants to the United States.

efforts of the police, state militia, and the thousand-strong " pick-handle brigade." This was an improvised militia under the command of a citizens' vigilance committee, and owed its name to the fact that each member was armed with a hickory pick handle.

Among the members of the pick-handle brigade was an Irish drayman, Denis Kearney by name. He was born in the county of Cork, Ireland, in 1847, and, after sailing the seas for some years, had come to California in 1868. He had picked up considerable information from newspapers, public meetings, political clubs, and other sources. He was a regular attendant at the meetings of the Lyceum for Self-Culture. He was especially temperate in his habits, and, when speaking at meetings, he took occasion to abuse the members of his own class for their laziness and shiftlessness. His remarks were consistently in favour of the employers and the Chinese.

But the July riots changed his attitude. He made application for admission to a section of the socialistic Workingmen's party of the United States, but its leaders, knowing Kearney's contempt for the working class, rejected the application.[6] Kearney then decided that he would organise a party of his own and forthwith formed the Workingmen's Trade and Labor Union of San Francisco, with J. G. Day as president, J. J. Hickey as treasurer, and himself as secretary. He delivered an address at the first meeting of the new party which the press characterised as " forcible in language and rather incendiary in sentiment." In the following election his organisation was practically unheard of. But becoming more and more violent, he found himself, within a short time, at the head of a considerable following. On September 23, he held his first meeting upon the sand-lots, which was attended by some 700 people. As had become his habit, he indulged in frenzied statement and concluded by declaring that San Francisco would meet the fate of Moscow unless something were done to alleviate the sufferings of the workers and drive the Chinese from California. The cry, " the Chinamen must go," now became the rallying

6 The story runs thus in the semi-annual report of the national secretary of the party, *National Socialist* (Cincinnati), Aug. 31, 1878.

slogan of the agitators and was soon echoed and re-echoed from one end of the State to the other.

On October 5, the next step was taken when the Workingmen's party of California was organised with Kearney as president, Day as vice-president, and H. L. Knight as secretary-treasurer.[7] Knight drew up the platform which was in part as follows:

"The object . . . is to unite all poor and workingmen and their friends into one political party, for the purpose of defending themselves against the dangerous encroachments of capital. . . .

"We propose to rid the country of cheap Chinese labor as soon as possible, and by all means in our power, because it tends still more to degrade labor and aggrandise capital.

"We propose to destroy land monopoly in our State by such laws as will make it possible.

"We propose to destroy the great money power of the rich by a system of taxation that will make great wealth impossible in the future. . . .

"When we have 10,000 members we shall have the sympathy and support of 20,000 other workingmen.

"The party will then wait upon all who employ Chinese and ask for their discharge, and it will mark as public enemies those who refuse to comply with their request.

"This party will exhaust all peaceable means of attaining its ends, but it will not be denied justice when it has the power to enforce it. It will encourage no riot or outrage, but it will not volunteer to repress, or put down, or arrest, or prosecute the hungry and impatient who manifest their hatred of the Chinamen by a crusade against 'John,' or those who employ him. Let those who raise the storm by their selfishness, suppress it themselves. If they dare raise the devil, let them meet him face to face. We will not help them." [8]

The party met with great success. The earnestness of the agitators in addressing two or three meetings every evening during the week and on Sundays at the sand-lots impressed people with their sincerity of purpose, and hundreds hastened to enrol themselves as members. The several socialist sections likewise were drawn into the agitation and joined the move-

---

[7] Day was a Canadian carpenter of Irish extraction. Knight was an Englishman. He came to the United States in 1842 and settled in Missouri, where he was admitted to the bar. He served through the Mexican War, coming to California in 1852, where he engaged in mining for three years and gave some attention to law.

[8] Cross, *History of the Labor Movement in California*, 157, MSS.

ment. Aspiring politicians also joined. Among the latter was a Dr. C. C. O'Donnell, a well-educated medical specialist of rather unenviable reputation but nevertheless a speaker of great force. The party also received steady and sympathetic publicity through the columns of the San Francisco *Chronicle*.[9]

The Sunday meetings upon the sand-lots continued to draw larger and larger crowds; the party organisation grew rapidly, and, in proportion, the utterances of the speakers became more radical and inflammatory. The Southern Pacific Railway came in for its share of abuse on account of employing Chinese. Finally, it was suggested that a meeting be held on " Nob Hill," the most fashionable district in the city.

After considerable hesitation on the part of the authorities, Kearney and his companions were arrested for inciting to riot and lodged in jail. The militia was held in readiness in case of disturbance. In view of these preparations, the unemployed quieted down. The arrested leaders were soon released by the court for lack of sufficient evidence, after they had written a self-humiliating letter of apology to the mayor. For a time thereafter the speeches at the sand-lots were remarkably mild and temperate, considering their character prior to the arrest of the leaders. On Thanksgiving Day, a procession of workers, variously estimated as having from 7,000 to 10,000 men in line, paraded the streets of San Francisco as a protest against the Chinese and in honour of the liberated sand-lot agitators. Organisations which took part were the trade unions of the plasterers, boot and shoemakers, tailors, coopers, printers, carpenters, pile drivers, the Scandinavian Association, the Austrian Benevolent Society, the Order of the Caucasians, and twelve ward clubs of the Workingmen's party.

That evening a meeting was held, attended by delegates from these associations and by delegates from without the city. Its purpose was to call a state convention at which nominations should be made for delegates to the constitutional convention which had been called to meet in 1879. Lack of harmony characterised the meeting, and the Sacramento delegation withdrew, claiming that it would not submit to the dictatorial

9 For a number of years intense rivalry had existed between the San Francisco *Call* and the *Chronicle*. When the *Call* took a very antagonistic attitude towards the workingmen's agitation, the *Chronicle* enlisted in its defence.

methods of Kearney, Knight, and Wellock.[10] For some time previous to this, Kearney had controlled the affairs of the organisation in a high-handed manner. Chairmen were deposed and meetings were broken up by his boisterous followers at his mere suggestion. Dissensions now increased and disruption seemed particularly near when, in addition, charges of corruption were made against Kearney. But Kearney proved equal to the situation. Clubs were disbanded at his command and members were expelled until the movem nt was once more under his control. It was at this time that ie reverted to the vituperative and violent language of the time before his arrest, for his cool and calm discourse could neither gain him new associates nor retain those already with him.

On January 3, 1878, about 500 unemployed men marched about the city and finally proceeded to the city hall where, headed by Kearney, a committee demanded that the mayor should give them work. Kearney declared that he could not keep his followers under control any longer unless they were given " work, bread, or a place in the county jail." Reply was made that the city authorities had no power to provide them with employment. Kearney became increasingly violent in his utterances. So incendiary did the agitation become that a secret committee of safety was formed among the leading citizens of San Francisco. On January 5, the grand jury indicted Kearney, Day, and four others on the charge of riot. The city was in an uproar and several companies of militia were kept under arms. The situation had become so critical that the San Francisco *Chronicle* reversed its position and came out strongly against the agitation. The board of supervisors, upon the recommendation of the mayor, petitioned the legislature to enact certain measures for the protection of the city. The mayor also issued a proclamation on January 17, declaring unlawful all assemblies of an incendiary or riotous nature and ordering the arrest of all persons taking part in them. Again, as before, seeing the authorities prepared to act, the agitators quieted down and awaited developments. On January 19 the governor signed a bill which had been rushed

10 Wellock was an English shoemaker and had served in the Crimean War. He came to the United States in 1873 and to California in 1877, and he achieved prominence during the time of Kearney's imprisonment.

through the legislature, later known as the "gag law," imposing extra heavy penalties for inciting to riot.

On January 21 the first state convention of the Workingmen's party of California met secretly in San Francisco with Frank Roney as temporary chairman.[11] The police had orders to break up the meeting, but, inasmuch as it was quiet and orderly, it was allowed to proceed. About 140 delegates were in attendance representing the different clubs of San Francisco, Oakland, Alameda, Petaluma, San Jose, Vallejo, Brooklyn, Mono County, and Siskiyou County. At this time there were about 25 unions in San Francisco with approximately 3,500 members, and several of these also sent delegates.

On the first day of the convention, it was announced that the trial of Kearney and his companions had resulted in an acquittal for all, and that the workingmen had elected their candidate for state senator at a special election in Alameda County. The second day of the convention was given to jollification. Kearney was made permanent chairman. During the next two days, a platform and constitution, drafted by Roney, and a set of resolutions were adopted. The platform declared that the government of the United States had fallen into the hands of the capitalists; that coolie labour was a curse to the land and should be restricted and abolished forever; that land should be held only for actual cultivation and settlement; and that a system of finance "consistent with the agricultural, manufacturing and mercantile industries, and requirements of the country uncontrolled by rings, brokers, and bankers," should be introduced. Further demands were that eight hours should be made the legal work day; that the farming-out of convict labour should be stopped; that all labour on public works should be performed by the day and at the current rate of wages; that the creation of millionaires and monopolists should be rendered impossible by a proper system of taxation, and that the

11 Roney was born in Belfast, Ireland, in 1841. Although the son of a wealthy contractor, he early allied himself with the Fenian movement. He was arrested, and upon promise not to return, he was sent to the United States by the British government. After removing to Omaha, he joined the moulders' union and later became president of the local organisation. He was active in the campaign of the National Labor Reform party in Nebraska. In 1874, he went to San Francisco and joined the anti-Chinese movement at the time of Kearney's first arrest.

fee system for the payment of public officers should be abolished. The agitation had shifted from attacks upon the Chinese to attacks upon capital and monopoly. The Chinese had ceased to flock into the country in large numbers owing to the antagonistic attitude of the Californians. Land and railroad monopolies furnished abundant material for new issues.

On February 19 a special election was held in Santa Clara County for the choice of senator and assemblyman which resulted in the workingmen electing their candidate for the latter against a combination of Republicans and Democrats. In March they elected their candidates for mayor and for several other offices in both Oakland and Sacramento. From this time, however, may be said to date the beginning of the decline of the Workingmen's party of California. It had become a factor in state and municipal affairs, and politicians now entered it with the object of obtaining offices or of using the organisation for the benefit of other political parties. The senator whom they elected in January in Alameda County disregarded from the first the principles of the party and refused to resign. Kearney and his friends were loudly accused of corruption, and a split became inevitable. On May 4 Kearney held a meeting of his faction, which deposed Roney, Knight, and others from the executive committee. The anti-Kearney faction also met, deposed Kearney as president of the party upon the grounds of corruption and despotic behaviour, and temporarily appointed Roney in his place.

As a result of the dissensions, two separate state conventions were called for May 16 for the purpose of nominating delegates to the constitutional convention. The county delegates were in doubt as to which faction they should join, but, after having heard the arguments of both, 20 joined the Kearney faction and 10 the opposition, while 9 refused to affiliate with either. The Kearney convention, after much discussion, passed a resolution declaring all officers of the party ineligible as candidates for any public office. The convention of the anti-Kearney faction was put poorly attended, and nominated only a few candidates. Its platform was radical and socialistic, while the Kearney platform was characterised by the press as being " as mild as a platform could well be."

In the campaign which followed, trouble continued between these factions of the party. The Democrats and Republicans joined forces and nominated a non-partisan ticket, hoping thereby to defeat the workingmen's candidates.

In the election for the constitutional convention which took place on June 19, 78 non-partisans were elected, 51 workingmen, 11 Republicans, 10 Democrats, and 2 independents. The workingmen carried San Francisco, Los Angeles, and Nevada City. In Los Angeles they had united with the Grangers. The defeat of the Kearneyites in Oakland, Sacramento, and San Jose was significant in view of their victory at preceding elections. The sand-lotters had been successful in the mining counties and in southern California. In the latter portion of the State, the loudest complaint had been made with regard to land monopoly and the inequality of taxation. In the central and northern counties less had been heard of these grievances. The party had also polled its heaviest vote in those counties which had suffered most from the drought of the preceding year.

Immediately following the election, Kearney went to Boston, primarily with the object of seeing what could be done towards organising a national party. He lent his support to Butler's campaign for governor, but after several violent addresses he was quickly repudiated by Butler. In his absence the movement began to quiet down. The people had begun to tire of the agitation and a slight revival in the business world had reduced the number of unemployed.

At the constitutional convention the workingmen allied themselves with the farmer element and introduced many propositions directed against the Chinese and the capitalists, such, for instance, as that no alien should be permitted to hold property in the State; that Chinese should not be allowed to peddle or carry on any mercantile business; that there should be only one legislative body; that land grabbing must be stopped. The greater portion of these propositions offered by the committee were rejected. However, a section was adopted providing that " no corporation now existing, or hereafter formed under the laws of this state, shall, after the adoption of this constitution, employ directly or indirectly, in any capacity, any Chinese or Mongolian."

The constitution as worked out by the convention was adopted by the people against the general opposition of the newspapers and of the business interests by a vote of 77,950 to 67,134. Kearney had canvassed the State in favour of it, ·while Knight had been sent out by the anti-Kearney faction to talk against it. This marked the last appearance of Knight in the sand-lot movement,[12] and also the end of his faction. The largest vote in favour of the constitution came from the northern and southern counties of the State. The agricultural counties which favoured its adoption were suffering from land monopoly and railways. The prosperous agricultural counties, as a unit, rejected it. The lumber counties, where trade was slack, voted for it. The balloting demonstrated beyond question that " hard times " had played an important part in its adoption.

In June, 1879, the state convention of the Workingmen's party of California met in San Francisco to nominate candidates for state and congressional offices. Kearney presided, but the proceedings were orderly. W. F. White, a wealthy rancher, was nominated for governor with W. R. Andrus, of Oakland, who had been elected in 1879 as mayor on the workingmen's ticket, as his running mate. During the ensuing campaign, the workingmen fused in many places with other parties and succeeded in electing 11 senators, 17 assemblymen, and a railway commissioner. In the legislature they were outnumbered only by the Republicans, but accomplished nothing of importance.

In the same year, the workingmen took part in their first municipal campaign in San Francisco. Their nominee for mayor was Reverend I. S. Kalloch, pastor of the Metropolitan Temple, a " people's church." Formerly, Kalloch had been strongly pro-Chinese, but he changed rather abruptly with the success of the Kearney agitation. On September 3, together with a number of workingmen's candidates, he was elected mayor by a safe majority. Through his entire term of office

---

12 He thereafter devoted himself exclusively to newspaper work.

Kalloch was opposed by the board of supervisors, only one of whom belonged to his party.

During the early months of 1880, another agitation, distinct from the Kearney movement in many respects, arose among the unemployed of San Francisco. Business was exceedingly dull, and large numbers of men were out of work. Immigration from the eastern States had been encouraged by false reports in the newspapers, with the result that many people had entered the State during the latter part of 1879. On January 18, 1880, a meeting was called by the painters' union with Thomas Bates, a socialist, as chairman, for the purpose of discussing the situation. Out of this grew a movement to enforce the clause in the new constitution which prohibited corporations from employing Chinese. Theretofore it had remained unenforced. Large numbers of men marched from factory to factory demanding the discharge of the Mongolians and threatening violence in case of refusal. Several of the leaders were members of the Socialist Labor party. Finally the legislature passed a law, in conformity with the constitution, later declared invalid,[13] prohibiting the employment of Chinese by corporations, and considerable numbers were discharged by several large corporations.

The agitation, however, continued and grew more violent and the speakers became more outspoken in their remarks, until the city was once more as excited as during the early days of the Kearney movement. A secret committee of safety was formed; business was brought to a standstill. The climax was reached in February when the board of health declared Chinatown a nuisance and decided that it should be abated. Now the business men in their turn threatened violence in case any attempt should be made to carry out the order. An ordinance increasing the police force was passed over the mayor's veto.

On March 11, Kearney and Gannon, a leader of the unemployed, were arrested for the use of incendiary language. Both were sentenced to six months' imprisonment but were later released by the Supreme Court on the ground that, although the city ordinance under which they had been arrested was valid, it did not cover the misdemeanor charged. The arrest and the

13 In re Tiburcio Parrott, 1 Fed. 481 (1880).

final decision helped to keep alive the Workingmen's party for a time.

But the organisation had lost the greater part of its earlier characteristics and had become a party of politicians only. In January, 1880, Kearney had attended the conference called by the greenbackers in Washington, D. C., and he came back an avowed greenbacker. But, in the meantime, the Democratic party in California had grown extremely weak and was eager to fuse and divide offices with any organisation having a chance of victory in the approaching elections. The result was that during the next few months a struggle ensued between the Democrats and the greenbackers for the control of the Workingmen's party of California.

On March 15 a convention was held by the Workingmen's party of San Francisco and fifteen freeholders were nominated, who, if elected, were to have served on the board having in charge the preparation of a new charter for the city. The list of nominees was composed largely, not of members of the party, but of a number of prominent Democrats and a few Republicans. A committee of 200 from the Citizens' Protective Union nominated a strong ticket in opposition to the workingmen's, and it received the endorsement of the Republicans. The expectation of violence at this election was not realised. The workingmen's candidates were overwhelmingly defeated, as they had been shortly before defeated in the municipal elections at Oakland, Sacramento, and San Jose. This in itself did much to break the spirit of the members of that organisation, so that the dissolution of the party was practically only a question of time.

On April 5 the executive committee met and elected delegates to the Greenback Labor convention in Chicago. This act aroused great opposition among the ward clubs and many openly affiliated with the Democratic party. The state convention met, May 17, with 100 delegates in attendance from 20 different counties. Upon the advice of Kearney, who was at that time in jail, delegates were chosen to the Greenback-Labor convention, notwithstanding the opposition coming from those supporting the Democrats. The greenback-Kearney delegates came, for the most part, from the interior counties.

The movement within the city also was split in twain as a result of the convention. Clubs were disbanded; others were reorganised. In June, Kearney went to Chicago and was made a member of the national executive committee of the Greenback party. During his absence the party moved still further on the way to disruption. The opposing faction met, deposed Kearney, and endorsed the national Democratic platform and candidates. The Workingmen's party nominated no ticket of its own, but fused throughout the State with the Democrats and greenbackers. The Workingmen's party of California was dead. During 1881–1883, Kearney spoke frequently at Sunday meetings on the sand-lots, but his remarks were cool and moderate and attracted little attention. After the campaign of 1880 he returned to his draying business, but again entered politics in 1881 as an active member of the Anti-Monopoly party. In 1882 he canvassed the State for the Democratic nominee for governor. In 1884 he abandoned politics and became a real estate agent and stock broker as well as the proprietor of an employment office. From that time until his death in 1907, he took no part in public affairs.

Had the unemployed in San Francisco, with their violent leaders, been the only class opposed to Chinese immigration, the movement would hardly have had any success. Beginning, however, in the early seventies, employers had started to join forces with the wage-earners in their opposition to the Chinese. They, too, had begun to feel the effects of the Chinese in industry. They had taught the aliens to make cigars, boots and shoes, clothing, and the like, and had been perfectly satisfied with the situation as long as the Chinese had been willing to work under the conditions and for the wages fixed by the white employers. Their attitude changed, however, when the Chinese themselves began to set up in business, to hire their fellow countrymen, and to sell their goods in direct competition with those manufactured by their former employers and instructors. It was useless to attempt to meet their prices. As one paper remarked, " a Chinese manufacturer has many advantages over an American in the employment of Chinese labor. In the first place they employ for at least half the wages, and then they get twice the amount of work out of their help. Hence, they can at any time undersell the American proprietor. In fact, in the boot and shoe trade, the white manufacturers are obliged to purchase the cheap grade of boots and shoes from the Chinese manufacturers. So that the nemesis of cheap labor is now affecting the white employers as well as the white mechanics and laborers." [14]

As soon as capital had enlisted against the Chinese, the press, public opinion, and legislatures showed a marvellous change of attitude. State laws and municipal ordinances were used to remedy the evil, but they were as a rule declared unconstitutional.[15] Next an appeal was made to Congress to prohibit the importation of Chinese. In 1876 the question became an issue of national importance. In that year, each of the national parties inserted an anti-Chinese plank in its platform. In the same year Congress appointed a commission to investigate the situation upon the coast, and, after examining a large number of witnesses, a voluminous report was submitted, recommending that immediate action be taken to restrict Chinese immigration.[16]

It was for this reason, namely, that it was an expression, an extreme one, to be sure, of the general sentiment in the State, that the Kearney agitation met with such singular success. Indeed, it led to far-reaching results. It served to emphasise the Chinese question as a subject of national importance and forced upon the Federal Government the necessity of abrogating the Burlingame Treaty. It was also the most active factor in the formation and adoption of the new constitution.

During the later seventies, owing to the Kearney agitation, the number of Chinese entering the United States had greatly decreased. Consequently, the opposition of the workingmen was for a time deadened. The ratification of the treaty of 1880, however, changed the situation completely. This treaty with China contained the provision that the government of the United States "may regulate, limit, or suspend" the coming

---

[14] *San Francisco Chronicle*, Apr. 27, 1873.

[15] In re Ah Fong, 3 Sawy. 144 (1874); Chu Lung *v.* Freeman, 92 U. S. 275 (1875); Ho Ah Kow *v.* Nunan, 5 Sawy. 552 (1879); In re Quong Woo, 13 Fed. 229 (1882); Yick Wo *v.* Hopkins, 118 U. S. 356 (1886); In re Tie Loy, 26 Fed. 611 (1886); In re Lee Sing et Al., 43 Fed. 359 (1890).

[16] *Reports of Committees of the Senate*, 44 Cong., 2 sess., 1876–1877, No. 689, vol. I.

of Chinese labourers, but "may not absolutely prohibit it." Every ship crossing the Pacific was filled with Chinese hastening to get into the United States before the gates should be closed against them. In the three years, 1880–1882, more than 57,000 were admitted, while in 1882 more than 39,000 arrived. Under such circumstances, it was not surprising that the anti-Chinese agitation was renewed.

But the new movement differed from the Kearney agitation. Prosperity had set in early in 1881. Unemployment fell off and labour organisations began to thrive. So it was that organised labour and not the unorganised mass of unemployed took up the agitation.

As early as March, 1878, as a result of an informal discussion by three delegates to the first state convention of the Workingmen's party of California, who also were members of the unions of their respective trades, there was organised the Representative Assembly of Trades and Labor Unions. The first meeting was attended by representatives from twelve trades. However, for the next three years, the organisation lacked vitality and leadership. It was not until July, 1881, when Frank Roney came as a delegate from the Seamen's Protective Union, that all this was changed. After he had severed connection with both the Kearney and anti-Kearney factions of the Workingmen's party, Roney became a socialist and an active trade unionist. Though not a sailor, he organised in September, 1880, the seamen's union which he represented. Under Roney's leadership, energetic action was taken to organise the unorganised trades, to bring about prison labour reform and, particularly to popularise the anti-Chinese labels of the cigar makers and shoemakers. These were the beginnings of the trade union label, which later became an important factor in the American labour movement.[17]

[17] In 1875 a cigar makers' union in San Francisco which was unaffiliated with the International Cigar Makers' Union, became incorporated under the laws of California, and adopted a stamp which it registered as its trade-mark. The stamp was issued by the union to employers who employed exclusively white labour. Spedden, "The Trade Union Label," in *Johns Hopkins University Publications* XXVIII, 9–10. This is the first known instance of the use of the union label by cigar makers. The earliest use of the union label, as far as is known, was made also in San Francisco in 1869, by a carpenters' eight-hour league, which furnished a stamp to all planing mills running on the eight-hour plan, so that they would be able to identify the work of the ten-hour mills. Lucile Eaves, *A History of California Labor Legislation*, 209.

With the idea of organising the opposition to the Chinese, the trades assembly called a state convention of labour and anti-Chinese organisations to be held in San Francisco, April 24, 1880. The meeting was attended by delegates from forty trade unions in the State. The outcome was the formation of a League of Deliverance with F. Roney as chairman. By the end of May, 13 branches of the League had been formed, especially in San Francisco, with a membership of more than 4,000.

The weapon most frequently used by the League was the boycott of Chinese-made goods. It was conducted systematically and with great effect. It was in this connection that the first boycott case was tried in a California court, resulting in the acquittal of the defendants and causing many factories to discharge their Mongolian help.

Meantime the movement for Chinese exclusion grew in intensity and became wide spread. It was urgently demanded by labour organisations throughout the country and by all the States west of the Rocky Mountains. The platforms of both national parties in 1880 contained planks pledging their candidates to its support. In 1882 the matter reached final solution in Congress. The fight for exclusion was led by the senators and representatives from California, who received ardent support from the members of the States west of the Rockies. The South also was in sympathy with the measure. The East, prompted by humanitarianism and business, opposed it. The bill, as finally passed, prohibited immigration of Chinese labourers for a period of twenty years. So eager had the Californians been over this first attempt at restriction by the Federal Government that the governor declared March 4 to be a state holiday in order that the people might thereby show approval of the acts of those congressmen and senators who had supported the measure. A monster demonstration was held in San Francisco under the auspices of the merchants and professional men. When President Arthur vetoed the bill, mainly on the ground that so long a period of suspension had not been contemplated by those negotiating the treaty of 1880, meetings of protest were held throughout the State, and for a time it seemed as though the agitation would become similar in character to that of the early days of the Kearney movement. However, Congress amended the bill by decreasing the period of suspension to ten years to take effect in August, 1882, and it became law.   With its passage, the League of Deliverance disbanded.

CHAPTER VI

FROM SOCIALISM TO ANARCHISM AND SYNDICALISM, 1876–1884

The Nationalised International. Preliminary union conference of all socialist organisations, 269. The Union Congress, 270. The Workingmen's party of the United States, 270. Resolution on political action, 270. Plan of organisation, 270. " Trade union " and " political " factions, 270. Phillip Van Patten, 272. New Haven experiment with politics, 272. Chicago election, 273. Factional differences, 273. Struggle for the *Labor Standard*, 274. Douai's effort of mediation, 275. Effect of the great strikes of 1877 on the factional struggle, 276. Part played by the socialists in the strike movement, 277.

Rush Into Politics. Election results, 277. Newark convention, 277. Control by the political faction, 278. Socialist Labor party, 278. Strength of the trade union faction in Chicago, 279. Success in the Chicago election, 279. Failure in Cincinnati, 279. Van Patten's attitude towards trade unions, 280. Workingmen's military organisations, 280. Autumn election of 1879, 282. Chicago — the principal socialist centre, 282. Influence in the state legislature, 283. Chicago municipal election of 1879, 284. Persistent pro-trade union attitude of the Chicago socialists, 284. Effect of prosperity, 284. National convention at Alleghany City, 284. Differences of opinion on a compromise with the greenbackers, 285. National greenback convention, 285. The " socialist " plank in the platform, 286. The double revolt: the " trade union " faction, and the revolutionists in the East, 287. Attitude of the *New Yorker Volkszeitung*, 287. Referendum vote, 288. Decrease in the greenback vote, 289. Struggle between the compromisers and non-compromisers in the socialist ranks, 289.

Evolution Towards Anarchism and " Syndicalism." Chicago and New York, 291. The national convention of the revolutionary socialists, 291. Affiliation with the International Working People's Association in London, 291. Attitude towards politics and trade unionism, 292. August Spies, 291. Proposed form or organisation, 292. Political action in Chicago once more, 292. Reorganisation in Chicago along revolutionary lines, 292. Johann Most and his philosophy, 293. The Pittsburgh convention and the *Manifesto*, 293. Crystallisation of a " syndicalist " philosophy in Chicago, 296. Attitude towards the state, trade unionism, politics, and violence, 294. A model " syndicalist " trade union, 296. The Red International. 298. Burnette G. Haskell and Joseph R. Buchanan, 298. Ebb of the Socialist Labor party, 300.

THE NATIONALISED INTERNATIONAL

ALTHOUGH the Pittsburgh convention of 1876 refused to endorse socialism, it proved a potent agency in favour of socialist unity. The same joint conference, which decided upon a common programme of action at the convention, drew up the articles of fusion.[1] The preliminary terms were a victory for the International since they embodied their attitude on trade unionism and politics, and, besides provided for an international council to maintain permanent connection with the labour organisations of Europe.[2]

The conference appointed a committee of two to serve as an intermediary between the organisations until the final settlement at a Union Congress to be held in Philadelphia. The congress met July 19, 1876, with the following delegates: F. A. Sorge and Otto Weydemeyer, from the International; Conrad A. Conzett, from the Labor party of Illinois; Charles Braun, from the Social Political Workingmen's Society of Cincinnati; and A. Strasser, A. Gabriel, and P. J. McGuire, from the Social Democratic party. The platform of the united party, called the Workingmen's party of the United States, contained a Declaration of Principles, taken from the General Statutes of the International, and a list of demands adopted from the platform of the Social Democratic party.[3] However, with regard to political action and trade unionism, the platform unequivocally took the position of the International. It said:

" The political action of the party is confined generally to obtaining legislative acts in the interest of the working class proper. It will not enter into a political campaign before being strong enough to exercise a perceptible influence, and then in the first place locally in the towns or cities, when demands of purely local character may be presented, providing they are not in conflict with the platform and principles of the party.

" We work for the organization of trades unions upon a national and international basis to ameliorate the condition of the working people and seek to spread therein the above principles." [4]

In the matter of the form of organisation, a concession was

1 The following organisations were represented at the conference: the International with 635 members, the Labor party of Illinois with 593, the Social Democratic party with 1,500, and the Social-Political Workingmen's Society of Cincinnati (German) with 250 members.

2 Chicago *Vorbote*, Apr. 21, 1876.

3 In this respect it resembled the platform adopted by the German socialist congress in 1875 at Gotha at which there took place a fusion of the Lassalleans and the Marxists. The fusion in Germany was a factor in accelerating the fusion in America.

4 *Labor Standard*, Feb. 24, 1877.

made to the Social Democratic party, which demanded a national organisation instead of an international.   The constitution provided for an Executive Committee and a Board of Control. Chicago was elected the seat of the former and Newark the seat of the latter.   A further concession to the Lassalleans was made in a resolution put forward by McGuire and opposed by Sorge, Strasser, Weydemeyer, and Conzett, empowering the executive committee to allow local sections to enter political campaigns when circumstances were very favourable.   The *Vorbote* in Chicago and the *Sozial-Demokrat* in New York were declared official organs, the name of the latter being changed to the *Arbeiterstimme*.   The English organ of the Social Democratic party, the *Socialist,* was treated likewise.   Its name was changed to *Labor Standard* and McDonnell of the United Workers was selected editor.

In order not to endanger union any further, the referendum vote of the membership on the resolutions of the congress was dispensed with, and the Workingmen's Party of the United States was launched immediately after the Congress.

The unification of the socialist factions in 1876 did not do away with the differences within the movement.   The two opposing factions, the Internationalist and the Lassallean, continued to exist as before.   However, their differences became more crystallised and were reduced, as it were, to their bare essence.   The fundamental difference, that between trade unionism, emphasised by the International, and political action, advocated by the Lassalleans, was no longer hidden beneath other distinctions lying nearer the surface.   The Internationalists had conceded to the Lassalleans that the labour movement must become nationalised in order to succeed; the Lassalleans, on their part, had conceded that the emancipation of labour might come through agencies different from co-operative societies with state credit.   Similarly, the old terms " Lassallean " and " Internationalist " gradually gave way to the simpler ones, " political " socialist and " trade union " socialist, which served to convey a better and more exact impression of the actual difference. The victory won by the " trade union " element in the negotiations for unity had been due mainly to the fact that the necessity for capturing the National Labor Convention had made its leadership imperative. The lasting predominance of the " trade union " element was therefore far from being assured.

This came to light soon after the selection of a National Executive Committee, which, in accordance with the constitution, was made by the sections in Chicago, the Union Congress having chosen that city as the seat of the board. The New Haven sections, numbering about a hundred members, decided by a majority of two votes to petition the board for permission to nominate candidates for the legislature. The *Labor Standard* and the *Vorbote* opposed it, but through the efforts of the national secretary, Phillip Van Patten, permission was finally granted.[5] Van Patten was a native American, coming from the middle class and was a leading figure in the socialist movement from 1876 to 1884. His sympathies from the very beginning were apparently with the political rather than with the trade union faction.

The outcome of the New Haven experiment was quite favourable, the ticket polling 640 votes.[6] It naturally tended to encourage the political faction throughout the country, so that the question of immediate political action became the foremost one in the party and the party organs. The example was followed in February, 1877, by the Cincinnati sections.[7] In Milwaukee, where Gustav Lyser, a former Lassallean, edited a paper, the sections formed a Social Democratic party with the object of taking part in the spring election. Even in Chicago, the centre of the trade union faction, the pressure in favour of participating in the next election became so strong that it could no longer be resisted.[8]

The political faction in Chicago was represented by former Lassalleans and by a group of English-speaking socialists. The former had their own organ, called first the *Sozialist* and later changed to the *Chicagoer Volkszeitung*. Knowing that the trade union faction, the *Vorbote* and its followers, would agree to enter politics only under extreme pressure, they called a mass meeting. This was attended by 600 or 700 people, and put through a resolution declaring for entry in the political campaign in the spring, irrespective of whether the national execu-

5 New York *Arbeiterstimme*, Nov. 26, 1876.
6 *Ibid.*
7 *Ibid.*, Feb. 25, 1877.
8 Chicago *Vorbote*, Mar. 10, 1877.

tive permitted it or not. Prominent in this action were Karl
Klinge, Kraus, and Winnen (former Lassalleans), and Albert
R. Parsons, who had recently joined the English-speaking section.[9] The *Vorbote* group, or the trade union faction, desiring
to avoid a split in the party, reluctantly gave in, and Parsons
was nominated at a general meeting of the sections as candidate
for alderman in the Fifteenth ward on a platform demanding
municipal ownership of public utilities, the abolition of the
contract system on city works, fair hours and fair wages for
city employés, and similar measures.[10]

The result of the election proved encouraging. Parsons
polled one-sixth of the total vote cast in his ward.[11] In Milwaukee the socialist ticket polled 1,500 votes and elected 2 aldermen, 2 supervisors, and 2 constables.[12] In Cincinnati the socialist vote reached 3,900, one-tenth of all the votes cast.

This success helped further to strengthen the political faction
in its discontent with the restrictions imposed by the Union
Congress. Already, in February, 1877, the German section in
New York had requested the German section in Newark to support a proposal that a party convention should be called at an
early date. The Newark section, which belonged to the trade
union faction, flatly refused, declaring that the status established
by the Union Congress needed no change.[13]

The situation was described in the correspondence which appeared in April, 1877, in the *Sozial-Demokrat,* the central organ
of the social democracy in Germany: [14]

" The unification of both socialist factions in America, which was
accomplished with enormous difficulty, is still in danger. . . . The
Lassalleans, and with them the younger immigrants, who are yet
novices in the labour movement, desire to enter the political arena
so as to acquire influence, by means of universal suffrage, first in the
municipality, then in the several states, and are consequently very
much dissatisfied with the decision of the Union Congress, which
prohibits the sections from participating in local elections before
they can feel certain of success, and even then only on a platform of
purely labour demands. The Internationalists and the older and
more experienced immigrants, on the other hand, foresee nothing

9 *Ibid.*
10 *Ibid.*, Mar. 17 and 24, 1877.
11 *Ibid.*, Apr. 14, 1877.
12 New York, *Arbeiterstimme,* Apr. 15, 1877.
13 *Ibid.*, Feb. 28, 1877.
14 Reprinted in the Chicago *Vorbote,* May 19, 1877.

but calamity if political action is begun at once. The former have small faith in trade unions and their efficacy; the latter expect salvation to come only from the trade unions. The former point to the example of the German socialists, the latter to that of the British trade unions. The former are represented in the *Arbeiterstimme* and in the German dailies of Chicago [the *Volkszeitung*] and Milwaukee [the *Sozialist*], as well as in the newly established English paper in Milwaukee [the *Emancipator*]; the latter in the *Vorbote* and *Labor Standard*. The former seek to get the small *bourgeoisie* interested in the party; the latter want to restrict it exclusively to wage-earners and expect only demoralisation to follow from a participation by still unproletarised small *bourgeois*. The former are seeking to change the party platform at another convention, the latter threaten to step out of the party should this occur. . . ."

For·a time, the *Arbeiterstimme* of New York, edited by Dr. Otto Walster, tried to occupy a neutral position. It opened its columns to both sides and accepted articles from John Schäfer, of the political faction, as well as from Adolph Strasser, who, notwithstanding his brief sojourn in the camp of the Lassalleans, was above all an advocate of trade unions. Finally, in May, 1877, it unequivocally put itself among the ranks of the political socialists.[15] "We consider that the trade-union movement in itself is sufficiently harmless but we also maintain that those trade unionists are extremely harmful who believe that this weapon [the trade union] is not a mere palliative, but possesses sufficient strength to bring about the abolition of the poverty, exploitation and oppression of the organised as well as of the unorganised labouring masses." McDonnell, the editor of the *Labor Standard* and the leader of the English-speaking socialists in the East, went to the opposite extreme. While favouring legislation, he declared that " as long as there are working people starving, it is utterly wrong to spend money on objects which bring no immediate relief to the toiler," and, further, that " political action must be of a practical character. To convince the masses that we are in earnest, we must always act for the material interests of the whole working class, never indulge in mere speculations. A mere canvass for some members of our own party will fail to attract the support that politi-

15 New York *Arbeiterstimme*, May 20, 1877.

cal [legislative] action on our part for some great measure such
as the reduction of the hours of labor would bring. . . ." [16]

The *Vorbote* in Chicago fully agreed with the *Labor Standard* on the supreme importance of trade unions, but was more
lenient with respect to immediate political action.[17]   This difference of opinion readily lends itself to explanation when we
recall that in Chicago the trade union socialists had been forced
to compromise with their "political" brethren and to take up
political action.   The National Executive Committee, influenced by Van Patten, was strongly in sympathy with the political faction.   It despatched P. J. McGuire on an extended tour
over the country, during which he made an effective agitation
for political action.   It was also zealous in supporting the
Arbeiterstimme, while it was only lukewarm toward the *Labor
Standard.*   The American section in New York even went as
far as to accuse Van Patten of intriguing to replace the *Labor
Standard* by the "political" Milwaukee *Emancipator* as the
official English organ of the party.

In the beginning of May, the controversy reached a critical
stage.   The *Labor Standard* suspended publication for a week,
and reappeared with the consent of the National Board of Control.[18]   It was still the official organ of the party but its ownership was transferred from the party to a private publishing association of which McDonnell was director.   This caused a
tempest in the camp of the political faction.   The business
manager of the *Arbeiterstimme,* who also acted as business manager for the *Labor Standard,* refused to deliver the books to the
new association.   The National Executive Committee felt in-
censed over the unconstitutional interference by the National
Board of Control and retaliated in an equally unconstitutional
manner by setting aside the Board which had its seat in Newark
and by calling upon the New Haven sections to elect its successor.   At the same time the National Executive Committee
submitted to a referendum vote, with its favourable recommendation, a call for a new party convention made [19] by the
political faction.

Adolph Douai attempted to arbitrate between the quarrelling

16 *Labor Standard,* Mar. 24, 1877.   18 *Labor Standard,* June 2, 1877.
17 Chicago *Vorbote,* Aug. 11, 1877.   19 New York *Arbeiterstimme,* June 3, 1877.

factions. At a general meeting of the New York sections, called for that purpose, he admitted that trade unions on the British pattern were imperfect, but he pointed out that, on the other hand, it was utterly impossible to adopt the tactics of the German Social Democracy, for "should we adopt immediate political action, our party would be in peril of being overrun by non-proletarian elements." [20] Douai's mission proved unsuccessful, for the opponents charged him with viewing matters too much through Sorge's spectacles. [21]

Meanwhile, a new factor, far more powerful than the arguments on either side, came to determine which element should have the upper hand in the party. The great strike of July, 1877, broke out and spread over the country. The Workingmen's party was taken completely unaware, but in numerous cities socialist sections or individual socialists made good use of this spontaneous outburst. In St. Louis, when the general excitement caused the shutting down of factories and slaughter houses, the socialists called a mass meeting and elected an executive committee to look after the interests of the workingmen. The panic of the authorities was so great that this committee, about whose membership nobody really knew anything, was able to hold undisputed sway over the city for more than a week. In Chicago, the socialist masses were the hardest sufferers. There the police did not wait for the rioting to begin, but broke into the hall where cabinet makers on strike were holding a mass meeting and unmercifully attacked the assembly, with the result that there were dead and wounded on both sides. [22] This unnecessary use of violence on the part of the police was remembered for many years afterwards and was partly responsible for the tactics of violence that the Chicago movement adopted at a later date.

The National Executive Committee ordered the sections to call mass meetings and to offer resolutions for an eight-hour law throughout the union, for the abolition of all conspiracy laws and for the purchase by the Federal Government of the railway and telegraph lines. [23] In Chicago, a mass meeting of 15,000 to 20,000 people had adopted a similar resolution. [24] In Brook-

20 Ibid., June 17, 1877.
21 Ibid.
22 Chicago Vorbote, Aug. 4, 1877.

23 New York Arbeiterstimme, Sept. 2, 1877.
24 Chicago Vorbote, July 28, 1877.

lyn, Newark, Paterson, and other cities [25] the socialists developed like activity. In Louisville, Kentucky, the German and English sections called a general labour convention and nominated 7 candidates for the legislature, of whom 5 were elected, and the ticket polled a total vote of 8,848 against 5,162 cast for the Democrats.[26]

THE RUSH INTO POLITICS

The outcome of the struggle within the party between the trade union and political factions was thus decided in favour of the latter by the political turn of the general labour movement. The sections began making preparations for the next campaign in spite of the decision of the Union Congress. The need for a new convention to revise the party's attitude toward political action became so pressing that the executive committee and the Board of Control jointly issued on October 14, 1877, a call for a convention that should meet in Newark on November 11,[27] notwithstanding the fact that the referendum had decided against a convention.[28]

Meanwhile, many of the local sections nominated candidates for the autumn election and met with considerable success. The vote was approximately as follows: in Chicago, 7,000; Cincinnati, 9,000; Buffalo, 6,000; Milwaukee, 1,500; New York, 1,800; Brooklyn, 1,200; New Haven, 1,600; and Detroit, 800.[29] In many cities the sections compromised with the greenbackers. In Louisville they headed the platform with a money plank; in Pittsburgh, they nominated a joint ticket. In Philadelphia and Baltimore the Workingmen's party was weak and the swollen labour vote went to the greenbackers.

The party convention met in Newark on December 26, 1877, several weeks later than the date that had been set in the call. Twenty-nine sections were represented: 17 German, 7 English, 3 Bohemian, 1 French, and 1 women's section. The inland sections, with few exceptions, were represented by proxies. Chicago sent A. R. Parsons and St. Louis, Albert Currlin. The

25 New York *Arbeiterstimme*, Aug. 5, 1877.
26 *Ibid.*, Aug. 19, 1877.
27 New York *Arbeiterstimme*, Oct. 14, 1877.
28 Chicago *Vorbote*, Sept. 1, 1877.

29 These are the figures given in the Chicago *Vorbote*, Nov. 3 and 17, 1877, and New York *Arbeiterstimme*, Nov. 18, 1877.

Labor Standard element kept away from the convention.   The report of the National Executive Committee stated that the total number of sections was 72, with approximately 7,000 members in good standing, that the party published 21 papers, of which the *Chicagoer Arbeiter-Zeitung* and the Philadelphia *Tageblatt* were dailies.

From the very beginning of the convention it was apparent that the political faction was in control.   A special committee, on examining the report of the National Executive Committee, reported that the latter was wrong when it stated that the former members of the Social Democratic party were the only ones dissatisfied with the decision of the Union Congress in 1876 to abstain from politics for the present.   The former members of the organisations in Milwaukee and Cincinnati, as well as a portion of the Labor party of Illinois, were also among the dissatisfied element.   The report was adopted by the convention, which further sustained the policy of the National Executive Committee with respect to the *Labor Standard,* and declared as the official organs of the party the *Arbeiterstimme,* the Bohemian daily *Delnicke Listy* in Cleveland, and an English paper which it was decided to establish in place of the *Labor Standard.*   The *Vorbote* in Chicago was punished for its adherence to the trade union faction by being removed from the list of the officially recognised papers.   Alexander Jonas was elected editor of the *Arbeiterstimme* in place of George Winter, who was temporary editor, after Otto Walster had resigned to become editor of the *Arbeiterstimme des Westens* in St. Louis.   The seat of the National Executive Committee was transferred to Cincinnati, with the provision, however, that Van Patten should continue as secretary.   The National Board of Control was left in Newark, and Alleghany City was chosen as the place of the next convention.

Further, the name of the party was changed to Socialist Labor party and the declaration of principles and the constitution were fundamentally remodelled.   These naturally affirmed that political action was the main function of the party, but included a provision that no man could be nominated for office if he had not been a party member for at least one year.   It was also decided that the party " should maintain friendly relations with the trade unions and should promote their formation upon socialistic principles," that there should be only one section in a locality, which could be subdivided further into ward and precinct organisations, but that business should be transacted only at the general meeting of the section. All sections of one State should form a state organisation [30] which should hold a convention before each state election. The national convention should meet at least once in two years and should select the seats of the National Executive Committee and the National Board of Control, the two highest agencies in the party.

Thus reorganised, it was thought that the Socialist Labor party was admirably fitted for its paramount function — the management of political campaigns.

The constitution which was adopted at the convention in Newark provided that a referendum vote of the sections should be taken on its decisions. The feeling in the party, however, was so overwhelmingly in favour of the new policy that the *Vorbote* [31] accepted it as a foregone conclusion. Chicago remained the stronghold of the trade union faction, but even there it was far from having complete control. For the English-speaking branch, which had first been organised by P. J. McGuire in 1876, and which had since steadily gained in strength under the leadership of Thomas J. Morgan, George Schilling, and A. R. Parsons, belonged to the political faction.

Meanwhile, the time for the spring election drew closer. The socialists made nominations in Chicago and Cincinnati, and in Milwaukee several of the candidates were endorsed by the old parties. The vote stood at about 8,000 in Chicago, one-seventh of the total vote cast, while it had been only one-eighth the autumn before, and two aldermen were elected.[32] In Cincinnati, the vote fell from 9,000 to 1,800.[33] The difference in the fate of the tickets in these cities is easily understood when we take into consideration that in Chicago over 100 trade unionists distributed socialist tickets on election day,[34] while in Cincinnati no such close connection with the trade unions existed.

30 The proceedings of the Newark convention are given in the Chicago *Vorbote*, Jan. 5, 1878; and in the New York *Arbeiterstimme*, Jan. 6, 1878. The *Labor Standard* passed it by in complete silence.
31 Jan. 12, 1878.

32 Chicago *Vorbote*, Apr. 13, 1878.
33 *Ibid*.
34 The Chicago *Vorbote* of June 22, 1878, enumerates over twenty trade unions in Chicago which had indorsed the Socialist Labor party.

It appears that the trade union socialists, who were opposed to immediate political action and accepted it only under pressure, were in a better position than their " political " brethren to secure a lasting political success.

In May, 1878, the National Executive Committee began publishing an English weekly in Cincinnati, the *National Socialist*. Van Patten was a steady contributor and controlled the policy of the paper. When McDonnell, with the followers of Ira Steward, launched the International Labor Union [35] in an attempt to organise the unskilled, Van Patten wrote: " The International Labor Union is far from perfect, and is unfortunately afflicted with a narrow-minded management. Its plans and its platform, however, are good, and it is easier to purify it by developing, than to stamp out and commence afresh, supposing the latter was entertained.   The men who have called it into existence are earnest, and with a few exceptions, honest." [36]

In contrast with Van Patten's lukewarm and reserved approval, the *Vorbote* gave the International Labor Union an enthusiastic welcome and declared that its formation was a triumph for the Socialist Labor party.[37]

The differences between the trade union faction in Chicago and the National Executive Committee soon reached an acute stage over the question of workingmen's military organisations. Such an organisation, called the Lehr und Wehr Verein, had been organised and incorporated by the Chicago German socialists in 1875 in protest against the policy of physical intimidation practised by the old political parties on election day.[38]   The need for such societies seemed to be more fully demonstrated in the atrocities committed by the police in Chicago during the strike of the cabinetmakers in July, 1877.   The example set in Chicago began to be imitated in other cities, so that finally the National Executive Committee grew alarmed, and on June 13, 1878, issued an address repudiating all socialist military organisations.[39]   At once the *Vorbote* came to the aid of socialist militarism.   It pointed out that the organisations might become useful if the ruling class should dare to restrict the right of free

35 See below, II, 308 *et seq.*
36 Cincinnati *National Socialist*, May 11, 1878.
37 Chicago *Vorbote*, July 13, 1878.
38 *Ibid.*, May 11, 1878.
39 Cincinnati *National Socialist*, June 22, 1878.

speech and of public meeting, or if the police should again commit atrocities against strikers as they had done in 1877. " Such," the *Vorbote* declared, " was the view of all those who cared nothing for being elected to office, but who kept at heart the immediate material betterment of the condition of the workingmen." [40]

Gustav Lyser was at that time editor of the *Vorbote,* after Conrad Conzett had left for Europe. Lyser, as was seen, had changed from an enemy of trade unions to an extreme trade union socialist. The *Vorbote* stood alone among the entire socialist press [41] in its defence of military organisations. The National Executive Committee, upheld by the majority of the sections, retaliated by repudiating the *Vorbote* as a party organ. One month later, the management of the paper passed into the hands of Paul Grottkau, one of the first refugees to America from the German anti-socialist law of 1878. The issue of military organisation was allowed to fall asleep, but the changed management by no means meant a radical change in the policy of the paper, for Grottkau had embraced the views of the trade union socialists as soon as he grew familiar with the situation. Evidently the trade union socialists were not impressed by the fear, which underlay the policy of Van Patten and the political faction, that a recognition of the military organisations would drive law-abiding voters away from the party.

The factional struggle continued unallayed, and Van Patten, in the semi-annual report of the National Executive Committee, complained bitterly. A temporary reconciliation was effected in the following September, when Van Patten was obliged to ask the Chicago section for aid in establishing an English paper in Chicago. The National Executive Committee had bad luck with its official organs. The numerous local papers — there were 19 such papers in 1878, among them 7 dailies — competed so successfully with the national organs that the New York *Arbeiterstimme* was compelled to cease publication in June, 1878. The official organ in the English language, the *National Socialist,* in Cincinnati, was also running at such a deficit that its publication had to be suspended. The *Arbeiterstimme* could well be dis-

40 Chicago *Vorbote,* June 29, 1878.
41 The Cincinnati *National Socialist,* May 4, 1876, enumerated 17 existing socialist papers: 7 dailies, 6 German and 1 Bohemian; 4 German weeklies; 4 English, 1 Bohemian, and 1 Scandinavian.

pensed with by the party, for its place was amply filled by the numerous local German papers. It was different, however, with the *National Socialist*. An English organ was necessary to carry on the agitation among the English-speaking workingmen. This consideration moved Van Patten to seek to obliterate his differences with the Chicago section, for Chicago, he thought, was the only place where an English organ could be sustained. His negotiations were crowned with success. The new English organ, called the *Socialist*, appeared in Chicago on September 14, 1878,[42] under the joint editorship of Frank Hirth, formerly editor of the Detroit *Socialist*, a paper sympathising with the trade-union faction, and A. R. Parsons.

At the next national and state elections, the socialists in Chicago polled 7,000 votes and elected 4 members to the legislature, 1 senator and 3 assemblymen.[43] In New York the previous vote of about 2,000 was now doubled. In St. Louis, 3 socialist representatives to the legislature were elected. But in Cincinnati, where the vote had been over 9,000 a year before and 1,800 six months before, it now fell to about 500. The complete fiasco in Cincinnati is explained by the fact that the vote in the autumn election of 1877, immediately following the big strikes, was unnaturally swollen, and that the Cincinnati socialists, belonging to the political faction, had established no connections with the trade unions. They therefore missed the opportunity of perpetuating in the latter the political discontent of 1877, with the inevitable result that they were now at the mercy of the receding wave of political enthusiasm. In fact, the Cincinnati trades council turned against the socialists and endorsed the Republican candidates.[44]

Chicago now became the undisputed centre of the socialist movement in the country. Its section numbered 870 members in good standing.[45] It published 4 socialist papers: 2 in the German language, the *Chicagoer Arbeiter-Zeitung* (daily) and the *Vorbote;* 1 in English, the *Socialist,* and 1 in Scandinavian, the *Nye Tid*. Peace reigned within the section. The political faction, represented by the English-speaking members, under Thomas J. Morgan's leadership, peacefully co-operated with the

42 The Chicago *Socialist* expired within a year.

43 Chicago *Vorbote*, Nov. 9, 1878.

44 Cincinnati *National Socialist*, Oct. 19, 1878.

45 Chicago *Vorbote*, Feb. 8, 1879.

trade union element, a fact which was largely due to the efforts of A. R. Parsons, who enjoyed the full confidence of both factions. The influence of the socialist members of the legislature was considerable. They succeeded in bringing about the appointment of a joint committee to investigate causes of industrial depression in the State. Karl Eberhardt, a socialist, was made chairman of the committee.[46] Thomas J. Morgan, one of the most influential men in the socialist section, appeared before the committee on behalf of the Socialist Labor party and the Chicago Trades Council. The intimate relations that existed between the trade unions and the socialists is further illustrated by the fact that A. R. Parsons was secretary of the trades council. Taking all these facts into consideration, it is not at all surprising that, at the next municipal election in April, 1879, the socialist vote rose to 11,800 and three aldermen were elected, in addition to the one elected the preceding year.[47] In Cincinnati the socialist vote was even less than it had been in the autumn.

The victories at the polls in Chicago, while naturally tending to bring the political faction into greater prominence, nevertheless caused no great change in the attitude of the trade union faction. On October 11, 1879, in connection with the forthcoming party congress, the *Vorbote* wrote as follows:

" The trade-union organisation always appears to us as the natural and fundamental organisation of the working class, and, being convinced that it should be entitled to all the support we can possibly give it, *for its own sake,* we cannot utter too strongly our feeling of protest, when here and there the over-zealous but unintelligent followers of the political labour movement desire to use the trade unions as mere auxiliaries for the Social-Democracy and demand that they should become socialistic in the sense in which that word applies to our political party."

The *Vorbote* declared in the same article that if it were obliged to choose between trade union and political action, its choice would invariably fall on the former. But we have no such alternative before us, it proceeded to say; therefore, we can be active in both spheres. Nevertheless, we must always place economic action above political.

46 *Ibid.*, Feb. 15, 1879.   47 *Ibid.*, Apr. 5, 1879.

The return of industrial prosperity in 1879 put an end to the socialist success at the polls in Chicago. At the autumn election in 1879, the socialist vote fell from 12,000 to 4,800. The *Vorbote* frankly acknowledged that the defeat was due, not to fraudulent practices by the other parties, but to the return of " good times." [48]   The situation was characterised by Van Patten as follows: [49]

" The result of the fall election shows little progress made toward uniting the workingmen.   Our party has gained slightly in New York, Detroit, Cincinnati,[50] and lost considerably in Chicago.   Were it not that we have succeeded in awakening a great revival among the trade unions of the West, we should feel discouraged at the slow growth of our political strength. . . .   The only reliable foundation to-day is the Trade Union organisation, and while political efforts of a spasmodic nature will often achieve temporary success, yet the only test of political strength is the extent to which trade union organization backs up the political movement."

Van Patten's admission does not signify that he accepted the position of the trade union faction.   Subsequent events will show that he sought salvation from a different source than trade unions.

The next national convention of the Socialist Labor party met in December, 1879, at Alleghany. City.[51]   The report of the national executive gave neither the number of sections nor the membership — a reliable proof of the diminution in the party's strength.   The protest raised by the Chicago German sub-section against the circular issued by the National Executive Committee with respect to the military organisations was disposed of by a compromise.   The convention praised the National Executive Committee for disclaiming all official connection between the party and such organisations, but censured it for calling upon individual party members to withdraw from them.   It also adopted a lukewarm resolution calling for the support of trade unions, and passed on to its chief business — the presidential campaign of 1880.

48 Chicago *Vorbote*, Nov. 8, 1879.
49 *Bulletin of the Social Labor Movement*, I, No. 2, November, 1879. This was issued by the National Executive Committee in Cincinnati, Ohio, in place of the deceased *Socialist* in Chicago.

50 In these cities the socialist vote had fallen off at previous elections.
51 It was attended by twenty-five delegates; Chicago sent Jeffers and Parsons.

There were three distinct currents of opinion at the convention. The delegates from Brooklyn and Philadelphia stood for a compromise with all liberal and labour organisations, not only in the selection of candidates, but, if necessary, also in framing a platform. The delegates from St. Louis, Chicago, and the Middle West generally advocated the sending of delegates to the greenback conference [52] and to the one called by Kearney,[53] with instructions, however, that they should use their utmost endeavours to secure the united support of all labour organisations and liberal elements for the socialist principles and platform and a socialist candidate. Failing in this, they were to withdraw from the conferences and nominate an independent socialist ticket. Lastly, the delegates from New York, Boston, and Alleghany City insisted that the socialist party should nominate candidates without reference to any other party.

The convention adopted none of these views in its entirety, but decided to nominate three men who should be voted upon by the sections, the one getting the largest number of votes to be presidential candidate and the next, vice-presidential candidate. It was further resolved that a special socialist convention be called in Chicago on the day when the Kearney conference was set to meet so as to influence it in the direction of socialism. The three nominees were Caleb Pink and Osborne Ward, of New York, and Orin A. Bishop, of Chicago. They were chosen, not by reason of their prominence in the movement, but because they were the most eligible among the small portion of the membership which satisfied the constitutional requirements of age and native birth.

After it had re-elected Van Patten as national secretary and transferred the seat of the National Executive Committee to Detroit, the convention adjourned.[54]

In spite of the fact that the Socialist Labor party had taken no official steps for representation at the greenback conference in Washington, to be held in January, 1880, the socialist element, as shown above, was there represented by A. R. Parsons, who went as a delegate from the Chicago Eight-Hour League.[55]

52 See above, II, 250.
53 See above, II, 249.
54 *Bulletin of the Social Labor Movement* (Detroit), January and February, 1880. (The Bulletin was transferred with this issue from Cincinnati to Detroit.)
55 *Ibid,*

Through a referendum vote, the Socialist Labour party also rescinded its former decision to proceed with the nomination of independent candidates, and decided to send delegates to the convention in Chicago called by the above conference.[56] At the convention the socialists had 44 delegates out of 756. The prominent leaders, such as Van Patten, Parsons, Douai, and McGuire were in attendance. Realising that they were too weak numerically to play an important rôle in the convention, they decided to centre their efforts upon the adoption of the following plank:

" We declare that land, light, air and water are the free gifts of nature to all mankind, and any law or custom of society that allows any person to monopolise more of these gifts than he has a right to, to the detriment of the rights of others, we earnestly condemn and seek to abolish." [57]

Even this colourless plank, which contained nothing specifically socialistic, proved unacceptable to the greenback leaders. Through a skilful use of parliamentary methods they succeeded in preventing a vote upon it until after the platform had been adopted and nominations made. Then it was adopted by a large majority, not, however, as a plank in the platform, for the greenback parliamentarians claimed that nothing could be added to the platform after nominations had been made, but merely as a special resolution of the convention which was " just as good." Notwithstanding this procedure, the socialist delegates met after the convention had adjourned and issued a declaration to the effect that the Socialist Labor party had a right to view with satisfaction the adoption of a radical platform and the nominations of Weaver and Chambers. However, should the national committee of the Greenback party under any pretext go back upon the land resolution, they would still continue to give their support to the greenback candidates, but would openly declare that their resolution had been barred from becoming a part of the platform through parliamentary trickery.[58]   The *New Yorker Volkszeitung* [59] likewise expressed full satisfaction with the effected compromise.

56 Chicago *Vorbote*, Apr. 24, 1880.
57 *Labor Review*, June, 1880. The *Bulletin of the Social Labor Movement* appeared under this name from March to June, 1880.
58 *Ibid.*
59 June 14, 1880.

But the delegates and the *Volkszeitung* voiced the sentiments of only one element in the Socialist Labor party. The trade union faction, which was keeping in the background while negotiations were carried on with the Greenback party, raised a cry of protest when the compromise was completed. Paul Grottkau, in the *Vorbote,* and Peterson, the editor of the Scandinavian paper, *Nye Tid,* at once started a passionate agitation for the repudiation of the compromise. The slump in the socialist vote in the autumn election of 1879 in Chicago had finally broken the moral prestige that the political faction enjoyed in that city. Also the disappointment with the outcome in the spring election of 1880 when, in spite of all predictions, the vote failed to rise again, helped to fix a well-settled sentiment against political action. This sentiment was further enforced by the fact that the only alderman who succeeded in getting re-elected at the latest election (by a majority of thirty-one votes) was kept out of his seat by the manipulation of a Democratic city council.[60]

These circumstances prompted the trade union element in the control of the German and Scandinavian subsections to take a firm stand against the greenback compromise which was, of course, supported by the political faction under the leadership of the American section. The latter, still having a majority on its side in the general meeting of the section in the city, retaliated by expelling Grottkau and Peterson from the party. The German and Scandinavian subsections, however, rallied strongly to their support and the factional struggle reached a high pitch. The American subsection then issued a call against its trade unionist opponents, and the conflict was justly described as one between the trade union and political factions of socialism.[61]

The protest against the compromise was not confined to Chicago. The section in New York had even preceded Chicago in

[60] He gained his seat one year later after a jury trial. Chicago *Vorbote,* Nov. 13, 1880. George A. Schilling said in his "History of the Labor Movement in Chicago," in *Life of Albert R. Parsons* (Parsons, 2d ed.), XXVIII, that this unlawful unseating of the socialist alderman "did more, perhaps, than all the other things combined to destroy the faith of the Socialists in Chicago in the efficiency of the ballot." However, as far as the trade union faction was concerned, the counting out of the socialist candidate merely helped to strengthen an aversion to politics which had existed in a more or less latent form throughout the seventies. Schilling had been, until 1882, a member of the political faction and naturally reflected in his recollections his sentiments at that time.

[61] Chicago *Vorbote,* July 17, 1880.

voicing their disapproval of the " deal." The delegate from New York, Bachman, at the Chicago convention had instructions to vote against it. The opposition in New York, however, differed substantially from that in Chicago in the manner in which it arrived at the attitude of non-compromise, if not in the attitude itself. In New York the anti-compromise faction did not coincide with the trade union faction. In fact, there, as will be seen, the trade union faction, together with McDonnell, had left the party as early as 1877, so that the line was drawn, not between the trade union and political socialists, but between the moderates on one side and the revolutionaries on the other. The moderates were grouped around the *New Yorker Volkszeitung* and the revolutionaries were for the most part refugees from the German anti-socialist law of 1878 and those under their influence. As stated above, the trade union socialists in Chicago had started with a general lack of enthusiasm for political action. They consequently felt averse to sacrificing the purity of their movement in exchange for the chimerical political advantage that the greenback compromise would bring. Added to this, though of lesser importance, was a more or less wide-spread revolutionary feeling caused mainly by the fraudulent unseating of the only alderman whom they had elected at the last election, as well as by the still burning memory of the police outrages of 1877, and by the influence of the few refugees from Germany. In New York, on the contrary, the opposition to the greenback compromise was due solely to a revolutionary sentiment. The revolutionaries there regarded trade unionism with the same unfavourable eyes that they cast on Van Patten's practical politics, for they believed that when allowed free rein both would equally lead the labour movement into the perilous channel of opportunism, and that both should, therefore, be reduced to the rank of mere auxiliaries to the social revolutionary agitation.

The result of the party referendum on this vexatious question became known in the middle of August. All sections except New York, Lawrence, Massachusetts, New Orleans, and the German and Scandinavian subsections of Chicago, voted as units in favour of the compromise. The membership vote was more evenly divided, the greenback candidates were endorsed by

608 votes against 396, and the platform by 521 votes against 455.[62]

The Chicago opponents of the greenback compromise were the first to raise the standard of rebellion. They gained control [63] of the local central committee one week after the results of the referendum had been made known, and started an agitation to elect provisionally a new executive committee and a board of control.[64] The New York section likewise refused to bow to the decision of the referendum and demanded a new party convention.[65] In order to appease the agitation, Van Patten wrote to the presidential candidate, General Weaver, inquiring whether he accepted the land plank. A letter came in from Chambers, the candidate for vice-president, in which absolute assurance was given that the land plank was heartily endorsed by Weaver and himself as well as by every greenbacker.[66] But this was hardly sufficient to put a stop to the rebellion. In fact, the New York section immediately passed a resolution declaring that the land plank was not socialistic since it allowed for private property in land, that Van Patten's letter to Weaver was entirely uncalled for, and that, therefore, the socialists ought not to vote for the greenback candidates.[67]

The outcome of the election was in full accord with the situation. In view of the " good times " the vote for Weaver and Chambers fell from the aggregate congressional vote of over 1,000,000 in 1878 to barely 300,000. The Socialist Labor party was beaten even more badly than the Greenback party. The compromise agreement had only covered the candidates for president and vice-president. All other candidates the socialists nominated independently. But dissensions broke out also over these nominations. In Chicago the anti-compromisers seceded and nominated A. R. Parsons, who had meantime come over to the trade union side, for assemblyman in the sixth district, against Christian Meier, the regular socialist candidate who was supported by Thomas J. Morgan and George A. Schilling, the leaders of the political compromisers. Meier

62 *Ibid.*, Aug. 21, 1880.
63 *Ibid.*, Sept. 4, 1880.
64 *Ibid.*, Oct. 16, 1880.
65 *Ibid.*, Sept. 11, 1880.
66 *New Yorker Volkszeitung*, Aug. 25, 1880.

67 *Bulletin of the Social Labor Movement*, September, 1880. The bulletin was resumed in September, 1880, and continued for three more months.

received 3,418 votes and Parsons only 495, since many *Vorbote*
socialists refrained from voting.[68] Neither was elected. In
New York there was only one socialist ticket in the field, put
forth by the " political " minority in the section, and it received
the normal vote of approximately 3,000. In St. Louis the anti-
compromise faction, headed by Albert Currlin, seceded from
the section with the result that the vote fell off considerably.[69]

The election of 1880 brought the political strength of socialism back to the point where it was prior to the political upheaval
of 1877. From this election also dates the development of the
socialist movement towards pure anarchism in the eastern cities,
towards anarchistic trade unionism, or a kind of a " syndicalism," in Chicago and the cities of the Middle West, and towards the new trade unionism of the American Federation of
Labor.

ANARCHISM AND " SYNDICALISM "

The Socialist Labor party emerged from the campaign of
1880 weakened in membership and divided into hostile factions.
The German, Bohemian, and Scandinavian subsections, and the
radical members in the English-speaking subsection in Chicago,
held a meeting immediately after the election, and resolved to
issue an address to all sections in the country recommending
the election of a new national executive committee. The same
meeting laid down a radical plan for future action in which
the strongest emphasis was laid upon trade unionism. A
permanent union was urged with the workingmen's military
organisation, and political action was favoured only in districts
where the socialists had a fair chance of being elected.[70] Following this, the central committee of the Chicago section issued,
in conjunction with the Agitation Committee of the Grand
Council of the Armed Organisations, a call [71] to " all revolutionists and armed workingmen's organisations in the country,"
pointing out the necessity of " getting ready to offer an armed
resistance to the invasions by the capitalist class and capitalist
legislatures." The English-speaking socialists in Chicago remained loyal to the National Executive Committee. They

68 Chicago *Vorbote*, Oct. 30, 1880.
69 *Bulletin of the Social Labor Move-*
ment, October and November, 1880.

70 Chicago *Vorbote*, Nov. 27, 1880.
71 *Ibid.*, Dec. 4, 1880.

held a meeting in the latter part of December,[72] at which they condemned the violent utterances of the address and declared that political action was the only reliable weapon of the workingmen.

In New York, as in Chicago, the movement was divided into two hostile factions, the revolutionary and the moderate. The former seceded from the Socialist Labor party and organised a social revolutionary club with Hasselman, Bachman, and Justus Schwab as the leading spirits.[73] A similar club, consisting mostly of newly arrived German immigrants, who were for the most part refugees escaping from the German anti-socialist law, was organised in Philadelphia.

An attempt to organise the revolutionary socialists on a national scale was made at a convention which met in Chicago, October 21, 1881. The original call came from New York, where the social revolutionary club had meantime affiliated with the International Working People's Association, the so-called Black International, having its headquarters in London, which had been organised in' July, 1881, by European anarchists. Delegates came also from Chicago, New York, Philadelphia, Boston, St. Louis, Louisville, Omaha, Milwaukee, Kansas City, Paterson, Jersey City, Jersey City Heights, Union Hill, and Hoboken. Justus Schwab of New York, and the four Chicago delegates, Winnen, Parsons, August Spies,[74] and Petersen, were the leading figures at the convention. In the discussion of the platform of the proposed national organisation, New York showed itself more radical than Chicago. Schwab condemned in unqualified terms all participation in political campaigns, while Spies, Winnen, and Parsons were

[72] *Ibid.*, Jan. 8, 1881.

[73] Hasselman had been expelled from the German Social Democratic party for denouncing parliamentarism. Bachman had been an advocate of the greenback compromise at the Chicago convention, but had now become more radical.

[74] August Vincent Theodore Spies, one of the Chicago anarchists, was born in 1855 at Friedewald, Kurhessen, Germany. His father was a government forester. He studied forestry at first, but was obliged to emigrate at the age of seventeen, after his father died. Landing in New York, he began to learn the trade of upholsterer. In 1872 he went to Chi-

cago and after several years set up in the furniture business for himself. His first interest in socialism was aroused in 1876, and the strikes of 1877 made him a convinced socialist. From that year until 1880 he was a member of the Socialist Labor party and ran for office on the ticket of that party in 1879 and 1880. Like other Chicago socialists he was a trade union socialist, laying the greatest emphasis upon trade union action. In 1880 he became business manager of the *Arbeiter Zeitung* and the *Vorbote*, and in 1881, editor. He carefully studied Marx, Proudhon, Buckle, and Morgan.

still in favour of the use of the ballot for agitational purposes. Schwab's attitude prevailed at the convention and the political plank was rejected. On the other hand, with regard to the trade union question, the Chicago delegates defeated Schwab, who felt lukewarm toward trade unions. The convention strongly recommended the organisation of trade unions upon progressive principles and promised active support to such trade unions as were already in existence. The convention further endorsed the London Congress of the International Working People's Association, and declared itself in favour of societies which "stand ready to render armed resistance to encroachments upon the rights of the workingmen." [75] The new national organisation was christened the Revolutionary Socialist party, and was intended to be a loose federation of autonomous groups with an information bureau located in Chicago to serve as the connecting link. The latter was to have a corresponding secretary for each language, with expenses covered by voluntary contributions from the groups. Each constituent group was left absolute master over its own activities, except that it was not supposed to come into conflict with the general programme and the resolutions of the federation.

Before the referendum vote on the decisions of the convention had been completed, the Chicago group, as yet not entirely satisfied with the voting down of the political plank, decided to try political action once more, and took part in the municipal campaign of the spring of 1882. However, it went into the election with a strictly revolutionary platform and refused to cooperate with the regular section of the Socialist Labor party, which was now dominated by English-speaking people and which remained loyal to the National Executive Committee. The revolutionaries nominated George A. Schilling, who had changed factions since the election of 1880, as candidate for mayor. Neither of the socialist tickets received an appreciable number of votes, since greater efforts were made on both sides to defeat the rival candidates than to win voters from older parties.

The campaign proved fatal to the section of the Socialist Labor party, but the effect upon the revolutionary socialists

75 Chicago *Vorbote*, Oct. 29, 1881.

was merely to destroy their last vestige of faith even in the agitational usefulness of political campaigns. Already in February, 1882, during the progress of the political campaign they had ratified the decisions of the October convention and definitely reorganised upon the principle of autonomous groups. Socialists in any part of the city might organise an unlimited number of groups with not less than ten members each, to be united by a central committee. Representation was likewise to be granted to radical trade unions. The decisions of the central committee were to be valid only when not objected to by any group at its first succeeding meeting. The prerogatives of the central committee were further limited by a maximum expenditure of $20 for any one object. Larger expenditures could be incurred only when authorised by a referendum vote of the groups. Each member paid 10 cents per month, of which only one-tenth went to the central committee.[76] The national information bureau, which the Chicago organisation was authorised by the convention to establish, was not organised until April, 1883, indicating the lack of cohesion among the revolutionary groups of the country. Indeed, the New York group, notwithstanding the fact that it had taken the lead in calling the convention of 1881, now hesitated to recognise the National Information Bureau. It became apparent therefore, that another national convention was required in order that the revolutionary movement in the country might become unified. A general vote of the groups designated such a convention to meet in Pittsburgh on October 19, 1883.

The delegates from Chicago at the Pittsburgh convention, Parsons, Spies, Meng, and Rau, represented the trade union wing of the social revolutionary movement in the country. Their ideas were shared *in toto* by the delegates from St. Louis, Milwaukee, Cleveland, Cincinnati, Omaha, and from the West in general. The social revolutionists from the East had now shown themselves as pure anarchists and were represented by Johann Most,[77] the only delegate from New York, who counted

76 *Ibid.*, Feb. 10, 1883.

77 Johann Most was born in Augsburg, Germany, in 1846. After a cheerless childhood and boyhood he left Germany in 1864, and, in 1868, he settled in Vienna. Two years later he was arrested for revolutionary propaganda and sentenced to five years' imprisonment, but was released in 1871, after a general political amnesty. He was, however, expelled from Austria soon after his release and, in June, 1871, we find him editing a

among his followers the delegates from Brooklyn, Philadelphia, Baltimore, and other cities in the East. Most's philosophy was decisively anarchistic. His ideal society was an agglomeration of loosely federated autonomous groups of producers. Each group followed one trade and owned its means of production. The groups directly interchanged products with the aid of paper money. Each group had the power to establish for itself either absolute communism or a system of wages for work done. No superior authority existed over the groups, the state and the church having been abolished. In the matter of tactics, Most was an ardent believer in the " propaganda by deed," that is, acts of violence against capitalists and officers of state and church. He denied that there could be even a temporary truce between anarchism and capitalism. His programme was, briefly, the execution of reactionaries and the confiscation of all capital by the people. Most did not believe in trade union action, as he did not believe in political action, but, while he opposed the latter with all the passion of his fiery nature, he was willing to make concessions regarding the former. His opposition to trade union action cost him the adherence of the revolutionary groups centering in Chicago, but, on the other hand, the social revolutionists in New York and other eastern cities became willing converts to his brand of anarchism, obviously for the reason that they had never before placed any emphasis upon economic organisation.

The work accomplished by the Pittsburgh congress was a compromise between the followers of Most and the Chicago faction. A resolution proposed by Spies was passed, which re-

paper in Chemnitz, Germany. He then belonged to the most radical wing of the Eisenacher (Marxian) party. During 1873, he again spent eight months in jail, and having gained his freedom he was elected to the Reichstag. He was arrested also in 1877 and again in 1878, this time in connection with the attempt made upon the life of William I. Upon his release he was compelled to leave Germany, and in December, 1878, he went to London, where he began publishing a weekly called *Die Freiheit*. His views were so extreme and violent that Liebknecht felt obliged to repudiate *Die Freiheit* on behalf of the Social Democratic party. Most became converted to anarchism in the same year, owing to the influence of a friend, an old Bakuninist, and was formally expelled from the German Social Democratic party at the party convention of 1880. In March, 1881, when Alexander II of Russia was assassinated, he wrote an editorial praising the deed, for which he was sentenced in London to a sixteen months' term in jail. He was released in October, 1882, and arrived in New York on December 12. The revolutionary faction of the socialists received him with open arms, and, after an agitational tour over the country, he settled down in New York to renew the publication of *Die Freiheit*.

ferred to trade unions fighting for the abolition of the wage system as the foundation of the future society. On the other hand, the manifesto which the congress issued *To the Workingmen of America,* was framed entirely in the spirit of Most's philosophy and contained no mention of trade union action. The manifesto, known as the *Pittsburgh Manifesto of the International Working People's Association,* started with a passionate review, very largely borrowed from the *Communist Manifesto,* of the miserable condition of the workers under capitalism. It condemned the state, the church, and even the present day-school system as barriers to their emancipation, affirming that these institutions would fall with the overthrow of capitalism. The struggle for reforms is futile:

" We could show by scores of illustrations that all attempts in the past to reform this monstrous system by peaceable means, such as the ballot, have been futile, and all such efforts in the future must necessarily be so. . . . The political institutions of our time are the agencies of the propertied class; their mission is the upholding of the privileges of their masters; any reform in your own behalf would curtail these privileges. . . . That they will not resign these privileges voluntarily we know. . . . Since we must then rely upon the kindness of our masters for whatever redress we have, and knowing that from them no good may be expected, there remains but one recourse — FORCE! . . .

" By force have our ancestors liberated themselves from political oppression, by force their children will have to liberate themselves from economic bondage. ' It is, therefore, your right, it is your duty,' says Jefferson —' to arms ! '

" What we would achieve is, therefore, plainly and simply:

" First: — Destruction of the existing class rule, by all means, *i.e.,* by energetic, relentless, revolutionary and international action.

" Second: — Establishment of a free society based upon co-operative organisation of production.

" Third: — Free exchange of equivalent products by and between the productive organizations without commerce and profit-mongery.

" Fourth: — Organisation of education on a secular, scientific and equal basis for both sexes.

" Fifth: — Equal rights for all without distinction of sex or race.

" Sixth: — Regulation of all public affairs by free contracts between the autonomous (independent) communes and associations, resting on a federalistic basis." [78]

[78] *The Alarm,* Oct. 4, 1884.

The Pittsburgh manifesto became the most important land-mark in the history of American anarchism, for, long after the organisation perfected at Pittsburgh had ceased to exist, it con-tinued to be generally accepted by anarchists as the clearest statement of their creed. The national federation established at Pittsburgh under the name of the International Working People's Association, or Black International, for short, became for a time, particularly after the Haymarket catastrophe, a veritable " bugaboo " of the terrified public. It took for its basis the autonomous group with a national information bureau as the connecting link. The Chicago pattern of local organisation was fully indorsed. Chicago was also authorised to elect the Information Bureau, which it did three weeks afterwards, naming August Spies as the English secretary, and Paul Grottkau, William Medon, and J. Micalonda as the German, French, and Bohemian secretaries respectively. The movement radiating from New York City, where Johann Most lived, was generally considered to express the official doctrines of the Black International. Chicago, how-ever, was the largest centre of the Black International, and also the place where, as pointed out above, the blending of anarch-ism and trade unionism produced a kind of a " syndicalism " which was not dissimilar from the French " syndicalism " of to-day. Its principles can best be seen in its representatives, August Spies and Albert R. Parsons, who, from 1883 to 1886, propagated in the *Vorbote* and *The Alarm* [79] the views which they had reached in 1883 of ideal society, trade union action (or direct action), political action, and the use of violence in strikes. Their ideal of future society was voluntary associa-tion. " No constitutions, laws or regulations are necessary to unite the people. Nor were unions ever produced by such things, they are brought in after the union is effected to pre-

[79] The first issue of *The Alarm* appeared on Oct. 4, 1884. Prior to 1884 a very prominent position in the Chicago move-ment was occupied by Paul Grottkau, an extremely radical refugee from the Ger-man anti-socialist law. He was an influ-ential speaker at meetings and a promi-nent contributor to the *Arbeiter-Zeitung*, where he advocated abstention from poli-tics and energetic trade union action. However, he parted company with Spies and Parsons after the Pittsburgh con-gress, when they changed from collectivis-tic socialism into communistic anarchism. After a brief struggle he left for Milwau-kee, where he became editor of a German paper, and managed in May, 1886, to be-come arrested as one of the authors of the notorious Bay View riot. He was de-clared guilty by the jury, but was let off by the judge with a mere nominal penalty.

vent disuniting, or to operate the union for other purposes. Do away with all contrivances for perpetuating unions and men will unite more readily and enthusiastically and accomplish infinitely more. We believe all rules and regulations only interfere with natural law to the disadvantage of mankind. We do not believe in State Socialism." [80]

What, however, made Spies' and Parson's anarchistic philosophy distinctly "syndicalistic" was their theory of the importance of trade unions. "The International recognises in the trade union the embryonic group of the future 'free society.' Every Trade Union is, *nolens volens,* an autonomous commune in process of incubation. The Trades Union is a necessity of capitalistic production, and will yet take its place by superseding it under the system of universal free co-operation. No, friends, it is not the unions but the methods which some of them employ with which the International finds fault, and as indifferently as it may be considered by some, the development of capitalism is hastening the day when all Trades Unions and Anarchists will of necessity become one and the same." [81]

A model trade union, in accordance with the "Chicago Idea" reached in 1883, was the Metal Workers' Federation Union of America, which was organised in 1885. It said in its *Declaration of Principles* as follows: "The Emancipation of Labor cannot be brought about whether by the regulation of the hours of labor or by the schedule of wages. The demands and struggles for higher wages or shorter hours, if granted, would only better the conditions of the wage-workers for a short time." The form of organisation of most of the trade unions as organised to-day is defective because they "are controlled by a few persons called an executive committee, who, however honest, are unable to see clearly, much less to instruct others as to the true position of the laboring masses." But, instead of the opportunism of the trade unions, the maxim should be adopted by the labour movement that "the entire abolition of the present system of society can alone emancipate the workers; being replaced by a new system, based upon co-operative organisation

---

80 *The Alarm*, Nov. 22, 1884. Precisely the same view was expressed by Spies in the Chicago *Vorbote*, Mar. 25, 1885.

81 *The Alarm*, April 4, 1885.

of production in a free society." To this end the trade union
should be so organised that "every member should be enabled
to do his part in the work of progress; the management not centralising in the few, but resting with the whole body of workers."
And further, "our organisation should be a school to educate
its members for the new condition of society, when the workers
will regulate their own affairs without any interference by the
few, who are always more capable to betray their cause." At
the same time "our organisation aims to secure for its members
such remunerations as will enable them to live as human beings
should live." But under no consideration should they resort
to politics. "Since the emancipation of the productive classes
must come by their own efforts, it is unwise to meddle in present politics." On the other hand, "all *direct* struggles of the
laboring masses have our fullest sympathy." [82]

Thus we find practically all the earmarks of present day
syndicalism in this call of the metal workers' union issued in
1885; a craving for a "free society" of which the trade union
is to be the formative cell, a distrust of centralised authority and
of leadership, a condemnation of political action, and an advocacy of direct action instead. Add to this the idea of the
"general strike," which at that time had not yet been theoreti-
cally developed, and of "sabotage," [83] and the *Declaration of
Principles* might pass for a syndicalist programme of the
twentieth century.

Nevertheless, although "syndicalism" as a philosophy had
been reached already in 1883, a "syndicalist" movement was
still wanting. This came with the general labour upheaval
during 1884-1887. [84]

Entirely distinct from the Black International or the International Working People's Association was the Red International or the "International Workingmen's Association," a
secret organisation established by Burnette G. Haskell, of San
Francisco, in 1881, and composed mostly of native Americans.
It derived its name "Red" from the red cards which were

[82] *The Alarm*, June 27, 1885. In Chicago there was an "armed section of the
Metal Workers' Union," with the object
to "prepare for the revolution by learning the use of arms." Chicago *Vorbote*,
June 23, 1885.

[83] See Pouget, *Le Sabotage*; Estey,
Revolutionary Syndicalism; Levine, *Labor
Movement in France*; and Brooks, *American Syndicalism; the I. W. W.*
[84] See below, II, 384 *et seq.*

issued to members and also because it advocated socialism instead of anarchism. However, like the Black International, it declared allegiance to the anarchistic International which was re-established at the London Congress in 1881 as the continuation of the old International Workingmen's Association.

The form of organisation was the so-called "closed group" system. This meant that each member of an original group of nine organised an additional group of nine; next, that each member of the new group in his turn organised a group of nine, and so forth, so that a member could have knowledge of the personnel of only two groups: the one to which he belonged himself and that which he himself had organised. The officers of a division, however, kept a record of all the members in the division. There were altogether two divisions: the Pacific Coast Division presided over by Haskell and the Rocky Mountain Division established by Joseph R. Buchanan, of Denver, in 1883. Each division was entirely autonomous so that, to this extent, the International conformed to the anarchistic principle of organisation.[85]

Haskell was of native parentage, a man with considerable means, and a lawyer. However, he never practised his profession. In January, 1882, he founded the San Francisco *Truth,* as a weekly organ of the anti-Chinese "League of Deliverance," and, owing to his great though erratic ability, it immediately became an influential sheet on the coast. Haskell viewed the anti-Chinese issue merely as a preliminary step to a radical overhauling of society, but refused to class himself with any of the existing schools, preferring to keep independent and to work towards the unification of all. While he kept the columns of his paper open alike to members of the Socialist Labor party, to greenbackers, to Black Internationalists, and to others, his own philosophy, as far as he may be said to have had a clearly defined philosophy, was state socialism combined with an opposition to either political action or violence as policies for the present. Instead, he advocated a long campaign of education in preparation for the coming social revolution. In this spirit were framed the programme and the Declaration of the Rights of Man.[86]

[85] Buchanan, *The Story of a Labor Agitator,* 254–289.　　[86] *Truth,* Sept. 15, 1883.

Buchanan, being absorbed as he was in his work for the Knights of Labor,[87] took a mere academic interest in the cause of the International, believing that for the present it should be confined to a few choice spirits rather than widely propagated among the working people. The number of such choice spirits, although including some of the prominent labour leaders of the country, hardly ever exceeded a thousand. Still it is true that the somewhat vague aspiration towards a better society, which the International suggests, had its roots directly in the contemporaneous labour movement and sprang from the conviction shared by many leaders of the time, that, though the labouring people might at times appear successful in their struggle, they were nevertheless incapable of securing lasting results.[88]

Alongside the two Internationals, the Socialist Labor party kept up an inconspicuous existence. After 1880, owing to the inroads made by anarchism, it had dwindled to a corporal's guard. It reached the lowest point in 1883, when there were only 30 sections with a total membership of about 1,500. A slight revival began in 1884. During this year 21 new sections were organised in the East and Middle West. In 1885 61 sections already existed. The centre of the movement was New York, with the daily *New Yorker Volkszeitung* edited by Alexander Jonas, and with Sergius Schevitsch, a Russian of noble birth, formerly in the diplomatic service of his country, and also for a time editor of the paper. The Socialist Labor party took no part in political campaigns until the political upheaval in New York in 1886.

87 See below, II, 367 *et seq.*
88 The Red International reached its highest point in 1886 and became amalga- mated with the Socialist Labor party in 1887.

CHAPTER VII

THE NEW TRADE UNIONISM, 1878–1884

From Socialism to Pure and Simple Trade Unionism. Two lines of trade union action, 302. Plan for the organisation of the unskilled: The International Labor Union, 302. "Internationalism" and "Stewardism," 302. Trade unionism and eight-hour legislative action, 303. Programme of the International Labor Union, 303. Success among textile workers, 304. The first convention, 305. Steps towards an international trade union organisation, 305. Failure of the International Labor Union, 306. International Cigar Makers' Union — the new model for the organisation of the skilled, 306. Strasser and Gompers, 307. Crystallisation of the pure and simple trade union philosophy, 308. Railroad brotherhoods, 309.

First Successes. The trades assemblies and their functions, economic, political, and legislative, 310. Building trades' councils — the first move towards industrialism, 312. Federations of the water-front trades in the South, 312. The Negro, 312. Formation of new national trade unions, 313. Their increase in membership, 1879–1883, 313. Their control over locals, 314. Their benefit features, 314. Their attitude towards legal incorporation, 314. Predominance of the foreign-speaking element in the trade unions, 315. The charge that the foreigners in the trade unions deprive the American boy of his opportunity in industry, 315. Strikes in 1880 and 1881, 316. Iron workers' strike in 1882, 316. The boycott, 316. New York *Tribune* boycott, 317.

Towards Federation. Attempts towards national federation since 1876, 318. Part played by the Knights of Labor in the last and successful attempt, 318. The Terre Haute conference, 318. Call for a convention, 320. Trade unions in the eighties and trade unions to-day, 320. The Pittsburgh convention of 1881, 321. The cause of the large representation of the Knights of Labor, 321. Formation of the Federation of Organised Trades and Labor Unions of the United States and Canada, 322. Attitude towards organising the unskilled, 323. Subordination of the city trades' assembly to the national trade union, 323. Legislative committee and the legislative programme, 324. The incorporation plank, 325. Shift from the co-operation argument to the one of trade agreements on the question of incorporation, 326. Second convention of the Federation, 326. Absence of the Knights of Labor and of the iron and steel workers, 326. Lack of interest in the Federation on the part of the trade unions, 327. The convention of 1883, 328. The first signs of friction with the Knights of Labor, 329. Attitude towards a protective tariff, 329. Miscellaneous resolutions, 330. Failure of the Federation as an organisation for obtaining legislation, 331.

THE former members of the International in New York and vicinity, unlike their colleagues in Chicago, did not remain with the Workingmen's party after the Newark convention, at which, as we have seen,[1] the programme had been changed to political action and the name to Socialist Labor party. Thereafter, they kept entirely aloof from the socialist movement, but devoted themselves exclusively to the economic organisation of labour. Two distinct lines of effort resulted from this. One group under McDonnell and Sorge entered into an alliance with the eight-hour advocates under Steward, McNeill, and Gunton [2] in an attempt to organise the unskilled into the International Labor Union. Another group headed by Adolph Strasser of the cigar makers' union, and later joined by P. J. McGuire, proceeded to regenerate and strengthen the trade unions of the skilled.

The International Labor Union was launched in the beginning of 1878, when McDonnell and McNeill organised a provisional central committee with members in eighteen different States, including A. R. Parsons and George Schilling, of Chicago; Otto Weydemeyer, of Pittsburgh; F. A. Sorge, of Hoboken; George Gunton and Ira Steward, of Massachusetts. The central committee acted through an executive board of seven, which included J. P. McDonnell, Carl Speyer, and George E. McNeill, the latter being president.

As is shown by the personnel of the officers, the new organisation represented the coming together of the two class-conscious programmes of the International and Steward's Eight-Hour League. Both had a socialist system of society for the final aim. But the socialism of Steward was not the collectivism of the International, but was, instead, a system of voluntary co-operation between employers and employés under which profit would ultimately be absorbed by wages. They differed in method of attainment even more than they did in the final aim. The International believed, as we have seen, in political action by a labour party that should grow out from, and be controlled

1 See above, II, 277 et seq.

2 George Gunton, textile worker, economist, and editor, was born in Cambridgeshire, England, in 1847. He emigrated to the United States in 1874, and for some time worked in factories in Massachusetts. Like McNeill, he was closely associated with Ira Steward and his Wealth and Progress, which appeared in 1887, was based upon Steward's unpublished writings. In 1890 Gunton became president of the Institute of Social Economics and editor of the Social Economist, the name of which was changed in 1896 to Gunton's Magazine. Gunton acted as an organiser of the International Labor Union in Fall River during 1878–1880. He subsequently severed connections with the labour movement and became one of the best-known defenders of the trusts.

by, the trade unions. It laid peculiar stress, therefore, upon the need for the immediate organisation of trade unions. Steward's eight-hour philosophy, held, on the contrary, neither to political action by a labour party nor to trade union action, but based the hopes for its millennium upon a general eight-hour law, which would have the effect of increasing the wants of the wage-earner and, therefore, his wages, until the latter had completely absorbed the employers' profits. In other words, the difference in methods preached by the two schools consisted in the fact that the International advocated for the present trade union action only, and, ultimately, a labour party, while the eight-hour school advocated as both an immediate and an ultimate programme a vigorous agitation in favour of a general eight-hour law, which politicians of all parties would not dare to disobey.

The International Labor Union accepted from Steward the theory of wages and from the International the idea of trade unionism. The platform was couched in the well-known Steward phraseology in the parts dealing with principles and demands:

" The wage system is a despotism under which the wage-worker is forced to sell his labor at such price and under such conditions as the employer of labor shall dictate. . . . That as the wealth of the world is distributed through the wage system, its better distribution must come through higher wages and better opportunities, until wages shall represent the earnings and not the necessities of labor; thus melting profit upon labor out of existence, and making cooperation, or self-employed labour, the natural and logical step from wages slavery to free labor. . . . The first step towards the emancipation of labor is a reduction of the hours of labor; that the added leisure produced by a reduction of the hours of labor will operate upon the natural causes that affect the habits and customs of the people, enlarging wants, stimulating ambition, decreasing idleness, and increasing wages. . . .

" We, therefore, severally agree to form ourselves into a Committee, known as the Provisional Central Committee of the International Labor Union, whose objects shall be to secure the following measures: The reduction of the hours of labour; higher wages; factory, mine and workshop inspection; abolition of the contract convict labor and truck systems; employers to be held responsible for accidents by neglected machinery; prohibition of child labor; the establishment of Labor Bureaus; labor propaganda by means of a labor press, labor lectures, the employment of a general organiser, and the final abolition of the wage system. . . ."

However, with respect to practical methods, Steward's legislative panacea completely gave way to the trade union idea of McDonnell and Sorge. The platform continues:

" The methods by which we propose to secure these measures are:
" 1st. The formation of an Amalgamated Union of labourers so that members of any calling can combine under a central head, and form a part of the Amalgamated Trades Unions.
" 2nd. The establishment of a general fund for benefit and protective purposes.
" 3rd. The organisation of all workingmen in their Trade Unions, and the creation of such Unions where none exist.
" 4th. The National and International Amalgamation of all Labor Unions." [3]

Notwithstanding the general favour of the labour press [4] for the plan of the International Labor Union, the organisation grew slowly at first. In July, 1878, the executive committee informed the Hoboken branch, known as Branch 3, that the total membership was only about 700.[5] But, later in the year when the textile mill operatives were organised by McDonnell in Paterson and by McNeill and Gunton in Fall River, the organisation began to grow so that in 1878 McNeill claimed a membership of nearly 8,000.[6] McDonnell came warmly to the support of a strike against a reduction in wages in a large cotton mill in Paterson, New Jersey, which began in June, 1878, and lasted over eight months. It was in connection with this strike that he was arrested and sent to jail on account of an article on the strike printed in his *Labor Standard,* which he had transferred to Paterson a few months before.[7]

That the International Labor Union became practically a mere union in the textile industry is shown by the attendance

---

[3] *Labor Standard,* Oct. 12, 1878.
[4] The Pittsburgh *National Labor Tribune,* Mar. 16, 1878, said: "The consummation of this comprehensive plan will be pregnant with results of the most lasting importance to the wage-workers in America, particularly, and generally throughout the civilised world of manufacturers. It is a plan that there is every reason to believe is eminently practical. . . ."

[5] " Report " of the meeting for July 10, 1878, in *Protokoll Buch* of Section 1 (Hoboken) of the International — later Branch 3 of the International Labor Union.
[6] *Depression in Labor and Business, House Miscellaneous Document,* 45 Cong., 3 sess., No. 29, p. 115.
[7] See above, II, 222, note.

at the first convention held in Paterson, December 28, 1878, where the overwhelming majority were textile workers from Fall River and Paterson.

Nevertheless the object of the union was broader. President McNeill reported to the committee that " the labor movement waits for the union of its leaders upon the single issue of the reduction of the hours of labor," and " that the labor movement has silently permeated the entire fabric of society; not only are the skilled mechanics concentrating their numbers but the unskilled, the manual labourers who heretofore have been without hope and without organisation, are fast learning from the experience of the past the necessity of combination. The International Labor Union presents a plan by which the unorganised masses and local unions can become affiliated." The convention fully accepted these views. It decided against any " political alliance or action," in favour " of reduction of the hours of labor and the establishment of National and State Bureaus of Statistics of Labor," and in favour of establishing a fund for the relief of the unemployed. The latter would be an " incentive to members of the cotton industries of New England to join the organisation " and would assist the work of propaganda by interesting " the wage-workers now unemployed." Finally, " arrangements were perfected for the admission of local unions and the organisation of the unskilled laborers." [8]

Strasser, the president of the cigar makers' union, attended as a visitor, advising the International Labor Union to " take steps to organise in their ranks the cotton operatives of New England and other districts with the cotton trade in England." Enlarging the scope of his advice, the convention resolved to " co-operate with Trades Unions of the United States in convening a congress of the Trade Organisations for the purpose of bringing about the National and International Amalgamation of the Trades Unions." The resolutions also contained the following: " That the International Labor Union of America be represented at the next Trades Congress of England, and we do hereby express to the Wage-workers of Great Britain our determination to stand by them in their hour of distress, and we call upon them to co-operate with us and with the National

8 *Labor Standard*, Jan. 4, 1879.

and International Trade Unions of this country in convening
an International Labor Congress of the World." [9]
McDonnell was the unanimous choice for delegate to England, but, like the other portions of the comprehensive programme of action worked out by the convention, his trip never
materialised. The union became involved in a series of strikes
in the textile industry, and, when they failed, a rapid decline
set in, so that by February, 1880, the membership fell off to
1400 or 1500,[10] and one year later it shrank to the single branch
in Hoboken where Sorge resided. The latter reorganised in
1883 as the International Labor Union of Hoboken, " to unite
the members of the old International Workingmen's Association and of the International Labor Union, for the purpose of
aiding the trade unions of New Jersey in attaining favourable
labour laws." [11] In 1887, when F. A. Sorge moved to Rochester, New York, it dissolved.

From the standpoint of labour organisation the significance
of the International Labor Union lies in the fact that it was
the first deliberately planned effort in this country to organise
on a comprehensive scale the unskilled wage-earners. Seven
or eight years later, the Order of the Knights of Labor succeeded incidentally for a time on a grand scale in such an undertaking, but the Order was favoured by a high tide of the labour
movement and by the greatly exaggerated notion of its strength
held by the masses of working people.

At the time when McDonnell was vainly attempting to build
up an organisation of the unskilled, Strasser and Samuel
Gompers succeeded in creating, in the reorganised International
Cigar Makers' Union, a model for the trade unions of the
skilled. Strasser had been elected president of the union in
1877, in the midst of the great strike in New York against the
tenement house system.[12]

The president of No. 144 of New York was at the time
Samuel Gompers, a young man of twenty-seven, who was born
in England and had come to America in 1863. In his endeavour to build up a model for the " new " unionism and in
his almost uninterrupted headship of that movement for over

9 Ibid.
10 Copy-book, 454.
11 Protokoll Buch of Section 1.
12 See above, II, 177, 178.

thirty years is indicated Gompers' truly representative character. Born of Dutch-Jewish parents in England in 1850, he typifies the cosmopolitan origins of American unionism. His early contact in the union of his trade with men like Strasser upon whom the ideas of Marx and the International Workingmen's Association had left an indelible stamp, gave him that grounding both in idealism and class consciousness which has produced many strong leaders of American unions and saved them from defection to other interests. Aggressive and uncompromising in a perpetual fight for the strongest possible position and power of trade unions, but always strong for collective agreements with the opposing employers, he displays the business tactics of organised labour. At the head of an organisation which denies itself power over its constituent unions, he has brought and held together the most widely divergent and often antagonistic unions, while permitting each to develop and even to change its character to fit the changing industrial conditions.

The dismal failure of the strike against the tenement house system had brought home to Strasser and Gompers the weakness of the plan of organisation of their union, as well as that of American trade unions in general.[13] They consequently resolved to rebuild their union upon the pattern of the British unions, although they firmly intended that it should remain a militant organisation. The change involved, first, complete authority over the local unions in the hands of the international officers; second, an increase in the membership dues for the purpose of building up a large fund; and, third, the adoption of a far-reaching benefit system in order to assure stability to the organisation. This was accomplished at the convention held in August, 1879. This convention simultaneously adopted the British idea of the " equalisation of funds," which gave the international officers the power to order a well-to-do local union to transfer a portion of its funds to another local union in financial straits.[14] With various modifications of the feature of " equalisation of funds," the system of government in the Cigar

13 See testimony by Gompers before the Industrial Commission at Washington, D. C., in Industrial Commission, *Report*, 1901, VII, 599.

14 *Cigar-Makers' Official Journal* (New York), Sept. 15, 1879.

Makers' International Union was later used as a model by the other national and international trade unions.

After the convention of 1879, the cigar makers' union increased its membership from 2,729 in 1879 to 4,440 in 1880 and 14,604 in 1881. Other unions grew at the same time, but at a much slower pace. The membership of the Typographical Union was 5,968 in 1879, 6,520 in 1880, and 7,931 in 1881; and the bricklayers' national union was 375 in 1879, 1,558 in 1880, and about the same in 1881. These figures indicate that the Cigar Makers' International Union was in a position sooner than other unions to take advantage of the turning industrial tide.

As Strasser, McDonnell, and McGuire [15] grew ever more deeply absorbed in the practical problems of the everyday struggle of the wage-earners for better conditions of employment, the socialistic portion of their original philosophy kept receding farther and farther into the background until they arrived at pure trade unionism. But their trade unionism differed vastly from that of Sylvis, Cameron, and Trevellick. They did not regard, like the trade union leaders of the sixties, combination into trade unions as a mere stepping stone to self-employment. Their grounding in the theory of class-conscious socialism acted as an inseparable barrier against middle-class philosophies, such as greenbackism and co-operation. At the same time their foreign birth and upbringing kept them from contact with the life of the great American middle class, the farmers and the small employers, the class which kept alive the philosophy of self-employment and voluntary co-operation.

The philosophy which these new leaders developed might be termed a philosophy of pure wage-consciousness. It signified a labour movement reduced to an opportunistic basis, accepting the existence of capitalism and having for its object the enlarging of the bargaining power of the wage-earner in the sale of his labour. It implied an attitude of aloofness from all those movements which aspire to replace the wage system by co-operation, whether voluntary or subsidised by government, whether greenbackism, socialism, or anarchism.

15 Peter J. McGuire was the last important accession of a socialist leader of the seventies to pure trade unionism. He organised the Brotherhood of Carpenters and Joiners in 1881, and was its general secretary for a quarter of a century.

Perhaps the most concise definition of this philosophy is to be found in Strasser's testimony before the Senate Committee on Education and Labor, in 1883: [16]

" Q. You are seeking to improve home matters first?

" A. Yes, sir, I look first to the trade I represent; I look first to cigars, to the interests of men who employ me to represent their interest.

" Chairman: I was only asking you in regard to your ultimate ends.

" Witness: We have no ultimate ends. We are going on from day to day. We are fighting only for immediate objects — objects that can be realised in a few years.

" By Mr. Call: Q. You want something better to eat and to wear, and better houses to live in?

" A. Yes, we want to dress better and to live better, and become better citizens generally.

" The Chairman: I see that you are a little sensitive lest it should be thought that you are a mere theoriser. I do not look upon you in that light at all.

" The Witness: Well, we say in our constitution that we are opposed to theorists, and I have to represent the organisation here. We are all practical men."

With the revival of business in 1879, this conception of militant but " pure and simple " trade unionism was accepted alike by the new national trade unions and by those which survived the depression. It was transmitted to the American Federation of Labor in 1881 at the time when it was formed under the name of Federation of Organised Trades and Labor Unions of the United States and Canada.

There were, however, several national labour organisations which came neither under the influence of these ideas nor of the new leaders. These were the three organisations of railway men which existed in 1879, the engineers, the firemen and the conductors, and to which was added a fourth, the brakemen's organisation of 1883. These organisations, more than any other American trade union, resembled the British unions formed in the fifties which in later years abandoned militancy

---

[16] Senate Committee on Education and Labor, *Report*, 1885, I, 460. Strasser showed a flicker of his old socialism at the convention of the American Federation of Labor in 1894 when he supported the adoption of the famous plank 10 of the proposed political programme of the Federation (*Proceedings*, 40,). However, his entire activity since 1877 bears out that it was but a last flicker of an old, almost extinct fire.

in support of a highly developed beneficiary policy. The high development of the beneficiary feature in the American railway unions was natural, since insurance companies ordinarily refuse to insure the lives of men who are engaged in railroad train service. During the seventies they were purely beneficiary organisations, although it was not until the nineties that insurance was made compulsory upon all members. They also retained the same characteristics through a part of the eighties. For this reason they kept aloof from the militant trade unions and did not affiliate with the Federation. The same policy of aloofness was continued also after they began to make wage demands, owing to their good strategic position in the railroad industry. To affiliate with the Federation would therefore have meant the forming of an entangling alliance with weak organisations which still had before them an uphill fight for recognition.

FIRST SUCCESSES

The first symptom of the upward trend in the labour movement was the rapid multiplication of the trades councils, variously known as trades councils, amalgamated trade and labour unions, trades assemblies, and the like. Practically all of these came into existence after 1879, since hardly any of the trades assemblies of the sixties had survived the depression. August Sartorius von Waltershausen, a contemporary observer, enumerated the following cities with a trades assembly during this period: New York, Chicago, Cincinnati, Detroit, San Francisco, Philadelphia, St. Louis, Washington, Pittsburgh, Boston, Cheyenne, Denver, Newark, Leadville, New Haven, Indianapolis, St. Joseph, St. Paul, Minneapolis, Columbus, (Ohio), Alleghany, Fall River, Milwaukee, Cleveland, Buffalo, Reading, and Portland (Ohio). Besides these there were trades assemblies extending over an entire industrial county like the trades assemblies of Essex County and of Passaic County, New Jersey, and Alleghany County, Pennsylvania. In New Orleans, Galveston, and Savannah, trade unions of coloured workmen existing in the water-front trades, were admitted to the trades assemblies on an equal footing with the other unions.[17]

17 Waltershausen, *Die Nordameri-kanischen Gewerkschaften unter dem* *Einfluss der fortschreitenden Produc-tionstechnik*, 135, 147.

In New Orleans this occurred at the initiative of the Typographical Union as early as 1881.[18]

The trades council played an important part during this period when national organisations existed in only 30 trades, while the number of trades organised locally in the large cities frequently reached 100.[19] The trade council, by uniting them all, was for the time being more representative of the labour movement than either the loosely affiliated national trade unions or the relatively unimportant Knights of Labor.[20]

The functions of the trades council were economic, legislative, and political. The numerous local unions without a national organisation derived from them the same support which a subordinate local union received from its national union. In only a few cities, however, was the council granted the right to levy compulsory strike assessments upon its constituent unions.[21] Generally it issued appeals for voluntary contributions which were, as a rule, liberally supplied. A trade union which refused aid to a sister union in a strike forfeited the right to demand similar assistance.[22]

Aside from direct pecuniary assistance during strikes, the trades council was a useful agency for mediation between the employers and a striking trade union. It naturally enjoyed greater authority than the individual union and was able to get a hearing from the employers where the latter could not. With the inauguration of the era of boycotts during 1883 and 1884, the trades council became the recognised leader of that movement. The New York Amalgamated Trades and Labor Union took the lead in enforcing boycotts, as it did also in independent political action and in promoting legislation. Several trades councils, as in Denver, succeeded in preventing the state legislature from enacting anti-labour conspiracy laws. Also, by

[18] Sorge, " Die Arbeiter Bewegung in den Vereinigten Staaten, 1877–1885," in *Neue Zeit*, 1891–1892, II, 244.

[19] The Tenth Census enumerates 2,440 local trade unions in the United States in 1880, of which not more than one-half were attached to national trade unions. Thirty of this number probably were city trades assemblies. Weeks, " Trade Societies," in U. S. *Census*, 1880, XX, 14–19.

[20] In a number of cities, as for instance, New York and Denver, the local assem-

blies of the Knights of Labor were represented in the trades councils.

[21] For instance, in San Francisco, The New York Amalgamated Trades and Labor Union had the right of making compulsory assessment until 1881. Waltershausen, *Die nordamerikanischen Gewerkschaften*, 138.

[22] *Ibid.*; quoted from the *Constitution of the Cincinnati Trades and Labor Assembly*.

advocating labour legislation, the formation of state bureaus of labour and state boards of mediation and arbitration, the trades council of the early eighties performed with considerable success the function which now belongs to the state federations of labour.

A special type of local central body which, for the first time, now began to acquire importance, was the building trades council. This differed entirely from the general councils of the period, since it took no part in political or legislative acts, nor in boycotts. It was rather a union of several trades working for different contractors on the same job — a federation for the purpose of sympathetic strikes — a move towards industrialism in organisation without the revolutionary tendency which the term in its present use implies. These councils developed the present type of the " business " man among trade union officials — the walking delegate. In New York City the council was composed of twenty-five unions. The bricklayers' union, the strongest in the council, conducted 29 strikes during the summer months of 1883, of which 27 were successful. Their wages were raised to $4 and $5 a day.[23] However, at this time the building trades councils were yet rare, and the building trades unions gave their support to the general city trades councils, a fact which contributed in no small degree to the strength of the latter.

Waltershausen [24] describes at length the operation of the federations of the water-front trades in the cotton-exporting ports of Savannah, New Orleans, and Galveston. These federations included unions of 'longshoremen, draymen, yardmen, cotton classers and markers, scale hands, weighers and re-weighers, pressmen and screwmen, no distinction being made between white and coloured in the matter of admittance to the union. By means of the sympathetic strike and of favourable state legislation, such as the law in Louisiana prohibiting sailors from strange vessels working in the port, these federations succeeded in reducing the working day to nine hours and in raising wages to $5 and $6 per day. In Galveston the conditions of employment were regulated by a written trade agreement

23 Senate Committee on Education and Labor *Report*, 1885, I, 813–817.

24 Waltershausen, *Die nordamerikanischen Gewerkschaften*, 142–148.

between the federation and the association of shipping merchants, but the agreement was one-sided, since the federation was in a position to exercise tyranny over the employers.

There existed also another type of city federation. This was the United German Trades, which was formed in New York, Chicago, Milwaukee, St. Louis, and other cities with a considerable German working population. These bodies stood in very close relation to the Socialist Labor party and they supported and spread the German labour and socialist papers.

As was said above, the national trade unions existed during this period in only about thirty trades. Eighteen of these had either retained a nucleus during the seventies or were first formed during that decade. The following is a list of the national unions in existence in 1880 with the year of formation: Typographical (1850), Hat Finishers' (1854), Iron Molders (1859), Locomotive Engineers (1863), Cigar makers (1864), Bricklayers and Masons (1865), Silk and Fur Hat Finishers (1866), Railway Conductors (1868), Coopers (1870), German Typographia (1873), Locomotive Firemen (1873), Horseshoers (1874), Furniture Workers (1873), Iron and Steel Workers (1876), Granite Cutters (1877), Lake Seamen (1878), Cotton Mill Spinners (1878), New England Boot and Shoe Lasters (1879).

In 1880 the western greenbottle blowers' national union was established; in 1881 the national unions of boilermakers and carpenters; in 1882, plasterers and metal-workers; in 1883, tailors, lithographers, wood-carvers, railroad brakemen, and silk-workers.

An illustration of the rapid growth in trade union membership during this period is given in the following figures: The bricklayers' union had 303 in 1880, 1,558 in 1881, 6,848 in 1882, 9,193 in 1883, each of these figures representing the membership in the month of January. The typographical union had 5,968 members in 1879, 6,520 in 1880, 7,931 in 1881, 10,439 in 1882, 12,273 in 1883. The cigar makers' union had 1,250 in 1879, 4,409 in 1880, 12,000 in 1881, 11,430 in 1882, 13,214 in 1883. The carpenters' and joiners' brotherhood had 2,042 in 1881, the year of its organisation, 3,780 in 1882, 3,293 in 1883. A comparison between the growth of the bricklayers', the typographical, and the cigar makers' unions, on the one hand, with the carpenters' union on the other, demonstrates that those unions which had retained during the seventies an organised nucleus, grew much more rapidly during the years of prosperity than the national unions which started anew.

The total trade union membership in the country, counting the three railway organisations and those organised only locally, amounted to between 200,000 and 225,000 in 1883 and probably was not below 300,000 in the beginning of 1885.[25]

The national trade unions of the early eighties differed but little in structure and policies from the unions of the sixties and seventies. Only five national unions, the cigar makers, the iron moulders, the granite cutters, the carpenters and joiners, and the German-American Typographia possessed benefit systems prior to 1887. The control over the local unions, except in the cigar makers' union remained imperfect; the latter continued to regulate apprenticeship, hours, and wages, to conduct strikes, and to negotiate with employers. The unions were eager to get trade agreements; they demanded Federal incorporation for the reason, as they thought, that official recognition by the United States would lead to recognition by employers [26] besides doing away with conspiracy laws of the several States and protecting their funds. But apart from the railway organisations, which, owing to their peculiar strategic position achieved recognition in the seventies, and the Amalgamated Association of Iron and Steel Workers, the first permanent system of local trade agreements was not adopted until

25 It was found impossible to obtain accurate membership figures for the first half of the eighties. P. J. McGuire, in his testimony before the Senate Committee on Education and Labor in 1883 (Report, 1885, I, 316), estimated the membership of 24 national trade unions at 250,000, but this is evidently an exaggeration, as revealed by a comparison of his estimated figures for several trade unions with the actual figures at hand. However, if we should add the membership of the unattached local unions, which was at that time particularly large, varying probably from 40,000 to 50,000, we might arrive at a total of 200,000 in 1883. In the beginning of 1885, Richard J. Hinton (Hin-

ton, "American Labor Organizations," in North-American Review, CXL, 48) estimated the total trade union membership at 436,000, placing the membership of unattached locals at approximately 75,000. Only a small portion of the figures upon which he based his estimate was official, the remainder having been taken from McGuire; so that 300,000 should be a liberal estimate for 1885.

26 See Senate Committee on Education and Labor, Report, 1885: testimony of P. J. McGuire of the carpenters, I, 324; of Adolph Strasser and Samuel Gompers of the cigar makers, 379, 461; and of John Jarrett of the Amalgamated Iron and Steel Workers, 1150.

1887 in the bricklaying trade of Chicago, and the first national trade agreement was not adopted until 1890 in the stove-moulding industry.

A distinguishing characteristic of the trade unions of this time was the predominance in them of the foreign element. The Illinois Bureau of Labor [27] describes the ethnical composition of the trade unions of that State during 1886, and states that 21 per cent were American, 33 per cent, German, 19 per cent, Irish, 10 per cent, British other than Irish, 12 per cent, Scandinavians, and the Poles, Bohemians, and Italians about 5 per cent. The strong predominance of the foreign element in the American trade unions should not appear unusual, since, owing to the breakdown of the apprenticeship system, the United States had been drawing its supply of skilled labour from abroad.

Colonel Richard T. Auchmuty, the pioneer worker for industrial schools and an authority on the situation in the building trades, said in a paper entitled: "Who are our Mechanics," read before the national convention of builders' exchanges in 1889:

"In the building trades, we have mechanics from England, Ireland, France, Italy, and Germany, and we have mechanics who are our own countrymen. Each nationality usually follows some particular trade. In New York, for instance, the stone masonry is mostly done by the sons of Italy; Englishmen and Irishmen lay the brick. When the heavy work of putting on the beams, or of framing and placing in position the roof trusses, begins, seldom an English word is spoken; the broad shoulders and brawny muscles of the German furnish the motive-power. Irishmen and Americans in about equal number do the carpenters' work. In the plumbing trade, where science is as needful as skill,— thanks, perhaps, to the interest the master plumbers have taken in the plumbing school — our own countrymen will soon have control. Where delicate artistic work is required, we find the Frenchman and the German. In all the trades, except the plumbing, we find that the best workmen, those who command the steadiest employment, are of foreign birth." [28]

Colonel Auchmuty charged the trade unions with responsibility for this situation, but Professor Bemis conclusively showed that the real cause was the unwillingness of the em-

[27] Illinois Bureau of Labor, *Report*, 1886, p. 227.
[28] *Trade Training* — an Address, 2.

ployer, who now no longer worked side by side with his journeymen, to assume the responsibility of training apprentices.[29]

The Tenth Census reports[30] the total number of strikes
and lockouts during 1880 as 762,[31] but gives detailed information only for 414, involving altogether 128,262 wage-earners.[32]

Strikes occurred much less frequently in 1881, since the
rapid rise in prices and the progress of organisation made for
concessions without them. In Ohio,[33] out of 463 reports on
conditions of employment, an increase in wages was stated in
202, but in only 25 cases of this number did strikes occur.
During the year 1882, however, there was a large number of
labour disputes. The partial failure of crops in the United
States in 1881 was followed in the spring of 1882 by an increase
in the cost of living. At the same time the employers were not
inclined to make advances in wages, for they were anticipating
a further decline in the market resulting from a diminished demand for their products on the part of the agricultural population. The most important strike of the year was the iron
workers' strike in the West. The iron workers' strike was declared on June 1, 1882 and lasted 16 weeks, tying up 116 establishments in Pennsylvania, Ohio, Indiana, West Virginia, Illinois, and Wisconsin, and involving about 35,000 men. A
sliding scale agreement between the Amalgamated Association
of Iron and Steel Workers and the iron-mill owners, based upon
the selling price of bar iron, had been in existence since 1865,
but now the association demanded a general increase of 15 to
25 per cent, in spite of the low market on bar iron, claiming that
the mills sold iron largely in other shapes and at advantageous
prices. The manufacturers of the affected regions acted as a
unit and the association was obliged to call off the strike on September 19.[34]

In general the trade unions met with no great success in

29 Bemis, " Trades Unions and Apprentices," in *American Journal of Social Science*, 1891, XXVIII, 116. He quoted the
Massachusetts Industrial Census of 1885
to the effect that in carpentering there
was only 1 apprentice to 62 journeymen,
in masonry, 1 to 105, in painting, 1 to
89, in plumbing, 1 to 44, etc., obviously
ratios far below those enforced by the
unions.

30 The Federal Department of Labor

did not begin its comprehensive statistics
of strikes until the year 1886, and the
first year covered was 1881.

31 This number includes only eighty-five
disputes definitely known as lockouts.

32 Weeks, " Strikes and Lockouts," in
U. S. *Census*, 1880, XX, 5, 6, 8, 10, 27.

33 Ohio Bureau of Labor, *Report*, 1881,
p. 195.

34 Pennsylvania Bureau of Labor, *Report*, 1882, pp. 174–190.

1882. In the State of Missouri, out of 43 strikes reported to the state bureau of labour, 13 only were successful and 26 ended in absolute failure. The stonecutters, masons, and bricklayers were most successful in their strikes, the moulders moderately so, but the other unions suffered defeat, notably the painters who lost 18 strikes out of 20.[35]

Notwithstanding these many defeats, the trade unions of the early eighties accomplished their mission with high success, especially west of the Alleghanies. If they did not win in many strikes, their very existence forced employers in many instances to pass on a share of prosperity to the employés without allowing strikes to occur.

The strike was the weapon *par excellence* of the trade unions during the early eighties, but already we find a more or less frequent resort to the boycott. The typographical union was the pioneer boycotter, and it first began its use in the West. The Milwaukee printers' union, as early as 1881, declared a boycott against a daily, the *Republican and News;* also against a saloon which subscribed to this paper. The boycott was successful and the publisher solved the problem by selling out to the *Sentinel.*[36]

The boycott which for the first time attracted nation-wide attention was the one declared by Typographical Union 6, of New York (" Big Six "), on December 18, 1883,[37] against the New York *Tribune.* The causes were the discharge of union men and the non-observance of a written agreement entered into one month previously between the foreman and the union, which the union understood to have been ratified by the owner, White-law Reid. The union established a special paper, the *Boycotter.* Operations were directed not only against the *Tribune* and its advertisers, but in the next year the boycott became a factor in the presidential campaign. The union declared against James G. Blaine, after the Republican national convention of 1884 had refused to repudiate the *Tribune* as its

---

[35] Missouri Labor Bureau, *Report,* 1882, pp. 122, 123.

[36] Wisconsin Bureau of Labor, *Report,* 1883–1884, pp. 149, 150.

[37] New York Bureau of Labor, *Report,* 1885, p. 356, says: " One of the earliest cases of boycotting of any magnitude in the United States — though not then known by that name — was the action taken by the New York Protective Association (comprising various trade unions) against the Duryea Glen Cove [starch] Manufacturing Company, some five or six years ago."

party organ.   Cleveland's plurality in the pivotal state of New York was so narrow that the boycott against the *Tribune* was a factor in deciding the election.   The labour organisations in the country, especially the Knights of Labor, took up enthusiastically the cause of " Big Six " and supported it until it terminated in August, 1892, with a victory for the union.[38]

However, the boycotts prior to 1884 were mere symptoms of the coming outburst which coincided during the following years with the remarkable growth of the Knights of Labor. The boycott was a weapon used much less by the trade unions than by the Knights of Labor.

TOWARDS FEDERATION

The national trade unions, isolated as they were from one another, felt the need of a common bond.   This they attempted to secure in the Federation of Organised Trades and Labor Unions of the United States and Canada, which was founded in Pittsburgh in November, 1881.

The last date of a national federation of skilled trades was 1873, when the national unions attempted to reorganise the National Labor Union on trade union lines.   The subsequent attempt of the Pittsburgh convention in 1876 brought no results, for it resolved itself into a battle between the socialists and the greenbackers.   The condition of depression during the seventies, and the disintegration of trade unions, nullified such attempts.   From time to time, one or another national union issued letters to the presidents of other unions urging the necessity of a national federation.   But not until the turn of the tide of prosperity could anything be accomplished.

The initiative which was finally crowned with success came apparently from a non-trade union source.   A disaffected group of the Knights of Labor, who desired to establish a rival order, called a conference for this purpose to meet August 2, 1881, at Terre Haute, Indiana.[39]   The conference was attended by J. E. Coughlin, president of the National Tanners' and Curriers' Union; E. Powers, general president of the Lake Seamen's

38 " History of Typographical Union 6," in New York Bureau of Labor, *Report,* 1911, p. 392.

39 Sorge, "Die Amerikanishe Arbeiter-Föderation," in *Neue Zeit,* 1895–1896, II, 236.

Union; Lyman A. Brant, International Typographical Union; P. J. McGuire, St. Louis Trades and Labor Assembly; T. Thompson, International Molders' Union, Dayton, Ohio; George W. Osborn, Springfield, Ohio; W. C. Pollner, Cleveland Trades Assembly; Samuel L. Leffingwell, Indianapolis Trades Assembly; J. R. Backus, Terre Haute Amalgamated Labor Union; and Mark W. Moore. Moore apparently represented the insurgent Knights of Labor.[40] The conference effected a temporary organisation, issued a call to all trades and labour unions of the United States and Canada, appointing as a standing committee, Lyman A. Brant, chairman and Mark W. Moore, corresponding secretary-treasurer. The framers of the call defined the objects for which the federation should be established in the following words:

". . . Only in such a body [a federation of trades] can proper action be taken to promote the general welfare of the industrial classes. There we can discuss and examine all questions affecting the national interests of each and every trade, and by a combination of forces secure that justice which isolated and separate trade and labor unions can never fully command.

" A national Trades Union Congress can prepare labour measures and agree upon laws they desire passed by the Congress of the United States; and a Congressional Labor Committee, after the manner of the Parliamentary Committee of Trades Unions in England, could be elected to urge and advance legislation at Washington on all such measures, and report to the various trades.

" In addition to this, an annual congress of trades unions could organise a systematic agitation to propagate trades union principles, and to impress the necessity of protective trade and labor organisations, and to encourage the formation of such unions and their amalgamation in trades assemblies. Thus we could elevate trades unionism and obtain for the working classes that respect for their rights, and that reward for their services, to which they are justly entitled.

" A federation of this character can be organised with a few simple rules and no salaried officers. The expenses of its management will be trivial and can be provided for by the Trades Union Congress.

" Impressed with the necessity of such a federation, and the im-

---

40 His name does not appear among the signers of the call issued by the conference, but as temporary secretary-treasurer. He spoke at the convention at Pittsburgh, and ended his report by the words: " Agitate! Educate! Consolidate! "— a rallying cry resembling closely the Agitate! Educate! Organise! of the Knights of Labor. First Annual Convention of the Federation of Organized Trades and Labor Unions of the United States and Canada, *Report*, 1881, pp. 7, 8.

portance of an International Trades Union Congress to perfect the organisation, we, the undersigned, delegates, in a preliminary national convention assembled at Terre Haute, Indiana, held August 2d, 1881, do hereby resolve to issue the following call:

" That all international and national unions, trades assemblies or councils, and local trades or labor unions are hereby invited to send delegates to an International Trades Union Congress, to be held in Pittsburgh, Pennsylvania, on Tuesday, November 15, 1881. Each local union will be entitled to one delegate for one hundred members or less, and one additional delegate for each additional five hundred members or major part thereof; also, one delegate for each inter- national or national union, and one delegate for each trades assembly or council."

The call was signed by nine delegates present. After the conference adjourned, the following names were added to the list: George Clark, president of the International Typo- graphical Union; P. F. Fitzpatrick, president of the iron moulders' union; John Kinnear, president of the Central Trade and Labor Assembly, Boston; and George Rodgers, president of the Chicago Trades Assembly.

The call explicitly stated that the object sought by the signers was primarily a national federation to look after the legisla- tive interests of trade unionists, and only secondarily to propa- gate the principles of trade unionism. It is easy to understand why the unions of the early eighties did not feel the need of a federation on economic lines. The main economic functions of the present American Federation of Labor are the assist- ance of national trade unions in organising their trades, the organisation of local unions where no national union exists, the adjustment of jurisdictional disputes, concerted action in matters of especial importance such as shorter hours, the " open shop," or boycotts. None of these functions would have been of material importance to the trade unions of the early eighties. Existing in well-defined trades, which were not affected by technical changes, they had no jurisdictional disputes; oper- ating at a period of great prosperity with full employment and rising wages, they did not realise a necessity for concerted action; the era of the boycotts had not yet begun. As for having a common agency to do the work of organising, it is true that the call mentioned it, but subsequent history showed that it carried little weight. The trade unions of the early eighties had no keen desire to organise any but the skilled workmen; and, since the competition of workmen in small towns had not yet made itself felt, each national trade union strove to organise primarily the workmen of its trade in the larger cities, a function for which its own means were adequate. Moreover, as yet the trade unionists felt no menace to their organisations from the Knights of Labor; in fact, they were in perfect harmony with the Knights. We can, therefore, understand why the unions sought in a national federation a mere legislative organisation, accepting as their model, as they stated in the Terre Haute call, the British Trades Union Congress.

The Pittsburgh convention was opened by Lyman A. Brant, of the typographical union, as chairman of the standing committee appointed at Terre Haute. It had a large and a varied attendance, 107 delegates being present, representing 8 national and international trade unions, 11 city trades councils, 42 local trade unions, 3 district assemblies of the Knights of Labor,[41] and 46 local assemblies of the Knights, including Local Assembly 300, which was in fact the national trade assembly of the window-glass workers. The national trade unions represented were the Amalgamated Association of Iron and Steel Workers by its president, John Jarrett; the cigar makers' union by Samuel Gompers; the coopers', by its president, Thomas Hennebery; the granite cutters', by John J. Thompson; the typographical, by Lyman A. Brant; the cotton and wool spinners, by Robert Howard; the lake seamen's union by Richard Powers, and the German American Typographia by Gustav Fowitz. The local trades assemblies were the Assembly of the Pacific Coast Trades and Labor Unions, and the assemblies of Chicago, Indianapolis, Boston, Detroit, St. Louis, Buffalo, New York, Cincinnati, Cleveland, and Milwaukee. Sixty-eight of the delegates, including mainly the Knights of Labor, came from the vicinity of Pittsburgh.[42] The large representation sent by the Knights was in part due to their fear lest the convention should organise a rival to their Order, a fear which had

[41] No. 3 of Pittsburgh by general secretary of the Knights of Labor, R. D. Layton; No. 2 of Unionville, N. J., and No. 39 of Clarksburg, W. Va.

[42] Among these was one coloured delegate.

some foundation, if we recall that the Terre Haute conference had originally been called for that purpose.

The question of the election of a permanent president gave rise to the first division of opinion. The committee on permanent organisation, one member from each State, with Robert Howard, of the mule spinners, as chairman, and W. H. Foster, of the Cincinnati Trades and Labor Assembly, as secretary, submitted a majority report recommending Samuel Gompers for president. The opposition submitted a minority report signed by five members, recommending Richard Powers of the lake seamen's union, Chicago, for the position. The issue was twofold: first, between the East and West, and second, between the socialists and their opponents. The latter were charged with having inserted in the Pittsburgh *Commercial-Gazette* an article containing the following: " The latter [Mr. Gompers] is the leader of the Socialist element, which is pretty well represented in the Congress, and one of the smartest men present. It is thought that an attempt will be made to capture the organisation for Mr. Gompers [for Permanent President] as the representative of the Socialists, and if such an attempt is made, whether it succeeds or not, there will likely be some lively work, as the delegates opposed to Socialism are determined not to be controlled by it. If the Socialists do not have their own way, they may bolt, as they have always done in the past. If they do bolt, the power of the proposed organisation will be so seriously crippled as to almost destroy its usefulness." [43]

But the " lively work " was spared, since both Gompers and Powers voluntarily ceded the place to John Jarrett of the Amalgamated Iron and Steel Workers, and were elected as vicepresidents.

The convention charged two special committees with framing a constitution and a declaration of principles. They were made up of fourteen members, one from each State. Samuel Gompers was chairman of the first committee and Samuel L. Leffingwell, of the second. Article I of the proposed constitution gave rise to a lengthy and interesting discussion. It stated that " this association shall be known as ' The Federation of Organised Trades Unions of the United States of America and Canada,' and shall consist of such Trades Unions as shall, after being duly admitted, conform to its rules and regulations, and pay all contributions required to carry out the objects of this Federation." [44]

The Knights of Labor delegates interpreted the restriction of membership to " Trades Unions " as amounting to an exclusion of the unskilled. The representative of the International Typographical Union supported the Knights, but on the other hand, Gompers (the cigar makers), Jarrett (the amalgamated iron and steel workers), Henneberry (the coopers), and Powers (the lake seamen) defended the wording as read. Gompers said that the committee had no intention " to exclude any working man who believes in and belongs to organised labor." [45] Jarrett said the same, but Henneberry definitely stated: " I am in favour of helping everybody and anybody, but let all trades join their respective national organisations." [46] Powers advanced the argument that the wording " Trades Unions " will keep out of the Federation political labor bodies which might try to force themselves into our future deliberations." [47] However, the article was amended to read " Trades and Labor Unions," thus meeting the objection of the champions of unskilled labour.

But the national trade unions succeeded in carrying their point in the matter of representation at the conventions. The committee's report gave them one vote for every 5,000 or less and one vote for every additional 5,000 members, or major fraction thereof. The local trades councils were given one vote each, but it was added that " no local Trade or Labor Union shall be entitled to a representation in the sessions of this Federation where International or National Unions of said craft exist, or where there are Trades Assemblies or Councils in the locality." [48] This plan was rejected, but neither was a substitute adopted which proposed to make the local trade union the basis of representation. The section was referred back to the committee and when it emerged it was so worded that no local trade union, whether affiliated with a national union or not, received any representation; local trades councils or assemblies got one vote each, but the representation of national trade unions was

[44] *Ibid.,* 16.   [45] *Ibid.*   [46] *Ibid.,* 17.   [47] *Ibid.*   [48] *Ibid.*

raised 1 vote for 1,000 members or less, 2 for 4,000, 3 for 8,000, and so on.

The constitution provided for a revenue to be derived from a *per capita* tax of 3 cents per member annually from each trade and labour union, trades assembly, or council affiliated with the federation. No president was provided for, but a legislative committee of five, including a federation secretary, were to be the only executive officers. Gompers received 32 votes for secretary on the first ballot, Crawford, his nearest opponent, 17, and Foster of Ohio, 16. This division was evidently determined by the same motives as at the time of electing a permanent president. On the third ballot the supporters of Crawford voted for Foster, who was elected by a vote of 99 to 31.

The platform revealed considerable difference of opinion, but by a narrow margin of three votes, President Jarrett forced through a declaration favouring a protective tariff, in spite of the protest of those who were either free traders (the delegates from the West) or of those who in order to avoid dissension did not desire to bring up the tariff question at all. Jarrett also ruled out of the proposed platform, as " being foreign to the purpose for which this convention was convened," two resolutions, one dealing with railway discrimination and extortion practised against small shippers and another demanding that the government reclaim the railway land grants forfeited by reason of non-fulfilment of contract and keep them henceforth as homes for actual settlers. The platform as adopted demanded: legal incorporation for trade unions, compulsory education for children, the prohibition of child labour before fourteen, uniform apprentice laws, the enforcement of the national eight-hour law, prison labour reform, abolition of the " truck " and " order " system, mechanics' lien, abolition of conspiracy laws as applied to labour organisations, a national bureau of labour statistics, a protective tariff for American labour, an anti-contract immigrant law, and recommended " all trades and labor organisations to secure proper representation in all lawmaking bodies by means of the ballot, and to use all honorable measures by which this result can be accomplished." [49]

[49] *Proceedings*, 4. Resolutions were also adopted expressing sympathy with the Irish people and greetings to the British trade unionists. Chinese immigration was condemned, the licensing of stationary engineers demanded, etc.

The plank of incorporation demanded " that an organisation of workingmen unto what is known as a Trades or Labor Union should have the right to the protection of their property in like manner as the property of all other persons and societies, and to accomplish this purpose we insist upon the passage of laws in the State Legislatures and in Congress for the incorporation of Trades Unions and similar labour organisations." [50] The desire expressed for incorporation is of extreme interest when compared with the opposite attitude of the present day. The motive behind it then was more than the mere securing of protection for trade union funds. A full enumeration of the other motives can be obtained from the testimony. of the labour leaders before the Senate Committee on Education and Labour in 1883. McGuire argued for a national law, mainly for the reason that such a law passed by Congress would remove the trade unions from the operation of the conspiracy laws that existed on the statute books of a number of States, notably New York and Pennsylvania. He pleaded that " if it [Congress] has not the power, it should assume the power; and, if necessary, amend the constitution to do it." [51]   Strasser raised the point of protection for union funds and gave as a second reason that it " will give our organisation more stability, and in that manner we shall be able to avoid strikes by perhaps settling with our employers, when otherwise we should be unable to do so, because when our employers know that we are to be legally recognised that will exercise such moral force upon them that they cannot avoid recognising us themselves." [52]   W. H. Foster stated that in Ohio the law provided for incorporation at a slight cost, but he wanted a national law to " legalise arbitration " by which he meant that " when a question of dispute arose between the employers and the employed, instead of having it as now, when the one often refuses to even acknowledge or discuss the question with the other, if they were required to submit the question to arbitration, or to meet on the same level before an impartial tribunal, there is no doubt but what the result would be more in our favor than. it is now, when very often public opinion cannot hear our cause." He,

50 *Ibid.*, 3.
51 Senate Committee on Education and Labor, *Report*, 1885, I, 326.
52 *Ibid.*, 461.

however, did not desire to have compulsory arbitration, but merely compulsory dealing with the union, or compulsory investigation by an impartial body, both parties to remain free to accept the reward, provided, however, "that once they do agree the agreement shall remain in force for a fixed period." [53] Like Foster, John Jarrett argued for an incorporation law before the committee, solely for its effect upon conciliation and arbitration.[54] He, too, was opposed to compulsory arbitration, but he showed that he had thought out the point less clearly than Foster.[55]

The above shows that the argument for incorporation had shifted from co-operation, the ground upon which it was urged during the sixties, to collective bargaining and arbitration — a change which denotes a fundamental change in the aim of the labour movement — from idealistic striving for self-employment to opportunistic trade unionism. The young and struggling trade unions of the early eighties saw only the good side of incorporation without its pitfalls; their subsequent experience with the courts converted them from exponents into ardent opponents of incorporation and of what Foster termed "legalised arbitration."

The second convention of the Federation met in Cleveland, November 21, 1882, with only nineteen delegates present. The reduction in numbers was due to the absence of the Knights of Labor and of the Association of Amalgamated Iron and Steel Workers, both of whom had been numerously represented in Pittsburgh. Eight national and international trade unions and ten trades' councils sent delegates. The former were the Amalgamated Society of Engineers, Machinists and Millwrights, the Brotherhood of Carpenters and Joiners of America, the Cigar Makers' International Union, the German American Typographia, the Granite Cutters' National Union,[56] the Lake Seamen's Union, the International Typographical Union, and the National Mule Spinners' Association. Each union had one delegate, except the cigar makers and the lake seamen, who were represented by two. The remaining delegates came from

53 *Ibid.*, 403.
54 *Ibid.*, 1150.
55 Gompers also spoke in favour of incorporation but gave no reasons.

56 The delegate of their union was Thomas H. Murch, a congressman from Maine, elected as a greenbacker in 1878.

the trades assemblies of Boston, Chicago, Cincinnati, Cleveland, Dayton, Detroit, District of Columbia, Indianapolis, New York, and the Pacific Coast.

Leffingwell of the Indianapolis Trades Assembly was chosen president, Gompers, vice-president, Congressman Murch, the English secretary, and Hugo Miller, of the German-American Typographia, the German secretary. The report of the legislative committee complained of meagre support from the trade unions which prevented the Federation from accomplishing any work. When the congressional committee was appointed, it sent a letter to Speaker Keifer, of the House of Representatives, suggesting names for the standing committee on education and labour, but the speaker did not even acknowledge the receipt of the letter. Richard Powers, of the Lake Seamen's Union, was sent to Washington in the interest of a seamen's safety bill, and he also helped to defeat a bill forbidding seamen to organise. Although he represented the Federation, his expenses were paid by his own union. Another mark of lack of interest in the Federation was shown by the fact that only one-half of the 5,000 copies of proceedings of the Pittsburgh convention were sold during the year. The Federation, with an annual budget of but $445.31, doubtless failed to justify the expectations of its organisers.

The convention gave attention to the tariff, to the eight-hour day, and to the land question. Frank Foster, of Boston, representing the International Typographical Union, moved to strike out the tariff plank in the constitution, on the ground that under the protective tariff, prosperity was not passed on to the workingmen. It was carried against one negative vote. An eighthour declaration, presented by the Chicago Trade and Labor Assembly and drawn up in the spirit of Ira Steward's teaching, was passed with the amendment, however, changing the wording from " the only " remedy to " a " remedy. Gompers felt lukewarm towards the declaration, for to him the eight-hour day meant providing more employment rather than raising the standard of living and thereby wages.[57] The land question was brought up in the form of a single-tax resolution offered by Grennell, of the Detroit trades assembly, but the general con-

[57] Federation of Organized Trades and Labor Unions, *Proceedings*, 1882, p. 17.

sensus of opinion, as expressed by Gompers, was the more so-cialistic view that " it is not the ownership of land that should be fought, but the doings of the capitalists we are organised to oppose." [58] The convention, however, recognised the Henry George agitation by recommending the study of the land question. Two planks were added to the platform, one opposing the contract system on public works and the other demanding employers' liability. Resolutions were adopted demanding the further restriction of Chinese immigration and extending an invitation to women's trade unions to affiliate with the Federation. The basis of representation was changed to admit, in addition to national trade unions and city trades councils, state or provincial federations of trades unions with two votes, district assemblies of the Knights of Labor [59] with one vote, and local trade unions also with one vote each, provided that " no local trade union shall be entitled to representation which has not been organised six months prior to the session of this body," a measure taken apparently to safeguard against politicians. The national trade union remained, of course, the basic unit of the Federation.

The convention adjourned on November 24, having re-elected W. H. Foster as secretary of the legislative committee, and Gompers, Howard, Edmonston, and Powers, members. Gompers was subsequently chosen by the committee as chairman and Powers as first vice-chairman.

The third convention of the Federation opened in New York City on August 21, 1883, with twenty-seven delegates. The same national trade unions as in the previous convention, with the exception of the granite cutters, were represented. Delegates from 5 city trades assemblies, 1 state assembly, the workingmen's assembly of the State of New York, 5 local trade unions, and a women's national labour league completed the roll. Gompers was chosen president, and the legislative committee made a report differing but little in contents from the report at the previous convention. The committee used Gabriel Edmonston, of the carpenters' brotherhood, who resided in Washington,

[58] *Ibid.*, 23.
[59] Richard Powers called attention to the fact that " an impression had gone out that this Congress ignored the Knights of Labor, when, on the contrary, it had decided that the Knights of Labor shall have an equal representation in the Federation." *Ibid.*, 27.

as a lobbyist before Congress,[60] and he introduced through Congressman Murch a bill for the incorporation of trade unions.[61] Considerable success in getting legislation was attained during the year by the trade unions in New York, New Jersey, Massachusetts, Michigan, and Maine, but the only credit that the Federation could claim was the one that its platform demanded all the measures enacted. The report referred to " over-zealous partisans who continued efforts detrimental to that harmony which should exist between labor organisations,"— a veiled attack on the Knights of Labor.

The convention discussed steps to be taken to make the Federation represent the entire labour movement. The committee on standing orders reported a resolution which called for the appointment of a special committee to " confer with the Knights of Labor, and other kindred labour organisations, with a view to a thorough unification and consolidation of the working people throughout the country." [62] Here the half-concealed animosity towards the Knights of Labor again revealed itself, for Gompers opposed too definite action and proposed instead that the legislative committee be instructed " to enter into immediate correspondence with the proper officers of national and international Labor organisations of all descriptions, for the purpose of obtaining their views upon what basis a more thorough unification of the Labor organisations may be accomplished." and to report to the next session of the Federation.[63] Finally a substitute resolution was passed, directing the legislative committee to appoint subcommittees to confer, etc., but the name of the Knights of Labor was not mentioned.[64]

No changes were made in the platform. The only interesting discussion in this connection was raised by a letter from Jarrett declaring that the iron and steel workers' union could no longer affiliate with the Federation because it had " passed a series of resolutions condemning tariff." [65] The legislative committee was thereupon authorised to reply that the action of the convention of 1882 signified not a condemnation of protec-

---

60 He received $15 for loss of time. The Federation was too poor to employ a regular lobbyist in Washington.

61 Senator Blair, of New Hampshire, introduced in the Senate a similar bill at the same session.

62 Federation of Organized Trades and Labor Unions, *Proceedings*, 1883, p. 10.

63 *Ibid.*, 11.

64 *Ibid.*

65 *Ibid.*, 18.

tion, but merely an expression of a desire to keep the Federation altogether out of the tariff controversy.[66]   However, the Amalgamated Association did not return to the Federation until 1887.[67]

The constitution, like the platform, was left unchanged, except that the membership of the legislative committee was increased to 9 so as to include 1 president, 6 vice-presidents, a secretary, and a treasurer.   But a notable advance was made in the method of legislative action.   A resolution was adopted ordering that " a committee be appointed to attend the next national conventions of the two great political parties, and in the name of the organised workmen of the United States demand the incorporation in their platform of principles their position on the enforcement of the eight-hour law, the incorporation of national trade organisations, and the establishment of a national bureau of labor statistics." [68]   The important resolutions passed were two on the hours of labour, one declaring " the question of shortening the hours of labor as paramount to all other questions at present "; [69] another recommending " to international, national, and local unions the necessity of shortening the hours of labor to eight hours per day "; [70] another resolution advocated government ownership of telegraph lines on the ground that the existing system practised discrimination and extortion toward the consumers and that under it " the law of demand of labor is controlled by one corporation "; a resolution endorsing the cigar makers' label was passed; another recommended the organisation of factory workers; and finally, an address was drafted to " Working Girls and Women " urging them to organise.   Upon the new legislative committee for

66 *Ibid.*, 20.

67 The Pittsburgh *National Labor Tribune* at the time constantly maintained that the weakness of the Federation was due to the position it had taken upon the tariff.   Since these first conventions the Federation has scrupulously been on guard against expressing any position upon tariff questions.   The convention of 1889 overwhelmingly voted down a resolution asking for an increase of duties upon imported cigars.   (American Federation of Labor, *Proceedings*, 1889, p. 24.)   In 1895 the same treatment befell a resolution presented by John B. Lennon, that " while the protective tariff policy of our

government continues " ready-made clothing should not be allowed to be brought in free of duty.   (*Ibid.*, 72, 73.)   Some of the national unions affiliated with the Federation, however, adopted an out-and-out stand in the protective tariff controversy.   The iron and steel workers' union on several occasions sent lobbyists to Washington to urge that steel be protected by high duties.   (Cleveland *Citizen*, Sept. 23, 1893.)

68 Federation of Organized Trades and Labor Unions, *Proceedings*, 1883, p. 11.

69 *Ibid.*, 17.

70 *Ibid.*, 16.

the year were: McLogan, of the Chicago Trade and Labor Assembly, president; Gompers, first vice-president; Frank H. Foster and Robert Howard, secretary and treasurer, respectively.

Immediately after the convention adjourned, the legislative committee, under instructions, made arrangements for a hearing before the Senate Committee on Education and Labor, which was at that time taking testimony on the relations between labour and capital.[71]

During 1884 it became evident that the Federation as a legislative organisation had proved a failure. Manifestly the trade unions felt no great interest in national legislation. Their indifference can be measured by the fact that the annual income of the Federation never exceeded $700 and that, excepting in 1881, none of its conventions represented more than one-fourth of the trade union membership of the country. Under such conditions the legislative influence of the Federation naturally was infinitesimal. The legislative committee carried out the instructions of the 1883 convention and sent communications to the national committees of the Republican and Democratic parties with the request that they should define their position upon the enforcement of the eight-hour law and other measures. The letters were not even answered. A subcommittee of the legislative committee appeared before the two political conventions, but met with no greater attention. The situation is described in Secretary Foster's report in the following words: " In presenting my report as secretary for the year past I am conscious that its chief interest will consist of the future possibilities it suggests rather than in its record of objects attained. The lack of funds has seriously crippled the work of the Federation, and this, coupled with an organisation lacking cohesiveness, has allowed small scope for effective expenditure of effort." [72] Altogether, notwithstanding the encouraging growth of local and national unions in the early eighties, the time was not yet ripe for a national federation.

[71] The committee published four volumes of testimony in 1885, but it never presented a report. The testimony elicited throws little light on the situation. Evidently the senators were unfamiliar with the subject, as is shown by the nature of their questions. The more important points in the testimony relating to the labour side of the inquiry were given above in connection with incorporation and the philosophy of trade unionism.

[72] *Ibid.*, 1884, p. 17.

CHAPTER VIII

END OF SECRECY IN THE KNIGHTS AND DEVIATION FROM FIRST PRINCIPLES, 1876–1884

Secrecy and the movement for centralisation, 332. District Assembly 1 and the convention at Philadelphia, 1876, 333. The National Labor League of North America, 333. District Assembly 3 and the convention at Pittsburgh, 333. Lull in the movement for centralisation, 334. The Knights and the railway strikes of 1877, 334. Other strikes, 334. The General Assembly at Reading, Pennsylvania, January 1, 1878, 334. Preamble, 335. "First Principles": Education, organisation, and co-operation, 335. The form of organisation, 337. Special convention on the secrecy question, June, 1878, 338. Referendum vote, 338. The Catholic Church and secrecy in the Knights, 339. The compromise in 1879, 339. Final abolition of secrecy in 1881, 339. Growth and fluctuation in membership, 1878–1880, 339. The resistance fund, 340. The compromise, 341. Compromise on political action, 341. Claims of the advocates of co-operation and education, 341. Demands of the trade union element within the Knights, 342. The national trade assembly, 343. Growth and fluctuation of membership, 1880–1883, 343. Component elements of the Knights, 344. Unattached local trade unions, 344. Weak national trade organisations, 345. Advantages to an incipient movement from affiliation with the Knights, 346. T. V. Powderly — Grand Master Workman in 1881, 347. Enthusiasm for strikes, 347. The telegraphers' strike in 1883, 348. Unorganised strikes, 349. The freight handlers' strike in New York, 349. Failure of the strikes conducted by the Knights, 349. Its effect on the fluctuation of membership, 350. The political faction, 351. Non-partisan politics, 351. Partiality of the general officers for co-operation, 351. Independent politics in the West, 352. Co-operative beginnings, 352. Attitude of the trades unions towards the Knights, 352. Their ,endeavour to turn the Knights back to "First Principles," 352. General summary, 1876–1884, 353.

AFTER the failure of the Pittsburgh convention of 1876 to consolidate the labour forces into a single national organisation, the movement for centralisation within the Order of the Knights of Labor gained accelerated pace. As said above,[1] the main impetus behind this movement was furnished by the secrecy issue which, since the Molly Maguire excitement was at its

[1] See above, II, 200 *et seq.*

height, became more pressing than ever. After much deliberation, District Assembly 1 decided to allow all assemblies to
vote on the question. The upshot was that a call was issued
to all assemblies whose addresses could be obtained, to meet in
convention in the city of Philadelphia on July 3, 1876, " for
the purpose of strengthening the Order for [by] a sound and
permanent organisation, also the promoting of peace, harmony,
and the welfare of its members." [2]

The convention called by District Assembly 1 met at Philadelphia as appointed. District Assembly 3 of Pittsburgh
failed, however, to send representatives, so that the convention
refrained from taking a decisive step in the matter of changing
the main principles and policies of the Order, including secrecy.

On the other hand, the greater portion of the session was
devoted to " strengthening the Order for a sound and permanent
organisation." The keynote of this convention was national
organisation. Upon this certainly all were agreed. Hence a
constitution was drawn up for a national body, and a committee
appointed to draft a constitution by which district assemblies
were to be governed, and the territory in which a district assembly should operate might be inviolable against any like assembly.
Thinking it might be necessary under certain emergencies to
make the name of the organisation known to the public, it was
designated as The National Labor League of North America.
The only power reserved to the League was control of the secret
ritual, which it could modify by a two-thirds vote. All other
powers remained vested in the district assemblies. A per capita
tax of 5 cents upon the membership was to constitute the sole
revenue of the League. The convention adjourned to meet
later in Pittsburgh, apparently with the intention of reconciling
the rebellious District Assembly 3.[3]

Meantime, District Assembly 3 called a national convention
of its own to meet at Pittsburgh. The attendance was entirely
from among its followers. District Assembly 1 and its adherents ignored the call. The convention assumed a conciliatory attitude by starting out on the presumption that a national
organisation had already been created in Philadelphia. To

2 Powderly, *Thirty Years of Labor*, 225.   call, the minutes of the convention, and
3 *Ibid.*, 225–232, gives verbatim the   the constitution adopted.

justify, however, its *raison d'être,* it took a decisive stand with regard to the matter of secrecy, resolved to make the name and objects of the Order public, changed the ritual so that a member of the Catholic Church might, " if he considers it his duty," confess to his father confessor, and decided in favour of incorporating the Order.

The Pittsburgh convention seemed to be satisfied after having asserted itself, and adjourned with the intention of meeting in Washington at a later date.   The matter of effective national organisation rested for over a year.   It was brought again into prominence by the great strikes of 1877 which taught the lesson that a wage movement without a central organisation and a strike fund was doomed to failure.   Powderly contends that the Order of the Knights of Labor as an organisation did not join in precipitating these strikes, although members were employed in the industries involved.   The Knights, on the contrary, aided in keeping the men from committing violence.   He also speaks of local assemblies in the coal fields striking without the consent of their district assembly.[4]   This, of course, shows that Knights of Labor were officially involved, although the district assembly was not consulted.   But, even granting that they were not involved officially, the fact alone that Knights as individuals took part is sufficient to prove that they saw the evil effects of lack of finances, a truth which was brought home to them with particular strength when the miners of the Lackawanna and Wyoming coal fields, strongholds of the Knights of Labor, were starved into submission.

Added to this was the question of taking an attitude toward the political labour movement which came immediately upon the heels of the big strikes, and also toward the question of secrecy which was still pressing for settlement.   This time the two rival district assemblies acted in unison, and District Assembly 3 consented that District Assembly 1 should issue a call for a convention to meet at Reading, January 1, 1878, " for the purpose of forming a Central Assembly . . . and also for the purpose of creating a Central Resistance Fund, Bureau of Statistics, Providing Revenue for the work of Organisation, estab-

4 *Ibid.,* 207–219.

lishment of an Official Register, giving number, place of meeting of each assembly, etc. Also the subject of making the name public. . . ." [5]

The convention at Reading finally achieved a central national organisation of the Knights of Labor and adopted a preamble and constitution, which, with minor changes, continued throughout the existence of the Order.

The delegates, who came from eleven district assemblies, while thoroughly representative, were actually sent by about one-half of the membership. Although, for unknown reasons District Assembly 3 was not represented, all of its followers sent delegates. The Order having worked secretly, it was difficult to know of the existence of all affiliated bodies. In addition, a considerable number did not have sufficient funds with which to finance the expenses of representatives, while a third factor was the scepticism of many as to the probable success of a national body.

The preamble recites how " wealth," with its development, has become so aggressive that " unless checked " it " will inevitably lead to the pauperisation and hopeless degradation of the toiling masses." Hence, if the toilers are " to enjoy the blessings of life " they must organise " every department of productive industry " in order to " check " the power of wealth and to put a stop to " unjust accumulation." The battle cry in this fight must be " moral worth, not wealth, the true standard of individual and national greatness." As the " action " of the toilers ought to be guided by " knowledge " it is necessary to know " the true condition of the producing masses "; therefore the Order demands " from the various governments the establishment of bureaus of labor statistics." Next in order comes the " establishment of co-operative institutions productive and distributive." Union of all trades, " education," and co-operation remained forever after the cardinal points in the Knights of Labor philosophy and were steadily referred to as the " First Principles," namely principles bequeathed to the Order by Uriah Stephens and the other " Founders."

The preamble further provides that the Order will stand for

5 *Ibid.*, 238.

the reservation of all lands for actual settlers; the "abrogation of all laws that do not bear equally upon capital and labor,
the removal of unjust technicalities, delays, and discriminations
in the administration of justice, and the adopting of measures
providing for the health and safety of those engaged in mining,
manufacturing, or building pursuits"; the enactment of a
weekly pay law, mechanics' lien law, and a law prohibiting child
labour under fourteen years of age; the abolition of the contract system on national, state, and municipal work, and of the
system of leasing out convicts; equal pay for equal work for
both sexes; reduction of hours of labor to eight per day; "the
substitution of arbitration for strikes, whenever and wherever
employers and employés are willing to meet on equitable
grounds"; the establishment of "a purely national circulating
medium, based upon the faith and resources of the nation, and
issued directly to the people, without the intervention of any
system of banking corporations, which money shall be a legal
tender in payment of all debts, public or private."

This preamble, which now replaced the ritual as the formula
of its principles and demands, was practically verbatim the
declaration of principles of the Industrial Brotherhood in 1874.[6]
It had then been prepared by Robert Schilling, who was now
a member of the committee on platform and resolutions. There
were, however, several planks on which the two platforms differed and these differences are very significant in determining
the philosophy of the Knights at this time. The preamble
totally omitted the plank of the Industrial Brotherhood, stating
that trade unions were effective "in regulating purely trade-
union matters,"[7] but it cautioned them that their influence
"upon all questions appertaining to the welfare of the masses
as a whole" must prove comparatively futile, without a closer
union. It omitted also the plank demanding the enactment of
apprenticeship laws. The reason for these omissions is obvious.
The Knights of Labor started out as the antithesis of the trade
unions in the form of organisation; and, similarly, it emphasised education, mutual aid, and co-operation rather than the
policy of restriction; hence the negative attitude on apprentice-

6 *Ibid*, 243–246. See above, II, 164, 165.
7 Chicago *Workingman's Advocate*, Apr. 24, 1875.

ship. This is explained in part also by the fact that the Order gathered into its ranks workingmen largely of the semi-skilled class to whom strict apprenticeship rules are of small consequence. Another significant difference is the modification of the money plank. While greenbackism was reaffirmed in principle, the Kellogg scheme of interchangeable bonds and paper money was omitted, reflecting the change that had taken place with regard to this matter in the greenback movement of the country. Other omissions were of less significance, namely, the planks demanding " a system of public markets " and systems of cheap transportation. These omissions indicate the waning influence of the Patrons of Husbandry.[8]

The constitution which was adopted provided for a highly centralised form of organisation. Just as the district assembly had absolute jurisdiction over its subordinate bodies, so the General Assembly of the Knights of Labor of North America, as the national body was styled, was given " full and final jurisdiction," and was made " the highest tribunal " of the Order. " It alone possesses the power and authority to make, amend, or repeal the fundamental and general laws and regulations of the Order; to finally decide all controversies arising in the Order; to issue all charters. . . . It can also tax the members of the Order for its maintenance." [9]

The district assembly was made the highest tribunal within its district, thus retaining its old function and powers, subordinate only to the General Assembly. The territory of a district assembly and the nature of its membership were left undefined, since there was no controversy on these matters at the time.[10] Local assemblies were to be " composed of not less than ten members at least three quarters of whom must be wage-workers; and this proportion shall be maintained for all time." [11]

The minimum initiation fee set at this time was 50 cents, and any person over eighteen years of age " working for wages, or who at any time worked for wages " could become a member. However, " no person who either sells, or makes his living by

8 See above, II. 112.
9 Constitution of the General Assembly, in General Assembly, *Proceedings*, 1878 (Reading), Art. I, Sec. 2, p. 29.

10 Constitution of the District Assembly, Art. I, Sec. 2, p. 35, in *ibid*.
11 Constitution of the Local Assembly, Art. I, Sec. 1, p. 36, in *ibid*.

the sale of, intoxicating drink, can be admitted, and no lawyer, doctor or banker can be admitted." [12]

No provision was made at this time in the constitution as to the body to which a local assembly owed its direct allegiance, and we find later considerable anarchy, because local assemblies were free to change affiliation at will. The clause allowing non-wage workers to join was later a means of bringing in large numbers of farmers, small merchants, and masters.

The matter of secrecy was discussed at a special convention held in June, 1878, in Philadelphia. It was called expressly for the purpose of considering the " expediency of making the name of the Order public, for the purpose of defending it from the fierce assaults and defamation made upon it by Press, Clergy, and Corporate Capital, and to take such further action as shall effectually meet with the GRAVE EMERGENCY." [13]

Secrecy was thoroughly discussed, but a two-thirds vote could not be raised [14] in favour of a resolution requiring the grand master workman and the general secretary " to give to D. A.'s [15] and to L. A.'s [16] under the jurisdiction of the G. A.[17] permission to make the name of the Order public, but only upon a request made by a two-thirds vote of such body." [18] It was decided, however, to submit to a referendum vote of the membership the questions, among others, of making the name of the Order public, and " of making such modifications in the initiatory exercises as will tend to remove the opposition coming from the church." [19] In the vote taken, the former question was decided upon favourably by a majority of those voting, but a majority of the locals were against making the name of the Order public. The latter question was rejected by a majority of both the votes and the locals.[20]

When a large number of the membership, the press, and the church demanded a change, and when the enemies of the Order libelled it because of its extreme secrecy, some action in the way of modification was inevitable. Consequently, the General Assembly of 1879 decided that any district assembly might,

---

12 *Ibid.*
13 General Assembly, *Proceedings*, 1878 (Special session, Philadelphia), 40.
14 The vote stood 9 for and 6 against the resolution. *Ibid.*, 42.
15 District Assemblies.

16 " Local Assemblies."
17 " General Assembly."
18 General Assembly, *Proceedings*, 1878 (Special session, Philadelphia), 42.
19 *Ibid.*, 44.
20 *Ibid.*, 1879 (St. Louis), 62, 63.

by a two-thirds vote, make the name of the Order public in its own district only.[21]　This was a compromise between those who believed secrecy no longer necessary for the success of the Order, and those who believed that " the veil of mystery was more potent for good than the education of the masses in an open organisation." [22]　However, the former insisted that making the name of the Order public would lead to an increase in membership.　The demand from those districts where the Catholic Church was dominant was also insistent against complete secrecy.　An unsuccessful attempt was made in 1880,[23] but in 1881 a resolution to make the name public throughout was carried by a vote of 28 to 6.[24]　The opposition this time came again from those who believed in the educational value of secrecy.　The provision, however, was still retained which forbade members from revealing any of the secret work of the assembly meetings, or from revealing " to any employer or other person the name or person of any one a member of the Order without permission of the member." [25]

The national organisation of the Knights of Labor did nothing in the nature of aggressive activity until 1880.　The district assemblies, and, in the absence of these, the individual local assemblies, took separate action on whatever policies they saw fit.　The sessions of the General Assembly in 1878 and 1879 were devoted, in the main, to perfecting the organisation and threshing out the future policies of the Order.　Strikes, politics, and co-operation were the prevailing issues, although some of the coal districts urged the adoption of a beneficial feature, not agreeing as to whether it should be a sick benefit, funeral, or burial, or all.　The membership doubled during these two years.　At the end of 1878 it was 9,287,[26] and at the end of 1879 it was 20,151.[27]　Reference has already been made to the enormous fluctuation in membership during the early years of the Order,[28] but apparently the situation did not change with national organisation.　During the year October, 1879,

21 *Ibid.*, 75.

22 Powderly, *Thirty Years of Labor*, 560.

23 General Assembly, *Proceedings*, 1880, pp. 193, 229.

24 *Ibid.*, 1881, pp. 292, 305.

25 *Adelphon Kruptos* (undated; probably printed in 1881), 13; also appears in *Adelphon Kruptos* (Toledo, Ohio, 1891), 16.

26 General Assembly, *Proceedings*, 1879 (Chicago), 116, 117.

27 *Ibid.*, 1880, pp. 214, 215.

28 See above, II, 199.

to October, 1880, although 18,104 members were initiated, 10,056 were suspended.[29]   The main cause for dissatisfaction was the neglect of the Order to take up any particular line of action.   Naturally, financial response was slow.

In accordance with the call for the Reading convention, a resistance fund was created, requiring each local " to set apart . . . each month, a sum equal to five cents each for every member upon the books." [30]   This resolution was adopted without opposition.   When the question was raised as to what purpose the fund should be put, there was much difference of opinion. The committee appointed to draw up this part of the constitution took it for granted that the fund was to be used for strike purposes only, and reported a clause embodying that view.[31] But a majority in the convention was opposed and believed that the fund should either not be touched at all, or put to such uses as co-operation,[32] propaganda, or mutual benefits.[33]   It was finally decided, after two and a half days' discussion, that the resistance fund should remain intact for the space of two years from January 1, 1878.   After that time it should be held for use and distribution under such laws and regulations as the General Assembly might then adopt.[34]

The struggle during those two years, which includes three regular sessions of the General Assembly, January, 1878 (Reading), January, 1879 (St. Louis), and September, 1879 (Chicago), centred around the disposition of the resistance fund. One element that was either preparing for, or in the midst of, a strike demanded that the fund be used for the support of strikes alone; another element, either not being in a position to start a strike,[35] or having gone through a disastrous one, demanded that the fund be appropriated either for co-operation or educational purposes, or both.   Then there was a sentiment in favour of using the money for mutual benefit purposes, coming mainly from coal communities where local assemblies were in the habit of providing burial expenses, sick and death benefits.

[29] *Proceedings*, 1880, pp. 214, 215.
[30] Constitution of the General Assembly, *Proceedings*, 1878 (Reading).
[31] *Ibid.*, 11, 12, 14.
[32] *Ibid.*, 1879 (Chicago), 120, 130.
[33] *Ibid.*, 106.
[34] Constitution of the General Assembly, Art. VIII, p. 32, in General Assembly, *Proceedings*, 1878 (Reading).
[35] Because such elements were located in an isolated community or composed of artisans of various trades in small towns. As we shall see later, this element was on the whole negligible during the succeeding period.

There was also a distinct educational element, led, in the main, by those who were active in politics, which held that it was through ignorance that the wage-earners did not support workingmen's tickets. An educational fund would enable the select to educate the rest of the workingmen to stand for their rights.

Since the Order, at the time, was not involved in any single important activity, the division of opinion was rather balanced, and a compromise was struck when, in 1880, the resistance fund was divided for the three purposes of strikes, co-operation, and education. Within a year or two, however, when the Order had plunged into numerous strikes, it was voted to use for their support the money set aside for co-operation and education.

As two-thirds of the demands in the preamble could be secured only through legislation, it is not surprising that the question of politics should consume a large portion of the time of each session. The attempt to commit the Order to political action manifested itself in several ways. It was first brought up at the session of January, 1879, when a resolution in favour of independent political action as an organisation was defeated.[36] It seems that a majority of the delegates favoured such action, while nearly all wished for political action in some form or another. The disagreement arose when it came to indorsing a political party. Hence, to satisfy all, it was voted that " local assemblies may take such political action in elections as shall be deemed by them best calculated to advance the interests of the Order." [37]

It seems that the response of local assemblies was not over-enthusiastic, for, at the following session, a resolution was introduced by the political actionists requiring local assemblies to " use their political power in all legislative elections," and reiterating " that it is left to the discretion of each L. A. to act with that Party in their vicinity, through which they can gain the most." Precautionary measures were taken to prevent disruption by providing that " in no case should an Assembly take political action in a campaign unless at least three-fourths of the attending members are united in supporting such action," [38] and that " no member shall, however, be compelled to vote with

36 General Assembly, *Proceedings*, 1879 (St. Louis), 49, 66.

37 *Ibid.*, 57, 67.
38 *Ibid.*, 1879 (Chicago), 120, 130.

the majority." Article X of the Constitution of the General Assembly was also amended at this time, extending the privilege of political action to district assemblies and requiring that when "political action is contemplated the regular business of the D. A. or L. A. shall be concluded, and the D. A. or L. A. regularly closed; and each Local in the D. A. and each member in the L. A. must have received previous notification before the proposed political action can be considered." [39]

This permission for subordinate bodies to determine on their own behalf which political party they should indorse, seemed to satisfy the various elements. If in one locality the sentiment was in favour of indorsing the Socialist or Greenback party, the assembly could do so without creating dissension in other localities where the sentiment might be in favour of indorsing individuals of either of the old parties. An attempt was also made by the political actionists to establish state assemblies, and either to abolish district assemblies or to make them subordinate to the state assembly. But this effort was not rewarded with success at the time.[40]

At the session of 1879 at St. Louis, the status of the local assembly and the latitude which trade union matters were to have, also received some further definition. The meaning of "sojourners" was defined as persons "of one trade initiated into an Assembly of another trade for the purpose of ultimately forming an Assembly of their own. During the continuance of their sojournership they are entitled to all the privileges of the Order, on such terms as the By-Laws of the Assembly may provide." [41]

At the session of 1879 another concession was made to the trade union element by providing "that trades organised as trades may select an executive officer of their own, who may have charge of their organisation, and organise Local Assemblies of the trade in any part of the country, and attach them to the D. A. controlling said trade . . . that trades so organised be allowed to hold delegate conventions on matters pertaining to their trades. . . ." [42] This virtually meant that national trade

---

[39] Constitution of the General Assembly, Art. X, p. 155, in General Assembly, *Proceedings*, 1879 (Chicago).

[40] *Proceedings*, 1879 (St. Louis), 49, 67.
[41] *Ibid.*, 69.
[42] *Ibid.*, 69, 72.

unions could be organised within the Order under the guise of district assemblies.

The trade element at this time was confined to districts where almost all were employed in the same industry, such as coal mining, and hence a district trade organisation met the need. The window-glass workers were the only members who had a national trade organisation. The activity of the window-glass workers in organising independent local assemblies in the territory of other district assemblies aroused the opposition of these assemblies, and, at the following session, a resolution was introduced not only forbidding the formation of national trade assemblies, but even compelling the dissolution of local trade assemblies, and requiring them thereafter to " admit workmen of all trades, and transact business in the interest of all trades represented." [43]

That part of the resolution which forbade the formation of national trade assemblies was adopted without much opposition. The second part of the resolution referring to local trade assemblies was refused adoption. Therefore, the status of local assemblies remained as before; they could be either a mixed or a trade assembly, but " must in all cases be subordinate to the D. A. in whose territory they may be located, and all laws permitting trade D. A.'s to interfere with the control of the other D. A.'s over any L. A. in their district are hereby rescinded." [44]

The window-glass workers, having a powerful trade union, refused to abide by the decision of the Order. Hence special dispensation was granted them to operate under the designation of Local Assembly 300 as a national trade union. On the other hand, weak trades which asked for a like privilege were denied it. In succeeding periods, as each trade became more conscious of its own problems, the struggle became intense, at times exceedingly bitter, and finally an important factor in the decline of the Knights of Labor.

With the advent of prosperity, the theoretical differences which were formulated during 1878–1879, were soon put to a practical test, although the Knights of Labor played but a subordinate part in the labour movement of the period of the early eighties. The membership was 20,151 in 1879, 28,136 in 1880,

---

[43] *Ibid.*, 1879 (Chicago), 98.   [44] *Ibid.*, 129.

19,422 in 1881, 42,517 in 1882, 51,914 in 1883, showing a steady and rapid growth, with the exception of the year 1881. But these figures are decidedly deceptive as a means of measuring the fighting strength of the Order, for the membership fluctuated widely, so that in the year 1883, when it reached 50,000, no less than one-half of this number passed out of the organisation.[45] The enormous fluctuation, while reducing the economic strength of the Order, brought large masses of people under its influence and prepared the ground for the upheaval in the middle of the eighties. It also brought the Order to the attention of the public press. The labour press gave the Order great publicity, but the Knights did not rely on gratuitous newspaper publicity. They set to work a host of lecturers, who held public meetings throughout the country, adding recruits and advertising the Order.

The membership figures indicate that the range of activity at this time was primarily in the industrial centres. Only a few of the organisers went in to the rural communities. The figures for 1883,[46] analysed by States and by sections in each State, warrant the conclusion that less than one-tenth of the membership came from non-industrial sections. Another conclusion that can be drawn is that the Order did very little actual organising. It endeavoured, instead, to gather together the various unattached local unions that had sprung into existence, and helped to resuscitate local unions that had been abandoned by their own national trade unions.[47] Likewise, trades which felt little outside competition, such as custom shoemakers, horse-car drivers, and newspaper printers, found the local trade assembly a convenient form of organisation. In large cities such trades were allowed to organise district assemblies for the city and vicinity, like District Assembly 64, embracing the printers of

45 The Boston *Daily Globe* speaks in 1880 of the "terribly powerful but undemonstrative" order of the Knights of Labor. In the fiscal year, 1880–1881, 7,947 were initiated, and 10,552 were suspended; 1881–1882, 23,415 were initiated and 7,557 were suspended; 1882–1883, 36,882 were initiated and 26,888 were suspended. Suspension meant the dropping of a member from the roll for a failure to pay dues. General Assembly, *Proceedings*, 1880, p. 215; 1881, p. 344; 1882, p. 391; 1883, p. 555.

46 General Assembly, *Proceedings*, 1883, p. 527.
47 For instance, as in the case of the Detroit Stove Molders' Union, which, in 1880 was "left in a demoralised condition . . . and yet no helping hand from the moulders' organisation was put out to assist them;" hence the Knights of Labor stepped in, "established a price list and got them a trade agreement." Pittsburgh *Journal of United Labor*, July, 1880.

Manhattan, Brooklyn, Jersey City, and vicinity. The miners belonged to the same category. Trade assemblies on racial or linguistic lines were also favoured by the Order, and many German, French, and Italian workingmen took advantage of the opportunity. In some localities and industries the workers found it advantageous to organise their locals by shops, in others by departments, and still in others by industries.

Likewise the Order helped to reorganise old national trade unions which were too weak to do the work alone. A good example is the old Knights of St. Crispin, which the Order organised into trade districts.[48] The case of the shoemakers illustrates one of the most distinctive advantages in the form of organisation of the Knights. In the old organisation of the Crispins, the skilled custom shoemakers and the machine shoemakers, although their interests were distinct, belonged to the same local unions. Now they could belong to different assemblies and yet be united in their district assembly. Another old union aided by the Knights of Labor at this time was the telegraphers. In 1882 a brotherhood of telegraphers existed in the West, but, as it was too weak to organise the entire trade, it joined the Order, which aided it in its undertaking.[49] There were many other trades which were unable to secure organisation through a broad area without external assistance. In such cases an appeal was made to the Knights of Labor and the Order joyously came " to the rescue." Some of the trades thus aided were the barbers, horse railway men, miners, railway men, such as shop-men, freight handlers, axe makers, trunk makers, harnessmakers. In 1882, the general secretary, in his annual address, gave the attitude of trade unions towards the Knights of Labor. " Many Trade Unions have also written me, stating that they were seriously meditating the propriety of coming over to us in a body, freely expressing the opinion that their proper place was in our Order." [50] On the other hand, the Order made overtures to the trade unions to affiliate themselves

---

[48] In May, 1883, a St. Crispin from Utica writes as follows: " We hold our local unions together for the good they have done. But we are in hopes that all the benefits we derive in the future will come through the noble order of the Knights of Labor, as nearly all employed in our business are members of the Noble Order. . . ." Philadelphia *Journal of United Labor*, May, 1883, p. 469.

[49] McNeill, *The Labor Movement: The Problem of To-day*, 391.

[50] General Assembly, *Proceedings*, 1882, p. 298.

with it, assuring them "that as members of the Knights of Labor they could protect the interests of their trade just the same as under their protective union, and at the same time receive all the advantages of organisation and association with all other branches of industry." [51]

The great benefit which an incipient trade movement derived from affiliating with the Knights of Labor becomes apparent when we consider the system of organising as practised by the Order. The financial condition of the trade itself would not permit the commissioning of organisers throughout the country to gather in members. On the other hand, the Order collectively, either through its national organisation, or through its subordinate geographic unit, the district assembly, could commission an organiser for all trades at the same time. In this way it was not even necessary to pay a specified salary. When an organiser was allowed to initiate all trades, the field in any industrial locality was large enough for a man to make a good living by receiving a small commission for each local organised. This was impossible when a man was assigned to organise one trade only, as he would find barely more than enough eligibles for one local at each stop. By allowing an organiser full sway among all trades, each community could easily support two or more professional organisers without feeling the burden. Generally these organisers were officers of the district assembly, and they also rendered aid in case of labour difficulties. Under this system, when the telegraphers sought to organise their trade, the only expense required was for stationery and a circular letter to the various district assemblies distributed throughout North America. This trade was organised at the same time under the auspices of District Assembly 53, San Francisco, District Assembly 49, New York, District Assembly 17, St. Louis, District Assembly 24, Chicago, etc.

Another difficulty encountered by single national trade unions was that of bringing into their fold "isolated workers in localities where the number of those employed at such trade was not sufficient to form a local body of their own," or where, for the time being, a sufficient number could not be interested. If affiliated with the Knights of Labor, this difficulty was " obviated," as they could join a mixed assembly until a sufficient number was secured to organise a separate trade.[52] That this was a practical difficulty encountered by national trade unions is evident. The mixed assembly acting as a recruiting ground for the trades, supplied a need vitally felt. When afterwards the rivalry grew intense between the Knights of Labor and the American Federation of Labor, the latter organisation found it important to provide for the federal labour union,— a local union identical with a mixed assembly.

With all this extreme heterogeneity in composition, the executive machinery of the Order ran smoothly. There was no change in officers except that the grand master workman, Uriah Stephens, owing to his old age, found it advisable to retire in favour of a younger and more active man. Through his recommendation, Terence V. Powderly,[53] active member of the Machinists' and Blacksmiths' Union during the early seventies and consequently a lineal descendant of the labour movement of that period, was chosen in his place. Powderly had also been elected mayor of Scranton, Pennsylvania, on a labour ticket in 1878, when the political labour movement swept over the entire country. The stamp of the sixties was unmistakably visible on Powderly throughout his entire career as the foremost labour leader in the country. Unlike Gompers, who came to supplant him before the public mind at a later date, he was foreign to the spirit of wage-consciousness. He was more closely akin to William H. Sylvis, who advocated trade union action as a mere preparation for co-operation. Herein, perhaps, lies the explanation of Powderly's sensitiveness to public opinion, as against Gompers' reliance solely on wage-earners.

The contest for office was not very acute, yet the Order was on a sound financial basis, and paid an annual salary of $750 to the general secretary.

The principal activity of the Knights of Labor during this period consisted in conducting strikes. These strikes did not differ in nature from those of the trade unions. They were not general strikes but each trade struck separately for better conditions of employment. The General Assembly of 1880 expressed itself in favour of strikes by voting to set aside 30 per cent of the Resistance Fund for their support.[54]   This was done notwithstanding the exhortation of the leaders to use the fund for co-operation and not to encourage strikes by their support.[55] The whole Order seems to have plunged into strikes.[56]   Even the mother district assembly, the one from which emanated all the inspiration and noble co-operative ideals of the Order, was itself caught in the whirl of pure strike action.   District Master Workman Thompson in his report of District Assembly 1, writes: " I am sorry to say that I found very few of the principles of our Order in practice.   In fact, there seems to be a general ignorance, or disregard of the principles of our organisation.   The older ideas of former trade organisations seem to predominate and control the actions of the locals generally." [57]

The most important Knights of Labor strike of this period was doubtless the telegraphers' strike in 1883.   The telegraphers had a national organisation in 1870, which soon collapsed.   In 1882 they again organised on a national basis and affiliated with the Order as District Assembly 45.   The strike was declared on June 19, 1883, against all commercial telegraph companies in the country, among which the Western Union, with about 4,000 operators, was by far the largest. The demands were one day's rest in seven, an eight-hour day shift and a seven-hour night shift, and a general increase of 15 per cent in wages.   The public and a large portion of the press gave their sympathy to the strikers, not so much on account of the oppressed condition of the telegraphers as of the general hatred that prevailed against Jay Gould, who controlled the Western Union Company.   This strike was the first in the eighties to call the attention of the general American public to the existence of a labour question, and received considerable attention at the hands of the Senate Committee on Education and Labor.[58]   By the end of July, over a month after the beginning of the strike, the men who escaped the blacklist went back to work on the old terms.

54 General   Assembly,   *Proceedings*, 1880, p. 246.
55 *Ibid.*, 172.
56 Philadelphia *Journal of United Labor*, June, 1882.

57 *Ibid.*, May, 1881, p. 117.
58 Senate Committee on Education and Labor, 1885, I, 102, 109, 892, 896; and II, 49, 52.

During 1882 there occurred a considerable number of unorganised strikes of unskilled and semi-skilled workmen, akin to the usual Knights of Labor strikes. A few succeeded, like the brick-makers' strike for higher wages in Chicago and vicinity, which tied up all building operations in the city for several weeks. But the greater number of them failed. The tanners and curriers in Chicago lost their strike, after standing out for seventy-two days.[59]

The freight-handlers' strike on the railroads centring in New York City, which occurred in the summer of 1882, was an unorganised strike of a similar nature. The men demanded an advance from 17 cents to 20 cents per hour, and, as the railways had recently declared an advance on freight going west, the public sympathised with the strikers. On July 17 an application was made to the court, accompanied by affidavits of merchants, shippers, and strikers, for a writ of mandamus against the New York Central & Hudson River and the New York, Lake Erie & Western Railroads, ordering them to perform their duties as common carriers with all reasonable despatch. The railways, operating with inexperienced strike-breakers, had allowed a large amount of freight to accumulate at the New York terminals. But even before the court had handed down a decision denying the writ, the railways secured a sufficient number of competent strike-breakers, and the strike collapsed.

The strikes of the Knights of Labor were failures in the large majority of cases. Two principal conditions conspired to bring this result. First, the Order operated mainly among the unorganised and the unskilled, an element which had no previous experience in the management of strikes and could easily be replaced by strike-breakers. Second, the form of organisation of the Knights, well adapted as it was to strikes on a large scale and to extensive boycotts, displayed an inherent weakness when it came to a strike of the members of a single trade against their employers. Such a strike soon becomes a test of organisation and of discipline, qualities which a mixed organisation like the district assembly of the Knights could not hope to possess in the same degree as a national trade union.

The dominant reason for the fluctuation of membership during this period was the numerous failures in strikes. After a lost strike the employers would persecute the leaders as well as the common strikers through the blacklist, and those who remained were compelled to sign the " iron-clad," and were constantly spied upon.[60]   Thus District Assembly 45, the national organisation of telegraphers with a membership of 3,561, dropped out of the Order after its unsuccessful strike of 1883.[61] Similarly, in the coal regions, entire district assemblies lapsed after a strike, such as District Assembly 33, Illinois.[62]   If whole district assemblies suffered as a result of strikes, very naturally for a like reason scores of locals lapsed.

Other locals and districts suffered in conflict with the employers, even without a strike. Some were detected while in process of organisation, and, through spies and threats, were forced to disband. The horse railway men of New York City suffered this fate. In 1883 they had an organisation of 600 men, but were reduced during this year to 13.[63]

Of course, the extreme strike policy adopted by the Order was not carried out without considerable opposition from within. This opposition consisted in part of the disappointed strikers, but it came mainly from the non-wage-earning element who desired that the Order should engage in greenbackism, socialism, anarchism, land reform, or co-operation, depending upon which school of thought the critic happened to represent. The greenbackers tried to secure an indorsement for their principles, but failed.[64]   The land reformers asked for the adoption of a plank abolishing the " private and corporate ownership in land," but received no encouragement.[65]   The co-operationists did their utmost to commit the Order to some definite co-operative policy, productive or distributive. They, too, were disappointed.[66] Nearly all of these reform elements combined in committing the Order indirectly to ideas or actions antagonistic to the prevailing trade union policy. In this they were but partially successful. Beginning with 1881, at every session an attempt was made to create state assemblies, some of the more radical

60 General Assembly, *Proceedings*, 1881, p. 290; 1883, p. 505.

61 *Ibid.*, 1883, p. 528; 1884, p. 796.

62 *Ibid.*, 1881, p. 333; 1882, p. 373.

63 McNeill, *The Labor Movement: The Problem of To-day*, 383.

64 General Assembly, *Proceedings*, 1880, p. 194; 1881, p. 309.

65 *Ibid.*, 1883, pp. 466, 499.

66 *Ibid.*, 1880, pp. 193, 196; 1881, pp. 299, 300.

advocating the substitution of state assemblies for district assemblies, or the organisation of district assemblies on congressional lines. But all resolutions to this effect were defeated.[67]   A resolution was also rejected calling upon members of the Order to " draw up petitions stating their grievances and present them to their respective Representatives in Congress." [68]   At this same session the General Assembly refused to adopt a resolution that steps " be taken by the various labor organisations to secure united action at the ballot, and favoring a convention of delegates from each labor organisation to draft a platform." [69]   Undoubtedly there existed a strong trend in favour of political action, but the wage-earners, who constituted the majority, looked keenly toward protective legislation, such as anti-prison labour laws, laws abolishing the truck-order system, prohibiting child labour, etc., and felt but lukewarm toward land reform or greenbackism; moreover, they expected to secure the desired legislation through non-partisan political action.

The position taken by the general officers is characteristic. In theory they doubtless were opposed to the deviation from " first principles " and favoured co-operation as against strikes. In 1881 the General Executive Board took it upon itself to insert into the constitution a compulsory article on co-operation.[70]   Yet in practical matters they felt obliged to follow the strike element and in 1883 Powderly was obliged to acknowledge that the strikes, and not co-operation, were responsible for the growth of the Order.   The difference between theory and practice had a beneficent influence upon the integrity of the Order since it kept both elements satisfied.   With respect to political action, Powderly reports that he aided both Republicans and Democrats in his locality, his criterion being that the good man was one who would work for the interest of labour.[71]

This position did not hinder several local organisations in

67 Ibid., 1881, p. 292.
68 Ibid., 1883, p. 503.
69 Ibid., 1883, pp. 463, 508.
70 The resolutions presented at the session of 1881 were of such magnitude that the convention authorised the General Executive Board to " compile and prepare the constitution," without any definite instructions on some important subjects.

The board took it upon itself to insert a compulsory article on co-operation (Constitution (1881), Art. VIII), levying upon each male member a sum of 10 cents, and 5 cents for each female.   Powderly, Thirty Years of Labor, 463–465.
71 General Assembly, Proceedings, 1883, p. 407.

the West from running independent labour candidates, as it did not prevent the locals in mill towns in Massachusetts and the miners in Kansas, Indiana, Missouri, and Ohio from embarking upon distributive and productive co-operation. Co-operation increased its following tremendously in 1883, as depression was setting in and strikes were proving to be failures. Most of these ventures were either merchandise stores or coal shafts, very little capital being required in opening a shaft.[72] Likewise, a strong demand for independent political action arose with the depression, which resulted in a multiplication of the local political attempts.

But while the opposition clamouring for a return to " first principles " was thus successfully put down within the Order, the same cry was heard from a different quarter. The growth of the Knights of Labor, which set out to bring together into one organisation all " productive labor," naturally looked disconcerting to the national trade unions. As yet the trade unions were not greatly menaced by the expansion of the Order.[73] It is true, the Order was organising cigar makers, printers, moulders, etc., but these generally were elements which the trade unions were either not desirous to get, such as semi-skilled workmen and machine operators, or isolated mechanics in small localities whom they were unable to reach. Besides, hardly any of the trade unions could as yet claim considerable shop control, so that rivalry for employment, which lies at the basis of acute rivalry between organisations, had not as yet arisen. This probably accounts for the conciliatory and indirect methods of the trade unions. The policy pursued was to praise the Order for the good educational work it was doing among the working people which was " the original object of the Order," and to caution it that stepping out of its legitimate bounds might prove fatal and impair its efficiency in its educational work. The following quotation from the *National Labor Tribune,* at this time the exponent of the national trade unions, gives their attitude very clearly: [74]

---

72 Philadelphia *Journal of United Labor,* November, 1882, p. 337.

73 A recorded instance of actual conflict during this period was the refusal in 1880 by the Iron Molders' International Union to recognise Knights of Labor cards issued to moulders. Most likely the latter were machine moulders whom the union was not eager to admit. General Assembly, *Proceedings,* 1880, p. 198.

74 Pittsburgh *National Labor Tribune,* July 7, 1883.

"It is well known that the Knights of Labor was not instituted with the view to action in the matter of regulating wages. The objects included education, the bettering of the material condition of the members by means of such schemes as co-operation, etc., and the elevation of labor by legislation through political action, but not taken, however, in a partisan way. The plan of the organisation did not include the management of strikes or aught else pertaining to wages and terms of labor, and it is not surprising, therefore, that the machinery has not proven equal to those occasions, when the Knights went outside of their original objects. It would be a blessing to all concerned if the Knights of Labor shall resolve to return to first principles and devote undivided attention thereto . . . lest all the labor be lost by being spread over too large an area.

"The coalescence of the respective trades by the organisation of the assemblies of each into its own union, and the representation of these bodies in a congress of the trades, would be an organisation in an effectively handleable condition — one that could take cognisance with the best results of wages and terms of labor."

Yet the feeling of animosity between the two great branches of the labour movement remained in abeyance until the labour upheaval of the middle of the decade.

If, now, we summarise our account of the confused and almost unnoticed struggles of labour organisations in the latter part of the seventies and the first part of the eighties, we shall find a real inheritance bequeathed to the succeeding years, the years of the Great Upheaval.

First of all, the bequest was intellectual rather than material. It consisted more of ideas than of organisations. The Order of the Knights of Labor, the Federation of Organised Trades and Labor Unions, and even the thirty or so national trade unions in existence in 1884, were in reality mere frameworks for future building. The intellectual accumulation during the period was, however, of exceedingly great importance. It was a period of theoretical differentiation and classification in respect to both general philosophies and practical methods.

At to philosophies, the half wage-conscious and half middle-class philosophy of the trade unionism of the sixties was entirely absent from the new trade union movement which started towards the end of the seventies. Yet that philosophy was preserved simon-pure in the Order of the Knights of Labor, which can be looked upon as the direct heir and successor to the unionism of Sylvis, Trevellick, and Cameron. The aspiring mechanic of the trade unions of the sixties had transmitted his faith in voluntary co-operation, social reform, and politics to the humbler and machine-menaced member of the Knights of Labor. But the new trade unionism got, in place of the lost philosophy, the wage-consciousness of Marx and the International, purged of its socialist ingredients.

Socialism had also undergone an evolution. Starting out with the trade union philosophy of the International of 1864, it successfully endured a brief but painful period of attempted inoculation with the " isms " of native American reformers of the intellectual class, only to be overcome later by the " politics-first " philosophy of Lassalleanism. Out of the strife and turmoil of factional struggle, the small group of Americanised Internationalists in the East withdrew to build up a potent trade union movement upon the basis of a wage-conscious but non-socialistic philosophy. Another group of Internationalists, much larger but also much more foreign-minded, with its centre in Chicago, remained true to socialism throughout all of its political vicissitudes, to begin, however, at the end of the decade a rapid evolution towards " syndicalism," or anarchistic trade unionism.

As to methods. The trade unions of the sixties had made their appeal exclusively to the skilled man, and they succeeded in time of prosperity. Their disintegration during the years of depression in the seventies reduced the skilled man to practically the same position as that of the unskilled, so that henceforth the appeal to organise was extended to him also. Although the wage-conscious and semi-socialistic appeal of the International Labor Union to the unskilled ended in failure, the Knights of Labor succeeded in accomplishing in the eighties what McDonnell and Sorge had failed to do in the seventies. But the new trade unions, like those of the sixties, restricted their appeal to the skilled mechanics. The experience of the seventies taught them to eschew politics, but in the Knights of Labor every political movement started by workmen or farmers was sure to find a warm response.

The working out of these theoretical and tactical lessons of
1876–1883, during the stirring events of 1884–1887, will bring
us to the clear-cut divisions of what may be called the modern
labour movement of the end of the century.

CHAPTER IX

THE GREAT UPHEAVAL, 1884-1886

New Economic Conditions. The difference between the labour movements in the early and the middle eighties, 357. The unskilled, 357.
Extension of the railways into the outlying districts, 358. Resultant intensification of competition among mechanics, 358. Industrial expansion,
358. Growth of cities, 359. Extension of the market and the supremacy
of the wholesale jobber, 359. Impossibility of trade agreements, 359.
Pools, 360. Immigration, 360. The exhaustion of the public domain, 360.
Peculiarities of the depression, 1883-1885, 361. Reduction in wages, 361.
Effect of the depression on the other economic classes, 362. The anti-
monopoly slogan, 362.

Strikes and Boycotts, 1884-1885. Fall River spinners' strike, 362. Troy
stove mounters' strike, 363. The Cincinnati cigar makers' strike, 363.
Hocking Valley coal miners' strike, 363. The vogue of the boycott, 364.
Extremes in boycotting, 365. Boycott statistics, 1884-1885, 365. Resumption of the strike movement, 366. The Saginaw Valley, Michigan,
strike, 366. Quarrymen's strike in Illinois, 367. Other strikes, 367. Shopmen's strikes on the Union Pacific in 1884, and the Knights of Labor, 367.
Joseph R. Buchanan, 367. The Gould railway strike in 1885, 368.
Gould's surrender, 369. Its enormous moral effect, 370. The general press
and the Order, 370. Keen public interest in the Order, 370. The New
York *Sun* "story," 371. Effect on Congress, 372. The contract immigrant
labour evil, 372. Situation in the glass-blowing industry, 372. The Knights
and the anti-contract labour law, 373. "The Knights of Labor — the
liberator of the oppressed," 373. Beginning of the upheaval, 373. Unrestrained class hatred, 374. Labour's refusal to arbitrate disputes, 374.
Readiness to commit violence, 374.

The Eight-Hour Issue and the Strike. Growth of trade unions, 375.
New trade unions formed, 1884-1885, 375. Convention of the Federation of
Organized Trades and Labor Unions, in 1884, 376. The eight-hour issue,
376. Invitation to the Knights to co-operate, 377. Referendum vote by the
affiliated organisations, 377. Advantage to the trade unions from the eight-
hour issue, 378. Lukewarmness of the national leaders of the Knights, 378.
Powderly's attitude, 378. Enthusiasm of the rank and file, 379. Pecuniary
interest of the Order's organisers in furthering the eight-hour agitation, 380. Marvellous increase in the membership of the Knights, 381.
Membership statistics for various States, 381. Racial composition, 382.
Composition by trades, 382. The pace of organisation in Illinois by
months, 382. The Southwest railway strike, 383. Its cause, 383. Its unusual violence, 383. Its failure, 384. The eight-hour strike, 384. Degree
of its immediate success, 384. Its ultimate failure, 385. Unequal prestige
of the Knights and the trade unions as a result of the strike, 385.

The Chicago Catastrophe. Effect of the Haymarket bomb on the eight-hour strike, 386. Spread of the " syndicalist " influence among the German trade unions in 1884, 387. Formation of the Central Labor Union, 387. Its relation to the "syndicalists," 387. Its declaration of principles, 388. Relation of individual trade unions to the " syndicalists " in Chicago and St. Louis, 388. Agitation among the English-speaking element, 389. *The Alarm*, 389. Strength of the Black International in Chicago and elsewhere, 390. Attitude of the Chicago Central Labor Union towards the eight-hour movement, 391. The Eight-Hour Association of Chicago, 391. The Mc-Cormick Reaper Company lockout, 392. Beginning of the eight-hour strike in Chicago, 392. Riot near the McCormick works, 392. The "revenge circular," 392. Meeting of protest on Haymarket Square, 393. The bomb, 393. The trial, 393. Attitude of the labour organisations, 394. Governor Altgeld's *Reasons for Pardoning Fielden*, et al., 393. Judge Gary's reply, 393.

NEW ECONOMIC CONDITIONS

THE organisation of labour during the early eighties was typical of a period of rising prices. It was practically restricted to skilled workmen, who organised to wrest from employers still better conditions than those which prosperity would have given under individual bargaining. The movement was essentially opportunistic and displayed no particular class feeling and no revolutionary tendencies. The solidarity of labour was not denied by the trade unions, but they did not try to reduce it to practice: each trade coped more or less successfully with its own employers. Even the Knights of Labor, the organisation *par excellence* of the solidarity of labour, was at this time, in so far as practical efforts went, merely a faint replica of the trade unions.

The situation radically changed during the depression of 1884-1885. The unskilled and the semi-skilled, affected as they were by wage reductions and unemployment even in a larger measure than the skilled, were drawn into the movement. Labour organisations assumed the nature of a real class movement. The idea of the solidarity of labour ceased to be merely verbal, and took on flesh and life; general strikes, sympathetic strikes, nation-wide boycotts, and nation-wide political movements became the order of the day. Although the upheaval came with the depression, it was the product of permanent and far-reaching economic changes which had taken place during the seventies and the early eighties.

The sixties had witnessed the first creation of a national

market, resulting from the consolidation of the principal railway lines into trunk lines and the opening up of transcontinental railway communication. The financial panic of 1873 put an end to rapid railway building, but nevertheless the total mileage constructed during the seventies amounted to 41,000. When we analyse the character of this construction, we discover that, while during the previous decade the large cities alone had become connected by railways, during the seventies railway communication was extended to a considerable number of smaller cities and towns in New England, the Middle States, and the Middle Western States. The 1,829 miles built in New England represented, in the main, short extensions, branches, or local roads; of the 11,492 miles constructed in New York, Pennsylvania, Ohio, Michigan, Indiana, Maryland, Delaware, New Jersey, and the District of Columbia, at least 7,000 went into short local roads or short extensions, and only about 3,000 into distinctly new roads. In the Southern States the new mileage was approximately 4,000. But the heaviest construction of the decade was in the Western States, where the railway opened up new regions for agricultural settlement.[1] The railway building in the seventies, therefore, operated both to bring the mechanics of the small towns into more direct competition with the machine production of the industrial centres, and to create for the latter an additional market in the new regions of the West.

The eighties were years of marvellous industrial expansion. For instance, *Bradstreet's*[2] estimates that one-tenth more wage-earners were employed in 1882 than during the census year of 1880. The dominant feature was the introduction of machinery upon an unprecedented scale.[3] Indeed, the factory system of production, for the first time, became general during the eighties. This is amply attested by the remarkable development in the production of machinery. In foundries and machine-shops the total capital invested increased two and a half times between 1880 and 1890. At the same time the aver-

1 Ringwalt, *Development of Transportation Systems in the United States*, 222–224.

2 Dec. 20, 1884.

3 The number of patents issued increased from an annual average of about 13,000 for the seventies to about 21,000 for the eighties. *Statistical Abstract of the United States*, 1915, p. 705.

age investment increased twofold for each establishment and 50 per cent for each employé.[4]

The factory system led to a large increase in the class of unskilled and semi-skilled labour, with inferior bargaining power. Accompanying this was the shifting of population from country to city. During the seventies the increase of 11,600,000 in the total population had raised the ratio of dwellers in cities having over 8,000 inhabitants 1.6 per cent.[5] On the other hand, during the eighties an increase of 12,500,000 brought up the ratio 6.6 per cent.[6] But there was still another change which added to the downward pressure on wages.

The wide areas over which manufactured products were now to be distributed called, more than ever before, for the services of the wholesaler. As the market extended, he sent out his travelling men, established business connections, and advertised the articles which bore his special trademark. His control of the market opened up credit with the banks, while the manufacturer, who with the exception of his patents, possessed only physical capital and no market opportunities, found it difficult to obtain credit. Moreover, the rapid introduction of machinery tied up all of his available capital and forced him to turn his products into money as rapidly as possible, with the inevitable result that the merchant had an enormous bargaining advantage over him. Had the extension of the market and the introduction of machinery proceeded at a less rapid pace, the manufacturer probably would have been able to obtain greater control over market opportunities. Also the larger credit which this would have given him, combined with the accumulation of his own capital, might have been sufficient to meet his needs. However, as the situation really developed, the jobber obtained a much superior bargaining power, and by playing off the competing manufacturers one against another, produced a cutthroat competition, low prices, low profits, and consequently a steady and insistent pressure upon wages.[7]

The manufacturers, on their part, frequently sought to

4 U. S. *Census*, 1890, *Compendium*, Pt. iii, 672–685.

5 From 20.93 per cent to 22.57 per cent. *U. S. Census*, 1890, I, p. lxv.

6 From 22.57 per cent to 29.20 per cent. *Ibid*.

7 A description of the functions of the wholesale jobber and a few historical glimpses may be found in J. H. Ritter, " Present Day Jobbing," in *Annals of the American Academy of Political and Social Science*, 1903, XXII, 451.

remedy the situation by combinations. The eighties were essentially a period of industrial pools. Henry D. Lloyd, who was first to raise in a forcible way a warning voice against the progress of monopoly in this country, enumerated, in 1884, pools in lumber, slaughtering and packing (in buying cattle), in bituminous coal mining, coke coal mining, stove manufacturing, matches, wall paper, crackers, burial cases, nails, barbed wire, pig iron, cotton fabrics (in the South), whiskey, and many others, besides the well-established monopolies in anthracite mining and oil refining.[8]

These pools, while they temporarily brought high profits, were constantly breaking up, but usually they were renewed after periods of cutthroat competition, so that they were an influence making for instability and insecurity. The bearing of this fact upon the labour situation becomes obvious when we take into account the basis of the trade agreement. No fixed agreement can survive for any length of time when prices are fixed alternately by combination and by cutthroat competition.

Other factors aggravating the situation were an unusually large immigration and the exhaustion of the public domain. The eighties were the banner decade of the entire century for immigration. The aggregate number of immigrants arriving was 5,246,613; two and a half millions larger than during the seventies and one million and a half larger than during the nineties. The eighties also witnessed the highest tide of immigration from Great Britain and the North of Europe and the beginnings of the tide of South and East European immigration.[9]

Simultaneously with the stocking up of the labour market by a record-breaking immigration, settlers were moving into the last unoccupied portion of the public domain. In a bulletin of the census for 1890 appear the following significant words: " Up to and including 1880 the country had a frontier of settlement, but at present the unsettled area has so been broken into

8 Lloyd, " Lords of Industry," in *North American Review* (1884), CXXXVIII, 536–553.

9 The number arriving from Great Britain was 1,462,839; from Germany, 1,452,-970; from Norway and Sweden, 568,362; from British North America, 392,802; from Austria, 353,719; from Italy, 307,-309; and from Russia, 265,088. *Statistical Abstract of the United States*, 1915, pp. 90, 91.

by isolated bodies of settlement that there can hardly be said to be a frontier line. In the discussion of its extent and its westward movement it cannot, therefore, any longer have a place in the census reports." [10]   American labour was now permanently shut up in the wage system.

Naturally, the depression of 1883–1885 made conditions still more unfavourable.   However, it had one redeeming feature by which it was distinguished from other depressions.   In the words of the report issued by the Federal Commissioner of Labor, " there has been a constant diminishing of profits until many industries have been conducted with little or no margin to those managing them, and a great lowering of wages in general . . . [but], on the whole, the volume of business of the country during the depressed period has been fairly satisfactory." [11]   The report placed the unemployment in manufacturing and mining at an average of 7.5 per cent during 1885 and, on this basis, estimated the total number of unemployed at about 168,750.[12]

Though the amount of unemployment was relatively small, reductions in wages were considerable.   *Bradstreet's* made an inquiry concerning wages in the beginning of 1885, and found that they had been cut 15 per cent on the average, ranging all the way from 40 per cent in coal mining to a very low percentage in the building trades.[13]   In the words of *Bradstreet's,* " among industrial wage-earners reductions in wages have been greatest where there have been no industrial organisations or weak ones.   Where trade unionism is strongest contract rates and united resistance have combined to retard the downward tendency of wages." [14]

Times continued hard during 1885, a slight improvement showing itself only during the last months of the year.   The years 1886 and 1887 were a period of gradual recovery, and normal conditions may be said to have returned about the middle of 1887.   Except in New England, the old wages were won again by the spring of 1887.[15]

But the wage-earners and employers were not the only suf-

---

10 U. S. *Census,* 1890, *Compendium,* Pt. i, XLVIII.

11 Bureau of Labor, *First Annual Report, Industrial Depression,* 75.

12 *Ibid.,* 65.

13 *Bradstreet's,* Mar. 14, 1885.

14 *Ibid.,* Dec. 20, 1884.

15 *Ibid.,* Apr. 9, 1887.

ferers. The agricultural classes, farm owners, tenant farmers, and farm labourers, also had their grievances. A large number of farmers suffered from exorbitant railroad charges or high interest rates on mortgages or low prices. These grievances affected especially the eastern and middle western farmers, while the tenant farmer in addition suffered from high rent and felt that his chances of becoming a farm proprietor were being diminished. As a result, the merchant found that his trade was decreased and that his earnings were reduced. Since all " producing classes " felt discontented, it is not surprising that they all readily responded when in 1886, the Order of the Knights of Labor directed its efforts to organise the " industrial masses " against " monopoly " in order " to prevent the benefits being monopolised by the few, and to secure for each member of society a full and just share of the wealth created by the labour of his hands." [16]

In other words, the activity of the Knights, after the beginning of the depression, marked the awakening of all democratic elements in society and their uniting in a common effort to combat plutocracy. The different groups used different means. The mechanic experimented with productive co-operation, the farmers, small employers, and merchants worked for legislation, and the unskilled and semi-skilled wage-earners in common with the mechanics took up strikes and boycotts. But a common sentiment animated them all — the sentiment of the struggle against monopoly.

STRIKES AND BOYCOTTS, 1884–1885

The year 1884 was one of decisive failure in strikes. They were practically all directed against reductions in wages and for the right of organisation. The most conspicuous strikes were those of the Fall River spinners, the Troy stove mounters, the Cincinnati cigar makers and the Hocking Valley miners.[17]

The Fall River strike against a reduction in wages affected

[16] Philadelphia *Journal of United Labor*, Feb. 25, 1886.

[17] The other strikes of importance during 1884 were: the Pittsburgh and Cincinnati moulders, the Troy and Albany stove moulders, the Buffalo bricklayers, the Buffalo 'longshoremen, the New York plumbers, the New York bricklayers and labourers, the New York brown stonecutters, the Colorado coal miners, the Pittsburgh miners, the Philadelphia carpet weavers, the Philadelphia shoemakers, the South Norwalk hatters, and the New Orleans car drivers.

over 5,000 spinners and other operatives in 10 cotton mills. After eighteen weeks it was defeated in June through the replacement of the strikers by Swedish strike-breakers. Fifty men were blacklisted, including Robert Howard, the secretary of the spinners' union and also secretary-treasurer of the Federation of Organised Trades and Labor Unions of the United States and Canada.[18]

The strike of the Troy stove mounters, to which John Swinton referred in an editorial as "the most important strike in this part of the country,"[19] resulted from the attempt of the United Stove Manufacturers' Association of that city to reduce wages 20 per cent and to compel the men to desert the union. Four hundred men were on strike from May until September, but in the end, notwithstanding the general support from labour organisations throughout the country, they succumbed and disbanded their union.[20]

The largest expenditure of money ever made up to this time by a labour organisation in a controversy with the employers was that of the Cigar Makers' International Union in a lockout in Cincinnati from March, 1884 to April, 1885. The union expended up to November, 1884, $140,000 in strike benefits. Nevertheless, it was defeated.[21]

But the strike which attracted the widest attention in labour circles as well as in the public press during 1884 was the famous strike of the coal miners in the Hocking Valley, Ohio. The ownership of the great majority of the mines in the Valley had been consolidated in 1883 in the hands of two companies, the Columbia and Hocking Coal Company, and the Ohio Coal Exchange, which had thus obtained the power to fix an arbitrary rate of wages. The western market for Hocking Valley coal began to be seriously threatened by the competition of the Pittsburgh operators and at the same time the shutdown of the local iron blast furnaces practically destroyed the local market. The companies, therefore, proposed to reduce the already meagre wages of the miners 10 cents per ton. The offer was indignantly refused and the Ohio State Miners' Union, of which

18 Howard, "Letter," in *John Swinton's Paper,* June 22, 1884.
19 *John Swinton's Paper,* July 13, 1884.
20 *Ibid.;* also Aug. 24, 1884.
21 *Ibid.,* Nov. 16, 1884.

John McBride was president, ordered the miners, nearly 4,000 in number, out on strike, June 22, 1884. Thereupon the companies adopted a rigid policy of opposition. The offered rate of wages was lowered another 10 cents to 50 cents per ton, and a return to work was made conditional upon the signing of an iron-clad contract abjuring membership in the union. Pinkerton detectives and state militia were immediately called in and the contest settled down to one of endurance. The strike was one of the longest in the mining industry. Expressions of sympathy and pecuniary aid came to the starving miners from many parts of the country, but, in view of the falling market, the companies could not be forced to surrender. After six months, having expended over $100,000 for strike benefits, the union ordered the men back to work upon the drastic conditions offered at the beginning of the strike.[22]

The failure of strikes brought into vogue the other weapon of labour — the boycott. But not until the latter part of 1884, when the failure of the strike as a weapon became apparent, did the boycott assume the nature of an epidemic. Early in 1885, John Swinton spoke of the boycott as " a new force in hand." [23] Besides the *Tribune* boycott, which continued over several years, the most notorious boycott in 1884 was the general boycott against the South Norwalk Hat Manufacturers, which grew out of the unsuccessful strike in 1884. The typographical union still occupied the lead, but Swinton enumerated a large number of other boycotts, such as the one declared by the Central Labor Union of New York against Ehret's beer for employing non-union men on the buildings, and the general boycott imposed by the executive board of the Knights of Labor upon the stoves, ranges, pots, and pokers of the John S. Perry Company of Troy, which had broken up the stove moulders' union in a recent strike.[24]

An instance of a perfect local boycott was the one in Orange, New Jersey, against Berg's hat factory, the only " unfair " factory among the twenty hat factories in the town. The boy-

22 *Ibid.*, Aug. 17, 1884; also Saliers, *The Coal Miners*, 13–23. See also Hocking Valley Investigating Committee of the General Assembly of the State of Ohio, *Proceedings* (Columbus, 1885).

23 *John Swinton's Paper*, Jan. 25, 1885.

24 *Ibid.*, Mar. 14, 1886. Successful after two years.

cotting union had the local dealers so well under control that brewers refused to furnish beer to saloon-keepers who sold drinks to strike-breakers employed in Berg's factory; and the co-operation of the other hat manufacturers is strikingly illustrated by the fact that one manufacturer discharged an employé for no other reason than that he lived with his brother who was "foul," that is, worked for Berg.[25]

It was during 1885 that the boycott reached the epidemic stage. A correspondent complained in Swinton's paper that "to be a sincere and systematic boycotter now, requires the carrying about of a catalogue of the different boycotted firms or articles; and, if you have a family, another catalogue is required for their use."[26] Nevertheless, in spite of the fact that the boycotts were promiscuously and indiscriminately used by local organisations and were neither regulated nor controlled by any central national organisation, they proved, on the whole, quite effective. *Bradstreet's* made a nation-wide inquiry into the boycott movement for 1884 and 1885, and from the published results the following can be learned.[27] The boycott movement was a truly national one, affecting the South and the far West as well as the East and Middle West. The number of boycotts during 1885 was nearly seven times as large as during 1884. Their number, excluding the 41 anti-Chinese boycotts on the Pacific Coast, was 196, of which 59 ended successfully, 23 were admittedly failures, and 114 were still pending. Nearly all of the boycotts either originated with, or were taken up by, the Knights of Labor. Of the trade unions only the typographical participated very heavily, with a total of 45 boy-

25 *Ibid.*, Apr. 5, 1885.
26 *Ibid.*, Aug. 23, 1885.
27 *Ibid.*, Dec. 19, 1885. The industries that were most affected by the boycott movement, next to newspapers, were as follows (*Bradstreet's*, Dec. 19, 1885):

Boycotted	Total No.	Claimed gained	Admitted lost	Still on
Cigar mfgrs. and dealers	26	11	5	10
Hat mfgrs. and dealers	22	4		18
Clothing dealers	14	1		13
Carpet mfgrs. and dealers	13		1	12
Nail mfgrs. and dealers	10			10
Dry goods dealers	7			7
Boot and shoe mfgrs. and dealers	7		1	6
Stove makers	5	3		2
Hotels and public houses	4	3		1
Breweries	4	3	1	
Excursion steamers	5	5		
Chinese employers	41	40	1	

cotts against newspapers, of which 13 were won, 10 were lost, and 21 were pending. The International Cigar Makers' Union was a distant second to the typographical, but it, on the whole, relied more on the label than on the boycott. The boycotts in New York City were very largely trade union boycotts, and to a minor extent also in Pittsburgh and western Pennsylvania. In each of these places they were successful. Practically in every case the boycott was also a secondary boycott, that is, persons disregarding a boycott were boycotted in turn.[28]

The strike, which had been overshadowed by the boycott during the latter half of 1884 and the first half of 1885, again came into prominence in the latter half of the year. This coincided with the beginning of an upward trend in general business conditions. The strikes of 1885, even more than those of the preceding year, were spontaneous outbreaks of unorganised masses. The general strike in the Saginaw Valley, Michigan, is typical of this movement. The legislature had enacted a general ten-hour law for all mills and manufacturing establishments, to become effective September 30, 1885.[29] However, the workmen in the lumber and shingle mills in the Saginaw Valley, among whom was a considerable foreign (mostly Polish) element, either were ignorant of the fact that the law did not go into effect at once, or were too impatient to wait. On July 6, practically without any previous organisation, they went out on strike for an immediate ten-hour day with the same pay as they already had. In a short time the strikers, marching in a body from mill to mill, everywhere demanding that the men quit work, had forced a shutdown in the entire lumber industry, numbering 17 shingle mills, 61 lumber mills, and 58 salt blocks attached to the latter, and employing altogether over 5,500 men. After the strike had started, T. B. Barry, a member of the executive board of the Knights of Labor, arrived and took charge. The employers imported over 150 Pinkerton detectives, and, besides, a large body of militia was constantly held in readiness. The strike lasted through July and August,

---

28 Ibid.

29 Like all of the general laws for shorter hours that the politicians in this period as well as in the earlier years felt themselves obliged to pass it contained the self-nullifying provision exempting from its operations all cases where a contract to the contrary was made. Michigan Bureau of Labor, Report, 1886, p. 130.

during which time prices on lumber and salt rose considerably. Apparently, the temptation to benefit from the high prices and the great determination exhibited by the strikers induced the employers to concede all the demands, and the strike was called off September 1.[30]

That the lowest strata of labour were drawn into the movement is demonstrated by the strike of 2,000 quarrymen at Lemont and Joliet, Illinois. The strikers were a polyglot mass of Swedes, Bohemians, Poles, Norwegians, and Welshmen. They demanded an increase of 25 per cent in their daily wage of one dollar and grew violent when the employers began importing Negro and other strike-breakers. Governor Oglesby ordered out the militia and the strike was broken up after several strikers and one woman had been killed in a riot. The correspondent in Swinton's paper ends his account by a sentence which may well be applied to a large number of the strikes of that time: "The miners were unorganised, and the strike has been a thing of confusion from first to last."[31] While violence and confusion characterised the movement of the unskilled and unorganised, and, in most of the cases, frustrated their efforts, the highly skilled and perfectly organised bricklayers, after a short strike, gained the nine-hour day in New York City.[32]

The frequent railway strikes were a notorious feature of the labour movement in 1885. There had been two strikes on the Union Pacific in 1884. The first one came entirely unorganised. The shopmen in Denver struck May 4, as a result of a wage reduction of 10 per cent, and requested Joseph R. Buchanan, editor of *The Labor Enquirer* of Denver and a prominent Knight of Labor, to manage the strike. He did this so well that inside of thirty-six hours every shop from Omaha to Ogden and upon all branch lines was on strike, and on the third day the order reducing the wages was recalled. This was the beginning of a strong organisation of the Knights of Labor on that road.[33] Its strength came to a test in August when the company ordered a reduction of the wages of 15 first-

---

[30] *Ibid.*, 92–126.
[31] *John Swinton's Paper*, May 10, 1885.
[32] Of the numerous other strikes, the street railway strikes in Chicago, New York, and St. Louis (of a very violent order in the case of the last named) during the summer and fall of 1885 attracted public attention.
[33] Buchanan, *The Story of a Labor Agitator*, 70–78.

class machinists at Ellis, Kansas, and discharged 20 men from the Denver shops for no reason, as the organisation claimed, excepting that they were prominent Knights of Labor. This strike ended also with complete success and served as a powerful advertisement of the Order in the territory of the Rocky Mountains.

A more notable event was the Gould railway strike in March, 1885. On February 26, a cut of 10 per cent was ordered in the wages of the shopmen of the Wabash road. A similar reduction had been made in October, 1884, on the Missouri, Kansas & Texas. Strikes occurred on the two roads, one on February 27 and the other March 9, and the strikers were joined by the men on the third Gould road, the Missouri Pacific, at all points where the two lines touched, making altogether over 4,500 men on strike. The " runners," that is, the locomotive engineers, firemen, brakemen, and conductors, supported the strikers, and to this fact more than to any other was due their speedy victory. The wages were restored and the strikers re-employed. The assemblies of the Union Pacific employés commissioned Buchanan to assist the Gould strikers and appropriated $30,000 to their support. He utilised the opportunity for organising railroad men's assemblies wherever he went during his extended trip over the striking roads. Such, as a rule, was the method of procedure characteristic of large numbers of the wage-earners at this time: They struck first and joined the Knights of Labor afterwards.

The practically unavoidable result of such a method was a second strike after a short interval in order to protect the existence of the organisation. The employer, who had been forced to surrender by the sudden strike, realised the weakness of the young organisation and endeavoured to nip it in the bud, by discharging as many leaders as he dared. The second strike on the Wabash railway, which began on August 18, 1885, was precisely of this nature. The road, now in the hands of a receiver, reduced the force of shopmen at Moberly, Missouri, to the lowest possible limit, which virtually meant a lockout of the members of the Knights of Labor in direct violation of the conditions of settlement of the preceding strike. The General Executive Board, after a futile attempt to have a conference with the receiver, issued a general order "to all assemblies on the Union Pacific and its branches and Gould's Southwestern system" to the effect that "all assemblies of the above lines of railway, all Knights of Labor in the employ of the Union Pacific and its branches and Gould Southwestern system, or any other railroad, must refuse to repair or handle in any manner Wabash rolling stock until further orders from the General Executive Board." [34] This order, had it been carried out, would have affected over 20,000 miles of railway and would have equalled the dimensions of the great railway strike of 1877. But Gould would not risk a general strike on his lines at this time. According to an appointment made between him and the executive board of the Knights of Labor, a conference was held between that board and the managers of the Missouri Pacific and the Wabash railroads, at which he threw his influence in favour of making concessions to the men. He assured the Knights that in all troubles he wanted the men to come directly to him, that he believed in labour organisations and in the arbitration of all difficulties, and that he "would always endeavour to do what was right." The Knights demanded the discharge of all new men hired in the Wabash shops since the beginning of the lockout, the reinstatement of all discharged men, the leaders being given priority, and an assurance that no discrimination against the members of the Order would be made in the future.[35] A settlement was finally made at another conference, and the receiver of the Wabash road agreed, under pressure by Jay Gould, to issue an order to the superintendents directing that they should, "in filling vacancies caused by the discharge of men for incompetency or by their leaving the service, give the old men the preference over strangers or new men, asking no questions as to whether they belong to the Knights of Labor or any other organisation." [36]

The significance of the second Wabash strike in the history of railway strikes was, that the railway brotherhoods (engineers, firemen, brakemen, and conductors) in contrast with their conduct during the first Wabash strike, now refused to lend any

34 *John Swinton's Paper*, Aug. 23, 1885.

35 *Ibid.*, Aug. 30, 1885.
36 *Ibid.*, Sept. 13, 1885.

aid to the striking shopmen, although many of the members were also Knights of Labor.

But far more important was the effect of the strike upon the general labour movement. Here a labour organisation for the first time dealt on an equal footing with the most powerful capitalist in the country. It forced Jay Gould to recognise it as a power equal to himself, a fact which he amply conceded when he declared his readiness to arbitrate all labour difficulties that might arise. The oppressed labouring masses finally discovered a champion which could curb the power of a man stronger even than the government itself. All the pent-up feeling of bitterness and resentment which had accumulated during the two years of depression, in consequence of the repeated cuts in wages and the intensified domination by employers, now found vent in a rush to organise under the banner of the powerful Knights of Labor. To the natural tendency on the part of the oppressed to exaggerate the power of a mysterious emancipator whom they suddenly find coming to their aid, there was added the influence of sensational reports in the public press. The newspapers especially took delight in exaggerating the powers and strength of the Order.

As early as 1883, Grand Master Workman Powderly complained of the exaggerated reports of the newspapers with respect to membership and activities.[37] The estimates of membership ranged from 500,000 to 5,000,000. In 1884 the general secretary reports that everywhere the press speaks of the Order.[38] Newspapers were always eager to give publicity to utterances of the leaders. When Powderly spoke in St. Paul and Minneapolis, the newspapers commented favourably and gave considerable space to what he said.[39] In Arkansas the legislature with only one dissenting vote,[40] granted Powderly the privilege of the house of representatives to deliver a speech upon the economic and labour problems of the day.

The general public also manifested a keen interest in the activities and growth of the Order. The New York Bureau of Statistics and Labor in 1889 declared: "That the public desires some information upon the subject of strikes is plainly

---

[37] General Assembly, *Proceedings*, 1883, p. 401.
[38] *Ibid.*, 1884, p. 586.
[39] Philadelphia *Journal of United Labor*, Aug. 10, 1885.
[40] *Ibid.*, Mar. 25, 1885.

evidenced by the prominence given the subject in the public prints during the past year and the eagerness with which even the most minute details regarding them have been followed, their movements watched, and all sorts of theories regarding this class of labor troubles accepted." [41]   Soon the newspapers tried to outdo each other in "scooping" labour news, and in the autumn of 1885 the New York *Sun* detailed one of its reporters to "get up a story of the strength and purposes of the Knights of Labor."   This story was copied by newspapers and magazines throughout the country and aided considerably in bringing the Knights of Labor into prominence.   The following extract illustrates the exaggerated notion of the power of the Knights.[42]

" Five men in this country control the chief interests of five hundred thousand workingmen, and can at any moment take the means of livelihood from two and a half millions of souls.   These men compose the executive board of the noble order of the Knights of Labor of America.   The ability of the president and cabinet to turn out all the men in the civil service, and to shift from one post to another the duties of the men in the army and navy, is a petty authority compared with that of these five Knights.   The authority of the late cardinal was, and that of the bishops of the Methodist Church is, narrow and prescribed, so far as material affairs are concerned, in comparison with that of these five rulers.

" They can stay the nimble touch of almost every telegraph operator ; can shut up most of the mills and factories, and can disable the railroads.   They can issue an edict against any manufactured goods so as to make their subjects cease buying them, and the tradesmen stop selling them.

" They can array labor against capital, putting labor on the offensive or the defensive, for quiet and stubborn self-protection, or for angry, organised assault, as they will."

The renown of the Order reached the most isolated communities.   Already in 1884 the general secretary-treasurer had reported that "numerous letters have been received from parties in Florida, Alabama, and North Carolina, asking instruction how to form assemblies." [43]   The tone of these letters indicates that the people seeking information had not come into contact

41 New York Bureau of Labor, *Report*, 1885, p. 199.

42 Powderly, *Thirty Years of Labor*, 494.

43 General Assembly, *Proceedings*, 1884, p. 580.

with the Knights of Labor, but must have learned of the Order through other channels.

Before long the Order was able to benefit by this publicity in quarters where the tale of its great power could but attract unqualified attention, namely, in Congress. The Knights of Labor led in the agitation for prohibiting the immigration of alien contract labourers. The problem of contract immigrant labour rapidly came to the front in 1884, when such labour began frequently to be used to defeat strikes. During the Hocking Valley miners' strike, the Coal Exchange of Ohio sent out agents to import 3,000 Hungarians or Italians.[44]   The Senate Committee on Education and Labor in its report on the Foran anti-contract labour bill which had come up from the House, stated that there were 2,000 Hungarian contract labourers in the Pennsylvania coke regions, and that contract labour was used in the construction of the Nickel Plate, Ohio River, and other railways in the Eastern, Southern, and Middle States.[45] A reporter on *John Swinton's Paper* approached an immigrant employment agency operating at Castle Garden, New York, ostensibly for the purpose of hiring contract labourers for an iron company, and was told that during the time this agency had been in the business, 14,000 contract Italians had been imported, of whom 6,000 had returned to Italy.[46]   The Hungarian consul in New York testified before the committee to the existence in Hungary of a bureau for recruiting contract labourers.   From the other testimony it appeared that the evil was most flagrant in coke making and bituminous coal mining, in railway construction and in glass-blowing.[47]

Twenty persons appeared to testify before the committee in favour of the bill, of whom all but 2 or 3 belonged to the Knights of Labor.   Local Assembly 300, the Window Glass Workers' Association, was represented by 8 speakers.   The other trades represented were the bituminous miners in Ohio and Pennsylvania and in the coke region, the cotton-mill operatives and the telegraphers.   A galaxy of the Knights of Labor leaders were present; Powderly, the grand master work-

---

44 *John Swinton's Paper*, July 20, 1884.
45 Senate Committee on Education and Labor, *Report*, 1883–1884, 48 Cong., 1 sess., No. 820.

46 House Committee on Labor, *Report*, 1883–1884, 48 Cong., 1 sess., No. 444.
47 *Ibid.*

man; Turner, the grand secretary; and Barry, a member of the executive board. The anti-contract labour law which was passed by Congress on February 2, 1885, therefore, was due almost entirely to the efforts of the Knights of Labor. The trade unions gave little active support, for to the skilled workingman the importation of contract Italian and Hungarian labourers was a matter of small importance; on the other hand, to the Knights of Labor with their vast contingent of unskilled, it was a strong menace. Although the law could not be enforced and had to be amended in 1887 in order to render it effective, its passage nevertheless attests the political influence already exercised by the Order in 1884. Having attained success in getting national legislation, it goes without saying that a corresponding success attended the work of state legislation. The subject that was agitated in a large number of States during 1883–1885 was prison labour. This again marks off this period as one of depression, for the competitive menace of prison labour is most strongly felt during such periods.

The outcome of the Gould strike of 1885 placed the Knights of Labor before the world as equal to the strongest capitalist combinations in the country. Added to this the dramatic exaggeration of the prowess of the Order by press and even by pulpit, and the success of the Order in Washington, were largely responsible for the psychological setting that called forth and surrounded the great upheaval of 1886. This upheaval meant more than the mere quickening of the pace of the movement begun in preceding years and decades. It signalled the appearance on the scene of a new class which had not hitherto found a place in the labour movement — the unskilled. All the peculiar characteristics of the dramatic events in 1886 and 1887, the highly feverish pace at which organisations grew, the nation-wide wave of strikes, particularly sympathetic strikes, the wide use of the boycott, the obliteration, apparently complete, of all lines that divided the labouring class, whether geographic or trade, the violence and turbulence which accompanied the movement — all of these were the signs of a great movement by the class of the unskilled, which had finally risen in rebellion. This movement, rising as an elemental protest against oppression and degradation, could be but feebly restrained by any considerations of expediency and prudence; nor, of course, could it be restrained by any lessons from experience. The movement bore in every way the aspect of a social war. A frenzied hatred of labour for capital was shown in every important strike. During the second Wabash strike, a convention of the employés on the Gould Southwestern system declared that "labor and capital have met in a deadly conflict" and pledged themselves to stand firmly by the Wabash employés, "sustaining them by . . . sympathy, money and . . . *lives, if necessary.*"[48] Extreme bitterness towards capital manifested itself in all the actions of the Knights of Labor, and wherever the leaders undertook to hold it within bounds they were generally discarded by their followers, and others who would lead as directed were placed in charge. The feeling of "give no quarter" is illustrated in the refusal to submit grievances to arbitration when the employés felt that they had the upper hand over their employers. Powderly wrote as follows in the beginning of 1886: "In some places where our Order is strong, the members refuse to arbitrate, simply because they *are strong.* Such a course is not in keeping with plank XXII of the declaration of principles of the Knights of Labor. One of the causes for complaint against employers has been that they refused to recognise the employees in the field of arbitration. Now that we are becoming powerful, we should not adopt the vices which organised labor has forced the employer to discard."[49] The secretary-treasurer complained at the same time that "seventy-five per cent of the strikes have taken place before even an attempt at arbitration was resorted to."[50]

The Saginaw Valley lumber strike in July, 1885, already referred to, illustrates the methods of intimidation used by striking workingmen. For several days the men marched from mill to mill forcing shutdowns by turning off the steam and banking the fires.[51] The idea of a sympathetic strike was so widespread that it penetrated even to Maine, where a strike was called against two lime-manufacturing firms because "they used

48 From a circular entitled *An Address,* dated at Moberly, Mo., Aug. 1, 1885.
49 Philadelphia *Journal of United Labor,* Jan. 25, 1886.

50 General Assembly, *Proceedings,* 1886, p. 46.
51 Michigan Bureau of Labor, *Report,* 1886, p. 94.

lime rock dug and hauled by men who were not members of the Knights of Labor." [52]

Many of the leaders of the Knights understood the danger created by this attitude of arrogance. The district master workman of District Assembly 30 wrote: "The danger is that in the excess of joy our members may imagine themselves invincible, and attempt to force measures that will result in injury to the cause." [53] But no warning from a leader, however high, was capable of restraining the combative rank and file.

But, if the origin and powerful sweep of this movement were largely spontaneous and elemental, the issues which it took up were supplied by the existing organisations — the trade unions and the Knights of Labor. These served also as the dykes between which the rapid streams were gathered, and if at times it seemed that they must burst under the pressure, still they gave form and direction to the movement and partly succeeded in introducing order where chaos had reigned.

THE EIGHT-HOUR ISSUE AND THE STRIKE

Since the depression of 1883 had not materially reduced the amount of employment, resistance to employers was not rendered entirely hopeless. Accordingly, the membership of labour organisations increased in many trades and localities. Yet some of the national trade unions, which had grown exceptionally strong during the preceding years of prosperity, were now losing members. For instance, the bricklayers' union decreased from 13,642 members at the end of 1883 to 8,600 in 1884 and increased only to 10,229 in 1885. On the other hand, the small carpenters' brotherhood grew from 3,293 in 1883 to 4,364 in 1884 and 5,789 in 1885. [54]

Several new national trade unions were organised during 1885: the table-knife grinders, the elastic-goring weavers, and the miners. Likewise there were organised numerous unions in trades where there was no national organisation. [55] As a

52 Maine Bureau of Labor, *Report*, 1886, p. 98.
53 Philadelphia *Journal of United Labor*, Aug. 10, 1885.
54 The carpenters' brotherhood first began to be tolerated by the employers about 1884–1885. *The Carpenter* (Indianapolis, Ind.), December, 1904.

55 In the state of New Jersey there were 3 new unions formed in 1883, 11 in 1884, and 15 in 1885. Among these were mainly independent local unions and locals in weak national unions. New Jersey Bureau of Labor, *Report*, 1887, pp. 37–41.

rule, it may be stated that during the depression, that portion of the working class which formerly had been either entirely unorganised or only partly organised came, in the matter of organisation, closely abreast of the trades which had enjoyed a strong organisation in the past.

But if the trade union movement, notwithstanding the depression, was growing apace, the Federation of Organised Trades and Labor Unions remained where it was and even declined. As already stated, it became apparent to the leaders that the organisation could not continue to exist if it remained a mere association for the purpose of legislation. So, at the convention of 1884, it was determined to infuse new life into the Federation by making it assume the leadership in a national movement for the eight-hour day.

The convention opened in Chicago, October 7, 1884, with 25 delegates from 8 national or international unions (the carpenters, amalgamated engineers, cigar makers, granite cutters, furniture workers, seamen's, typographical, and tailors), 4 city federations (Chicago, Cincinnati, Washington, and Minneapolis), 1 State federation (Illinois), 1 local assembly of the Knights of Labor (No. 280, Cincinnati), and 6 local trade unions. Gompers was absent and also Frank K. Foster, the secretary of the Federation. A salient question brought up, in addition to the inauguration of a concerted movement for the eight-hour day, was the power of the Federation to grant strike benefits. Both propositions were of such a nature that, had they been adopted, they would have transformed the Federation from a purely legislative organisation into a predominantly economic one. The eight-hour question was raised by Gabriel Edmonston, the representative of the carpenters' brotherhood, in the form of the following resolution: " *Resolved,* By the Federation of Organised Trades and Labor Unions of the United States and Canada, that eight hours shall constitute a legal day's labour from and after May 1, 1886, and that we recommend to labor organisations throughout this jurisdiction that they so direct their laws as to conform to this resolution by the time named." [56] It was passed by the convention in this

---

[56] Federation of Organized Trades and Labor Unions of the United States and Canada, *Proceedings,* 1884, p. 24.

form by a vote of 23 to 2.[57]   It was further decided that "the incoming Legislative Committee be instructed to extend an invitation to the Knights of Labor to co-operate in the general movement to establish the eight-hour reform." [58]

The entire membership of the trade unions affiliated with the Federation in 1884 seems to have been considerably less than 50,000.   Assuredly a general strike on May 1, 1886, for the eight-hour day was an ambitious programme for such an organisation.

The proposal that the Federation should dispense strike benefits came up from the Cigar Makers' International Union, which pledged 2 per cent of its total revenue toward a strike fund, providing the majority of the affiliated organisations did likewise.[59]   Since this involved an amendment to the constitution, the convention decided to refer it to all organisations for a referendum vote by their membership.[60]

The eight-hour declaration was coolly received even at the hands of the trade unions affiliated with the Federation.   So few unions acted upon the strike benefit proposal that the convention of 1885 did not venture to adopt it.   In consequence the Federation was unable to expend a dollar in aid of the strike.   By the time of the convention of 1885 only the Brotherhood of Carpenters and Joiners had voted upon the amendment.   They adopted it by a vote of 2,197 to 310,[61] although the large local unions of Washington, Chicago, and San Francisco failed to vote upon the question.   Nevertheless the convention of 1885 changed but slightly from the position taken in the preceding year.   It again declared that the eight-hour work-day should begin on May 1, 1886; but at the same time it requested all affiliated unions which did not intend to enforce it to assist financially such organisations as should strike for a reduction of hours.[62]   Shortly after the adjournment of the convention, the referendum vote of the cigar makers was taken. The vote stood 2,640 to 1,389 for the establishment of the eight-hour day.[63]   The German-American Typographia, however, seems to have been the only other national trade union which followed the cigar makers.

57 *Ibid.*, 25.
58 *Ibid.*, 81.
59 *Ibid.*, 14.
60 *Ibid.*, 80.

61 *Ibid.*, 1885, p. 17.
62 *Ibid.*, 20.
63 *Cigar Makers' Official Journal*, December, 1885.

That notwithstanding their apathy the trade unions seem to have profited considerably from the eight-hour movement is shown by the statistics available for their growth during 1885 and the first part of 1886. In Illinois, of the 279 trade unions reporting on July 1, 1886, 140 were organised after January 1, 1885. They brought in 21,055 new members, not counting the simultaneous increase in the membership of the old unions. The organisation of new unions in 1886 by months was as follows: 6 in January, 7 in February, 17 in March, 28 in April, 11 in May, 3 in June, and 2 in July; a total of 75. The heavy organisation of new unions took place in March and April immediately preceding the eight-hour strike, and the sudden drop after the strike proves that for the trade unions, this issue was of paramount importance.[64]

The success or failure of the eight-hour movement largely depended upon the assistance of the Knights of Labor. In the General Assembly of 1885 a resolution was offered pledging the support of the Order to the Federation of trades in its movement to establish the eight-hour day on May 1, 1886.[65]   Scant consideration was given to the resolution. On the eve of the eight-hour strike the general officers of the Knights adopted an attitude of hostility toward the movement. On March 13, 1886, Grand Master Workman Powderly issued a secret circular in which he advised the Knights not to rush into the eight-hour movement. At the Richmond General Assembly later in the year, Powderly tried to justify his course upon the plea that " the education which must always precede intelligent action had not been given to those most in need of it, because no definite, business-like plan for the inauguration of the eight-hour movement had been mapped out."[66]   This plea has merit insofar as the Federation of trades had failed to provide financial means to conduct such a wide-spread strike as was planned. Nor did the Federation succeed in advertising the movement

---

64 There were on July 1, 1886, 328 trade unions in the State with a total membership of 61,904, and, including the 96 railroad men's lodges with 9,024 members and the 56 coal miners' lodges with 7,840, there remain 176 trade unions with a total membership of 45,040. Fully 88 per cent lived in Cook County. Seventeen per cent were at the same time members of the Knights of Labor. These figures are estimates based on data from 279 trade unions which reported in detail. Illinois Bureau of Labor, *Report*, 1886, pp. 165–230.

65 General Assembly, *Proceedings*, 1885, p. 125.

66 *Ibid.*, 1886, p. 39.

among the workingmen. To this must doubtless be added, however, a feeling of jealousy on the part of the officers of the Knights of Labor on account of the gratuitous advertising which the Federation was receiving through its championship of the eight-hour movement. By the winter of 1885–1886, also, the relations between several of the trade unions belonging to the Federation and the Knights of Labor were strained. Furthermore, Powderly did not look upon the eight-hour day as a panacea for social ills. His point of view is clearly expressed in his *Thirty Years of Labor,* published in 1889: " To talk of reducing the hours of labor without reducing the power of machinery to oppress instead of to benefit, is a waste of energy. What men gain through a reduction of hours will be taken from them in another way while the age of iron continues. . . . The advocates of the eight-hour system must go beyond a reduction of the number of hours a man must work and [must] labor for the establishment of a just and humane system of land ownership, control of machinery, railroads, and telegraphs, as well as an equitable currency system before he will be able to retain the vantage ground gained when the hours of labour are reduced to eight per day." [67]

But if the slogan had failed to arouse the enthusiasm of the national leaders of the Knights, it nevertheless found ready response in the ranks. The great class of the unskilled and unorganised, who, owing to the events in that year, had come to look upon the Knights of Labor as the all-powerful liberator of the labouring masses from oppression, now eagerly seized upon this demand as the issue upon which the first battle with capital should be fought. The new members and, even more, the prospective ones, could not be aware of Powderly's negative attitude to the whole agitation as expressed by him in secret circulars to the assemblies. At the same time the universal condemnation of the eight-hour demand by the general press during the months preceding May 1, 1886, could but heighten its claims for them. Another powerful factor in disseminating the idea was the paid organisers of the Knights of Labor. The Federation was financially unable to put a single organiser in the field in aid of this movement, but in the Knights of Labor,

[67] Powderly, *Thirty Years of Labor,* 514.

owing to the system of local payment and the lack of central control over organisers, the latter found it profitable for themselves to agitate the popular eight-hour issue as a means of organising new assemblies.

The aim of the Knights of Labor was to build up a closely knitted organisation, and one means of accomplishing this would have been to give the General Assembly complete control over the organisers. But the General Assembly never secured this control, although other measures, even more restrictive, designed to bring the organisation under the control of the General Assembly, were adopted at nearly every session. As the matter stood in 1885 there were four organisers at large, directly appointed by the grand master workman, and a large number of district organisers, each recommended by a district assembly and confirmed by the grand master workman. The pay as provided by the constitution was $3 per day and mileage not to exceed 4 cents per mile.[68] The commissions of all organisers automatically expired at each session of the General Assembly, so that a district organiser naturally depended for continuation in office upon the good will of his district assembly which possessed the recommending power. The representation of each district assembly in the General Assembly was, moreover, proportionate to its membership, so that the organiser was more frequently inclined to act in accord with the desires of the district assembly than with those of the grand master workman who constantly, and very properly, warned against over-zealous and too rapid organisation of new assemblies. Powderly issued a characteristic warning early in 1886: " Our organisers, as a rule, are careful and painstaking, but once in a while we have trouble with some of them, who, over-zealous and anxious to do good work, organise too quickly. Organisers must not take in a body of men who are engaged in a strike or about to embark in a strike. If they need advice or counsel, give it to them, but the Knights of Labor must not in future be charged with sins of which they are not guilty." [69] At the regular session of the General Assembly in October of the same year he asserted that the car drivers in St. Louis organised under a promise from

[68] General Assembly, *Constitution* (1882), Art. IX, Sec. 14.

[69] Philadelphia *Journal of United Labor*, Feb. 10, 1886.

the organiser that they would receive unstinted aid in case of a strike, and that they were on strike even before they received their charter.[70]

The trouble with the organisers in St. Louis was no doubt aggravated by the fact that District Assembly 17 of St. Louis provided in its by-laws for the election of organisers at a rate of pay different from that provided for in the constitution of the General Assembly. It paid its organisers $6 for each new local organised, and $5 for every local reorganised.[71] This provision was virtually an encouragement to an unscrupulous organiser to violate the provision of the General Assembly constitution which said that an organiser must not offer special inducements to former members to rejoin the Order.[72]

Still, as far as the Knights of Labor were concerned, the eight-hour issue was merely a slogan that the new and rapidly multiplying membership chanced to seize upon. It was not itself the impetus. That had been given by the industrial depression of 1884–1885. American labour movements have never experienced such a rush of organisation as the one in the latter part of 1885 and during 1886. In a remarkably short time — in a few months — over 600,000 people living practically in every State in the Union united in one organisation. The Knights grew from 989 local assemblies with 104,066 members in good standing in July, 1885,[73] to 5,892 assemblies with 702,924 members in July, 1886. The greatest portion of this growth occurred after January 1, 1886. In the state of New York there were, in July, 1886, about 110,000 members (60,809 in District Assembly 49 of New York City alone), in Pennsylvania, 95,000 (51,557 in District Assembly 1, Philadelphia alone), in Massachusetts, 90,000 (81,191 in District Assembly 30, Boston), and in Illinois, 32,000.[74]

In the state of Illinois, for which detailed information for that year is available, there were 204 local assemblies with 34,974 members,[75] of which 65 per cent were found in Cook County alone. One hundred and forty-nine assemblies were

70 General Assembly, *Proceedings*, 1886, p. 38.

71 District Assembly 17, St. Louis, *Constitution and By-laws*, Art. VII.

72 General Assembly, *Constitution* (1881), Art. IX, Sec. 13.

73 The membership in 1884 was 60,811.

74 General Assembly, *Proceedings*, 1886, pp. 326–328.

75 Illinois Bureau of Labor, *Report*, 231–243. Only 4 per cent of the total number were non-wage-earners.

mixed, that is, comprised members of different trades and of the unskilled, and only 55 were trade assemblies. Reckoned according to country of birth the membership was 45 per cent American, 16 per cent German, 13 per cent Irish, 10 per cent British, and 5 per cent Scandinavian. The largest occupational groups in Illinois were the following: day labourers, 7,498; coal miners, 3,557; garment workers, 1,987; packing-house men, 1,780; brickmakers, 1,394; machinists, 1,222; iron moulders, (machine moulders), 1,203; coopers, 930; painters and paper hangers, 816; box factory men, 506; shoemakers, 934; rolling-mill labourers, 404; watch factory workers, 394; the remainder being distributed among more than 100 occupations. Evidently those who were lacking in bargaining strength, whether for the reason that they were unskilled or little skilled or because they were menaced by machinery, looked to the Knights of Labor as their deliverers. The history of the years immediately preceding throws light upon the forces impelling them to organise.

Half of the assemblies in Illinois and three-fourths of the membership were organised after January 1, 1885 — 50 assemblies during the year 1885, and 94 from January to July, 1886. The progress during 1886 by months was as follows: 11 assemblies were organised in January; 19 in February; 14 in March; 29 in April; 23 in May; and 3 in June. Yet high figures for April and May do not necessarily prove that the eight-hour agitation and strike had been the paramount factor, for, although this agitation did not spread outside of Chicago, the number organised after January 1 in that city was only 37, while for the rest of the State it was 57. Moreover, in the autumn of 1886, the number of Knights in Cook County (Chicago) was double that in July; in other words, in Chicago the growth had been most rapid after the May strike.[76] Nevertheless, the Knights throughout the country furnished a large proportion of the strikers for the eight-hour day. Shortly, however, before this strike broke out, the country's attention was for a time monopolised in another direction by the Southwest strike.

At the settlement of the first strike on the Gould system in March, 1885, the employés were assured that the road would

76 *Ibid.*, 221.

institute no discriminations against the Knights of Labor. However, it is apparent that a series of petty discriminations was indulged in by minor officials, which kept the men in a state of unrest. It culminated in the discharge of a foreman, a member of the Knights, from the car shop at Marshall, Texas, on the Texas and Pacific road, which had shortly before passed into the hands of a receiver. The strike broke out over the entire road on March 1, 1886. It is necessary, however, to note that the Knights of Labor themselves were meditating aggressive action ten months before the strike. District Assembly 101, the organisation embracing the employés on the Southwest system, held a convention on January 10, and authorised the officers to call a strike at any time they might find opportunity to enforce the two following demands: first, the recognition of the Order; and second, a daily wage of $1.50 for the unskilled. The latter demand is peculiarly characteristic of the Knights of Labor and of the feeling of labour solidarity that prevailed in the movement. But evidently the organisation preferred to make the issue turn on discrimination against the members. Another peculiarity which marked off this strike as the beginning of a new era was the facility with which it led to a sympathetic strike on the Missouri-Pacific and all leased and operated lines, which broke out simultaneously over the entire system, March 6. This strike affected more than 5,000 miles of railway situated in Missouri, Kansas, Arkansas, Indian Territory, and Nebraska. The strikers did not content themselves with mere picketing, but actually took possession of the railroad property and by a systematic "killing" of engines, that is, removing some indispensable part, effectively stopped all the freight traffic. The number of men actively on strike was in the neighbourhood of 9,000, including practically all of the shopmen, yardmen, and section gangs. The engineers, firemen, brakemen, and conductors took no active part and had to be forced to leave their posts under threats from the strikers.

The leader, District Master Workman Martin Irons, accurately represented the feelings of the strikers. Personally honest and probably well-meaning, his attitude was overbearing and tyrannical. With him as with those who followed him, a strike was not a more or less drastic means of forcing a better labour contract, but necessarily assumed the aspect of a crusade against capital. Hence all compromise, and any policy of give and take, were absolutely excluded.

Negotiations were conducted by Jay Gould and Powderly to submit the dispute to arbitration, but they failed, and after two months of sporadic violence, the strike spent itself and came to an end. It left, however, a profound impression upon the public mind, second only to the impression made by the great railway strike of 1877, and a congressional committee was appointed to investigate the whole matter.[77]

The Southwest strike terminated on May 3. On May 1, preceding, the general eight-hour strike began.

The preparatory agitation assumed large proportions in March. The main argument for the shorter day was work for the unemployed. With the exception of the cigar makers, it was left wholly in the hands of local organisations. The Knights of Labor figured far less prominently than the trade unions, and, among the latter, the building trades and the German-speaking furniture workers and cigar makers stood in the front ranks of the movement. Evidently Powderly's secret circular did not fail to exercise a strong restraining effect. Nevertheless, *Bradstreet's*[78] estimated that no fewer than 340,000 men took part in the movement: 190,000 actually struck, only 42,000 of this number with success, and 150,000 secured shorter hours without a strike. Thus the total number of those who succeeded with or without strikes was something less than 200,000.

It should be noted, however, that the eight-hour movement very early changed, for the most part, into a shorter-hour movement, only the cigar makers and a majority in the building trades having consistently adhered to the demand for eight hours. Of those to whom shorter hours were granted without a strike, 35,000 were Chicago packing-house employés (Knights of Labor), 19,500 were cigar makers (15,000 in New York), 22,000 were in the building trades (Washington, New York, Chicago, and Baltimore accounting for 18,000), 8,200 were tobacco factory workers (5,000 at Baltimore), 3,300 were furniture workers (3,000 at Grand Rapids), 3,300 were machinists

---

[77] " Investigation of Labor Troubles in Missouri, Arkansas, Texas, and Illinois," in *House of Representatives Report*, 49 Cong., 2 sess., No. 4174.
[78] May 15, 1886.

(2,000 at Chicago).[79] The centre of the strike was in Chicago with 80,000 [80] participants. New York followed with 45,000 strikers, Cincinnati with 32,000, Baltimore with 9,000, Milwaukee with 7,000, Boston with 4,700, Pittsburgh with 4,250, Detroit with 3,000, St. Louis with 2,000, Washington with 1,500, and from all other cities, 13,000, making a total of 198,450.[81]

Of the total number of those who, after a strike, succeeded in getting a shorter day, 10,000 were in Cincinnati (out of 32,000 who struck), and, distinguished by trades, 5,000 were in the building trades (1,000 in New York and 1,000 in Newark), 1,000 were piano makers (New York), 3,200 were machinists (3,000 in New York), 1,900 were agricultural implement makers, and the remainder came from miscellaneous trades.[82]

Even those who for the present succeeded, whether with or without strikes, soon lost the concession. *Bradstreet's* stated in January, 1887, that " the best available information respecting the outcome of the wide-spread short-hour strikes of May and of October, 1886,[83] points to a conspicuous failure. Those who gained and have retained the rule permitting shorter hours of labour daily, have in many instances sacrificed a corresponding portion of wages, or have consented to piece work or to work by the hour. It may be fairly assumed . . . that so far as the payment of former wages for a shorter day's work is concerned the grand total of those retaining the concession will not exceed, if it equals, 15,000." [84] *Bradstreet's* had reported a loss of nearly one-third of the concessions one month after the strike, and a prediction that " the aggregates will probably fall away still further as competition presses on the short-hour employers." [85]

The Knights of Labor and the trade unions emerged from the strike with unequal prestige. Powderly's circular, while it did not stop the Knights from participating, tended to place the Order in an unfavourable light before the working class. It is

79 *Bradstreet's*, May 8, 1886.
80 *Ibid.*, June 12, 1886.
81 *Ibid.*
82 *Ibid.*, May 8, 1886.
83 This latter was the Chicago packers' lockout against the retention of the eight-hour system which had been granted in May without a strike.
84 *Bradstreet's*, Jan. 8, 1887.
85 *Ibid.*, June 12, 1886.

true this did not tell immediately, as the Order stood at the height of its strength in 1886, but, subsequently, when the movement subsided, it furnished to the trade unions an invaluable talking point. On the other hand, the trade unions were always able to point back with satisfaction to their record in May, 1886. Moreover, notwithstanding Powderly's position against the strike, the press and the general public charged the Order with responsibility for the crimes laid at the doors of organised labour, notably the Haymarket bomb, and praised the trade unions by way of contrast. Though such a view was wholly inaccurate with regard to the May strike, the press and the public were correct when they instinctively scented the greater danger to the established social order as coming from the solidarity of all labour rather than from the trade unions.

THE CHICAGO CATASTROPHE

The failure of four-fifths of those who struck was in large measure due to the fatal bomb exploded May 3 on Haymarket Square in Chicago. Samuel Gompers afterwards testified: " The effect of that bomb was that it not only killed the policemen, but it killed our eight-hour movement for that year and for a few years after, notwithstanding we had absolutely no connection with these people." [86]

The Chicago bomb and its effect on the labour movement crystallised as it were the emotional and intellectual connection between the Upheaval and the early American " syndicalism." [87] What many of the Knights of Labor were practising during the Upheaval in a less tragic manner and without stopping to look for a theoretical justification, the Chicago anarchists or, to be more correct, syndicalists, had elevated into a well rounded-out system of thought. Both Syndicalism and the Upheaval were related chapters in the revolutionary movement of the eighties.

Notwithstanding the emphasis which the Chicago revolutionists laid upon trade union action, their influence among the trade unions in the city prior to 1884 was infinitesimal, even among the German unions. Prosperity was a weak culture for

86 Industrial Commission, *Report*, VII, 623.
87 See above, II, 296 *et seq.*

revolutionary teachings.   Thus we find that at a labour demonstration which the socialists organised in August, 1883, only a few German trade unions, the typographical, the furniture workers, and the house carpenters, besides the Lehr und Wehr Verein officially participated.   Nor, apparently, did any trade union avail itself prior to 1884 of the invitation to send delegates to the central committee of the Black International.   However, the advent of depression radically altered the situation.   In February, 1884, the local Progressive Cigar Makers' Union held a mass meeting to discuss the comprehensive programme for labour legislation recommended to the legislature by Governor McLane of Maryland.   Thomas J. Morgan and Waltheich, members of the Socialist Labor party, spoke in favour of the programme, and Spies and Grottkau against it.   The latter secured the adoption of a resolution which declared " that the only means whereby the emancipation of mankind can be brought about is the open rebellion of the robbed class in all parts of the country against the existing economic and political institutions." [88]

The same union took the initiative in organising a new progressive central trade union body.   In June, 1884, it issued a call to the unions in the city to secede from the conservative Amalgamated Trades and Labor Assembly and to form a central labour union with a progressive policy.   The German unions of metal workers, carpenters and joiners, cabinet makers, and butchers sent delegates.   At first the growth of the new central body was slow.   One year after its formation the majority of the trade unions in the city were still affiliated with the old central body, but towards the end of 1885 the strength of the rival bodies became considerably less uneven — the Central Labor Union having 13 unions, mostly German, some of which, however, were the largest in the city, and the Amalgamated Trades and Labor Assembly counting 19 affiliated unions.

From the time of its formation the Central Labor Union was on exceedingly friendly terms with the central committee of the Black International and took part in the processions which the latter organised from time to time.   In June, 1884, the following trade unions participated in such a procession

88 Chicago *Vorbote*, Feb. 20, 1884.

and listened to speeches by Parsons: custom tailors, Typographical No. 9, carpenters, tanners, butchers, cabinet makers, and Progressive Cigar Makers.[89]   In October the Central Labor Union adopted a declaration of principles, which, starting out with the assertion that land is a social heritage, that labour creates all wealth, that there can be no harmony between capital and labour, and that strikes as at present conducted by trade unions are doomed to fail, declared that it was " the sacred duty of every workingman to cut loose from all capitalist political parties and to devote his entire energy to his trades or labour union . . . in order to stand ready to resist the encroachment by the ruling class upon our liberties." The recommendation to cut loose from politics and to devote their entire energy to the trade or labour union meant something very different from a return to " pure and simple " trade unionism. This is evidenced by the fact that at a public debate held between the Central Labor Union and its rival, the Amalgamated Trades and Labor Assembly, the former openly took its position with the Black International.[90]

Many of the individual trade unions went even further. The officers of the carpenters' and joiners' union admitted, in reply to an attack in the New York *Der Sozialist,* that but few of its 368 members were not anarchists. This union had been formed in October, 1884, with 40 members, as a rival to the regular union affiliated with the Brotherhood of Carpenters and Joiners of America. It became the nucleus of an attempted international union intended to be an extremely decentralised organisation, in accordance with the anarchistic aversion to centralised power.[91]   As seen above, a similar union was established by metal workers, of whom, in addition, a considerable number formed themselves into an Armed Section of the Metal Workers' Union of Chicago, with the object to " prepare for the revolution by learning how to use arms." [92]   The headquarters, however, of the revolutionary metal workers' movement were not in Chicago, but in St. Louis.[93]

[89] *Ibid.,* July 2, 1884.

[90] *The Alarm,* Feb. 7, 1885. The Socialist Labor party members remained with the Amalgamated Trades and Labor Assembly.

[91] Chicago *Vorbote,* Mar. 4, 1885, and May 20, 1885.

[92] *Ibid.,* June 23, 1885. See above, II, 297, 298. A revolutionary cigar makers' union was formed in the same month.

[93] In St. Louis a Central Labor Union,

During the summer and autumn of 1885 the principal activity of the Chicago Central Labor Union was agitational. It conducted mass meetings and processions. On the Sunday preceding Labor Day, it organised a grand march to offset the Labor Day parade of the Amalgamated Trades and Labor Assembly, which had secured Mayor Harrison and the labour congressman, Martin A. Foran, as speakers. The number of participants at the revolutionary parade was estimated at 10,000,[94] but this figure is doubtless strongly overdrawn, since the daily papers in Chicago made no mention of it. Indeed, the revolutionary movement did not become a matter of general public attention until Thanksgiving Day of 1885, when a great parade occurred at Chicago in which the principal figures were the English-speaking element and the unemployed, who had been organised by Parsons and his aides. As long as the movement consisted mainly of the German trade unions, the public took little notice of it.

The English-speaking element was organised, not in trade unions, but in " groups of the International." The centre of this movement was occupied by the editorial staff of *The Alarm*. The first copy of the paper, which appeared October 9, 1884, contained, besides the Pittsburgh manifesto, several editorials by A. R. Parsons, and an article " dedicated to tramps," by Lucy E. Parsons, which closed with the words *" Learn the use of the explosives."* The " tramps," that is, the unemployed, who grew particularly numerous in 1884, the year of the lowest depression, proved to be very responsive at this time. Thanksgiving Day of 1884, Parsons had organised a procession of about 5,000,[95] largely composed of the unemployed. The procession halted in Market Square and was addressed by Parsons, Spies, Griffin, and Schwab. The *Chicagoer Arbeiter-Zeitung* [96] commented upon it in the following words : " Yesterday took place the birth of a new phase in the social struggle. Hitherto the revolutionary movement has been restricted to the better situ-

modelled upon the Chicago pattern, was established in January, 1885, in opposition to an existing trades council which was accused of being under the influence of politicians. The Central Labor Union was composed of nine German and four English-speaking trade unions and had for its main object the agitation of the eight-hour day. *Die Parole* (St. Louis), Feb. 3, 1886.

94 Estimated by the Chicago *Vorbote*.
95 Estimated by the Chicago *Vorbote*.
96 Nov. 28, 1884.

ated and the more intelligent German, Bohemian and Danish workingmen. . . . Since yesterday this is no longer the case. Yesterday, the typically American working class carried the red flag through the streets and thereby proclaimed its solidarity with the international proletariat." About this time there existed in Chicago 13 groups of the Black International, including " one vigorous English speaking organisation," with a total membership of over 1,000. The English-speaking, or American, group had been organised by Parsons in November, 1883, with but 5 members; its agitation was at first comparatively without results, but after the appearance of *The Alarm,* it soon became the most active group in the city. In October, 1884, its membership was 45 and in April, 1885, it increased to 90.[97] It held two mass meetings every week and periodically sent out such agitators as Spies, Parsons, Griffin, and Gorsuch on speaking tours over the country. Largely as a result of their efforts, American groups were in existence in June, 1885, in Alleghany City, Kansas City, Cincinnati, Chicago, St. Louis, Covington (Kentucky), New York City, Cleveland, and Philadelphia, and, during the following month, Parsons alone organised 8 American groups in Missouri, Kansas, and Nebraska.

The movement among the foreign nationalities kept pace with the American. In November, 1885, there were 11 Bohemian groups in the country, and the total number of groups reached over 100, located in 43 different cities. The total membership does not lend itself to a ready estimate since the information bureau published no statistics. Assuming, however, the average membership of a group to be between 50 and 70, the total membership of the Black International at that time was about 5,000 or 6,000, and of this number about 1,000 were English-speaking.[98]

Chicago with its 2,000 organised Internationalists at the end of 1885 remained throughout the entire life of the Black International the city where the movement had its deepest roots,

---

[97] *The Alarm,* May 16, 1885.

[98] Eight papers were published under the auspices of the International: 1 in English, *The Alarm;* 5 in German, the New York *Die Freiheit,* the *Chicagoer Arbeiter-Zeitung, Fackel,* and *Vorbote,* in Chicago, and *Die Parole,* in St. Louis; and 2 in Bohemian, the Chicago *Bondoucnost* and the New York *Proletar.*

where the best brains of the organisation were centred, and the only city where the English-speaking wage-earners of the kind then filling the ranks of the Knights of Labor were attracted into the revolutionary movement. This movement reached its climax in the spring of 1886 at the time of the general labour movement for the eight-hour day, and met its tragic collapse at Haymarket Square.

The Central Labor Union began an active agitation for the eight-hour day in November, 1885. Its attitude and motives were quite characteristic and they strongly differentiated the revolutionary trade unions from the other trade unions and the Knights of Labor. A resolution introduced by Spies at a meeting in October was adopted " with enthusiasm." It ended as follows: [99] " Be it Resolved, That we urgently call upon the wage-earning class to arm itself in order to be able to put forth against their exploiters such an argument which alone can be effective: *Violence,* and further be it Resolved, that notwithstanding that we expect very little from the introduction of the eight-hour day, we firmly promise to assist our more backward brethren in this class struggle with all means and power at our disposal, so long as they will continue to show an open and resolute front to our common oppressors, the aristocratic vagabonds and the exploiters. Our war-cry is ' Death to the foes of the human race.' "

The Central Labor Union had already outstripped the Amalgamated Trades and Labor Assembly and consisted in April, 1886, of 22 unions, including the 11 largest ones in the city.[1] True to the spirit of the above declaration, it did not take the initiative in the eight-hour struggle but allowed an Eight-Hour Association of Chicago, which was specially organised for this purpose, to lead the movement. This association was organised in November and comprised the Amalgamated Trades and Labor Assembly, the Socialist Labor party, socialists (who

[99] Chicago *Vorbote,* Oct. 14, 1885.

[1] These unions were as follows: Typographical No. 9, Fringe and Tassel Workers, Fresco Painters, Furniture Workers (Pullman), Bakers No. 10, South Side Bakers' Union, Lumber Workers, Hand Labor Union, Hod Carriers' Union, Brewers and Malters, Beer Barrel Coopers, Brickmakers, International Carpenters, International Carpenters (Bohemian), Independent Carpenters and Joiners, Carpenters and Joiners (Lake View), Wagon Workers, Harness Makers, Butchers, Progressive Cigar Makers, Metal Workers, No. 1, 2, 3, and the Metal Workers' Union (Pullman). Chicago *Vorbote,* Apr. 24, 1886.

remained loyal to the Assembly), and the Knights of Labor. Yet, when the movement was well under way, the Central Labor Union generously contributed its share. On the Sunday preceding the first of May it organised an eight-hour monster demonstration, in which 25,000 took part, with addresses by Parsons, Spies, Fielden, and Schwab. The Internationalists also took an active part in the struggle against the McCormick Harvester Works, which had begun several months earlier but shaded into the eight-hour movement. In the middle of February, the McCormick trouble took on the form of a lockout, following upon the demand of the men that the company should stop its discrimination against their fellows who had been identified with a former strike at the same plant. On March 2, Parsons and Schwab addressed a meeting of the locked-out men to protest against the employment of detectives, and they addressed several other meetings at subsequent dates.

Meanwhile, the general eight-hour movement in the city started out with good promise. About 40,000 employés struck on the first day of May and the number was almost doubled within four days. Of these, 10,000 were lumber-shovers and labourers, 10,000 metal workers, 20,500 clothing workers, 7,000 furniture workers and upholsterers, and 2,500 employés of the Pullman shops.[2] Indeed, the movement assumed larger proportions in Chicago than elsewhere in the country and the outcome would probably have been proportionately successful, had it not been for the tragic event on the fourth of the month.

On the third of May, a group of striking lumber-shovers held a meeting near the McCormick reaper works and were addressed by Spies. About this time strike-breakers employed in these works began to leave for their homes, and were attacked by some of the bystanders at the meeting. The police arrived in large numbers and, upon being received with stones, fired and killed four and wounded many. Burning with indignation Spies rushed to his office where he prepared and issued a call for revenge which contained the words: " Workingmen, arm yourselves and appear in full force." A mass meeting of 3,000 met at 7:30 P. M. on the following day, May 4, on Haymarket Square, to protest against the shooting by the police. The

2 *Bradstreet's*, May 15, 1886.

meeting was addressed first by Spies, then by Parsons, the latter confining himself to the eight-hour question. Fielden spoke last. Meanwhile a threatening rainstorm dispersed the crowd, leaving a few hundred to listen to Fielden's speech. Mayor Harrison, who had attended for the purpose of influencing the meeting to maintain order, also left with the bulk of the crowd. Soon after, a squad of 180 police formed in line and began to advance upon the remaining crowd. Fielden cried out aloud to the captain that this was a peaceable meeting. While the captain was turning around to give an order, a bomb was hurled at the police, killing a sergeant and throwing about sixty to the ground. The police immediately opened fire. On the next day, Spies as well as six other Internationalists, were arrested.[3] Albert R. Parsons escaped but gave himself up during the trial.

It is unnecessary to describe here the period of police terror in Chicago, the hysterical attitude of the press, or the state of panic that came over the inhabitants of the city. Nor is it necessary to deal in detail with the trial of the accused anarchists. One view of it was expressed by Governor John P. Altgeld in 1893 in his *Reasons for Pardoning Fielden, Neebe, and Schwab,* which elicited a reply from the presiding judge.[4]

3 They were Michael Schwab, Adolph Fischer, George Engel, Louis Lingg, immigrants from Germany; Oscar Neebe, an American of German parentage, and Samuel Fielden, an Englishman. Three other men, Waller, Schrader, and Seliger, were arrested and later turned informers.

4 Governor Altgeld pointed out that the jury had been drawn in an unusual way, namely, Judge Gary appointing a special bailiff to go out and summon such men as he, the bailiff, chose, instead of having a number of names drawn out of a box that contained many hundred names; that the judge by his ruling had made it extremely difficult for the lawyer for the defendants to get consideration for his charge that the jury had been packed; that the judge through adroit questioning of the prospective jurors had made it possible for many to be placed upon the jury who candidly admitted their prejudice against the defendants, including a relative of one of the victims of bomb; that the State had never discovered who threw the bomb and that the judge had admitted that he ruled without precedent when he denied a motion for a new trial on the ground that it sufficed that the defendants had incited large masses of people to violence, even though they had left the commission of the crime to individual whim as to place and time; and finally that the personal bearing of the judge had been extremely unfair throughout the trial.

Judge Joseph E. Gary replied in defence of the verdict, pointing out that the defendants had been sentenced not because they were anarchists, but because they were parties to the murder. He quoted from his charge to the jury at the trial: "The conviction proceeds upon the ground . . . that they had generally by speech and print advised large classes . . . to commit murder, and have left the commission, the time, and place, and when, to the individual will and whim or caprice, or whatever it may be, of each individual man who listened to their advice, and that in consequence of that advice, in pursuance of that advice, and influenced by that advice, somebody, not known, did throw the bomb that caused Degan's death." ("The Chicago Anarchists of 1886: The Crime, the Trial and the Punishment," in

The jury handed in a verdict declaring Spies, Schwab, Fielden, Parsons, Fischer, Engel, and Lingg guilty of the murder of Patrolman M. J. Degan and imposed a death sentence. Oscar W. Neebe was declared guilty of the same crime and sentenced to imprisonment for fifteen years. The case was carried to the Supreme Court, and there was affirmed in the autumn of 1887.[5] On November 10, Lingg committed suicide; the sentence of Fielden and Schwab was commuted to imprisonment for life, and Parsons, Fischer, Engel, and Spies were hanged November 11, 1887.

The labour organisations throughout the country, while condemning violence on principle, pleaded for mercy to the sentenced men. The convention of the American Federation of Labor adopted a resolution in this sense, and the feeling was the same among the Knights of Labor, particularly on behalf of Parsons who had been a Knight for over ten years. However, Powderly, who always showed fear lest the general public should suspect the Order of abetting violence, threw his personal influence into the scale and prevented a similar resolution from being adopted by the General Assembly of the Knights of Labor. After the Chicago tragedy, the Black International practically collapsed. The workingmen who supported it in the West withdrew and the organisation shrank to a mere handful of intellectuals.

Century Magazine (New York), April, 1893, XXIII, 835.)

[5] Spies et al. *v.* The People, 122 Ill. 2 (1887).

CHAPTER X

THE AFTERMATH, 1886–1887

The Knights and the Federation. New national trade unions, 396. Efforts of the Knights to annex the skilled unions in order to strengthen the bargaining power of the unskilled, 397. Resistance of the skilled, 397. Situation in the early eighties, 397. Beginning of aggression, 398. District Assembly 49 of New York, 399. Conflict with the International Cigar Makers' Union, 399. The split in the latter, 399. The support of the secessionists by District Assembly 49, 400. The strike in New York in January, 1886, 400. Settlement with District Assembly 49, 400. Fusion of the seceders from the International Cigar Makers' Union with District Assembly 49, 401. Widening of the struggle, 401. Gompers' leadership, 401. General appeal to the trade unions, 402. Conflicts between the Knights and other trade unions, 402. Trade union conference in Philadelphia, 403. The " address," 404. Proposed treaty, 405. Reply of the Knights, 406. Refusal of the skilled trades to be used as a lever by the unskilled, 407. Further negotiations, 407. Declaration of war by the Knights, 409. Impetus for complete unification of the trade unions, 409. Convention of the Federation of Organized Trades and Labor Unions in 1886, 409. The American Federation of Labor, 410. Its paramount activity — economic, 410. Another effort for a settlement, 411. The outcome, 411. Arbitrary action of District Assembly 49 of New York, 412. Return of the secessionist cigar makers to the International Union, 412. The Orders' new conciliatory attitude, 412. Non-conciliatory attitude of the unions, 413.

Subsidence of the Knights. Beginning of the backward tide in the Order, 413. The employers' reaction, 414. Forms of employers' associations, 414. Their aim, 414. Their refusal to arbitrate, 415. The means for the suppression of the Order, 415. The Knights' and the employers' attitude towards trade agreements, 416. Control over strikes in the Order, 416. Control over boycotts, 417. Strikes during the second half of 1886, 417. The Troy laundry workers' lockout, 418. The knit goods industry lockout, 418. Chicago packing industry lockout, 418. Powderly's weakness, 420. Longshoremen's strike in New York in 1887, 420. Its spread, 420. Its consequences, 421. Falling off of the Order's membership, 422. Recession of the wave of the unskilled, 422. Growing predominance of the middle-class element in the Order, 423. Success of the trade unions, 423. Chicago bricklayers' strike, 423. The employers' association and the trade agreement, 424. Situation in the bituminous coal industry, 425. National Federation of Miners and Mine Laborers, 425. Relations with the Order, 425. The " interstate " trade agreement, 426. Drift towards trade union organisation within the Order, 427. History of the national trade assemblies, 1880–1885, 427. Fluctuation of the Order's policy, 427. Its cause, 427. The victory of the national trade assembly idea, 428.

KNIGHTS AND FEDERATION

DURING 1886 the combined membership of labour organisations was exceptionally strong and for the first time came near the million mark.[1] The Knights of Labor had a membership of 700,000 and the trade unions at least 250,000,[2] the former composed largely of the unskilled and the latter of the skilled. Still, the leaders of the Knights realised that mere numbers were not sufficient to defeat the employers and that control over the skilled, and consequently the more strategic occupations, was required before the unskilled and semi-skilled could expect to march to victory. Hence, parallel to the tremendous growth of the Knights in 1886, there was a constantly growing effort to absorb the existing trade unions for the purpose of making them subservient to the interests of the less skilled elements. It was mainly this that produced the bitter conflict between the Knights and the trade unions during 1886 and 1887. Neither the jealousy aroused by the success of the unions nor the opposite aims of labour solidarity and trade separatism gives an adequate explanation of this conflict. The one, of course, aggravated the situation by introducing a feeling of personal bitterness, and the other furnished an appealing argument to each side. But the struggle was one between groups within the working class, in which the small but more skilled group fought for independence of the larger but weaker group of the unskilled and semi-skilled. The skilled men stood for the right to use their advantage of skill and efficient organisation in order to wrest the maximum

[1] This number was not reached again until 1900.

[2] It is extremely difficult and hazardous to make an estimate of the total numerical strength of the trade unions at this time. The Federation of Labor claimed in 1886 that there were 600,000 trade unionists organised, but the statistical table showing the growth since 1881, published in 1912, gives only 140,000 as the strength in 1886. However, adding the membership of the railway organisations and the bricklayers' national union, which were then, as now, unaffiliated, and the unnumbered local trade unions without a national organisation, it is safe to estimate the membership at 250,000. The following national trade unions were formed in 1886: the National Union of Brewery Workers, the Metal Polishers', Buffers', Platers' and Brass Workers' International Union, the Order of Railroad Telegraphers, the Machinists' National League, the National League of Musicians, the International Musical Union, the Protective Fraternity of Printers, the Tailors' Progressive Union, the Mutual Association of Railroad Switchmen of North America, and the Glass-blowers of North America (split off from District Assembly 149 and rejoined the latter in 1889). The following were organised in 1887: the Brotherhood of Painters and Decorators, the Horse Collar Makers' National Union, the Building Laborers' National Union, the Saddle and Harness Makers' National Association, the Silk Workers' National Union, the Umbrella, Pipe and Cane Workers' National Union, the Paving Cutters' National Union, the Pattern Makers' League, and the Brotherhood of Section Foremen.

amount of concessions for themselves. The Knights of Labor endeavoured to annex the skilled men in order that the advantage from their exceptional fighting strength might lift up the unskilled and semi-skilled. From the viewpoint of a struggle between principles, this was indeed a clash between the principle of solidarity of labour and that of trade separatism, but, in reality, each of the principles reflected only the special interest of a certain portion of the working class. Just as the trade unions, when they fought for trade autonomy, really refused to consider the unskilled men, so the Knights of Labor were insensible to the fact that their scheme would retard the progress of the skilled trades.

The conflict was held in abeyance during the early eighties. The trade unions were by far the strongest organisations in the field and scented no particular danger when here or there the Knights formed an assembly either contiguous to the sphere of a trade union (such as organising the machine moulders whom the union ignored) or even encroaching upon it (such as the organisation of an assembly of iron workers at Braddock, which included unskilled as well as some tonnage men).[3]   The Federation of Organised Trades and Labor Unions and the Knights of Labor mutually endeavoured to remain on as friendly terms as possible. We have had occasion to note that the Federation in 1880 extended to district assemblies of the Knights an invitation to affiliate, and again, as we saw in 1884, it invited the Order to co-operate in the eight-hour movement. This friendly feeling was largely reciprocated by the Knights of Labor. The General Assembly in 1882 ordered a communication to be sent to the Amalgamated Association of Iron and Steel Workers with the assurance that the Order would not admit a seceding faction from that union. The next General Assembly voted against recognising a printers' trade district and rejected the proposal of District Assembly 64 (practically composed only of printers), that all printers should be required to join it.[4]   The assembly also authorised the appointment of a committee to draw up a platform for an alliance of the various labour unions of the

---

[3] Fitch, *The Steel Workers*, 111. Fitch shows how the existence of two rival organisations weakened the strength of the iron workers at Braddock.

[4] General Assembly, *Proceedings*, 1883, pp. 467, 508.

country, having power to confer with the representatives of existing unions.[5]

Even with the expansion of the Order, beginning in 1884, when the local assemblies grew aggressive towards trade unions, the General Assembly for a long time maintained this friendly attitude.   In 1884 a resolution was passed, as follows: " No local Assembly of the Order, or any of its members, shall antagonise any trade and labor organisation, or any of its members if known to be faithful workers in the cause of labor, by refusing to work with those holding membership cards in any factory and non-co-operative industry under the control of the Knights of Labor." [6]   In 1885 the General Executive Board ruled that District Assembly 41, Baltimore, could not force one of its locals to refrain from sending delegates to the convention of the Federation of Organised Trades and Labor Unions.[7] The General Assembly of 1885 decided that Local Assembly 3834 under District Assembly 1, formerly a local union affiliated with the granite cutters' national union, should return to that organisation provided this could be done without a fine or humiliating conditions,[8] and that the label of the Knights of Labor should never be placed upon goods manufactured at less than union prices.

However, complaints made by trade unions became numerous after 1884.   The *Furniture Workers' Journal* accused the furniture workers' assembly at Grand Rapids of trying to win over the members of the union in that place, on the plea that its dues were lower than those of the union.   The *Journal* claimed that the same situation existed in several other localities.   *John Swinton's Paper* reported early in 1885 from Philadelphia that " the open unions are quietly fighting the Knights of Labor, who in return break up organised unions by taking out a few men and organising an Assembly." [9]   The greatness of the drawing power of the Order is illustrated by the fact that during 1885–1886 several local unions in such a highly skilled trade as that of custom tailors went over bodily to the Knights. This had almost ruined the national union.[10]

5 *Ibid.*, 467, 506.
6 *Ibid.*, 1884, pp. 707, 787.
7 *Ibid.*, 1885, p. 73.
8 *Ibid.*, 140.

9 *John Swinton's Paper*, Mar. 1, 1885.
10 *American Federationist*, 1902, IX, 599.

The Knights were in nearly every case the aggressors; only such a powerful trade union as the Brotherhood of Locomotive Engineers could afford to issue the aggressive order of Grand Chief Engineer Arthur, during the Wabash strike in 1885, that all members withdraw from the Knights of Labor.[11] He soon thereafter declared that the brotherhood was not a labour organisation.

It is significant that among the local organisations inimical to trade unions, District Assembly 49, of New York, should prove the most relentless. This assembly in 1887 [12] during the 'longshoremen's and coal-miners' strike, did not hesitate to tie up the industries of the entire city for the sake of securing the demands of several hundred unskilled workingmen. The action of the assembly furnishes another proof that the conflict between the Knights and the trade unions was really one between the classes of the unskilled and the skilled.[13]

Though District Assembly 49, New York, came into conflict with not a few of the trade unions in that city, its battle royal was fought with the cigar makers' unions. There were at this time two rival national unions in the cigar making trade, the International and the Progressive, and the aggressive interference by the Knights of Labor created a series of situations of such complexity that at times they almost resembled some of the most involved problems with which modern European diplomacy has been obliged to deal. The split in the cigar makers' union, dating from 1881, occurred in No. 144, New York, turning on the policy of the international officers, which was to support candidates of the existing parties who pledged themselves to the prohibition of tenement house work. The socialist element in the union at first tried to block this policy, but carried the fight over into the next election of officers where it won by electing a socialist as president of No. 144. He was, however, immediately suspended by Strasser, the international president, on the ground that he was a manufacturer and consequently ineligible.

11 General Assembly, *Proceedings*, 1885, p. 88.

12 See below, II, 420–422.

13 This district assembly was managed by a mysterious " Home Club " of which it can definitely be stated only that it endeavoured to wipe out the trade unions and that it was later charged with acquiring control of the entire Order at the special session of the General Assembly in May, 1886, when it effected a reconciliation with Powderly, whom it had formerly opposed. Buchanan, *The Story of a Labor Agitator*, 301.

But the socialists refused to submit either to the suspension of this chosen officer or to the order issued by the international executive board to turn over the funds to the union pending a new election. They formally seceded by assuming the name, Progressive Union No. 1. The Progressive Union grew very rapidly because it took in the tenement house workers and adopted lower dues than those of the International Union. It soon spread outside of New York and thus became in fact, as well as in name, a rival national union to the older organisation. Naturally its membership was recruited from among the socialists and the recent immigrants, who also were largely tenement-house workers.[14] Efforts at reconciliation were repeatedly made, and in December, 1885, a small part of the Progressives united with the International. Strasser stated in January, 1886, that the trade union element had come back to the fold " under the resolutions of the Rochester Conference and the restrictions adopted at the last Convention," but that the " anarchists " and the " tenement-house scum " still continued to form a union of their own.[15] However, the " anarchists " and the " tenement-house scum " constituted nearly the entire membership of the Progressive Union.

As early as 1883, District Assembly 49 took a hand in the struggle to support the Progressive Union.[16] But the most active aggression came with the beginning of 1886, when District Assembly 49, its membership multiplying by leaps and bounds, gained great confidence in its own prowess. On January 2, 1886, the manufacturers' association, embracing fourteen firms, declared a reduction in wages. Both the International and the Progressive unions refused to submit, and, in consequence, the association started a lockout which threw out of work about 10,000 employés. However, the intense rivalry between the unions made durable co-operation impossible, and ten weeks later the Progressive Union, with the aid of the Central Labor Union, entered into an agreement with the employers.

14 The above facts are taken from a document presented by Local Assembly 2814, Knights of Labor, to District Assembly 49, giving the Progressive Cigar Makers' version (Leaflet in library of University of Wisconsin), and from a special report by Strasser in the " Proceedings of the Convention of the International Union in 1883," supplement to the *Cigar Makers' Official Journal*, 5–10.

15 *Cigar Makers' Official Journal*, January, 1886.

16 Philadelphia *Journal of United Labor*, December, 1883, p. 609.

The other union continued the strike. Thereupon the manufacturers applied to District Assembly 49 for settlement and
for the label of the Knights of Labor. District Assembly 49
readily met the proposal, gave them the white [17] label, and besides allowed the use of the newly introduced bunching machine in exchange for a promise to abolish tenement-house
work.[18] Neither the International nor the Progressive cigar
makers desired to accept the machine. But the Progressive
Union could ill afford to go against its powerful ally, District
Assembly 49. On the contrary it felt so hard-pressed by its
rival that on March 14, 1886, it decided to join District Assembly 49 as a body and become Local Assembly 2814 with 7,000
members.[19]

The events in New York at once let loose the dogs of war.
Already in 1885 the International Union and the Order had
come into conflict over the label. In February, 1886, the International Union instituted a general boycott on all cigars which
did not bear the label of that union, including those which bore
the Knights of Labor label.[20] Similar struggles developed in
a large number of cities, notably in Milwaukee and Syracuse.
There is ample proof that each side " scabbed " on the other.

The conflict between the Knights of Labor and the cigar
makers' union brought to a climax the sporadic struggle that
had been going on between the Order and the trade unions.
The trade unions finally awakened to a sense of the danger
from the rapidly growing Order. The common danger created
unity of feeling, and the indifference previously felt for federated action now gave way to a desire for closer union.

Another highly important effect of this conflict was the
ascendency in the trade union movement of Samuel Gompers as

[17] The Knights of Labor label was
white, while the International Cigar Makers' Union used the blue label.

[18] It is extremely interesting to note
the agreement with regard to the bunching
machine. The patentee was made a party
to it and both he and the manufacturers
agreed that the latter should pay a specified royalty to District Assembly 49 for the
use of the machine. (New York Bureau
of Labor, *Report*, 1886, p. 524.) The
" bunching machine " did the work of
four or five hands in the bunching department.

[19] *The Order and the Cigarmakers*

(pamphlet), published July 2, 1886, sets
forth the Knights of Labor side. The
other side was given in the *Cigar Makers'
Official Journal*, March, 1886. A number of international cigar makers in New
York, including Gompers, organised into
a local assembly, to enable themselves to
give the Knights of Labor label to friendly
employers. This assembly was suspended
by the General Executive Board after a
hearing in March, 1886. General Assembly, *Proceedings*, 1886, p. 28, 29.

[20] Philadelphia *Journal of United Labor*, Feb. 25, 1886.

the foremost leader. Gompers had first achieved prominence in 1881 at the time of the organisation of the Federation of Organised Trades and Labor Unions. But not until the situation created by the conflict with the Knights of Labor did he get his first real opportunity, both to demonstrate his inborn capacity for leadership, and to train and develop that capacity by overcoming what was perhaps the most serious problem that ever confronted American organised labour.

Gompers was the leading emissary sent out early in 1886 by the cigar makers' union to agitate in favour of a closer federation with other unions.[21] The appeal found a ready response. McGuire, of the carpenters' brotherhood, stated before the special meeting of the General Assembly in May, 1886, that from 150 to 160 unions had grievances against the Knights of Labor, and these included iron moulders, brick makers, bakers, miners, printers, carpenters, and granite cutters.[22] In granite cutting the national union engaged in a controversy over a boycott with District Assembly 99 of Providence.[23] On the other hand, the Seamen's Benevolent Union of the Great Lakes, being hard pressed by the employers, voluntarily joined the Order in the expectation that this might gain for it recognition from the vessel owners.[24] The glass industry was practically under the control of the Knights of Labor. In addition to the window-glass blowers' organisation, Local Assembly 300, both the Druggist Ware Glass Blowers' League of America and the Western Green Bottle Blowers' League became district assemblies in 1886.[25] The Flint Glass Workers' Union, on the other hand, came into violent conflict with the Order when the latter admitted a seceding faction from that union.[26]

From the standpoint of the trade unions fighting for preservation, the voluntary assimilation of the weaker unions spelled no less danger than the attempted forcible assimilation of the cigar makers' and the granite cutters' unions. Already the convention of the Federation of Organised Trades and Labor

[21] Keller and Kirschner were others. J. S. Kirschner, " Statement," in *American Federationist*, 1901, VIII, 470.

[22] General Assembly *Proceedings*, 1886, p. 51.

[23] *John Swinton's Paper*, Feb. 28, 1886.

[24] Philadelphia *Journal of United Labor*, Aug. 20, 1887.

[25] McCabe, "The Standard Rate in American Trade Unions," in *Johns Hopkins University Studies*, XXX, 155.

[26] Pennsylvania Bureau of Labor, *Report*, 1888, F. p. 18, *et seq.*

Unions in 1885, at a secret session, had instructed the secretary to raise the question with Powderly. Powderly replied in a friendly and reassuring tone, but, as the report of the legislative committee at the convention of 1886 put it: " Mr. Powderly's power for good was sadly overestimated by the delegates to the last session of the Federation." [27]

The agitation carried on by the emissaries of the cigar makers' union bore fruit and in the spring of 1886, P. J. McGuire, of the carpenters, A. Strasser, of the cigar makers, P. J. Fitzpatrick, of the iron moulders, Jonah Dyer, of the granite cutters, and W. H. Foster, secretary of the Federation of Organised Trades and Labor Unions, issued a call for a general trade union conference in Philadelphia on May 17. Besides the above named unions, it was attended by the officers of the Amalgamated Association of Iron and Steel Workers, the typographical union, the National Federation of Coal Miners and Labourers, the Amalgamated Association of Coal Miners and Labourers, Boiler Makers' International Union, Lasters' Protective Union of New England, German-American Typographia, Tailors' National Union, Nailers' National Union, Bricklayers' and Masons' International Union, Stereotypers' Association and McKay Shoe Stitchers' Union of New England. [28] For the first time in the eighties, did the combined trade union movement of the entire country come together for common action. What the drawing power of the legislative programme put forth by the Federation of Organised Trades and Labor Unions fell short of accomplishing, the common menace from the Knights was sufficiently strong to realise.

William H. Weihe, of the iron and steel workers, was made chairman and William H. Foster and P. J. McGuire, secretaries of the conference. A proposed treaty of peace with the Knights of Labor was then drawn up and McGuire, Weihe, Strasser, Fitzpatrick, Chris Evans (of the miners), and Daniel P. Boyer (of the printers) were selected as a committee to con-

[27] American Federation of Labor, *Proceedings*, 1886, p. 9.

[28] Letters of sympathy were received from the Druggist Glass Blowers' Union, Western District, the Glass Workers, Eastern District, United States Wool Hat Finishers' Union, the Telegraphers' National Association, the National Silk Hat Finishers' Association, the United Piano Makers' Union, the Ohio Valley Trades Assembly, the American Flint Glass Workers, Carpenters, Amalgamated Machinists and Engineers, and the Spinners' Union. *Cigar Makers' Official Journal*, June, 1886.

duct negotiations with the Order. It was also voted that the conference of the executive officers of the national trade unions should meet annually thereafter.

The conference stated " the conviction of the chief officers of the National and International Unions here assembled that, inasmuch as trades unions have a historical basis, and in view of the success that has attended their efforts in the past, we hold that they should strictly preserve their distinct and individual autonomy, and that we do not deem it advisable for any trade union to be controlled by or to join the Knights of Labor in a body, believing that trades unions are best qualified to regulate their own internal trade affairs. Nevertheless, we recognise the solidarity of all labor interests." That the trade union conception of the " solidarity of all labor interests," however, meant no promise of active support to the unskilled class can plainly be seen from the address to the trade unions issued later, which described their task as follows: " Through the development of industry and the aggregation of capital, the tendency is to monopolise the business of the country. Hence the various trades have been affected by the introduction of machinery, the sub-division of labor, the use of women's and children's labor and the lack of an apprentice system, so that the skilled trades were rapidly sinking to the level of pauper labor. To protect the skilled labor of America from being reduced to beggary, and to sustain the standard of American workmanship and skill, the trades unions of America have been established." The address goes on to say that " When they [the trade unions] are founded on such grounds, there need be no fears of their destruction, nor need there be any antagonism between them and the Knights of Labor." The last conclusion, though it may have been entirely legitimate and in strict conformity with abstract logic and justice, went, nevertheless, contrary to the concrete logic of the situation. The trade unions could hardly expect that the Knights of Labor at a critical period such as this, when the fate of their movement was hanging in the balance, could allow the skilled men to remain within the narrow circle of their special trade interests. It was, therefore, a matter of natural sequence that, using the words of the resolution passed by the conference, it became " the avowed purpose of a certain element of the Knights of Labor to destroy the trades unions." [29]

But though the trade unions seem to have failed to grasp the nature of the class struggle conducted by the Knights of Labor, and, therefore, viewed the latter merely as an encroaching organisation, no one can deny that they were acting within their right when they strenuously opposed the policy of forcible assimilation applied by the Knights of Labor. The proposed treaty of peace drawn up by the conference as the basis for future negotiations read as follows:

" First, That in any branch of labor having a national or international organisation, the Knights of Labor shall not initiate any person or form any assembly of persons following said organised craft or calling without the consent of the nearest national or international union affected.

" Second, That no person shall be admitted to the Knights of Labor who works for less than the regular scale of wages fixed by the union of his craft, and none shall be admitted to membership in the Knights of Labor who have ever been convicted of ' scabbing,' ' ratting,' embezzlement or any other offence against the union of his trade or calling until exonerated by the same.

" Third, That the charter of any Knight of Labor Assembly of any trade having a national or international union shall be revoked and the members of the same be requested to join a mixed assembly or form a local union under the jurisdiction of their respective national or international trades unions.

" Fourth, That any organizer of the Knights of Labor who endeavours to induce trades unions to disband, or tampers with their growth or privileges, shall have his commission forthwith revoked.

" Fifth, That whenever a strike or lockout of any trade unionists is in progress no assembly or district assembly of the Knights of Labor shall interfere until the difficulty is settled to the satisfaction of the trades unions affected.

" Sixth, That the Knights of Labor shall not establish nor issue any trade mark or label in competition with any trade mark or label now issued or that may hereafter be issued by any national or international trades union." [30]

The General Assembly met in special session, May 25, 1886, at Cleveland. The prime object of this session was to settle the question of the relation to the trade unions. Powderly remained neutral. Nearly one-third of the delegates were trade

unionists.   Nevertheless the delegates from District Assembly
49 [31] laboured so diligently that it required four days to secure
the passage of an address to " Brothers in the Cause of Labor." [32]   The executive board laid the proposed treaty before
the convention and the trade union's special committee was given
a hearing before the committee on the state of the Order.   The
treaty was rejected, but a conciliatory address, largely the work
of George E. McNeill and Frank K. Foster, with approval by
Powderly, was issued " To the Officers and Members of all National and International Trades' Unions of the United States
and Canada," as follows:

" We recognise the service rendered to humanity and the cause of
labor by trades-union organisations, but believe that the time has
come, or is fast approaching, when all who earn their bread *by the
sweat of their brow* shall be enrolled under one general head, as we
are controlled by one common law — the law of our necessities; and
we will gladly welcome to our ranks or to protection under our banner any organisation requesting admission.   And to such organisations as believe that their craftsmen are better protected under their
present form of government, we pledge ourselves, as members of the
great army of labor, to co-operate with them in every honourable
effort to achieve the success which we are unitedly organised to obtain; and to this end we have appointed a Special Committee to confer with a like committee of any National or International Trades
Union which shall desire to confer with us on the settlement of any
difficulties that may occur between the members of the several organisations."

The practical aspects of the co-operation were to be, according to the address, the interchange of working cards, " the adoption of some plan by which all labour organisations could be protected from unfair men, men expelled, suspended, under fine,
or guilty of taking places of union men or Knights of
Labor while on strike or while locked out from work," the
adoption of a uniform standard of hours and wages throughout each trade whether controlled by a trade union or by the
Knights of Labor, and finally, a system of joint conferences

[31] The General Assembly passed a resolution offered by T. B. McGuire, the representative of District Assembly 49 of
New York, instructing the General Executive Board to issue a general order to the
effect that the " members support and
protect all labels or trade-marks issued by
the Knights of Labor, in preference to
any other trade-mark or label.   Any member who refuses to obey shall be guilty of
violation of obligation."   General Assembly, *Proceedings*, 1886, p. 73.

[32] Buchanan, *The Story of a Labor Agitator*, 301.

and of common action against employers, provided that " in the settlement of any difficulties between employers and employees, the organisations represented in the establishment shall be parties to the terms of settlement." [33]

Obviously, the majority of the Knights of Labor preferred that the trade unions should affiliate with them. It cannot be said, however, that this preference sprang from the mere desire for expansion common to all organisations. The address that the convention ordered to be sent to the president of the Amalgamated Association of Iron and Steel Workers shows that the expansionist policy of the Knights was dictated by its solicitude for the interests of unskilled labour. It said in part: " In the use of the wonderful inventions . . . your organisation plays a most important part. Naturally it embraces within its ranks a very large proportion of laborers of a high grade of skill and intelligence. With this skill of hand, guided by intelligent thought, comes the right to demand that excess of compensation paid to skilled above the unskilled labor. But the unskilled labor must receive attention, or in the hour of difficulty the employer will not hesitate to use it to depress the compensation you now receive. That skilled or unskilled labor may no longer be found unorganised, we ask of you to annex your grand and powerful corps to the main army that we may fight the battle under one flag." [34]

But apparently the skilled iron workers evinced no desire to be pressed into the service of lifting up the unskilled, for when a special committee of the Knights of Labor submitted the proposal to the convention of the amalgamated association, it was voted down practically unanimously.[35] It met with like treatment at the national conventions of the typographical union,[36] the plumbers, steam and gas fitters,[37] the flint glass workers, the coal miners, the stationary engineers, and at the hands of the New York telegraphers, German confectioners, and the jewelers.[38]

During the summer months of 1886 the conflict between the trade unions and the Order was held in abeyance pending nego-

33 General Assembly, *Proceedings*, 1886, p. 53.
34 *Ibd.*, 38.
35 *Carpenter*, June, 1886.

36 *Ibid.*
37 *John Swinton's Paper*, Sept. 19, 1886.
38 *Carpenter*, October, 1886.

tiations. The committee appointed at the Philadelphia trade union conference convened again at Philadelphia on September 29 and held a joint meeting with Powderly and the executive board of the Knights of Labor regarding the appointment by the latter of a special negotiating committee. Powderly's position was unsatisfactory. Nevertheless, the trade union leaders decided to postpone action until after the meeting of the General Assembly at Richmond, Virginia, in October, 1886, and to meet again at Columbus, in December.[39]

The Richmond General Assembly, which met October 9, presented a unique spectacle. It was thoroughly typical of the great labour upheaval at its highest point. The number of the delegates had more than quadrupled since the session in May, 658 delegates representing a constituency of over 700,000. The overwhelming majority were attending a convention for the first time. They possessed no parliamentary experience and totally lacked cohesiveness. Consequently, District Assembly 49, New York, the leader of the " union haters " with its 61 delegates bound by the unit rule, found it a comparatively easy matter to dictate the proceedings of the assembly, particularly since it secured the co-operation of Charles H. Litchman, the most influential leader in District Assembly 30, Massachusetts, with 75 votes.[40]   Powderly, who had been at all previous sessions independent of any combination and thoroughly out of sympathy with the Napoleonic tendencies of District Assembly 49, was now lined up with the latter.

Here is how Joseph R. Buchanan, of Denver, the leader of the minority faction which favoured amicable relations with the trade unions, describes the Richmond session:

" It was at Richmond that the seal of approval was placed upon the acts of those members who had been bending every energy since the Cleveland special session to bring an open warfare between the order and the trades-unions. The contest between the exclusivists and the bi-organisation representatives was fierce, and it never waned for one moment during the two weeks of the session. The bitterness of feeling engendered by the strife between these two elements entered into

39 *Cigar Makers' Official Journal*, October, 1886.

40 Litchman was elected general secretary for two years with an annual salary of $2,000. This office was created at this session; formerly the duties had been performed by the secretary-treasurer. Powderly's salary was raised to $5,000, and the term of office was lengthened to two years.

every matter of any consequence which came before the body. . . .
While the question at issue was the Knights against the whole trades-
union movement, the discussions covering every possible phase of
the subject, one trade only was named in the action taken by the General Assembly — the cigar makers. A resolution was adopted ordering all members of the order who were also members of the Cigar
Makers' International Union to withdraw from the latter organisation; failure to comply with said order meaning forfeiture of
membership in the Order of the Knights of Labor. The majority
by which the resolution was adopted was not, comparatively, large,
but it was enough; and the greatest labor organisation up to that
time known in this country received its mortal wound at Richmond.
. . . Powderly . . . was unequivocally with the anti-unionists.
This was Mr. Powderly's first serious mistake as General Master
Workman, though he had been criticised because of his course in the
Southwestern strike and during the eight-hour movement of May 1,
1886. . . . The General Master Workman desired harmony in the
order, and he permitted himself to be deceived into the belief that
harmony could be secured by killing the influence of the trades-
unionists who were Knights." [41]

The open declaration of war by the Knights furnished the
last impetus necessary for the complete unification of the trade
unions already begun at the Philadelphia conference. The conference of the trade union officials scheduled for Columbus,
Ohio, in December, 1886, came together on the eighth of the
month. The legislative committee of the Federation of Organised Trades and Labor Unions changed the place of meeting
of the annual convention from St. Louis to Columbus, where
it met on the seventh. The report of the legislative committee,
of which Samuel Gompers was chairman, reviewed with satisfaction the part the organisation had played in the eight-hour
strikes. The movement had greatly stimulated the growth of
trade unions, which had doubled their membership during the
year. It would have been more successful but for the fickle
attitude of the "leading members of the Knights of Labor."
Among the legislative achievements of the year were the establishment of bureaus of labour statistics in several States, child
labour laws, etc. An important place was occupied by the new
Federal law for the incorporation of trade unions. The report
saw in it a recognition of the "principle of the lawful character

41 Buchanan, *The Story of a Labor Agitator*, 313–316.

of Trades Unions, a principle we have been contending for years," though "the law is not what was desired, covering only those organisations which have, or may remove their headquarters to the District of Columbia, or any of the Territories of the United States." [42]

The delegates to the convention of the Federation attended in a body the conference of the trade union officials, the latter representing 25 organisations claiming to represent "316,469 members in good standing." [43]

On the second day, having effected a permanent organisation, the conference declared itself as the first annual convention of the American Federation of Labor and devoted the three remaining days of the session to the constitution and to the relations with the Knights of Labor.

A committee was appointed to meet with a similar committee chosen by the convention of the Federation of Organised Trades and Labor Unions and the latter consented to merge itself with the American Federation of Labor.

The new federation was not to be, like its predecessor, a mere association for legislation, but was entrusted with important economic functions. The national or international trade union was made the sole basic unit, and local unions remained entitled to independent representation only in trades where no national union existed. [44] The place of the former legislative commit-

[42] Federation of Organized Trades and Labor Unions of the United States and Canada, *Proceedings*, 1886, p. 8.

[43] American Federation of Labor, *Proceedings*, 1886, p. 16. P. J. McGuire, the chosen secretary, said to a reporter on *John Swinton's Paper*, Dec. 19, 1886: "It is not a membership merely on paper, but is proven by the most recent official reports of the organisation. We spent a day and a half of our time in obtaining these reports from the delegates." Still the statistics published by the American Federation of Labor in 1912 estimate the membership in 1886 at about 140,000. Twelve national or international unions were as follows: the Iron Molders' National Union, the Typographical International Union, the German-American Typographia, the Granite Cutters' National Union, the New England Lasters' National Union, the Furniture Workers' National Union, the National Federation of Miners and Mine Laborers, the Journeymen Tailors' National Union, the Journeymen

Barbers' National Union, the Metal Workmen's National Union, the Brotherhood of Carpenters and Joiners, and the Cigarmakers' International Union. The following were city trades' councils: The United German Trades of New York, the Baltimore Federation of Labor, the Philadelphia Central Labor Union, Chicago Trades' Assembly, the Essex County (New York) Trades' Assembly and the St. Louis Trades' Assembly, and the following local trade unions: Bricklayers No. 1, Cincinnati, United Order of Carpenters of New York City, New York Stereotypers' Union, Waiters' No. 1, the New York Mutual Benevolent and Protective Society of Operative Painters, the Journeymen Barbers' Protective Union of New York, and the International Boatmen's No. 1 of New York.

[44] The dominance of the national union was further guaranteed at the convention of 1887 by a provision that in case a roll call is demanded each delegate, except those of city or state federations, may cast

tee was taken by a president, two vice-presidents, a secretary, and a treasurer, together forming an executive council, with the following duties: first, to watch legislation; second, to organise new local and national trade unions; third, while recognising "the right of each trade to manage its own affairs," to secure the unification of all labour organisations; fourth, to pass upon boycotts instituted by the affiliated organisations; and fifth, in cases of strikes and lockouts, to issue after an investigation, general appeals for voluntary financial contributions in aid of the organisation involved. The revenue of the Federation was to be derived from charter fees and from a per capita tax of one-half cent per month for each member in good standing. The president's salary was fixed at $1,000 per annum.

Bitter feeling towards the Knights of Labor at once manifested itself, when the delegate from the window-glass workers' association was refused a seat on the ground that "said organisation is affiliated with the Knights of Labor, and is not a Trade Union within the meaning of the call for the Convention." [45] Another attempt was made to negotiate with the Order, and a special committee of the convention met December 11 with a committee of the Knights of Labor. The meeting led to no results, since the trade unions would be satisfied with nothing less than the acceptance of the treaty, and the Knights of Labor took the attitude that they not only did not have the right to consider it again after it had been rejected by the General Assembly, but that they would refuse to make a definite promise that organisers should not interfere in strikes ordered by trade unions or should not try to organise assemblies from among the members of trade unions.[46] Thereupon the Federation in its turn unanimously declared war upon the Knights and announced the decision to carry hostilities into the enemy's territory: "We condemn the acts [of the Knights] above recited, and call upon all workingmen to join the Unions of their respective trades, and urge the formation of National and International Unions and the centralisation of all under one head, the American Federation of Labor." [47] Along with

one vote for every one hundred members which he represents.

45 American Federation of Labor, *Proceedings*, 1886, p. 18.

46 General Assembly, *Proceedings*, 1887, 1444-1447.

47 American Federation of Labor, *Proceedings*, 1886, p. 23.

this went a resolution, likewise unanimously adopted, refusing
to patronise the label of the Knights of Labor.[48]   After electing Samuel Gompers as president, P. F. Fitzpatrick, of the iron
moulders, first vice-president, J. W. Smith, of the journeymen
tailors', second vice-president, P. J. McGuire, of the carpenters,
secretary, and Gabriel Edmonston, also of the carpenters,
treasurer, the convention adjourned to meet the following year
at Baltimore.

Although the negotiations between the Knights and the trade
unions were rendered fruitless by the arrogance of the trade
unions on the one side, and by the apparent indifference of the
Order on the other, the fact that out of the conflict had arisen
a closely knitted trade union federation practically guaranteed
that in the future a bridle would be put upon the aggressiveness
of the organisers of the Knights.   Of course, District Assembly
49 made the fullest use of the victory at Richmond, and pushed
its anti-trade union policy to extremes.   It even ordered the
members of the Progressive Cigar Makers' Union, its faithful
ally against the International Cigar Makers' Union, which had
become affiliated as Local Assembly 2814, in March, 1886, either
to leave the Order or to give up their union.   This arbitrary
action was too much even for the Progressives, and, rather than
submit, they reunited with the International Union, their bitter enemy of the past six years.[49]

However, the Order as a whole, by the time of the next session of the General Assembly at Minneapolis in October, 1887,
clearly saw its mistake, and Powderly handed down a belated
decision declaring unconstitutional the action taken at Richmond which expelled all members of the International Cigar
Makers' Union.   The decision was upheld by the General Assembly.[50]   Besides the growing strength of the Federation, this
change of policy must have contributed also to the decreasing
membership of the Order, which had fallen off one-third in one

48 *Ibid.*
49 *John Swinton's Paper*, Aug. 1, 1886;
Cigar Makers' Official Journal, September,
1886, p. 2; and a circular by District Assembly 49, date not given.   An important
ground for friction was supplied by the
dissatisfaction on the part of the progressives with the acceptance of the bunching
machine upon which the Knights insisted,
and on account of which District Assembly
49 was receiving a royalty.   Growing out
of this was an order issued Dec. 14, 1886,
by District Assembly 49 to its affiliated
local assemblies to withdraw from the
Central Labor Union.
50 General Assembly, *Proceedings*, 1887,
pp. 1528–1531, 1822.

year.   But the Order's conciliatory attitude met with but little response.   The trade unions, now feeling their advantage, were not prone to accept the outstretched hand.   The Amalgamated Association of Iron and Steel Workers had ordered that none of its members should belong to the Knights of Labor after April 1, 1888.[51]   At the convention of the American Federation of Labour in December, 1887, a report was adopted which said: " The attitude of the Knights of Labor towards many of the trades unions connected with the American Federation of Labor has been anything but friendly. . . . While we agree that a conflict is not desirable on our part, we also believe that the party or power which seeks to exterminate the trades unions of the country should be met with unrelenting opposition, whether that power consists of millionaire employers or men who title themselves Knights of Labor." [52]   Gompers, in the presidential report, recalled that the Knights of Labor had been present at the Pittsburgh convention in 1881, where the Federation of Organised Trades and Labor Unions had been established, and added: " Let us hope that the near future will bring them back to the fold, so that all having the grand purposes in view, as understood and advocated by the American Federation of Labor, may work for their realisation." [53]

THE SUBSIDENCE OF THE KNIGHTS

As a basis for this hope Gompers said: " It is noticeable that a great reaction and a steady disintegration is going on in most all organisations of labor which are not formed upon the basis that the experience of past failures teaches, namely, the benevolent as well as the protective features in the unions." [54]

He was not in the least exaggerating.   At the end of 1887 the disintegration in the Knights of Labor had reached an advanced stage.   The tide of the uprising, which in half a year had carried the Order from 150,000 to over 700,000 members, began to ebb before the beginning of 1887 and the membership had diminished to 510,351 by July 1.   While a share of this

51 Chicago *Labor Enquirer*, June 25, 1887.

52 American Federation of Labor, *Proceedings*, 1887, pp. 25, 26.

53 *Ibid.*, 11.

54 *Ibid.*

retrogression may have been due to the natural reaction of large masses of people who had been suddenly set in motion without experience, a more immediate cause came from the employers. Profiting by the lessons of May, they organised strong associations and began a policy of discriminations and lockouts, directed mainly against the Knights. "Since May last," said John Swinton in September, "many corporations and Employers' Associations have been resorting to all sorts of unusual expedients to break up the labor organisations whose strength has become so great within the past two or three years. Sometimes they attack them in the front, but more often on the flanks or in the rear. Sometimes they make an assault in force, and sometimes lay siege to the works; but more often they seek to carry their point by petty subterfuges that can be carried on for a long time without arousing resistance." [55]

The form of organisation of these employers' associations clearly indicated that their main object was the defeat of the Knights. They were organised sectionally and nationally, but the opposing force, the district assembly, operated over only a limited area. In small localities, where the power of the Knights was especially great, all employers regardless of industry joined in one association. But in large manufacturing centres, where the rich corporation prevailed, they included the employers of only one industry as, for instance, the association of shoe manufacturers of Worcester County, Massachusetts, or the Manufacturing Knit Goods Association of New York State.[56] An exception to this rule was the state employers' association in Rhode Island, which was a general association.

The common object of these associations was to eradicate whatever form of organisation existed among the wage-earners. For instance, the association of shirt manufacturers of Jamesburg, New Jersey, locked out 2,000 employés when it was discovered that they had joined the Knights.[57] Likewise the manufacturers of silver goods of New York, Brooklyn, and Providence formed an association and locked out 1,200 men for joining the Knights.[58] It is therefore not surprising that the

[55] *John Swinton's Paper*, Sept. 5, 1886.
[56] Philadelphia *Journal of United Labor*, Jan. 22, 1887, and Apr. 2, 1887.
[57] New Jersey Bureau of Labor, *Report*, 1886, p. 200.
[58] Philadelphia *Journal of United Labor*, Apr. 30, 1887.

associations generally refused to negotiate with the Order and to arbitrate disputes. In an appeal for aid issued by the Knights of Labor in 1886, instances where employers refused to negotiate were cited in Georgia, Massachusetts, Delaware, Montana, Pennsylvania, Maryland, New Jersey, and Mississippi.[59] Out of 76 attempts at arbitration investigated by the Illinois Bureau of Labour, 38 offers were rejected — 6 by labour and 32 by capital.[60] The New York commissioner of labour affirmed that the irreconcilable attitude of the employers was " the first obstacle in the way of successful introduction of arbitration." [61] Trade agreements, where they were entered into, were held no more sacred by the employers than by the rank and file of the Knights. For instance, the association of leather manufacturers of Newark, New Jersey, which had entered into a trade agreement with the leather workers' council of the Knights, selected one of its members to violate it, assisted him in the hire of strike-breakers, turned over to him a large portion of the work of the other members, and forthwith ordered a systematic discharge of the organised men.[62]

Other important elements in this policy of repression were the blacklist, the " iron-clad," and the use of Pinkerton detectives. The following is a typical case. The Champion Reaper Company of Springfield, Ohio, locked out its 1,200 employés upon discovering that they were members of the Knights, and, with the exception of a small number who were blacklisted, the remainder were permitted to return to work upon signing an " iron-clad " oath never to belong to a labour organisation. The common use of the blacklist is confirmed by the bureaus of labour of Ohio, Connecticut, Pennsylvania, and New Jersey.

The Pinkerton detectives, who had first begun to specialise in labour disputes during the seventies, now became an almost indispensable factor. A confidential circular sent around by the Pinkerton agency to employers, announced that " corporations or individuals desirous of ascertaining the feeling of their employees, and whether they are likely to engage in strikes or

---

[59] Circular entitled *Appeal for Aid* (Philadelphia, Sept. 10, 1886).

[60] Illinois Bureau of Labor, *Report*, 1886, p. 419.

[61] New York Bureau of Labor, *Report*, 1885, p. 366.

[62] Philadelphia *Journal of United Labor*, Sept. 24, 1887. This is corroborated by accounts in local papers.

are joining any secret labor organisations with a view of compelling terms from corporations or employers, can obtain, on application to the superintendent of either of the offices, a detective suitable to associate with their employees and obtain this information." [63]

Notwithstanding the wide-spread and bitter hostility between the employers and the Knights, the movement resulted in a considerable number of trade agreements with employers' associations and with individual employers. The national officers of the Order strongly urged the idea of conciliation and trade agreement. In 1885 they induced the General Assembly to declare in favour of compulsory arbitration.[64] Ralph Beaumont, chief lobbyist for the Order before Congress, explained the long-continued and steady demand for the incorporation of trade unions on the ground that it would give the Order a legal right to speak for its members in the proceedings of compulsory arbitration.[65] It is true that, when, following the Southwest and eight-hour strikes, the leaders realised that public opinion had turned against the Knights, the demand for compulsory arbitration was rescinded.[66] Still there can be no better proof of the strong partiality of the leaders in the Order for trade agreements.

Trade agreements multiplied, especially beginning with 1887. They generally provided for the recognition of the Order and of the authority of its chosen committees, prohibited discrimination against Knights, and obligated the employer to submit to arbitration in the case of disagreement with his employés. They included no closed-shop provision, and the employer retained the right to discharge Knights for any good cause, except incompetence, in which case he had to arbitrate. Other agreements also included specific provisions for wages and hours.

However, the trade agreement was the exception; the rule was the strike and the lock-out.

The control over strikes was an important question for the organisation. As in previous years, contributions to the " de-

63 This circular fell into the hands of Joseph R. Buchanan, who made it public. Philadelphia *Journal of United Labor*, Nov. 25, 1885.

64 General Assembly, *Proceedings*, 1885, p. 164.

65 Philadelphia *Journal of United Labor*, Sept. 10, 1887.

66 General Assembly, *Proceedings*, Special Session, 1886, p. 41.

fence" fund were compulsory, and each district assembly administered the fund separately. Each one, however, was liable to an assessment by the General Executive Board for the relief of any district assembly whose funds had been exhausted by reason of lockouts or strikes.[67] But this provision was in no case carried out, for each district assembly had its fund constantly depleted by its own strikes. The complete control of strikes by district assemblies was at once a source of strength and of weakness for the Order; of strength, because the local freedom to strike aided the extension of the organisation; of weakness, because it prevented concentrated efforts by the Order as a whole. But prior to the great mass movement of 1886, the dark side of local strike autonomy was not yet obvious. The Order was more careful in the matter of the boycott. Absolute local autonomy in boycotting stood more open to abuse than it did in striking, since the boycott had a tendency to spread beyond local limits and was inexpensive to its originators. So in 1885, the General Executive Board was given jurisdiction over all boycotts that were not strictly local. The General Assembly adopted a rule providing that as long as a boycott affected no one outside of the territory of a local, district, or state assembly, these respective units should retain "the privilege to institute a boycott." In all other cases the approval of the general executive board was made imperative.[68]

The disputes during the second half of 1886 ended, for the most part, disastrously to labour. The number of men involved in 7 months, as estimated by *Bradstreet's,* was 97,300. Of these, about 75,300 were in 9 great lockouts, of whom 54,000 suffered defeat[69] at the hands of associated employers. The most important lockouts were against 15,000 laundry workers at Troy, New York, in June, 20,000 Chicago packing-house workers, and 20,000 knitters at Cohoes and Amsterdam, New York, both in October.

[67] General Assembly *Constitution* (1884), Art. XV, Sec. 5.

[68] General Assembly, *Proceedings,* 1885, p. 162.

[69] Exclusive of the small disputes which *Bradstreet's* did not tabulate. The total number of strikers in 1886, as given by *Bradstreet's,* was 448,000, and of the locked-out, 80,000, but these figures were raised to 499,489 for strikers and 101,980 for lockouts in the reports of the Federal department of labor. However, *Bradstreet's* figures are summarised by months and are accompanied by a more or less detailed description of the disputes, and are, therefore, to be preferred for the present use. *Bradstreet's,* Jan. 8, 1887.

The Troy lockout grew out of a strike on May 15, 1886, for higher wages by 180 women. These women had been organised shortly before as the "Joan of Arc" assembly of the Knights of Labor. Immediately the employers, who sensed in this demand the beginning of a general movement, united in a manufacturers' association and, on May 18, declared a general lockout against the members of the Knights of Labor. Although only one-sixth of those employed in the industry were Knights, the others left work. After five weeks, General Secretary Hayes accepted the price list presented by the manufacturers' association and the lockout and strike were called off.[70]

The lockout in the knit goods industry at Amsterdam and Cohoes, New York, arose on the ground that an apprentice had been promoted to take charge of a new machine. There existed a contract previously entered into by Barry, of the executive board of the Knights of Labor, and the trade manufacturers' association of fifty-eight leading firms, which provided for the open shop and gave to the employer the unlimited right of discharging and promoting men. However, the district master workman of District Assembly 104 declared that his assembly had not been a party to the agreement, and, notwithstanding Powderly's injunction, declared a strike against the mill. This immediately led to a general lockout of the Knights, October 16. Barry and T. B. McGuire, the latter of District Assembly 49, took charge of the dispute and succeeded for over five months in preventing a large portion of the locked-out from going back to work on the conditions prescribed by the employers. Early in May, 1887, the strike was declared off.[71]

More wide-spread attention than either the Troy or Cohoes lockout was attracted by the lockout of 20,000 Chicago butcher workmen. These men had obtained the eight-hour day without a strike during May. A short time thereafter, upon the initiative of Armour & Company, the employers formed a packers' association and, in the beginning of October, notified the men of a return to the ten-hour day on October 11. They justified this action on the ground that they could not compete with Cincinnati and Kansas City, which operated on the ten-hour system.

On October 8, the men, who were organised in District Assemblies 27 and 54, suspended work, and the memorable lockout began. The negotiations were conducted by T. P. Barry, who had been especially commissioned by the General Assembly then in session in Richmond, and M. J. Butler, the master workman of District Assembly 54. The packers' association, however, rejected all offers of compromise and, October 18, Barry ordered the men to work on the ten-hour basis. But the dispute in October, which was marked by a complete lack of ill feeling on the part of the men and was one of the most peaceable labour disputes of the year, was in reality a mere prelude to a second disturbance which broke out in the plant of Swift & Company, on November 2, and became general throughout the stock yards on November 6. The men demanded a return to the eight-hour day, but the packers' association, which was not joined by Swift & Company, who formerly had kept aloof, not only refused to give up the ten-hour day, but declared that they would employ no Knights of Labor in the future. The Knights retaliated by declaring a boycott on the meat of Armour & Company. The behaviour of the men was now no longer peaceable, as before, and the employers took extra precautions by prevailing upon the governor to send two regiments of militia in addition to the several hundred Pinkerton detectives employed by the association. To all appearances, the men were slowly gaining over the employers, for, on November 10, the packers' association rescinded its decision not to employ Knights, when suddenly on November 15, like a thunderbolt out of a clear sky, a telegram arrived from Powderly ordering the men back to work. Powderly had refused to consider the reports from Barry and Carlton, the members of the General Executive Board who were on the ground, but, as was charged by Barry, was guided instead by the advice of a priest who had appealed to him to call off the strike and thus put an end to the suffering of the men and their families.[72]

The outcome of the Chicago packing-house lockout not only aided materially in reducing the organisation in Chicago, but it had a demoralising effect elsewhere. It taught the lesson that the centralised form of government in the Order, which meant

[72] Compiled from the Chicago *Times* and other general papers; also *John Swinton's Paper*, Nov. 14, 1886; the Denver *Labor Enquirer*, Nov. 20 and 27, and Dec. 25, 1886.

practically a one-man government, was bound up with the greatest danger. Powderly did not possess the aggressive qualifications required for a successful leader in strikes. His eight-hour circular, his telegram in the Chicago lockout, and his later refusal to allow the Order to plead for mercy for the condemned Chicago anarchists,[73] show that, in his reverence for public opinion and especially the opinion of the general press, he had come to overlook the sentiments of the masses whom he led. At a time when his organisation was coming to the front as the fighting organisation of a new class, he endeavoured to play the diplomatist rather than the fighting general.

The Chicago packers' lockout showed in an unfavourable light the centralised form of government. It remained for the great New York strike in January, 1887, to reveal the drawbacks and inefficiency of the mixed district assembly.

The strike began as two separate strikes, one by coal handlers at the Jersey ports supplying New York with coal, and the other by 'longshoremen on the New York water front, both starting on January 1, 1887. Eighty-five coal handlers employed by the Philadelphia & Reading Railroad Company, members of the Knights of Labor, struck against a reduction of 2½ cents an hour in the wages of the "top-men," and were joined by the trimmers with grievances of their own. Soon the strike spread to the other roads, and the number of striking coal-handlers reached 3,000. The 'longshoremen's strike was begun by 200 men, employed by the Old Dominion Steamship Company, against a reduction in wages and the hiring of cheap men by the week. The strikers were not organised, but the Ocean Association, Knights of Labor, took up their case and was assisted by the 'longshoremen's union. Both strikes soon widened out through a series of sympathetic strikes of related trades and finally became united into one. The Ocean Association, Knights of Labor, declared a boycott on the freight of the Old Dominion Company, and this was strictly obeyed by all of the 'longshoremen's unions. The International Boatmen's Union refused to allow their boats to be used for "scab coal" or to permit their members to steer the companies' boats. The

73 At the General Assembly of the Knights of Labor at Minneapolis held in October, 1887.

'longshoremen joined the boatmen in refusing to handle coal,
and the shovellers followed.   Then the grain handlers on both
floating and stationary elevators refused to load ships with grain
on which there was scab coal, and the bag-sewers stood with
them.   The 'longshoremen now resolved to go out and refused
to work on ships which received scab coal, and finally they decided to stop work altogether on all kinds of craft in the harbour
until the trouble should be settled.   The strike spirit spread to
a large number of freight handlers working for railroads along
the river front, so that in the last week of January the number
of strikers in New York, Brooklyn, and New Jersey reached
approximately 28,000: 13,000 'longshoremen, 1,000 boatmen,
6,000 grain handlers, 7,500 coal-handlers, and 400 bag-sewers.
Master Workman Quinn, with his *aides de camp* in District
Assembly 49, was in complete control of the strike from the beginning and had the active sympathy of the Central Labor
Union and the trade unions.

On February 11, August Corbin, president and receiver of
the Philadelphia & Reading Railroad Company, fearing a strike
by the miners working in the coal mines operated by that road,
settled with District Assembly 49 and restored to the eighty-
five coal-handlers, the original strikers, their former rate of
wages.   District Assembly 49 felt impelled to accept such a
trivial settlement for two reasons.   The coal strike, which drove
up the price of coal to the consumer, was very unpopular, and
the strike itself had begun to weaken when the brewers and stationary engineers had refused to come out on the demand of
the assembly.   The situation was thus unchanged, as far as the
coal handlers employed by the other companies, the 'longshoremen, and the many thousands of men who went out on sympathetic strike, were concerned.   The men began to return to
work by the thousands and the entire strike collapsed.[74]   Swinton attributed the failure to the grave blundering of the committee leaders in District Assembly 49, who, instead of calling
out the railroad men and thus stopping all traffic at once, ordered out the engineers and brewers, who could help but little
and stood to sacrifice their agreements with their employers.
Although Swinton ordinarily refrained from taking sides in the

[74] New York Bureau of Labor, *Report*, 1887, pp. 327–385.

internal fights of the labour movement, he summarised the outcome of this strike as follows: [75]   " We do most sincerely regret the unfortunate collapse of the great strikes along shore. . . . We are not surprised to hear of the deep and wide dissatisfaction with those braggarts and bunglers who so often forced themselves to the front as ' strike managers ' for District Assembly 49, and whose final subterfuges were the laughing stock of the satanic press; but it is to be regretted that the powerful District must be made to suffer through such obtrusive incompetency as we have seen.   We trust that the organised labor of New York will never again be damaged as it has been by such displays.   Tens of thousands of poor men made sacrifices during the strike, without either whining or boasting."

The determined attack and stubborn resistance of the employers' associations after the strikes of May, 1886, coupled with the incompetence displayed by the leaders, caused the turn of the tide in the labour movement in the first half of 1887.   This, however, manifested itself during 1887 exclusively in the large cities, where the movement had borne in the purest form the character of an uprising of the class of the unskilled and where the hardest battles were fought with the employers.   District Assembly 49, New York, fell from its membership of 60,809, in June, 1886, to 32,826 in July, 1887.   During the same interval, District Assembly 1, Philadelphia, decreased from 51,557 to 11,294 and District Assembly 30 Boston, from 81,197 to 31,644.   In Chicago there were about 40,000 Knights immediately before the packers' strike in October, 1886, and only about 17,000 on July 1, 1887.   The falling off of the largest district assemblies in 10 large cities practically equalled the total loss of the Order, which amounted approximately to 191,000, of whom not more than 20,000 [76] can be accounted for as having withdrawn to trade assemblies, national or district.   At the same time the membership of the smallest district assemblies, which were for the most part located in small cities, remained stationary and, outside of the national and district trade assemblies which were formed by separation from mixed district assemblies, thirty-seven new district assemblies were formed,

[75] *John Swinton's Paper*, Feb. 20, 1887.
[76] The total membership of the national   and the district trade assemblies in July, 1887, reached over 50,000.

also mostly in small localities. In addition, state assemblies were added in Alabama, Florida, Georgia, Indiana, Kansas, Mississippi, Nebraska, North Carolina, Ohio, West Virginia, and Wisconsin, with an average membership of about 2,000 each. Balancing these new extensions, however, was a decrease from 122,027 to 61,936 in the total membership of the local assemblies directly affiliated with the General Assembly.[77]

It thus becomes clear that, by the middle of 1887, the Great Upheaval of the unskilled and semi-skilled portions of the working class had already subsided beneath the strength of the combined employers and the centralisation and unwieldiness of their own organisation. After 1887 the Knights of Labor lost their hold upon the large cities with their wage-conscious and largely foreign population, and became an organisation predominantly of country people, of mechanics, small merchants, and farmers, an element more or less purely American and decidedly middle-class in its philosophy. This change serves, more than anything else, to account for the subsequent close affiliation between the Order and the " Farmers' Alliance," as well as for the whole-hearted support which it gave to the People's party.

In contrast to the Knights of Labor, the trade unions met with some success in strikes and lockouts. The great lockout of the building trades in Chicago, May, 1887, although it ended in defeat, nevertheless showed the superiority of the trade union form of organisation. It came about when the bricklayers' union, without consulting the employers, adopted a resolution providing for the payment of wages at the end of each week and

---

[77] The following shows the decrease in membership in good standing of ten district assemblies from July, 1886, to July, 1887:

No. of D. A.	Name of City	Membership, July 1, '86	Membership, July 1, '87	Decrease
1	Philadelphia	51,557	11,294	40,263
24	Chicago	12,868	10,483	2,385
30	Boston	81,191	31,644	49,547
41	Baltimore	18,297	7,549	10,748
49	New York City	60,809	32,826	27,983
51	Newark	10,958	4,766	6,192
77	Lynn, Mass.	10,838	2,450	8,388
86	Portland	19,493	4,930	14,563
95	Hartford	14,148	5,622	8,526
99	Providence	11,512	1,735	9,777

Total decrease 178,372

Proceedings, 1886, pp. 326–328, and *Proceedings*, 1887, pp. 1847–1850.

on Saturday. This trivial demand, coming as one among many manifestations of the tyrannical policy pursued by the union, served to unite all associations of employers in the city and they ordered a general lockout of all the building trades, affecting 30,000 men.[78] The bricklayers' union had considered itself so strongly entrenched that it not only had refused to affiliate with the building trades' council of the city, but also had regarded its affiliation with the Bricklayers' International Union as an "entangling alliance." It was obliged to go into the struggle practically single-handed. On the other hand there was perfect unanimity among the employers. The Illinois Association of Architects and the material-men's association acted together with the other masters' associations in support of the master masons' association. The lockout lasted from May 10 to June 11, and ended in the defeat of the union, which was obliged to give up the closed shop. But the most important outcome was a written trade agreement providing for the regular annual election of a standing committee of arbitration with full power to "hear all evidence in complaint and grievances . . . and which shall finally decide all questions submitted, and shall certify by the umpire such decisions to the respective organisations "; and, further, " work shall go on continuously, and all parties interested shall be governed by the award made or decisions rendered." [79]   This system remained in vogue until 1897.

The Chicago lockout was materially helped by the national association of builders, a federation of builders' exchanges embracing general contractors, sub-contractors, and material-men, which had been established through the efforts of William H. Sayward of Boston, in January, 1887, avowedly as a result of the aggressive movement of the unions in the building trades during 1886. The strongest evidence of the progress made by these unions may be found in the attitude of the National Association of Builders. While it expressly declared in the preamble against the closed shop, it urged at the same time the policy of recognising the unions.[80]   Contrast with this the ir-

---

78 The carpenters had shortly before gained the eight-hour day with reduced wages and 3,000 hod-carriers were still on strike for higher wages.

79 Second Annual Convention of National Association of Builders of America, *Proceedings*, 1888, p. 21.

80 *Ibid.*, 1887, p. 110.

reconcilable attitude of the employers who formed associations in the industries organised by the Knights of Labor. While the superiority of the position of the building trades' union was largely due to the intrinsic advantages of the industry, such as the absence of national competition between employers and the high skill demanded from the employés, still the trade union form of organisation could but gain in the esteem of the labouring masses.

Another instance of the rather tentative success of trade unionism in achieving a trade agreement system occurred in the bituminous mining industry.[81] During the early eighties the miners in what is known as the central competitive field [82] were organised either as assemblies of the Knights of Labor or as state unions, but all of these were of short duration and succumbed after strikes. The miners in this region were still in the main English-speaking or had come from North European countries. The leaders of the miners' unions thoroughly understood the necessity for organisation upon a national scale. In the general assemblies of the Knights of Labor in 1880 and 1881 an unsuccessful effort was made to secure the appointment of a special salaried organiser for the coal miners of the country. In 1883 the General Assembly made provision for such an organiser. Finally, in 1885, the National Federation of Miners and Mine Laborers of the United States was formed at a convention attended by delegates from local unions in Pennsylvania, West Virginia, Ohio, Indiana, Illinois, Iowa, and Kansas. It was an organisation independent of the Knights of Labor and was brought into existence through the refusal by the General Executive Board to allow the coal miners to form a national trade assembly.[83] Within a year after the organisation of this federation, the Knights of Labor chartered a national trade assembly of the coal miners, known as National Trade Assembly 135.[84] The miners had desired the establish-

81 In the following account of the early trade agreement system in the bituminous mining industry the author drew largely from an unpublished monograph by E. E. Witte, *Unionism Among Coal Miners in the United States, 1880–1910.*

82 Includes western Pennsylvania, West Virginia, Ohio, Indiana, Illinois, and, in a less recognised degree, also Michigan, southeast Kentucky, and Iowa. During the eighties, Pennsylvania produced one-half of the total bituminous coal mined in the country, Ohio was second, and Illinois, Maryland, Missouri, West Virginia, Iowa, Indiana, and Kentucky followed in the order named.

83 United Mine Workers, *Proceedings,* 1911, I, 581.

84 Roy, *History of the Coal Miners,* 263.

ment of a national union, because, as stated in the preamble to the constitution of the national federation, " neither district nor State unions can regulate the markets to which their coal is shipped." [85]   In 1886, however, they had not one but two unions claiming national jurisdiction. In most mining districts both organisations were represented, yet, in spite of their intense rivalry, the two co-operated in a sufficient measure to become joint parties to an interstate trade agreement with the mine operators in a conference at Columbus, Ohio, January, 1886. This conference was attended by operators from Pennsylvania, Ohio, Indiana, and Illinois, and perhaps, also from West Virginia.[86] Representatives of the miners were present from all these States, and also from Maryland.

As a result of the deliberations of this conference an interstate agreement was drawn up between the miners and the operators, covering the wages which were to prevail throughout the central competitive field from May 1, 1886, to April 30, 1887. The scale established would seem to have been dictated by the wish to give the markets of the central competitive field to the Ohio operators.[87]   That Ohio was favoured in the scale established by this first interstate conference can be explained by the fact that more than half of the operators present came from Ohio, and that the chief strength of the miners' union, also, lay in that State. To prevent friction over the interpretation of the interstate agreement, a board of arbitration and conciliation was established.[88] This board consisted of 5 miners and 5 operators chosen at large, and 1 miner and 1 operator from each of the States of this field. Such a board of arbitration and conciliation was provided for in all of the interstate agreements of the period of the eighties. During the entire period of the existence of this board, its secretary was Chris Evans, who served, also, in the same capacity for the miners' union. This system of interstate trade agreement, in spite of the cutthroat competition raging between operators, was maintained for Pennsylvania and Ohio practically until 1890, Illinois having been lost in 1887, and Indiana, in 1888. It formed

85 U. S. Bureau of Labor, *Eleventh Special Report* on " Regulation and Restriction of Output," 386.

86 Roy, *History of the Coal Miners*, 256.

87 This conclusion is based upon the scale of mining rates for the year printed in the report on the " Regulation and Restriction of Output," 387.

88 *American   Federationist*, August, 1894, p. 115.

the real predecessor of the system established in 1898 and in vogue at the present time.

The apparent superiority of the trade union form of organisation over the mixed organisation, as revealed by events in 1886 and 1887, strengthened the tendency on the part of the more skilled and better organised trades in the Knights of Labor to separate themselves from the mixed district assemblies and to create national trade assemblies. Just as the struggle between the Knights of Labor and the trade unions on the outside had been fundamentally a struggle between the unskilled and the skilled portions of the wage-earning class, so the aspiration toward the national trade assembly within the Order represented the effort of the more or less skilled men for emancipation from the dominance of the unskilled. The ups and downs of the struggle bear out this conclusion.

Prior to 1884 several national trade assemblies existed under the guise either of a local assembly, such as Local Assembly 300, which, as we have seen, was a national organisation of window-glass workers admitted in 1880, or of a trade district, as for instance, District Assembly 45, the national union of telegraphers which became affiliated in 1883. During 1884, shortly before the rush of the unskilled into the Order, the ideas of the skilled men were gradually receiving recognition. In accordance with this the General Assembly of 1884 specifically authorised the formation of national trade assemblies. During the next year, however, with the predominance acquired by the unskilled, the policy changed. Powderly in his address at the General Assembly in 1885, said: "I do not favour the establishment of any more National Trade Districts; they are a step backward in the direction of the old form of trade union. . . . We should discourage them in the future." [89]

So it continued until the defeat of the mixed district assemblies or, in other words, of the unskilled class, in the struggle with the employers. With the withdrawal of a very large portion of this class, as shown by the membership figures for 1887, the demand for the national trade assembly revived, and there soon began a veritable rush to organise by trades. The stampede was strongest in the city of New York where the incompe-

[89] General Assembly, *Proceedings*, 1885, p. 25.

tence of the mixed District Assembly 49 had become patent. At the General Assembly in 1887, 22 national trade and district assemblies were represented with a total membership of over 52,000 (out of 511,000), of which number 21,230 were coal miners organised in National Trade Assembly 135 and over 17,000 were distributed among the various organisations in New York and Brooklyn.[90] The report of the New Jersey Bureau of Labor for 1887 enumerates the following trades in the Knights of Labor organised as national trade assemblies: axe and edge tool makers, bookbinders, cigar makers, file makers, garment cutters, hatters, iron and steel workers, leather workers, lithographers, machinery constructors, miners, painters, paper hangers, plumbers, gas and steam-fitters, potters, seamen, silk workers, surface railroad men, steam railroad employés, glass blowers, shoemakers, stationary engineers and firemen, textile workers, and printers.[91]

All these national and district trade assemblies had been organised under the rules adopted in 1884, which merely provided that the General Executive Board " may " grant the permission, and furthermore that each local assembly must obtain from the district assembly to which it belongs the permission to join a national trade assembly. At the General Assembly in 1887 at Minneapolis, the rules were amended in the sense that it was made obligatory upon the General Executive Board to grant such a permission, and the consent of the district assembly was not only no longer required, but it was even made compulsory upon all local trade assemblies to withdraw from the mixed district and to enter the national trade assembly as soon as one was established in a particular trade. The national trade assembly was also given full authority in the matter of initiation fee, strikes, apprenticeship regulations, etc., limited only by the provisions of the general constitution of the Order.[92]

Thus the claims of the skilled men finally achieved full recognition from the Knights of Labor, and P. J. McGuire was not far from right when he asserted in October, 1887, that " the Knights of Labor are now taking lessons from the Trade

90 General Assembly, *Proceedings*, 1887, pp. 1847–1850.
91 New Jersey Bureau of Labor, *Report*, 1887, p. 9.
92 General Assembly, *Proceedings*, 1887, p. 1800.

Unions, and are forming themselves on National Trade District lines, which are simply the skeletons of trade unions without either their flesh or blood." [93]   He would not have been wrong had he predicted that the national trade assemblies would soon break away from the Order.

[93] *Carpenter*, October, 1887, p. 4.

CHAPTER XI

THE FAILURE OF CO-OPERATION, 1884–1887

Attitude towards co-operation of the several component elements of the Knights of Labor, 430. The inheritance from the sixties, 430. Powderly's attitude, 431. Co-operation in the early eighties, 431. Centralised co-operation, 432. Change to decentralised co-operation, 432. Statistics and nature of the co-operative enterprises, 433. Sectional distribution, 434. Co-operation among the coopers in Minneapolis, 434. The General Co-operative Board, 435. John Samuel, 435. Difficulties of the Board, 436. Participation by the Order, 436. The failure of the movement, 437. Its causes, 437. The lesson for the future, 438.

ALTHOUGH strikes and boycotts undoubtedly were the chief recruiting activities of the Knights, the deliberately planned policy of the Order, as a whole, was directed chiefly to co-operation. Occupying, as it did the foreground in the official programme of the Order, co-operation had also the additional merit of being well suited to the period of industrial depression when strikes were failing. The new and unskilled membership, though interested only in industrial warfare against employers, had no desire to quarrel with the official philosophy of the organisation to which it looked for economic salvation.

The active champions of co-operation, however, came from the older membership. Among these, first in importance were the machine-menaced mechanics, notably the machinists and shoemakers, whose national trade organisations of the sixties and seventies had disappeared. They furnished the national leaders, such as Powderly, formerly a member of the machinists' and blacksmiths' national union, and Beaumont and Litchman, former members of the order of the Knights of St. Crispin. They also supplied the official philosophy of the Order. In their control they formed in every way the connecting link between the movement in the eighties and that of the trade unions of the sixties. The trade unionist of the sixties had been by nature a small employer rather than a wage-earner. He had not only aspired to become an employer in the future, but, in many instances, he actually employed unskilled helpers for wages. It was, therefore, natural that he should have favoured measures, such as cheap money and co-operation, which he thought would help in raising him up to the status of employer. On this account he was willing to extend political aid to the farmers, for he felt that he belonged potentially, if not actually, to the class of independent producers. These ideas of the sixties were carried over to the eighties by the leaders of the Knights. They found ready response among the small-town skilled mechanics and purely middle-class elements, represented by the small merchants, petty employers, and farmers, who had succeeded in finding their way into the Order.

Powderly, in each of his reports to the General Assembly, consistently urged that practical steps be taken toward co-operation.[1] The movers for co-operation had witnessed the downfall of the decentralised productive co-operation of the sixties, and the plan now espoused was a centralised one. Its motto was: "Co-operation of the Order, by the Order and for the Order." It started out with the organisation of consumers to create a market for the productive establishments that were to follow. The entire undertaking was to be financed from the dues of the membership of the Order, and, of course, was to be under its control.[2]

Notwithstanding the exhortations by Powderly, the Order was slow in taking up co-operation. In 1882 a general co-operative board was elected to work out a plan of action, but it never reported, and a new board was chosen in its place at the assembly of 1883. In that year, the first practical step was taken in the purchase by the Order of a coal mine at Cannelburg, Indiana, with the idea of selling the coal at reduced prices to the members.[3]

Soon, however, a thorough change of sentiment with regard to the whole matter of co-operation took place, contemporaneously with the industrial depression and the great and unsuccessful strikes. The rank and file, which had hitherto been indifferent, now seized upon the idea with enthusiasm. A member of Local Assembly 1279, West Virginia, writes: "Co-

[1] See above, II, 351.
[2] General Assembly, *Proceedings*, 1884, p. 601.
[3] *Ibid.*, 625–640.

operation is what we want, as strikes have proved a failure here and broke up our Order very near every time. The members here are tired of strikes, they want to try something else." [4]

The Illinois commissioner of labour writes that wage-earners "are not infrequently forced into [co-operation] . . . by reason of discriminations against them by employers. Especially is this true of productive enterprises, many of which are the direct result of unsuccessful strikes and the blacklisting which has followed them. . . ." [5] The enthusiasm ran so high in Lynn, Massachusetts, that it was found necessary to raise the shares of the Knights of Labor Co-operative Shoe Company to $100 in order to prevent a large influx of "unsuitable members." [6] In 1885 Powderly complained that "many of our members grow impatient and unreasonable because every avenue of the Order does not lead to co-operation." [7]

The demand for immediate attempts at co-operation, which manifested itself about this time among the rank and file in practically every section of the country, caused an important modification in the official doctrine of the Order. Under the older plan of centralised action, it would have taken years before a large portion of the membership could realise any considerable benefit. This was now dropped and the decentralised plan was adopted. Local assemblies and, more frequently groups of members with the financial aid of their assembly, now began to establish work shops, and, to a lesser extent, stores. Most of the enterprises were managed by the stockholders, although, in some cases, the assemblies managed the plants. One notable illustration of management by the organisation was that of District Assembly 49, New York. The management was conducted with the utmost secrecy. The holders of shares were not given either a voice or a vote. The money was invested by a committee chosen by District Assembly 49. No interest was paid on the stock, but the shares were to be redeemed in the course of time and the ownership of the plant to remain with the employés. On the basis of this

---

[4] Philadelphia *Journal of United Labor*, Jan. 1, 1884.

[5] Illinois Bureau of Labor, *Report*, 1886, p. 461.

[6] Bemis, "Co-operation in New England," in *Johns Hopkins University Studies*, 1886, VI, 87.

[7] General Assembly, *Proceedings*, 1885, p. 22.

plan, District Assembly 49 formed the Solidarity Co-operative Association of the Knights of Labor, which association sold shares without designating in what industry the money would be invested. The committee on co-operation invested the money as it saw fit. With this power, the committee sought to establish a complete co-operative scheme, and they financed a cigar factory, fancy leather goods shop, plumbing shop, publishing association, printing shop, watch-case factory, building association, marketing association, etc.[8] The plan was worked out by Victor Drury, a Frenchman, who had migrated as a refugee after the Paris Commune in 1871. As a former Blanquist, he retained a strong predilection for secrecy. He was also responsible for the secret " Home Club " which ruled District Assembly 49.

Most of the co-operative enterprises were conducted on a small scale. Incomplete statistics warrant the conclusion that the average amount invested per establishment was about $10,-000.[9] From the data gathered it seems that co-operation reached its highest point in 1886, although it had not completely spent itself by the end of 1887.[10] The largest number of ventures were in mining, cooperage, and shoes. These industries paid the poorest wages and their employés were the most harshly treated. A comparatively small amount of capital was required to organise such establishments.

[8] Bemis, " Co-operation in the Middle States," in *Johns Hopkins University Studies*, 1888, VI, 162.

[9] Illinois Bureau of Labor, *Report*, 1886, pp. 457–460.

[10] Following is an incomplete list of the co-operative ventures of this period:

Mining	22	Laundries	2
Coopers	15	Carpets	1
Shoes	14	Bakers	1
Clothing	8	Leather	1
Foundries	8	Leather goods	1
Soap	6	Plumbing	1
Furniture workers	5	Harness	1
Cigar	5	Watch case	1
Glass	5	Pipes	1
Knitting	3	Brass works	1
Nail mills	3	Pottery	1
Tobacco	3	Wagon	1
Planing mills	3	Refining	1
Tailoring	2	Caskets	1
Hats	2	Brooms	1
Printing	2	Pottery	1
Agricultural implements	2	Ice	1
Painters	2	Packing	1
Matches	2		
Baking powder	2	Total	185
Carpentering	2		

The large majority of co-operative enterprises were located in the Central and Eastern States. Amos G. Warner, who in 1888 investigated co-operation in the Middle West, writes: ". . . the great majority of organised laborers in this section of the country believe in co-operation, and are making very practical and very vigorous efforts to help forward 'the cause.' "[11]

The movement was rather weak on the Pacific coast and in the Southern States. The lukewarmness toward co-operation on the Pacific coast is explained by Shinn, as follows: " The Pacific Coast states and territories have been so prosperous, and their immense natural resources have offered such unusual opportunities to individual labour, that the principles of co-operation have not made much headway as yet, and, perhaps, cannot for years to come. The working classes are far from being ready for such organisations." [12] With the exception of Maryland, the reason for the lack of a wide-spread movement toward co-operation in the South is accounted for by its late industrial development.[13]

Dr. Albert Shaw, who in 1888 personally investigated the co-operative movement of the coopers in Minneapolis, brings out its middle-class nature in the following words:

" It may be worth while to remark that co-operation is not a religion with these coopers. . . . One of them might withdraw with his savings and set himself up as the proprietor of a boss shop without the slightest twinge of conscience or the remotest chance of being charged with the sin of apostasy. . . . Any cooper is ready to bid farewell to his berth . . . when something better clearly presents itself. They believe heartily in co-operation, because the system benefits and elevates workingmen; but they are not on bad terms with society as they find it about them, and are entirely willing to step out of the ranks of handicraftsmen and wage-workers whenever opportunity permits. They recognise no impassable gulf severing industrial and social classes. Their advancement to the dignity of capitalists, employers or brain-workers, is not a repudiation of the co-operative system, but the highest possible compliment they could pay

11 Warner, " Three Phases of Co-operation in the West," in *Johns Hopkins University Studies*, 1888, VI, 395. Randall, " Co-operation in Maryland and the South," *ibid.*, 494, and Bemis, " Co-operation in the Middle States," *ibid.*, 86, show the existence of a similar enthusiasm for co-operation in those sections.

12 Shinn, " Co-operation on the Pacific Coast," in *Johns Hopkins University Studies*, 1888, VI, 447.

13 Randall, " Co-operation in Maryland and the South," *ibid.*, 489.

it. . . . So far as I know, the movement has never had a social philosopher or a hobby-riding ' reformer ' connected with it, and nobody who ever thought of idealising it into a cult." [14]

This characterisation applied fully to the few co-operative enterprises, which, like that of the coopers in Minneapolis, were already past the stage of the bare struggle for existence. The general movement, however, was idealistic, and aimed at broad social reform. Still, it is safe to say that the coopers had merely carried to the logical end what was the general tendency in all efforts toward productive co-operation.

With the spontaneous development of the co-operative movement in 1884, the rôle of the central authority of the Order changed correspondingly. The leading member of the General Co-operative Board was now John Samuel, whose ardour for decentralised productive co-operation had not been cooled by his experience with the movement during the sixties and seventies. The duty of the General Co-operative Board was to educate the members of the Order in the principles of co-operation, to aid by information and otherwise prospective or actual participators in co-operation; in brief, to co-ordinate the co-operative movement within the Order, as the central co-operative board of England was doing. Hence the board issued forms of constitution and laws which, with a few modifications, could be adopted by any locality. The board also published articles on the dangers and pitfalls in co-operative ventures, such as granting credit, poor management, etc., as well as numerous articles on specific kinds of co-operation.

In its effort to co-ordinate co-operation, the label of the Knights of Labor was granted for the use of co-operative goods,[15] and an agitation was steadily conducted to induce purchasers to give a preference to co-operative products.[16]

Perhaps the most delicate function of the Order was the granting of financial aid to local co-operative enterprises. This matter was left to the General Executive Board with the approval of the General Co-operative Board. No definite fund was established for this purpose, but it was within the power

14 *Ibid.*, 239.
15 General Assembly, *Proceedings*, 1886, p. 290.
16 *Ibid.*, 1887, pp. 1685, 1825.

of the General Executive Board to decide how much, and to whom, aid should be granted. Naturally, with co-operative projects planned throughout the country in time of depression, the appeals for help were overwhelmingly heavy. Although the requests were numerous, the Order granted aid in but a few instances, and only in cases where locked-out- and victimised members were involved. How insistent these demands became is clearly seen from the following characteristic notice issued by the secretary of the General Co-operative Board:

" The Co-operative Board would require the resources of some of our millionaires to be sufficient for the demands upon them; and the calls for a visit to see and examine this and that, from the Atlantic to the Pacific, would take the time of several Secretaries. Kind friends and dear brethren, this thing of expecting help in starting a carp pond, a dairy, or a machine shop, is a great mistake. The Co-operativé Fund would soon become a nuisance as well as a nonentity. Halt! Give us a rest, in the name of Brotherhood and humane charity. If you have printed plans of co-operative stores or shops, or other enterprises, send me a copy; if you have ideas of value, please forward them; or if you think the present co-operative law, as found in the Constitution, can be amended, send us your propositions. But do not look for aid such a long way from home. If your plans are feasible, the best place to look for help must be near home. Self-help is the surest as well as the best help. . . . I must respectfully give notice that I am utterly unable to grant help in any way to parties wishing loans from the Co-operative Fund." [17]

The co-operative movement reached such large proportions in 1886 and the demand for aid was so insistent that, in the session of 1886, $10,000 quarterly was set aside for the use of the General Co-operative Board.[18] This fund was never actually created or used, as the demands upon the Order for other purposes were too large. Another attempt to establish a fund was made in 1887, but by this time the general funds of the Order were' so depleted that the proposition was rejected.[19]

The Order also provided rules for the governing of co-operative enterprises, such as the safekeeping of funds, giving preference to members for employment, and division of profits.[20]

[17] Philadelphia *Journal of United Labor*, Apr. 25, 1886.
[18] General Assembly, *Proceedings*, 1886, p. 292.
[19] *Ibid.*, 1887, pp. 1750, 1753.
[20] *Constitution of the General Assembly*, 1886, Art. VIII, p. 16.

As a scheme of industrial regeneration, co-operation, as we know, never materialised. As a means of enabling some enterprising and ambitious wage-earners to become independent or self-employed, co-operation proved fairly successful. The form which the success took, however, proved detrimental to the very purpose for which co-operation was intended. It seems that the successful co-operative establishments sooner or later became joint stock companies.[21]

The causes which brought on the failure of most of the co-operative enterprises were many. Hasty action, the selection of inefficient managers, internal dissensions, lack of capital, injudicious borrowing of money at high rates of interest upon the mortgage of the plant, and finally discriminations instigated by competitors. Railroads were heavy offenders, by delaying side tracks, on some pretence or other, refusing to furnish cars, or refusing to haul them.[22] The Union Mining Company of Cannelburg, Indiana, owned and operated by the Order, as its sole experiment of the centralised kind, met this fate. After expending $20,000 in equipping the mines, purchasing land, laying tracks, cutting and sawing timber on the land, and mining $1,000 worth of coal, they were compelled to lie idle for nine months before the railroad company saw fit to connect their switch with the main track. When they were ready to ship their product, it was learned that their coal could be utilised for the manufacture of gas only, and that contracts for supply of such coal were let in July, nine months from the time of connecting the switch with the main track. In addition, the company was informed that it must supply itself with a switch-engine to do the switching of the cars from its mine to the main track, at an additional cost of $4,000. When this was accomplished they had to enter "the market in competition with a bitter opponent who has been fighting [them] since the opening of the mine." Having exhausted their funds and not seeing their way clear to secure additional funds for the purchase of a locomotive and to tide over the nine months before any contracts for coal could be entered into, they sold out.[23]

---

21 The famous co-operative coopers' shops in Minneapolis finally ended in this manner.

22 *Journal of United Labor*, Nov. 12, 1887.

23 General Assembly, *Proceedings*, 1885, p. 92.

Another form of opposition to which manufacturers resorted was that of pressure upon machinery manufacturers and wholesalers of raw material to prevent sales to the co-operators.[24]

Thus three or four years after it had first begun, the co-operative movement had passed the full cycle of life, and both the centralised and decentralised forms had succumbed.   The fact that it was the Knights of Labor that fathered the movement, while the trade unions practically kept aloof from it, shows both the weaker bargaining power of their membership and the middle-class psychology of their leaders.

The failure was definite and final.   Not since this time has the American labour movement ventured upon co-operation.   The year 1888 marks the closing of the age of middle-class " panaceas," and consequently the beginning of the wage-conscious period.   The failure was not due to external causes only.   Indeed, it was foredoomed, thanks to the form which it assumed.   In England, where the great co-operative movement, started by the Rochdale pioneers, was of the distributive kind, it remained independent of the wage question or trade unionism.   There the co-operative and the trade union organisations grew side by side and, although they drew recruits from the same constituency, never came seriously into collision.   In the United States, however, the co-operative attempts were not distributive but, for the most part, productive.   When the co-operators lowered the price of their product in order to build up a market, the wages of the workers who continued to work for private employers were immediately affected for the worse.   Hence the Order, when it endeavoured to practise both co-operation and trade unionism, was driving its teams in opposite directions.   The difficulties were further enhanced by the fact that its financial means were limited so that any diversion of funds for co-operative ends weakened its trade union action, and vice versa.   After 1888 the Order never obtained another opportunity to choose between the two, but the trade unions were in a position to benefit by the lesson and, as a result, eschewed co-operation.

24 Such was the case of the Co-operative Furniture Company of Baltimore.   Randall, " Co-operation in Maryland and the South," in *Johns Hopkins University Studies*, 498.

CHAPTER XII

THE POLITICAL UPHEAVAL, 1886-1887

The Greenback Labor party, 440. The Butler campaign, 440. New political outlook, 441. New York Central Labor Union, 441. Its radical declaration of principles, 442. Early activities, 442. The conspiracy law, 443. Campaign of 1882, 444. The Theiss boycott case, 444. Decision to go into politics, 445. Henry George's life and philosophy, 446. Comparison with John Swinton, 447. California experiences, 447. The "new agrarianism," 448. Availability as a candidate, 448. The platform, 449. Attitude of the socialists, 449. Democratic nomination, 450. The George-Hewitt campaign, 450. The *Leader*, 451. The general press, 451. Hewitt's view of the struggle, 452. George's view of the struggle, 452. Reverend Dr. McGlynn, 453. Attitude of the Catholic Church, 453. Powderly's attitude, 453 The vote, 453. Effect on the old parties, 454. Beginning of friction with the socialists, 454. The choice of a name for the party, 455. "Land and labor" clubs, 455. The county convention and the party constitution, 455. Call for a state convention, 456. Opposition of the socialists, 456. Their capture of the *Leader*, 456. The *Standard* and the attack upon the Catholic hierarchy, 456. The Anti-poverty Society, 456. George's attitude towards the purely labour demands, 457. McMackin's ruling on the eligibility of socialists to membership, 457. Struggle in the assembly districts, 458. Attitude of the trade unions, 458. Gompers' attitude, 458. Unseating of the socialist delegates at the state convention, 459. The new platform, 460. Revolt of the socialists, 460. Progressive Labor party, 460. Swinton's nomination, 461. The vote, 461. Causes of the failure of the movement, 461. Political movement outside of New York, 461. Labour tickets, 462. Labour platforms, 462. Success in the elections, 462. Attitude of the Federation, 463. Powderly's attitude, 464. Efforts for national organisations, 464. The national convention in Cincinnati, 465. National Union Labor party, 465. Labour's attitude towards the new party, 465. Spring elections of 1887, 466. Autumn election of 1887, 466. Spring elections of 1888, 467. The Chicago Socialists, 467. The Union Labor party presidential nomination, 468. The United Labor party, 468. Predominance of the farmers in the Union Labor party, 468. Apostasy of many labour leaders, 468. Powderly's secret circular, 469. The vote, 469. The order of the Videttes, 469.

THE indifference of the wage-earners to independent politics, displayed by the greenback vote of 1880,[1] continued until 1886. In 1882 an attempt was made in Pennsylvania, where labour was still taking a part in the management of the Greenback

---

[1] See above, II, 251.

Labour party, to resuscitate the movement by nominating Thomas J. Armstrong, the editor of the *National Labour Tribune,* for governor on the greenback ticket. But the result was most disappointing. In so far as the greenback movement was still in existence, it was a movement of farmers, not of wage-earners. Gradually the greenback issues were losing their last grip and were being supplanted by the issue of anti-monopoly. By the middle of 1883 the anti-monopoly movement had become general enough to warrant the calling of a national conference. Joseph R. Buchanan enthusiastically supported the idea, although the greenbackers were generally opposed. He attended such a conference on July 4, 1883, as a representative of the Anti-Monopoly or People's party of Colorado and found that the delegates " were nearly all farmers." [2] As a result of the conference, a nominating convention met at Chicago on May 19, 1884, and nominated Benjamin F. Butler for president. The remnants of the Greenback party met a fortnight later and, after much discussion, indorsed him.

The campaign was conducted with still less energy than that of 1880. Butler, who was then governor of Massachusetts, having been elected in 1882 by a combination of Democrats and greenbackers, was looking for the Democratic nomination. He remained undecided for a time as to whether he should openly accept the nomination of the greenbackers, and did so only after the Democrats had nominated Cleveland. Moreover, his choice of campaign managers was displeasing to the rank and file of the party, and it served to enhance the doubt which had been excited by his conduct in accepting the nomination, of the genuineness of his canvass.

The vote polled was almost negligible — 135,000, or about 1.33 per cent of the total, as against 350,000 [3] polled in 1880, and some 15,000 less than that polled by the prohibition candidate. A very large percentage of the Butler vote was drawn from the wage-workers, owing to his popularity among the labouring people, and as a result of the distinct bid for the labour vote made in the platform. Obviously, however, only a por-

[2] Chicago *Labor Enquirer,* July 11, 1883.

[3] Not including the 42,000 polled by the Butler electors at large in Michigan, where the rest of the electoral ticket was nominated jointly by the Democratic and Greenback parties.

tion of the members of labour organisations voted for him. Typographical Union 6 of New York conducted an extensive campaign in labour circles on behalf of Cleveland, since Blaine was supported by the boycotted New York *Tribune*. Foran, ex-president of the coopers, and Farquhar, ex-president of the typographical union, were elected to Congress as Democrats, in Cleveland and Buffalo, respectively. There was also the usual small number of labour-union members elected to state legislatures on old party tickets.

The insignificant vote polled by Butler completed the process of dissolving the loose organisations of diverse elements known variously as the " National," the " Anti-Monopoly," and the " People's party "— a process which had been going on with but little interruption since 1878. However, the sudden growth of the vote in Milwaukee, Wisconsin, where the movement had virtually disappeared in 1880, may be taken as a distant herald of another political upheaval.

This came on the heels of the economic disturbance of 1886. Many factors contributed toward it. These were the disastrous strikes of the year, such as the Southwest strike, the eight-hour strike, and the Chicago building workmen's strike; the wholesale conviction of union members on criminal charges of boycotts, conspiracy, intimidation, and rioting; the turning of public opinion against labour as a result of the Haymarket bomb, and the identification in the minds of many people of the Knights of Labor and the trade unionists with the anarchists; the enactment in this year of much legislation designed to restrict the freedom of action of labour organisations; and finally, the presence of a large non-wage-earning element among the Knights of Labor, an element which was able to assert itself only through political action. The political movement reached its culminating point in New York City, in the autumn of 1886. There it was directed by the Central Labor Union, which was often termed the Parliament of Organised Labour.[4]

This organisation had grown out of a mass meeting called early in 1882 by Robert Blissert, a journeyman tailor and

4 For the following account of the political movement in New York, I am indebted to the manuscript of P. A. Speek, "The Single Tax and the Labor Movement,"

University of Wisconsin, *Bulletin*, Economic and Political Science Series, Vol. VIII, No. 3.

refugee from Ireland, "for the purpose of sending greetings to the workers of Ireland in their struggle against English landlordism." [5] The first meeting on February 11, 1882, was attended by delegates from fourteen trade unions, with a majority of the German element, and was addressed by Philip Van Patten, the national secretary of the Socialist Labour party. The predominance of the socialist element is clearly shown in the declaration of principles. It asserted that "there can be no harmony between capital and labour under the present industrial system, for the simple reason that capital, in its modern character, consists very largely of rent, interest and profits wrongfully extorted from the producer"; and ended by pointing out "as the sacred duty of every honorable laboring man to sever his affiliations with all political parties of the capitalists, and to devote his energy and attention to the organisation of his Trade and .Labor Union, and the concentration of all Unions into one solid body for the purpose of assisting each other in all struggles — political or industrial — to resist every attempt of the ruling classes directed against our liberties, and to extend our fraternal hand to the wage earners of our land and to all nations of the globe that struggle for the same independence." [6]

The radical tenor of this declaration and especially its emphasis upon the international character of the labour movement were directly due to the influence of the two leading elements in the organisation, the German socialists and the political refugees from Ireland. The declaration remained unaltered until the end of the eighties.

The Central Labor Union immediately took its place at the head of the city central organisations of the country. During the celebrated freight-handlers' strike in New York in July, 1882, it raised a fund of $60,000 for the strikers. It put into operation one of the first boycotts in the eighties, namely, that against an anti-union firm of gold beaters in Philadelphia, in April, 1882. Besides popularising the boycott, the Central Labor Union, upon the motion of P. J. McGuire, for the first time called a labour holiday on the first Monday in September, 1882. This was afterwards taken up by the Knights and the

---

[5] *John Swinton's Paper*, Feb. 28, 1886.   [6] Central Labor Union, *Constitution*.

Federation of Labor and made legally " Labour Day " in several States. In 1882, the Central Labor Union also made its début in politics. This was provoked by the incorporation into the penal code of the State of seven stringent anti-conspiracy statutes.

In 1870 New York had passed a law which provided that strikes for higher wages or shorter hours should not be considered conspiracies. However, in 1881–1882, when the penal code was revised, it was found that the conspiracy law was widened both directly and indirectly. It provided that an agreement to commit a crime was a misdemeanor and also a criminal conspiracy. The list of actions which constituted a crime was widened considerably. It specifically enumerated the forms of picketing that should constitute intimidation. It declared a misdemeanor the breach of " contract of service or hiring . . . either alone or in combination with others," in cases when it might result in danger to life or in bodily injury or would " expose valuable property to destruction or serious injury." Furthermore, there was a general provision enacted to the effect that a person who " commits any act which seriously injures the person or property of another, or which seriously disturbs or endangers the public peace or health, or which openly outrages public decency, for which no other punishment is expressly prescribed by this Code, is guilty of a misdemeanor." [7] Each of the enumerated misdemeanors could be punished by one year's imprisonment and $500 fine. Finally, in regard to extortion, which was defined as the " obtaining of property from another without his consent, induced by wrongful use of force or fear, or under colour of official right," a maximum penalty of five years was given. It was under this last clause that the famous boycott cases of 1886 were decided. Swinton asserted at the time that the clause had been smuggled into the penal code by the committee appointed to codify existing laws, and that the legislature when it adopted the code, acted in total ignorance of it.[8]

The leaders of labour organisations felt the greatest apprehension on account of the clause which dealt with picketing.

[7] New York Bureau of Labor, *Report*, 1887, p. 669.
[8] *John Swinton's Paper*, July 11, 1886.

They feared that peaceful boycotting would be construed as an act injurious to trade or commerce, and that refusal to work with a strike-breaker would be regarded as intimidation.[9]

Candidates were nominated in 1882 in 4 congressional districts (Louis F. Post [10] in the fourth), in 11 aldermanic districts, and in 11 assembly districts. The total vote cast was only about 10,000. Charges of bribery were freely made and were believed, so that the enthusiasm for independent political action waned.

After 1882 the Central Labor Union became a purely economic organisation. It assumed undisputed leadership of the strike and boycott movements of the city. It maintained friendly relations with the Knights of Labor, and even counted among its affiliated organisations many of the assemblies of the Knights. With the beginning of the upward trend in the labour movement early in 1885 it grew in proportion. The number of affiliated organisations had so increased that in order to expedite business, related trades were grouped into sections and, in July, 1886, there were 10 sections with a total of 207 unions as follows: building trades with 39 unions; iron and metal, 18; food products, 16; clothing, 16; furniture, 14; printing, 13; tobacco, 9; textile, 8; clerks, 6; and miscellaneous, 68.[11] The total membership was estimated by an unfriendly writer at 40,000,[12] and was probably 50,000.

While the Central Labor Union took no active part in the eight-hour movement, the widest attention was attracted by its activity on behalf of the boycott, since for the first time in the eighties it brought organised labour prominently in conflict with the courts. In March, 1886, the Carl Sahm Club of musicians (a local assembly of the Knights of Labor under the jurisdiction of District Assembly 49) declared a boycott, after an unsuccessful strike, against George Theiss, a proprietor of a music and beer garden. The waiters' and bar-tenders' unions, which also had grievances against Theiss, joined in, and, upon their appeal, the Central Labor Union declared a general boycott

9 Expressed by P. J. McGuire at a meeting of the Central Labor Union in October, 1882. New York *Workman*, Oct. 16, 1882.

10 A prominent disciple of Henry George, for many years editor of the *Public* (the single tax weekly in Chicago), and since 1913 assistant secretary of labor at Washington.

11 New York *Sun*, July 19, 1886.

12 *Ibid.*, Sept. 19, 1886.

against Theiss' place. The boycott was conducted with great energy. Pickets were stationed near the establishment to warn customers away. Several arrests were made, but resulted in no convictions. Finally, George Ehret, a brewer, and a certain baker from whom Theiss bought beer and bread, fearing that the sales of their goods would fall off owing to the boycott, arranged for a meeting between Theiss and a committee representing the boycotters and the Central Labor Union. The meeting resulted in a written settlement, the last clause of which required Theiss to pay $1,000 to cover the expenses of the boycott, and the money was afterwards paid.[13]

Soon after this, however, Theiss brought suit against the members of the union committees charging them with intimidation and extortion. The judge, George C. Barrett, in his charge to the jury, conceded that striking, picketing, and boycotting as such were not prohibited by law, if not accompanied by force, threats, or intimidation. But in the case under consideration the action of the pickets in advising passers-by not to patronise the establishment, and in distributing boycott circulars, constituted intimidation. Also, since the $1,000 was obtained by fear induced by a threat to continue the unlawful injury to Theiss' property inflicted by the " boycott," the case was one of extortion covered by the penal code. It made no difference whether the money was appropriated by the defendants for personal use or whether it was turned over to their organisations. The jury, which reflected the current public opinion against boycotts, found all of the 5 defendants guilty of extortion, and Judge Barrett sentenced them to prison for terms ranging from 1 year and 6 months to 3 years and 8 months.[14]

The Theiss case, coming as it did at a time of general restlessness of labour, and closely after the defeat of the eight-hour movement, greatly hastened the growth of the sentiment for an independent labour party. During 1885 independent politics had been made a subject of lively discussion at the meetings of

13 *John Swinton's Paper*, July 11, 1886.

14 People *v.* Wilzig, 4 N. Y. Crim. 403 (1886); People *v.* Kostka, 4 N. Y. Crim. 429 (1886); New York Bureau of Labor, *Report*, 1886, p. 752. The sentences were all commuted Oct. 9, 1886, by Governor David B. Hill, to imprisonment for the term of 100 days, from July 3, 1886, to Oct. 11, 1886.

the Central Labor Union and also of the affiliated organisations, but the sides were equally matched. On the evening of
the last day of the trial, the delegates of the Socialist Labor
party, the cigar makers', bar-tenders', and waiters' unions, and
of the Carl Sahm Club met and called a mass meeting to protest against the conviction of the boycotters. A few days later
the Central Labor Union endorsed the call.

The mass meeting was held at Coopers' Union on July 7.
The speakers, among them John Swinton and S. E. Schevitsch,
the editor of the socialist *New Yorker Volkszeitung,* all urged
political action. On July 11, the Central Labor Union met.
A resolution was introduced and seconded by socialists, that a
committee be appointed to devise ways and means for forming
an independent labour party. It was carried, and at the next
meeting the committee presented a plan to extend an invitation
to all labour and labour reform organisations, labour unions,
Knights of Labor, greenbackers, anti-monopolists, socialists,
and land reformers to send delegates to a labour conference on
August 5, 1886, at Clarendon Hall.

The conference was composed of 402 delegates from 165 organisations with an aggregate membership of 50,000.[15] The
Socialist Labor party as well as others was represented as a
bona fide labour organisation. Again the socialists took the
lead on the side of independent politics and met with little opposition save from the delegates of Typographical Union 6.
The resolution was carried by a vote of 362 to 40. A committee on permanent organisation resulted, with John Mc-
Mackin, of the painters, for chairman, and James P. Archibald,
of the paper hangers, for secretary. At the next conference it
was decided to form an independent labour party of New York
and vicinity, and a platform was presented, consisting almost
entirely of purely labour demands. For a technical reason,
the platform was not passed upon at this meeting. Meantime
the committee was in search of a candidate for mayor in the
election of the next autumn, and the choice fell on Henry George.

Henry George, although he had started his career as a printer,
was not a product of the labour movement. His influence was
quite in contrast with that of another printer who also at that

15 Post and Leubuscher, *The George-Hewitt Campaign,* 6.

time belonged to the "intellectuals"—John Swinton. Swinton [16] saw around him the complexity of the social and economic life in the East, with its diversity of interests and struggles and its no less diversity of social evils. He, therefore, ruled out as obviously inadequate any theory of economic development based upon any one fundamental idea, and naturally came to embrace doctrines of empiricism. George, on the contrary, did not approach the labour movement with the empirical spirit of Swinton. He came with a ready-made theory and the labour movement appealed to him merely as a vehicle for the spread of his single-tax teaching. His dogmatism was largely the result of environment. Born in Philadelphia in 1839, he went to San Francisco after he had learned the printer's trade. He therefore began his philosophical experience on what was then the economic frontier, where as yet there was little manufacturing, but mainly mining and agricultural pursuits having a direct dependence upon natural resources. Wages were high, owing to the abundance of these resources, offering rich alternative opportunities to the wage-earner. When the first transcontinental railroad was completed in 1869 and a rapid growth of population began, the free land was quickly pre-empted by speculators, the price of land soared up, and wages simultaneously fell. George drew the conclusion that wages had declined because the land owner was now exacting a high rent for the use of the land. He also ascribed to high rent the similar effect on profits, whose similarity to wages he could see in a community where the independent miners commonly spoke of washing their "wages" out of the soil. Futhermore, George keenly observed the severe industrial depression which struck California in 1877 and served to confirm the idea already ripened in his mind that the monopolisation of the land by withholding it from use both reduced "wages," and decreased the opportunities for employment.[17] Thus, the observation of conditions in California led George to explain the exploitation of labour and the lack of employment by a single cause, the monopolisation of land.

Although primarily an outgrowth of the economic evolution

16 See above, II, 220, note.
17 His book on *Progress and Poverty* was first published in 1880.

of California the single-tax philosophy was given an enthusiastic acceptance among many of the "intellectuals" in the industrial East. The single-tax programme seemed admirably to meet the urban rent problem. It also appealed to those who, while keenly aware of the existing evils in industrial society, preferred a solution on individualistic lines. Indeed, the single-tax philosophy had enjoyed in the cities of the East much the same persuasive power that had been enjoyed by the agrarian philosophy of the homestead movement which originated there during the forties.[18]   Henry George was the spiritual heir of George Henry Evans, the agrarian thinker and leader during the forties. Both advocated "agrarianism," yet a comparison between them will yield no less a contrast than would a comparison of the agricultural and largely unoccupied United States of Clay and Calhoun with the industrialised and settled country of Blaine and Cleveland. "Vote yourself a farm" was a practical kind of agrarianism when the existence of an apparently inexhaustible public domain logically suggested an "extensive" solution of the labour problem, a mere opening up of the land to the energetic wage-earner seeking, as his own employer, for an opportunity to apply his labour force to the resources of nature. At a time, however, when the railway had nearly abolished the available supply of free land, and when industry had concentrated huge populations in the cities, the "agrarian" solution of the labour question had to be of the "intensive" order, namely, the opening up of opportunities to the labourer by means of an indirect pressure upon the owner of the natural resources through the power of taxation.

George was a most suitable candidate for the Labor party. A man with an international reputation, exceedingly popular in labour circles, especially among the Irish, owing to his work in Ireland, he was at the same time unaffiliated with any group or organisation in the labour movement. George was willing to accept the nomination, but stipulated that at least 30,000 voters should pledge themselves, over their signatures, to vote for him. The conference enthusiastically accepted his condition, and the work of gathering the signatures was begun at once. The platform presented first was quietly dropped, al-

[18] See above, I, 522, et seq.

though it met with general approval, and George was asked to write his own platform. Such being the case, the new platform naturally made the single tax the issue. The labour demands were compressed into one plank. They were the reform of court procedure so that "the practice of drawing grand jurors from one class should cease, and the requirements of a property qualification for trial jurors should be abolished"; the stopping of the "officious intermeddling of the police with peaceful assemblages"; the enforcement of the laws for safety and the sanitary inspection of buildings; the abolition of contract labour on public work, and equal pay for equal work without distinction of sex on such work. Another plank dealt with over-crowding in tenements, but the remedy advanced was not regulation of buildings but the single-tax idea of abolishing all taxes on buildings and substituting heavy taxation of land values irrespective of improvements. The remaining four planks advanced the single tax, demanded the government ownership of railways and telegraphs, and dealt with the existing political corruption.[19]

From the standpoint of labour, therefore, the platform was not satisfactory, for the single tax was hardly understood by the workingmen. But so great was the popularity of the man and so bright the chances for success that this was overlooked. Even the socialists, from whom the harshest criticism might have been expected, raised no protest.

The socialist movement had recovered from the blow dealt it by anarchism about 1884.[20] As in previous years, it was divided into two factions, a "trade union" faction and a "political" one. The former, with the *New Yorker Volkszeitung* as its organ, favoured the postponement of political action and the continuation of active work in and on behalf of the trade unions; the political faction, represented by the National Executive Committee of the party and its newly established organ, *Der Sozialist,* under the leadership of V. L. Rosenberg, preferred independent political action to participation in the trade union movement. The trade union faction was able, with the help of the German unions, to play an important part in the Central Labor Union, where it carried on a steady agitation

[19] *The George-Hewitt Campaign,* 14.   [20] See above, II, 300.

in favour of a labour party by the trade unions. So that when finally in 1886 such a party was launched, the trade union faction felt inclined to overlook the deficiencies in the platform from the socialist standpoint and even to welcome the issue of the single tax as "partial socialism." As a matter of fact, the trade union faction expected from the first that the movement would eventually turn into a socialistic channel. The opposite faction, the political one, although it still held that political action should be carried on by the Socialist Labor party and not by the trade unions, felt so strongly inspired by the great possibilities suddenly opening up, that, notwithstanding its control over the National Executive Committee, it allowed the trade union faction full sway and even refrained from criticism.

The nominating convention met September 23, with 409 delegates from 175 organisations. The George platform was adopted and George was nominated for mayor by a vote of 360 to 49.

On October 1, a mass meeting was held in Chickering Hall of several thousand radical middle-class and professional people to ratify George's candidacy. Among those who took part in its debates were Professor Daniel De Leon and Father McGlynn. A joint mass meeting of the professional and labour people was held on October 5, 1886, at Cooper Union. In full view of the audience were placed the rolls containing the 39,000 signatures of voters for Henry George's candidacy for mayor. George officially accepted the nomination and the memorable campaign opened.

The Democrats who had heretofore been divided into two factions, Tammany Hall and the County Democracy, united upon Abram S. Hewitt, a member of the latter. Hewitt was a large iron manufacturer of the firm founded by Peter Cooper and had been congressman from New York. The Republicans nominated Theodore Roosevelt.

The George-Hewitt campaign — for from the very beginning the campaign became a contest between these two only — marks one of the most spectacular and romantic epochs in the history of the labour movement in America. It was also the culminating point in the great labour upheaval. The enthusiasm of the labouring people reached its highest pitch. They felt that, baffled and defeated as they were in their economic struggle, they were now nearing victory in the struggle for the control of government. A considerable campaign fund was speedily formed by an assessment of 25 cents per capita upon the members of each union. Besides, money was coming in from collections at campaign meetings and from individual donations. Sympathisers among professional people also contributed liberally and organised numerous Henry George clubs. A daily paper, the *Leader,* was issued, for which the Central Labor Union gave $1,000, the carpenters, $1,500, and other affiliated unions, $100 each. It was edited by Louis F. Post, counsel of the Central Labor Union, with the collaboration of many unpaid writers upon other papers who gave their spare time to the cause. Its circulation was 30,000 on the first day and reached 52,000 on the second; so that it was almost self-supporting. The *New Yorker Volkszeitung,* and, during a part of the campaign until the opposition of the Catholic Church developed, the *Irish World,* were the only other papers which supported George.

Against them was pitted the powerful press of the city of New York. When the movement was still in its initial stage, the press tried to counteract it with ridicule. When, however, George was named and his election became probable, a bitter and concerted attack was opened upon him. In this the *Daily Illustrated Graphic,* the *Evening Post,* and *Harper's Weekly,* especially excelled. " Revolutionist," and " Apostle of anarchy and destruction" were not the harshest epithets hurled at him. On the other side, George's campaign was of the most unusual nature for New York. Mass meetings were numerous and large. Most of them were held in the open air, usually on the street corners. From the system by which one speaker followed another, speaking at several meeting places in a night, the labour campaign got its nickname of the " tailboard campaign." The common people, women and men, gathered in hundreds and often thousands around a truck from which the shifting speakers addressed the crowd. The speakers were volunteers, including representatives of the liberal professions, lawyers, physicians, teachers, ministers, and labour leaders. At such mass meetings George did most of his campaigning, making several speeches a night, once as many as eleven.[21] The single tax and the prevailing political corruption were favourite topics.

Of the two opponents of George, Hewitt had by far a clearer conception of the significance of the campaign than Roosevelt. In his speech of acceptance, Hewitt squarely stated the issue in the following words:

"A new issue has . . . been suddenly sprung upon this community. An attempt is being made to organise one class of our citizens against all other classes, and to place the Government of the city in the hands of men willing to represent the special interests of this class [labour], to the exclusion of the just rights of the other classes. . . . Between capitalists, or those who control capital, and laborers, there may be a conflict of interests, which, like all other disputes, must be adjusted by mutual concessions, or by the operation of the law. . . . With more experience and better education, the evils of strikes, lockouts, and boycotts will pass away. Conciliation and arbitration will take place of denunciation and hostility." [22]

George denied the class nature of the movement, and replied in his first public letter to Hewitt:

"You have heard so much of the working-class that you evidently forget that the ' working-class ' is in reality not a class, but *the mass,* and that any political movement in which they engage is not that of one class against other classes, but, as one English statesman has happily phrased it, a movement of the ' masses against the classes.' . . . I do not stand as the candidate of the hand-workers alone. Among the men who have given me the most democratic nomination given to an American citizen in our time are not wholly hand-workers, but working-men of all kinds — editors, reporters, teachers, clergymen, artists, authors, physicians, store-keepers, merchants — in short, representatives of all classes of men who earn their living by the exertion of their hand and head." [23]

An exchange of public letters between Hewitt and George followed. Hewitt criticised the single tax as " robbery " but avoided all reference to the existing political corruption. He also rejected George's offer of a public debate. Hewitt's letters and speeches accomplished their purpose; he succeeded in frightening the business men.

21 *The George-Hewitt Campaign,* 106.   22 *Ibid.,* 31–37.   23 *Ibid.,* 46–50.

Among the non-labour supporters of George, the greatest attention was attracted by Father McGlynn, a Catholic priest.
Owing to his great popularity among Catholics, his public advocacy of the single tax and of George's candidacy he was considered by the Democrats as a source of great danger. With
the view of counteracting it, the chairman of Tammany Hall's
committee on resolutions addressed a letter to Thomas S. Pres-
ton, vicar-general of the Catholic Church, asking if it were true
that the Catholic clergymen were in favour of Henry George.
The reply brought the anticipated assurance that the great
majority of the Catholic clergy strongly condemned and
would " deeply regret the election of Mr. George to any position of influence." The letter was given the widest circulation.
It was distributed in front of Catholic churches and among
Catholic worshippers on their return from service. The press
also gave it wide publicity.

Shortly before election day, the Democratic politicians
spread the rumor that Powderly was opposed to George's candidacy. At the beginning of the campaign Powderly had decided to take no part, but, seeing that his attitude was misin-
terpreted into an indication of opposition to George, he ordered
a mass meeting called in New York on the eve of the election
and came out in his speech strongly in favour of the independent
candidates.

The vote cast was 90,000 for Hewitt, 68,000 for George, and
60,000 for Roosevelt. There is sufficient ground for the belief
that George was counted out of thousands of votes. The nature of the George voters can be sufficiently gathered from an
analysis of the pledges to vote for him.[24] An apparently
trustworthy investigation was made by a representative of the
Sun. He drew the conclusion that the vast majority were not
simply wage-earners, but also naturalised immigrants, mainly
Irish, Germans, and Bohemians, the native element being in
the minority. While the Irish were divided between George
and Hewitt, the majority of the German element had gone over
to Henry George.[25]

The outcome was hailed as a victory by George and his sup-

[24] Although no longer solicited after the
nomination was made, the pledges spon-
taneously continued to pour in, reaching a
total of 42,500.

[25] New York *Sun*, Oct. 22, 1886.

porters, and this view was also taken by the general press. It assured the continuance of the labour party, and inspired labour with an ambition for success on a larger scale in the future. The effect upon the old parties is shown by labour laws passed at the legislative session of 1887, creating a board of mediation and arbitration, regulating tenement houses, providing for the labelling and marketing of convict-made goods, perfecting the mechanics' lien, regulating employment of women and children, regulating the hours of labour on street, surface, and elevated railroads, and finally amending the notorious penal code by prohibiting employers, singly or combined, from coercing employés not to join a labour organisation.[26]

Soon after the election, cleavage began in the movement. The single taxers aspired to place the party entirely upon a single tax basis and in doing so came to disregard its labour character. In fact, since they were aspiring to make the party one of all producing classes against the landlords and special privilege, a specific labour character, or what amounted to the same, a class character, appeared to them as out of harmony with their philosophy and seemed tactically imprudent. The extreme popularity of Henry George among the wage-earners facilitated the task. But active opposition came from the socialists. To these, the nature of the movement as one of wage-earners had been the only ground for joining, as they believed that a labour party once formed would by the logic of events be forced to accept socialism. Consequently, the success of the designs of the single taxers would have meant their dismal failure. Although their influence among the labour people was far less than that of Henry George, their control of the German unions, their compactness of organisation, and skilful leadership in the person of Schevitsch, made them a force not to be despised. At first both sides carefully avoided open rupture.

The leaders close to Henry George called a mass meeting at Cooper Union on November 6, and, as a result, a temporary executive committee of three, Father McGlynn, John McMackin, and James Redpath, one of the editors of the *North American Review,* was appointed to establish the Progressive Democracy, as the party was named, on a permanent basis.

26 New York Bureau of Labor, *Report,* 1887, pp. 736-776.

The committee on laws of the Central Labor Union was recognised as the committee on laws of the party. This committee worked out a provisional constitution. On November 9, the district organisers of the Central Labor Union met. They rejected the name Progressive Democracy as well as Land and Labor party, favoured by none, but named the party the United Labor party. They also decided to call a county convention on January 6, 1887, in which each assembly district was to be represented by one delegate for each 200 votes cast on November 2 — altogether 340 delegates. Meanwhile, an organisation was to be established in each assembly district.

The committee of three continued its work along parallel lines by organising " Land and Labor Clubs," organisations, which, although they contained a considerable portion of wage-earners among their membership, were led solely by intellectuals. On the other hand, the assembly district organisations were manned and led by wage-earners.

The county convention met on the appointed day. Three hundred and twenty of the 340 delegates were wage-earners.[27] McMackin was elected chairman. Committees on organisation and constitution were elected. The former contained the socialists, Hugo Vogt, Lucien Sanial, and Daniel De Leon. The latter, Richard T. Hinton, H. Emrich, socialists, and James P. Archibald, the recording secretary of the Central Labor Union. The Clarendon Hall platform was reaffirmed and also the name United Labor party. The constitution provided for election district organisations, assembly district organisations, a county general committee, and a county executive board. It included a clause stating that no person " shall be eligible to membership . . . unless . . . he has severed all connections with all other political parties, organisations and clubs." [28] It was under this clause that the socialists were later expelled.

County organisations were also formed in Kings (Brooklyn), Albany, Erie (Buffalo), and several other counties in the State. The organisation of land and labour clubs was energetically carried on, and fifteen existed in New York alone.

27 Quoted from the *New Yorker Voltszeitung* by the New York *Standard*, Jan. 22, 1887.
28 New York *Leader*, Jan. 22, 1887.

In May, 1887, a joint call was issued by the state convention committees of the general committee of the counties of New York and Kings, and by the land and labour committee, for a state convention in Syracuse on August 17. The call specified three issues, the taxation of land values, currency reform, and the government ownership of railways.[29]

The total omission of labour demands in the call caused the socialists to break into open criticism of Henry George and the management of the party. The criticism was at first mild, but grew more severe during June and July. As early as January, 1887, the socialists had managed to gain the control of the *Leader* principally through a shrewd redistribution of the stock in the *Leader* publication company among a large number of their members. They elected Schevitsch editor in place of Post, so that now when the conflict with the single taxers had come into the open, they had a daily English organ to defend their side. Almost in reply to the capture of the *Leader* by the socialists, came the announcement of the publication of a weekly paper, *The Standard,* edited by George, the first issue appearing on January 8, 1887. In this issue George published a vigorous attack upon the hierarchy of the Catholic Church, provoked by what he considered harsh and unjust treatment of Father McGlynn. In November, 1886, Archbishop Corrigan had published a letter condemning the single tax as anti-Christian, and McGlynn had publicly criticised this letter. In reply, he was ordered to Rome to defend himself. Upon his refusal on the ground of ill health, he was indefinitely suspended. The incident helped to keep the movement before the public eye probably as much as the mayoralty campaign. As his popularity increased rather than decreased even among Catholics, McGlynn became a valuable aid to George. In March, 1887, he formed the Anti-poverty Society, a single-tax organisation upon a religious basis. The enrolment of members was large, the majority of McGlynn's former parishioners, mostly Irish wage-earners, joining, and also a number of intellectuals of all creeds. Upon his second refusal to go to Rome, McGlynn was excommunicated in July, but was given forty days' grace. Shortly before that time expired, the Anti-

29 *Ibid.,* May 5, 1887.

poverty Society organised a protest parade, in which about 25,-
000 people, mostly Catholic wage-earners, took part.

The antagonism between George and the socialists grew
from day to day. In June *The Standard* opened up a discussion concerning the word "Labor" in the party's title.
George was displeased with the term because it had "narrow
associations and would handicap the new movement with the
notion that it [was] merely a class movement." He preferred
either Free Soil or Free Land. McGlynn shared his view
and offered the "Commonwealth" party as a substitute. The
socialists stubbornly defended the term "Labor" and, in a
less emphatic way, the trade unionists did the same. The
election of delegates to the state convention began in July.
Here and there appeared instructions to delegates to defend the
term "Labor" in the party's name, to emphasise "Labor
demands" in the platform, and to nominate a "straight labor
ticket." This was attributed by the single taxers to the influence of the socialists and, in consequence, the breach grew
wider and wider. In the middle of July the rumour spread
that the socialists would be ousted from the United Labor
party on the ground that they at the same time belonged to
another party — the Socialist Labor party. Thereupon the
socialists demanded that the county executive committee issue
a ruling on the eligibility of socialists to membership. The
committee met on July 29, and unanimously decided that the
socialists were eligible to membership.[30] Encouraged by this,
the socialists began to push their views and candidates and
the election of their delegates still more energetically, so that
the general press heralded the news that, repeating the case of
the *Leader,* the socialists were about to capture the United
Labor party.

George and the single taxers felt that this placed the future
of the movement at stake. On August 5 the county general
committee met. The decision of the executive committee was
made a subject of lively discussion and Chairman McMackin
was asked to rule upon the eligibility of the socialists. Although in his capacity of chairman of the executive committee
he had shortly before voted in favour of the socialists, he now

30 New York *Standard,* Aug. 13, 1887.

ruled against them, and was sustained by a considerable majority.[31]

War was now openly declared. The twenty-four assembly district organisations became as many battle fields preparatory to the battle royal at the state convention at Syracuse. Ten districts protested against the ousting of the socialists, 7 approved of McMackin's ruling, 4 expressed no opinion, and in 3 districts rival delegations to Syracuse were elected. The majority of the districts adopted resolutions urging that " Labor " should be retained in the party's name and labour demands in the platform. The attitude of the trade unions as a whole was similar. While all were united in the desire for a labour platform and a purely labour party, the position on the expulsion of the socialists was bound to be undecided, as the majority were influenced by the consideration of harmony in the party and especially between them and Henry George. Naturally, the German unions favoured the socialists. Schevitsch stated at the Syracuse convention that 12 unions with an aggregate membership of 17,000 condemned the expulsion.[32] But on the other hand, the entire building trades section of the Central Labor Union, with a membership of 40,000 (including several large German unions which favoured the socialists), upheld McMackin.[33] The leaders in the Central Labor Union tried to avoid bringing up the question for discussion and succeeded in doing so by a tie vote.[34]

The attitude of Gompers, whose position was that of a sympathising outsider, was characteristic. He said: " The labour movement, to succeed politically, must work for present and tangible results. While keeping in view a lofty ideal, we must advance towards it through practical steps, taken with intelligent regard for pressing needs. I believe with the most advanced thinkers as to ultimate ends, including the abolition of the wage-system. . . ." However, " as many of us understand it, Mr. George's theory of land taxation does not promise present reform, nor an ultimate solution." [35]

The attitude of the parties immediately concerned in the conflict was the following. The New York section of the So-

31 New York *Leader*, Aug. 5, 1887.   34 New York *Standard*, Aug. 20, 1887.
32 *Ibid.*, Aug. 18, 1887.   35 New York *Leader*, July 25, 1887.
33 *Public* (Chicago), Nov. 17, 1911.

cialist Labor party held a meeting which declared that it was
not a political party in the sense of the clause in the constitution of the United Labor party, and emphatically denied having had any intention whatsoever of capturing that party.
The *Leader* justly accounted for the expulsion on the ground
that George feared that the voters might believe the statements
of the general press that his party in reality was socialistic.
It proposed a reconciliation on the basis of a return to the
status prior to McMackin's ruling, promising, however, that
the socialist organisation would officially declare that it was
not a political party. George, on his part, remained irreconcilable. "The question between State or German Socialism
and the ideas of that great party of equal rights and individual freedom which is now beginning to rise all over the land,
may as well, since the Socialists have raised it, be settled
now." [36] His view was shared by McGlynn and other single
taxers.

The state convention met on the appointed day with 180
delegates. Those from the assembly districts, namely, the
workingmen's delegates, were nearly evenly divided on the question of admitting socialists. But the balance was turned in
favour of the irreconcilable single taxers' attitude by the presence of a considerable number of delegates from land and labour clubs. Louis F. Post was elected temporary chairman by
91 votes against 61 cast for Frank Ferrell, a prominent labour
leader from New York who was supported by the socialists
and their sympathisers. The committee on credentials brought
in two reports. The majority report, signed by 15 members,
was against the admission of the 6 socialist delegates who still
held their connection with the Socialist Labor party, on the
ground that the decision of the highest executive authority
(Chairman McMackin) was binding. The minority report,
signed by 8 members, favoured the admission of the socialists.
A heated debate ensued. Schevitsch was the principal speaker
for the socialists. He warned the convention not to antagonise the workingmen in large industrial cities and condemned
as demagoguery the endeavour made to represent the issue as
one between American and foreign ideas.[37] A compromise

36 *Ibid.*, Aug. 4, 1887. 37 New York *Standard*, Aug. 27, 1887.

resolution was introduced, giving each contesting delegate one-half vote upon the promise of the Socialist Labor party at its next convention to declare that it was not a political party. Against the compromise proposed, George himself took the floor. He said: "The greatest danger that could befall the party would not be the separation of its elements . . . but would be a continuance within its ranks of incongruous elements. . . . This is the question we must settle. We cannot compromise." [38] McGlynn spoke in the same vein. The vote was 94 to 59 against the socialists.

The platform adopted took special pains to disavow any leaning toward socialism. Of course, the single tax was made the principal issue. The platform included also a demand for currency reform, municipal ownership of public utilities, and a list of labour and democracy demands.[39] McMackin was elected permanent chairman of the party. Among the five candidates named for office at the coming election, there was no wage-earner. George received the nomination for secretary of state.

Soon after the Syracuse convention, the socialists in New York called a conference to form a new labour party. It was attended by delegates from 56 trade unions, 31 political organisations in New York and Brooklyn, and from 15 sections of the Socialist Labor party from New York and vicinity. The conference launched a Progressive Labor party. The platform declared that the emancipation of the working class will be accomplished only by the workingmen themselves, " through the establishment, as demanded by the Knights of Labor, of co-operative institutions, such as will tend to supersede the wage system by the introducing of a co-operative industrial system." [40] The platform specifically enumerated a long list of labour demands, and prudently introduced the socialist wedge in the form of a demand for the public ownership of means of communication and transportation and other public utilities; it also demanded reforms in taxation, namely a tax upon unimproved land and a progressive income tax. The national convention of the Socialist Labor party, held in Buffalo at the

38 *Ibid.*
39 New York *World*, Aug. 20, 1887.
40 New York *Leader*, Sept. 9, 1887.

end of September, officially sanctioned participation by socialists in labour parties. The Central Labor Union condemned
the Progressive Labor party by a vote of 52 to 44, the votes of
the building trades being wholly against the party.

The party held a state convention the last week of September and nominated John Swinton for secretary of state, and
other candidates. Swinton refused on the ground of ill health,
but later agreed to be a candidate for the state senate in the
seventh senatorial district in New York City. The campaign
was enlivened by a public debate between George and
Schevitsch at which Gompers, in the capacity of a person neutral to the contest, presided.

The outcome of the election proved disappointing to both
parties. George's vote in New York City fell from 68,000 in
the previous November to 37,000. In the whole State it was
72,000. The Progressive Labor party polled only 5,000 in
the State, and 2,900 were cast for Swinton for state senator
as against 2,300 cast for the United Labor party candidate,
out of a total of 24,000. There seem to be several causes for
this outcome. The dissensions in the movement apparently
robbed it of the prospect to win. With this a portion of the
enthusiasm was gone. Moreover, as mentioned before, the
legislative session of 1887 had yielded a most abundant crop
of labour laws. Another potent influence was the improved
industrial conditions, which, having started on the up-grade in
the early part of 1886, reached a normal state in the middle
of 1887. And last, but not least, the labour upheaval had
spent its force by the middle of 1887. After the election, the
United Labor party rapidly dwindled to a small group of land
reformers. George abandoned it in 1888 and supported Cleveland for president. McGlynn remained until 1889 when the
party finally disappeared.

The political movement outside of New York [41] passed
through a similar cycle. In the autumn election of 1886, independent labour candidates were run in many places under
various party names. In Boston the workingmen's candidates
were upon the Central Labor Union ticket. The labour party

[41] In the following account the author
drew from an unpublished monograph by
E. E. Witte, *Union Labor Parties, 1884–
1889.*

was known in Baltimore as the Industrial party, in Wisconsin as the People's party, and in Chicago as the Union Labor party. In other localities the workingmen's candidates ran simply upon labour or "Knight of Labor" tickets. In many places they were directly nominated by the local assemblies of the Knights. In others they owed their nomination to a convention in which the Knights of Labor, the trade unions, and frequently also miscellaneous reform organisations took part. Nowhere does there seem to have been in these campaigns the slightest friction between the Knights and the trade unions. In many cases there was co-operation also between organised labour and the remnants of the Greenback party and other farmers' organisations, such as the Agricultural Wheel, in Arkansas, and the Farmers' Alliance, in Texas. Similarly, socialist sections gave their support to the labour tickets. Nowhere does there seem to have been a socialist ticket in the field where labour organisations had their candidates. The platform in each case laid the greatest stress on labour demands. For instance, the People's party of Wisconsin demanded the prohibition of child labour, the abolition of the contract system on public work, the prevention of competition between convict and free labour, the enactment of a weekly-payment law, more adequate safety legislation, an improved Federal contract labour law, and the reduction of the hours of labour proportional to the improvement of machinery. Most of the platforms seem, also, to have reiterated the greenback demand for currency reform. The Wisconsin platform demanded the increase of currency proportional to the growth of industry, and the issue of greenbacks by the government to "the people" at not above 3 per cent interest. All of the platforms, also, had a land plank. The most common demand was for the prohibition of alien land holding. The Wisconsin platform asked for the public ownership of land, a graduated income tax, and the reform of patent laws.

The showing made at the election surpassed even all expectations. The vote in Chicago, where the ferocity of the persecution of the anarchists was keenly felt and resented by the labour people, was almost 25,000 out of a total of 92,000. A state senator and several assemblymen were elected. In Milwaukee the People's party ticket polled 13,000, carrying the county. It elected one state senator, six assemblymen, and one congressman. The labour municipal tickets won out in Lynn, Massachusetts, Rutland, Vermont, Nangatuck and South Norwalk, Connecticut, Key West, Florida, and Richmond, Virginia. In Leadville, Colorado, the Knights of Labor elected one state senator and three assemblymen. In Illinois, outside of Chicago, five labour or greenback assemblymen were elected. In Newark, New Jersey, the independent labour candidates for Congress polled 6,300 votes, and one assemblyman was elected. In St. Louis the workingmen's ticket polled about 7,000. In the sixth congressional district of Kentucky, the labour candidate received so many votes that he contested the seat of Speaker Carlisle. There was, however, no Republican opponent. A like situation enabled the Knights of Labor candidate in the sixth Virginia congressional district to win out. Very poor showing, on the other hand, was made by the labour tickets in Maine, Connecticut, Boston, and Baltimore. Independent greenback candidates everywhere fared even worse than unsuccessful labour candidates. Many labour men ran upon old party tickets, in most cases upon the Democratic ticket. In Cleveland, Martin A. Foran was re-elected to Congress as a Democrat; so was B. F. Shively, a "pioneer Knight of Labor," in Indiana. In Massachusetts Robert Howard was again elected state senator as a Democrat and one Knight of Labor was elected to the legislature on the same ticket. Likewise, several Knights were elected in New York, Connecticut, and one in Paterson, New Jersey. In St. Louis two Knights were successful upon the Republican ticket.

With this singular success the attitude of the Federation of Organised Trades and Labor Unions toward politics was changed. In 1885, the Federation convention had voted down a resolution declaring in favour of the foundation of " a strict workingmen's party." [42] After the elections of 1886, however, the legislative committee of the Federation declared: " We regard with pleasure the recent political action of the organised workingmen of the country, and by which they have demonstrated that they are determined to exhibit their political power.

[42] Federation of Organized Trades and Labor Unions of the United States and Canada, *Proceedings*, 1885, p. 30.

We, in full accord therewith, recommend to organised labour throughout the country that they persist in their recent efforts to the end that labour may achieve its just rights through the exercise of its political powers." [43] The convention of the Federation endorsed this recommendation in a resolution urging " a most generous support to the independent political movement of the workingmen." [44] Grand Master Workman Powderly of the Knights of Labor, however, continued to oppose independent political action. Answering the invitation to speak to the " Workingmen's Convention " at Philadelphia, he advised it " not to take any action as a party." [45] His was a lone protest, however, and passed quite unheeded by labour.

Immediately after the elections of 1886 steps were taken everywhere to give permanence to the temporary organisations called into being by the exigencies of these campaigns. A move had already been made as early as the summer of 1886 to effect the organisation of a national independent labour party. The Chicago *Express,* upon the " request of over 500 petitioners," had issued a call to the " Knights of Labor, the Farmers' Alliance, the Farmers' and Laborers' Co-operative Union, Wheelers, Grangers, Greenbackers, Corn-Planters, Anti-Monopolists," to send representatives to a convention to be held at Indianapolis, September 1, 1886, to organise a political party, " under which to enroll the industrial vote of the nation." Representatives from six States were at the Indianapolis convention. Nothing was done by this convention except to call another convention to meet at Cincinnati, February 22, 1887. Immediately after the November elections, *John Swinton's Paper* began urging that as many labour organisations as possible should be represented at this Cincinnati convention, because labour could not create any great national political movement in this country without the aid of the farmers.[46] Alliance in politics with the farmers had already been effected by the Knights of Labor in Arkansas and Texas. The convention of the National Farmers' Alliance of November, 1886, also declared in favour of a " union of the farmers with the labor

[43] *Ibid.,* 1886, p. 9.
[44] *Ibid.,* 20.

[45] *John Swinton's Paper,* Dec. 26, 1886.
[46] *Ibid.,* Nov. 14, 1886.

organisations to ameliorate all evils oppressing both classes in common." [47]

Comparatively few of the 458 delegates who attended the Cincinnati convention were workingmen. Farmers distinctly predominated among the delegates; and although most of the farmer delegates were members of the Knights of Labor, the convention was in no sense controlled by wage-earners. A few of the delegates represented labour organisations of cities in the Middle West, but there were almost no representatives of the workingmen of the East. This Cincinnati convention organised the National Union Labor party. All of the members of the national executive committee elected were farmers. The platform, however, endorsed substantially all of the distinctly wage-earners' demands of the preamble of the Knights. Among these demands was a plank calling for the reduction of hours of labour commensurate with the improvements effected in machinery. Immediately after the organisation of the Union Labor party, the national executive committee of the Greenback Labor party declared the latter organisation dissolved. Very promptly, also, the new party put several lecturers into the field to increase its membership.

Organised labour, however, was not at all united as to whether it should merge its political movement with this new party. In the Middle Western cities this was done quite readily. In Philadelphia, Baltimore, San Francisco, and to some extent in Cincinnati, bitter dissensions were called forth by this proposal. The New York United Labor party decided to have nothing to do with the new organisation, because it had rejected a single-tax plank. *John Swinton's Paper,* on the other hand, favoured the new party, and was instrumental in starting a few Union Labor party sections in New York in opposition to the United Labor party. The quarrel grew so bitter that Swinton accused the United Labor party managers of having " sold out " to old-party machines in the preceding autumn election. By July, 1887, the situation was such that the Milwaukee labour party voted to rescind its action in changing its names from the People's party to the Union Labor party, until

47 *Ibid.,* Dec. 5, 1886.

"the Union Labor and United Labor parties have gathered into one common camp." [48]

The municipal elections of the spring of 1887, however, did not mark any falling off in the interest taken by organised labour in independent politics. Union Labor party, Knights of Labor, or labour tickets were in the field in at least fifty-nine localities, including Chicago, Philadelphia, Cincinnati, Indianapolis, East St. Louis, St. Louis, Milwaukee, Dubuque, Kansas City (Missouri), Denver, and San Diego (California).

Probably the most important contest of the independent labour forces in the spring of 1887, was the general municipal election in Chicago. Such was the fear of a Union Labor party triumph that the old parties combined upon a fusion ticket. The labour candidates were most violently denounced as anarchists and cutthroats. The expectation that the labour party would carry the city did not come true; the labour ticket polled 25,000 votes as against 52,000 for the fusion forces. In Milwaukee, also, the labour forces were opposed by a fusion ticket. Against the combined old parties the Union Labor judicial candidates swept the city of Milwaukee, though the country vote of the county defeated them. Nine of the aldermen elected were labour candidates. In Cincinnati the Union Labor candidate for mayor came within 600 votes of being elected, leading the Democratic candidates by above 5,000 votes. The labour ticket won out in at least nineteen more localities, mostly in the Middle West. In Paterson, New Jersey, the labour ticket lost by only 300 votes. Philadelphia, Kansas City, St. Louis and Denver were the places where the showing of labour was most disappointing.

By the autumn of 1887 the independent labour party movement was clearly losing strength. One of the chief factors in its decline was the bitter dissension which almost everywhere broke out in the independent labour party forces. In Chicago the Union Labor party was split in two in the autumn election of 1887. The one faction bargained with the Democrats, while the other openly advocated socialism. In Cincinnati, also, there was a split in the labour party as early as May, 1887. Buchanan's comment upon the situation as it presented itself

48 *Ibid.*, July 17, 1887.

in the autumn of the year is significant. In giving his analysis
of what the difficulty with the independent labour party movement had been, he stated: "Men representing a dozen different shades of opinion have come together ostensibly to pool
their issues and amalgamate the elements variedly represented.
When they have come to write the 'union' platform . . .
each one claimed that he had the cure-all. . . . Well, the upshot of the business has been a few truces, and the stronger
faction has written the platform, while the rest have gone home
sore-headed." [49]

Out of the autumn elections of 1887 organised labour could,
indeed, get little comfort. The Union Labor party ran state
tickets in Massachusetts, New York, Pennsylvania, Ohio, Kentucky, and Iowa. In Ohio the party made its best showing,
polling 25,000 votes. The "labor" candidate for governor
received but 600 votes in Massachusetts. In Pennsylvania the
party could muster less than 9,000 votes. In New York the
Union Labor party barely commanded 1,000 votes. The
United Labor party, with Henry George as candidate for
secretary of state, also made a disappointing showing. In the
prairie States the Union Labor party fared much better than
in the industrial centres. The elections of autumn made it
clear that the wave of independent political activity by the
wage-earners had about spent its force. The Union Labor
party had dismally failed to secure the votes of the workingmen
of the cities.

The spring elections of 1888 were almost as disappointing
to labour as those of the preceding autumn. In Chicago there
was again the old split between the socialists and the conserva-
tives. The socialists ran their own Radical Labor party
ticket, but secured only 3,600 votes. The United Labor
party made combinations with the Democrats in all wards
where this could be arranged. Where it ran its own candidates
it made no better showing than did the socialists. In Kansas
City, also, the socialist and "labor" forces opposed each other.
The "labor" ticket polled 900 votes as against 2,000 in 1887.
Dubuque, carried by the "labor" forces in 1887, now turned
them out of office. In Milwaukee the Union Labor party

made a determined effort to elect its city ticket. Against it
was arrayed an old party fusion ticket, as well as independent
socialist candidates. The socialist ticket was responsible for
the defeat of the Union Labor party. The " Citizen's " ticket
secured a plurality of but 900 votes, while the socialist vote
was almost 1,000. In Galesburg, Illinois, organised labour
scored its only victory in independent politics during the spring
of 1888. At that place two striking engineers on the Burlington railway were elected as aldermen.

The spring elections of 1888 show that the socialists had
withdrawn their support from the independent labour party
forces. In Denver and Philadelphia the socialists seem to have
captured the labour party organisation, but they could not get
any very considerable support from the wage-earners. Personal animosities were another element of disruption within
the labour forces almost everywhere. The Chicago labour party
seems to have been the worst sufferer in this respect.

In the presidential election of the autumn of 1888 organised
labour split its forces. In May the United and the Union Labor parties held their conventions simultaneously in Cincinnati. The efforts made to unite them, however, proved un-
availing, because the United Labor party would not recede
from its advocacy of the single tax. It named Robert H.
Cowdrey for president, while the Union Labor party candidate was A. J. Streeter, the president of the northern Farmers'
Alliance. Late in the campaign the United Labor party withdrew from the struggle, except in New York. The Union
Labor party of the campaign of 1888 was distinctly a farmers' party, although its platform contained most of the planks
of the preamble of the Knights of Labor. In Kansas, where
the Union Labor party got its largest vote, not a single mechanic was upon its ticket. Nor did organised labour give its
support to this party. Many of the most prominent leaders
of organised labour served as old-party campaigners in this election. Charles Litchman, secretary of the Knights of Labor,
John Jarrett, ex-president of the iron and steel workers, and
John Campbell, of the glass-workers, were stump speakers for
Harrison. The window-glass workers' union, Local Assembly
300, Knights of Labor, made a considerable contribution to

the Republican campaign fund. Henry George, on the other hand, worked for the election of Cleveland. The independent labour party organisations in most cities, also, were mere annexes of one or the other of the old parties. During the campaign, Powderly said: "There is no Knights of Labor ticket in the field, and the ticket through which the most practical results can be secured is the ticket which the Knights of Labor should support." [50]

The activity of labour leaders on behalf of old-party candidates in the campaign of 1888 was a source of much trouble within the unions. A later secret circular of the General Executive Board of the Knights of Labor made the claim that the partisan political activity of several of its officers in the presidential campaign of 1888 cost the Order no less than 100,000 members. In Cleveland the trades assembly had become so much of a "Democratic side-show," that a rival central labour union was organised. As early as February, 1888, a determined effort was made in the Chicago Trades and Labor Assembly to bar all unions whose main activity lay in the political field. The independent political movement of organised labour had by this time reached the stage of utter collapse.

Streeter, the Union Labor party nominee, received almost no votes in industrial centres in the election of 1888. Milwaukee with several thousand votes for Streeter was the one large city in which the Union Labor party showed any strength. The 38,000 votes cast for Streeter in Kansas, 29,000 in Texas, 19,000 in Missouri, and 11,000 in Arkansas, must be contrasted with the few votes he polled in the industrial States.

While the Union Labor party gained no support from the workingmen of the cities on the strength of its name and platform, these proved a decided handicap with the farmer voters. Its candidates were denounced as being anarchists. Less than three weeks before the election an exposé of the Order of the Videttes made the rounds of the Kansas press. The Order of the Videttes was represented as the controlling inner ring of the Union Labor party. The overthrow of all law and order was claimed to be the aim of this Order, though its pretended

50 Pittsburgh *Trades Journal*, Sept. 15, 1888. The account of the political movement outside of New York was compiled from a large number of local labour and of farmers' papers, including *John Swinton's Paper*.

ritual read like that of any other secret fraternal organisation. In fact, it is doubtful whether such an organisation as the Order of Videttes ever existed. About a week after the exposé of the ritual, a story was circulated that an express package, marked "glass, handle with care," consigned to Winfield, Kansas, exploded while being handled by the agent at Coffeyville. As the state headquarters of the Union Labor party were at Winfield, the claim was made that the Coffeyville express package contained dynamite intended for the Order of the Videttes. In Arkansas similar charges seem to have been made in this campaign against the Union Labor party.

CHAPTER XIII

REORGANISATION, 1888–1896

The Perfection of the Class Alignment. Decreased influence of industrial fluctuations, 472. The trade agreement idea, 472. The huge corporation, 473. The courts, 473.

The Progress of the Trade Unions. New unions, 473. Increase in membership, 474. Strikes during 1888, 474. The Burlington strike, 474. Resumption of the eight-hour struggle, 475. Action of the convention of the Federation in 1888, 475. The agitational campaign, 475. Selection of the carpenters as the entering wedge, 476. Their success, 477. Unwise selection of the miners to follow the carpenters, 477. End of the eight-hour movement, 478. General appraisal of the movement, 478. Backwardness of the bricklayers on the shorter hours question, 478. The trade-agreement idea in the building trades, 479. The closed shop, 479. The stove moulders' agreement, 480. Peculiarity of the industry from the marketing standpoint, 480. The Stove Founders' National Defense Association, 480. The St. Louis strike, 481. Further strikes, 481. The national trade agreement of 1890, 481.

The Liquidation of the Knights of Labor. Decrease in membership, 1886–1890, 482. Relative increase in importance of the rural membership, 482. Increasing aversion to strikes, 483. Relations to the Federation, 483. Grievances of the trade unions, 483. Rival local trade organisations, 483. Mutual "scabbing," 484. Refusal of the Order to participate in the eight-hour movement of 1890, 484. Final efforts for a reconciliation, 485. Their failure, 485. Withdrawal from the Order of the national trade asemblies, 486. Shoemakers, 486. Machinists, 486. Spinners, 486. Situation in the coal mining industry, 487. The United Mine Workers of America, 487. Situation in the beer-brewing industry, 488. Increasing predominance of politics and of the farmer element in the Order, 488. The Southern Farmers' Alliance, 488. Pivotal rôle of the merchant in the Southern economy, 488. Northern Farmers' Alliance, 489. The Shreveport session of the Southern Alliance, 1887, 490. The Agricultural Wheel, 490. Session of the Southern Alliance in 1889, and the abandonment of co-operation for legislative reform, 490. Alliance with the Knights of Labor, 491. The common programme, 491. Middle-class character of the Knights, 492. Political successes in 1890, 492. The Knights and an independent reform party, 493. Cincinnati convention in 1891 and the People's party, 493. Omaha convention in 1892, 494. Election of J. R. Sovereign as Grand Master Workman of the Knights, 494. His farmer philosophy, 494.

The Reverses of the Trade Unions. Neglect of legislation by the Federation, 495. The Homestead strike, 495. Negotiations for a new scale of wages, 496. Battle with the Pinkertons, 497. Defeat of the union and the elimination of unionism, 497. The miners' strike at Cœur d'Alène, 497. Quelling the strike, 498. The switchmen's strike in Buffalo, 498. Its fail-

ure, 498.   Coal miners' strike in Tennessee, 498.   Its failure, 499.   The lesson, 499.   Gompers' view, 499.   The stimulus to industrial unionism, 500.
Eugene V. Debs and the American Railway Union, 500.   The panic of
1893, 501.   Gompers' hopeful view, 501.
    Trade Unions and the Courts.   The miners' strike, 501.   The Pullman
strike, 502.   Court injunctions, 502.   Violence, 502.   Arrests for contempt
of court, 502.   The Pullman boycott, 503.   The general managers' association, 503.   Attitude of the Federation, 503.   End of the strike, 503.
The court record of the labour unions during the eighties, 504.   The evolution of the doctrines of conspiracy as applied to labour disputes, 504.
Real significance of Commonwealth v. Hunt (1842), 504.   The first injunctions, 505.   Legal justifications, 505.   The Sherman law and the Interstate Commerce Act, 505.   Stages in the evolution of the doctrine that the
right to do business is property, 505.   The part of the doctrine of conspiracy in the theory of the injunction, 507.   Injunctions during the
eighties, 507.   The " blanket injunction," 507.   The Ann Arbor injunction,
507.   The Debs case, 508.   Statutes against " labour conspiracies," 508.
    The Latest Attempt towards a Labour Party.   The causes of the change
on the question of politics, 509.   Convention of the Federation in 1892,
509.   " Political programme," 509.   Gompers' attitude in 1893, 511.   The
disputed plank 10, 511.   Referendum vote, 511.   Sporadic political efforts
in 1894, 511.   Their failure, 512.   Gompers' attack on the " political programme," 512.   The "legislative programme" at the convention in 1894,
512.   Attitude of the convention in 1895, 513.   The Federation and the
campaign of 1896, 514.
    The Socialists and Labour Organisations.   The factional struggle, 1887–
1889, 514.   Final victory of the trade union faction, 515.   Its hope of winning the Federation over to socialism, 516.   Relation to the New York Central labour bodies, 516.   Central Labor Federation, 516   The socialist
question at the convention of the Federation in 1890, 517   Daniel De Leon
and the new tactics, 517   The United Hebrew Trades, 518.   Socialists and
the Knights of Labor, 518.   Socialist Trade and Labor Alliance, 519.   Concluding summary, 519.

By the end of the eighties the labour movement had attained
such a degree of class organisation that, compared with former
years, a transition from prosperity to depression no longer led
to appreciable change in its character.   Formerly it had centred on economic or trade union action during prosperity and
then abruptly changed to panaceas and politics with the descent
of depression.   Now the movement, notwithstanding changes
in membership, became stable in the alignment of classes.   Industrial development ceased to be completely overshadowed by
periodic fluctuations of markets.   The new factors of a more
permanent nature, which revealed themselves after the year
1888, were the national trade agreement, beginning with the
stove-moulding industry; the large manufacturing corporation

with its enormous fighting capacity, which came to light in the Homestead strike against the Carnegie Steel Company; the restraining power of the courts against labour, which found expression in injunctions; and the application of the Federal commerce and anti-trust laws to labour organisations. The moulders' trade agreement, after 1891, furnished the labour movement with a concrete ideal and showed what a well organised national union is capable of attaining in a standardised competitive industry. The Homestead strike of 1892 gave a glimpse of the crushing power of the coming trust. The railway strikes of 1893–1894 demonstrated that the employers had obtained a powerful ally in the courts. Each of these new factors, both favourable and unfavourable, served to draw more clearly and more permanently the line of class division.

THE PROGRESS OF TRADE UNIONS

The Great Upheaval of 1886 had suddenly swelled the membership of trade unions, and consequently, during several years following, notwithstanding the prosperity in industry, further growth was bound to proceed at a slower rate.[1] In his presidential address at the convention of the American Federation of Labor held in December, 1888, at St. Louis, Gompers said:[2] " In the past year, when the tendency in all other directions of the labour movement to disintegration of membership has been going on and interest in their organisation laxing,[3] we may justly pride ourselves when we know that the trade union movement has not only maintained but actually increased its numerical strength."

However, this increase had not been large and, in some instances, there had been an actual loss. The Cigar Makers'

[1] The following new unions were organised: in 1888 the Machinists' International Association, the United Brotherhood of Paper Makers of America, the International Association of Sheet Metal Workers, the Steam and Hot Water Fitters' and Helpers' National Association; and in 1889 the International Brotherhood of Blacksmiths, the Atlantic Coast Seamen's Union, the National Letter Carriers' Association, the International Printing Pressmen's and Assistants' Union, the Wire Weavers' Protective Association of America, the Varnishers' Hard Wood and Piano Makers' International Union, the United Association of Plumbers, Gas Fitters, Steam Fitters and Steam Fitters' Helpers of the United States and Canada, the Coal Miners' and Coal Laborers' National Progressive Union, the Boot and Shoe Workers' International Union, the Tin and Sheet Iron Workers' International Association, and the Sailors' and Firemen's International Amalgamated Society.

[2] American Federation of Labor, *Proceedings*, 1888, p. 10.

[3] Referring to the Knights of Labor.

International Union had 20,566 members in 1887, 17,199 in 1888, 17,555 in 1889, but increased in 1890 to 24,624.[4] The typographical union had 19,190 members in 1887, 17,491 in 1888, and regained its former strength in 1889, when the figure reached 21,120.[5] The bricklayers' union (unaffiliated with the Federation) had a more regular growth; 16,489 members in 1887, 20,110 in 1888, 21,348 in 1889, and 24,022 in 1890.[6] But the most rapidly growing union was the Brotherhood of Carpenters' and Joiners'; its membership was 5,789 in 1885, 21,423 in 1886, and 53,769 in 1890.[7]

The statistics of strikes during the latter eighties, like the figures of membership, show that after the strenuous years from 1885 to 1887 the labour movement had entered a more or less quiet stage in its history. *Bradstreet's* places the number of strikers during 1888 at 211,016, as against 345,073 in 1887, but while only 37.9 per cent of all strikers succeeded in 1887, 50.2 per cent succeeded in 1888.[8]

Most prominent among the strikes was the one of 60,000 iron and steel workers in Pennsylvania, Ohio, and the West, which was carried to a successful conclusion against a strong combination of employers. The Amalgamated Association of Iron and Steel Workers stood at the zenith of its power about this time, and was able, in 1889, with the mere threat of a strike, to dictate terms to the Carnegie Steel companies. The most noted and the last great strike of a railway brotherhood was the one of the locomotive engineers on the Chicago, Burlington & Quincy Railroad. The strike was begun jointly on February 27, 1888, by the brotherhoods of locomotive engineers and locomotive firemen. The main demands were made by the engineers, who asked for the abandonment of the system of classification and for a new wage scale. Two months previously, the Knights of Labor had declared a miners' strike against the Philadelphia & Reading Railroad Company, employing 80,000 anthracite miners, and the strike had been accompanied by a sympathetic strike of engineers and firemen

---

4 Industrial Commission, *Report*, 1901, XVII, 280.

5 Barnett, *The Printers*, 376.

6 These figures are taken from an unpublished history of the union.

7 Industrial Commission, *Report*, 1901, XVII, 128.

8 *Bradstreet's*, Jan. 26, 1889. The figures given by the United States Bureau of Labor, *Report*, are 379,676 for 1887, and 147,704 for 1888.

belonging to the Order. The members of the brotherhoods had filled their places and in retaliation the former Reading engineers and firemen now came and took the places of the Burlington strikers, so that on March 15 the company claimed to have a full contingent of employés. The brotherhoods ordered a boycott upon the Burlington cars, which was partly enforced, but they were finally compelled to submit. The strike was not officially called off until January 3, 1889. Notwithstanding the defeat of the strike, the damage to the railway was enormous, and neither the railways of the country nor the brotherhoods since that date have permitted a serious strike of their members to occur.

The lull in the trade union movement was broken at the convention of the Federation in December, 1888, which declared that a general demand should be made for the eight-hour day on May 1, 1890.[9] The vote upon this resolution stood 38 to 8. The chief advocates of the resolution were the delegates of the carpenters, who announced that they were instructed to work for a general adoption of the eight-hour day in 1890.[10] The boiler makers, the typographical union, the furniture workers, and the granite cutters cast their votes against the resolution. To carry through the programme, the convention once more referred to the affiliated unions the question of making the American Federation of Labor a strike benefit organisation. The co-operation of all labour organisations in the eight-hour movement was also requested. The executive council was instructed to issue pamphlets giving arguments for the establishment of the eight-hour day and to arrange for mass meetings throughout the country in the interest of the movement.[11] Another resolution declared in favour of establishing eight-hour leagues composed of non-wage-earners in all localities.[12]

In pursuance of these instructions the Executive Council of the Federation at once inaugurated an aggressive campaign. For the first time in its history it employed special salaried or-

---

9 American Federation of Labor, *Proceedings*, 1888, p. 28. In the following account of the eight-hour movement in 1890 the author drew largely from an unpublished monograph by E. E. Witte, *The*

American Federation of Labor and the Eight-Hour Day.
10 *Ibid.*, 22.
11 *Ibid.*, 28.
12 *Ibid.*, 84.

ganisers. Two pamphlets [13] were issued and widely distributed. On every important holiday mass meetings were held in the larger cities. On Labour Day, 1889, no less than 420 such mass meetings were held throughout the country.[14] Yet it seems clear that the movement inaugurated by the convention of 1888 attracted much less public attention than that of 1886. Again the Knights of Labor came out against it.[15]

The convention of the Federation of 1889 materially modified the plan of campaign. The idea of a general strike for the eight-hour day in May, 1890, was abandoned, but the Executive Council was authorised to select one union, which alone should move for this object. After it had won out another union was to be selected, and so on until all organised labourers should have gained their demand. To assist the union selected to lead in the fight, the Executive Council was authorised to levy a special assessment of 2 cents per week per member for a period of five weeks upon all affiliated unions.[16] This strike benefit amendment to the constitution was opposed by the representatives of the typographical, granite cutters, and tailors' unions, who were at this time committed to a nine-hour day, believing the eight-hour day unattainable.[17]

In March, 1890, the Executive Council selected the carpenters as the union which should make the demand on May 1, 1890. At the same time the United Mine Workers [18] were selected to move for the eight-hour day after the carpenters should have won their demands. To aid the carpenters, the special assessment provided for the convention of 1889 was levied. Though many unions failed to pay their quota, the assessment netted the carpenters a considerable sum. Organisers, also, were commissioned to help the carpenters.[19]

The choice of the carpenters as the union to lead the fight for the eight-hour day was indeed fortunate. Beginning with 1886, that union had a rapid growth and was now the largest union affiliated with the Federation. For several years it had

13 The Eight-Hour Day Primer, by George E. McNeill, and The Economic and Social Importance of the Eight-Hour Movement, by George Gunton.
14 American Federation of Labor, Proceedings, 1889, p. 15.
15 Ibid., 30.
16 Ibid., 32.

17 Ibid., 32.
18 Formed in 1890 through the amalgamation of the National Trades Assembly 135 of the Knights of Labor and the National Progressive Union.
19 American Federation of Labor, Proceedings, 1890, p. 13.

been accumulating funds for the eight-hour day, and, when the movement was inaugurated in May, 1890, it achieved a large measure of success. According to Secretary P. J. McGuire, it won the eight-hour day in 137 cities, and gained a nine-hour day in most other places.[20] The carpenters kept up their struggle to make the eight-hour day universal. In 1892 their convention declared that strikes for that purpose should be given preference over all other movements.[21]

Contrary to the original plan, the miners' strike for the eight-hour day, which was to follow that of the carpenters, did not materialise. After the carpenters had so generally won their demand, it was too late for the miners to take up the battle in the same year. The convention of the Federation in 1890, therefore, designated them as the union which should move for the eight-hour day on May 1, 1891. The convention directed, also, that a special assessment of the same amount as that levied for the carpenters should be collected for the miners.[22] However, the contemplated movement came to naught. The selection of the miners to undertake the fight at this time was a fatal mistake. Less than one-tenth of the coal miners of the country were then organised. With the constant decline in coal prices, the miners' union had for years been losing ground. The selection of the other applicant for undertaking the movement in 1891, the typographical union, would appear to have been a preferable choice. Some months before May 1, 1891, the United Mine Workers had become involved in a disastrous strike in the Connellsville coke region. In this emergency the Executive Council of the Federation was asked to levy immediately the assessment authorised by the convention of 1890 in aid of the miners' eight-hour movement. This the Council refused to do. The United Mine Workers in their turn now refused to strike for the eight-hour day on May 1, 1891. A strike at that time, in fact, President Gompers admitted, would

20 Gompers, " Report," in *ibid.*

21 *Carpenter*, September, 1892. In the midst of the period of depression, the carpenters' convention of 1894 declared that the time was most opportune for establishing the eight-hour day universally, since contractors would not object to it while work was slack. (*Carpenter*, October, 1894.) Nevertheless, they made very little progress for a long time after 1890. During the succeeding period of depression the union lost one-half of its membership. In consequence it lost in many places the shorter hours won in 1890. Cleveland *Citizen*, Nov. 9, 1895.

22 American Federation of Labor, *Proceedings*, 1890, pp. 40–42,

have been useless, since the operators had accumulated large stores of coal in anticipation of the strike, of which they had been warned so long in advance.[23]

The convention of the Federation in 1891 was asked to give its support to an eight-hour movement in 1892 by the bakers' union, and to a struggle for the nine-hour day by the typographical union. The convention, however, voted to leave to the Executive Council the choice of the union to lead the next effort.[24] The latter in turn found the time inopportune for beginning another struggle. The next convention, in 1892, merely instructed the Executive Council to keep up agitation for the eight-hour work-day, and especially to prepare some union to lead the next fight.

In this manner the eight-hour movement inaugurated by the convention of 1888 came to an end. Apart from the strike of the carpenters in 1890, it had not led to any general movement to gain the eight-hour work-day. During these years, however, the percentage of strikes for a reduction of the hours of labour was much greater than at any other time after 1886. In the reports of President Gompers during these years, it was claimed that hundreds of thousands of workingmen had won reduced hours of labour through these movements. Notable progress was made, not only by the carpenters, but by other unions in the building trades. By 1891 the eight-hour day had been secured for all branches of the industry in Chicago, St. Louis, Denver, Indianapolis, and San Francisco. In New York and Brooklyn the carpenters, stone cutters, painters, and plasterers worked eight hours, while the bricklayers, masons, and plumbers worked nine. In St. Paul the bricklayers alone worked nine hours, the remaining trades, eight.[25] The backwardness of the bricklayers in these cities was due to their policy of aloofness from the general labour movement. Their national convention in 1890 declared, with regard to the eight-hour movement inaugurated by the Federation, that " the interests of the country are not yet of such a nature as would warrant our departure from our present effective system . . . and the time has not yet come when we could with safety and propriety make such

23 *Ibid.*, 1891, p. 12.
24 *Ibid.*, 45.
25 Convention of the National Associa-   tion of Builders, *Proceedings*, 1891, p. 162.

demand, and [we desire] to retain our autonomy in all matters which pertain to our welfare as a trade." [26]

It is significant that in 1891, when President Gompers asked the affiliated national unions to name the three things upon which the American Federation of Labor should concentrate its efforts, every one of them included among these the reduction of hours of labour.[27] It is no less significant that throughout the eighties the argument of Ira Steward that shorter hours would lead to increased wages by raising the standard of life, receded into the background before the theory of "making work." Gompers declared in 1887 that "the answer to all opponents to the reduction of the hours of labor could well be given in these words: 'that so long as there is one man who seeks employment and cannot obtain it, the hours of labor are too long.'"[28] He expounded this philosophy of the eight-hour movement at greater length to the convention of 1889. In speaking of "the hundreds of thousands of our fellows, who, through the ever-increasing inventions and improvements in the modern methods of production, are rendered 'superfluous,'" he said, "we must find employment for our wretched Brothers and Sisters by reducing the hours of labor or we will be overwhelmed and destroyed."[29] Again in his report of 1893, he urged that "the only method by which a practical, just and safe equilibrium can be maintained in the industrial world for the fast and ever increasing introduction of machinery, is a commensurate reduction in the hours of labor."[30]

The system of the settlement of trade disputes by arbitration, which had been advocated by William H. Sayward, the secretary of the National Builders' Association since its inception, was formally approved by the association in 1890. However, it carried a provision for the open shop and against the sympathetic strike,[31] and the trade unions were not desirous even of giving it a trial. The exception to this rule also was the brick-

26 Quoted from official records in manuscript history of the union. In 1886 the bricklayers had similarly refused to participate in the eight-hour movement and demanded instead, the nine-hour day, which they secured.

27 American Federation of Labor, Proceedings, 1891, p. 13.

28 Ibid., 1887, p. 10.

29 Ibid., 1889, p. 16.

30 Ibid., 1893, p. 11.

31 Stockton in his study of the closed shop in American trade unions said: "The campaign for the closed shop was carried on among a large number of unions between 1885 and 1893. The strong closed-shop unions already mentioned [during the seventies: the Iron and Steel Workers, Granite Cutters, Cigarmakers, Hatters, Printers, Moulders, and Brick-

layers, who entered into a written agreement with the master masons' association in Boston in 1890.[32]

While one of the earliest stable trade agreements in a conspicuous trade covering a local field was the bricklayers' agreement in Chicago in 1887, the era of trade agreements really dates from the national system established in the stove foundry industry in 1891. It is true that the iron and steel workers had worked under a national trade agreement since 1866. However, the trade was so exceptionally strong that its example had no power to make other trades aspire with confidence towards the same.[33]

The stove industry had early reached a high degree of development and organisation. There had existed since 1872 the National Association of Stove Manufacturers, an organisation dealing with prices, and embracing in its membership the largest stove manufacturers of the country. The stove foundrymen, therefore, unlike the manufacturers in practically all other industries, controlled in a large measure their own market. Furthermore, the product had been completely standardised and reduced to a piece-work basis, and machinery had not taken the place of the moulders' skill. It consequently was no mere accident that the stove industry was the first to develop a system of permanent industrial peace. But, on the other hand, this was not automatically established as soon as the favourable external conditions were provided. In reality, only after years of struggle, of strikes and lockouts, and after the two sides had fought each other " to a standstill " was the system finally installed.

The eighties abounded in stove moulders' strikes, and in 1886 the national union began to render effective aid. The Stove Founders' National Defense Association was formed in 1886 as an employers' association, with its membership recruited from the mercantile association of stove manufacturers. The Defense Association aimed at a national labour policy; it was

---

layers] were joined by the Lasters, Glass Bottle Blowers, Window Glass Workers, Flint Glass Workers, Machinists, and many local unions in the metal, printing, building and miscellaneous trades. In a few of the building trades unions, as, for example the Painters, the closed shop, was practically obligatory on the local

unions." " The Closed Shop in American Trade Unions," in *Johns Hopkins University Studies*, 1911, XXIX, 39–40.

[32] W. H. Sayward. in Industrial Commission, *Report*, 1900, VII, 841–860.

[33] The trade agreements in the glass trades partook of the same exceptional character as in the iron and steel trades.

organised for " resistance against any unjust demands of their workmen, and such other purposes as may from time to time prove or appear to be necessary for the benefit of the members thereof as employers of labor." [34]   Thus, after 1886, the alignment was made national on both sides.   The great battle, however, was fought the next year.

March 8, 1887, the employés of the Bridge and Beach Manufacturing Company in St. Louis struck for an advance in wages and the struggle at once became one between the international union and the National Defense Association.   The St. Louis company sent its patterns to foundries in other districts, but the union successfully prevented their use.   This occasioned a series of strikes in the West and of lockouts in the East, affecting altogether about 5,000 moulders.   It continued thus until June, when the St. Louis patterns were recalled, the Defense Association having provided the company with a sufficient number of strike-breakers.   Each side was in a position to claim the victory for itself, so evenly matched were the opposing forces.

During the next four years, disputes in Association plants were rare.   In August, 1890, a strike took place in Pittsburgh, and, for the first time in the history of the industry, it was settled by a written trade agreement with the local union.   This supported the idea of a national trade agreement between the two organisations.   After the dispute of 1887, negotiations with this object were from time to time conducted, the Defense Association invariably taking the initiative.   Finally, the national convention of the union in 1890 appointed a committee to meet in conference with a like committee of the Defense Association. The conference took place March 25, 1891, and worked out a complete plan of government for the stove-moulding industry, including legislative, executive, and judicial branches.   Every year two committees of three members each, chosen respectively by the union and the association, were to meet in conference and to draw up general laws for the year.   In case of a dispute arising in a locality, if the parties immediately concerned were unable to arrive at common terms, the chief executives of both

[34] Commons and Frey, " Conciliation and Arbitration in the Stove Industry," in   Bureau of Labor, *Bulletin*, Jan. 1906, p. 143.

organisations, the president of the union, and the president of the association, were to step in and try to effect an adjustment. If, however, they too failed, a conference committee composed of an equal number of members from each side was to be called in and its findings were to be final. As in every well-constituted government, the parties were enjoined from engaging in hostilities while the matter at dispute was being dealt with by the duly appointed authorities. Each organisation obligated itself to exercise " police authority " over its constituents, enforcing obedience to the " government." The endorsement of the plan by both organisations was practically unanimous and has continued in operation without interruption until the present day.[35]

THE LIQUIDATION OF THE KNIGHTS OF LABOR

The progress made by the building trades, particularly the carpenters, the dominance achieved by the Amalgamated Association of Iron and Steel Workers, and the establishment of the stove moulders' national trade agreement were the high-water marks in 1891 of the unions of skilled men. On the other hand, the Knights of Labor were rapidly declining. They fell from a membership of 700,000 in 1886 to 500,982 in 1887, 259,578 in 1888, 220,607 in 1889, and 100,-000 in 1890. Of the greatest significance was the decrease in the large cities. In 1886 the aggregate membership in the 20 largest cities of 150,000 inhabitants and over [36] amounted to about 309,000; in 1887 to about 195,000; and in 1888 it had fallen to about 82,000. In percentages of the total membership, the decrease was from about 44 per cent in 1886 to 38 per cent in 1887 and finally to about 31 per cent in 1888.[37] No detailed membership statistics were published after 1888, but it is safe to assume that the same tendency continued at work. This assumption appears particularly warranted in view of the close alliance between the Order and the farmers' organisations after 1889, and the rapid growth of the American Federation of Labor in the large cities.

35 For further details see *ibid.*
36 According to U. S. *Census*, 1890.
37 These figures and percentages are compiled from the official membership figures published with the General Assembly, *Proceedings*.

With the loss of a foothold in the cities the strike era of the Knights of Labor came to an end. Henceforth, although small strikes continued to occur nearly as often as before, long strikes came at infrequent intervals. After the unsuccessful strike of 35,000 coal miners and railroad men against the Philadelphia & Reading Railroad Company early in 1888, the Order engaged in no conspicuous strike until August, 1890, when it conducted another unsuccessful strike against the New York Central & Hudson River Railroad Company.[38] The general officers of the Order endeavoured to prevent this strike in accordance with their attitude towards strikes in general. The decline in membership, the contest with the trade unions, and the recourse to politics were reducing their energy as a strike organisation.

After 1887, the bulk of the unskilled labourers having left the Order, the struggle between the Knights and the trade unions ceased to be one between the unskilled and skilled portions of the wage-earning class for control of the labour movement, and became instead a mere fight between two rival organisations. The grievance of the trade unions was stated by the convention of 1889, as follows: [39] " Much of the trouble has been occasioned by the organisation of National trade districts of the Knights of Labor in crafts where national and international unions already exist. Not only has the creation of this dual authority been productive of evil results, but too often the National trade districts have been made the dumping ground for men who have been branded as unfair by the trade unions." Indeed, numerous illustrations can be adduced where

---

[38] The New York Central Road had been known since the sixties as the fairest employer among railways. The Vanderbilt policy toward the organisations of employés had been one of cordial toleration. In consequence the system was entirely unaffected by the strike of 1877. When the Knights of Labor appeared, the same liberal policy was pursued. However, a change occurred about 1890 and the railroad began to discharge men for no other reason, as the employés believed, than activity in the organisation. The matter came to a climax in August, 1890, while President Chauncey Depew was absent in Europe, after fifty-five men had been discharged. Powderly counselled the men to await the time of the Columbian Exposi-

tion in 1893 or the presidential year of 1892. But, notwithstanding this advice, which was also reinforced by the warning that the Order was not in a position to render any strike assistance, 2,500 switchmen, brakemen, yardmen, freight-handlers and clerks struck on August 8. The strike succeeded in tying up the passenger traffic between New York and Albany for three days and also caused a considerable freight blockade. It was, however, speedily defeated, primarily because the firemen and locomotive engineers refused to strike in sympathy. General Assembly, *Proceedings*, 1890, pp. 4–10; also *Bradstreet's*, Aug. 16 and 23, 1890.

[39] American Federation of Labor, *Proceedings*, 1889, 36–38.

disaffected local unions of an international or national union joined the Knights of Labor in order to win an ally for their cause.[40] On the other hand, the Knights of Labor pointed out that they were doing useful work by organising the mechanics in the small towns. The General Assembly of 1892 authorised the employment of an organiser to form mixed local assemblies of building trades in cities of 25,000 and less.[41] It also pointed to numerous cases where the trade unions had committed similar acts.[42] The breaking up of the Knights of Labor strike on the Philadelphia & Reading Railroad by engineers and firemen who were members of the brotherhoods in January, 1888, and the retaliatory action of the Reading men in the Chicago, Burlington & Quincy strike during the fall of 1888 were salient illustrations of the internecine war raging within the labour movement.

The relations between the Federation and the Order were no better than those existing between their respective parts. The Federation, having decided at its convention in 1888 in favour of a renewed eight-hour movement, naturally desired to obtain the co-operation of the Knights. Several meetings for this purpose were held between the national officers of both organisations. At a conference, held on October 14, the representatives of the Knights " pointed out that it appeared to them to be essential, before the necessary unity of action could be obtained which would insure success, that, as far as possible, the unfortunate disputes and misunderstandings between labor bodies should be arranged and terminated," [43] and proposed an

---

[40] National Trade Assembly 217, Steel and Iron Workers, was organised as a rival to the Amalgamated Association. (Pittsburgh *National Labor Tribune*, Feb. 11, 1888.) In Chicago the Knights of Labor organised a rival carpenters' council. (Chicago *Labor Enquirer*, Apr. 14, 1888.) During 1890–1891 there was considerable trouble between the bakers' union and the Knights of Labor, chiefly because the former demanded the closed shop. (Philadelphia *Journal of the Knights of Labor*, June 4, 1891.) In New York City the United Order of Carpenters, a rival to the Brotherhood, joined the Knights of Labor in July, 1890. The Progressive Carpenters' Union, another rival organisation, had done so earlier. (*Ibid.*, July 10, 1890.) The Painters'

union of Pittsburgh left the national union to join the Knights of Labor. *Ibid.*, Aug. 6, 1891.
[41] General Assembly, *Proceedings*, 1892, p. 80.
[42] The New York Central Labor Union declared as fair a carpet firm which was boycotted by the Knights of Labor. (Philadelphia *Journal of United Labor*, May 5, 1888.) The iron moulders' union praised the Fuller and Warren Co. as a friend of labour, against which the Knights of Labor had been carrying on a boycott since 1884; and numerous other instances. (*Ibid.*, Apr. 21, 1888.)
[43] " Report of General Executive Board," in General Assembly, *Proceedings*, 1889, p. 36.

agreement upon the basis of the interchange of cards, the mutual endorsement of labels and the reciprocal promise to refrain from organising scabs.[44] To this Gompers and McGuire moved as a counter proposal that the Knights of Labor should revoke the charters of all trade assemblies, national and local, in exchange for which the Federation would urge its members to join mixed assemblies of the Order.[45] As was to be expected, the conference resulted in nothing.

The General Assembly, which met November 12, 1889, refused actively to co-operate with the Federation in the eight-hour movement on the mere formal ground that " no plan has been submitted to the General Assembly by Mr. Gompers." [46] The convention of the American Federation of Labor, which met immediately after, December 10, 1889, decided that thereafter no conferences should be held with representatives of the Knights of Labor,[47] and issued an " Address to the Working People of America." This address said in part: " The success of the short hour cause is of too vast import to be imperilled by policies of masterly inaction or acrobatic posing. The march toward the eight-hour goal must not be halted at the behest of the middleman. . . . Experience has also proven that the wage-earner is the natural and proper guardian of the wage-earners' right. . . . Professions of harmony and platitudes of peace are a poor recompense for the attempted weakening of the trade union column." [48] With regard to future relations with the Knights, the address went on to say: " With the original educational purpose of the Knights of Labor, as vested in mixed assemblies, the trade unionists of America were and are in sympathy. The evidence of this fact is to be found in the large number of trade unionists who worked zealously for the building up of the Order in its early period of growth, but who were forced to leave that organisation when ambitious and unscrupulous persons sought to trench upon the rightful prerogatives of the trade unions and subordinate the legitimate labor movement to the aggrandisement of personal ambition." [49]

44 *Ibid.*
45 American Federation of Labor, *Proceedings*, 1889, p. 14.
46 General Assembly, *Proceedings*, 1889, p. 52.
47 American Federation of Labor, *Proceedings*, 1889, p. 21.
48 *Ibid.*, 38.
49 *Ibid.*, 37.

The same result attended the attempt to bring together the Federation and the Knights in 1891,[50] and again, upon the initiative of Joseph R. Buchanan,[51] in 1894, as well as the last attempt made by the brewery workmen's union in 1895.[52]

Notwithstanding the fact that much of the trouble between the Federation and the Knights had been occasioned by the organisation of national trade assemblies, the latter had no strong feeling of loyalty to the Order. This was due to many causes, one of the chief being the obstruction they met on the part of the mixed district assemblies. The case of the shoemakers illustrates this admirably. The Shoemakers' National Trade Assembly 216 was formed in 1887. It met with considerable trouble in gathering up the shoemakers' local assemblies scattered among the various district assemblies. The trouble grew acute in Cincinnati where District Assembly 48, contrary to the rule adopted by the General Assembly of 1887, persistently refused to allow the transfer of its shoemaker locals. Since the national officers of the Knights were disposed to render little aid, National Trade Assembly 216 seceded in February, 1889, and formed the Boot and Shoe Workers' International Union.[53]

Another cause for leaving the Knights of Labor was named by the general officers of National Trade Assembly 198, which had been organised in March 1887, and consisted of pattern makers, foundrymen, blacksmiths, machinists, boiler makers, and the respective helpers of each. In May, 1888, they wrote: "The odium which the Order has gained is damaging to us. We will have to cut loose from the Knights of Labor before the employers will meet us or respect us in any way."[54] In accordance with this the national trade assembly of machinists became the next year the National Association of Machinists.[55] Another illustration is provided by the mule spinners' association, which had unanimously withdrawn from the Knights of Labor. "The principal cause for the withdrawal was the heavy expense of membership in the Knights compared with the benefit received."[56] An instance of a later date is supplied by

50 *Ibid.*, 1891, p. 47.
51 *Ibid.*, 1894, p. 14.
52 *Ibid.*, 1895, p. 95.
53 From a leaflet issued in 1889 by President Skeffington of the union.

54 *Journal of United Labor*, May 19, 1888.
55 National Association of Machinists, *Constitution* 1890, 1.
56 *Carpenter*, May, 1888.

the Carriage and Wagon Workers' International Union, which was organised in 1891 out of District Trade Assembly 247 of the Knights of Labor.[57]

Thus, through a gradual process of secession the unions of the semi-skilled machine trades, which had their origin in the Knights of Labor, found their way into the Federation, converting the latter from an organisation primarily of skilled men into one more representative of the entire labour movement.

A peculiar situation existed in the coal-mining industry. National Trade Assembly 135 had, in 1889, a membership of over 10,000 in 16 States, and the Coal Miners' and Laborers' National Progressive Union a somewhat smaller membership, mainly in the central competitive region.[58] A minority of National Trade Assembly 135, headed by National Master Workman William T. Lewis, had seceded in December, 1888, from the Knights of Labor in order to join the National Progressive Union, naming in justification of its action the persistent interference by District Assembly 15 in the Reading anthracite region and District Assembly 11 in the coke region, in which actions they had been supported by Powderly.[59] Notwithstanding the hostile feeling aroused, both organisations had managed to co-operate at the annual interstate conferences held with the employers. But the downward course that unionism took in the coal-mining industry during 1889 and 1890 finally brought the two organisations into closer union and they formed through amalgamation the United Mine Workers of America. The new organisation had a peculiar status: It continued to be affiliated with the Order as a secret organisation under the name of National Trade Assembly 135, but at the same time it functioned as an open and independent trade union affiliated with the American Federation of Labor. Since it was doing its important work in the latter capacity, the membership was gradually giving up allegiance to the Order, so that the latter expelled it in 1894.[60] A similar double

---

[57] Industrial Commission, *Report*, 1901, XVII, 209.

[58] This region includes the Pittsburgh district in Pennsylvania, West Virginia, Ohio, Indiana, Illinois, Iowa, southeastern Kentucky, and Michigan.

[59] Pittsburgh *National Labor Tribune*, Nov. 17, 1888.

[60] *Secret Circular of the Knights of Labor*, Dec. 17, 1894.

allegiance was maintained for a time by the International Union of United Brewery Workmen of America. Originally an open non-secret trade union, having received a charter from the Federation in 1887, it allowed a large number of its locals to remain in the Knights of Labor, and in 1893 became affiliated with the Order as a national trade district. The especial cause at work in the case of the brewery workmen was the important assistance the Order might render in their boycott against the national organisation of brewery owners. This long established organisation had originally been called into existence as a manufacturers' organisation for the purpose of influencing legislation, but became in 1886 also an association of employers. It began, in 1888, a struggle against the brewery workmen's union by declaring a lockout to which the union replied by a nation-wide boycott, which lasted fourteen years. The brewery workmen maintained their dual affiliation until 1896, when, partly as a result of friction with independent brewery workmen's organisations within the Order, but mainly owing to a threat by the Federation to revoke its charter, they severed connection with the Knights.[61]

The withdrawal from the Knights of the nationally organised trades served to strengthen the tendency, already apparent with the shift of membership, towards politics and the farmers. The Farmers' and Laborers' Union of America, which in 1889 had organised in eighteen States and territories with a membership of fully a million [62] was originated by a group of farmers in Texas in the middle of the seventies, mainly in order to protect the land tillers against " land sharks." By 1878 it had spread to three counties and a State Alliance was formed. It went to pieces as a result of greenback party politics, but was revived in 1879 as a non-political organisation with co-operative buying and selling as one of its features. The organisation was secret and admitted women but excluded Negroes. In the middle of the eighties, co-operative buying and selling became its principal activity and the movement was directed primarily against the domination of the merchant.

The merchant was the pivotal figure in the economy of the

61 Schlüter, *The Brewing Industry and the Brewery Workers' Movement in America*, 142–204, 212–219.

62 Dunning, *The Farmers' Alliance History and Agricultural Digest*, 95.

South after the War. The small planters and the farmers were too poor to finance their crops, and therefore were obliged to resort to the merchant for loans. He willingly advanced them money, but only on mortgage upon the future crop, with the outcome that he obtained the right to prescribe what the farmer should raise. Naturally he found it to his advantage to insist upon cotton as the only crop, because that would enable him, first, to make a profit upon a larger amount of cotton, and then an additional profit upon the wheat, bacon, and other supplies which he sold to the farmers at exorbitant prices. The organised farmers in Texas tried to meet this situation by a state exchange, a joint stock association which gathered from the members their individual notes and used them as collateral in buying the quantities of supplies that they ordered.[63]

In January, 1887, the Farmers' Alliance of Texas, in conjunction with the Farmers' Union of Louisiana, an organisation with a similar career, formed the National Farmers' Alliance and Co-operative Union of America with a programme consisting mainly of propaganda, education, and mutual benefits.[64] The marketing side of the work was to remain with the state organisations. Dr. C. W. Macune, president of the alliance of Texas, was chosen national president.

There had existed since October, 1880, a national farmers' alliance in the wheat region of the Northwest, which had, in 1887, state alliances in Dakota, Illinois, Iowa, Kansas, Minnesota, Nebraska, Ohio, Washington, and Wisconsin. This national alliance, known as the Northern Alliance, organised by such men as Streeter of Illinois, the presidential candidate of the Greenback Union Labor party in 1888, was primarily a political organisation,[65] particularly active in the politics of the Dakotas and Minnesota.[66] As the National Farmers' Alliance and Co-operative Union, or the Southern Alliance, desired at this time to remain on a strictly " business," or co-operative basis, fusion of the two sister organisations was impossible.[67]

63 *Ibid.*, 85.

64 *Ibid.*, 58. The National Alliance took out a Federal charter under the law of 1885. The Texas State Alliance had been incorporated in 1880 in that State.

65 *History of the Farmers' Alliance, the Agricultural Wheel*, etc., edited and compiled under the auspices of the St. Louis *Journal of Agriculture*, 1890, 237–247.

66 Dunning, *Farmers' Alliance History*, 306, 307.

67 President Macune said in his address to the Shreveport, La., convention: " It

The first regular session of the Southern Alliance was held at Shrevesport, Louisiana, October, 1887, and included delegates from Mississippi, Arkansas, Florida, North Carolina, Alabama, Louisana, Missouri, Tennessee, and Texas.[68] At the convention preliminary preparations were made for amalgamation with the Agricultural Wheel. Like the Southern Alliance, this organisation, which arose in Arkansas in February, 1882, was a protest against exploitation by the merchant. It soon extended into Tennessee, Kentucky, Wisconsin, Texas, Alabama, Mississippi, Missouri, and Indian Territory. The national " Wheel " was organised in July, 1886. Although it had as its object emancipation from the merchant, the Wheel did not launch into co-operative buying and selling, but agitated a greater diversification of crops in place of cotton. In addition it had a comprehensive list of legislative demands, principally relating to legal tender currency, taxation, and usury laws.[69] In 1887 it claimed a membership of 500,000.

The convention at St. Louis in September, 1889, was the first to bring the farmers' movement before the country. At this convention the Alliance completed its amalgamation with the Wheel and received the affiliation of the Farmers' Alliance of Kansas, which had hitherto been a part of the Alliance of the North, thereby achieving a membership in 18 States, estimated at 1,000,000. But far more significant was the advance in policy. Mere co-operation and education were recognised as insufficient. As ex-President Macune, now editor of the *National Economist* at Washington, pointed out, the financial class by the mere device of arbitrary contraction of the currency when the farmer came on the market as a seller, and of expanding it when he came as a buyer, was in a position

was, after a full investigation, decided that the organisation as it existed in Texas and the States of the South, to which it had spread from and by the authority of the Texas alliance, could accomplish nothing by joining the National Farmers' Alliance of the Northwest, and in view of the fact that the cotton belt of America was a circumscribed country, there was a necessity for a national organisation of those residing in the cotton belt, to the end that the whole world of cotton-raisers might be united for self-protection. . . . It was, therefore, decided to organise, in connection with Louisiana, a National Farmers' Alliance and Co-operative Union of America. . . . Let the Alliance be a business organisation for business purposes, and as such, necessarily secret, and as secret, necessarily strictly non-political." *Ibid.*, 68–70.

[68] *Ibid.*, 66.

[69] *History of the Farmers' Alliance*, etc., edited and compiled under the auspices of the St. Louis *Journal of Agriculture*, 1890, pp. 113–144.

to neutralise every advantage that accrued to the farmer from co-operation. As a result of such manipulation, Macune estimated that the farmer was swindled out of 50 per cent of his legitimate income.[70] To remedy this situation the St. Louis convention brought out a financial measure known as the sub-treasury plank, which came to be regarded as the pet project of the Alliance. Put in a nutshell, this measure provided that the government should warehouse non-perishable farm products and upon these as security should loan to the producer 80 per cent of the market value of the goods in legal tender money at the nominal rate of 1 per cent interest. It is evident that the intention of the fathers of this measure was to make the volume of currency automatically expand during the season of marketing the crops and consequently to enhance agricultural prices at that time.

The shift of the Alliance from co-operation to legislative reform brought it face to face with the question of the mode of political action. The St. Louis convention favoured both an active participation in the primary elections of the old parties and an energetic lobbying activity in Washington. In this convention the first formal covenant was made between the Alliance and the Knights of Labor. T. V. Powderly, A. W. Wright, and Ralph Beaumont, of the Knights, were present at St. Louis and entered into an agreement with a committee representing the Alliance, which read in part as follows:

" The undersigned committee representing the Knights of Labor, having read the demands of the National Farmers' Alliance and Industrial Union, which are embodied in this agreement, hereby endorse the same on behalf of the Knights of Labor, and for the purpose of giving practical effect to the demands herein set forth, the legislative committees of both organisations will act in concert before Congress for the purpose of securing the enactment of laws in harmony with the demands mutually agreed. And it is further agreed, in order to carry out these objects, we will support for office only such men as can be depended upon to enact these principles in statute law, uninfluenced by party caucus."

The demands upon which both the Alliance and the Knights agreed were: first, the abolition of national banks and the issue

70 Dunning, *Farmers' Alliance History*, 111, 112.

of legal tender treasury notes in lieu of national bank notes, regulating the amount needed on a per capita basis as the business of the country increased; second, the prohibition of dealing in futures; third, the free and unlimited coinage of silver; fourth, the prohibition of alien land ownership and the reclaiming by the government of land granted to railroads but not actually in use; fifth, equitable and just taxation and economy in government; sixth, the issue of a sufficient amount of fractional paper currency to facilitate exchange through the mails, and seventh, government ownership of the means of communication and transportation. A clause provided for the mutual recognition of labels.[71]

This list of demands speaks volumes for the mental subjection of the Knights of Labor to the farmers' movement. None of these demands may be called a strictly labour demand, and, even if certain of them tended to benefit labour, such a benefit would be merely incidental and of minor importance. Currency inflation might make for a larger amount of employment, but in 1889, when industry had already recovered from the preceding depression, the matter of employment was a minor problem. The same might be said of the demand for reclaiming the excess of land granted to the railroads with its expected draining-off of the labour market. There remains only one demand that might lead to a tangible benefit to labour, the government ownership of railroads and telegraphs, which although primarily designed to give the farmer cheaper rates, might also considerably improve the condition of railroad labour.

We can fully understand this total absence of wage consciousness on the part of the Knights of Labor only by taking account of the shift of membership, just mentioned, from the unskilled class in the large cities of the East to the class of mechanics and small merchants in the smaller cities and country towns who depended upon the farmer for a living, and also the gradual withdrawal of the nationally organised trades.

The year 1890 was eventful in the history of the farmers' movement. The autumn election brought the first political successes. Tillman was elected governor of South Carolina, and, in Kansas, though the independent Alliance candidate for gov-

71 *Ibid.*, 122.

ernor fell short of election by only 10,000 votes, the control of
the legislature was secured in both branches and a senator and
congressmen were elected, among them John H. Davis, a member of the National Executive Board of the Knights of Labor.
Success also attended the political efforts in North Carolina
and Georgia, and somewhat less success in Nebraska and the
Dakotas.[72] On the other hand, their lobbying activity in Congress met with failure. The Fifty-first Congress paid scant
attention to the measures which the Alliance and the Knights
jointly introduced. The success in the election, coupled with
the failure in Congress, tended to strengthen the third-party
feeling. It grew particularly strong in the West, but was
comparatively weak in the South, where action through the
Democratic party was naturally preferred.

The General Assembly of the Knights of Labor in November, 1890, by a vote of 53 against 12, put itself upon record
in favour of an independent political party,[73] and at the next
convention of the Alliance at Ocala, Florida, in December,
1890, the General Executive Board, headed by Powderly, attended in a body, and exerted an influence in this direction.
However, President Polk and the other leaders of the Alliance
did not desire to risk their strong organisation [74] in the attempt, but preferred to see the third party started under different auspices. To this effect a national Citizens' Alliance
was formed at the convention, with J. D. Holden, of Kansas,
president; Ralph Beaumont, of New York, secretary, and L. P.
Wild of Washington, treasurer. Beaumont was the head of
the lobbying committee of the Knights at Washington and
Wild was also a member of the Order.

The Citizens' Alliance and the Knights of Labor jointly
issued a call for a national political convention to meet in Cincinnati in February, 1891, but, since the call was coolly received by the Alliance, and the Knights of Labor also experienced a change of heart, the convention was postponed until
May. Meanwhile, a general conference was held in Washing-

---

72 The organisations in Nebraska and
the Dakotas had seceded from the Alliance
in the Northwest and joined the Southern
Alliance.

73 General Assembly, *Proceedings*, 1890,
p. 71.

74 At Ocala, the Farmers' Mutual Benefit Society, formed in 1883 and 150,000
strong, joined the movement; also the coloured farmers' alliance, with a membership claimed to be 1,200,000.

ton, January 21, 1891, as an attempt to form a permanent confederation of all " industrial " organisations: the Alliance, the Farmers' Mutual Benefit Association, the Patrons of Husbandry, the coloured Alliance, and the Knights of Labor. Nothing tangible, however, resulted.

The political convention, which was originally called by the Citizens' Alliance and the Knights of Labor met, in Cincinnati, May 19, 1891, and resulted in the preliminary organisation of the People's party. The Knights of Labor took little part in the proceedings, Powderly being present, not in his official capacity, but as a mere sympathiser. One-fourth of the delegation was from Kansas alone, and more than three-fourths were from the six States of Kansas, Ohio, Indiana, Illinois, Missouri, and Nebraska. The East was entirely unrepresented. A nominating national convention met July 4, 1892, at Omaha, formulated a platform, and nominated General Weaver, of Iowa, for president and General Field, of Virginia, for vice-president. The subtreasury scheme formed the main plank of the platform, which included also the other Alliance demands. But in order to attract the labour vote, several strictly labour planks were added: the restriction of undesirable immigration, the reduction of the hours of labour on government work, and the condemnation of Pinkertons. The industrial organisations, which met in Washington in January, 1891, including the Knights of Labor, decided not to become the official sponsors of the party, but their unofficial support remained unequivocal.

At the General Assembly in November, 1893, when its membership had fallen to 74,635, the national organisation of the Knights took the final step away from the wage-earners' movement. James R. Sovereign, a farmer editor from Iowa, succeeded through a temporary alliance with the socialist delegates,[75] in supplanting Powderly for the office of grand master workman. In which direction the Order was steering under Sovereign will appear from the following portion of his report to the General Assembly of 1894:[76]

" The Order of the Knights of Labor is not so much intended to

75 See below, II, 519.
76 General Assembly, *Proceedings*, 1894, p. 1.

adjust the relationship between the employer and employe as to adjust natural resources and productive facilities to the common interests of the whole people, that all who wish may work for themselves, independent of large employing corporations and companies. It is not founded on the question of adjusting wages, but on the question of abolishing the wage-system and the establishment of a co-operative industrial system. When its real mission is accomplished, poverty will be reduced to a minimum and the land dotted over with peaceful, happy homes. Then, and not till then, will the Order die."

REVERSES OF THE TRADE UNIONS

While the Knights of Labor, its membership dwindling and its industrial strength a matter of the past, was resorting to political action, the trade unions, at the height of their power in 1891, persistently refused to follow their example.[77] The American Federation of Labor was at this period, more than during any other, a purely economic organisation. Even in the legislative lobbying of the Federation for labour measures, these years were sterile. The only time when the Federation seems to have been officially represented before a congressional committee, was in 1888, through President Gompers.[78] In 1890 a motion to maintain a permanent lobby in Washington during the session of Congress was defeated.[79] In lieu thereof the convention of 1891 adopted instructions to the Executive Council to send copies of all resolutions approved to every member of Congress.[80]

The political self-complacency of the trade unions came to an abrupt end in 1892. The big and disastrous strikes in that year of the iron and steel workers at Homestead, of the switchmen in Buffalo, and of the miners in Tennessee and Cœur d'Alène, proved to organised labour the overwhelming strength of the employing class.

In the Homestead strike the labour movement faced for the first time a really modern manufacturing corporation with its practically boundless resources of war. The Amalgamated Association of Iron and Steel Workers in 1891 with a membership of 24,068 was the strongest trade union in the entire

---

77 The attitude of the Federation was expressed by Gompers at the convention in 1891. American Federation of Labor, *Proceedings*, 1891, p. 15.

78 *Ibid.*, 1888, p. 12.
79 *Ibid.*, 1890, p. 30.
80 *Ibid.*, 1891, p. 36.

history of the American labour movement. Prior to 1889 the relations between the union and the Carnegie firm had been invariably friendly. In January, 1889, H. C. Frick, who, as owner of the largest coke manufacturing plant, had acquired the reputation of a bitter opponent of organised labour, became chairman of Carnegie Brothers & Company. In the same year, owing to his assumption of management, as the union men believed, the first dispute occurred between them and the company. Although the agreement was finally renewed for three years on terms dictated by the association, the controversy left a disturbing impression upon the minds of the men, since, during the course of the negotiations, Frick had demanded the dissolution of the union.

Negotiations for the new scale presented to the company began in February, 1892. A few weeks later the company presented a scale to the men providing for a reduction, and, besides, demanding that the date of the termination of the scale be changed from July 1 to January 1. A number of conferences were held without result; and on May 30 the company submitted an ultimatum to the effect that if the scale were not signed by June 29, they would treat with the men as individuals. At a final conference which was held on June 23, the company raised its offer from $22 per ton to $23 as the minimum base of the scale, and the union lowered its demand from $25, the rate formerly paid, to $24. But no agreement could be reached on this point nor on others, and the strike began June 29 upon the definite issue of the preservation of the union.

Even before the negotiations were broken up, Frick had arranged with the Pinkerton agency for 300 men to serve as guards. These men arrived at a station on the Ohio River below Pittsburgh near midnight of July 5. Here they embarked on barges and were towed up the river to Pittsburgh and taken up the Monongahela River to Homestead, which they approached about four o'clock on the morning of July 6. The workmen had been warned of their coming, and, when the boat reached the landing back of the steel works, nearly the whole town was there to meet them and to prevent their landing. Passion ran high. The men armed themselves with guns and gave the Pinkertons a pitched battle. When the day was over, at least half a dozen men on both sides had been killed and a number were seriously wounded. The Pinkertons were defeated and driven away, and, although there was no more disorder of any sort, the state militia appeared in Homestead on July 12 and remained for several months.

The strike which began in Homestead soon spread to other mills. The Carnegie mills at 29th and 33d Streets, Pittsburgh, went out on strike in sympathy. Duquesne, non-union from the beginning, was organised in July, and most of the men came out on strike for a few weeks. Other mills in Pittsburgh having no connection with the Carnegie Steel Company went on strike. The strike at Homestead was finally declared off on November 20, and most of the men went back to their old positions as non-union men. The treasury of the union was depleted, winter was coming, and it was finally decided to consider the battle lost.

The defeat meant not only the loss by the union of the Homestead plant but the elimination of unionism in most of the mills in the Pittsburgh region. Where the great Carnegie Company led, the others had to follow.[81] The power of the union was henceforth broken and the labour movement learned the lesson that even its strongest organisation was unable to withstand an onslaught by the modern corporation.[82]

July 11, the same day that the militia arrived at Homestead, a pitched battle was fought between the organised miners of the Cœur d'Alène district of Idaho and the strike-breakers who came to take their places. The silver mine which was the scene of this battle was the richest in the district and was owned by a number of prominent eastern capitalists. The continuous drop in the price of silver on the market caused the management to make periodic reductions in the wages of the miners, which finally culminated in a strike. The miners, being well armed and having the advantage of numbers, after a bloody fight seized the property and drove the strike-breakers

81 Fitch, "Unionism in the Iron and Steel Industry," in *Political Science Quarterly*, 1909, XXIV, 71–78.

82 The Homestead strike proved to be a potent factor in the presidential campaign of 1892, since it demonstrated to wage-earners that tariff protection was inadequate to protect them in their rights. It added, therefore, considerable vigour to Cleveland's free trade campaign.

out of the district.   In the course of the battle a large quartz
mill was destroyed by an explosion.   The governor, his own
forces being utterly inadequate, called upon the President, and
on June 12 Federal troops were ordered to Cœur d'Alène, mar-
tial law was declared, and the strike came to an end.

The strike of the switchmen in the Buffalo railway yards
occurred on August 13.   The legislature had shortly before
passed a ten-hour law for railway men, which contained, however, a sufficient loophole to enable the railways to render it
inoperative.   Basing themselves upon this law, the switchmen
struck for a ten-hour day.   At first the strikers had the upper
hand and succeeded in stopping completely the movement of
freight.   The proximity of the November election made the
authorities reluctant to take energetic action.   Finally, however, the railway officials prevailed upon the sheriff to apply to
the governor for troops, and, on August 18, several thousand
state troops arrived at Buffalo.   Effective picketing being no
longer possible, the national officers of the switchmen's union
asked for a conference with the national officers of the brotherhoods of engineers, firemen, conductors, and trainmen, to consider the proposition of a sympathetic strike.   But it came to
nothing, since Arthur, of the engineers, refused to appear, and
the other organisations, though willing to aid the switchmen,
could not decide to act without the engineers.   On August 24,
the strike was consequently called off.

Simultaneously with the breaking out of the strike in Buffalo, the miners in Tracy City, Tennessee, seized the mines,
and, after an ineffectual resistance by the guards, set at liberty 300 convicts who were working there under the leasing
system.   The same was done two days later, on August 15,
in the iron mines of Inman, on August 17 in the coal mines
of Oliver Springs, and on August 18 in Coal Creek — in the
latter after a hard fight.   The Tennessee miners were organised as Knights of Labor.   Destructive competition from
cheap convict labour had for years been their chief grievance,
in addition to the more common miners' grievances centering
around the company store, the right to have a check weigh-
man, and the like.   Trouble in acute form had started in Coal
Creek in April of the year before, when the miners armed

themselves, drove the prisoners out of the mines, and escorted them back to prison in Knoxville. The governor entered into negotiations with the miners, and, upon his promise to call a special session of the legislature to enact for the mines a modification in the prison-labour system, they agreed to a *status quo* and the convicts were allowed to return to the mines pending the enactment of the new legislation. The governor kept his promise, but the political influence of the convict-leasing companies was sufficiently strong to defeat all action, and the miners, having grown desperate, again took the matter into their own hands and set free 1,500 prisoners in Coal Creek. They were the more able to do so, as they took good care to maintain friendly relations with the militia. This happened in 1891.

During 1892 the militia was permanently stationed in the mining districts, and friction with the miners had time to arise. The operations which began with the liberation of the prisoners in Tracy City, on August 13, were followed by a serious war between the militia and the armed miners. In several instances entire train loads of militia were taken captive and disarmed, but the final victory was with the militia. The mines were retaken from the miners and the prisoners were put back to work.[83]

Each of the strikes of 1892 served as an instructive lesson to the labour movement. The Homestead strike forcibly demonstrated the unconquerable fighting strength of the modern large corporation. Similarly, the strikes in Buffalo, Cœur d'Alène, and Tennessee showed the far-reaching control which the employing class exercised over government, both state and national.

Gompers, in his report to the Philadelphia convention of the Federation in December, 1892, asked the question, " Shall we change our methods ? " and answered it as follows:

" Many of our earnest friends in the labor movement . . . look upon some of the recent defeats and predict the annihilation of the economic effort of organised labor — or the impotency of the economic organisations, the trade unions — to cope with the great power of concentrated wealth. . . . It is not true that the economic ef-

---

[83] See contemporary account of the strikes during 1892, by Sorge, in *Neue* *Zeit*, 1891–1892, II, 740, 782; 1892–1893, I, 236, 270.

fort has been a failure, nor that the usefulness of the economic organisation is at an end. It is true that in several instances they have been defeated; but though defeated, they are not conquered; the very fact that the monopolistic and capitalist class having assumed the aggressive, and after defeating the toilers in several contests, the wage-workers of our country have maintained their organisations is the best proof of the power, influence and permanency of the trade unions. They have not been routed, they have merely retreated, and await a better opportunity to obtain the improved conditions which for the time they were deprived of. . . . What the toilers need at this time is to answer the bitterness and vindictiveness of the oppressors with Organisation." [84]

The events of 1892 stimulated the development of industrial unionism, that is, the union of all crafts in an industry into one organisation. It had been practised by the Knights of Labor, but since in the Order it was rather a step backward from the official doctrine of the solidarity of all labour through co-operative industry, it did not at that time attract the attention of the radical element in the movement. The brewers' national union became an industrial union at the national convention of 1887, when it extended the organisation to beer-drivers, coopers, engineers, firemen, and malsters. The industrial form of the organisation had been of material aid to the brewery workmen in their fourteen-year long boycott.[85] The unions of the coal miners during the eighties and nineties also were in many localities industrial unions. It was not until 1898, however, that the United Mine Workers systematically began to organise workmen in the industry who were not miners or their helpers.

In 1893, following the Cœur d'Alène trouble, the several unions in the metalliferous mining industry came together in a convention and formed the Western Federation of Miners as an industrial union. Similarly, after the switchmen's strike in Buffalo, Eugene V. Debs, the secretary-treasurer of the Brotherhood of Locomotive Firemen, resigned his office and devoted himself to an agitation in favour of a close federation of all railway organisations. In June, 1893, he formed the American Railway Union, an industrial union of all railway

[84] American Federation of Labor, *Proceedings*, 1892, p. 12.
[85] Schlüter, *The Brewing Industry and the Brewery Workers' Movement in America*, 219, 220. See also above, II, 488.

employés. In the following year it had 465 local lodges and claimed a membership of 150,000.[86] The brotherhoods were hostile to the new movement.

In the summer of 1893 the panic, which had been threatening ever since the Baring failure in 1890, came. The panic and the ensuing crisis may be regarded as the acid test which conclusively proved the strength and stability of the American labour movement. Gompers in his presidential report at the convention of 1893, following the depression, said: "It is noteworthy, that while in every previous industrial crisis the trade unions were literally mowed down and swept out of existence, the unions now in existence have manifested, not only the powers of resistance, but of stability and permanency," [87] and he assigned as the most prominent cause the system of high dues and benefits which had come into vogue in a large number of trade unions. He said: "Beyond doubt the superficial motive of continued membership in unions organised upon this basis was the monetary benefits the members were entitled to; but be that as it may, the results are the same, that is, *membership is maintained, the organisation remains intact during dull periods of industry, and is prepared to take advantage of the first sign of an industrial revival.*" [88] Gompers may have exaggerated the power of resistance of the unions, but their holding power upon the membership cannot be disputed: The aggregate membership of all unions affiliated with the Federation remained near the mark of 275,000 throughout the period from 1893 to 1897.[89]

TRADE UNIONS AND THE COURTS

The year 1894 was exceptional for labour disturbances. The number of employés involved reached nearly 750,000, surpassing even the mark set in 1886. However, in contradistinction to 1886, the movement was defensive. It also resulted in greater failure. The strike of the coal miners and the Pullman strike were the most important ones. The United Mine Workers began their strike in Ohio on April 21. The

---

[86] Report on the Chicago strike of June and July, 1894; see United States Strike Commission, *Report*, 1895, p. 130.

[87] American Federation of Labor, *Proceedings*, 1893, p. 12.
[88] *Ibid.*
[89] *Ibid.*, 1912, p. 81.

membership did not exceed 20,000, but about 125,000 struck. At first the demand was made that wages should be restored to the level at which they were in May, 1893. But within a month the union in most regions was struggling to prevent a further reduction in wages. By the end of July, the strike was lost.

The Pullman strike began May 11, 1894, and grew out of a demand of certain employés in the shops of the Pullman Palace Car Company, situated at Pullman, Illinois, for a restoration of the wages paid during the previous year. In March, 1894, the Pullman employés had voted to join the American Railway Union. Between June 9 and June 26 the latter held a convention in Chicago. The Pullman matter was publicly discussed before and after its committee reported their interviews with the Pullman Company. On June 21, the delegates under instructions from their local unions, feeling confident after a victory over the Great Northern in April, unanimously voted that the members should stop handling Pullman cars on June 26 unless the Pullman Company would consent to arbitration. On June 26 the railway strike began. It was a purely sympathetic strike as no demands were made. The union found itself pitted against the general managers' association, representing twenty-four roads centring or terminating in Chicago, which were bound by contracts with the Pullman Company. The association had been organised in 1886, its main business being to determine a common policy as to traffic and freight rates, but incidentally it dealt also with wages. The strike soon spread over an enormous territory. Many of the members of the brotherhoods joined in, although their organisations were opposed to the strike. The lawless element in Chicago took advantage of the opportunity to rob, burn, and plunder, so that the scenes of the great railway strike of 1877 were now repeated. The damages in losses of property and business to the country have been estimated at $80,000,000. On July 7, E. V. Debs, president, and other principal officers of the American Railway Union were indicted, arrested, and held under $10,000 bail. On July 13 they were attacked for contempt of the United States court in disobeying an injunction which enjoined them, together with other things, from compelling, or by threats, inducing railway employés to strike. The strike had already been weakening for some days. On July 12, at the request of the American Railway Union, about twenty-five of the executive officers of national and international labor unions affiliated with the American Federation of Labor met in conference in Chicago to discuss the situation. Debs appeared and urged a general strike by all labour organisations. But the conference decided that " it would be unwise and disastrous to the interests of labor to extend the strike any further than it had already gone," [90] and advised the strikers to return to work. On July 13, the American Railway Union, through the mayor of Chicago, offered the general managers' association to declare the strike off, provided the men should be restored to their former positions without prejudice, except in cases where they had been convicted of crime. But the association refused to deal with the union. The strike was already virtually beaten by the combined moral effect of the indictment of the leaders and of the arrival in Chicago of United States troops which President Cleveland sent in spite of the protest of Governor Altgeld of Illinois.[91]

The labour organisations were taught two important lessons. First, that nothing can be gained through revolutionary striking, for the government was sufficiently strong to cope with it; and second, that the employers had obtained a formidable ally in the courts.

The bitterness of the industrial struggle during the eighties made it inevitable that the labour movement should acquire an extensive police and court record. It was during that decade that charges like " inciting to riot," " obstructing the streets," " intimidation," and " trespass " were first extensively used in connection with labour disputes. Convictions were frequent and penalties often severe. What attitude the courts at that time took towards labour violence was shown most strikingly, even if in too extreme a form to be entirely typical, in the case of the Chicago anarchists.

In addition to arrests and punishment for violence and rioting, which were, after all, nothing but ordinary police cases

[90] Gompers, " Report," in American Federation of Labor, *Proceedings*, 1894, p. 12.

[91] United States Strike Commission, *Report* (on the Chicago strike of June and July, 1894).

magnified to an unusual degree by the intensity of the industrial struggle and the excited state of public opinion, the courts
gave a new lease of life to the doctrine of conspiracy as affecting labour disputes.[92]   During the eighties there seem to have
been more conspiracy cases than during all the rest of the
century.   It was especially in 1886 and 1887 that organised
labour found court interference a factor.   At this time there
was also passed voluminous state legislation strengthening the
application of the common law doctrine of conspiracy to labour
disputes.   The conviction of the New York boycotters in
1886[93] and many similar, though less widely known, convictions of participants in strikes and boycotts, were obtained
upon this ground.   Yet this novel use made of the doctrine of
conspiracy was not necessarily as complete a revolution in the
heretofore prevailing practice as is commonly supposed.   In
reality the much heralded case of Commonwealth v. Hunt, decided by the Supreme Judicial Court of Massachusetts in 1842,
had never been wholly accepted.   True, that a part of the
decision which affirmed that a trade union was legal *per se* was
not questioned, but in so far as the decision legalised the closed
shop and aimed to free the trade union of the charge of conspiracy regardless of the means used, Commonwealth v. Hunt
remained, as a matter of fact, an isolated case.[94]

Where the eighties actually witnessed a revolution in the
doctrine of conspiracy was in the totally new use made of it
by the courts when they began to issue injunctions in labour
cases.   Injunctions were an old remedy, but not until the
eighties did they figure in the struggles between labour and
capital.   In England an injunction was issued in a labour dispute as early as 1868; [95] but this case was not noticed in the
United States, and had nothing whatever to do with the use of
injunctions in this country.   When and where the first labour
injunction was issued in the United States is not known.   An
injunction was applied for in a New York case as early as 1880,
but was denied.[96]   An injunction was granted in Iowa in

---

92 The following account of legal doctrines is largely taken from a monograph
in preparation by Edwin E. Witte on *The
Courts in Labor Disputes.*
93 See above, II, 445.

94 See above, I, 441, 442.
95 Springhead Spinning Co. v. Riley,
L. R. 6E. 551 (1868).
96 Johnson Harvester Co. v. Meinhardt,
60 How. Pr. 171.

1884,[97] but not until the Southwest railway strike in 1886 were injunctions used extensively.[98] By 1890 the public had yet heard little of injunctions in connection with labour disputes, but such use was already fortified by numerous precedents.

The first injunctions that attained wide publicity were those issued by Federal courts during the strike of engineers against the Chicago, Burlington & Quincy Railway,[99] in 1888, and during the railway strikes of the early nineties. Justification for these injunctions was found in the provisions of the Interstate Commerce Act and the Sherman Anti-Trust Act. Often the state courts used these Federal cases as precedents, in disregard of the fact that there the issuance of injunctions was based upon special statutes. In other cases the more logical course was followed of justifying the issuance of injunctions upon grounds of equity. But most of the acts which the courts enjoined strikers from doing were already prohibited by the criminal laws. Hence organised labour objected that these injunctions violated the old principle that equity will not interfere to prevent crime. No such difficulties arose when the issuance of injunctions was justified as a measure for the protection of property. In the Debs case,[1] when the Supreme Court of the United States passed upon the issuance of injunctions in labour disputes, it had recourse to this theory.

But the theory of protection to property also presented some difficulties. The problem was to establish the principle of irreparable injury to the complainant's property. This was a simple matter when the strikers were guilty of trespass, arson, or sabotage. Then they damaged the complainant's physical property, and since they were usually men against whom judgments are worthless, any injury they might do was irreparable. But these were exceptional cases. Usually injunctions were sought to prevent not violence, but strikes, picketing, or boycotting. What is threatened by strikes and picketing is not

[97] Keystone Coal Co. v. Davis, Circuit Court, Boone County, Iowa (Dec. 8, 1884). Text given in the Iowa Bureau of Labor, Report, 1885, p. 155. Powderly, Thirty Years of Labor, 442, 443, states that injunctions were issued in 1883 at Kent, Ohio, and at Baltimore.

[98] " Official History of the Great Strike of 1886 on the Southwestern Railroad System," in Missouri Bureau of Labor, Report, 1886, p. 34.

[99] Chicago, Burlington, etc., R. R. Co. v. Union Pacific R. R. Co., U. S. Dist. Ct., D. Neb. (1888).

[1] In re Debs, 158 U. S. 564 (1895).

the employer's physical property, but the relations he has established as an employer of labour, summed up in his expectancy of retaining the services of old employés and of obtaining new ones. Boycotting, obviously, has no connection with acts of violence against physical property, but is designed merely to undermine the profitable relations which the employer has developed with his customers. These expectancies are advantages enjoyed by established businesses over new competitors, and are usually transferable and have market value. For these reasons they are now recognised as property in the law of good will and unfair competition for customers, having been first formulated about the middle of the nineteenth century. '

The first case which recognised these expectancies of a labour market was Walker v. Cronin,[2] decided by the Massachusetts Supreme Judicial Court in 1871. It held that the plaintiff was entitled to recover damages from the defendants, certain union officials, because they had induced his employés, who were free to quit at will, to leave his employment, and had also been instrumental in preventing him from getting new employés. But as yet these expectancies were not considered property in the full sense of the word. A transitional case is that of Brace Bros. v. Evans in 1888.[3] In that case an injunction against a boycott was justified on the ground that the value of the complainant's physical property was being destroyed when the market was cut off. Here the expectancies based upon relations with customers and employés were thought of as giving value to the physical property, but they were not yet recognised as a distinct asset which in itself justifies the issuance of injunctions.

This next step was taken in the Barr[4] case in New Jersey in 1893. Since then there have been frequent statements in labour injunction cases to the effect that both the expectancies based upon the merchant-function and the expectancies based upon the employer-function are property.[5]

2 107 Mass. 555 (1871).
3 5 Pa. Co. Ct. 163 (1888).
4 Barr v. Trades' Council, 53 N. J. E. 101, 30 Atl. 881 (1894).
5 Eureka Foundry Co. v. Lehker, 13 Ohio N. P. 398 (1902); Underhill v. Murphy, 117 Ky. 640, 78 S. W. 482 (1904); Purvis v. Carpenters, 214 Pa. St. 348, 63 Atl. 585 (1906); Sailors' Union v. Hammond Lumber Co., 156 Fed. 450 (1908); Buck's Stove and Range Co. v. A. F. of L., 36 Wash. L. Rep. 882 (1908); Newton Co. v. Erickson, 126 N. Y. Supp. 949 (1911).

But the recognition of " probable expectancies " as property was not in itself sufficient to complete the chain of reasoning that justifies injunctions in labour disputes. It is well established that no recovery can be had for losses due to the exercise by others of that which they have a lawful right to do. Hence the employers were obliged to charge that the strikes and boycotts were undertaken in pursuance of an unlawful conspiracy. Thus the old conspiracy doctrine was combined with the new theory, and " malicious " interference with " probable expectancies " was held unlawful. Earlier conspiracy had been thought of as a criminal offence, now it was primarily a civil wrong. The emphasis had been upon the danger to the public, now it was the destruction of the employers' business. Occasionally the court went so far as to say that all interference with the business of employers is unlawful. The better view developed was that interference is *prima facie* unlawful, but may be justified. But even this view placed the burden of proof upon the workingmen. It actually meant that the court held the conduct of the workingmen to be lawful only when it sympathised with their demands.

During the eighties, despite the far-reaching development of legal theories on labour disputes, the issuance of injunctions was merely sporadic, but a veritable crop came up during 1893–1894. Only the best-known injunctions can be here noted. The injunctions issued in the course of the Southwest railway strike in 1886 and the Burlington strike in 1888 have already received mention. An injunction was also issued by a Federal court during the miners' strike at Cœur d'Alène, Idaho, in 1892.[6] A famous injunction was the one of Judges Taft and Ricks in 1893, which directed the engineers who were employed by connecting railways to handle the cars of the Ann Arbor and Michigan railway, whose engineers were on strike.[7] This order elicited much criticism because it came close to requiring men to work against their will. This was followed by the injunction of Judge Jenkins in the Northern Pacific case, which directly prohibited the quitting of work.[8]

[6] Cœur d'Alène Mining Co. *v.* Miners' Union, 51 Fed. 260 (1892).

[7] Toledo, etc., Co. *v.* Pennsylvania Co., 54 Fed. 730 (1893).

[8] Farmers' Loan and Trust Co. *v.* N. P. R. Co., 60 Fed. 803 (1894).

From this injunction the defendants took an appeal, with the result that in Arthur *v.* Oakes [9] it was once for all established that the quitting of work may not be enjoined.

During the Pullman strike numerous injunctions, most sweeping in character, were issued by the Federal courts, upon the initiative of the Department of Justice.[10] Under the injunction which was issued in Chicago arose the famous contempt case against Eugene V. Debs, which was carried to the Supreme Court of the United States. The decision of the court in this case [11] is notable, because it covered the main points of doubt above mentioned and placed the use of injunctions in labour disputes upon a firm legal basis.

Another famous decision of the Supreme Court growing out of the railway strikes of the early nineties was in the Lennon case [12] in 1897. Therein the court held that all persons who have actual notice of the issuance of an injunction are bound to obey its terms, although the order may not be especially directed to them nor served upon them. Thus was sanctioned the so-called " blanket injunction."

During the eighties there was much new legislation applicable to labour disputes. The first laws against boycotting and blacklisting, and the first laws which prohibited discrimination against members who belonged to a union, were passed during this decade. At this time also were passed the first laws to promote voluntary arbitration, and most of the laws which allow unions to incorporate. Only in New York and Maryland were the conspiracy laws repealed. Four States enacted such laws and many States passed laws against intimidation.[13] Statutes, however, played at that time, as they do now, but a secondary rôle. The only statute which proved of much importance was the Sherman Anti-Trust Act. When Congress passed this act in 1890, few people thought it had application to labour unions.

9 63 **Fed.** 310 (1894).

10 **So. Cal. Ry. Co.** *v.* **Rutherford, 62 Fed.** 796 (1894) ; **U. S.** *v.* **Elliott** *et al.,* 62 **Fed.** 801 (1894) ; **Thomas** *v.* **Cincinnati N. O. & T. P. R. Co.**— In re Phelan, 62 **Fed**: 803 (1894) ; **U. S.** *v.* **Alger, 62 Fed.** 824 (1894) ; **U. S.** *v.* **Debs, 64 Fed.** 724 (1894). The newspapers of the time show that injunctions like these were issued by the Federal courts in all districts affected by the strike.

11 In re Debs, 158 U. S. 564 (1895).

12 In re Lennon, 166 U. S. 548 (1897).

13 Nearly all of the laws passed since 1880, which relate to the doctrines of conspiracy in industrial disputes, are still in force. For a summary of the laws, see " Strikes and Lockouts," in Commissioner of Labor, *Third Annual Report,* 1887, 1146–1164; and " Strikes and Lockouts," in *Sixteenth Annual Report,* 1901, 986–1036.

In 1893–1894, however this act was successfully invoked in several labour controversies, notably in the Debs case.[14]

THE LATEST ATTEMPT TOWARD A LABOUR PARTY

Defeats in strikes, depression in trade, a rapidly falling labour market, and court prosecutions were powerful allies of those socialistic and radical leaders inside the Federation who aspired to convert it from a mere economic organisation into an economic political one and to make it embark upon the sea of independent politics.

A change of position upon the question of politics was foreshadowed in the resolutions adopted by the convention of the Federation in 1892. Two of the leading planks of the Populist platform — the initiative and referendum and government ownership of the telegraph and telephone system — were indorsed.[15] Even more significant was the instruction given to the Executive Council, " to use their best endeavour to carry on a vigorous campaign of education by appointing organisers, lecturers, and supplying economic literature to affiliated organisations in order to widen the scope of usefulness of the trade unions in the direction of political action. But," the resolution continued, " we wish the distinction to be made that partisan politics should not be confounded with the business of the trade unions." [16]

The convention of 1893 is memorable in that it submitted to the consideration of affiliated unions a " political programme." [17] The preamble to the programme recited that the English trade unions had recently launched upon independent politics " as auxiliary to their economic action." The eleven planks of the programme demanded: compulsory education; the initiative; a legal eight-hour work-day; governmental inspection of mines and workshops; abolition of the sweating system; employers' liability laws; abolition of the contract system upon public work; municipal ownership of electric light,

---

14 U. S. v. Workmen's Council, 54 Fed. 994, 57 Fed. 85 (1893); Waterhouse v. Comer, 55 Fed. 149 (1893); Toledo, etc., R. R. Co. v. Pennsylvania R. R. Co., 54 Fed. 730 (1893); U. S. v. Alger, 62 Fed. 824 (1894); U. S. v. Debs, 64 Fed. 724 (1894); In re Grand Jury, 62 Fed. 840 (1894).

15 American Federation of Labor, *Proceedings*, 1892, p. 43.

16 *Ibid*.

17 *Ibid*., 1892, 36.

gas, street railway, and water systems; the nationalisation of telegraphs, telephones, railroads, and mines; "the collective ownership by the people of all means of production and distribution"; and the referendum upon all legislation. The programme was submitted by Thomas J. Morgan, a socialist from Chicago, representing the International Machinists' Union, and received a more than passive support from Gompers [18] and P. J. McGuire.[19]   Only one real test vote upon the political programme was had in this convention. It came upon a motion to strike out the recommendation to affiliated unions to give the programme their "favourable consideration." The vote against the recommendation was 1,253 to 1,182. McGuire voted with the majority and Gompers refrained from voting. Very strangely, the conservative typographical union voted solidly to recommend "favorable consideration." With this recommendation stricken out, the submission of the programme was carried by the overwhelming vote of 2,244 to 67.

Several other resolutions adopted by the convention of 1893 are of significance in this connection. One of these instructed the Executive Council to bring about an alliance with the farmers' organisations "to the end that the best interests of all may be served." [20]   Another resolution renewed the demand for the nationalisation of the telegraph system.[21] Finally there was a declaration in favour of the free coinage of silver as "one of the means of relieving the present monetary stringency, and of a return to national prosperity." [22]   The Federation had been officially represented at the bi-metallic convention in Chicago during the summer, although there had been no previous endorsement of bi-metallism.[23]

Immediately after the convention of 1893 affiliated unions began to give their endorsement to the political programme.

[18] He said in the presidential address: ". . . An intelligent use of the ballot by the toilers in their own interest must largely contribute to lighten the burthens of our economic struggles. Let us elect men from the ranks of labor to represent us in Congress and the Legislatures whenever and wherever the opportunity presents itself. Let us never be recreant to our trust, and, regardless of political affiliations or predilections, always vote against those who are inimical to the interests of labor." *Ibid.*, 1893, p. 12.

[19] McGuire favoured an alliance with the People's party. To him the existing depression and the demonetisation of silver were but parts of a great conspiracy "to bring American labor to the pauperised condition of the workers of foreign lands." *Carpenter*, August, 1893.
[20] American Federation of Labor, *Proceedings*, 1893, 37.
[21] *Ibid.*, 34.
[22] *Ibid.*, 60.
[23] Cleveland *Citizen*, Aug. 12, 1893.

Not until comparatively late did any opposition make itself manifest. Then it took the form of a demand by such conservative leaders as Gompers, McGuire, and Strasser, that plank 10, with its pledge in favour of " the collective ownership by the people of all means of production and distribution," be stricken out. Only the bakers' union seems to have rejected the programme in its entirety. The typographical union and the web-weavers' union voted to strike out plank 10. The carpenters approved plank 10, but with the amendment, " as the people elect to operate." Only a partial list can be given of the unions which unconditionally endorsed the political programme. The list includes the United Mine Workers, iron and steel workers, lasters, tailors, wood workers, flint glassworkers, brewery workmen, painters, furniture workers, streetrailway employés, waiters, shoe workers, textile workers, mule spinners, machinists, and the German-American typographical union. The cigar makers' union by a referendum vote approved every plank of the political programme, but the result of the vote was not given out until after the convention of the Federation. The programme was approved, also, by the state federations of labour in Maine, Rhode Island, New York, Ohio, Michigan, Wisconsin, Illinois, Missouri, Kansas, Nebraska, and Montana. It also had the endorsement of city centrals in Baltimore, New Haven, Cleveland, Toledo, Lansing, Saginaw, Grand Rapids, and Milwaukee.

During 1894 the trade unions were active participants in politics. Of course, the Federation, pending the referendum on the programme, refrained from partisan politics and confined itself to agitation and lobbying for favoured measures. But many of these were clearly different from such strictly trade union legislative measures, as shorter hours, restricting immigration, or granting freedom from legal prosecution to trade unions. Thus in the summer the Executive Council, in co-operation with the Bi-Metallic League, issued a number of circulars on behalf of the free coinage of silver.[24] It also lobbied actively on behalf of the bill providing for the nationalisation of the telegraph and the telephone system. On the other hand, the representatives of the Federation in the peace confer-

---

[24] American Federation of Labor, *Proceedings*, 1894, p. 14,

ence with the Knights of Labor of the summer of 1894 declined to go upon record as favouring an endorsement of the People's party, on the ground that their instructions did not cover this point.[25]

Locally, however, the trade unions were unequivocally in politics. A very large number of members were candidates for office. A majority of them ran upon the People's party, or " Populist " ticket. In many localities the trade unions virtually were part of the Populist party machinery. In November, 1894, the *Federationist* gave a list of more than 300 union members, candidates for some elective office.[26]   Only a half dozen of these, however, were elected.

It was mainly to these local failures that Gompers pointed in his presidential address at the convention of 1894 as an argument against the adoption of the political programme by the Federation.[27]   His attitude clearly foreshadowed the destiny of the programme at the convention.   The first attack was made upon the preamble, upon the ground that the statement therein that the English trade unions had declared for independent political action was false.   By a vote of 1,345 to 861 the convention struck out the preamble.   The real fight, however, was over plank 10, endorsing socialism.   Upon motion of the typographical union, a substitute was adopted, calling for the " abolition of the monopoly system of land holding and the substitution therefor a title of occupancy and use only."[28]   Some of the delegates seem to have interpreted this substitute as a declaration for the single tax; but the majority of those who voted in its favour probably acted upon the principle, " anything to beat socialism."   The delegates of the painters, and part of the representatives of the mine workers, the iron and steel workers, the tailors, and the lasters, voted for the substitute, although their unions had endorsed the entire political programme.   Upon the rejection of the preamble all but one of the

25 *American Federationist*, 1894, I, 262, 267.
26 *Ibid.*, 205.
27 " During the past year the trade unions in many localities plunged into the political arena by nominating their candidates for public office, and sad as it may be to record, it is nevertheless true, that in each of these localities politically they were defeated and the trade-union movement more or less divided and disrupted. What the results would be if such a movement were inaugurated under the auspices of the American Federation of Labor, involving it and all our affiliated organisations, is too portentous for contemplation." American Federation of Labor, *Proceedings*, 1894, p. 15,
28 *Ibid.*, 38–43.

cigar makers' delegates voted with the majority, explaining their vote upon the ground that their instruction covered only the "platform," but not the "preamble." [29] None of the other ten planks of the programme was materially altered, except that a declaration in favour of the repeal of conspiracy laws was added. A motion to endorse the amended platform as a whole, however, was voted down, 735 to 1,173. With the majority were a large number of delegates who had supported plank 10, including the entire delegations of the moulders, carpenters, painters (one faction), bakers, and 'longshoremen, and one delegate each of the lasters and of the mine workers. The convention, however, once more placed the Federation upon record as favouring the free coinage of silver.[30] This action was taken in spite of the refusal of the convention of the typographical union a few months before to endorse free coinage.[31] In revenge, the defeated socialists combined with the supporters of McBride of the mine workers and elected him president instead of Gompers. The headquarters of the Federation were moved from Washington to Indianapolis.

Immediately after the adjournment of the convention of 1894, a hot dispute arose as to whether the amended political programme had been adopted, when each plank in turn had been approved. President McBride stated in his report that the convention had adopted the programme. The convention of 1895, however, voted to construe the action of the preceding year as a rejection of the entire programme.[32] Next it voted to treat the "platform" as embodying the "legislative demands" of the Federation. Under the caption "Legislative Platform," the amended "platform" was printed for several years thereafter in every number of the *American Federationist*.

In the convention of 1895 a resolution, presented by a socialist, came up. It declared that it was the duty of the trade unions to organise an independent labour party. In lieu thereof, the convention by a vote of 1,460 to 158, adopted a resolution: "That it is clearly the duty of union workingmen to use their franchise so as to protect and advance the class interests of the men and women of labor and their children.

29 Holyoke *Labor*, Dec. 29, 1894.
30 American Federation of Labor, *Proceedings*, 1894, p. 29.
31 Cleveland *Citizen*, Oct. 20, 1894.
32 American Federation of Labor, *Proceedings*, 1895, pp. 80–82.

That the interests of the workers as a class is of paramount importance to party interests. That the class interests of labour demand labour measures in preference to party measures, and, we, therefore, recommend to the workers more independent voting outside of party lines." [33]

The American Federation of Labor was once more almost drawn into the whirlpool of partisan politics during the presidential campaign of 1896. Three successive conventions had declared in favour of the free coinage of silver; and now the Democratic party had come out for free coinage. In this situation very many prominent trade union leaders declared publicly for Bryan. President Gompers, however, issued a warning to all affiliated unions to keep out of partisan politics. [34] Notwithstanding this, Secretary McGraith at the next convention of the Federation, charged President Gompers with acting in collusion with the Democratic headquarters throughout the campaign in aid of Bryan's candidacy. [35] After a lengthy secret session, the convention approved the conduct of Gompers. [36]

Free silver continued to be endorsed annually down to the convention of 1898, when the return of industrial prosperity and rising prices put an end to it as a demand advocated by labour. [37] The failure to direct the labour movement into a labour party gave proof of the strength achieved by the trade union movement. Henceforth the demand for a labour party was confined to the socialists.

SOCIALISTS AND LABOUR ORGANISATIONS, 1888-1896

The socialists viewed their participation in the labour parties of 1886–1888 primarily as a means of winning the trade unions to socialism. Failing in this, they reacted against trade unions in general. It is true that the *New Yorker Volkszeitung* and a majority of the German section in New York now favoured a

---

[33] *Ibid.*, 96.
[34] *Hollister's Eight-Hour Herald* (Chicago), Oct. 20, 1896.
[35] *Ibid.*, Jan. 12, 1897.
[36] American Federation of Labor, *Proceedings*, 1896, pp. 59–61. A similar case came up involving William O. Pomeroy, a prominent Chicago trade union leader, who was accused of having used his official position in McKinley's interest. The convention refused to allow him to

take his seat. *Ibid.*, 35–40.
[37] As might be expected, the free silver demand had caused a great amount of dissatisfaction within the Federation. For instance, the *Bakers' Journal*, edited by Weissman, a supporter of McKinley, declared after the convention of 1896 that free coinage " promises to become the rock upon which the ship of trade unionism may wreck." Quoted in *Hollister's Eight-Hour Herald*, Jan. 12, 1897.

still closer identification with the trade union movement and even the complete abandonment of political action by the Socialist Labor party for the present. But the opposite faction was now in the saddle. V. L. Rosenberg, editor of the official party organ, deplored the fact that too much energy was spent on trade unions to the detriment of the agitation for socialism,[38] and the general meeting of the section in New York decided, though by a narrow majority, to enter the campaign of 1888 under socialist colours undisguised. The turning of the scale in favour of the political faction was due mainly to the English-speaking members.[39] However, the ascendency of Rosenberg and the political faction was short-lived. The small socialist vote cast in the election (2,580 in New York City), coming, as it did, after the heavy labour vote of the preceding years, proved a decided disappointment. At the same time, the step of the American Federation of Labor in starting the eight-hour movement in 1888 helped to revive the spirits of the " trade-union " faction. The latter was now in position to justify alliance with the trade unions by pointing to the aggressive tactics of the Federation. The disappointing outcome of the municipal elections in the spring of 1889 [40] added still further to the strength of the *Volkszeitung* and the trade union faction.

Still, the National Executive Committee persisted in its opposition toward trade unions. *Der Sozialist,* though giving general approval to the eight-hour movement, hedged it around with so many qualifications that the sincere trade unionists in the socialist ranks were bound to revolt.

On September 10, 1889, the general section of New York held a meeting and by a practically unanimous vote recalled Rosenberg and a majority of the National Executive Committee, electing Sergius Schevitsch and others in their places. This move was of doubtful legality. However that may be, a large majority of the party acquiesced in the New York revolution and the trade union faction again found itself at the helm. The national convention held on October 12 in Chicago legalised the New York *coup d'état.* It promised to co-operate in

38 *Der Sozialist,* Apr. 28, 1888.
39 *Ibid.,* Sept. 29, 1888.
40 The vote was 167 in Chicago, 420 in Milwaukee, and 104 in Jersey City. *Der Sozialist,* Apr. 13, 1889.

organising trade unions in case the unions resolved to form a labour party, and it granted unqualified and enthusiastic endorsement to the eight-hour movement. The platform as well as the constitution were overhauled. The preamble was entirely rewritten by Lucien Sanial and remodelled after the Declaration of Independence. The Lassallean demand for state credit to co-operative associations was struck out.

Only a small number of sections remained loyal to Rosenberg. Their convention met on October 2, decided for vigorous and immediate political action, revoked the clause in the constitution, which demanded that at least two-thirds of the members of each section should be wage-earners, and passed by in complete silence the subject of trade unions. The section in Cincinnati was the leading one of this faction and, for this reason, the organisation was known as the Socialist Labor party of the "Cincinnati persuasion." It continued down to 1897, when it amalgamated with the Debs-Berger Social Democracy of America.

The regular Socialist Labor party, of which the trade union faction was now in undisputed control, abstained from any participation at the state election in New York in the fall of 1889, for the reason that the trade unions were still unprepared for political action. The relations with the Federation of Labor were extremely friendly, and, in March 1890, the Executive Council of the Federation appointed the well-known socialist, Paul Grottkau, traveling agitator for the eight-hour movement, along with George E. McNeill.

In New York City the socialists were unable to keep on friendly terms with the old established central body of trade unions, the Central Labor Union, which became famous during the George campaign. The latter had, during 1888, fallen under the influence of the Knights of Labor and the conservative trade unions, and, as the socialists charged, of corrupt politicians also. The socialists had therefore organised the Central Labor Federation in February, 1889, which received a charter from the American Federation of Labor. In December, 1889, the Central Labor Federation effected a reconciliation with the Central Labor Union and fused with it. However, the lukewarmness of the Central Labor

Union toward the eight-hour movement and principally
the suspicion of political corruption drove the socialists
for a second time to secession, and in June, 1890, they
resurrected the Central Labor Federation. Soon the socialists were given cause to doubt the friendship of the
American Federation of Labor, for it refused a charter to
the Central Labor Federation on the ground that it had affiliated with itself besides thirty-eight trade unions, also the
section of the Socialist Labor party. The matter was thoroughly threshed out in a nine-hour debate at the convention of
the Federation at Detroit in December, 1890. The outcome
was that Lucien Sanial, who held credentials from the Central
Labor Federation, was refused a seat. Ultimately, the Socialist Labor party withdrew from the central labour bodies
in the sixteen cities [41] in which it had hitherto been represented.

The socialists felt disappointed, but still maintained their
hope of winning over the American Federation of Labor to
socialism. In 1891, however, Weissman, of the bakers' union,
with encouragement from Gompers, organised the Federation
of Labor of New York, which purported to be free from any
political influence, socialist as well as any other. This placed
a third central body alongside the Central Labor Union and
the Central Labor Federation. In 1892, after lengthy negotiations between the three bodies, the Central Labor Union
and the Federation of Labor amalgamated, but the socialistic
Central Labor Federation decided to remain independent.

The conflict considerably cooled the hopes of the socialists
for an easy conquest of the American Federation of Labor.
However, the mild methods were not replaced by more aggressive ones until the control of the party had solidified in the
hands of Daniel De Leon,[42] about 1892. Under De Leon's
leadership the party adopted more vigorous tactics. In 1892

41 Baltimore, Brooklyn, Chicago, Cleve-
land, Dayton, Detroit, Evansville (Ind.),
Hudson County, Paterson, New Haven,
New York, Philadelphia, Pittsburgh,
Providence, Sandusky, and Sheboygan
(Wis.). In practically every case these
were organisations of German trade un-
ions,

42 De Leon was born in Curaçao, Dutch
West Indies, in 1852. He came to the
United States from Europe in 1872,
studied law at the Columbia Law School,
and subsequently became a lecturer on
diplomacy at the Columbia University.
He was active in the Henry George campaign of 1886, joined the Knights of Labor in 1888, and became interested in
nationalism in 1889. In 1890 he joined
the Socialist Labor party and founded
the weekly *People* in 1892. He died in
1915.

it nominated for the first time a presidential ticket. The candidates were Simon Wing, a photographer of Boston and an old abolitionist, and Charles Matchett, a New York telephone mechanician, prominent among the Knights of Labor. Both were recent recruits to the Socialist Labor party. The ticket polled 21,157 votes, of which 18,147 were cast in the state of New York, including 6,100 in New York City. With regard to labour organisation the policy was still more aggressive. At the national convention in July, 1893, the opinion was generally shared that it was sheer utopianism to look for a natural transformation of the American Federation of Labor into a labour party. In order that the latter might come into existence, energetic action on the part of the socialists was required.

Energetic measures were, however, first tried on the Knights of Labor, and the instrument was the United Hebrew Trades. The United Hebrew Trades [43] had been organised in 1888 as the central body of the Jewish trade unions in New York. There had existed from 1884 to 1887 a Jewish Workmen's Society, the first labour organisation of the Russian immigrants of that race. Along with propaganda for socialism, it aided in the organisation of unions in the Jewish trades. But by 1888 all of these, except the printers' union, had gone to pieces. They were mostly in the needle trades, and the rock upon which they split was the Jewish sweat-shop workman's easy elevation from wage-earner to sweat-shop boss.

The United Hebrew Trades, starting with only 1 union in 1888, had, 2 years later, 40 affiliated unions with 13,500 members. The largest unions were those of the tailors and cloak makers, each running well into the thousands. During 1892 its strength fell off, mainly owing to the ardent agitation [44] for the socialist ticket in the presidential campaign, which drew off from trade union work many of the more energetic members. But in 1893 it again recovered and retained some strength until weakened by the business depression. The Jewish unions conducted many memorable wage struggles from 1888 to 1893, notably those of the cloak makers' union. This union

---

[43] In the following account of the early Jewish labour movement the author drew largely from an unpublished monograph by Wm. M. Leiserson, *The Jewish Labor Movement in New York.*

[44] The Jews cast 1,500 socialist votes in New York, or one-fourth of the total.

achieved enormous strength, based on the closed shop, during 1890, but fell asunder after the conviction of its leader, Joseph Barondess, in 1891, on a charge of extortion.

The United Hebrew Trades joined the Knights of Labor in 1893 and De Leon at once became a power in the famous but declining District Assembly 49 of New York. He and several other socialists were elected among the delegates to the General Assembly of 1893, where they combined with Powderly's enemies and elected Sovereign grand master workman. The socialists carried the election of officers in District Assembly 49 in 1894 and had 8 delegates out of a total of 63 at the General Assembly of 1894. Sovereign saw their strength, and, as the socialists afterwards claimed, promised to appoint Lucien Sanial as editor of the *Journal of the Knights of Labor*. As he did not comply with his alleged promise and as the socialists were at the same time beaten also in the American Federation of Labor,[45] the Socialist Trade and Labour Alliance was started in December, 1895, as a rival to all existing non-socialistic labour organisations. The socialistic Central Labor Federation of New York, Brooklyn, and Newark, the United Hebrew Trades, and District Assembly 49, with an aggregate membership of about 15,000, merged into the new organisation. However, it proved a failure, and the only outcome, apart from a socialist vote for president of 36,564 in 1896, was the irreparable loss of the socialist cause within the American Federation of Labor.

With the returning prosperity in the latter nineties, the formative stage of trade unionism was complete. The wage-earning class was permanently separated from the middle-class. Wage consciousness permanently displaced middle-class panaceas, such as productive co-operation, currency, and land reform. The separation from the outside was accompanied by a closing up of the ranks within. Yet the new solidarity was not the emotional solidarity of the Knights of Labor, but a solidarity expressing itself in the co-operation of the national trade unions within the Federation and with the growing industrial unionism. Alongside developed a recognition of partnership with the employers — not the partnership of the in-

45 See above, II, 512, 513.

dividual employé with his employer, as preached by the " social harmony " advocates — but the partnership of the wage-
earning class, organised in a national trade or industrial union,
with the employing class, organised in a national employers'
association. This recognition of partnership took full cog-
nizance of the existing antagonism between the two classes but
proposed to bridge it by the trade agreement.

The ideal of the trade agreement was the main achievement
of the nineties. It led the way from an industrial system which
alternately was either despotism or anarchy to a constitutional
form of government in industry. Without the trade agreement the labour movement could hardly come to eschew " panaceas " and to reconstitute itself upon the basis of opportunism.
The coming in of the trade agreement, whether national, sectional, or local, was also the chief factor in stabilising the movement against industrial depressions.

But one should not overlook the other agencies in the labour
struggle which made their appearance about the same time,
namely, the trusts and court injunctions. Enriched on the one
side by the lessons of the past and by the possession of a concrete goal in the trade agreement, but pressed on the other side
by a new form of legal attack and by the growing consolidation
of industry, the labour movement in 1897 had started upon a
career of new power and new difficulty.

CHAPTER XIV

RECENT DEVELOPMENTS (FROM 1896)

Industrial Prosperity and the Growth of the Federation. The extension into new regions and into hitherto untouched trades, 522. Lack of success among the unskilled, 523. The Industrial Workers of the World, 523. The floaters and foreign-speaking workingmen, 523. Success of the miners, 523. The garment workers' unions, 524. Progress of the trade-agreement idea, 524. Its test during the anthracite miners' strike in 1902, 525. The manufacturers' control over access to the market, 525. The trust and its effect on unionism, 526. The "open shop movement," 526. Structural iron industry, 526. Trade-agreement outlook, 527. Awakening of the public to the existence of a labour question, 527. Evolution of public opinion since the eighties, 528. The public and labour legislation, 528. Organised labour's luke-warmness toward labour legislation, 529. Its cause, 529. Its effect on the administration of labour laws, 530. The courts, 530. The Danbury Hatters', the Adair, and Buck's Stove and Range cases, 530, The failure of lobbying, 531. "Reward your friends and punish your enemies," 531. Alliance with the Democrats, 531. The socialists, 532. Effect of litigation and politics on economic organisation, 533. Problem of the unskilled, 533. Three forms of industrialism, 533. The "one big union," 533. Industrialism of the middle stratum, 534. "Craft industrialism," 534. The National Building Trades' Council, 535. The Structural Building Trades' Alliance and the theory of "basic" unions, 535. The Building Trades' Department, 536. Other departments, 536. Forced amalgamations, 537. The new conception of "craft autonomy," 537. Probable future structure of American labour organisations, 537. The "concerted movement," 537.

BEGINNING in 1898 a distinctly new period emerged, but its facts are so recent that they belong more to a discussion of current problems than to a record of history. It remains only to connect them in a general way with the movements of preceding years.

In 1898 industrial prosperity returned, and with it, a rapid expansion of labour organisations. At no time in its history, not excepting the throbbing year of 1886, did labour organisation make such important gains as during the next five years. True, in none of these years did the labour movement add over half a million members as it had done in that memorable year; nevertheless, from the standpoint of permanency of achievement, the upheaval during the eighties can scarcely be classed with that which began in the late nineties.

During 1898 the membership of the American Federation of Labor remained practically stationary, but during 1899 it increased by about 70,000 (to about 350,000); in 1900, it increased by 200,000; in 1901, by 240,000; in 1902, by 247,000; in 1903, by 441,000; and in 1904, by 209,000, bringing up the total to 1,676,000. In 1905 a backward tide set in, and the membership decreased nearly 200,000 during that year. It remained practically stationary until 1910, when the upward movement was resumed, finally bringing the membership up to 2,371,434 in 1917. If we include organisations unaffiliated with the Federation, such as bricklayers,[1] the four railway brotherhoods,[2] and, prior to 1911, the Western Federation of Miners, the average increase in union membership would be about 131,000 per year for 17 years.[3]

Accompanying this numerical growth was an extension of organisation into heretofore untouched trades and amongst the unskilled, as well as a branching out into new geographical regions, the South and the West. There were 92 new national or international trade unions organised between 1897 and 1904, while some index of the growth of organisation among the unskilled is found in the 4,636 so-called " federal labour unions," the " mixed " locals chartered directly by the American Federation of Labor and the local labour unions unaffiliated with any national trade union, which were organised during the same period. Though the Federation was not unmindful of the un-

---

[1] The International Union of Bricklayers, Masons and Plasterers of America, numbering over 80,000 members, joined the Federation in 1916.

[2] Although the organisations of the locomotive engineers, firemen, conductors, and trainmen take no part in the economic struggles of the Federation, they give it their unqualified support in the matter of obtaining favourable legislation.

[3] Prof. George E. Barnett, upon the basis of an independent investigation, gives the total membership of all labour organisations, including those which are unaffiliated with the Federation, by years as follows:

1897	444,500
1898	497,100
1899	604,100
1900	865,400
1901	1,123,600
1902	1,374,300
1903	1,912,900
1904	2,072,600
1905	1,945,000
1906	1,906,300
1907	2,077,600
1908	2,090,400
1909	2,003,100
1910	2,138,000
1911	2,336,500
1912	2,440,800
1913	2,701,000
1914	2,674,400

(" Growth of Labor Organizations," in *Quarterly Journal of Economics*, XXX, 846, Appendix.)

skilled, still, during this period it brought into its fold principally the upper strata of semi-skilled labour. In 1905 it did not comprise to any extent either the totally unskilled, or the partially skilled foreign-speaking workmen, with the exception of the miners. In other words, those below the level of the skilled trades, which did gain admittance, were principally the same elements which had asserted their claim to organisation during the stormy period of the Knights of Labor. The new accretions to the American wage-earning class since the eighties, the East and South Europeans, on one hand, and the ever-growing contingent of " floaters " of native and North and West European stock, on the other, had to await a new upheaval somewhat similar to that of the eighties in order to make felt their claims to organisation.

During 1912 and 1913 it appeared to some as though such an upheaval was close at hand; it seemed as though a successor of both the Knights of Labor and the Chicago syndicalists was created in the Industrial Workers of the World. The latter had been organised by socialists in 1905 as a rival of the American Federation of Labor, but split into two factions, two years later, on the question of political action. The trade union element refusing to remain affiliated with either faction, the movement languished until 1912, when the non-political faction suddenly became an important factor. Its clamourous début in the industrial East, the strikes by non-English-speaking workers in the textile mills of Lawrence, Paterson, and Little Falls on the one hand, and on the other hand, the less tangible but no less desperate strikes of casual labourers which occurred from time to time in the West, bore for the outside observer a marked resemblance to the Great Upheaval in the eighties. Furthermore, the trained eyes of the leaders of the Federation espied in the Industrial Workers of the World a new rival which could best be met on its own ground by organising within the Federation the very same elements to which it especially addressed itself. Accordingly at the convention of 1912, held in Rochester, the problem of organising the unskilled occupied a place near the head of the list. The miners' national union picked up in earnest the gauntlet thrown down by the new revolutionary organisation and succeeded in building up in the anthracite coal region a large organisation of foreigners, which in point of fighting ability and permanence did not lag behind the organisation in other districts where the percentage of foreigners was smaller.

Aside from the miners, the extension of organisation into these fields made slight progress. After the unsuccessful Paterson strikes the star of the Industrial Workers of the World set as rapidly as it had risen, and the organisation rapidly retrogressed. At no time did it roll up a membership of more than 60,000 as compared with the maximum membership of 750,000 of the Knights of Labor. With this dangerous rival all but extinct, the problem of organising the unskilled has lost much of its urgency and, largely because too many of its recent attainments in that direction have ended in failure, the Federation again perforce remains, with the striking exceptions of the miners' and garment workers' organisations, mainly the organisation of the upper and medium strata among the native and Americanised wage-earners.

The remarkable growth in numbers and the remarkable capacity to hold them in spite of depression which the American labour movement has displayed since 1900, very evidently accounts for the economic strength of the trade unions, a strength which they showed in a most striking manner when they prevented large reduction in wages during the hard times following the financial panic of 1907. But even a more striking proof of their progress is found in the remarkable spread of trade agreements. The idea of a joint partnership between organised labour and organised capital, which, ever since the fifties, had been struggling for acceptance, finally came to fruition. Indeed, so complete, so full of enthusiasm was this newly discovered reciprocal understanding that the scarcely interrupted prosperity from 1898 to 1904 may with fitness be called a honeymoon period of capital and labour.

Owing to the depression of the nineties, the moulders' agreement with the National Stove Defense Association remained for eight years a lone road-post pointing the way which other industries were soon to follow. Another great stride in the same direction was taken in 1898, at the time of the settlement of a general strike in the so-called central competitive bituminous coal district, whose forerunner we have seen in the imperfect agreement of 1886.[4] The settlement of 1898 was a distinct gain for unskilled immigrant labour and industrial unionism. It was followed shortly by national and district trade agreements in iron moulding, other than stoves, stove mounting and brass polishing, the machine industry, newspaper and book and job printing, the pottery industry, the overalls industry, and the shipping industry of the Great Lakes, and also by innumerable local trade agreements in building and other industries. However, the climax of the trade agreement enthusiasm was not reached until 1902, when, during the anthracite coal strike, John Mitchell refused, in spite of the strongest possible pressure, to order a sympathetic strike of the bituminous coal miners who had a time agreement with the operators, and gave as his ground that it would constitute a breach of faith with the employers. Here, again, the trade agreement, brought about by arbitration, redounded to the benefit of the immigrant.

The new trade agreement era meant more than the advent of constitutionalism in the relations between labour and capital; it signified that the bargaining strength of employer and employé were more nearly equalised in the organised trades. What enabled this state of equilibrium to be more or less permanent in character were the fundamental changes which had taken place in the control over access to the market. The struggle between the jobber and the manufacturer had been largely won by the latter. The manufacturer had either reached out directly to the ultimate consumer or else, by means of control over patents or trade-marks, had succeeded in reducing the merchant-capitalist to a position which more nearly resembled that of an agent working on a commission than that of the quondam industrial ruler. The immediate outcome was an increase in the margin of the manufacturer's profits. The anxiety of operating at a loss thus removed, the manufacturer was materially and psychologically ready, if necessary, to assume time obligations with reference to wages and other working conditions. The recognition of the union and the trade agreement logically followed.

If the emancipation of the manufacturer from control by

4 See above, II, 425 et seq.

the jobber was thus perhaps a strong aid in the movement for trade agreements, the result was entirely different wherever the manufacturer effected his liberation by means of a "trust." As soon as the trust became the sole employer of labour in an industry, the relations between labour and capital were thrown almost invariably into the state of affairs which had preceded any organisation of labour whatsoever. By abolishing competition among employers for labour and by giving the employer unlimited power to hold out against a strike, "trustification" destroyed every bargaining advantage which labour ever enjoyed. The results were not late in making their appearance. The trade agreement was practically abolished in the steel industry after the formation of the United States Steel Corporation in 1901. Similarly, in 1907, soon after the Steel Trust had become the dominant influence in the carrying trade on the Great Lakes, the agreement between the Lake Carriers' Association and the 'longshoremen came to an end. The case of the bridge and structural iron erecting industry is identical.

But the trust was not the only restraining factor. The abrupt growth of trade union control over industry caused many employers to react strongly against the unaccustomed restrictions. Especially was the opposition strong against the closed shop policy of the unions. Accordingly, the "open shop movement," conducted for the most part by establishments independent of trusts, endeavoured during 1902–1908 to undo much that had been accomplished during 1900–1905. Yet its success has far from measured up to its efforts. Some trade agreements were not renewed, especially where they had suffered from imperfect administrative machinery, but the unions were not destroyed, and in many cases, not even weakened. Only in the bridge and structural iron erecting industry, the only "trustified" industry where the union remained strongly entrenched for a time, did the open shop movement achieve a full measure of success and this was followed by the union adopting terrorist methods. At present the general tendency seems to be in the direction of more rather than fewer trade agreements. Since 1910 the trade agreement has made rapid progress in industries which are manned almost exclusively by immigrants, such as the needle trades. It is indeed in the

women's garment industries, starting under the name of the
" protocol," that copartnership between organised capital and
organised labour reached its highest constitutional development.

At present the trade agreement is one of the most generally
accepted principles in the American labour movement. It is
professed by the " pure and simple " trade unionists and by
the great majority of their socialist opponents. Those who
reject it are a very small minority composed principally of the
sympathisers with the Industrial Workers of the World. However, it is not to be understood that by accepting the principle
of the trade agreement the labour movement has committed
itself to unlimited arbitration of industrial disputes. The
basic idea of the trade agreement is that of collective bargaining rather than arbitration. The two terms are not always
distinguished, but the essential difference is that in the trade
agreement proper no outside party intervenes to settle the dispute and make an award. The agreement is made by direct
negotiation between the two organised groups, and the sanction
which each holds over the head of the other is the strike or
lockout. If no agreement can be reached, the labour organisation, as much as the employers' association, insists on its right
to refuse arbitration, whether it be " voluntary " or so-called
" compulsory." [5]

Along with the recognition of the unions by organised employers there came the recognition by the public of the existence of a labour question as a phenomenon of normal and everyday social life. Heretofore the labour question had forced
itself upon the attention of the public merely for brief moments
and then invariably in a catastrophic setting. Such was the
case in 1877, 1886, and again in 1894. This was due partly
to the absence of any considerable body of non-partisan writers
on social and political subjects, who, in Europe, are aptly called
" publicists " ; and it was due in part to the somewhat deliberate self-sufficiency of the trade union movement after it had
achieved complete wage-consciousness. It was not until the
great anthracite coal strike of 1902, with the threatened spectacular interference by President Roosevelt and the widely dis-

[5] See Commons and Andrews, *Principles of Labor Legislation*, chap. iii.

cussed award by the public commission of arbitration, that the
public at large became accustomed to view the labour question
in a matter-of-course, non-hysterical light. Also one year
earlier, in 1901, the formation of the National Civic Federation, with the prime purpose of promoting trade agreements,
had signified the awakening of the most far-sighted members
of the business and financial class to the importance of a peaceable solution of the labour question. Since then the labour
question has held the public stage practically without interruption, though the interest it has aroused has of necessity fluctuated.

Probably nothing has contributed to bring the labour question to the front as much as the periodically recurring threats
of railway strikes in connection with demands made by the
brotherhoods of railway employés upon the companies. The
overwhelming public interest in averting such strikes has led
to Federal legislation providing for mediation and conciliation, and lending the aid of government to strengthen systems
of trade agreements which, on some of the roads, have existed
for several decades. In the summer of 1916, when neither
private negotiations nor Federal mediation seemed to be able
to avert a general strike by the four brotherhoods for the eight-
hour day, Congress enacted, upon the recommendation of the
President, the legal eight-hour day for engineers, firemen, conductors, and brakemen, and this was afterwards sustained by
the United States Supreme Court.[6]

A clear gauge of the growth of popular education on the
labour question is given by the McNamara dynamite case.
What a difference between the attitude of the public toward this
case of extreme and premeditated violence and its attitude
towards the suspected Chicago anarchists! In 1886, bloody revenge and suppression were violently demanded. In 1912 nothing more drastic was heard than a demand for an impartial investigation of the causes of the labour unrest, with a view to
the prevention of future conflicts, and scarcely any call for
revenge or any disaster to the labour movement as a whole.

The aroused sympathetic interest of the public in the labour
question is beginning to produce results also in the field of la-

6 Wilson v. New, 37, Sup. Ct. 298 (1917).

bour legislation. During the last half dozen years, two-thirds of the States have adopted the principle of workmen's compensation for all industrial accidents, preparing in this manner a fertile ground for the important movement for industrial safety. Other protective regulations have been the prohibition by the Federal taxing power of the use of an industrial poison, the provision in several States of one day's rest in seven, the beginning of effective prohibition of night work, of maximum limits upon the length of the working day, and of minimum wage laws for women. This legislation differs from the class legislation demanded by workingmen during preceding periods in that it bases itself entirely upon police power, a power which, as a result of the spreading understanding of the labour problem, and the persistent demand coming from the public as well as from organised labour, has become so broadened in scope that much which, a decade or two ago, would have been ruled out of court as class legislation, has recently been held to be warranted under the Federal and the state constitutions.[7]

Nor is it amiss to emphasise the rôle of the public in bringing this legislation about. American trade unions are unique in that, of the labour movements in the whole world, with the sole exception of the French Confédération Générale du Travail, they make the least demand upon the government along the line of legal protection to labour. Owing to the constitutional separation of powers between the executive, the legislative, and the judiciary, and especially owing to the existence of the four dozen different state governments, each a law unto itself, American labour leaders have for the most part become convinced, after long and discouraging experience with unconstitutional and unenforceable labour laws, that only through trade unions can the wage-earner secure protection worthy of the name. In the shadow of this mistrust of governmental action, there developed a nervous fear lest by legislative meddling, however well intentioned, trade union action would be hampered. Hence the Federation is generally opposed to legislation on wages and hours, except as affecting women and children. It is for this reason that it desires to have trade union members in all the public offices dealing with labour, and, on the whole,

---

7 See Commons and Andrews, *Principles of Labor Legislation.*

remains indifferent to the consideration of efficiency in the administration of labour laws. At present this attitude towards the State is supported by the bulk of the voting strength of organised labour, especially of unions most typical of the strength of the American labour movement, such as the highly organised building trades and the railway brotherhoods.[8]

As the American labour movement has become adjusted to a purely economic horizon, it follows that it will undertake political action only when its freedom of economic action becomes threatened. The recollection of the many trade unions in the past wrecked on the rocks of political intrigue undoubtedly is another factor militating against participation in politics.

When employers discovered that they could not place complete reliance upon the executive officers of the democratically controlled state, they turned to the courts for protection. The latter responded by developing a code of trade union law, which, having for its cornerstone a resurrected doctrine of malicious conspiracy as applied to labour combinations and, for its weapon, the injunction, proceeded to outlaw the boycott, to materially circumscribe the right to strike, and even to turn against labour the Federal statutes which had been originally directed against railway and industrial monopoly.

The height of this development, which had begun in the eighties and continued during the nineties, was reached in the well-known Danbury Hatters' case, passed upon by the United States Supreme Court early in 1908.[9] The Sherman anti-trust law, of 1890, had been applied in labour cases in the past, notably in the Pullman boycott case, but never in a civil suit for damages against the individual members of a trade union. In this case the significant thing was not that a few union leaders were to be punished with short terms of imprisonment, but that the life savings of several hundreds of the members were attached to satisfy the staggering triple

---

[8] The acceptance by the railway brotherhoods and the American Federation of Labor of the Adamson Act of 1916 does not necessarily contradict this conclusion. The law was an expedient adopted by the President and Congress to avert a threatened general railway strike, after conciliation and mediation had both failed. The final settlement, in the spring of 1917, was arrived at as a result of negotiation between the railways and the brotherhoods, shortly before the decision by the United States Supreme Court on the constitutionality of the Adamson Act.

[9] For the several stages of this case, see Loewe v. Lawlor, 208 U. S. 274 (1908); Lawlor v. Loewe, 209 Fed. 721 (1913), 235 U. S. 522 (1914).

damages awarded the employer under the anti-trust law. Close upon the outlawing of the boycott in the Danbury hatters' case, came the Adair decision,[10] which in effect legalised "blacklisting" of employés by employers. A few months later, the courts dealt another blow to the boycott in the Buck's Stove and Range case, when Gompers, Morrison, and Mitchell were sentenced to imprisonment, ranging from six months to one year, for disregarding the court's injunction against the boycott of the St. Louis firm.[11]

After the middle of the nineties the Federation had had an official legislative programme, but only as a minor feature. The legislative committee would urge, at each session of Congress, the passage of certain labour bills, notably bills affecting the legal status of the trade unions; and state federations would urge similar measures upon state legislatures. A considerable degree of success was attained in the latter, but practically the result was that employers learned to invoke the interference of the Federal courts. At Washington the labour bills were passed by the House of Representatives at several sessions of Congress, but invariably failed in the Senate. About 1904, owing to the activity of the National Association of Manufacturers and related organisations, the employers' control became consolidated also in the House. Wish as it might, the Federation could no longer remain a purely economic organisation. It was obliged to seek influence in elections.

The first attempt was made in the congressional campaign of 1906. The method was the identical one which had been used by George Henry Evans in the homestead movement and had been urged by Ira Steward in the movement for the eight-hour day, "reward your friends and punish your enemies." And, though some of the hostile Congressmen were not defeated for office, their majorities were considerably reduced. In 1908 the method of "questioning" was applied to the conventions of the two great parties, and the Democratic party was endorsed.[12] At the elections of 1910 and 1912 the Demo-

10 Adair v. U. S., 208 U. S. 161 (1908).
11 For the several stages of this case, see 35 Wash. L. Rep. 747 (1908); 36 Wash. L. Rep. 828 (1908); 37 Wash. L. Rep. 706 (1909); 221 U. S. 418 (1911); 233 U. S. 604 (1914).
12 See "Official Circular" signed by President Gompers, in American Federationist, November, 1908, pp. 955–957.

crats were again endorsed.[13] The Democratic victories resulted in the passage of legislation which, whatever its real
worth after the courts shall have passed upon it, at present
seems to satisfy the Federation leaders. The eight-hour law on
public contract work, the seamen's law, and the creation of a
Department of Labor with a seat in the Cabinet, were unqualified gains, but considerable uncertainty attaches to the
value of the Clayton Act which was designed, in addition to
other things, to redefine the status of trade unions before the
law. Not until the courts have interpreted these provisions
can there be had an authoritative estimate of labour's success
in regaining its freedom of collective action. The defiant attitude assumed by the Federation at its convention in 1916
on the question of the legal interference with labour organisations seems to indicate that organised labour will scarcely be
contented with a compromise.

The political activity of the American Federation of Labor
should be sharply distinguished from that of the Socialist party
of America. Socialists welcomed the former, as they expected
that it would become the forerunner of an independent labour
party or else of a standing alliance between the Federation and
their party, such as exists in Germany. So far these expectations have failed to come true; and indications are lacking that
they may do so in the near future. So long as the majority
of the American trade unions refuse to make labour legislation
a cornerstone in their programme, so long as their chief concern with politics remains merely to protect their freedom of
economic action, just so long, it seems, they will lack an adequate incentive for forming an independent labour party.

Since 1900 socialism has been making rapid progress in the
labour ranks. In the last four years it has succeeded in gaining the support of the important unions of the miners and the
machinists. It now commands about one-third of the votes at
the annual conventions of the Federation, coming, to a large
extent, from the "industrial unions," and it has reached a
million votes at national elections. The old-time struggle between the rival ideas of political and economic socialism, which
dates back to the time of the Lassallean movement and the In-

13 *Ibid.*, October, 1912, pp. 804–814.

ternational, in some measure finds a modern counterpart in the
rivalry between the political socialists and the syndicalist
movement.

Socialism has acquired a considerable following also among
the native-born educated classes, and has gained some noted
converts among the rising class of American "publicists,"
which, in certain respects, enables it to exercise an influence in
the community, which is not to be measured only by its polling
strength. The notable though brief socialist administrations
in Milwaukee and Schenectady have demonstrated that, at last,
after nearly sixty years of effort to become acclimatised, there
is such a thing as an "American" socialism.

Whatever the direct success or failure, it cannot be doubted
that litigation and political and legislative activity led to undesirable consequences in the fields of economic action proper.
Litigation absorbed a considerable portion of the Federation's
income. Legislative and political action, while less costly from
the financial standpoint, perhaps proved even a greater burden
from the standpoint of organisation. It diverted the attention
of the active men in the Federation from the work of organising
new trades. The inevitable outcome of the slackening economic activity of the Federation was the failure to spread out
in the field where organisation was most needed, namely among
the unskilled. This was also due in part to the conviction of
many that the unskilled and foreign element would, for some
reason, remain unresponsive to the kind of appeal which they
were in a position to make, and further, that when organised
such organisation would be short-lived. The unskilled were
practically let alone by the Federation after 1904. Thus the
field was clear for the revolutionary industrialist movement of
syndicalism.

But there may be traced out three kinds of industrialism,
each answering the demands of a particular stratum of the
wage-earning class. The class lowest in the scale, the unskilled
and "floaters," conceives industrialism as "one big union,"
where not only trade but even industrial distinctions are virtually ignored with reference to action against employers, if
not also with reference to the principle of organisation. In
the eighties, it was this class that saw in the Knights of Labor

its saviour, and it is this same class that recently responded to the Industrial Workers of the World. The native floater in the West and the unskilled foreigner in the East are equally responsive to the appeal to storm capitalism in a successive series of revolts under the banner of the " one big union." Uniting in its ranks the workers with the least experience in organisation and with none in political action, the " one big union " pins its faith upon assault rather than " armed peace," upon the strike without the trade agreement, and has no faith whatsoever in political or legislative action. Such is syndical- ism — the industrialism of the immigrant unskilled and native floating classes, whose power is spectacular but not continuous.

Another form of industrialism is that of the middle stratum of the Federation — trades which are moderately skilled and have had considerable experience in organisation, such as the brewers and miners. They realise that, in order to attain an equal footing with the employers, they must present a front co-extensive with the employers' association, which means that all trades in an industry must act under one direction. Hence they strive to assimilate the engineers and machinists, whose labour is essential to the continuance of the operation of the plant. They thus reproduce on a minor scale the attempt of the Knights of Labor during the eighties to engulf the more skilled trade unions.

At the same time the relatively unprivileged position of these trades makes them keenly alive to the danger from below, from the unskilled whom the employer may break into their jobs in case of strikes. They therefore favour taking such into the organisation. Their industrialism is consequently caused perhaps more by their own trade considerations than by the al- truistic desire to uplift the unskilled, although they realise that the organisation of the unskilled is required by the broader interests of the wage-earning class. However, their long ex- perience in matters of organisation teaches them that the " one big union " would be a poor medium. Their accumulated ex- perience likewise has a moderating influence on their economic activity, and they are consequently among the strongest sup- porters inside the American Federation of Labor of the trade agreement. Nevertheless, opportunistic though they are in the industrial field, their position is not sufficiently favoured above the unskilled to make them satisfied with the wage system. Hence, they are mostly controlled by socialists and are strongly in favour of political action through the Socialist party. This form of industrialism may consequently be called " socialist industrialism." In the annual conventions of the Federation, " industrialists " are practically synonymous with socialists and they control about one-third of the total vote.

But there is still another form of industrialism, that of the upper stratum. Long before industrialism had entered the national arena as the economic creed of syndicalists and socialists, the unions of the skilled began to evolve an industrialism of their own. This species may properly be termed craft industrialism, as it seeks merely to unite on an efficient basis the fighting strength of the unions of the skilled trades by devising a method for speedy solution of jurisdictional disputes between overlapping unions and by reducing the sympathetic strike to a science. This movement first manifested itself in the early eighties in the form of local building trades' councils, which especially devoted themselves to sympathetic strikes. This local industrialism grew, after a fashion, to national dimensions in the form of the International Building Trades Council organised in St. Louis in 1897. The latter proved, however, ineffective, since, having for its basic unit the local building trades' council, it inevitably came into conflict with the national unions in the building trades. For the same reason it was barred from obtaining the recognition of the American Federation of Labor. The date of the real birth of craft industrialism on a national scale was therefore deferred to 1903, when the Structural Building Trades Alliance was founded. The formation of the Alliance marks an event of supreme importance, not only because for the first time it united for common action all the important national unions in the building industry, but especially because it promulgated a new principle which, if generally adopted, was apparently destined to revolutionise the structure of American labour organisations. The Alliance purported to be a federation of the " basic " trades in the industry, and in reality it did represent an *entente* of the big and aggressive unions. These were moved to federate, not only for the purpose of forcing the struggle against the employers, but also of expanding at the expense of the "non-basic" or weak unions, besides seeking to annihilate the last vestiges of the International Building Trades Council. The Brotherhood of Carpenters and Joiners, probably the most aggressive union in the American Federation of Labor, was the leader in this movement. From the standpoint of the Federation, the Structural Alliance was at best an extra-legal organisation, as it did not receive the latter's formal sanction, but the Federation could scarcely afford to ignore it as it had ignored the International Building Trades Council. Thus in 1908 the Alliance was legitimatised and made the first "Department" of the American Federation of Labor under the name of Building Trades Department, with the settlement of jurisdictional disputes as its main function. It was followed by departments of metal trades, of railway employés, of miners, and by a "label" department.

It is not, however, open to much doubt that the Department was not a very successful custodian of the trade autonomy principle, as announced in the well-known "Scranton Declaration" adopted in 1901 at the convention held in Scranton, Pennsylvania. Jurisdictional disputes are caused either by a technical change, which plays havoc with official "jurisdiction" or else by a plain desire on the part of the stronger union to encroach upon the province of the weaker one. When the former was the case and the struggle happened to be between unions of equal strength and influence, it generally terminated in a compromise. When, however, the combatants were two unions of unequal strength, the doctrine of the supremacy of "basic unions" was generally made to prevail in the end. Such was the outcome of the struggle between carpenters and joiners on the one side and the wood workers on the other, and also between the plumbers and steam fitters. In each case it ended in the forced amalgamation of the weaker union with the stronger one, upon the principle that there must be only one union in each "basic" trade. In the case of the steamfitters, which was settled finally at the convention at Rochester in 1912, the American Federation of Labor gave what might be interpreted as an official sanction of the new doctrine.

Notwithstanding these official lapses from the principle of trade autonomy, the socialist industrialists were still compelled to abide by the letter and the spirit of the Scranton declaration. The effect of such a policy on the coming American industrialism may be twofold. It may resemble less closely the brewers' or the miners' unions than the industrial unions of Germany. In the former all who work for the same employer belong to one organisation, but in the latter all who work upon the same kind of material, such as wood, metal, etc., belong together. Or, the future development of the "Department" may enable the strong "basic" unions to undertake concerted action against employers, while each retains its own autonomy. Such, indeed, is the notable "concerted movement" of the railway brotherhoods, which during the past ten years has begun to set a type for craft industrialism. It is not at all unlikely that the strenuous opposition which the four brotherhoods have met on the part of the railways during the concerted movement for the eight-hour day in the summer of 1916, especially in view of the turn toward legislation which this matter took with the passage of the Adamson law, might lead to a more or less permanent affiliation between these hitherto unaffiliated organisations and the American Federation of Labor.

BIBLIOGRAPHY

BIBLIOGRAPHY

General Survey, 541. Colonial and Federal Beginnings, 548. Citizenship, 555. Trade Unionism, 561. Humanitarianism, 566. Nationalisation, 571. Upheaval and Reorganisation, 576.

GENERAL SURVEY

IN no country has the value of strictly economic records been sufficiently appreciated, whether by the government or by private associations and least of all in America. As far as colonial industrial conditions and policies are concerned, with the special organisations of those days such as guilds, voluntary associations to raise capital, to develop markets, and to enlist governmental support for domestic producers, the economic historian is able to draw, in common with the general historian, upon such sources as Colonial Records, local histories, and publications of historical societies.

For the succeeding periods, and especially on the subject of the early labour struggles, there has been until recently scarcely any collected documentary material. The first state bureau of labour statistics in the United States was established in Massachusetts in 1869 and the Federal Bureau first came into existence in 1884. In their reports there are a few cursory studies of labour events and conditions during earlier years, such as the incomplete chronology of strikes since 1825, given for Massachusetts in the Massachusetts Bureau of Labor Statistics, *Eleventh Annual Report,* 1880, pp. 3–71; the account of "Strikes and Lockouts occurring Prior to 1881 in the United States," in the Commissioner of Labor, *Third Annual Report,* 1887, pp. 1029–1108; the similar one for Pennsylvania since 1835 in Secretary of Internal Affairs, *Annual Report,* 1880–1881 (Harrisburg, 1882), Pt. III, *Industrial Statistics,* IX, 262–391; and the list of eleven (instead of seventeen) labour conspiracy cases prior to 1842 enumerated in the United States Bureau of Labor, *Sixteenth Annual Report,* 1901, pp.

873–986. *A Documentary History of the Early Organizations of Printers* was prepared by Ethelbert Stewart (United States Bureau of Labor, Bulletin No. 61, 1905), and is the pioneer work in the field.

In 1886, when Professor Richard T. Ely, of the University of Wisconsin, then of Johns Hopkins University, published his *Labor Movement in America,* he said in the preface: " I offer this book merely as a sketch which will, I trust, some day be followed by a book worthy of the title History of Labor in the New World." During the following two decades, keeping this aim in mind, Professor Ely made notes and memoranda for this larger work and especially spared neither effort nor expense in collecting material for that book. As a result, he found himself in possession of a unique collection of labour literature which had outgrown the capacity of a private house and had begun to involve an expense beyond his private resources. For a time the Wisconsin Historical Society housed and cared for the Collection and assisted in its enlargement. With the growth of the Collection and the possibilities of still further enlargement, the expense involved becoming greater, with the approval of Dr. Reuben Gold Thwaites, Secretary of the Wisconsin Historical Society, the Collection, after examination by Mr. Clement W. Andrews, the librarian, was turned over to the John Crerar Library of Chicago.

The management of the Crerar Library evinced special interest in this field of work and undertook to care for and increase the collection. In addition, it agreed to the condition that Dr. Ely and his co-workers at Madison should have the right to borrow or use at Madison any part of the Collection needed in the prosecution of his undertaking.

By letters and personal interviews with prominent men throughout the country, Professor Ely strove to secure the organisation of a society for industrial research. As a result of his initiative and the personal interest as well as material support of Messrs. V. Everit Macy (treasurer), Robert Hunter, Robert Fulton Cutting, Justice Henry Dugro, and William English Walling, of New York, Stanley McCormick and Charles R. Crane, of Chicago, and others, the American Bureau of Industrial Research was organised with headquarters in Madison, Wisconsin.

Dr. Ely's collection was turned over to the Crerar before the American Bureau was established. But this event changed the situation and made it advisable to form as large a collection in Madison as possible, and in this effort the University of Wisconsin and the State Historical Society have co-operated, with the result that in Madison and Chicago are now unrivalled collections and their use is available for the work of all investigators.

A survey of the field revealed an unexpected wealth of hitherto unknown sources in the form of pamphlets and files of newspapers published in the interest of early labour organisations. Some of the newspapers in question had not hitherto been consulted at any time, so far as the librarians in charge were aware, and in one library, *The Man,* a daily labour paper, published in co-operation with the Trades' Union of New York in 1834 and 1835, was discovered literally buried beneath the accumulations of seventy years. Some of the most important material, however, has not been found in libraries, but has been obtained by searching dusty old bookshops in many cities, and by begging or buying personal collections from aged labour leaders — a part of the work carried on largely by Dr. John B. Andrews, Dr. Helen L. Sumner, and Mrs. W. H. Lighty. Many others also aided generously and loyally, and their help is highly appreciated even if they are too many to be named in this connection. The collection thus made is now in the libraries of the University of Wisconsin and of the State Historical Society of Wisconsin, both of which have given valuable co-operation.

An important collection is the one secured through the efforts of Dr. R. T. Ely from Mr. Herman Schlüter who became interested in the work of the Bureau. William English Walling, of New York, contributed a generous sum toward the purchase price of this collection. It not only contains material covering the history of practically all the organisations of German-speaking workingmen in the United States, socialistic, trade union, benevolent as well as co-operative in early days, but presents also a rich collection of materials and documents pertaining to the early history of the socialist movement in Germany. Many of the documents in this collection came to Mr. Schlüter from the late F. A. Sorge, surnamed the " Father of American Socialism," a personal friend of Marx and Engels, and their " official " representative in this country. Especially noteworthy among the " Sorge Documents " are the letter copy-book of the North American Federation of the International Workingmen's Association, 1869–1876, and a transcription of the letters and addresses which were sent by Sorge, in his capacity of General Secretary of the International Workingmen's Association, 1872–1876, to the national organisations of the International in Europe.

Another important collection in possession of the American Bureau of Industrial Research is the Henry Demarest Lloyd Collection abounding in material on co-operation and the socialist movement during the nineties. A unique document obtained by the Bureau is a complete file of *Die Republik der Arbeiter* (probably the only one in existence) (New York, 1850–1855), edited by Wilhelm Weitling, the famous communist. This came from the Philadelphia Freie Gemeinde.

Among the rarer and more important documents secured by the Bureau, in addition to those already mentioned, are: the Chicago *Workingman's Advocate,* 1864–1876; *Fincher's Trades' Review,* Philadelphia, 1863–1866, the *Practical Christian,* edited by Adin Ballou, 1860–1880, and the John Samuel Collection on Co-operation, composed of manuscripts, letters, and scrapbooks.

Practically all the large libraries of the country were visited by John B. Andrews, Helen L. Sumner, and Professor Commons. In October, 1906, the Bureau sent out to nearly 500 libraries a printed finding list containing the names of about 160 labour papers and papers sympathetic to labour published in the United States before 1872. By means of this list a number of valuable papers, of which no record had previously been found, were located.

As it was impossible to borrow these newspapers and it would be expensive to study them with the care they deserved in their scattered situations, it was decided to take transcripts from their most important articles and to abstract notes of the less important. As a result, the Bureau now possesses a card catalogue, each card presenting either a brief statement of a labour event or else a summary of an article on a labour subject to be found in other libraries, as well as half a dozen large-sized filing cases of transcribed articles.

In view of the rarity of the sources and the interest manifested by economists and historians, the idea was suggested of publishing the material, in so far as it might be considered to have documentary value, in such form as to be available for students, economists, and historians. The outcome was the *Documentary History of American Industrial Society* (Cleveland, 1910). Of the ten volumes of this *Documentary History,* two, edited by U. B. Phillips, are devoted to *Plantation and Frontier,* 1649–1863; two (and a supplement), edited by J. R. Commons and E. A. Gilmore, to *Labor Conspiracy Cases,* 1806–1842; two, to *Labor Movement,* 1820–1840; two to *Labor Movement,* 1840–1860, and two, to *Labor Movement,* 1860–1880. The last volume contains a *Finding List of Sources Quoted* for seventy libraries. About one-tenth of the transcribed material in possession of the Bureau, selected for its typical value, found a place on the pages of the *Documentary History.*

Since the eighties, facilities for writing labour history began more or less to approximate those commanded by the general historian, owing to the output of the various labour bureaus and to frequent governmental investigations into labour conditions and labour troubles. The most convenient index of Federal documents is the *Checklist of United States Public Documents,* 1789–1909 (Vol. I, 1911) prepared by the Superintendent of Documents, Washington. For state publications, the most valuable is the " *Index of Economic Material in Documents of the States of the United States* prepared by Adelaide R. Hasse (Carnegie Institution of Washington, *Publications,* 1907–1915). This index has thus far been compiled for thirteen states. There is also an *Index of All Reports issued by Bureaus of Labor Statistics in the United States Prior to March 1, 1902,* published by the United States Department of Labor (Washington, 1902). Unfortunately there does not exist a similar useful index for the period since 1902.

An exceedingly useful *Trial Bibliography of American Trade-Union Publications* was prepared by the Economic Seminary of the *Johns Hopkins University*, and edited by Dr. G. E. Barnett (Baltimore, 1904), of which a second revised edition also appeared (Baltimore, 1907). It is far more than a mere enumeration of titles, as it is combined with a finding list which comprises the Johns Hopkins University Library, the Library of the Federal Department of Labor, the John Crerar Library (Chicago), the Library of Congress, and the central office of the particular union or federation. The Division of Bibliography of the Library of Congress published a *Select List of Books (with reference to periodicals) on Labor, particularly relating to strikes* (Washington, 1903). The State Historical Society of Wisconsin, *Bulletin of Information,* No. 77 (Madison, 1915) describes the *Collection on Labor and Socialism in the Wisconsin State Historical Library.*

American historians, until within the last ten or fifteen years, were wholly unconscious of the existence of a permanent labour question. It was only following such catastrophic events as the railway strikes of 1877, the anarchist bombs in Chicago, and the Pullman strike of 1894, that the labour movement temporarily forced itself upon their attention. The workingmen's political movement during the thirties is treated in John Bach Mcmaster's *History of the People of the United States* (New York, 1900), V, 84–108, and VI, 80–101 (New York, 1906). The movement from the forties to the seventies was practically unnoticed by the historians, with the exception of its humanitarian and intellectual offshoots during the forties and fifties. The labour movement during the Civil War is treated in E. D. Fite, *Social and Industrial Conditions in the North during the Civil War* (New York, 1910), 182–212. E. E. Sparks in his *National Development, 1877–1885* (New York, 1907), Vol. XXIII of The American Nation Series, has a chapter on the labour movement, 1875–1885. There is a similar chapter on the movement, 1884–1888, in D. R. Dewey, *National Problems, 1885–1897* (New York, 1907), Vol. XXIV, and a part of a chapter in J. H. Latane, *America as a World Power,* 1897–1907 (New York, 1907), Vol. XXV of the same series, on the movement since 1895.

If labour history still remains a field practically untilled by the general historian, important beginnings have already been made by the economists. Dr. Richard T. Ely's *Labor Movement in America* (Baltimore, 1886) gives a valuable sketch of the events of the labour movement prior to 1886, the first ever attempted. The justly deserved reputation of his book rests on this and, to a still greater extent, on the attitude of the author towards his subject. This attitude, namely a strictly objective point of view, combined with broad sympathies for the labouring class struggling for recognition in a democracy, was entirely novel in America when Dr. Ely published his book, but it has since been adopted by a majority of American economic writers.

Of great value is also the work by August Sartorius Freih. v. Waltershausen, a trained German economist who travelled in the United States during 1880 and 1881, *Die nordamerikanischen Gewerkschaften unter dem Einfluss der fortschreitenden Productionstechnik* (Berlin, 1886).

F. A. Sorge, the foremost leader of the International Workingmen's Association in America, deserves well of the student of labour history. Although he had for several decades himself taken a leading part in the American labour movement, his historical work leaves little to be desired as far as objectiveness is concerned. He published a series of articles on American labour history, 1850–1896, in the *Neue Zeit* (Stuttgart) between 1890 and 1895.

George E. McNeill's *The Labor Movement — The Problem of To-day* (Boston and New York, 1887) contains an account of the history of the labour movement as a whole from early times to 1886, separate accounts of the histories of a number of trades, and a semi-historical, semi-expository treatment of the following labour problems: labour legislation, co-operation, arbitration, Chinese immigration, industrial education, the land question, and unemployment.

The bibliographies in the following pages include only publications which have been actually cited in the text of the several parts of these volumes. Besides these citations a very large number of papers and pamphlets had been examined but no citation is actually made to them. A complete bibliography of the periods covered in these volumes would constitute a good-sized volume in itself.

PART I. COLONIAL AND FEDERAL BEGINNINGS TO 1827

Most of the primary and secondary sources upon which the description and analysis of Colonial industrial conditions and policies is based and which require critical treatment have been reviewed either in the bibliographies of Johnson's *History of Foreign and Domestic Commerce in the United States,* or Clark's *History of Manufactures in the United States.* Evidently an attempt to appraise them here would be but repetition.

However, several classes of sources have thus far received scant consideration. Such are the semi-official documents like city annals, of which Munsell's *Annals of Albany* is an illustration, and descriptive manuals, like Mease's *The Picture of Philadelphia,* which contain authentic records of significant local events, as well as descriptions of the numerous organised activities of the inhabitants. Similarly, advertisements in city directories are especially useful for the study of commercial phases of economic life.

Extensive search, but with limited success, was also made for proceedings and other official records of economic organisations. Among those discovered were *The Annals of the General Society of Mechanics and Tradesmen* of the City of New York, and the *Ordinances, By-Laws and Resolutions of the Carpenters' Company.* The rules, correspondence with kindred societies, and other items contained in these documents, often made it possible better to comprehend complex economic situations, as well as to gauge the extent to which these associations co-operated in furthering matters vital to their existence.

There is also lacking the systematic publication of private records, such as business accounts and correspondence, similar to those contained in U. B. Phillips' *Plantation and Frontier* mentioned above.

Of what might be termed semi-documentary sources, local histories are, of course, most useful. Appreciative historic sketches of early industrial organisations also belong to this class of sources. However, only one, Bett's *Carpenters' Hall and its Historic Memories,* has been found.

It is from sources such as enumerated above that the most instructive material for Colonial economic history must be derived. Without them the economic historian must rely solely upon his imagination in his endeavour to picture and interpret many of the controlling forces of Colonial economic life.

Unfortunately, with the exception of local histories and city directories, these sources have not been collected extensively. A large part of them are probably extant in manuscript form, and in the possession of persons who do not appreciate their historical significance. A properly directed search should yield as bountiful a harvest as did the searches of the American Bureau of Industrial Research in allied fields.

Since this is the dormant period in American labour history and only two trades had continuous organisations, trade union sources are naturally few. By way of secondary accounts chronicling the activities of wage earners in general, we have the essentially sketchy but fruitful account in McMaster's *History of the People of the United States;* Ethelbert Stewart's article on *Two Forgotten Decades in the History of Labor Organisations, 1820–1840;* and Glocker's *Trade Unionism in Baltimore Before the War of 1812,* a Johns Hopkins University Seminary Report. Each of these has been of unusual help in shedding light on the extent and nature of early unions. They have also rendered yeoman service by furnishing clues to newspaper sources which invariably contained valuable accounts of important labour activities. McMaster's history was especially helpful for this purpose. Without the aid of this pioneer work many of the early labour organisations would probably not have been located.

We also have secondary accounts of one of the two trades that had reached the stage of continuous organisation. The *Printers' Circular* reproduced "A Historical Sketch of the Philadelphia Typographical Society, 1802–1811," written by contemporary members, and following the method common to untrained historical writers. Professor Geo. E. Barnett's scholarly history of *" The Printers "* is the other secondary source, and, being accepted as the final work on the history of that trade, needs no evaluation here.

For the printers the primary sources are plentiful. Fortunately Professor Barnett had the minutes of the *Philadelphia Typographical Society, 1802–1811,* and of the *New York Typographical Society, 1809–1818,* typewritten and a copy deposited with the Johns Hopkins University Library, thus making them available to all students. Ethelbert Stewart's *A Documentary History of the Early Organisations of Printers,* and George A. Stevens' work on *New York Typographical Union No. 6,* are conscientious compilations of documents illuminatingly explained, illustrating both the formal and human phases of the early printers' organisations.

Unfortunately none of the official trade union records of the cordwainers could be located. If it were not for the testimony in the conspiracy cases, reprinted in volumes III and IV of the *Documentary History of American Industrial Society,* we should entirely lack a comprehensive record of their activities. However, this voluminous testimony amply depicts the nature of their grievances, demands, policies, and point of view.

Unlike the succeeding periods, this dormant period in the history of American labour naturally has no trade union organs. Nevertheless, the scattered newspaper accounts, especially those of the Jeffersonian press; the controversial testimony, vitriolic arguments of attorneys and vindictive instructions of judges; the " spicy " minutes of the printers — all these sources when brought together give us a vivid and realistic picture of the prevailing spirit of that time which witnessed the uprising of a new, virile and constantly ascending class.

I. PUBLIC DOCUMENTS.

J. Munsell. *The Annals of Albany* (Albany, 1852), III.
Boston Directory of 1823.
An Act to condense all the Ordinances, By-Laws, and Resolutions of the Carpenters Corporation, now in force into one law (1807). Copy in Wisconsin Historical Society Collection, *Philadelphia Miscellaneous Pamphlets,* VI.
An Act to Incorporate the Carpenters Company of the City and County of Philadelphia (Philadelphia, 1827). Copy in Wis-

consin Historical Society Collection, *Philadelphia Miscellaneous Pamphlets*, VI.

The Public Records of the Colony of Connecticut, from 1636–1665 (Hartford, 1850) ; 1665–1678 (1852) ; 1744–1750 (1876).

Archives of Maryland, Proceedings and Acts of the General Assembly of Maryland (Baltimore, 1883), I, II, III, V, VII, XVII, XIX, XXVI, XXIX.

Laws of the Commonwealth of Massachusetts (Boston, 1815).

Private and Special Statutes of the Commonwealth of Massachusetts, 1822–1830 (Boston, 1837).

The Colonial Laws of Massachusetts, with supplements 1660–1672 (Boston, 1889).

Acts and Resolves of the Province of the Massachusetts Bay (Boston, 1869), I, III.

Records of the Governor and Company of the Massachusetts Bay in New England (Boston, 1853), Vol. I, II, III, IV, V.

Laws of New Hampshire, Province Period, 1702–1745 (Concord, 1913), II.

Records of the Colony or Jurisdiction of New Haven, 1653–1665 (Hartford, 1858).

Stevens, George A. *New York Typographical Union No. 6*, in Bureau of Labor Statistics, Annual Report, 1911, of the New York State Department of Labor.

Minutes of the Common Council of the City of New York (Vol. I, New York, 1905).

Colonial Laws of New York (Vols. I and V, Albany, 1894).

Laws of the State of New York Passed at the Twenty-eighth Session of the Legislature (Albany, 1805).

Private Laws of the State of New York (Albany, 1808).

Colonial Records of North Carolina (Vols. VII, VIII, XV, XVII, Raleigh, 1890).

Acts of the General Assembly of the Commonwealth of Pennsylvania (Harrisburg, 1824).

Statutes at Large of Pennsylvania (Vols. II, III, XII, XIII, Harrisburg, 1908).

Records of the Colony of Rhode Island and Providence Plantations in New England (Vols. IV, VIII, and IX, Providence, 1859).

Stewart, Ethelbert. *A Documentary History of the Early Organizations of Printers*, in Bureau of Labor Bulletin, No. 61 (Washington, 1905).

United States Commissioner of Labor, *Report on Strikes and Lockouts* (Washington, 1887).

Acts Passed at a General Assembly of the Commonwealth of Virginia (Richmond, 1811).

The Statutes at Large; being a collection of all the Laws of Virginia (Vols. I, II, and VI, ed. by Wm. H. Hening, New York, 1823).

II. BOOKS, ARTICLES AND PAMPHLETS.

Abbott, Edith. *Women in Industry* (New York, 1910).

Ames, Herman V. *Some Peculiar Laws and Customs of Colonial Days, A Paper read before the Pennsylvania Society of the Order of the Founders and Patriots of America* (1905).

Anderson, A. *Historical and Chronological Deductions of the Origin of Commerce* (Dublin, 1790).

Babcock, Kendrick C. *The Rise of American Nationality, 1811–1819* (New York, 1906, Vol. XIII of the American Nation Series).

Barnett, G. E. *The Printers,* in Publications of the American Economic Association, October, 1909 (Vol. X, Cambridge, Mass., 1909).

Basset, J. S. *The Federalist System* (New York, 1906, Vol. XI, of the American Nation Series).

Beard, C. A. *An Economic Interpretation of the Constitution of the United States* (New York, 1913).

Becker, C. L. *Beginnings of the American People* (Boston, 1915, Vol. I of the Riverside History of the United States).

———· *The History of Political parties in the Province of New York,* University of Wisconsin *Bulletin, No. 286* (Madison, 1909).

Betts, Richard K. *Carpenters' Hall and Its Historic Memories* (rev. ed., published by the Company, Philadelphia, 1893). Copy of pamphlet is in Wisconsin Historical Library Collection.

Bishop, J. L. *A History of American Manufactures from 1608 to 1860* (3d ed., rev. and enlarged, Vols. I, II, III and IV, Philadelphia, 1868).

Bogart, E. L. *The Economic History of the United States* (New York, 1907).

Bruce, R. A. *Economic History of Virginia in the Seventeenth Century* (Vols. I and II, New York, 1896).

Bücher, Karl. *Die Entstehungen der Volkswirtschaft* (Tübingen, 1901). *Industrial Evolution* (translated by S. M. Wickett, New York, 1907).

Callender, G. S. *Selections from the Economic History of the United States, 1765–1860* (New York, 1909).

Channing, Edward. *A History of the United States* (Vol. III, New York, 1912).

Coman, Katharine. *The Industrial History of the United States* (new and rev. ed., New York, 1910).

Commons, J. R. *Labor and Administration* (New York, 1913).

——— *Types of American Labor Organizations — The Teamsters of Chicago,* in *Quarterly Journal of Economics,* XIX, 400.

Commons and Andrews. *Principles of Labor Legislation* (New York, 1916).

Coxe, Tench. *A View of the United States of America* (Philadelphia, 1794).

Dewey, Davis R. *Financial History of the United States* (5th ed., New York, 1915, American Citizen Series).

Ely, R. T. *Studies in the Evolution of Industrial Society* (New York, 1903).

Engels, Frederick. *The Origin of the Family, Private Property, and the State* (translated by Ernest Untermann, Chicago, 1902).

Force, Peter. *Tracts and Other Papers,* relating principally to the Origin, Settlement, and Progress of the Colonies in North America (Vol. III, Washington, 1844).

Glocker, T. W. *Trade Unionism in Baltimore before the War of 1812,* in Johns Hopkins University, *Circular,* No. 196 (Baltimore, April, 1907).

Hazard, Blanche E. *Organization of the Boot and Shoe Industry in Massachusetts before 1875,* in *Quarterly Journal of Economics,* XXVII.

Hobson, J. A. *The Evolution of Modern Capitalism* (new and rev. ed., New York, 1913).

Howard, G. E. *Preliminaries of the Revolution* (New York, 1905, Vol. VIII of The American Nation Series).

Johnson, David N. *Sketches of Lynn* (Lynn, 1880).

Johnson, Edward. *Wonder Working Providence of Sions Saviour in New England,* in Massachusetts Historical Society, *Collections* (2d ser. Vol. VIII, Boston, 1826), also reprinted in *Original Narratives of Early American History* (J. Franklin Jameson, ed., New York, 1910).

Johnson, E. R., and collaborators, *History of Domestic and Foreign Commerce of the United States* (2 vols., Washington, D. C., 1915).

Johnston, Henry P. *New York after the Revolution,* in *Magazine of American History,* XXIX, 305.

Killikelly, Sarah H. *The History of Pittsburgh* (Pittsburgh, 1906).

Lewis, Alanzo. *The History of Lynn* (Boston, 1829).

Lord, Eleanor L. *Industrial Experiments in the British Colonies of North America,* in *Johns Hopkins University Studies* (extra Vol. XVII, Baltimore, 1898).

McMaster, J. B. *A History of the People of the United States from the Revolution to the Civil War* (Vols. I to V, New York, 1901).

——— *A Century of Social Betterment, Atlantic Monthly,* LXXIX, 23.

Massachusetts Historical Society, *Collections* (2d ser. Boston, MDCCCXLVI).

Marx, Karl. *Capital.* (3 vols., Kerr edition, Chicago, 1909).

—— *A Contribution to the Critique of Political Economy* (translated by N. I. Stone, New York, 1904).

Marx and Engels. *Manifesto of the Communist Party.*

Mease, James. *The Picture of Philadelphia* (Philadelphia, 1811).

Annals of the General Society of Mechanics and Tradesmen of the City of New York, from 1785 to 1880 (New York, 1882).

Morgan, Forrest (editor-in-chief). *Connecticut as a Colony and as a State* (Vol. II, Hartford, 1902).

Morgan, Lewis H. *Ancient Society* (New York, 1877).

New York Typographical Society. *MS. Minutes* (1809-1818, in Johns Hopkins University Library).

Nystrom, P. H. *The Economics of Retailing* (New York, 1913).

O'Callaghan, E. B. *Calendar of Historical Manuscripts in the office of the Secretary of State, Albany, N. Y.* (English Manuscripts, Pt. II, Albany, 1866).

Pasko, W. W. *American Dictionary of Printing and Bookmaking* (New York, 1894).

Philadelphia Typographical Society. *MS. Minutes,* (1802–1811, in Johns Hopkins University Library).

A Historical Sketch of the Philadelphia Typographical Society, in *Printers' Circular* ('Philadelphia, 1867).

Schmoller, Gustav. *Grundriss der Allgemeinen Volkswirtschaftslehre, Vol. II* (Leipzig, 1904).

—— *The Mercantile System and Its Historical Significance* (New York, 1896).

Seligman, E. R. A. *The Economic Interpretation of History* (New York, 1912).

Simons, A. M. *Social Forces in American History* (New York, 1911).

Smith, Thomas E. V. *The City of New York in the Year of Washington's Inauguration, 1789* (New York, 1899).

Stewart, Ethelbert. *Two Forgotten Decades in the History of Labor Organizations, 1820–1840,* in *American Federationist,* XX, 518.

Sumner, William G. *A History of American Currency* (New York, 1876).

Taussig, F. W. *The Tariff History of the United States* (6th ed., New York, 1914).

Turner, F. J. *Rise of the New West* (New York, 1906, Vol. XIV of the American Nation Series).

Unwin, George. *Industrial Organization in the Sixteenth and Seventeenth Centuries* (Oxford, 1904).

Van Rensselaer, Mrs. Schuyler. *History of the City of New York in the Seventeenth Century* (2 vols., New York, 1909).

Vandervelde, Emile. *Collectivism and Industrial Evolution* (translated by C. H. Kerr, Chicago, 1901).

Waltershausen, A. Sartorius Freih. v. *Die nordamerikanischen Gewerkschaften, unter dem Einfluss der fortschreitenden Productionstechnik* (Berlin, 1886).

Webb, Sidney and Beatrice. *The History of Trade Unionism* (new ed., New York, 1902).

Weeden, William B. *Economic and Social History of New England* (Vols. I and II, New York, 1890).

Wilson, James Grant. *The Memorial History of the City of New York* (Vol. III, New York, 1893).

III. PAPERS.

The American Museum (Philadelphia), printed by Mathew Carey, Vol. III.

Aurora and General Advertiser (Philadelphia), 1803, 1805, 1806.

Charleston City (North Carolina) *Gazette,* 1825.

Columbian Centinel (Boston), 1825.

Dunlap's American Daily Advertiser (Philadelphia), 1791.

Federal Gazette (Baltimore), 1800.

Federal Intelligencer and Baltimore Gazette (Baltimore), 1795.

Freeman's Journal (Philadelphia), 1825.

The General Advertiser (Philadelphia), 1791.

National Advocate (New York), 1823.

National Gazette (New York), 1824.

New York *Evening Post,* 1825.

Niles' Weekly Register (Baltimore), 1812.

Providence (Rhode Island) *Patriot,* 1825.

PART II. CITIZENSHIP — 1827–1833

The secondary sources for this period are very meagre. A history of the Working Men's party in New York was written by one of its most prominent leaders, George Henry Evans, and published in a monthly magazine (*The Radical,* 1841–1843, " History of the Working Men's Party "). Another by Hobart Berrian is entitled *The Origin and Rise of the Working Men's Party* (Washington, n. d., ca. 1841). John B. McMaster treats of the workingmen's movement in his *History of the People of the United States* (New York, 1900), volume V, 84–108, but he attaches too much significance to the " intellectuals " in the movement. George E. McNeill in his *The*

Labor Movement: The Problem of To-day (Boston, 1887) and
Professor R. T. Ely in his *The Labor Movement in America*
(New York, 1886) also treat at some length of the working-
men's parties of 1827 to 1833.

A brief summary of this period entitled "Labor Organizations and Labor Politics, 1827–1837," based in part on the
material used by the writer, was published by Professor John
R. Commons in the *Quarterly Journal of Economics,* 1907,
XXI, 323–329. A discussion of the working class origins of
the public school system in America, also based in part upon
this material, is contained in Frank Tracy Carlton, *Economic
Influences upon Educational Progress in the United States,
1820–1850,* University of Wisconsin, *Bulletin,* Economics and
Political Science Series, Vol. IV, No. 1 (Madison, 1908). The
Webbs' *History of Trade Unionism* (London, 1911) Chap. II,
102–161, deals with the contemporary movement in England,
and offers a valuable historical perspective.

By far the most valuable sources of information for this
period have been the few existing files of papers published
during these years. The newspapers and periodicals may be
roughly divided into two classes, those which were sympathetic
and those which were hostile towards the labour movement.
Among the sympathetic papers the most important were the
Baltimore *Republican,* the *Morning Herald* [1] and the *Evening
Post* of New York, the *Pennsylvanian* and the *Public Ledger*
of Philadelphia, the Boston *Transcript,*[2] and the *Washingtonian* of Washington, D. C. The chief papers opposed to the
labour movement during this period were the New York *Journal of Commerce,* the Philadelphia *National Gazette,* the Boston *Courier,* the Albany *Argus,* and the *United States Telegraph* of Washington. Other general papers which from time
to time printed labour news were *Niles' Weekly Register,* of
Baltimore; the *American Sentinel,* the *Freeman's Journal,* the
Democratic Press, the *Free Trade Advocate, Poulson's American Daily Advertiser,* the Pennsylvania *Inquirer,* the Philadelphia *Gazette,* the United States *Gazette,* and the *Banner of*

---

[1] This was a predecessor, published in
1830, of the *Herald,* started by James
Gordon Bennett in 1835.

[2] The Boston *Transcript* was favourable

to the labour movement until 1864, when
it changed its attitude as the result of a
printers' strike.

the Constitution, of Philadelphia; the *American,* the *Commercial Advertiser,* the *Morning Courier and New York Enquirer,* and the *Mercury,* of New York; the *Independent Chronicle and Boston Patriot,* the *Chronicle,* the *Columbian Centinel,* the *Daily Advertiser and Patriot,* the *People's Magazine,* and the *New England Weekly Review,* of Boston; the *Mercury* and *Journal,* of Lowell; the Troy *Farmer's Register;* and the Rochester *Craftsman* and *Examiner.* The amount of attention given to the movement by the contemporary press proves that it loomed large in the everyday life of the times.

More or less complete files of ten labour papers which appeared during this period have been located and examined. Of these six belong exclusively to the years of political activity before 1832; one was published during these years and also during the later trade union movement; and three of lesser importance — *The Co-operator,* of Utica, 1832–1833, the *State Herald; the Manufacturers' and Mechanics' Advocate,* of Portsmouth, New Hampshire, 1831–1833, and the *Working Men's Shield* of Cincinnati, 1832–1833,— belong to the period just after the political movement had disappeared. The New York *Anti-Auctioneer,* 1828, was a campaign sheet published by a political organisation of master mechanics.

The first distinctly labour paper ever published in the United States, and perhaps the first in the world, was the *Journeyman Mechanics' Advocate,* started in Philadelphia in June or July, 1827.[3] It appears, however, to have been short lived, and the first labour paper of which any numbers are now in existence is the *Mechanics' Free Press,* which was first published on January 12, 1828, in Philadelphia. Even this antedated by two years the first issue of a similar journal in England.[4] The earliest number preserved is dated April 12, 1828, and the latest April 3, 1831, when a change of management was announced. The paper was still in existence as late as October, 1831,[5] but it was then said to have " become degenerate."

The most important of the labour papers published during the political movement, of which files have been preserved, was

[3] *Democratic Press* (Philadelphia), June 20, 1827.
[4] Webb, *History of Trade Unionism in England,* 107.
[5] New York *Working Man's Advocate,* Oct. 8, 1831.

The Working Man's Advocate, of New York, the first number of which was issued on October 31, 1829, and which was edited from that date until 1836 by George H. Evans, the prominent land reformer. During 1830 a daily edition was published under the title New York *Daily Sentinel,* and a semi-weekly, a few numbers of which are preserved, under the title New York *Daily Sentinel and Working Man's Advocate.*

The Delaware *Free Press,* published at Wilmington, Delaware, during 1830 and perhaps later, was in part a free-thought publication and in part an organ of the workingmen's political movement of that State. It quoted from labour papers in other sections and was in turn quoted by them.

The other four labour papers published during the political period of which copies have been found are the *Working Man's Gazette* of Woodstock, Vermont, 1830–1831, a small weekly; the *Mechanics' Press* of Utica, 1829–1830; the *Farmers', Mechanics' and Workingmen's Advocate* of Albany, 1830–1831, and the New York *Free Enquirer,* 1828–1835,[6] The latter, though primarily a free-thought publication, also distinctly championed the workingmen's party, as did both of its chief editors during its early years, Frances Wright and Robert Dale Owen.

Echoes of the Citizenship Period are also found in the labour press of the succeeding trade union period, in *The Man,* 1834–1835, and the *National Trades' Union,* 1834–1836, of New York; the *National Laborer,* 1836–1837, and the *Radical Reformer and Working Man's Advocate,* 1835, of Philadelphia.

But the labour papers of this period which have been preserved are few in comparison with those which have been lost. From various sources a list has been secured of seventy-four labour or professedly labour papers supposed to have been issued between 1827 and 1837, *i.e.,* during the political period and the ensuing trade union period. Of these, twenty-two may be considered as doubtful, that is, either as established papers which took up the workingmen's cause only by way of temporary protest or as mere imposters designed to divide the workingmen. Fifty-two true labour papers, however, one or

6 The *Free Enquirer* contained labour news only during 1829–1832.

more numbers of which are positively known to have been issued, are completely lost. This list includes all of the labour papers published at Boston, Baltimore, and Washington. It includes, moreover, papers published in all parts of the country, from New York to Cincinnati and from Portland, Maine, to Charleston, South Carolina.

A helpful source of information was a collection of scrapbooks of newspaper clippings made between 1828 and 1839 by Mathew Carey, the father of the economist and the first American investigator and ardent champion of working women. This collection is preserved in the Ridgway Branch of the Library Company in Philadelphia under the general title Carey's *Excerpta, Select Excerpta* or *Scraps*. Unfortunately these clippings are undated and are not even labelled with the names of the papers from which they were taken.

Public Documents, Books and Pamphlets.

Address of the Association of Mechanics and Other Working Men of the City of Washington to the Operatives throughout the United States (Washington, printed at the office of the *National Journal* by Wm. Duncan, 1830).

Address of the General Executive Committee of the Mechanics and Other Working Men of the City of New York, read at a General Meeting of Working Men held at West Chester House, Bowery (New York, 1830).

Address of the Majority of the General Executive Committee of the Mechanics and Other Working Men of the City of New York (New York, 1830).

Beard, C. A. *Economic Origins of Jeffersonian Democracy* (New York, 1915).

Bourne, W. O. *History of the Public School Society of the City of New York* (New York, 1879).

Bradford, Alden. *Biographical Notices of Distinguished Men in New England* (Boston, 1842).

Commons, J. R. *"Junior Republic," American Journal of Sociology,* November, 1897, and January, 1898.

Evans, F. W. *Autobiography of a Shaker* (Mount Lebanon, New York, 1869).

Gilbert, Amos. *Memoirs of Frances Wright* (Cincinnati, 1855).

Greeley, H. *Recollections of a Busy Life* (New York, 1868).

Luther, Seth. *An Address to the Working Men of New England* (Cambridge, Massachusetts, 1832).

McMaster, J. B. *The Acquisition of Political, Social and Industrial Rights of Man in America* (Cleveland, 1903).

Massachusetts Bureau of Statistics of Labor, *Eleventh Annual Report,* " Strikes in Massachusetts " (Boston, 1880).

Montgomery, James A. *Practical Detail of the Cotton Manufacture of the United States of America* (New York, 1840).

Owen, Robert Dale. *Threading My Way* (New York, 1874).

Paine, Thomas. *Agrarian Justice as Opposed to Agrarian Law and to Agrarian Monopoly* (London, 1797).

Pennsylvania *Acts of the General Assembly of the Commonwealth,* "Militia Law of 1822," (Harrisburg, 1822).

Pierce, F. C. *Foster Genealogy* (Chicago, 1899).

Political Essays, October 1, 1831, by the New York Association for Gratuitous Distribution of Discussions on Political Economy.

Prison Discipline Society. *Reports,* 1829–1835 (Boston).

Public School Society of New York, *Twenty-seventh and Twenty-eighth Annual Reports of the Trustees* (1832–1833).

Proceedings of a Meeting of Mechanics and Other Working Men Held at New York on December 29, 1829 (New York, 1830).

Proceedings of the Working Men's Convention (Boston, 1833).

Proceedings of the Working Men's State Convention at Salina, New York (Auburn, New York, 1830).

Report on the Production and Manufacture of Cotton, by the Convention of the Friends of Domestic Industry (New York, 1832).

Richardson, James D. *A Compilation of the Messages and Papers of the Presidents, 1789–1897* (Vols. II and III, Washington, 1896).

Secrist, H. *" The Anti-Auction Movement of 1828,"* Annals of *Wisconsin Academy,* Vol. XVII, No. 2.

Sharpless, Isaac. *Two Centuries of Pennsylvania History* (Philadelphia, 1909).

Skidmore, Thomas. *The Rights of Man to Property* (New York, 1829).

Sumner, H. L. *" History of Women in Industry in the United States,"* Sen. Doc., 61st Cong. 2d sess. No. 645 (Washington, 1910).

Thorpe, F. N. *The Federal and State Constitutions* (Washington, 1909).

To the Working Men of New England (Boston, Aug. 11, 1832).

Trumbull, Levi R. *A History of Industrial Paterson* (Paterson, New Jersey, 1882).

United States Bureau of Labor. *Report on Condition of Woman and Child Wage Earners,* Vol. IX.

United States Census, 1820, 1830, 1840, 1910.

Whitcomb, Samuel, Jr. *Address Before the Working Men's Society of Dedham* (Boston, 1831).
Wright, Frances. *Views of Society and Manners in America* (London, 1821).
Young, John R. *Memorial History of the City of Philadelphia* (2 vols., New York, 1895, 1898).

PART III. TRADE UNIONISM, 1833–1839

The history of the movement contained in these chapters is based almost entirely upon the labour papers that sprang up with it. The New York, Philadelphia, and Baltimore trades' unions established papers of their own; the Boston Trades' Union chose the *New England Artisan,* the organ of the New England Association of Farmers, Mechanics, and Other Working Men, as its official paper; and the Washington Trades' Union published its minutes in the *Washingtonian.* The National Trades' Union had its official organ in the *National Trades' Union,* a weekly, established in New York City in 1834, and published during this and the following year by Ely Moore, president of the organisation, and the first labour member of Congress.

Unfortunately the New York, Philadelphia, and Baltimore trades' union papers are among the twenty-one or more labour papers published from 1833 to 1839 that have not been located. Their loss is partly compensated, however, in the possession of other trades' union papers, some of which begin where others ended, thus making the story more or less complete. The New York *Union* did not appear until 1836, but before that time the Trades' Union published its proceedings in the *National Trades' Union,* which has been preserved by Ely Moore, of Lawrence, Kansas, a son of the editor, and which constitutes an invaluable source of information not only for the Trades' Union of New York City, but for the National Trades' Union and the trade union movement at large. The Philadelphia *Trades' Union* was started in 1834 and probably ran until 1836, when the *National Laborer* appeared. The latter paper was published from March, 1836, to March, 1837, by the National Society for the Diffusion of Useful Knowledge, and edited by Thomas Hogan, president of the

Trades' Union during a part of this time. The Baltimore *Trades' Union* was probably not started until 1836, but the record of the organisation it represented is partly preserved in a friendly paper, the Baltimore *Republican and Commercial Advertiser.*

Other labour papers, not necessarily trades' union papers, published during the time were the *Radical Reformer* and *Working Man's Advocate* in Philadelphia in 1835, the *Working Man's Advocate* in New York from 1829 to 1836, and *The Man* in the same city during 1834 and 1835. *The Man* was a daily penny paper and together with the *Working Man's Advocate* was published by George Henry Evans.

Valuable sources of information are also the papers friendly to labour at this time. These were the Baltimore *Republican and Commercial Advertiser,* already mentioned, the *Pennsylvanian,* and the *Public Ledger* of Philadelphia, and the *Morning Courier and New York Enquirer,* the *Evening Post,* the *Plaindealer* and the *New Era* of New York.

The hostile papers also throw some light on the movement, particularly the Boston *Courier,* the New York *Journal of Commerce,* the Albany *Argus,* the Philadelphia *National Gazette and Literary Register,* and the Washington *United States Telegraph.*

Other papers consulted, of a more general character were the *Essex Tribune,* the Lynn *Record,* the Boston *Transcript,* the *Evening Transcript, American, Commercial Advertiser,* and *Daily Advertiser* of New York, *Hazard's Register* of Philadelphia, *Niles' Weekly Register* of Baltimore, and the *Commercial Bulletin and Missouri Literary Register* of St. Louis.

Papers which properly belong to the political period, 1827–1833, were also referred to. These are the *Delaware Free Press,* published in Wilmington, Delaware, during 1830, the New York *Daily Sentinel and Working Man's Advocate,* a semi-weekly edition of the *Working Man's Advocate* published during the same year, and particularly the *Mechanics' Free Press* published in Philadelphia from 1828 to 1831.[1]

In addition to volumes V and VI of the *Documentary History of American Industrial Society,* edited by Professor Com-

---

[1] For a fuller account of these papers, see Bibliography: Citizenship, 1827–1833, 455 *et seq.*

mons and Helen L. Sumner, the only other collection of original sources is Ethelbert Stewart's *Documentary History of Early Organizations of Printers*.[2] The principal secondary source is Barnett's exhaustive treatise, *The Printers, A Study in American Trade Unionism*.[3] Evans Woollen, in *Labor Troubles Between 1834 and 1837*[4] discusses the labour problems of the time, but hardly mentions the organisations described here.

I. PUBLIC DOCUMENTS.

Documents Relative to the Manufactures in the United States, House Document, 22 Cong., I sess., No. 3081 (1803).

Laws of Pennsylvania, 1828–1829.

Manual of Councils of Philadelphia (Philadelphia, 1907–1908).

Messages and Papers of Philadelphia (Philadelphia, 1907–1908).

Messages and Papers of Presidents, 1789–1897, III. *Miscellaneous Documents* of the House of Representatives (1895).

Revised Statutes of New York, 1829.

Stewart, Ethelbert. *A Documentary History of the Early Organizations of the Printers*, in *Bulletin* of the United States Department of Labor, XI, 857–1033 (1905).

Report of the Commissioners Appointed by the Governor under the "Act Concerning State Prisons," Assembly Document (New York, 1835), No. 135.

Report of the Commissioners on the Penal Code of Pennsylvania, in *Senate Journal*, 1827–1828.

Report of Gershom Powers, Agent and Keeper of the State Prison at Auburn to the Legislature, Assembly Document (Albany, 1828), No. 135.

United States Bureau of Labor, *Sixteenth Annual Report*, "Strikes and Lockouts" (1887).

United States Census, 1880. History and Present Condition of the Newspaper and Periodical Press of the United States.

United States Census, 1880. Report on the Agencies of Transportation in the United States.

United States *House Journal*, 24 Cong. 1st sess. (1835).

United States Immigration Commission. *Report, Sen. Doc.*, 61 Cong., 3d sess., No. 750, IX, XXXIX.

United States Secretary of the Treasury on the State of Finances. *Report*, 1827–1838, 1863.

United States *Senate Document*, 24 Cong. 2d sess., No. 5, "Immigration" (Washington, 1836).

2 United States Department of Labor, *Bulletin*, 1905, Vol. XI.

3 *American Economic Association Quarterly*, 1909, 3rd ser., Vol. X.

4 *Yale Review*, 1892, pp. 87–100.

United States. *Statistical Abstract, 1915.*
Wright, Carroll D. *Report on the Factory System in the United States, United States Census,* 1880, II.

II. Books and Pamphlets.

Abbott, Edith. *Women in Industry* (New York and London, 1910).
Bogart, E. L. *The Economic History of the United States* (New York, 1907).
Byrdsall, F. *The History of the Loco-Foco or Equal Rights Party* (New York, 1842).
Commonwealth v. Hunt, *Thacher's Criminal Cases;* 4 Metcalf III.
Carey, M. *Appeal to the Wealthy of the Land* (Philadelphia, 1833).
Coggeshall, William T. *An Essay on Newspapers, Historical and Statistical,* read before the Ohio Historical Association at Zanesville, January 17, 1855 (Columbus, Ohio, 1855).
Coman, Katharine. *The Industrial History of the United States* (New York, 1905).
Derby, J. C. *Fifty Years among Authors, Books and Publishers* (New York, 1884).
Desmond, H. J. *The Know-Nothing Party* (Washington, 1905).
Dewey, D. R. *Financial History of the United States* (New York, 1905).
Finch, John. *Rise and Progress of the General Trades' Union of the City of New York and its Vicinity, with an Address to the Mechanics of the City of New York and Throughout the United States* (New York, 1833, Pamphlet).
Harper, Henry J. *The House of Harper* (New York and London, 1912).
Hudson, Frederick. *Journalism in the United States, from 1690 to 1872* (New York, 1873).
Journeymen Cabinet-Makers of the City of Philadelphia. *Constitution* (Philadelphia, 1829).
Kerr, R. W. *Government Printing Office with a Brief Record of the Public Printing for a Century, 1789–1881* (Lancaster, Pa., 1881).
Knox, John J. *History of Banking in the United States* (New York, 1900).
Laws of the State of New York, 1785, 1795, 1805, 1815, 1825, 1835, 1836.
Luther, Seth. *Address to the Working Men of New England* (Boston, 1832).
Myers, Gustavus. *The History of Tammany Hall* (New York, 1901).

National Typographical Society. *Proceedings, together with the Constitution for a National Typographical Society* (Washington, 1836).

On the Prisons of Philadelphia, by An European (Philadelphia, 1796).

One Hundred Years of Publishing, 1785–1885 (Philadelphia, 1885).

People v. Fisher et al., 14 *Wendell* 10 (1835).

Poor, Henry V. *Manual of Railroads of the United States* (New York, 1881).

Prison Discipline Society, Board of Managers, *Annual Report, 1827–1835* (Boston).

Proceedings of the Government and Citizens of Philadelphia on the Reduction of the Hours of Labor and Increase of Wages (Boston, 1835, Pamphlet).

Putnam, G. H. *George Palmer Putnam, A Memoir* (New York and London, 1912).

Report on the Production and Manufacture of Cotton, 1832, New York Convention of the Friends of Domestic Industry.

Scharf, J. T. *Chronicles of Baltimore* (Baltimore, 1874).

Schouler, James S. *History of the United States of America* (New York, 1908–1913).

Tanner, H. S. *A Description of the Canals and Rail Roads of the United States* (New York, 1840).

United States. *Reports* of the Secretary of the Treasury, 1829–1844.

White, George S. *Memoirs of Samuel Slater, the Father of American Manufactures, connected with a History of the Rise and Progress of the Cotton Manufacture in England and America* (Philadelphia, 1836).

Winsor, Justin. *Memorial History of Boston* (Boston, 1881), III.

III. GENERAL PAPERS.

Albany Argus, semi-weekly, 1833–1837.

American (New York), daily, 1836.

American Sentinel (Philadelphia), daily, 1833–1835.

Baltimore Republican and Commercial Advertiser, daily, 1833–1839.

Banner of the Constitution (Washington, New York, Philadelphia), weekly, 1829–1832.

Columbian Centinel (Boston), 1829.

Commercial Bulletin and Missouri Literary Register (St. Louis), weekly, 1835.

Courier (Boston), daily, 1833–1839.

Daily Evening Transcript (Boston), 1833–1836.

Democratic Press (Philadelphia), daily, 1829.
Evening Post (New York), daily, 1835–1839.
Evening Transcript (New York), daily, 1834–1836.
Lynn Record, daily, 1834.
Morning Courier and New York Enquirer, daily, 1833–1836.
National Gazette and Literary Register (Philadelphia), semi-weekly, 1838–1839.
New Era (New York), weekly, 1837.
New York *Journal of Commerce,* daily, 1833–1839.
Niles' Weekly Register (Baltimore), 1835–1838.
Pennsylvanian (Philadelphia), daily, 1835–1838.
Plaindealer (New York), weekly, 1836.
Poulson's American Daily Advertiser (Philadelphia), 1828–1833.
Public Ledger (Philadelphia), daily, 1836–1838.
Register of Pennsylvania (Philadelphia), daily, 1833–1839.
United States Telegraph (Washington), semi-weekly, 1834–1835.
Washingtonian, daily, 1836.

The following labour papers have been preserved: (See the Bibliography for the preceding period for a fuller statement on the labour papers during the thirties.)

Delaware Free Press, weekly, 1830.
Co-operator (Utica, N. Y.), weekly, 1832–1833.
Mechanics Free Press (Philadelphia), weekly, 1828–1831.
The Man (New York), weekly, 1834–1835.
National Laborer (Philadelphia), weekly, 1836–1837.
National Trades' Union (New York), weekly, 1836–1837.
Radical Reformer and Working Man's Advocate (Philadelphia), weekly, 1836.
Working Man's Advocate (New York), weekly, 1829–1836.

PART IV. HUMANITARIANISM

The bibliography of this period consists chiefly of contemporary sources, many of which are quoted in the *Documentary History of American Industrial Society.* These contemporary sources may be roughly divided into three classes: the newspaper press, the reform press, and public documents.

The newspaper press, then as now, contained current news items which, taken together, afford a fairly definite picture of the economic conditions of the time and of the labour and reform movements which were initiated for the purpose of changing these conditions. A part of the press, such as the New York *Herald,* opposed all reforms and reformers and tolerated organisations of the workers themselves only as the lesser of two evils; a much larger part were indifferent chroniclers, without criticism or approval, of the events which happened in industrial life from day to day; and a few, led by the New York *Tribune,* not only served as open forums for all of the isms of the time, but took an active editorial stand on many of the labour issues which arose during the period.

The reform press was as varied in content as the issues which they advocated. Each new ism was heralded by a paper, a pamphlet, or a book. Like the reforms which they advocated, the papers were short-lived; the series of pamphlets were equally short; and the books serve as monuments or as milestones, according as they were entirely forgotten or helped to influence the public opinion which crystallised into action then or later. The *Working Man's Advocate* and the *Republik der Arbeiter* are good examples of reform papers. The *Proceedings of the Industrial Congress* of any given year illustrate the propagandist pamphlets of the time. Of the reform publications which attained the dignity of books, Albert Brisbane's *The Social Destiny of Man,* or *Association and Reorganisation of Industry* (Philadelphia, 1840) and E. Kellogg's *Labor and Other Capital; the Rights of Each Secured and the Wrongs of Both Eradicated* (New York, 1849) serve as examples.

Public documents referred to in this section consist chiefly of legislative reports such as the New York *Assembly Journal* for a given year of the *Laws* of the state in question. A few special documentary reports were consulted, such as the *Report of the Committee on Internal Health* (Boston City *Document,* No. 66, 1849).

Trade union records of the period are not numerous and consist mainly of the minutes of the meetings of local organisations. None of these is in separate published form.

Secondary sources consist of biographical publications such as Horace Greeley's *Recollections of a Busy Life* (New York, 1868); and special historical treatises like Gustavus Myers' *History of Tammany Hall* (New York, 1901), and Herman

Schlüter's *Die Anfänge der deutschen Arbeiterbewegung in Amerika* (*Stuttgart*, 1907). The secondary literature of the period is very limited.

I. PUBLIC DOCUMENTS.

Commissioner of Labor. *Ninth Annual Report*, 1893, "Building and Loan Associations."
Laws of California, 1853.
Laws of Maine, 1848.
Laws of New Hampshire, 1847.
Laws of New York, 1853.
Laws of Ohio, 1852.
Laws of Pennsylvania, 1848, 1855.
Laws of Rhode Island, 1853.
"Co-operation in Massachusetts," in Massachusetts Bureau of Labor Statistics, *Report*, 1877, pp. 51–137.
Massachusetts *House Documents*, Nos. 50 and 81, 1845.
Massachusetts *House Reports*, 1853, No. 122; 1855, No. 180.
Massachusetts *Senate Document*, 1855, No. 107.
New Hampshire Bureau of Labor, *Report*, 1894.
New Hampshire *House Journal*, 1846.
New Hampshire *Senate Journal*, 1847.
"The Policy of Our Labor Organisations," in New Jersey Bureau of Labor, *Report*, 1887, pp. 77–86.
New York *Assembly Document*, 1848, No. 78.
New York *Assembly Journal*, 1847, 1848, 1850, 1852, and 1853.
Pennsylvania *House Journal* (1846).
Pennsylvania *Senate Journal*, 1837.
Rhode Island *Report* of an Investigation into Child Labor, 1853.
Wisconsin *Assembly Journal*, 1848 and 1851.
Wisconsin *Senate Journal*, 1849.

II. BOOKS AND PAMPHLETS.

Andrews, Stephen P. *Cost the Limit of Price* (New York, 1852).
—— *True Constitution of Government* (New York, 1882).
Appleton's *Cyclopedia of American Biography*.
Arthur, P. M. "Rise of Railway Organization," in George E. McNeill, *The Labor Movement* (Boston, 1887), 312ff.
Bailie, William. *Josiah Warren* (Boston, 1906).
Bartlett, D. W. *Modern Agitators* (New York, 1856).
Bemis, E. W. Co-operation in New England, in American Economic Association, *Publications* (Baltimore, 1886).
Brisbane, Albert. *Concise Exposition of the Doctrine of Association* (New York, 1844).

Brisbane, Albert. *Social Destiny of Man* (Philadelphia, 1840).
—— *A Mental Biography by His Wife* (Boston, 1893).
Bromwell, William T. *History of Immigration* (New York, 1856).
Brownson, Henry F. *Orestes Brownson's Early Life* (Detroit, 1898).
Brownson, Orestes. *Collected Works* (Detroit, 1882–1907).
—— *The Convert, or Leaves from My Experience* (New York, 1857).
—— "The Labouring Classes," in *Boston Quarterly Review*, 1840, III.
Butterfield, C. W. *History of Fond du Lac County, Wisconsin* (Chicago, 1880).
Campbell, John. *A Theory of Equality; or, the Way to Make Every Man Act Honestly* (Philadelphia, 1848).
—— *Negro-Mania* (Philadelphia, 1851).
Clark, F. C. "A Neglected Socialist," in American Academy of Political and Social Science, *Annals*, 1894–1895, V, 718–739.
Commons, J. R. "An Idealistic Interpretation of History," in *Labor and Administration* (New York, 1913) ; same, entitled "Horace Greeley and the Working Class Origins of the Republican Party," in *Political Science Quarterly*, 1909, XXIV, 468–488.
Cooke, G. W. *The Poets of Transcendentalism* (Boston, 1903).
Curtis. "Report" in *Transactions* of the American Medical Association (Boston, 1849).
Curtis, Francis. *History of the Republican Party* (2 vols., New York, 1904).
Devyr, Thomas A. *Our National Rights* (n. p., n. d.).
"Dwellings and Schools for the Poor," in *North American Review*, 1852, LXXIV, 464–489.
Ely, R. T. *French and German Socialism* (New York, 1883).
Evans, F. W. *Autobiography of a Shaker* (Mount Lebanon, N. Y., 1869).
Forney, J. W. *Anecdotes of Public Men* (New York, 1873–1881).
Kellogg, Edward. *Labor and Other Capital: the Rights of Each Secured and Wrongs of Both Eradicated* (New York, 1849).
Kingsbury, Susan. *Labor Laws and their Enforcement, with Special Reference to Massachusetts* (New York, 1911).
Lockwood, G. B. *The New Harmony Movement* (New York, 1905).
Masquerier, Lewis. *Sociology: or the Reconstruction of Society, Government, and Property* (New York, 1877).
Minutes of the Cigar Maker's Society of Baltimore, 1856. In Library of Johns Hopkins University.
Myers, Gustavus. *History of Tammany Hall* (New York, 1901).
Murray, David. "The Anti-Rent Episode in the State of New

York," in *Annual Report* of the American Historical Society, 1896, I, 139–173.

National Cotton Mule Spinners' Association of America, *Constitution and By-laws* (1890).

Noyes, John H. *History of American Socialisms* (Philadelphia, 1870).

Parton, James. *The Life of Horace Greeley* (Boston, 1872).

Persons, C. E. "The Early History of Factory Legislation in Massachusetts: From 1825 to the Passage of the Ten-Hour Law in 1874," in *Labor Laws and their Enforcement, with special reference to Massachusetts* (New York, 1911), 1–124.

Schlüter, Herman. *Lincoln, Labor and Slavery* (New York, 1913).

Podmore, E. P. *Robert Owen* (2 vols., London, 1906).

Weitling, Wilhelm. *Das Evangelium eines armen Sünders* (Bern, 1845).

———— *Garantien der Harmonie und Freiheit* (New York, 1879).

Wrigley, Edward. *The Working Man's Way to Wealth* (Philadelphia, 1872).

III. PAPERS.

The Awl (Lynn, Mass.), weekly, 1844–1846.

Bee (Albany), daily, 1845.

Pittsburgh *Chronicle,* daily, 1850.

Pittsburgh *Daily Commercial Journal,* 1848.

New York *Evening Post,* 1841.

New York *Globe,* daily, 1850.

Harbinger (Boston and New York), weekly, 1845–1849.

New York *Herald,* daily, 1850.

Mechanic (Fall River), weekly, 1844.

The Herald of the New Moral World (New York), weekly, 1841.

Nonpareil (Cincinnati), weekly, 1851.

Philadelphia *North American and United States Gazette,* daily, 1854.

People's Paper (Cincinnati), weekly, 1843.

Phalanx (New York), weekly, 1843–1845; continued as *Harbinger.*

Public Ledger (Philadelphia), daily, 1844–1848.

Pittsburgh *Daily Morning Post,* 1848–1849, 1853.

Quaker City (Philadelphia), daily, 1849.

Die Reform (New York), weekly, 1853–1854.

Republik der Arbeiter (New York), weekly, 1850–1855.

Spirit of the Age (New York), weekly, 1849–1850.

Baltimore *Sun,* daily, 1855.

New York *Sun,* daily, 1853.

New York *Times,* daily, 1853–1857.

New York *Tribune,* daily, 1842–1857.
New York *Weekly Tribune,* 1845–1853.
Voice of Industry (Fitchburg and Lowell, Mass.), weekly, 1845–1847.
Volks-Tribun (New York), weekly, 1846.
Working Man's Advocate (New York), weekly, 1844–1848.
Young America (New York), weekly, 1845–1848.

PART V. NATIONALISATION, 1858–1877

The secondary sources are George E. McNeill, *The Labor Movement — The Problem of To-day,* especially chapter V, " The Progress of the Movement From 1861–1886 "; also T. V. Powderly in *Thirty Years of Labor* (Columbus, Ohio, 1889), 18–130. Excellent accounts are found also in R. T. Ely, *The Labor Movement in America,* 69–91, and in a series of articles by F. A. Sorge, in the *Neue Zeit* (Stuttgart), 1890–1891, II, 397, 438; 1891–1892, I, 69, 110, 172, 206, 651.

This period witnessed the establishment of a labour press upon a lasting foundation. No less than one hundred and twenty daily, weekly and monthly journals of labour reform appeared during the decade 1863–1873.[1] *Fincher's Trades' Review,* Philadelphia, 1863–1866, was the paramount trade union paper and perhaps the most influential paper of the entire period. The labour organ of the West, the Chicago *Workingman's Advocate,* 1864–1876, laid particular stress on labour politics. The Boston *Daily Evening Voice,* 1864–1867, was the organ of the New England labour movement with its emphasis on shorter hours. The files of the *Workingman's Advocate* contain the proceedings of all the annual conventions of the National Labor Union, which are reproduced in Vol. IX of the *Documentary History of American Industrial Society.*[2]

I. PUBLIC DOCUMENTS.

Chinese Immigration. An address to the people of the United States on the social, moral and political effect of Chinese immigration. Prepared by a committee of the Senate of California. 45th Congress, 1st sess., *House Miscellaneous Document,* No. 9.

[1] *Doc. Hist.,* X, 142.
[2] A more comprehensive description of the labour press is to be found in Chapter II of Part V, II, 15 *et seq.*

California *Laws,* 1865–1866, 1868.
Commonwealth *v.* John Kehoe et al. (Pottsville, 1876).
Connecticut *Laws,* 1867.
First Annual Report of the Bureau of Labor Statistics (Columbus, Ohio, 1878).
House Journal, 29th Cong., 1st sess.; 39th Cong., 1st sess.
Illinois Public *Laws,* 1867.
Industrial Commission *Report* (Washington, 1901), VII and XVII.
In Matter Jacobs, 98 New York 98 (1895).
Massachusetts *Acts and Resolves,* 1866.
Massachusetts *House Documents,* 1865, No. 259; 1866, No. 98; 1867, No. 44.
Missouri *Laws,* 1867.
Ninetieth General Assembly of the State of New Jersey, *Minutes of Votes and Proceedings* (1866).
New York *Laws,* 1867.
Ohio *House Journal,* 1866.
Pennsylvania *Report* (Harrisburg, 1878), of the Joint Special Committee of the Legislature of Pennsylvania on Contract Convict Labor, with accompanying Testimony. January 16, 1878.
Pennsylvania *House Journal,* 1866.
Report (Harrisburg, 1878) of Committee appointed by the Pennsylvania General Assembly to investigate the Railroad Riots in July, 1877.
Senate Committee on Education and Labor, *Report on Relations between Capital and Labor* (Washington, 1885), I.
United States Bureau of Education *Circulars of Information* (Washington, 1872), " Relation of Education to Labor."
United States Session *Laws,* 38th Cong., 1st sess.; 41st Cong., 1st sess.
United States Session *Laws,* 41st Cong., 1st sess., Appendix.
United States *Statutes* at Large, 37th Cong., 2d sess.
United States *Statutes* at Large, 38th Cong., 1st sess.
United States *Statutes* at Large, 40th Cong., 2d sess.
United States *Statutes* at Large, 42d Cong., 2d sess., Appendix.
Wisconsin *Laws,* 1867.
Wholesale Prices, 1890–1912, Bureau of Labor Statistics, *Bulletin,* No. 114 (Washington, 1913).
Wright, Carroll D. *Apprenticeship System in its Relation to Industrial Education,* United States *Bulletin of Education,* No. 6 (Washington, 1908).
Young, Edward. *Labor in Europe and America: a special report on the Rates of Wages, the Cost of Subsistence, and the Condition of the Working Classes* (Washington, 1875). United States Treasury Department, Bureau of Statistics.

II. BOOKS AND PAMPHLETS

Archcroft's Railway Directory (New York, 1865).

Bemis, E. W. "Co-operation in New England," in American Economic Association, *Publications* (Baltimore, 1886–1887), I, 335–464. Also in *Johns Hopkins University Studies* (Baltimore, 1888), VI.

Campbell, Alexander C. *The True American System of Finance* (Chicago, 1864).

—— *The True Greenback, or the Way to Pay the National Debt without Taxes and Emancipate Labor* (Chicago, 1868).

Chamberlain, E. M. *Sovereigns of Industry* (Boston, 1875).

Cigar Makers' International Union, *Proceedings*, 1864, 1865, 1866, 1867. Typewritten Record at Johns Hopkins University Library.

Cooper, Peter. "Autobiography," in *Old South Leaflets* (Boston, 1904). General Series, VI, No. 147.

Coopers' International Union, *Proceedings,* 1871 (Cleveland, 1871).

Coulter, J. L. "Organizations among the Farmers of the United States," in *Yale Review,* 1909, XVIII, 277–298.

Crowe, Robert. *The Reminiscences of R. Crowe, the Octogenarian Tailor* (New York, 1903).

Dacus, J. A. *Annals of the Great Strikes in the United States* (Chicago, 1877).

Dewees, F. P. *The Molly Maguires* (Philadelphia, 1877).

Farnam, H. W. "Die Amerikanischen Gewerkvereine," in *Schriften des Vereins für Socialpolitik* (Leipzig, 1879), XVIII.

Fitch, J. A. "Unionism in the Iron and Steel Industry," in *Political Science Quarterly,* 1909, XXIV, 57–79.

Gladden, Washington. *Working people and their employers* (Boston, 1876).

Greene, William B. *Mutual Banking: Showing the Radical Deficiency of the Present Circulating Medium* (Boston, 1870).

—— *Socialistic, Communistic, Materialistic and Financial Fragments* (Boston, 1875).

Harper, Ida Husted. *Life and Work of Susan B. Anthony* (2 vols., Indianapolis and Kansas City, 1898–1899).

Heywood, Ezra Hoar. *The Great Strike* (Princeton, Mass., 1878).

—— *Yours or Mine* (Princeton, Mass., 1876).

International Iron Molders' Union, *Proceedings,* 1864, 1865, 1867, 1868 (Philadelphia).

Kelley, Oliver Hudson. *Origin and Progress of the order of the Patrons of Husbandry in the United States; a history from 1866 to 1873* (Philadelphia, 1875).

Kennedy, J. B. "Beneficiary Features of American Trade Unions," in *Johns Hopkins University Studies* (Baltimore, 1908), XXVI.

Knox, J. J. *United States Notes* (New York, 1888).

Grand International Division of the Brotherhood of Locomotive Engineers, *Proceedings,* 1864 (Indianapolis, 1864).

Grand International Division of the Brotherhood of Locomotive Engineers, *Minutes* (Rochester, N. Y., 1866), Special Session, Rochester, June, 1866.

Grand International Division of the Brotherhood of Locomotive Engineers, *Minutes* (Fort Wayne, Ind., 1867), Cincinnati, October, 1867.

Grand International Division of the Brotherhood of Locomotive Engineers, *Minutes* (Fort Wayne, 1868), Chicago, October, 1868.

McCabe, James. *History of the Grange Movement* (Chicago, 1874).

National Union of Machinists and Blacksmiths of the United States of America, *Proceedings* (New York, 1868), Baltimore, November, 1860.

International Union of Machinists and Blacksmiths of the United States of America, *Proceedings* (Philadelphia, 1862), Pittsburgh, 1861.

McNeill, George E. *Factory Children* (Boston, 1875).

Martin, E. W. *History of the Great Riots* (Philadelphia, 1877).

Mitchell, W. C. " Gold, Prices and Wages under the Greenback Standard," in University of California *Publications* (Berkeley, 1908).

Motley, J. M. " Apprenticeship in American Trade Unions," *Johns Hopkins University Studies* (Baltimore, 1907), XXV.

National Labor Union, *Proceedings* ('Philadelphia, 1868), New York, 1868.

New York Chamber of Commerce, *Special Reports,* 1864–1865.

Orvis, John. *A plan for the Organization and Management of Co-operative Stores and Boards of Trade under the Auspices of the Order of Sovereigns of Industry* (Worcester, Mass., 1876).

Penny, Virginia. *Five hundred Employments adapted to Women, Married or Single with the Average Rate of Pay in each* (Philadelphia, n. d.).

Phillips, Wendell. *The Foundation of the Labor Movement. The Labor Inertia* (Boston, 1871).

———— *Labor Question* (Boston, 1884).

———— *Speech to the working men of Boston and Vicinity* (Nov. 2, 1885).

———— *Speeches, Lectures and Letters* (2d ser., Boston, 1891).

Pinkerton, A. *Strikes, Communists, Tramps and Detectives* (New York, 1900).

Rhodes, J. F. *History of the United States* (New York, 1895), III.

—— "Molly Maguires in the Anthracite Region of Pennsylvania," in *American Historical Review*, 1909–1910, XV, 547–561.

Rogers, Edward H. *Autobiography*. Manuscript in possession of the American Bureau of Industrial Research, Madison, Wis.

—— *Eight Hours a Day's Work* (Boston, 1872).

Roy, A. *History of the Coal Miners of the United States* (Columbus, Ohio, 1902).

Shaw, Albert. "Co-operation in a Western City," in American Economic Association, *Publications* (Baltimore, 1886–1887); also in *Johns Hopkins University Studies* (Baltimore, 1888), VI.

Spencer, E. E. *Address before Prospect Union* (n. p., 1895).

Steward, Ira. *The Eight-Hour Movement* (Boston, 1865).

—— *Poverty* (Boston, 1873).

Sylvis, J. C. *The Life, Speeches, Labors and Essays of William H. Sylvis* (Philadelphia, 1872).

International Typographical Union, *Proceedings* (Detroit, 1864), of the tenth, eleventh and twelfth sessions, held at New York, Cleveland, and Louisville, Kentucky, May 5, 1862, May 4, 1863, and May 2, 1864, respectively.

National Typographical Union, *Proceedings* (Detroit, 1865), Philadelphia, June, 1865.

National Typographical Union, *Proceedings* (Boston, 1866), fourteenth session, Chicago, June, 1866.

III. PAPERS.

Washington *Daily Chronicle*, 1869.
Philadelphia *Enquirer*, daily, 1861–1862.
New York *Herald*, daily, 1865–1869.
New York *Times*, daily, 1874–1876.
Chicago *Tribune*, daily, 1876–1879.
Detroit *Tribune*, daily, 1864.
New York *Tribune*, daily, 1861–1866.

IV. LABOUR PAPERS

American Workman (Boston), 1868–1872.
Cooper's Monthly Journal (Cleveland, Ohio), 1870–1874.
Daily Evening Voice (Boston), 1864–1867.
Fincher's Trades' Review, (Philadelphia), 1863–1866.
Engineer's Journal (Cleveland), 1869–1871.

Equity (Boston), 1874–1875.
Machinists' and Blacksmiths' Monthly Journal (Cleveland), 1872.
Miners' National Record (Cleveland), 1875–1876.
National Labor Tribune (Pittsburgh), 1875–1877.
Pomeroy's Democrat (Chicago), 1877.
The Printer (New York), 1864.
Printers' Circular (Philadelphia), 1866.
Welcome Workman (Philadelphia), 1867–1868.
Workingman's Advocate (Chicago), 1864–1877.

PART VI.   UPHEAVAL AND REORGANISATION, 1876–1897

The secondary sources for this period naturally are more abundant than for previous periods.   Dr. Ely's *Labor Movement in America,* published in 1886, during the climax of the upheaval, gives a contemporary appraisal by a trained eye of the social forces then at work.   Waltershausen's *Die nordamerikanischen Gewerkschaften,* etc., and his *Der moderne Sozialismus in den Vereinigten Staaten von America* (Berlin, 1890) are also exceedingly helpful.   Although he was clearly wrong in his conclusion that as a result of the growth of factory system of production, the mixed organisation of labour as typified by the Knights of Labor will come to prevail over separate organisation by trades, he none the less deserves to be classed among the keenest observers of American industrial life.   His treatment of the subject is comprehensive and objective, although the book on socialism might benefit by a closer organisation of the material.   A valuable cross-section description of the American labour movement during a period for which the then existing material is most meagre, namely, the later seventies, is found in Professor Henry W. Farnam's " Die Amerikanischen Gewerkvereine," in *Schriften des Vereins fur Sozialpolitik* (Leipzig, 1879.), 1–39.

Sorge's contribution is particularly valuable for this period. He published one series of articles in the Stuttgart *Neue Zeit* (1891–1892, I, 206, 388; II, 197, 239, 268, 324, 453, and 495; 1894–1895, II, 196, 234, 272, 304, and 330; 1895–1896, II, 101, 132, 236, 262), as a connected history of the labour movement in America from 1877 to 1896, and another series in the same publication (1891–1892, II, 740 and 782; 1892–1893, I, 236 and 270, II, 326; 1894–1895, I, 14, 43, 71, 111,

147), currently describing labour events from 1892 to 1895. Morris Hillquit's *History of Socialism in the United States* (New York, 1903) is the only work on the subject in the English language. As a piece of historical research it is not as good as the above mentioned, but it is valuable for the period after 1890, when the author was able to draw upon personal observation and experience.

George E. McNeill's *The Labor Movement — The Problem of To-day* contains several valuable chapters on this period, especially chapters IX on the textile trades, X on the miners, XV on the Knights of Labor, and the end of V on the International Labor Union. Terence V. Powderly's *Thirty Years of Labor* (Columbus, Ohio, 1889) is semi-historical and semi-rhetorical. It contains valuable information on the beginnings of the Knights of Labor. The book is valuable as a mirror of the state of mind of the foremost leader of the Knights of Labor at a time when his authority was still unshaken although already questioned. A short "History of the Labor Movement in Chicago" was written by George A. Schilling and published in the *Life of Albert R. Parsons* (Chicago, 1903). Schilling relates the events which led up to the Haymarket catastrophe from the point of view of one who was an adherent of the "political" faction in socialism.

There is no lack of public documents dealing with the subject of labour organisation during this period. The *Census* of 1880 published statistics on strikes and labour organisations for that year. (*Tenth Census,* XX, "Report on Statistics of Wages . . . with Supplementary Reports on . . . Trade Societies, and Strikes, and Lockouts," Washington, 1886). The first attempt towards a comprehensive inquiry into labour conditions in the United States was made by the Senate Committee on Education and Labor in 1883. The Committee published four volumes of testimony in 1885, but it never presented a report.[1] The testimony elicited, while important in many respects, is too fragmentary in nature to be of great value. The first successful comprehensive labour investigation was carried through by the Industrial Commission which

---

[1] Nor were the published volumes of testimony included in the regular congressional set.

was appointed by President McKinley in 1898. The nineteen volumes of report and testimony (Washington, 1900, 1901, and 1902) while naturally paying the closest attention to the current and recent events of that time, abound also in material pertaining to the history of labour during the eighties and nineties.

The following are the more important special government reports:

"Report of the Joint Special Committee to Investigate Chinese Immigration," *Senate Document,* 44th Cong., 2d sess., 1876–1877, No. 689 (Washington, 1877); "Depression in Labor and Business," *House Document,* 45th Cong., 3rd sess., 1878–1879, No. 29; "Report on Importation of Contract Labor," *Senate Document,* 48th Cong., 1st sess., 1883–1884, No. 820; "Report on Importation of Foreign Contract Labor," *House Document,* 48th Cong., 1st sess., 1883–1884, No. 444; "Report of House Select Committee on Labor Troubles in Missouri, Arkansas, Kansas and Texas," *House Document,* 49th Cong., 2d sess., 1886–1887, No. 4174; "Report of House Select Committee on Existing Labor Troubles in Pennsylvania," *House Document,* 50th Cong., 2d sess., 1888–1889, No. 4147; "Report of Senate Select Committee on Employment of Armed Guards," etc., *Senate Document,* 52d Cong., 2d sess., 1892–1893, No. 1280; *Report of the United States Strike Commission on the Chicago Strike of June and July, 1894* (Washington, 1895); the same in *Senate Document,* 53d Cong., 3d sess., 1894–1895, No. 7; and the *Proceedings of the Hocking Valley Investigating Committee of the General Assembly of the State of Ohio* (Columbus, O., 1885).

But of the greatest importance are, of course, the reports of the national and state bureaus of labour. The Bureau of Labor at Washington was created in 1884 as a part of the Department of the Interior. It became an independent Department of Labor in 1888, which in 1905, was merged into the newly created Department of Commerce and Labor. In 1912, with the re-establishment of the Department of Labor and with the creation of the Office of Secretary of Labor, it became the Bureau of Labor Statistics in that Department.

The following is the order in which the several state bureaus of labour issued their first reports:

1870 — Massachusetts;   1873 — Pennsylvania;   1877 — Kentucky and Ohio;   1878 — New Jersey;   1879 — Indiana and Missouri; 1881 — Illinois; 1883 — New York; 1884 — California, Michigan, and Wisconsin; 1885 — Connecticut, Iowa, Kansas, and Maryland; 1887 — Maine, North Carolina, and Rhode Island; 1888 — Colorado, Minnesota, and Nebraska; 1890 — West Virginia, North Dakota, and Arkansas; 1892 — Tennessee; 1893 — Montana and New Hampshire; 1894 — Utah.

I. PUBLIC DOCUMENTS.

United States — *First Annual Report of the Commisioner of Labor,* March, 1886, " Industrial Depressions."
  Third Annual Report, 1887, " Strikes and Lockouts."
  Tenth Annual Report, 1894, " Strikes and Lockouts."
  Sixteenth Annual Report, 1901, " Strikes and Lockouts."
  Third Special Report, 1893, "Analysis and Index of all Reports issued by Bureaus of Labor Statistics in the United States Prior to November 1, 1892."
  Eleventh Special Report, 1904, " Regulation and Restriction of Output " prepared under the supervision of John R. Commons.
  " Conciliation in the Stove Industry," John P. Frey and John R. Commons, *Bulletin of the Bureau of Labor,* XII, Jan., 1906, 124–196.
California — *Third Biennial Report,* 1887–1888, " Trades Unions and Labor Organizations," 109–192.
Colorado — *First Biennial Report,* 1887–1888, " The Labor Movement," 70–108.
Connecticut — *Third Annual Report,* 1887, " Labor Organizations in Connecticut," 353–379.
Illinois — *Second Biennial Report,* " Strikes in Chicago and Vicinity," 261–286.
  Fourth Biennial Report, 1885–1886, " Trade and Labor Organizations in Illinois," 145–163; " The Eight-Hour Movement in Chicago, May, 1886," 466–498.
Kansas — *Second Annual Report,* 1886, " The Southwestern Strike," 21–72.
Maine — *Statistics of the Industries of Maine for 1886,* " Labor Troubles," 95–105.
Massachusetts — *Twelfth Annual Report,* 1881, " Industrial Arbitration and Conciliation," 5–75.
  Thirteenth Annual Report, 1882, " Fall River, Lowell, and Lawrence," 193–415.
  Sixteenth Annual Report, 1885, " Pullman," Joint Report of the Commissioners of the Various Bureaus of Statistics of Labor in the United States, 3–26.
Michigan — *Third Annual Report,* 1886, " Strikes in Michigan, March 1 to December 1, 1885," 83–134.

Missouri — *Fourth Annual Report*, 1882, " Strike Statistics," 121–123.

    Eighth Annual Report, 1886, " The Official History of 1886 Strike on the Southwestern Railway System," Appendix, 5–117.

New Jersey — *Tenth Annual Report*, 1887, " Labor Organization in America and England," 3–64.

New York — *Third Annual Report*, 1885, " Strikes," 195–330; " Boycotts," 331–362; " Labor Organizations," 539–605.

    Fourth Annual Report, 1886, " Strikes," 411–710; " Boycotting," 713–806.

    Fifth Annual Report, 1887, " Strikes of 1887," 39–517; " Boycotts," 522–552; " Conspiracy prosecutions and conspiracy laws," 565–700; " Labor Laws of 1886 and 1887," 703–776.

    Annual Report, 1911, " New York Typographical Union No. 6."

Ohio — *Third Annual Report*, 1879, " Trade and Labor Organizations," 258–262.

    Fifth Annual Report, 1881, " Trade and Labor Organizations," 97–100.

    Seventh Annual Report, 1883, " Labor Troubles," 213–254.

Pennsylvania — *Tenth Annual Report*, 1881–1882, " Labor Troubles in Pennsylvania, 1882," 144–192.

Rhode Island — *Second Annual Report*, 1888, " Labor Organizations," 86–97.

Wisconsin — *First Biennial Report*, 1883–1884, " Trade and Labor Unions," 119–139.

    Second Biennial Report, 1885–1886, " Strikes and Industrial Disturbances," 238–313; " The Eight-Hour Day," 314–371; " Boycotting in Wisconsin," 377–390.

Eleventh Census Compendium, 1890.

United States, *Statistical Abstract,* 1915.

II. BOOKS AND PAMPHLETS.

Adelphon Kruptos. (n. p., 1881) ; *same* (Toledo, 1891).

Altgeld, John P. *The Eight-Hour Movement.* An address delivered before the Brotherhood of United Labor at the Armory in Chicago, February 22, 1890.

" An Address " (Moberly, Mo., 1885, Leaflet).

An Argument in favor of a Legislative Enactment to Abolish the Tenement House Cigar Factories in New York and Brooklyn (New York, 1882).

" Appeal to Aid " (Philadelphia, 1886, Leaflet).

Ashworth, J. H. " The Helper and American Trade Unions," *Johns Hopkins University Studies* (Baltimore, 1915), XXXIII.

Aveling, E. B. and E. M. *The Working Class Movement in America* (London, 1891).
Bemis, E. W. " Co-operation in the Middle States," *Johns Hopkins University Studies* (Baltimore, 1888), VI.
—— " Co-operation in New England," *Johns Hopkins University Studies* (Baltimore, 1888), VI.
—— " Relation of labor organizations to the American boy and to trade instruction," *Annals of the American Academy,* 1894, V, 209–241.
—— " Trades Unions and Apprentices," *American Journal of Social Science,* 1890, XXVIII, 108–125.
Buchanan, J. R. *The Story of a Labor Agitator* (New York, 1903).
Constitution and By-Laws of District Assembly 17 (St. Louis, Leaflet).
Constitution of the Central Labor Union (New York, 1887).
Constitution of the Junior Sons of '76 (Leaflet).
Dunning, N. A. *The Farmers' Alliance History and Agricultural Digest* (Washington, 1891).
Farnam, H. W. " Die Amerikanischen Gewerkvereine," in *Schriften des Vereins für Sozialpolitik* (Leipzig, 1879), XVIII, 1–38.
Fitch, J. A. *The Steel Workers* (New York, 1911).
—— " Unionism in the Iron and Steel Industry," *Political Science Quarterly,* 1909, XXIV, 71–78.
George, Henry. *The Condition of Labor, an Open Letter to Pope Leo XIII* (New York, 1891).
—— *The Crime of Poverty.* Address delivered at Burlington, Iowa, April 1, 1885, under the auspices of the Burlington Assembly, Knights of Labor, No. 3135 (Burlington, 1885).
—— *Progress and Poverty* (New York, 1880).
George, Henry, Jr. *The Life of Henry George, by His Son* (2 vols., New York, 1904).
Gunton, George. *Wealth and Progress . . . the Economic Philosophy of the Eight-Hour Movement* (New York, 1887).
Hardy, S. M. " Quantity of Money and Prices," in *Journal of Political Economy,* 1894–1895, III, 145–168.
Hewitt, Abram S. *The Emancipation of Labor.* Speech delivered in the House of Representatives, April 30, 1884 (Washington, 1884).
Hinton, R. F. " American Labor Organizations," *North American Review,* 1885, CXL, 48.
History of the Farmers' Alliance, the Agricultural Wheel, etc., edited and compiled under the auspices of the St. Louis *Journal of Agriculture* (1890).
Holyoake, George Jacob. *Among the Americans* (London, 1881).

Huebner, Grover G. *Blacklisting,* Wisconsin Free Library Commission, Legislative Reference Department, *Comparative Legislation Bulletin,* No. 10 (Madison, 1906).
——— *Boycotting,* Wisconsin Free Library Commission, Legislative Reference Department, *Comparative Legislation Bulletin,* No. 9 (Madison, 1906).
Jonas, Alexander. *Eight-Hour Standard Working Day* (New York, n. d.).
Kennedy, J. B. "Beneficiary Features of American Trade Unions, *Johns Hopkins University Studies* (Baltimore, 1908), XXVI.
Kirk, William, "National Labor Federations in the United States," *Johns Hopkins University Studies* (Baltimore, 1906), XXIV.
Libby, O. G. "A Study of the Greenback Movement, 1876–1884," in *Transactions of Wisconsin Academy of Sciences, Arts and Letters,* 1898–1899, XII, 530–543.
Lloyd, H. D. "Lords of Industry," in *North American Review,* 1884, CXXXVIII, 535–553.
——— *The Safety of the Future Lies in Organized Labor.* A Paper Read before the 13th Annual Convention of the American Federation of Labor (Chicago, 1893).
——— *A Strike of Millionaires against Miners* (Chicago, 1890).
McCabe, D. A. "The Standard Rate in American Trade Unions," *Johns Hopkins University Studies* (Baltimore, 1912), XXX.
McNeill, George E. *Eight-Hour Primer, the Fact, Theory and the Argument* (Published by American Federation of Labor, New York, n. d.).
——— *The Philosophy of the Labor Movement.* Read before International Labor Congress (Washington, n. d.).
——— *Trade Union Ideals,* in American Economic Association Publications, Ser. 3, IV, No. 1, pp. 211–229, 248–268 (New York, 1903).
Motley, F. M. "Apprenticeship in American Trade Unions," *Johns Hopkins University Studies* (Baltimore, 1907), XXV.
Old Ritual of the Knights of Labor (n. p., n. d.).
Perry, J. S. *Prison Labor; with Tables Showing the Proportion of Convict to Citizen Labor, in the Prisons of the State of New York, and of the United States* (Albany, 1885).
Pinkerton, Allan. *Strikers, Communists, Tramps and Detectives* (New York, 1900).
Post, L. F., and Leubuscher, F. C. *An Account of the George-Hewitt Campaign* (New York, 1886).
Proceedings of the Annual Conventions of the American Federation of Labor, 1886–1915.
Proceedings of the Annual Conventions of the Federation of Organized Trades and Labor Unions, 1881–1886.

Proceedings of the Annual Conventions of the National Associa-tion of Builders' Exchanges, 1887–1895.

Proceedings of the Sessions of the General Assembly of the Knights of Labor, 1878–1897.

Proceedings of the Twenty-Second Annual Convention of United Mine Workers of America (Indianapolis, 1911).

Randall, D. R. " Co-operation in Maryland and the South," *Johns Hopkins University Studies* (Baltimore, 1888), VI.

The Record of Benjamin F. Butler, Compiled from the Original Sources (Boston, 1883).

Ringwalt, J. L. *Development of Transportation Systems in the United States* (Philadelphia, 1888).

Ritter, J. H. " Present Day Jobbing," in *Annals of the American Academy of Political and Social Science,* 1903, XXII, 451.

Roy, Andrew. *A History of Coal Miners in the United States* (Co-lumbus, Ohio, n. d.).

Sakolski, A. M. " The Finances of American Trade Unions," *Johns Hopkins University Studies* (Baltimore, 1906), XXIV.

Salmons, C. H. *The Burlington Strike* (Aurora, Illinois, 1889).

Samuel, J. *Collection of Manuscripts, Letters, and Scrap-books on Co-operation.*

——— *How to Organize Co-operative Societies, with Constitution, Rules, etc. In Local or District Assemblies* (St. Louis, n. d.).

——— *Tracts for the Times. Co-operation the only Hope for American Wage-Earners* (St. Louis, n. d.).

Schlüter, H. *The Brewing Industry and the Brewery Workers' Movement in America* (Cincinnati, 1910).

Secret Circular of the Knights of Labor (n. p., December, 1894).

Shaw, Albert. " Co-operation in the Northwest," *Johns Hopkins University Studies* (Baltimore, 1888), VI.

Shinn, C. H. " Co-operation on the Pacific Coast," *Johns Hopkins University Studies* (Baltimore, 1888), VI.

Spedden, E. R. " The Trade Union Label," *Johns Hopkins Uni-versity Studies* (Baltimore, 1910), XXVIII.

Stockton, F. T. " The Closed Shop in American Trade Unions," *Johns Hopkins University Studies* (Baltimore, 1911), XXIX.

Studnitz, Arthur von. *Nordamerikanische Arbeiterverhältnisse* (Leipzig, 1879).

Swinton, John. *Live, Burning Questions* (Stockton, Cal., 1885).

——— *Striking for Life* (New York, 1894).

Warner, A. G. " Three Phases of Co-operation in the West," *Johns Hopkins University Studies* (Baltimore, 1888), VI.

Waters, Robert. *Career and Conversation of John Swinton, Jour-nalist, Orator, Economist* (Chicago, 1902).

Whitney, N. R. " Jurisdiction in American Building-Trades Unions," *Johns Hopkins University Studies* (Baltimore, 1914), XXXII.

Wolfe, F. E. "Admission to American Trade Unions," *Johns Hopkins University Studies* (Baltimore, 1912), XXX.
Wolman, Leo. "The Boycott in American Trade Unions," *Johns Hopkins University Studies* (Baltimore, 1916), XXXIV.
Wright, Carroll D. *Industrial Conciliation and Arbitration* (Boston, 1881).
—— *A Manual of Distributive Co-operation* (Boston, 1885).

III. SOCIALISM AND ANARCHISM.

Altgeld, John Peter. *Reasons for Pardoning Fielden, Neebe and Schwab* (Springfield, Illinois, 1893).
An die Leser und Theilhaber der Arbeiter-Zeitung (New York, 1874).
August Spies, et al. *v.* The People, etc. In the Supreme Court of Illinois. *Brief and Argument* on application for writ of error to the Criminal Court, Cook County, and that the same be made a supersedeas. 151 pp. Leonard Swett, of Counsel (Chicago, 1887).
Brooks, J. G. *American Syndicalism; the I. W. W.* (New York, 1913).
Constitution of the Socialist Trade and Labor Alliance of the United States and Canada, adopted at its first convention held in New York city, June 29th to July 2d, 1896 (New York, 1896).
Copy-book of the International Workingmen's Association, 1869–1876; see General Bibliography.
Douai, Adolph. *Hard Times* (Chicago, 1877).
Eltzbacher, Paul. *Anarchism* (translation, New York, 1908).
Ely, R. T. *French and German Socialism* (New York, 1883).
—— "Recent American Socialism," *Johns Hopkins University Studies* (Baltimore, 1885), III, 229–304.
Engels, Frederick. *The Labor Movement in America* (New York, 1887).
Estey, J. *Revolutionary Syndicalism, an Exposition and a Criticism* (London, 1913).
Gary, Joseph E. "The Chicago Anarchists of 1886: The Crime, the Trial, and the Punishment," *The Century Magazine*, 1892–1893, XXIII, 803–837.
General Rules and Administrative Regulations of the International Working Men's Association (London, 1871).
General Rules of the Association of United Workers of America (New York, 1874).
Gronlund, Lawrence. *Insufficiency of Henry George's Theory* (New York, 1887).
The Haymarket Speeches (Chicago, 1886).

Hunter, Robert. *Violence and the Labor Movement* (New York, 1914).

Jaeckh, G. *Die Internationale* (Leipzig, 1904).

Lassalle, Ferdinand. *Open Letter to the National Labor Association of Germany* (Translation, New York, 1879).

Levine, L. *The Labor Movement in France* (New York, 1912).

Lum, Dyer D. *A Concise History of the Great Trial of the Chicago Anarchists in 1886* (Chicago, n. d.).

Most, Johann. *August Rheinsdorf und die Propaganda der That* (New York, 1890).

The New Democracy, or *Political Commonwealth*. "Declaration of principles and plan of organization (on a communistic basis)" (New York, 1869).

Offizielles protokoll der 5ten National-Konvention der Sozialistischen Arbeiter Partei von Nord-Amerika (New York, 1886).

Parsons, A. R. *Anarchism: Its Philosophy and Scientific Basis. As Defined by Some of Its Apostles* (Chicago, 1887).

Platform and Constitution of the Socialist Labor Party, adopted by the national convention held at Baltimore (New York, 1884).

Proceedings of the First Congress of the American Confederation of the International Workingmen's Association (New York, 1872).

Proceedings of the First Congress of the North American Federation of the International Workingmen's Association, held in Philadelphia, 1872.

Protokoll Buch des Allgemeinen Deutschen Arbeiter Vereins (Manuscript in Library of the Rand School of Social Science in New York).

Protokoll des Kommunistischen Klubs in New York, 1857–1867 (Manuscript in Library of the Rand School of Social Science in New York).

Book of Minutes of Section 1 (Hoboken) of the International Labor Union. Bound with Copy-Book of the International Workingmen's Association.

Protokoll des 5ten Allgemeinen Kongresses der Internationalen Arbeiter Association (The Hague, September, 1872), *Sorge Manuscripts.*

Report of Proceedings of the National Convention of the Socialist Labor Party, held at Buffalo, New York, September 17–21, 1887 (New York, 1887).

Constitution and Plan of Organisation of Social Party of New York and Vicinity (New York, 1868).

Platform, Constitution and Resolutions, Adopted at the National Congress of the Workingmen's Party of the United States, held at Newark, New Jersey, December, 1877 (Cincinnati, 1878).

Sorge, F. A. *Briefe und Auszuge aus Briefen von Joh. Phil.*

Becker, Jos. Dietzgen, Fr. Engels, K. Marx u. a. and F. A. Sorge, u. andere (Stuttgart, 1906).
——— *Collection of Manuscript Documents on the History of the International Workingmen's Association;* see General Bibliography.
Stiebeling, George C. *Ein Beitrag zur Geschichte der Internationale in Nord-Amerika* (New York, 1874).
Woodhull, Victoria Claflin. *Speech on the Principles of Social Freedom* (New York, 1874).
Proceedings of the Union Congress, held at Philadelphia on the 19th–22d day of July, 1876 (New York, 1876).
Zacher, Georg. *Die rothe Internationale* (Berlin, 1885).

IV.   PAPERS.

Bradstreet's (New York), weekly, 1880–1896.
The Sun (New York), 1886–1887.
Chicago Times, daily, 1886–1887.
New York Times, daily, 1875–1879.
Revolution (New York), weekly, 1868–1870.
San Francisco Evening Bulletin, daily, 1876–1878.
San Francisco Chronicle, daily, 1873–1879.

V.   LABOUR PAPERS.

American Federationist (Washington, D. C.), monthly, 1894–1915.
Carpenter (Indianapolis), monthly, 1886–1897.
Cigar Makers' Official Journal (New York, Buffalo, Chicago), monthly, 1876–1890.
Daily Evening Voice (Boston), 1866–1869.
Hollister's Eight-Hour Herald (Chicago), 1896–1897.
John Swinton's Paper (New York), weekly, 1883–1887.
Journal of United Labor (Pittsburgh, Philadelphia), bi-monthly, 1880–1889.
Journal of the Knights of Labor (Philadelphia, Washington), weekly. 1890–1893. (Successor to *Journal of United Labor.*)
The Labor Enquirer (Denver and Chicago), weekly, 1883–1888.
Labor Standard (New York, Boston, Fall River and Paterson), weekly, 1876–1889.
National Labor Tribune (Pittsburgh), weekly, 1874–1890.
The Standard (New York), weekly, 1887–1890.
Trades Journal (Pittsburgh), weekly, 1888–1890.
Truth (San Francisco), weekly, 1882–1884.
The Workingman's Advocate (Chicago), weekly, 1875–1876.
Workman (New York), weekly, 1882.

VI. SOCIALIST AND ANARCHIST PAPERS.

Arbeiterstimme (New York), weekly, 1876–1878.
Arbeiter-Zeitung (New York), weekly, 1873–1875.
Bulletin of Social Labor Movement (Detroit), monthly, 1880–1881.
Chicagoer Arbeiter-Zeitung, daily, 1887–1888.
The Cleveland Citizen, weekly, 1893–1899.
Der Deutsche Arbeiter (Chicago), weekly, 1870.
Die Arbeiter-Union (New York), weekly, 1866–1870.
Holyoke *Labor* (Holyoke, Massachusetts), weekly, 1894–1896.
Leader (New York), 1886–1887.
National Socialist (Cincinnati), weekly, 1870–1879.
New Yorker Arbeiter-Zeitung, weekly, 1864–1865.
New Yorker Volkszeitung, daily, 1888–1895.
Die Parole (St. Louis), weekly, 1884–1886.
Sozial-Demokrat (New York), weekly, 1874–1878.
Der Sozialist (New York), weekly, 1885–1892.
The Alarm (Chicago), weekly, 1884–1886.
Vorbote (Chicago), weekly, 1874–1888.
Vorwärts (New York), weekly, 1893–1894.
Woodhull and Claflin's Weekly (New York), 1872–1874.

INDEX

INDEX

A

Adelphon Kruptos, Knights of Labor, II, 339.

Advertising, by Knights of Labor, II, 344; descriptive of marketing methods, I, 61; in cordwainers' controversy, I, 58–60; commission stores, I, 94, 95; warehouses, I, 100; weapon against journeymen societies, I, 134.

Agrarianism, Influence: German land reformers, I, 535; on government policy, I, 562, 563; on Industrial Congresses, I, 548, 550, 551; National Reform Association, I, 531; New England Workingmen's Association, I, 537, 538; on trade unionism, I, 531, 532, 577, 578. —

Opinions: Kriege, I, 534; labour, I, 244, 245, 248; Owen, I, 243; press, I, 532, 533; public, I, 211, 239, 271, 273, 275, 293, 363.

Theories: inalienability of land, I, 523, 524; new, I, 522, 523; II, 448; Skidmore, I, 236–238, 243; supremacy of individualism, I, 524.

Agricultural Wheel, activities, II, 490.

Alarm, The, anarchist paper, II, 296, 389.

Albany, coopers fix prices, I, 61; surveyor of weights appointed, I, 47; trade society, I, 72; typographical society, I, 113; workingmen's party, I, 261, 267.

Alimoners, in Columbia Typographical Society, I, 137.

Alleghany City Convention, compromise with Greenbackers, II, 285.

Allen, Samuel C., in Massachusetts politics, I, 315, 316.

Altgeld, John P., II, 393, 503.

Amalgamated Trades and Labor Assembly, Central Labor Union, II, 387–389, 391; Eight-Hour association, II, 391.

American Federation of Labor, Anarchism: Haymarket Square bomb, II, 394; industrial unionism, II, 500; Industrial Workers of the World, II, 523; industrialism, II, 534.

Conditions: depression, II, 501; future, II, 537; growth, II, 410n, 522, 524; organisation, II, 410, 411, 534; revolutionary strikes, II, 503; solidarity, II, 519, 520.

Conventions: Federation of Organised Trades and Labor Unions, II, 309, 318, 322–326; 1888, II, 475; 1892, II, 509; 1893, II, 509–511; 1895, II, 513.

Knights of Labor, II, 411, 413, 483–488.

Legislation and politics: Adamson Act, II, 530n; campaign of 1896, II, 514; congressional campaign, 1906, II, 531; labour legislation, II, 512, 513, 529; political action, II, 509; 512n.

Policies: aims, II, 479; bimetallism, II, 511, 514n; economic functions, II, 320, 495; eight-hour campaign, II, 476, 515; opportunism, I, 17; tariff, II, 330n.

Socialism, II, 516–519.

Trade Unions: brewery workers, II, 488; coal miners, II, 487; craft autonomy, II, 536; trades' assembly, II, 22; unskilled, II, 523, 533.

See also, Federation of Organised Trades and Labor Unions of United States and Canada.

American Federationist, legislative programme, II, 513.

Ammon, Robert H., strikes, 1877, II, 186, 190.

Anarchism, æsthetic individualism, I, 494; agrarianism, I, 523; Andrews, Stephen Pearl, I, 517, 518; co-operative marketing, I, 95, 96; doctrines, I, 16, 17, 20,

21; evolution, I, 14; Masquerier, I, 532; Most, Johann, II, 294; Pittsburgh Convention, 1883, II, 293; Pittsburgh Manifesto, II, 295, 296; politics, II, 292, 293; Proudhonism, II, 139; Red International, II, 299, 300; socialism, II, 290; syndicalism, II, 297; ticket exchange, I, 511; unionism, II, 292, 293; Weitling's bank of exchange, I, 514, 515.
See also, International, Black; Transcendentalism.
Anarchists, see Andrews; Bakunin; Brisbane; Fourier; Tucker; Warren; Weitling.
Ancient Order of United Workmen, II, 196.
Andrews, Stephen Pearl, anarchist, I, 17, 516–518, 556; II, 210.
Anthony, Susan B., II, 127, 129.
Anti-monopoly Party, Kearney, a leader, II, 264; nominations, 1884, II, 440.
Anti-Poverty Society, organised, II, 456.
Apprenticeship, Conditions: becomes child labour, I, 339–341; a custom, I, 125; division of labour, II, 81; education, I, 77, 78; employers shirk responsibility, II, 316; moulders, II, 50; printing trade, I, 115, 116, 448, 451; runaway apprentices, I, 114, 115.
Regulation: demands, I, 104, 341, 342; limitation of numbers, II, 82; reformers, I, 595, 596; uniform laws, I, 56; II, 83, 238; 324; union, I, 590–595, 613n; II, 82–84.
Arbeiter Union, Die, organised, II, 223, 225.
Arbeiter Union Publishing Association, established, II, 223; paper under Douai, II, 224.
Arbeiterstimme, policy, II, 274, 278; ceases publication, II, 281.
Arbeiterstimme des Westens, Walster editor, II, 278.
Arbeiter-Zeitung, established, II, 216; fight for control, II, 221; discontinued, II, 222.
Arbitration, collective bargaining, II, 527; compulsory, II, 326; employers' associations, II, 414, 415; labour, II, 374, 384; cabinet-makers, I, 337; Rochester Congress, II, 165.
Archibald, James P., II, 446, 455.
Armour and Company, form employers' association, II, 418.
Armstrong, Thomas J., II, 247, 440.
Arthur, P. M., II, 67, 68.
Arthur, President, vetoed Chinese Exclusion Act, II, 267.
Arthur v. Oakes, decision, II, 508.
Association, advocates, I, 502; convention, 1844, I, 503; failure, I, 506; Fourierism, I, 499, 500; Greeley, I, 500, 501; Industrial Congresses, I, 550; New England Working Men's Association, I, 538; phalanxes organised, I, 505, 506; predecessors, I, 504; press, I, 501, 502; unitary dwellings, I, 520.
See also, Fourierism.
" Association," term for local union, I, 14.
Association of Working People of New Castle County, organised, I, 287; spring election in 1830, I, 288, 289; end, I, 289, 290.
Athenian Society of Baltimore, I, 92; opens warehouse, I, 94.
Atkinson, James A., at Cleveland Congress, II, 161.
Auction system, opposition, I, 278, 279, 231n.
Auchmuty, Richard T., on apprenticeship, II, 315.
Australia, influence of free land, I, 4.
Austria, International Workingmen's Association, II, 215; socialist strife, II, 221.

B

Bagley, Sarah G., I, 539, 539n.
Bakunin, Michael, anarchist, I, 17; II, 205, 214, 215.
Baltimore, co-operation, II, 438n; *Daily Press* founded, I, 617; labour party, I, 277; printers, I, 109; strikes, I, 386, 387, 419, 478–484; tailors, I, 109; trade societies, I, 473; trades' union, I, 358, 359; unemployment, I, 135.
See also Cordwainers of Baltimore; Typographical Society, Baltimore.
Baltimore Athenian Society, I, 92;

opens warehouse, I, 94; sales, I, 98.

Banking System, see Financial System.

Bargaining Power, Classes: conflict, I, 49, 50, 56, 64, 87; harmony, I, 48, 49; origin, I, 6, 26–29; solidarity, II, 519, 520; vertical separation, I, 57.

Collective: arbitration, II, 325, 414–417, 527; benevolent societies, I, 87; corporations, I, 541, 542; II, 496, 497, 499; employers' associations, I, 132–134, 403, 404; II, 32, 33; guilds, I, 7, 72, 73; method, I, 121–123; monopoly, II, 6, 526; pools, I, 359; trade agreements, I, 15, 606, 607; II, 307, 308, 314, 315, 525, 527; trade union, I, 9, 90, 105–107, 113–115, 350, 352–368, 374, 589, 599–607; II, 32, 33, 373, 374, 426; trades' assemblies, II, 22–26, 36–39, 310–313.

Conditions: Chinese, II, 141, 146, 148–150; cigar makers and the mould, II, 71, 72; depression, I, 456, 457; factory system, II, 76, 77; immigration, I, 10, 597, 616; II, 116–118; itinerant to custom-order stage, I, 34–36; machinery, I, 491, 492; markets, extension of, I, 440, 441; Negro, II, 114; printing trade, "two-thirders" in, I, 448; railways, II, 6; retail shop to wholesale-order stage, I, 61, 62.

Government Regulation: bounties, I, 38; Chinese exclusion act, II, 260, 261, 267, 268; employers control, II, 498, 499; guilds, I, 46–48; imprisonment for debt, I, 178–180; legal tender acts, II, 14, 15; loans and tax emptions, I, 37; manufacturers' monopoly, I, 40; price and wage, I, 50–53; protective tariffs, I, 41–44, 75; raw materials, I, 38; subsidised mechanics, I, 37; war revenue law, II, 69.

Individual: apprenticeship, I, 340, 590–595; book publishers, I, 447, 448; mechanics, I, 25, 36, 37, 57, 175, 220, 339, 340; II, 6; merchants, I, 63, 64, 72; merchant capitalist, I, 101, 102,

106; method, I, 121–123; price bargain, I, 29, 70; price-wage bargain, I, 32, 33; price and wage regulations, I, 50–52; puddler, II, 80; quality regulations, I, 48, 49; unskilled, II, 359, 397.

Methods: blacklist, II, 64; boycott, I, 600; closed shop, I, 130–132, 522, 596, 598.

See also, Arbitration; Boycott; Chinese; Competition; Convict labour; Women in labour movement; Employers' associations; Immigration; Industrial congresses; Industrial cycles; Negro; Strikes; Trade agreements; Wages.

Barondess, Joseph, United Hebrew Trades, II, 519.

Barr case, injunction, II, 506.

Barry, T. B., II, 366, 373.

Bates, Thomas, socialist, II, 262.

Beaumont, Ralph, II, 242, 244, 491, 493.

Beck, William, ticket exchange, I, 511.

Becker, Johann Philipp, Swiss socialist, II, 207.

Benefits, Conditions: depressions, I, 614; union stability, I, 136, 137; II, 307, 501.

Systems: II, 314; death, I, 124; sickness, I, 124, 125; strike, I, 122–124, 585; II, 70.

Union: benevolent societies, I, 83–87; cabinet-makers, I, 336; cigar makers, I, 336; house painters, I, 608; in sixties, II, 175; locomotive engineers, II, 68.

Benevolent Societies, aggressiveness, I, 578–580; early, I, 85; incorporation, I, 86, 87.

Bennett, James Gordon, industrial congresses, I, 554, 560.

Berger, Victor, socialist, II, 516.

Be-spoke, term, I, 36.

Bi-Metallic League, American Federation of Labor, II, 511.

Black International, see International, Black.

Blacklist, employers' associations, I, 403; Fall River cotton mills, II, 362; New York tailors, I, 408; Paterson strike, I, 421; policy, II, 195; railways, II, 64;

secret organization to fight, II, 239.
Blaine, James G., opposed by Typographical Union, II, 317, 318.
Blair, George, II, 163, 235, 236, 242.
Blissert, Robert, and Central Labor Union, II, 441, 442.
Boot and Shoe Workers' International Union, organised, II, 486.
Boston, Associated Housewrights, I, 76; bread assize, I, 54, 55; carpenters, I, 118, 388; II, 158–162; Columbian Charitable Society, I, 77; Eight-Hour League, II, 140; election, II, 142; Faustus Association, I, 77; Labor Reform Association, II, 91; Mechanics Institute, I, 78; New England Working Men's Convention, I, 537; Prison Discipline Society, I, 178–180; shoemakers, I, 36, 45–47, 109; strikes, I, 388, 478–484; II, 158–162.
Bounties, to encourage manufactures, I, 38, 39.
Bovay, Alvin E., I, 537, 547.
Boycott, Cases: Armour Company, II, 419; boarding houses, I, 130; brewery workers, II, 488; Buck's Stove and Range, II, 531; Chinese-made goods, II, 267; Danbury Hatters, II, 530; Duryea Glen Cove Company, II, 317n; in 1884, 1885, II, 364, 365; New York Tribune, II, 317, 318; Pullman, II, 502; Theiss boycott, II, 445.
Legal Theory: business is property, II, 506.
Union Practice: New York Central Labor Union, II, 444; trades' assemblies, II, 22–25, 311; trades' union, I, 364; union weapon, I, 600; II, 442.
Boycotter, The, established, II, 317.
Brace Bros. v. Evans, boycott case, II, 506.
Brandt, Lyman A., II, 319, 321.
Bread Assize, I, 52, 53.
Bricklayers' National Union, and American Federation of Labor, II, 522n; established, II, 213; growth, II, 308, 375; lockout, II, 423–425.
Brisbane, Albert, I, 17, 497, 498, 499, 500, 505, 525, 538, 544, 547; II, 138.

Brooklyn, labour party, I, 277.
Brownson, Orestes A., I, 260, 494–496.
Buchanan, Joseph R., II, 299, 300, 367, 368, 408, 409, 416n, 466, 467.
Bücher, Karl, cited, I, 20, 26, 27, 33.
Buffalo, conspiracy case, I, 164, 165; labour party, II, 277; switchmen's strike, II, 498.
Building Trades, associations, I, 519–521, 574; early organisations, I, 67–69; industrial stages, I, 66; itinerant worker, I, 67; piece work and contract work, I, 67; price bargain, I, 70; trades' council, I, 68; II, 312, 515.
See also, Carpenters.
Burlingame Treaty with China, abrogation demanded, II, 238, 250; passed, II, 150; ratified, II, 265.
Butler, Benjamin F., II, 246, 260, 440, 441.

C

Cabinet-Makers of Philadelphia, Pennsylvania Society of Journeymen, co-operation, I, 467; organisation, I, 99, 336, 337.
Cabinet-makers, United, Arbeiter Union, II, 223; convict labour, I, 155; eight-hour movement, II, 225; prejudice against I. W. A., II, 226.
California, anti-Chinese agitation, II, 146, 149–151, 262; constitutional convention, II, 260, 261; eight-hour movement, II, 147; industrial situation in the sixties, II, 147; Mechanics' State Council, II, 148; ten-hour law, I, 544.
See also, Chinese; Workingmen's Party of California.
Cameron, A. C., II, 99, 115, 119, 124, 129, 132, 133, 145, 149, 152, 166.
Campbell, Alexander, II, 120, 122, 123, 126.
Campbell, John, I, 516, 595; II, 468.
Capital Punishment, demand for abolition, I, 299; in New York, I, 345.
Capitalist - wholesaler, separation from retailer, I, 7.

Carey, Mathew, I, 73, 354, 356, 415, 416, 447.

Carl, Conrad, II, 207, 216, 221, 225.

Carnegie Brothers and Company, Homestead strike, II, 495–497.

Carpenters, Organisation: Carpenters' and Joiners' Brotherhood, II, 313, 326, 376, 377, 388; Carpenters' Company of Philadelphia, I, 68, 78, 80–82, 84, 97; conventions, I, 453; II, 326; growth, II, 313, 375; strikes, I, 127, 128, 186–189, 388–397; II, 476; unions, I, 110; II, 20, 477n.

   Programme: anarchism, II, 388; apprenticeship, I, 342; co-operation, I, 97; hours, II, 377, 476; trade agreement, I, 608; wages, I, 582.

Cary, Samuel F., II, 125, 130, 149, 171, 244.

Catholic Church, on co-operation, I, 571; Henry George, II, 453; Knights of Labor, II, 201, 331; opposition to, I, 415; II, 456.
   See also, McGlynn, Father.

Central bodies, term, I, 15.

Central Labor Federation, New York, organised, II, 516, 517.

Central labor union, term, I, 15.

Central Labor Union, Chicago: agitation, II, 389; composition, II, 391n; eight-hour day, II, 391; organisation, II, 387; principles, II, 388.

   New York: activities, II, 441–443; boycott, II, 444, 445; the Leader, II, 451; political action, II, 446; principles, II, 442; Progressive Democracy, II, 455; Progressive Labor Party, II, 401; socialism, II, 517.

   St. Louis: II, 389n.

Channing, William H., I, 502, 503, 538, 547.

Charleston, bakers, I, 53, 54; Columbian Charitable Society, I, 77.

Chicago, anarchism, II, 209, 298n, 386–393; socialism, II, 279n, 282, 283, 285, 287n; strikes, II, 367n, 419; trade unionism, II, 279; Trade and Labor Assembly, II, 327, 331.
   See also Central Labor Union; International, Black.

Chicagoer Arbeiter-Zeitung, II, 282; unemployed, II, 389.

Chicagoer Volkszeitung, Lassallean organ, II, 272.

Child Labour, Conditions: apprenticeship, I, 339–341; education, I, 182, 183; hours, I, 174, 175, 542; factories, I, 320, 321, 331, 428, 432; textile industry, I, 172, 173.

   Laws: demanded by Greenback Party, II, 251; demanded by Illinois Labor Party, II, 228; by Knights of Labor, II, 336; by New England Association of Farmers, Mechanics, and Other Workingmen, I, 318; in Pennsylvania, I, 331; limitation on hours, I, 542–544; Pittsburgh convention, 1881, II, 324.

Chinese, Burlingame treaty, II, 150; California agitation, II, 252–268; congressional investigation, II, 265; Crispins, II, 141; Federal Exclusion Act, II, 151, 252, 267, 268; immigration, II, 266, 328; National Labor Union, II, 149, 150; Rochester Congress, II, 165; strike breakism, II, 146, 149; trade unionism, II, 158; unemployment, II, 148.

Cigar Makers' Union, International, Activities: apprenticeship, I, 593; II, 84; benefits, II, 71, 73, 175n, 377; boycotts, II, 366; conspiracy case, Kingston, II, 70; strikes, II, 70–74, 177, 178, 307, 363; war revenue law, II, 68, 69; women, II, 363.

   Organisation: conventions, I, 621; II, 69, 72, 73, 321, 326; established, II, 313; federation, II, 402; government, II, 314; growth, II, 47, 70, 176, 308, 313, 473; reorganised, II, 45, 306; split, II, 399, 400, 412.
   See also, Gompers, Samuel.

Cigar Makers' Union, Progressive, formed, II, 400; joins District Assembly 49, II, 401; labour legislation, II, 387; unites with International Union, II, 412.

Cincinnati, co-operative marketing, I, 96, 99; National Labor Union, Congress, II, 209; socialism, II, 273, 277, 282; tailors organise, I, 352.

Citizens' Alliance, organised, II, 493; Cincinnati convention, 1891, II, 494.

Citizens' Protective Union, San Francisco, II, 263.
Citizenship, education, I, 181–184, 223–229, 283; Mechanics' Union of Trade Associations, I, 190, 299, 300; progress, I, 331, 332; representation, I, 232, 233; suffrage, I, 175–178; theories, I, 13, 14, 170–172, 300–303, 324, 382–385.
Civil War, depression, II, 9, 10; labour, I, 4; II, 10–12; unions, II, 13.
Claflin, Tennessee, suffragist, II, 211.
Class Antagonism, Indications: Chartist clubs, I, 564, 565; city industrial congresses, I, 544; education, I, 323; hatred, II, 373; politics, I, 234, 292, 304, 305.
  Theories: I, 120; Brisbane, I, 499; Evans, I, 525; origin, I, 26–29; Owen, I, 525; price bargain, I, 29; versus race struggle, II, 253–268; Weitling, I, 513.
Clayton Act, II, 532.
Cleveland, Grover, election, II, 318; sends troops in Pullman strike, II, 503.
Closed shop, Carpenters' Company of Philadelphia, I, 81; Commonwealth v. Hunt decision, I, 412; employers' associations, I, 404; immigrants excluded, I, 10; theory, I, 130–132; unions, II, 479n.
Collins, John A., I, 504; II, 157.
Colman, Reverend Henry, I, 321, 323, 324.
Colorado, Greenbackism, II, 248.
Commerford, John, I, 263n, 429, 434, 531.
Commission stores, development, I, 100; inadequacy, I, 101; private, I, 94.
Common law, conspiracy cases, I, 139, 143; opinions, I, 147, 148.
Commonwealth v. Carlisle, conspiracy case, I, 163.
Commonwealth v. Hunt, conspiracy case, II, 504.
Communist Club, International, II, 206, 207; Social Party, II, 208, 209.
Communist Manifesto, and Communist Club, II, 207.

Competition, Conditions: control, I, 57–61, 68; cut-throat, II, 359; equalised, I, 112; evils, I, 45, 46; immigration, I, 9, 10; international labour, II, 86; machinery, I, 491; markets, extension of, I, 41, 440, 441; II, 5, 6, 44, 148; mechanics, II, 358; merchant-capitalist system, I, 102, 104, 339; monopoly, I, 219; pools, II, 360; shoe industry, II, 76, 77; wage, I, 621.
  Kinds: Chinese, II, 149, 264, 265; convict labour, I, 155, 443, 492; foreign, I, 72, 154; inferior workers, I, 114; Negro, II, 113.
  Opinions: Andrews, S. P., I, 518; Brisbane, I, 499; Greeley, I, 548.
Connecticut, greenbackism, II, 245; hours of labour, I, 543; II, 108; price regulation, I, 50; unions, II, 19; wage regulation, I, 51.
Conservation, natural resources, I, 4; raw materials, I, 39.
  See also, Land Policy.
Conspiracy, Administrative Problems: commercial appeals, I, 149–152; employers aided, II, 503; judges antagonistic to labour, I, 152; jurors, occupations of, I, 147; political issues, I, 146–149; power, II, 473.
  Cases: Arthur v. Oakes, II, 507; Baltimore weavers, I, 419; Barr, II, 506; Brace Brothers v. Evans, II, 506; Buck's Stove and Range, II, 531; Buffalo tailors, I, 164, 165; Commonwealth v. Carlisle, I, 163; Commonwealth v. Hunt, I, 411, 412; II, 504; cordwainers, I, 138–146; Danbury hatters, II, 530; Debs, II, 502, 503, 508; Gaul, II, 123; Geneva shoemakers, I, 406, 407; in 1829–1842, I, 405; in 1835, I, 372, 373; in 1853–1854, I, 611, 612; in 1859, I, 612; Kingston, II, 70; Lennon, II, 508; New York hatters', I, 164; New York tailors', I, 337, 408; Siney and Parks, II, 180, 181n; Thompsonville, I, 313, 314; Walker v. Cronin, II, 506; weavers, I, 314n.
  Judicial Theory: business is property, II, 505, 506; combination to improve conditions, I, 140,

141, 144; common law, I, 139, 146–149; injunctions, II, 502, 503, 505–509; legal issues, I, 139, 146; II, 504; public injury, I, 146; unlawful means, I, 143–145.

Legislation: II, 324; Clayton Act, II, 532; in 1877, II, 191; incorporation of unions, II, 314; Interstate Commerce Act, II, 505; New York law, II, 23n, 443; Sherman Anti-trust Act, II, 505, 508, 509, 530.

Opinions: employers', I, 405; labours', I, 162, 299, 409, 410, 443; II, 276.

Constitution, federal, I, 4, 74, 75; incorporation, II, 326; of 1787, II, 7.

Contract immigrant labour, legislation, II, 373; protested, II, 372.

Convict labour, abolition demanded, I, 282, 369n, 370n; competition, I, 155, 339, 344–347, 443, 460, 491; introduction, I, 103; investigation, I, 369; labour, I, 432; II, 37.

Conzett, Conrad, II, 230, 230n, 270, 271, 281.

Cook, Noah, I, 243, 248, 260n.

Cooper, Peter, I, 19; II, 240, 271, 271n.

Co-operation, Endorsed: Cleveland Congress, II, 161; Illinois Labor Party, II, 228, 230; Labor Congress, 1866, II, 107; Labor Congress, 1867, II, 118, 119; New England Working Men's Association, I, 539; New York Industrial Congress, I, 555, 556; socialists, I, 14; II, 231, 237; Sovereigns of Industry, II, 171–175; syndicalism, II, 297, 298; trades' assembly, II, 23, 37; trades' union, I, 378, 436.

Theories: Andrews, S. P., I, 518; banking reform, I, 510; collective bargaining, II, 326; Greeley's profit-sharing, I, 507; Lassalle, II, 206; Owen, I, 549; profit-sharing, I, 508; retaliatory, I, 127, 128; Rochdale plan, II, 40, 110, 205; Schulze-Delitzsch's system, II, 206, 223; self employment, I, 128–130; substitute for strikes, I, 466, 565, 566; voluntary, II, 302;

Weitling's bank of exchange, I, 18, 513, 514, 566.

Ventures: building associations, I, 519–521, 574; coopers, II, 76, 435, 437n; credit, I, 97, 98; Crispins, II, 79, 140, 141, 152, 153; distributive, I, 95–100, 508, 509, 571–573; II, 39; European, I, 99, 100; failure, I, 570, 573; II, 151, 437, 438; farmers, II, 489–491; furniture company, II, 438n; German, I, 567, 568; II, 223n; in 1836, I, 467–469; in 1868, II, 124; in eighties, II, 431, 433n; in New England, I, 573; iron workers, I, 565, 569; II, 53–56; Knights of Labor, II, 335, 351, 352, 430–438; newspaper publication, I, 371; need, I, 10; II, 113; productive, I, 57, 58–60, 75, 76, 85, 98, 568; II, 41, 53–56, 110–112; sectional distribution, II, 434; statistics, II, 433; tailors, I, 353, 569.

Coopers' Union, International, apprenticeship, II, 84; co-operation, II, 76; federation, II, 157; Foran, II, 75; growth, II, 75, 176; machinery, II, 74; organised, II, 46, 75, 313; Schilling, II, 76.

Cordwainers, apprenticeship, I, 341; collective bargaining, II, 121, 122; closed shop, I, 130–132, 411, 598; competition, I, 58–60; conspiracy, I, 65, 131, 138–152; co-operation, I, 97, 99, 441–443, 467; courts, I, 134; employer membership, I, 118, 120; minimum wage demands, I, 117; organise, I, 109, 114; prices, I, 64.

Cordwainers of Baltimore, conspiracy case, I, 138, 139; union, I, 114.

Cordwainers, New York Journeymen, closed shop theory, I, 131, 132; conspiracy cases, I, 138, 140, 143, 144; employer members expelled, I, 119, 120; grievances, I, 352; members, I, 105; organise, I, 352; strikes, I, 124, 126, 383; women shoe binders, I, 383.

Cordwainers of Philadelphia, benefits, I, 123, 125, 136; boycott, I, 130; collective bargaining, I,

121, 122, 133; conspiracy case, I, 138–141; co-operation, I, 97, 99, 128–130; depression, I, 456; organise, I, 58, 109, 114, 132, 357; prices reduced, I, 65; strikes, I, 126, 376, 392, 398, 399.

Cordwainers, Pittsburgh, apprenticeship, I, 117; benefits, I, 123, 125; collective bargaining, I, 121; conspiracy cases, I, 138, 144–146; minimum wage demand, I, 117; prices regulated, I, 60, 64.

Corrigan, Archbishop, condemns single-tax, II, 456.

Cotton Mill Spinners' Union, established, II, 313.

Cox, Trench, cited, I, 91.

Credit Societies, I, 81, 82.

Credit System, see Financial System.

Crittenden Compromise, labour's support, II, 11; provisions, II, 11n.

Cummings, Samuel P., II, 138, 140, 142, 145.

Curtis, Josiah, M.D., hours of labour, I, 541.

Custom-order Stage, building trade, I, 66; capital, I, 54; competition, I, 44, 45; protective legislation, I, 46–48; transition from itinerant, I, 34–36.

D

Daily Evening Voice, II, 17; eight-hour day, II, 31; supported by trades' assembly, II, 24.

Danbury Hatters, case, II, 530.

Daniels, Newell, organised Knights of Saint Crispin, II, 77.

Davis, John M., II, 199, 200n, 202, 235, 243, 246, 493.

Davis, William M., cited, II, 195.

Day, H. H., I, 19; II, 126, 153, 155, 169, 170.

Day, J. G., II, 254, 255n, 257.

Debs, Eugene V., II, 500–503, 508.

Delaware, militia law, I, 330, 331; political action, I, 287–289; political demand, I, 299, 300; unions, 1863–1864, II, 19.

Delaware Free Press, I, 288n.

De Leon, Daniel, II, 455, 517, 519.

Delnicke Listy, official labour organ, II, 278.

Denmark, International Working-men's Association, II, 215.

Depression, see Industrial Cycles.

Detroit, labour party, II, 277.

Deutsche Arbeiter Union, of National Labor Union, II, 209.

Devyr, Thomas A., I, 532, 532n.

Division of labour, apprenticeship, II, 81; effect on national unions, II, 44.

Domestic Economy, market theory, I, 26.

Donnelly, Ignatius, Greenback Party, II, 170.

Douai, Adolph, II, 149, 224, 224n, 225, 275, 276, 286.

Douglass, Dr. Charles, I, 360, 380, 426, 428, 434.

Drury, Victor, co-operation, II, 433.

E

Earle, William H., organises Sovereigns of Industry, II, 172.

Eberhardt, Karl, cited, II, 283.

Eccarius, J. George, II, 132, 212.

Edmonston, Gabriel, II, 328, 329, 411.

Education, children in factories, I, 182–184, 322; compulsory, II, 228, 229, 323, 324; Knights of Labor, II, 335, 441; labour demands, I, 223, 224, 296, 299–301, 313, 318, 321–324, 327, 328, 427, 432, 470; opposition, I, 229, 230; Owen's plan, I, 247, 248, 249, 252, 273; Philadelphia report, I, 226, 227, 228; public, I, 12, 170, 181, 182, 224, 258, 274, 286.

See also, Industrial Education.

Eight-hour Day, Demanded: American Federation of Labor, II, 376, 377, 485; Boston Eight-Hour League, II, 140; Boston Labor Reform Association, I, 91; California labour, 1865, II, 147, 148; Central Labor Union, II, 391; Chicago Eight-Hour League, II, 250, 285, 286, 391, 392; Cleveland, convention, II, 324; eight-hour leagues, II, 95; Greenback Party, II, 250; Knights of Labor, II, 336, 378, 379, 485; Labor Congress, 1866, 1867, II, 95, 118; machinists, II, 57, 58; Massachusetts

Eight-Hour League, I, 92; National Labor Party, II, 209; National Labor Union, II, 113; New York Assembly, II, 95; New York convention, II, 330; Pittsburgh convention, II, 238, 324; Rochester convention, II, 165; Social Party, II, 208; socialists, II, 276; Workingmen's Party of California, II, 258.

Legislation: congress, II, 104, 105; government employés, II, 124; Massachusetts, II, 105–107; President Johnson, II, 104; state, II, 105, 107–109.

Status: adoption, first instance of, II, 87; bricklayers, II, 476, 478, 479n; brotherhoods win, II, 528; cabinet makers, II, 225; carpenters, II, 424n, 477n; failure, causes for, II, 109, 110; gains, II, 378, 384; Haymarket bomb, II, 386; in 1878, II, 177; soldiers, return of, II, 94; strikes, II, 385, 418, 475, 476, 477.

Theories: employers' associations, II, 30, 31; greenbackism versus, II, 139, 140; make work, II, 479; "Stewardism," II, 89–91, 303.

Emancipator, Milwaukee, socialist organ, II, 275.

Emerson, Ralph W., individualism, I, 494.

Employers' Associations, Attitude: apprenticeship, II, 51; blacklist, I, 403; closed shop, I, 404; conspiracy, I, 406–410; eight-hour movement, II, 30, 31; "exclusive" agreements, II, 32; Knights of Labor, II, 414; machinists, II, 56, 57; merchants' associations, I, 132, 133; moulders, II, 49; trade agreements, II, 33; unionism, I, 133, 134; II, 26, 27, 28, 44.

Organisation: central bodies, I, 403, 404; Boston Master Mechanics, II, 30; builders, II, 424; disintegration, II, 55; in Michigan, II, 26–29; New York Master Builders' Association, II, 29, 30; Northwestern Publishers' Association, II, 61; packers, II, 418; spread, I, 401, 402; stove manufacturers, II, 50–55.

English, William, I, 196n, 425, 426, 461.

Engineers, Machinists and Millwrights, Amalgamated Society of, Cleveland convention, II, 326; Pittsburgh convention, II, 321.

England, conspiracy laws, I, 125; feudalism, I, 142; International Workingmen's Association, II, 213, 215; textile workers, I, 111; trade unionists, II, 205.

Erie, Pennsylvania, People's Party, I, 207.

Europe, co-operation, I, 99, 100; guilds, I, 36; International Workingmen's Associations, II, 215; socialists of, I, 18; socialists from, II, 196.

Evans, Chris, II, 403, 426.

Evans, George Henry, I, 5, 234, 237, 242, 243, 461, 522–524, 525, 527–531, 537, 559.

F

Factory Inspection, plank in state labour party platform in New York, II, 242.

Factory System, Brownson, I, 495; condition, I, 320, 544; in New England, I, 305, 306; in Paterson, I, 420, 421; opposition, I, 320, 321, 331, 428, 429; shoe makers, II, 37; strikes, I, 418, 419, 420, 422, 423; trades' union, I, 374, 418; women, I, 422.

Farmers' Alliance, Northern: activities, II, 489; Southern: co-operation for legislative reform, II, 490, 491; join Knights of Labor, II, 491; organised, II, 488–490; programme, II, 492.

Farmers' and Laborers' Union of America, organised, II, 488.

Farmer-consumer, favours protection, I, 41.

Faustus Association, fosters inventions, I, 77.

Federalists, conspiracy laws, I, 139, 141.

Federation of Labor of New York, organised, II, 517.

Federation of Organised Trades and Labor Unions, conventions, II, 321–328, 376, 403; **Knights** of Labor, II, 397; organised, II, 309, 318; political action, II, 463, 464; trade unions, II, 327.

Fehrenbatch, John, II, 157, 159, 175, 176.

Fellenberg, Emmanuel von, school at Hofwyl, I, 247, 328.

Ferral, John, I, 312n, 390–392, 427, 429, 430, 531.

Ferrell, Frank, United Labor Party, II, 459.

Fielden, Samuel, Chicago anarchist, Haymarket Square, II, 393, 394.

Financial System, Conditions: contraction of currency, II, 151; co-operation, I, 97, 98, 510; II, 112; extension, I, 7, 91, 92, 101, 102; failures of banks, I, 454; Andrew Jackson, I, 347, 348; legal tender acts, II, 14, 15; politics, II, 142; " rag " money, I, 349.

Opinions: Junior Sons of '76, II, 201, 202; labour, I, 180, 181, 296, 297, 298, 318–320, 330, 459; opposition, I, 220, 276, 277; Trades' Union, I, 435.

Reforms: abolition of national banks, II, 209, 236; Beck's ticket exchange, I, 511; Kellogg's, I, 519; Muhlenberg, I, 460; Proudhonism, II, 139; Weitling's bank of exchange, I, 514.

Finch, John, organises trades' union, I, 358.

Fincher, Jonathan C., II, 7, 8, 15, 24, 25, 39, 56, 93, 97, 126, 128.

Fincher's Trades' Review, circulation, II, 16; established, II, 15; on co-operation, II, 110, 111; on local unions, II, 17–21; on moulder's organisation, II, 49; on Rochdale plan, II, 40.

Fischer, Adolph, Chicago anarchist, II, 393.

Fitzpatrick, P. F., II, 320, 412.

Foran, Martin A., cooper, I, 19; II, 75, 75n, 152, 157, 159, 176, 389, 463.

Ford, Ebenezer, and Working Men's Party, I, 242, 255.

Foster, Frank, II, 327, 331.

Foster, W. A., II, 322, 324, 325, 328, 403, 406.

Fourierism, American, II, 204;

principles, I, 496, 497; production, I, 498, 499.
See also, Brisbane; Association.

Fourier, Charles, co-operative anarchist, I, 17, 18; principles, I, 496, 497.

France, solidarisme, I, 17.

Franklin, Benjamin, establishes loan fund for mechanics, I, 79, 80; organised printers, I, 87.

Franklin Institute, industrial education, I, 78.

French Revolution, effect on industry, I, 134.

Frick, H. C., Homestead strike, II, 496, 497.

Furniture Workers' National Union, established, II, 226, 313; Knights of Labor, II, 398.

G

Gag law, threatened, II, 257, 258.

Garment Cutters' Union, opposed Knights of Labor, II, 197.

Garrison, William Lloyd, slavery, I, 525.

Gary, Joseph E., Judge, trial of anarchists, II, 393, 394.

George, Henry, I, 563; II, 446–454, 457–461, 469.

Georgia, legal day, I, 544; regulates profits, I, 51.

German Social Democratic Workingmen's Union, joins International, II, 209, 210.

German Workingmen's Alliance, programme, II, 204.

German Workingmen's Union, General, Lassallean programme, II, 207, 208; Social Party, II, 208, 209; Union in Germany, II, 208.

Germany, Franco-Prussian War and socialism, II, 225; International Workingmen's Association, II, 215.

Gibson, C. William, II, 102, 112, 115, 116, 126.

Gilchrist, Robert P., II, 10, 34, 145.

Gleicheit, Die, Austrian socialist's organ, II, 221.

Gilmore, William, Trades' union leader, I, 470.

Gold, discovery, I, 12.

Gompers, Samuel, II, 176, 306, 307, 321–329, 331, 347, 402, 409, 412, 458, 473, 478, 479, 485, 499,

500, 501, 510, 510n, 512, 512n, 514, 517, 531, 531n.

Gould, Jay, II, 369, 370, 384.

Government ownership, and American Federation of Labor, II, 509–511; of railroads advocated, II, 228, 231, 276.

Granite Cutters' National Union, Cleveland convention, 1882, II, 326; established, II, 313; Pittsburgh convention, 1881, II, 321.

Greeley, Horace, I, 17, 170, 171, 500, 507, 533, 538, 544, 544n, 548, 570, 576, 577, 588, 604.

Green, General Duff, I, 342, 445, 448, 449.

Greenbackism, Conditions: depression, II, 122, 123, 170; prosperity, II, 249.

In Labour Congresses: II, 119–124, 128, 165, 245.

In Politics: California, II, 263; congressional election of 1878, II, 245, 246; democrats, II, 249; "Greenback and Labor" combination, II, 243; National Nominating Convention, II, 250; New York, II, 242; Ohio, II, 248; Pennsylvania, II, 247; Pomeroy clubs, II, 246; West, II, 244.

Theories: anarchism versus, II, 121; Douai, II, 224; Kelloggism, II, 120; Proudhonism, II, 139; socialism versus, II, 196, 237–239, 285–290; trade unionism versus, II, 223.

Greenback Labor Party, National, Butler campaign, II, 440; failure, II, 251; in 1882, II, 439, 440; in Pennsylvania, II, 242, 243; national convention, II, 285; organised, II, 241–247.

Greenback Party, 1874–1877, conventions, II, 168–170; Peter Cooper, II, 171; depression, II, 170; power, II, 196, 197.

Grottkau, Paul, II, 281, 287, 296, 387, 516.

Guilds, breaking up, I, 8; charters, I, 46, 48; European, I, 77; organisation, I, 7; revival of principle, I, 492.

Gunton, George, II, 302n, 304.

H

Hague, The, Congress of International Workingmen's Association, II, 213, 215.

Hales, John, London General Council, II, 212, 213.

Hanna, Mark, trade agreement, II, 180.

Harding, William, II, 96, 99, 116, 119.

Hardy, Thomas, common law, I, 148.

Haskell, Burnette G., II, 298, 299.

Hat Finishers Union, established, II, 313.

Hatters of the City of Philadelphia, I, 157.

Haymarket bomb, II, 392–394; eight-hour strike, II, 386.

Hebrew Trades, United, and Knights of Labor, II, 519; organised in New York, II, 518.

Heighton, William, education, I, 226.

Hennebery, Thomas, at Pittsburgh convention, II, 321, 323.

Herttell, Thomas, abolition of imprisonment for debt, I, 328, 329.

Hewitt, Abram S., campaign, II, 450–452.

Heywood, Ezra A., anarchist, II, 126, 138, 138n.

Hinchcliffe, John, II, 17, 97, 99, 103, 115, 126, 152, 170.

Hine, Lucius A., I, 533; II, 128.

Hinton, Richard, II, 314n, 455.

Historical periods, characterised, I, 11–13; philosophies, I, 13, 14.

Hobson, J. A., production theory, I, 28.

Hogan. Thomas, I, 360, 425, 434, 461.

Horseshoers' Union, established, II, 313.

Homestead movement, see Land Policy.

Homework, Bücher's use of the term, I, 33; merchant-capitalist stage, I, 103.

Hours of Labour, bakers', I, 162; Boston ship carpenters, I, 311, 312, 325; building trades, I, 188; carpenters, I, 69; in 1839, I, 172; labour parties, I, 331; National Trades' Union, I, 433, 536; New England Working Men's Association, I, 537, 539; printers, I, 118; public employment, I, 192, 393–395; public opinion, I, 174, 175; strikes for shorter, I, 158–162, 183, 186–

189, 386–392; II, 367; sunrise
to sunset system, I, 158, 171,
174, 186, 189n, 544; ten-hour
movement, I, 110, 159n, 235,
303, 307, 324, 366n, 384.
Legislation, legislative investigation, I, 436, 437, 540; ten-hour
law in New Hampshire, I, 541,
542; in New York, I, 542, 543;
in Pennsylvania, I, 543; in
other states, I, 543–545.
Theories: citizenship, I, 170–172,
384, 385; make-work, I, 545,
546.
See also, Eight-Hour Day.
Housewrights of Boston, promote
inventions, I, 76.
Howard, Robert, II, 321, 322, 328,
331, 463.
Humanitarianism, anti-Chinise agitation, II, 267; apprenticeship,
I, 595; co-operation, I, 565;
high-water mark, I, 564; hours
of labour, I, 536, 541; in 1837,
I, 12; in forties, I, 14; unionism, I, 576.
See also, Agrarianism; Association; Co-operation; Land Policy; Transcendentalism.
Hungary, Bureau for recruiting
contract labourers, II, 372.

I

Illinois, eight hour day, II, 108;
Knights of Labor, II, 381, 382;
unions, 1863, 1864, II, 19.
Immigration, decrease, 1855, 1856,
I, 616; increase, I, 413, 488,
489.
Character: change, I, 489, 490;
Chinese, II, 149, 150; contract,
II, 117, 118, 131, 324, 372, 373,
413, 414; German forty-eighters, II, 204; in eighties, II,
360, 523.
Effects: competition, I, 9, 10; II,
86, 149, 150; hours of labour, I,
544; riots, I, 412, 415; strikes,
I, 597; II, 117, 179; trade union
membership, II, 315.
Imprisonment for Debt, abolition,
I, 221, 281, 296–298, 318;
wage-earner, I, 177–180, 221n.
Incorporation of unions, before Congress, II, 328; early attitude
toward, II, 314; Farmers' Alliance, II, 489n; law, II, 409;

labour conventions, II, 165, 324,
325, 330; Charles Wilson's plan,
II, 66, 67.
Industrialism, first move, II, 312;
forms, II, 534, 535.
Industrialists, in Columbia Typographical Society, I, 137.
Industrial Brotherhood, beginning,
II, 196.
Industrial Congresses, 1845–1856,
aims, I, 558; bargain for votes,
I, 559; city, I, 551, 552, 557;
land reformers control, I, 550,
551; organised, I, 548; Owen's
world convention, I, 549.
Cleveland, 1873: call, II, 159;
constitution, II, 160; co-operation, II, 161; panic, II, 161;
political action, II, 161; trade
unionism, II, 160; representation, II, 159.
Indianapolis: constitution, II,
167; trade unions, II, 166.
New York, 1850: bargain for
votes, I, 559; control, I, 555,
561, 562; organised, I, 552;
purpose, I, 554; representation,
I, 553; trade unionism, I, 557.
Rochester, 1874: arbitration, II,
165; constitution, II, 162;
greenbackism, II, 164, 165; Industrial Brotherhood, II, 163,
164; political action, II, 166;
representation, II, 162.
Industrial Cycles, Depression: apprenticeship, II, 84; bank failures, 1837, I, 454, 455; causes,
II, 283; food riots, 1837, I, 12,
463, 464; greenbackism, II, 122,
168, 170, 245, 248, 249; in California, II, 147, 148, 253, 267;
in 1829, I, 170; in 1833, I, 351;
in 1837–1852, I, 488, 489, 492;
in 1847, I, 564; in 1854, 1855,
I, 613–615; in 1857, II, 5; in
1861, II, 9, 10; in 1866–1868,
II, 115, 123, 124; in 1873–1879,
II, 195, 219, 220; in 1877, II,
185; in 1883–1885, II, 361, 362;
in 1893, II, 501; influence, I,
10; II, 472; Lassalleanism, II,
227, 228; prison labour, I, 369;
Sovereigns of Industry, II, 175;
strikes, I, 381, 382; unionism, I,
134–138, 456, 460, 614, 615; II,
46, 47, 161, 166, 175.
Prosperity: apprenticeship, II, 84;
in 1835, I, 348, 351; in 1862, II,

14, 15; in 1869, II, 55; in 1898, II, 521; influence, I, 10; II, 472; political action, I, 326; II, 143; socialism, II, 284; strikes, I, 381, 382.

Industrial Education, apprenticeship, I, 77, 78; demand, I, 284, 300, 301, 322; funds, I, 84, 85; labour, I, 226, 228, 328.

Industrial Workers of the World, I, 17; industrialism, II, 533, 534; organised, II, 523; trade agreement, II, 527.

Infidelity, workingman accused, I, 211–213, 254, 272, 273, 290, 293.

Ingersoll, Jared, in Philadelphia conspiracy case, I, 139.

Injunctions, see Conspiracy.

Intellectuals, term explained, I, 19, 20; welcome International, II, 210.

See also, Andrews, Stephen Pearl; Brisbane; Cooper, Peter; Day, H. H.; Foran, Martin A.; George, Henry; Greeley, H.; Hinchcliffe; Kellogg, Edward; Lloyd, Henry D.; McNeill, George E.; Moore, Ely; Owen, Robert; Owen, Robert Dale; Sorge, F. A.; Steward, Ira; Swinton, John; Warren, Josiah; Wright, Frances.

International, Black, Central Labor Union, II, 387; Chicago, II, 390; collapse, II, 394; Haymarket Square bomb, II, 393, 394; information bureau, II, 296; organised, II, 291; Pittsburgh Convention, II, 293–296.

International, Bohemian Section, formed, II, 209, 390.

International, French Section, formed, II, 209.

International, Red, established, II, 298–299; Socialist Labor Party, II, 300n.

International Working People's Association, see International, Black.

Interstate Commerce Act, injunctions, II, 505.

International Labor Union, convention, II, 305; failure, II, 306; organised, II, 302; programme, II, 303, 304; textile workers, II, 304; unskilled, II, 280.

International Workingmen's Association, Organisation: American Confederation, II, 213; American forerunners, II, 206, 207; Bakunin and Marx, II, 214, 215; central committee, II, 210, 211; councils, II, 212, 213, 215; European federations, II, 216, 269, 270, 271; nationalisation, II, 231, 269–271; National Labor Union, II, 131; North American Federation, II, 214; organs, II, 221, 222, 230, 390n; sections, II, 209, 210, 216, 217; secessionists, II, 217, 233; unemployed, II, 219, 220; Union Congress, II, 270; United Workers of America affiliate, II, 222.

Theories: II, 86, 87, 302, 303; immigration, II, 131, 132; Lassalleanisation, II, 228, 229; political action, II, 205, 218, 219; trade unionism, II, 205, 223–226, 233, 234.

See also, Bakunin, Michael; Carl, Conrad; Claflin, Tennessee; Hales, John; Marx, Karl; Sorge, F. A.; Stiebling, George C.; Woodhull, Victoria; Workingmen's Party of United States.

Iowa, Greenbackism, II, 244, 248.

Irish World, The, supports Henry George, II, 451.

Iron and Steel Workers, Amalgamated Association of, and A. F. of L., II, 329; established, II, 313; Homestead strike, II, 495, 497; long strike, II, 181, 184, 185; organised, II, 179; trade agreement, II, 179–181.

Iron Moulders, see Molders International Union.

Irons, Martin, Southwest strike, II, 383.

Italy, contract labourers, II, 372.

Itinerancy, Bücher's use of the term, I, 33; competition, I, 45, 48, 49, 67; wages, I, 51, 52.

Inventions, encouraged, I, 76, 77.

J

Jackson, Alexander, J. W., I, 430, 434.

Jackson, Andrew, I, 269, 270, 347, 348.

Jarrett, John, II, 321–325, 329, 468.

Jessup, William J., II, 108, 113, 115, 116, 123, 124, 126, 133, 211.

Johnson, Andrew, I, 103, 104, 124, 562.

John Swinton's Paper, boycott, II, 364, 365; contract labour, II, 372; National Union Labor Party, II, 465; strikes, II, 363; trade unions and the Knights, II, 414.

Jonas, Alexander, II, 278, 300.

Journeyman, Conditions: bricklayers, I, 405; class conflict, I, 64; competition, control, I, 57; competition, convicts, I, 155, 344–347; competition, women, I, 342–344; merchant-capitalist system, I, 339, 379; politics, I, 234; printing trade, I, 446, 447, 448; Weitling, I, 514.
Demands: apprenticeship, I, 339, 340–342, 590–595; ten-hour day, I, 159–162, 234, 310.

Junior Sons of '76, call national labour convention, II, 201, 202, 235; organised, II, 196, 201; platform, II, 202n.

Jurassian Federation, Bakunin's stronghold, II, 215.

K

Kalloch, I. S. Reverend, mayor of San Francisco, II, 261, 262.

Kearney, Denis, II, 249, 250, 254–264.

Kellogg, Edward, I, 20, 519, 556; II, 119–121, 225.

Kelley, O. H., and Patrons of Husbandry, II, 172.

Kennady, A. M., II, 113, 147, 147n, 148.

Kentucky, unions, 1863, 1864, II, 19.

Klinge, Karl, socialist, II, 228, 230, 273.

Knight, H. L., II, 255, 259, 261.

Knights of Labor, Conventions: Cincinnati, 1891, II, 494; Cleveland, 1882, II, 326; District Assembly 1 at Philadelphia, 1876, II, 333; District Assembly 3 at Pittsburgh, II, 333; Minneapolis General Assembly, II, 412, 413; Omaha, 1892, II, 494; Pittsburgh, 1876, II, 236, 239; Pittsburgh, 1881, II, 321, 322; Reading, II, 335; Richmond, II, 408; Terre Haute, II, 318–320.
Organisation: assemblies, II, 197, 199–201; beginnings, II, 196,

197; centralisation, II, 334; elements, II, 344, 345, 382, 482, 488, 492; form, II, 339; growth, II, 339, 344, 350, 381, 396, 413, 414, 422, 423, 482; Ocean Association, II, 420; resistance fund, II, 340, 341; sojourners, II, 198; Southern Farmers' Alliance, II, 489, 491.
Policies: arbitration, 11, 374; boycott, II, 317, 364, 365, 419, 444; Catholic Church, II, 339; co-operation, I, 18; II, 351, 352, 430–438; eight-hour movement, II, 378, 379, 392, 485; immigration, II, 372, 373; monopoly, II, 362; political action, II, 243, 351, 462, 463, 488, 493; principles, II, 198, 335, 495; secrecy, II, 201, 232, 338, 339; socialism, II, 519; strikes, II, 200, 334, 347–350, 367–369, 383, 384, 394, 416, 417, 419, 420–422, 483, 483n, 498, 499.
Trade Unions: American Federation of Labor, II, 484, 488; attitude, II, 352; brewery workers, II, 488; conflict, II, 397–399, 402, 405, 406, 409, 484; federation, II, 328, 329; machinists, II, 486; miners, II, 425, 426, 487; moulders, II, 344n, 401n; movement within, II, 342, 346, 427; trade assemblies, II, 428, 486; trade councils, II, 311n.
See also, Powderly, Terence V.; Sovereign, James R.

Knights of Saint Crispin, aims, II, 77; apprenticeship, II, 84; Chinese labour, II, 141, 149; co-operation, II, 79, 140, 141, 152; eight-hour day, II, 140; factory system, II, 76, 77; green hands, II, 77; in seventies, II, 152, 153; Knights of Labor, II, 200, 345; membership, II, 177; organised, II, 77; Phillips, Thomas, II, 39, 40n; political action, II, 140; strikes, II, 77, 78.

Kommunistischen Klub in New York, II, 207n.

Kriege, Herman, and land reform, I, 534, 535.

L

Label, anti-Chinese, II, 266, 267,

401; cigar makers, II, 266n, 401n; endorsed, II, 330; Knights of Labor, II, 401n, 435.

Labour Congresses, 1866: co-operation, II, 101; eight-hour question, II, 98; land question, II, 100, 101; organisation, II, 101, 102; political action, II, 99; representation, II, 96, 97; trade unionism, II, 98; women in industry, II, 101.

1867: constitution, II, 116; cooperation, II, 118, 119; eight-hour day, II, 118; greenbackism, II, 119; immigration, II, 116–118; Negro, II, 118; principles, II, 122; representation, II, 115.

1868: greenbackism, 11, 128; political action, II, 125, 129; representation, II, 126; strikes, II, 129; women present, II, 127, 128.

1869: acts, II, 134, 135n; effect of Sylvis' death, II, 134; representation, II, 133.

1870: Chinese problem, II, 146; constitution, II, 146; Negro question, II, 144, 145; political action, II, 145, 146; representation, II, 144.

Labour Conventions, National, Alleghany City, 1879, II, 284, 285; Baltimore Congress, 1866, II, 96; carpenters, 1836, I, 452; cigar makers, 1864, 11, 69; Cincinnati, 1887, II, 464, 465; Cincinnati, 1891, II, 494; Cleveland, 1873, II, 159–161; Cleveland, 1875, II, 169; Cleveland, 1882, II, 326–328; Columbus, 1886, II, 409–412; combmakers, 1836, I, 452; currency reformers, 1878, II, 244; Indianapolis, 1874, II, 166–168; industrial, 1870, II, 153; Knights of Labor, II, 333, 334, 407, 493; Labor Congress, 1867, II, 115–122; 1868, II, 125, 130; 1869, II, 133; 1870, II, 144–147; loom weavers, 1836, I, 453; Louisville, 1864, II, 35, 36; Machinists and Blacksmiths, 1861, II, 13; National Trades' Union, 1834, I, 425–429; National Trades' Union, 1835, I, 430–433; National Trades' Union, 1836, I, 433–436; Newark, 1877, II, 277–279; New York, 1883,

II, 328; nominating, 1876, II, 170; Omaha, 1892, II, 494; Philadelphia, 1861, II, 11; Philadelphia, 1886, II, 403; Pittsburgh, 1876, II, 236; Pittsburgh, 1881, II, 321–326; Pittsburgh, 1883, II, 293–296; Rochester, 1874, II, 162–165; St. Louis farmers, 1889, II, 490–492; Terre Haute, 1881, II, 318–320; Typographical Union, 1837, I, 450, 453; Tyrone, 1875, II, 235.

Labour Papers, *American Banker and Workingmen's Leader*, II, 16; *Arbeiter*, II, 16; *Baltimore Trades' Union*, I, 360; Chicago, II, 282; *Chicagoer Arbeiter-Zeitung*, II, 282; *Daily Press*, I, 617; II, 17, 23; depression, I, 456; in 1863–1873, II, 15–17; *International Labor Union*, II, 304; *Journal*, I, 248; *Mechanic's Own*, II, 16; *Miner and Artisan*, II, 17; *National Labourer*, I, 360, 375; *National Trades' Union*, I, 360; *New England Artisan*, I, 360; *New England Mechanic*, II, 16; official, I, 360; II, 278, 281; *People's Rights*, I, 527; *Philadelphia Trades' Union*, I, 360; *Portland Mechanic*, I, 291; *Practical Politician and Workingmen's Advocate*, I, 291; *Reform, Die*, I, 618; *Republik der Arbeiter*, I, 507; revolutionary, I, 564; *Sentinel*, I, 248, 268; *Soziale Republik*, II, 16; *Subterranean*, I, 527; *Washingtonian*, I, 360; *Working Man's Advocate*, II, 16; *Working Man's National Advocate*, II, 618; Working Man's Party, I, 268; *Young America*, I, 530.

See also, *Alarm, The; Arbeiterstimme; Arbeiterstimme des Westens; Arbeiter-Zeitung; Boycotter, The; Daily Evening Voice; Delaware Free Press; Delnicke Listy; Emancipator*, Milwaukee; *Fincher's Trades' Review; Gleicheit, Die; John Swinton's Paper; Labor Standard; Leader, The; Mechanics' Free Press; Milwaukee Sozialist; National Socialist; New Yorker Volkszeitung; Nye Tid;*

Socialist; Sozial-Demokrat; Sozialist, Der; Standard, The; Tageblatt, Philadelphia; *Vorbote; Woodhull and Claflin's Weekly.*

Labour Party, early attempts to form, I, 17, 18.

Labor Party of Illinois: Lassallean ideas, II, 227; International, II, 233; organisation, II, 228; political action, II, 229, 230; trade unionism, II, 228; Union Congress, II, 270.
See also *Vorbote.*

Labor Party of Newark, joins Social Democrat Party of N. A., II, 230.

Labor Standard, control, II, 275; Newark convention, II, 278; socialist organ, II, 271; trade unionism, II, 274.

Laissez-faire, argument of journeymen, I, 150.

Lake Seamen's Union, Cleveland convention, II, 326; established, II, 313; Terre Haute Conference, II, 318.
See also, Powers, Richard.

Land Policy, Bovay's, I, 549; class struggle, I, 4; free land, I, 4, 526; II, 360; government, I, 562; Hine, II, 128; homestead law, 1862, I, 562; immigration, I, 489; Industrial Congresses, I, 550, 551, 557, 558, 561; II, 100, 101; Kriege, I, 534, 535; manufacturers, I, 562; rents, limitation of, I, 558; single-tax resolution, II, 327; slave holders, I, 563; Trades' Union, I, 428, 433; western ideas, I, 563.
See also, Agrarianism.

Lassalle, Ferdinand, II, 205–207.

Lassalleanism, Campbell's money reform, II, 121; Chicago, II, 272, 273; depression, II, 227, 228; German, II, 207; German Workingmen's Union, General, II, 207; Marxism, II, 270, 271; political action, II, 206, 271; trade unionism, II, 271–274.
See also, Klinge, Karl; Labor Party of Illinois; Lyser, Gustav; McGuire, P. J.; Schlägel, E.; Social Democratic Party of North America; Strasser, Adolph.

Layton, R. D., and Knights of Labor, II, 321n.

Leader, The, George-Hewitt campaign, II, 451; socialism, II, 451, 459.

League of Deliverance, boycott of Chinese goods, II, 267.

Leffingwell, Samuel L., Cleveland convention, 1882, II, 321; Pittsburgh convention, 1881, II, 322; Terre Haute convention, II, 319.

Legal tender acts, see Financial system.

Lehr and Wehr Verein, militarism, II, 280, 387.

Liebknecht, Wilhelm, German correspondent of Arbeiter Zeitung, II, 221.

Litchman, Charles H., II, 79, 250, 408n, 468.

Lloyd, Henry D., I, 19; warns against monopoly, II, 360.

Lockouts, Boston printers, II, 17; Boston ship-carpenters, II, 312; brewery workers, II, 488; Champion Reaper Company, II, 415; Chicago brick layers, II, 423–425; Chicago packing industry, II, 385n, 418, 419; in 1886, II, 417n; Jamestown, II, 414; knit goods, II, 418; McCormick Reaper Company, II, 392; Moberly, Missouri, II, 368, 369; Philadelphia cordwainers, I, 122; policy, II, 195; Troy, II, 418.

Locomotive Engineers, Brotherhood of, Arthur, P. M., II, 67, 68; benefit system, II, 68; Brotherhood of the Footboard, II, 62; growth, II, 47; incorporation, II, 66; organised, II, 62; piece work, II, 62; railway consolidation, II, 61, 62; strike on Michigan Southern, II, 64, 65; Wilson, II, 63, 67.

Lottery System, demand for abolition, I, 223.

Lowell, factory system, I, 429; politics, I, 316.

Lowell Female Labor Reform Association, hours of labour, I, 539.

Lucker, Labor Congress, 1868, II, 126; on conspiracy, II, 133.

Luther, Seth, I, 312, 319, 325, 380, 422n.

Lynn, shoemakers of, I, 102, 105; women organise, I, 355.

Lyser, Gustav, II, 232, 233, 272, 281.

M

MacFarlane, Robert, and prison labour, I, 492.
McBride, John, II, 199, 364, 513.
McCormick Harvester Company, lockout, II, 392.
McDonald, Mary, II, 127, 129.
McDonnell, J. P., II, 222, 226, 271, 274, 280, 288, 302, 304, 306, 308.
McGlynn, Father, II, 453–461.
McGuire, P. J., II, 231n, 232, 235, 270, 271, 275, 279, 286, 302, 308n, 314n, 319, 325, 403, 404, 412, 418, 428, 442, 510n.
McLaughlin, William J., II, 138, 140, 142.
McMakin, John, II, 446, 454, 455, 457.
McNamara, dynamite case, II, 528.
McNeill, George E., I, 19; II, 92n, 138–142, 163,·165, 184.
Machinery, introduction, II, 44, 75, 358; in shoe industry, II, 76, 77.
See also, Bargaining Power; Competition.
Machinists and Blacksmiths, National Union of, apprenticeship, II, 84; co-operation, II, 112; depression, II, 9, 10; eight-hour movement, II, 57, 58, 89, 95; federation, II, 157; grievances, II, 8; growth, II, 9, 20, 45, 47, 176; intellectual ascendency, II, 56; Knights of Labor, II, 200; Labor Congress, 1866, II, 13; national trades' assembly, II, 39; New York picketing bill, II, 23n; organised, II, 6, 9; Pittsburgh convention, 1861, II, 13; revival, 1870, II, 58; strike against Baldwin Locomotive Works, II, 9.
Macune, Dr. C. W., II, 489, 491.
Maine, Charitable Mechanics Association, I, 79; Greenbackism, II, 245; monopoly grants, I, 40; subsidised steel industry, I, 37; ten-hour law, I, 54; unions, 1863–1864, II, 19.
Market, theories of Schmoller and Bücher, I, 26, 27; versus production theories, I, 26–29.
Markets, Extension of, Development: causes, I, 6; canals, I, 438, 439;

Civil War, II, 22; colonial period, I, 5, 6, 28; domestic market propaganda, I, 73, 89, 91, 92; historical view, I, 6; itinerant to custom-order stage, I, 36, 37; railroads, I, 8, 153, 154, 439; II, 3–5, 61, 148, 358; retail shop to wholesale-order period, I, 61–63.
Influence: agriculture, I, 32, 33; apprenticeship, II, 81; California industries, II, 148; class antagonism, I, 26–28, 106; competition, commodity, I, 440; competition, labour, I, 440, 441; II, 43, 44; contracts, I, 29; co-operation, I, 95–100; export trade, I, 149; locomotive engineers, I, 101–104, 338; moulders' trade, II, 6; national trade union, I, 441; production, I, 71; typographical union, II, 58; wholesale jobber, II, 359.
Marx, Karl, I, 20, 26–29, 44; II, 204, 205, 207, 214, 215.
Maryland, trade regulations, I, 4; unions, 1863, 1864, II, 19.
Massachusetts, bread assize, I, 52, 55; bounties granted, I, 37, 38, 39, 43; child labour investigation, I, 331; Chinese labour, II, 149; Greenbackism, II, 246; lottery conducted, I, 93; Mechanics' Association, I, 73; monopolies granted, I, 40; politics, I, 315–318; II, 92, 102, 138–144; price regulation, I, 50–52; quality regulation, I, 47; ten-hour movement, I, 546; unemployment, 1837, I, 457; unions, 1863, 1864, I, 19, 20; women cigar makers, I, 343.
See also, Boston.
Masquerier, Lewis, I, 523, 531, 532, 547.
Master Mechanics' Benevolent Society, benefits, I, 85.
Mazzini, Joseph, harmony of capital and labour, II, 205.
Mechanics of Boston, Associated, I, 74.
Mechanics and Manufacturers, Association of, Providence, promote inventions, I, 76, 77.
Mechanics and Tradesmen, General Society of, I, 72; activities, I, 81; credit facilities, I, 89; in-

corporated, I, 84; letter to Associated Mechanics of Boston, I, 74.

Mechanics and Tradesmen of the County of Kings, incorporation, I, 86, 87.

Mechanics of Massachusetts, Association of, I, 73, 77.

Mechanics' Free Press, circulation, I, 205; election results, I, 204, 213, 215; influence, I, 207, 210; mechanics' lien law, I, 220, 280; political action, I, 239; Workingmen's Measures, I, 217, 218.

Mechanics' liens, I, 12; II, 324; agitation, I, 220, 221, 279, 296, 297, 318; Knights of Labor, II, 336; labour parties, I, 329.

Mechanics' Union of Trade Associations, I, 15; decline, I, 191, 192; politics, I, 191; purposes, I, 190.

Merchants' Associations, and employers' associations, I, 132, 133.

Merchant-capitalist, apprenticeship, I, 339–341; ascendency, I, 104, 154; coming, I, 101, 102; convict labour, I, 344–347; cordwainers, I, 441; labour-cost theory of exchange, I, 510; master and journeymen unite against, I, 379; production, I, 338, 339; retailer, I, 17; ship-building industry, I, 309, 310; shoe industry, II, 78; sweating introduced, I, 102, 103; Weitling, I, 543.

Metal Workers' Federation Union of America, model syndicalist union, II, 297, 298.

Metal Workers Union, Armed Section of, II, 388.

Meyer, Siegfried, II, 207, 209.

Micalonda, J., and Black International, II, 296.

Militarism, socialist, II, 280, 281, 284.

Militia system, abolition demanded, I, 281, 282, 296, 298, 318; burden, I, 180; in Pennsylvania, 1822, I, 221, 222.

Miller, Joseph D., I, 434, 470.

Milwaukee, Knights of St. Crispin organised, II, 77; socialism, II, 273, 274, 277, 533.

Milwaukee, *Sozialist*, II, 233.

Mine Workers of America, United, organisation, II, 487, 500.

Miners and Mine Laborers of United States, National Federation of, interstate agreement, II, 426; organised, II, 425.

Miners' Benevolent and Protective Association, II, 211.

Miners' National Association, and Knights of Labor, II, 200.

Ming, Alexander, Sr., I, 240, 245.

Minimum Wage, demanded, I, 104, 117, 118; first strike for, I, 25.

Missouri, Greenbackism, II, 248; unions, 1863, 1864, II, 19.

Mitchell, John, and education, I, 226.

Molders' International Union, Iron, apprenticeship, II, 50, 84; benefits, II, 175n; co-operation, II, 53–56; employers' associations, II, 49; epitomizes labour movement, II, 48; growth, II, 45, 46; Knights of Labor, II, 352n; Labor Congress, 1866, II, 96; lethargy of 1861, 1862, II, 14; locals, II, 120; New York picketing bill, II, 23n; organised, II, 5, 7, 313; strikes, II, 51, 52, 56; war activities, II, 49; weakness, II, 7.

Molly Maguires, Ancient Order of Hibernians, II, 181, 187; "long strike," II, 184, 185; McParlan, James, II, 184; organised, II, 196; politics, II, 183; secrecy, II, 201; trial, II, 185; violence, II, 181, 183, 184n.

Monopoly, abolition demanded, I, 218, 219, 296, 298, 318, 458, 459; corporations, I, 458, 459; grants, I, 40, 43, 44.

Moore, Ely, I, 20, 360, 367n, 369–371, 394, 425, 461, 463.

Morgan, Thomas J., II, 279, 282, 283, 289, 387, 509.

Most, Johann, 293n, 294.

Muhlenberg, Henry A., I, 459, 460, 461.

Mule Spinners' Association, National, at Cleveland convention, 1882, II, 326.

Murch, Thompson, II, 245, 249, 327, 329.

Musicians' Union, I, 8; similarity to guilds, I, 55.

Mutual loans, by early protective organisations, I, 81, 82.

Myers, Isaac I., Negro labour movement, II, 137, 144, 145.

N

Napoleonic wars, depression following, I, 134–138.

National economy, I, 26, 27.

National Labor Congress, of 1874, II, 196.

National Laborer, cited, I, 99; on co-operation, I, 468.

National Labor Union, after 1870, II, 153; *Die Arbeiter Union* affiliates, II, 223; Chinese question, II, 149, 150; conventions, II, 142, 153–155, 227; disintegration, II, 155, 157; eight-hour day, II, 87, 94, 142; greenbackism, II, 123, 224; immigration, II, 116–118; in 1867, II, 112; International Workingmen's Association, II, 86, 87, 131, 132, 206, 208, 209; labour congresses, II, 96–102, 115–118, 125–130, 133, 134, 144–147; Negro, II, 137; New England Labour Reform League, II, 139; organised, II, 86; political action, II, 141, 145, 146; trade unionism, II, 152; Sylvis, II, 130, 131; Trevellick, II, 137, 138.

National Party, demands, II, 245; Greenback platform, II, 241; organised, II, 244, 245.

National Reform Association, need for organisation, I, 547.
  See also, Industrial Congress.

National Socialist, policy, II, 280; publication suspended, II, 281.

National Union Labor Party, order of the Videttes, II, 469, 470; organised, II, 465; political results, II, 466–470.

Neebe, Oscar, pardoned, II, 393.

Negro, anti-slavery agitation, I, 4, 12; labour problem, II, 114, 116, 118, 135, 619; organisation, II, 135, 136, 137, 145, 312; Republican party, II, 136, 145, 146.

Newark, Workingmen's Party Convention, II, 277, 278.

New Democracy, platform, II, 210; failure and reorganisation, II, 210, 211.

New England, banks, I, 348; child labour, I, 320, 321; education, I, 300, 321–324; greenbackism, II, 245; ship-building, I, 309, 310; ten-hour movement, I, 325;

women in factories, I, 422; workingmen's movement, I, 290–293, 298, 299.
  See also, Boston; Connecticut; Massachusetts; New Hampshire; Rhode Island; Vermont.

New England Association of Farmers, Mechanics, and Other Workingmen, aims, I, 306, 307, 318, 319; banking system, I, 319, 320; child labour, I, 320, 321; class lines, I, 304; conventions, I, 308, 309, 312–315; education, I, 183, 184, 321–324; factory conditions, I, 305, 306, 320, 321, 331; organised, I, 302, 306, 314, 315; political action, I, 309, 315; Thompsonville case, I, 313; trades' unions, I, 314.

New England Boot and Shoe Lasters, established, II, 313.

New England Labour Reform League, convention, 1869, II, 138; eight-hour day, II, 139; Proudhonism and the Intellectuals, II, 139.

New England Society for the Promotion of Manufactures and Mechanic Arts, sales, I, 98.

New England Working Men's Association, 1844–1849, associationists control, I, 538; conventions, I, 537–540; co-operation, I, 539; political action, I, 539; ten-hour day, I, 537–540.

New Hampshire, Greenbackism, II, 244; ten-hour law, I, 541; trade restrictions, I, 39; unions, 1863, 1864, II, 19.

New Haven, labour party, II, 277; trade restrictions, I, 39.

New Jersey, bounties, I, 39, 92; education, 1835, I, 182; eight-hour law, II, 107; lotteries, I, 93; political action, II, 286; unions, 1863, 1864, II, 19.

New York, apprenticeship, I, 77, 78; bread assize, I, 52–54; Central Labor Union, II, 441; city assembly, I, 456; city industrial congresses, I, 552, 553; commission stores, I, 94; conspiracy cases, I, 164, 409, 410; coopers, I, 56; corporations, I, 458; education, I, 328; eight-hour day, II, 108; employers' associations, I, 402, 404; General Society of Mechanics and Tradesmen, I, 72,

81; greenbackism, II, 240, 242, 246, 248; housing conditions, I, 490, 491; labour party, II, 277; mechanics' liens, I, 329; militia law, I, 330; politics in 1835, I, 461–465; printers, I, 50, 109, 112, 113, 133, 134, 580, 581; prison reform, I, 346; unemployment, I, 135, 457; rag money, I, 349; rents, I, 349; riots, I, 415, 416, 417; socialism, II, 282; social party, II, 207–209; state Workingmen's Assembly, II, 211; strikes, I, 53, 54, 55, 110, 111, 157, 365, 382, 383, 395–397, 478–484, 576; II, 151, 178, 367n; ten hour bill, I, 542, 543; Trades and Labour Council, II, 226; Trades' Union Convention, I, 425, 430; unionism, I, 109, 337, 358, 363, 364, 366; II, 19, 20; United Labor Party, II, 455; women organise, I, 356.
See also, Cordwainers; New York Journeymen; Typographical Society; Working Men's Party.
New York Amalgamated Trades and Labor Union, enforced boycotts, II, 311.
New Yorker Volkszeitung, greenbackism, II, 286, 287, 288; Henry George, II, 451; socialism, II, 300, 449.
Nye Tid, Chicago socialist paper, II, 282; agitates against Greenback compromise, II, 287.

O

Ohio, eight-hour law, II, 107; greenbackism, II, 241, 247; tenhour law, I, 543.
Ohio, State Miners' Union, and Hocking Valley Strike, II, 363.
Open Shop, and the trust, II, 526.
Open Union, ineffective weapon, II, 195.
Orvis, John, II, 138, 173.
Owen Robert, I, 14, 173, 493, 494, 538, 548, 549.
Owen, Robert Dale, I, 20, 226n, 240, 240n, 242, 243, 247–253, 260n, 272, 273n.
Owenism, I, 14; revival, I, 504.

P

Panics, see Industrial Cycles.
Parsons, Albert R., anarchist, II, 250n, 273, 279, 282, 283, 284n, 289, 291, 296, 302, 389, 390, 392–394.
Parsons, Lucy E., and tramps, II, 389.
Paterson, cotton operatives' strike, I, 418.
Patrons of Husbandry, II, 196.
Pennsylvania, banking reform, I, 330; bounties granted, I, 37, 38, 39, 42; cabinet makers, I, 99, 336, 337, 467; child labour, I, 331; education, I, 223–229, 328; eight-hour law, II, 108; factory workers, II, 375, 419, 420; Franklin Institute, I, 78; greenbackism, II, 242, 244, 245, 247; militia law, I, 221, 222; Molly Maguires, II, 181–185; politics, I, 195, 459–461; price regulation, I, 50; ten-hour legislation, I, 543; unions, II, 19, 20.
See also, Philadelphia; Working Men's Party.
Pennsylvania Society to Encourage Manufactures, I, 74; extends credit, I, 91, 92; opens warehouse, I, 94.
Peoples' Party, organised, II, 494; platform, II, 509; trade unions, II, 512.
People's Party of Erie, Pennsylvania, organised, I, 207.
People's Party of Wisconsin, platform, II, 462.
Personal Rights, against property rights, I, 12.
Phelps, Alfred W., II, 113, 115, 118, 126.
Philadelphia, banks, I, 219n; cabinet makers, I, 336, 337; carpenters, I, 68, 78, 80–82, 84, 97, 118, 127, 128; commission stores, I, 94; conventions, I, 214, 333, 434, 470, 471; II, 11, 209, 270; co-operation, I, 96, 97, 467–469; education, I, 226, 227, 469; employers' associations, I, 402, 403; greenbackism, II, 247; lotteries, I, 93; marketing agency, I, 100; population, I, 176n, 490; riots, I, 407; strikes, I, 25, 69, 186–189, 383, 389–392, 397–399, 399–401, 417, 478–484, 576; trade

unionism, I, 109, 114, 169, 184,
189–191, 351, 352, 359, 363, 375;
II, 24–26, 277; unemployment,
I, 135; women organise, I, 343,
355.
See also, Cordwainers of Phila-
delphia.
Philadelphia Aurora, defends cord-
wainers, I, 142.
Philadelphia Domestic Society, I,
92; dividends, I, 99; opens
warehouse, I, 94.
Philadelphia Journeymen House
Painters' Association, and
trades' assembly, II, 24.
Philadelphia Society of Master
Cordwainers, purpose, I, 132;
purpose changed, I, 133, 134.
Phillips, Thomas, II, 16, 39n, 40,
110.
Phillips, Wendell, II, 88n, 102, 138,
140, 142, 143, 144n, 155.
Pinkerton detectives, strike breakers,
II, 186, 366, 415, 496, 497.
Pittsburgh, conventions, II, 292,
321–326, 333; labour party, II,
277.
Pittsburgh and Vicinity Manufacturing Association, co-operative
marketing, I, 95; dividends, I,
99; sales, I, 98.
See also, Cordwainers of Pittsburgh.
Pittsburgh Manifesto of International Working People's Association, II, 295.
Political Commonwealth, see New
Democracy.
Political Action, Beginning, I, 18.
Elections: 1830, I, 262–268,
287–289, 290–294; 1832, I, 269;
1836, 1837, I, 465, 466; 1866,
II, 102; 1876, II, 171; 1877, II,
273, 277, 279; 1878, II, 245,
246; 1879, II, 282–284; 1880,
II, 290; 1886, II, 462, 463;
1887, II, 466–470.
Issues: agrarianism, I, 531; anti-
monopoly, II, 168; Chinese, II,
260–262; class antagonism, I,
192, 193; eight-hour day, I,
103–109; financial reform, II,
142; greenbackism, II, 242, 243,
250; in 1828, I, 216; in 1830,
I, 217, 221–229; in 1877, I, 274–
284; in 1892, II, 518; land reform, I, 535; Lassalleanism, II,
227–234; religion, I, 272, 273;

Stewardism, II, 91; ten-hour
day, I, 537–539.
Massachusetts: 1833, 1834, I,
315–317; 1865, II, 92; 1869, II,
141, 142; 1876, II, 143, 144.
New Jersey, I, 287.
New York: 1829, I, 238–240;
1830, I, 232; 1835, I, 461–465;
1877, II, 242.
Ohio: II, 248.
Opinions: farmers' alliance, II,
489; Lassalle, II, 206; newspapers, I, 144; Schilling, Robert, II, 163; socialist, II, 278,
279, 449; Walsh, I, 528.
Organised Labour: American Federation of Labor, II, 509, 529;
Central Labor Union, II, 444,
446; convention action, I, 558–
560; II, 99, 100, 129, 130, 153,
154, 155, 161, 238, 324, 327;
Crispins, II, 140, 153; Federation of Organised Trades, II,
463, 464; International Workingmen's Association, II, 218,
219, 250; Knights of Labor, II,
341, 350–352, 488, 492–493; Mechanics' Union of Trade Associations, I, 191; Molly Maguires,
II, 183; National Labor Union,
II, 114; trade union, II, 152,
158, 317; trades' assemblies, II,
23, 38; trades' union, I, 361,
410, 411, 426.
Pennsylvania: 1828, I, 195, 459–
461; II, 247.
Philadelphia, II, 93.
Political Parties, anti-monopoly, II,
264; Equal Rights, I, 463–465;
Erie People's, I, 207, 208; Fe-
male Labor Reform Association,
I, 533; Independent Party,
Massachusetts, II, 141; Loco-
Foco Party, I, 462; National
Party of California, II, 255–
261; National Party of Ohio,
II, 241.
See also, Association of Working
People of New Castle County;
Citizens' Alliance; Greenback
Labor Party, National; Green-
back Party; Labor Party of
Illinois; Labor Party of New-
ark; League of Deliverance;
National Party; National Re-
form Association; National
Union Labor Party; New
Democracy; New England Asso-

ciation of Farmers, Mechanics, and Other Workingmen; New England Working Men's Association; People's Party; People's Party of Erie, Pennsylvania; People's Party of Wisconsin; Progressive Democracy; Progressive Labor Party; Radical Labor Party; Revolutionary Socialist Party; Social Democratic Party; Social Democratic Party of North America; Social Party; Socialist Labor Party; United Labor Party; Working Men's Party; Workingmen's Party of California; Workingmen's Party of the United States.

Pomeroy, Mark, editor *Pomeroy's Democrat*, II, 246.

Pools, in eighties, II, 360.

Populist movement, see People's Party.

Portsmouth, trade society, I, 72.

Post, Louis F., II, 451, 459.

Powderly, Terence V., II, 56, 163n, 166, 345n, 347, 351, 352, 370, 372, 374, 378, 379, 384, 408n, 412, 419, 427, 430, 431, 452, 464, 469, 483n, 491, 494.

Powers, Richard, II, 318, 321, 322, 323, 327, 328.

Prices, bread assize, I, 52, 53; building associations, I, 574; Civil War, II, 5; conflict, I, 49; competition, I, 63, 64; co-operation, II, 37; coopers, I, 56; employers' associations, II, 27; fluctuating, I, 11; II, 6; greenbackism, II, 121; in 1835, I, 348, 349; in 1836, I, 396, 397, 398, 435; in 1853, I, 488; labour cost theory of exchange, I, 510; legal tender acts, 1862, II, 14, 15; merchant-capitalist, I, 102, 106; merchants' associations, I, 133; price bargain dominates wage bargain, I, 70; regulation, I, 7, 50–52, 58–61, 68, 69; rents, I, 491; term, I, 50; unionism, I, 488; wages, I, 150, 396, 415, 416, 435, 582, 600; II, 15, 110; Warren's time stores, I, 511; Weitling's bank of exchange, I, 514.

Price-wage bargain, I, 22–36.

Printers, collective bargaining, I, 122; employer membership, I, 118; grievances, I, 114; locals, I, 112, 113, 135, 136; organise, I, 109; prices, I, 112. See also, Typographical Societies.

Prison Labour, see Convict Labour.

Prison Reform, Auburn model, I, 346; in twenties, I, 345.

Producers' Exchange Association, I, 96.

Production, Brisbane, I, 499; cheap methods, I, 154, 155; Engels' theory, I, 27–29; foreign competition, I, 72; Hobson's theory, I, 28; inventions, I, 76, 77; market theory, I, 26–29; markets, I, 6, 71; Marxian theory, I, 26–29; merchant-capitalist, I, 338–340; methods improved, I, 76; sweat shop, I, 102–104; Vandervelde's theory, I, 26–29.

Progressive Democracy, established, II, 454; named United Labor Party, II, 455.

Progressive Labor Party, platform, II, 460; nominate Swinton, II, 461.

Property, in business, II, 505, 506; factor in industrial evolution, I, 28, 29.

Property rights against personal rights, I, 12.

Property values, influenced by immigration, I, 10.

Prosperity, see Industrial Cycles.

Protectionism, I, 10, 17; apprenticeship, I, 56; arguments, I, 42; bounties, I, 37, 38; capitalistic system, I, 44; courts favour manufacturers, I, 149; domestic and Tradesmen, I, 72, 81; General Society of Mechanics and Tradesmen, I, 72, 81; guilds, I, 46–48; Homestead strike, II, 497n; limited, I, 43, 44; manufacturers' monopolies, I, 40; non-importation agreements, I, 40, 41, 72; Pennsylvania Society to Encourage Manufactures, I, 74; producers revolt, I, 49, 50; tariff, I, 41–44, 74, 104; II, 220, 237, 294, 295, 298, 324, 327, 329; tariff and child labour, I, 319; tariff and factory system, I, 429; tariff and wages, I, 443; tariff war, II, 14.

See also, Closed shop; Conspiracy; Employers' association.
Providence, Association of Mechanics and Manufacturers, I, 72, 76.
Provident Society of House Carpenters', I, 85.
Pullman Company, strike, II, 502.
Putnam, Mary Kellogg, II, 126, 127.

R

Race problem, I, 10; versus class problem, II, 252–257, 259.
See also, anti-Chinese Agitation; Negro.
Radical Labor Party, Chicago, II, 467.
Railroad Brotherhood, II, 309; Adamson Act, II, 530n; Locomotive Engineers, II, 313; Locomotive Firemen, II, 313; Railroad Conductors, II, 186, 187, 313; theories, II, 309, 310.
Railways, see Markets, Extension of.
Railway Union, American, organised, II, 500, 501; Pullman strike, II, 502, 503, 508.
Rand School of Social Sciences, II, 207, 209.
Redpath, James, establishes Progressive Democracy, II, 454.
Referendum, advocated, 1850, II, 210.
Reid, Whitelaw, *Tribune* boycott, II, 317.
Representative Assembly of Trades and Labor Unions, organised in California, II, 266.
Republik der Arbeiter, on co-operation, I, 567.
Retail merchant, advantage, I, 102.
Retail-shop stage, competition, I, 57; co-operation, I, 96; journeymen, I, 56–60; price-maintenance, I, 60, 61; transition to wholesale order period, I, 61, 62.
Revolutionary Socialist Party, organised, II, 292.
Revolutionary War, depression following, I, 83; improvements following, I, 61; industry protected, I, 41, 42; Non-Importation Act, I, 72.
Rhode Island, protective tariff, I, 42; subsidised cloth industry, I, 37; suffrage, I, 319; ten-hour

law, I, 543; unions, 1863–1864, II, 19.
Riots, anti-Catholic, I, 415; anti-Chinese, II, 253; dock hands, I, 417; food, 1837, I, 463, 464; gag law, II, 257, 258; Haymarket Square, II, 392–394; Martinsburg, II, 187, 188; Milwaukee, II, 296; of 1877, II, 276; Philadelphia coal heavers, I, 377; Pittsburgh, 1877, II, 188–190; railway construction hands, I, 416; Tompkins Square, II, 220.
Robinson, William D., and locomotive engineers, II, 63, 67.
Rochdale plan of co-operation, II, 205; in America, II, 40; Sovereigns of Industry, II, 173.
Roney, Frank, II, 258, 258n, 259, 266.
Roosevelt, Clinton, I, 463, 549.
Root, General Erastus, in New York politics, I, 264–266.
Rosenberg, V. L., socialist leader, II, 515, 516.
Roy, Andrew, miner, II, 248.
Ryckman, Lewis W., I, 537, 538, 548, 549.

S

Sabotage, early syndicalism, II, 298.
Saffin, William, II, 152, 157.
Sailors, strikes, I, 110, 111.
Samuel, John, co-operationist, II, 25, 25n, 435.
Sand-lot meetings, California, II, 253, 255, 256.
San Francisco *Chronicle*, organ of Workingmen's Party of California, II, 256; opposes Workingmen's Party of California, II, 251.
San Francisco, Citizens' Protective Union, II, 263; municipal election, II, 261, 262.
Sanial, Lucien, II, 455, 515, 517, 519.
Sayward, William H., II, 424, 479.
Schäfer, John, political socialist, II, 274.
Schewitsch, Sergius E., socialist, II, 300, 446, 454, 456, 458, 459, 515.
Schilling, George, supports political-socialists, II, 279, 289.
Schilling, Robert, II, 76, 161, 163,

164, 165, 168, 170, 241, 244, 302, 336.

Schlägel, E., Lassallean, II, 99, 102, 115.

Schmoller, Gustav, I, 20, 26, 27.

Schulze-Delitzsch, system of Co-operation, see Co-operation.

Schwab, Justus, revolutionary socialist, II, 291.

Schwab, Michael, pardoned, II, 393.

Scranton, elects Powderly mayor, II, 245.

Seamen's Protective Union, under Roney's leadership, II, 266.

Seamen's Safety Bill, and Richard Powers, II, 327.

Shaw, Justice, Commonwealth v. Hunt decision, I, 411, 412.

Sherman Anti-Trust Act, Danbury Hatters' Case, II, 530; Debs case, II, 502, 503, 508; injunctions, II, 505; unions, II, 508, 509.

See also, Conspiracy.

Ship-builders, strike, I, 110.

Ship Carpenters' and Caulkers' National Union, and Knights of Labor, II, 200.

Shoe Industry, cheap labour stage, I, 103; collective bargaining, I, 121; cordwainers controversy, I, 58; Lynn, I, 102, 105; organisation, I, 109, 114; retail shop period, I, 62.

See also, Cordwainers; Shoemakers of Boston; Strikes.

Shoemakers' National Assembly, secede from Knights, II, 486.

Shoemakers of Boston, charter, I, 36, 47; fight competition, I, 45, 46.

Silk and Fur Hat Finishers' Union, established, II, 313.

Simpson, Stephen, I, 211n, 228.

Siney, John, II, 138, 152, 169, 180.

Single-tax, advocated, II, 327; Catholic Church, II, 456; Henry George, II, 448; socialism, II, 457-460.

Skidmore, Thomas, agrarian, I, 234-240, 242, 243-245, 269n, 271, 362.

Socialism, Conditions: Chicago, II, 282, 283; depression, I, 619; factional struggle, II, 233, 270, 449, 515, 516; Franco-Prussian War and German movement, II, 225; progress since 1900, II,

532, 533; strikes, II, 253, 276, 277.

Connection with: American Federation of Labor, II, 512; Communist Club, II, 206, 207; General German Workingmen's Union, II, 207, 208; Knights of Labor, II, 519; New York central labour bodies, II, 517; Pittsburgh convention, 1881, II, 322; Progressive Labor Party, II, 460; Radical Labor Party, II, 467, 468; Red International, II, 300n; Strasser, II, 309n; trade unions, II, 202, 225, 226, 279n, 281, 308n, 514; United Hebrew Trades, II, 518; Weydemeyer, I, 617, 618.

Theories: anarchism, II, 290-300; eight-hour movement, II, 391; evolution, I, 14, 21; II, 196, 204, 354; German forty-eighters, II, 204; greenbackism, II, 237, 239, 286-289; Henry George movement, II, 454-457; Lassalle, II, 205, 206; Marx, II, 205, 214, 215; militarism, II, 280, 281; political action versus trade union action, II, 218, 219, 271, 272-275, 278-280, 283, 284, 287n, 301-309; voluntary, II, 210.

See also, Becker, Johann; Berger, Victor; Carl, Conrad; Communist Club; De Leon, Daniel; Douai, Adolph; Eberhardt, Karl; German Workingmen's Union, General; German Social Democratic Workingmen's Union; Grottkau, Paul; Lassalle, Ferdinand; Lassalleanism; Marx, Karl; Meyer, Siegfried; National Labor Union; Rosenberg, V. L.; Social Party; Sorge, F. A.; Strasser, Adolph; Weydemeyer, Joseph.

Socialist, established in Chicago, II, 282.

Socialist Labor Party, convention, II, 284, 285; De Leon, II, 517, 518; ebb, II, 300; factions, II, 291, 450, 516; greenbackism, II, 286-288; New York Central labour bodies, II, 517; organised, II, 278, 519; political action, II, 277-290, 401; principles, II, 278, 279, 446; Red In-

ternational, II, 300n; United Labor Party, II, 451.
See also, Workingmen's Party of the United States.
Social Democratic Party, dissatisfied, II, 278; factional differences, II, 271; first labour convention, II, 202; Milwaukee election, II, 273, 277; organised, II, 218, 271; Union Congress, II, 270.
Social Democratic Party of North America, conventions, II, 231, 233, 235, 237, 238; organised, II, 230; unionism, II, 232.
See also, *Sozial-Demokrat.*
Social Party, failure and re-organisation, II, 209; of New York, II, 207; programme, II, 208.
Social-Republicans, and General German Workingmen's Union, II, 207.
"Society," term for trade union, I, 14.
"Sojourners," in Knights of Labor, II, 198, 342.
Solidarisme, I, 17.
Sons of Vulcan, Amalgamated Association of Iron and Steel Workers, II, 174; bargaining advantage of puddler, II, 80; growth, II, 47; sliding scale agreement, II, 80.
Sorge, F. A., I, 19, 207n, 209, 209n, 210, 211, 214–216, 216n, 221, 270, 276, 302, 304.
Sovereign, James R., II, 494, 495, 519.
Sovereigns of Industry, activities, II, 173, 174; constitution, II, 173; co-operation, II, 171, 172; failure, II, 175; Industrial Congresses, II, 163, 175; membership, 1874–1877, II, 173; origin, II, 172, 196; purposes, II, 172; trade unions, II, 174.
Sozial-Demokrat, advocates Lassellean platform, II, 234; becomes *Arbeiterstimme,* II, 271; Otto Walster editor, II, 233; party organ, II, 232.
See also, *Arbeiterstimme.*
Sozialist, Der, advocates political action, II, 449; eight-hour movement, II, 515.
Speyer, Carl, and International Labor Union, II, 302.

Speyer, J. G., and Trades and Labour Council, II, 226.
Spies, August, anarchist, II, 290, 291n, 294, 296, 387, 392–394.
St. Louis, central labour union, II, 389n; socialism, II, 282; strikes, II, 367n; tailors organise, I, 352, 353.
St. Patrick's Benefit Society, I, 85.
Standard, The, and Catholic Church, II, 456.
Stanton, Elizabeth Cady, at Labor Congress, 1868, II, 127.
Stevens, Uriah Smith, II, 197, 197n, 244, 247, 335, 347.
Steward, Ira, II, 16, 56, 86, 87, 89, 91, 92, 106, 138, 139, 140, 143, 280, 302, 303.
Stiebling, George C., II, 210, 216, 217, 232.
Stone Cutters' Company, established, I, 69; protects quality of goods, I, 83.
Stove Founders' National Defense Association, policy, II, 480, 481.
Stove Manufacturers, National Association of, arbitration, II, 480.
Strasser, Adolph, II, 217, 217n, 218, 231, 270, 271, 274, 302, 305, 306, 308, 309, 309n, 325, 400, 403, 404.
Streeter, A. J., II, 468, 469, 490.
Strikes, Conditions: Chinese, II, 146, 149; funds, I, 123, 124, 442; II, 59, 70, 311; immigration, I, 488, 597; injunction, II, 505–508; markets, I, 440, 441; store-order payment, I, 488; violence, I, 412; walking delegates, I, 126.
List: Baldwin Locomotive Works, II, 9; bakers, 1741, I, 53, 54; bookbinders, I, 399; bricklayers, II, 33, 123, 152, 312; Burlington, II, 474, 475, 507; carpenters, I, 69, 127, 128, 158–162, 186–189, 388, 389, 430, 466; II, 476, 477; cartmen, I, 55; cigar makers, II, 71, 72, 177, 178, 306, 363, 400; closed shop, I, 412; coal heavers, I, 417; collateral, I, 126; cordwainers, I, 105, 109, 128, 140, 144, 398, 399; during Civil War, II, 23; early, I, 25, 109, 111; eight-hour, II, 156, 385, 476–478; factory operatives, I, 419, 420; freight handlers, II, 349; general, I,

389–392; II, 298, 366; hatters, I, 338; Homestead, II, 473, 495–497; in 1833–1837, I, 478–484; in 1850–1852, I, 576, 597; in 1853, 1854, I, 607n; in 1877, II, 276; in 1880, 1881, II, 316; in 1886, II, 417, 417n, 418; in 1888, II, 474; longshoremen, II, 420–422; miners, II, 184, 185, 334, 363, 478, 497, 498, 499, 501, 508, 525, 528; moulders, I, 565; II, 7, 51, 52, 316; navy yards, I, 394, 395; packing industry, II, 419; printers, I, 136, 137, 412n, 450, 552, 612; quarrymen, II, 367; railroad, I, 622; II, 64, 186–190, 196, 334, 367–369, 382–384, 502, 503, 508, 528; stove mounters, II, 363, 481; switch-men, II, 498; sympathetic, I, 585; tailors, I, 163, 164, 337, 368, 408, 409, 576; telegraphers, II, 384; ten-hour, I, 386, 387; textile, I, 183; II, 178, 304, 362, 363, 418, 420–423, 523, 524; wage, I, 156, 157, 381–383, 395–399; weavers, I, 313; women, I, 356, 418, 420–423.

Opinions: agrarianism, I, 522; employers' associations, II, 31, 51, 52; Greeley, Horace, I, 576; Knights of Labor, II, 347–350; labour congresses, II, 98, 123, 129, 160; public, II, 190; St. Crispin, II, 77–78; socialism, II, 253, 276; trades' union, I, 363, 364, 371, 375, 377.

Suffrage, caucus system, I, 233; democracy, I, 177, 178; exten-sion, I, 175, 318, 319; man-hood, I, 5, 20; personal rights versus property rights, I, 12; woman's, I, 297; II, 129, 211.

Sunday laws, repeal advocated, II, 208.

Syndicalism, Central Labor Union, II, 387, 388; German trade unions, II, 386, 387; Spies and Parsons, II, 297.
See also, International, Black.

Sweating, introduction, I, 7, 102–104; unions, I, 104–107; women, I, 354.

Swinton, John, I, 19; II, 220, 363, 364, 365, 446, 447, 461.

Sylvis, Ben F., at industrial con-vention, 1871, II, 154.

Sylvis, William H., II, 6, 7, 11, 12, 23, 25, 39, 49, 51, 53, 82n, 96, 111, 115, 116, 118, 119, 124, 125, 126, 129, 130, 131, 133, 137, 237n.

Syndicalism, meaning, I, 15, 16.
See also, Anarchism.

T

Tageblatt, Philadelphia, labour daily, II, 278.

Tailors, organise in St. Louis, I, 352; strike, 1850, I, 597.
See also, Tailors, Benevolent Soci-ety of Journeymen.

Tailors, Benevolent Society of Jour-neymen, employment, I, 339; transformation, I, 337.

Tailoresses of New York, strike, I, 156.

Tanners' and Curriers' Union, Na-tional, II, 318.

Tariff, see Protectionism.

Tax Exemptions, stimulate business, I, 37.

Taylor, Daniel B., at New York In-dustrial congress, I, 554n.

Teamsters' Union, I, 8.

Telegraphers, aided by Knights of Labor, II, 345.

Tenement House, cigar making, II, 178.

Tennessee, coal miners' strike, II, 498, 499; unions, in 1864, II, 19.

Terre Haute, conference, II, 318–320.

Textile workers, organise, I, 111.

Thompsonville, conspiracy case, I, 313, 314.

Townsend, Robert, I, 411, 425, 427, 429, 463.

Trade agreements, anthracite min-ers, II, 525; arbitration versus, II, 527; bituminous miners, II, 179–181, 425; building trades, II, 479, 480; employers, II, 33, 415, 416, 424; "exclusive," II, 32; impossibility, II, 359; Na-tional Civic Federation, II, 528; puddler's sliding scale, II, 80, 179; spread, II, 524; stove moulders, II, 480, 481, 482; theory, I, 14, 15; II, 520; trust, II, 526; unions, II, 33, 36.
See also, Bargaining Power.

Trade Courts, early protective or-ganisations, I, 80, 81.

Trade Societies, date of appearance, 1833–1837, I, 472–477.

Trades' and Labor Council of New York, organised, II, 226.

Trades' Assemblies, boycott, II, 22, 23, 24; convention, II, 35, 36, 38, 95; co-operation, II, 23; disappearance, II, 177; employers' associations, II, 26, 27; federation, II, 34, 38, 39, 94, 96; functions, II, 23, 311, 312; International Industrial, II, 36–39; multiplication, II, 310; Philadelphia, II, 24–26, 39; politics, II, 38.

Trades' Union, beginning, I, 12, 358, 365–368, 424; child labour, I, 428, 432; conspiracy, I, 408, 409; conventions, I, 424, 430–437, 469–471; co-operation, I, 468; education, I, 427, 432; employers, I, 368, 371, 372; factory workers, I, 374, 418, 428, 429; finances, I, 434; growth, I, 358, 359, 379, 380; hours of labour, I, 433, 536; influence, I, 438; jurisdictional disputes, I, 376, 377; land policy, I, 428; labour press, I, 360; Mechanics' Union, I, 375; membership, I, 424; need, I, 357; organisation, I, 427, 431; politics, I, 361, 362, 426, 427; prison labour, I, 369–371; riots, I, 377, 378; speculation, I, 435; strikes, I, 363, 371, 390; Tammany, I, 461, 462; term, I, 14; women's labour, I, 436, 437.

Trainmen's Union, organised, II, 186.

Transcendentalism, colonies, I, 505; forms, I, 494.

See also, Anarchism.

Transportation, see Markets, Extension of.

Trevellick, Richard, II, 16, 29, 29n, 35, 115, 118, 122, 124, 126, 129, 130, 131, 133, 137, 150, 152, 153, 168, 170, 244.

Tribune, New York, boycotted, II, 317.

Troup, Alexander H., II, 97, 99, 126, 133, 170.

Truck and order system, abolition, II, 324.

Truth, The, Haskell, II, 299.

Tucker, Benjamin R., individualistic anarchist, I, 17.

Tucker, Gideon J., greenback candidate, II, 246, 247.

Typographia, German - American, Cleveland convention, 1882, II, 326; established, II, 313; socialism, II, 226.

See also, Fowitz, Gustav.

Typographical Association, National, cause for organisation, I, 340.

Typographical Society, Albany, I, 113; Baltimore, I, 115.

Typographical Society, Franklin, I, 109; aided, I, 112; wage scale, I, 126.

Typographical Society, National, apprenticeship policy, I, 451; book publisher, I, 447, 448; capitalism, political, I, 444–446; conventions, I, 450, 452; locals, 1836, I, 443; organisation, I, 620, 621; "two-thirders," I, 448, 449; wage policy, I, 451.

Typographical Society, New York, apprenticeship, I, 116; benefits, I, 124, 125, 137; collective bargaining, I, 603; depression, I, 136, 456; education, I, 249, 250; employers, I, 119; evolution, I, 335, 336; grievances, I, 114, 115; incorporation, I, 86, 109; minimum wage, I, 131; scabs, I, 131.

See also, Strikes.

Typographical Society, Philadelphia, apprenticeship, I, 116; benefits, I, 85; collective bargaining, I, 120, 121; competition of women, I, 343, 344; co-operation with New York local, I, 113; evolution, I, 335; Franklin Society, I, 112; organise, I, 109.

See also, Strikes.

Typographical Society, Washington, apprenticeship, I, 342; Duff Green, I, 450; economic purpose, I, 137; strike, I, 451; women labour, I, 344.

Typographical Union, International, apprenticeship, II, 83; boycott, II, 317, 365; conditional membership, II, 58; conventions, II, 97, 319, 326; established, II, 58, 313; federation, II, 60, 61, 157; growth, II, 45, 1.1, 308, 313; Negro, II, 135, 311; Northwestern Publishers' Association, II, 61; political action,

II, 318; strike fund, II, 59, 60.
See also, Strikes.

U

Unemployment, Chinese, II, 148, 262, 263; Civil War, II, 10, 13; currency policies, II, 123; hours of labour, I, 234; in 1829, I, 170, 171; in 1837, I, 457, 458; in 1857–1863, I, 488; II, 204; in 1869, II, 123; in 1873, II, 219; in 1877, II, 253, 257; legal tender acts, 1862, II, 15; organisation of Chicago unemployed, II, 200; Parsons, A. R., II, 389; riot of Tompkins Square, II, 220; union employment offices, I, 587, 588; Weitling's bank of exchange, I, 514.
Union Congress, Chicago as centre, II, 272; Philadelphia, II, 270; restrictions, II, 273, 278.
Union Society of Carpenters, I, 110.
Union Trade Society of Journeymen Tailors, competition of women, I, 344; organised, I, 337.
United Cabinet Makers, New York, II, 208.
United German Benefit Society, I, 84.
United German Trades, type of city federation, II, 313.
United Labor Party, conventions, II, 455, 456, 459; dwindles, II, 491; in 1887 elections, II, 467; platform, II, 460; single tax, II, 468; socialists, II, 457, 458; Union Labor Party, II, 465.
United Workers of America, II, 222, 223, 234.
Universal Brotherhood, The, II, 196.
Unskilled, Condition, 1829, I, 171; Conflict with skilled; cigar makers, II, 400, 401; District Assembly 49, II, 399; in shoe industry, II, 77; iron workers, II, 407; Knights and trade unionists, II, 396–398, 403, 404, 427.
Organisation: attitude, II, 323; class hate, II, 374; failure, II, 427; Illinois quarrymen's strike, II, 367; in 1884, 1885, II, 357, 362; International Labor Union, II, 280, 302; unemployed, II, 389, 390.
Riots: I, 412, 416, 417.
See also, Factory System; Indus-

trial Workers of the World; Knights of Labor.

V

Van Buren, issues ten-hour order, I, 395.
Van Patten Phillip, II, 272–286.
Virginia, mechanics aided, I, 40, 43; monopoly grants, I, 40, 43; tariff, I, 42; unions, 1863, 1864, II, 19.
Vorbote, official organ, II, 228, 271; on anarchism, II, 296; on co-operation, II, 230; on greenbackism, II, 287; on International Labor Union, II, 280; on militarism, II, 281; on trade unionism, II, 230, 275, 283.

W

Wages, Conditions: banks, I, 459; bread assize, I, 52, 53; cheap labour, I, 347; Chinese labour, II, 264, 265; combination to raise, I, 140–143; contract work, I, 67, 68; co-operation, II, 53; depression, I, 456, 457, 614, 615; II, 185, 361; employers' associations, II, 27, 28; free land, I, 527; growth of cities, II, 359; in 1850, I, 582; in 1854, I, 610, 611; merchant-capitalist, I, 339; monopoly, I, 219; piece work, I, 67, 583, 584; prices, I, 150, 396, 415, 435, 600; II, 15, 110; regulation, I, 7, 50–52, 85, 86, 87, 126, 580, 583; scarcity of labour, I, 128; strikes, I, 110, 111, 156, 363, 381–383, 395–401, 418, 422, 432, 424n, 441, 599; II, 78, 178, 184, 186, 312, 362–364, 367, 368, 496; sunrise to sunset day, I, 171, 172; tariff, I, 443; ten-hour day, I, 311; trade agreement, I, 607; trades' union, I, 7, 358, 433; unionism, modern, I, 575, 613; II, 18, 20, 177.
Occupations: apprentices, I, 592; carpenters, I, 359; cigar makers, I, 621; cigar makers, women, I, 343; construction gangs, I, 415; cordwainers, I, 442; cotton operatives, I, 111; engineers, locomotive, II, 62; house painters, I, 608; labour-

ers, city, I, 415, 416; machinists, II, 57; moulders, II, 49, 51, 52; printers, I, 448, 451, 580, 581; puddlers, I, 552; women, I, 354, 355, 442, 443. Theories: abolition, II, 295; Andrews, S. P., I, 518; collective bargaining, I, 603, 604; price-bargain and wage-bargain, I, 70; Steward, II, 89, 90, 303.

Wage-work, Bücher's use of term, I, 33.

Walker, Amasa, and hours of labour, II, 107.

Walker, Isaac P., I, 551, 558n, 561.

Walker v. Cronin, and expectancy as property, II, 506.

Walking delegates, first, I, 126.

Walls, H. J., I, 162, 176.

Walsh, Mike, I, 527, 528–530, 537, 561.

Walster, Otto, II, 232, 274, 278.

Waltershausen, August Sartorius von, cited, II, 310, 311, 312.

Ward, Osborne, at Alleghany convention, II, 285.

Warehouses, marketing agencies, I, 93, 94; co-operative, I, 95–99; development, I, 100; inadequacy, I, 101.

Warren, Josiah, I, 17, 18, 96, 99, 494, 511; II, 138.

Weavers' Union, organised, I, 156.

Weitling movement, programme, II, 204.

Weitling, Wilhelm, I, 17, 512, 513, 514, 515, 566, 577.

Welch, William, Philadelphia cordwainer, I, 60.

West, William, II, 210, 213.

Western Federation of Miners, industrial union, II, 500.

Western Greenbottle Blowers' National Union, established, II, 313.

Weydemeyer, Joseph, I, 617, 617n, 618; II, 204, 207, 227.

Weydemeyer, Otto, II, 237, 270, 271, 302.

Whaley, J. C. C., II, 102, 112, 115, 116, 129.

Wholesale jobber, appearance, II, 5; legal tender acts, II, 14; supremacy, II, 359.

Wholesale-order period, building trades, I, 66; class struggle, I, 65, 66; markets, I, 61–63; merchant-capitalist follows, I, 103;

production, I, 71; retail-shop period, I, 61, 62.

Wilson, Charles, locomotive engineer, II, 63–68.

Window Glass Workers' Association, protest against contract immigrant labour, II, 372.

Windt, John, and George Henry Evans, I, 527.

Winn, A. M., II, 147, 148n, 149, 162.

Wisconsin eight-hour law, II, 108; greenbackism, II, 244, 248; People's Party, II, 462, 463; unions, 1864, II, 19.

Wolf, George, I, 459, 460.

Wollstonecraft, Mary, in Lowell strike, I, 423.

Women in labour movement, at labour conventions, I, 555; II, 101, 127, 133, 277, 328, 330; competition, I, 339, 342, 343, 436, 437, 595; co-operation, I, 566; equal pay for equal work, II, 114; hours, I, 540, 542, 543; in factories, I, 156, 172–174, 422; organisation, I, 350, 351, 353, 355, 356, 443; II, 128, 328, 418; strikes, I, 418–423; trade union regulation, I, 596; wages, I, 344, 354.

See also, Anthony, Susan B.; Bagley, Sarah G.; Claflin, Tennessee; McDonald, Mary; Parsons, Lucy; Putnam, Mary Kellogg; Stanton, Elizabeth Cady; Wollstonecraft, Mary; Woodhull, Victoria; Wright, Frances.

Woodhull, Victoria, suffragist, II, 210, 211.

Woodhull and Claflin's Weekly, organ American section of I. W. A., II, 211, 212.

Workingmen's Advocate, The, character, II, 16; on education, I, 250–252; Tammany, I, 270; trades' assembly supports, II, 24.

Working Men's Party, Issues: agrarianism, I, 211–213, 271–273; banking system, I, 330; education, I, 251, 252, 274, 299, 300, 327, 328; imprisonment for debt, I, 328; in 1828, I, 216; in 1829, 1830, I, 217, 218–229, 274–284, 295–299; mechanics' liens, I, 329; tariff, I, 294, 295; woman's suffrage, I, 297.

Organisation: candidates, I, 203, 208, 209, 210; class alignment, I, 234; committee of fifty, I, 237, 238, 243, 244; conventions, I, 196, 197, 201, 263–265, 266; democracy, I, 331, 332; election strength, I, 198, 199, 203–216, 239–241, 266–269; growth, I, 195, 205, 206, 207, 223, 244, 246, 255–262; old parties, I, 199–202, 210, 211.
See also, New England Working Men's Association.
Workingmen's Party of California, conventions, II, 256, 257, 258; election strength, II, 259–262; end, II, 264; greenbackism, II, 263, 264; platform, II, 255; sand-lot meetings, II, 255, 256; split, II, 259, 260.
See also, Kearney, Denis.
Workingmen's Party of the United States, factions, II, 271–274; organisation, II, 271; political action, II, 270, 272, 277–290; strikes, II, 276, 277.
See also, Socialist Labor Party.
Workingmen's Trade and Labor Union of San Francisco, organised, II, 254.
Wright, Frances, I, 19, 213, 240, 240n, 250, 272, 284n, 293.
Wright, James L., II, 25, 25n, 236, 243, 247.

CPSIA information can be obtained at www.ICGtesting.com
Printed in the USA
LVOW060148140112

263863LV00001B/60/A